THIRD E

Henretta Brownlee Brody Ware Johnson

Documents Collection

America*s History

Volume 2 SINCE 1865

Douglas Bukowski

Stephen J. Kneeshaw
College of the Ozarks

Louis S. Gerteis
University of Missouri–St. Louis

Worth Publishers

Documents Collection by Douglas Bukowski, Stephen Kneeshaw,
and Louis S. Gerteis

to accompany
Henretta, Brownlee, Brody, Ware, and Johnson:
America's History, Volume 2 since 1865, Third Edition

ISBN: 1–57259–224–9

Printing: 2 3 4 5   Year: 01 00 99 98

Cover: John Sloan, *Six O'Clock, Winter,* c. 1912. Oil on canvas,
26 × 32". The Phillips Collection, Washington, D.C. Acquired 1922.
(Detail)

Most credits and acknowledgments appear with the documents. Some changes, however, appear in
"Credits and Acknowledgments," page 443. This listing constitutes a continuation of the copyright page.

Worth Publishers
33 Irving Place
New York, NY 10003

Preface

Volume 2 of the *Documents Collection* brings together over 180 primary source documents to enrich the study of *America's History*. In addition to key speeches, laws, contemporary accounts, letters, oral histories, autobiographies, and other written documents, the collection includes political cartoons, statistical tables, figures, and photographs that shed light on all aspects of political, social, economic, and cultural history.

The *Collection* follows the chapter organization of the textbook. The ten or so documents in each chapter are grouped into two or three sets corresponding to the main headings of the textbook chapter. Each set begins with an introduction that places that group of documents in their wider historical context. The individual documents follow, each with its own headnote and questions. The document set concludes with three Questions for Further Thought designed to help students to see connections among the documents and how the documents illustrate or exemplify larger themes.

The *Collection* has been designed for maximum flexibility of use. Because headnotes and questions accompany each document, instructors who want to focus on a particular document can do so, while those who wish to explore a section in depth can assign a complete document set. Some of the documents provide interesting comparisons and contrasts to specific American Voices excerpts in the textbook, for example.

For documents-based courses or courses with a special focus, the *Instructor's Resource Manual* to accompany *America's History* contains more than 100 *additional* documents that can be reproduced as student handouts. These collections of documents have been designed to help your students learn to read and interpret the rich diversity of source materials used in American history today.

Contents

P A R T **5**

The Modern State and Society, 1914–1945

★   ★   ★

CHAPTER *16*

The Union Reconstructed 1865–1877

★　　　★　　　★

Presidential Restoration

Planning for Reconstruction began to take shape in December 1863 (see text p. 486), when President Lincoln laid out his ideas in a presidential proclamation. His pronouncement opened a debate that became the central issue in American politics for more than a decade (see text pp. 486–494). The power struggle that followed led to a collision between the executive and legislative branches of government, the displacement of presidential Reconstruction by Congressional Reconstruction, and the first impeachment of a president of the United States, a process that nearly resulted in the removal of President Andrew Johnson, Lincoln's successor (Document 16-1).

Reconstruction involved fundamental questions: Who had the primary responsibility for Reconstruction: the president or Congress? What should the basic aims of Reconstruction be: reunion of the nation as quickly as possible or reunion only after ensuring that the South would remain loyal (Document 16-2)? Congress made its views known in the Wade-Davis bill of July 2, 1864, and then in its strongly negative reaction to Lincoln's veto of the bill (see text p. 487). Lincoln realized that he had to strike a compromise with Congress on Reconstruction, but Johnson did not, setting the stage for a dramatic confrontation with Congress (see text pp. 488–489).

Other fundamental questions about Reconstruction involved determining the place African-Americans would have in the United States (Documents 16-3 and 16-4), especially in the former slave states, and deciding whether the federal government should take measures to prevent the restoration of slavery or a facsimile of slavery. What about the place and role of Unionists in the South?

A number of factors were critical to the way these questions were answered. The first was the Constitution, which set the ground rules by which Americans governed themselves and therefore guided the way in which they dealt with Reconstruction. The second factor was the deep commitment of Americans to private property and their belief that the government should play only a limited role in daily life. The third was the profoundly held idea of self-government, or the belief that the only legitimate governments were those chosen freely by the governed. The fourth was the critical role racism played in both the South and the North. The fifth factor was the strong emotions that followed four years of bloody and expensive war, emotions that were compounded by this country's long history of sectionalism.

16-1 Andrew Johnson's Plan of Reconstruction (1865)

As the Civil War came to an end, Lincoln's successor, Andrew Johnson, moved quickly to implement his plan for Reconstruction, which differed little from Lincoln's plan (see text p. 486). Johnson acted largely on his own, without much consultation with Congress. In particular, he ignored Congress's demand for a harsher policy toward the former Confederate states (see text pp. 488–489).

On May 29, 1865, President Johnson set forth his plan in two presidential proclamations. In the first he promised amnesty to all rebels who would swear an oath of future loyalty, except for certain high-ranking officials and officers of the Confederacy, who had to petition for a presidential pardon.

In the second proclamation, which appears below, Johnson announced the creation of a provisional government for North Carolina. After appointing William W. Holden, a North Carolina Unionist who had opposed secession, as the provisional governor, Johnson described the means by which that state could be restored to the Union. Johnson intended this plan to serve as a model for the other seceded states, hoping that all could be restored before Congress reconvened in December.

Johnson's approach to Reconstruction was very different from that proposed by the Wade-Davis bill (see text p. 487), which stipulated that more than 50 percent of the voters who were qualified in 1860 in each southern state had to be able to prove their past loyalty and swear future loyalty to the Union. Johnson and Congress also differed about allowing former Confederate leaders to participate in Reconstruction and in government. Presidents Lincoln and Johnson envisioned temporary disqualification; Congress favored permanent disqualification (see text pp. 486–487).

Source: In James D. Richardson, ed., *A Compilation of the Messages and Papers of the Presidents* (Washington, D.C.: U.S. Government Printing Office, 1896–1899), vol. 6, pp. 312–313.

Whereas the fourth section of the fourth article of the Constitution of the United States declares that the United States shall guarantee to every State in the Union a republican form of government and shall protect each of them against invasion and domestic violence; and

Whereas the President of the United States is by the Constitution made Commander in Chief of the Army and Navy, as well as chief civil executive officer of the United States, and is bound by solemn oath faithfully to execute the office of President of the United States and to take care that the laws be faithfully executed; and

Whereas the rebellion which has been waged by a portion of the people of the United States against the properly constituted authorities of the Government . . . and

Whereas it becomes necessary and proper to carry out and enforce the obligations of the United States to the people of North Carolina in securing them in the enjoyment of a republican form of government:

Now, therefore, in obedience to the high and solemn duties imposed upon me by the Constitution of the United States and for the purpose of enabling the loyal people of said State to organize a State government whereby justice may be established, domestic tranquillity insured, and loyal citizens protected in all their rights of life, liberty, and property, I, Andrew Johnson, President of the United States and Commander in Chief of the Army and Navy of the United States, do hereby appoint William W. Holden provisional governor of the State of North Carolina, whose duty it shall be, at the earliest practicable period, to prescribe such rules and regulations as may be necessary and proper for convening a convention composed of delegates to be chosen by that portion of the people of said State who are loyal to the United States, and no others, for the purpose of altering or amending the constitution thereof, and with authority to exercise within the limits of said State all the powers necessary and proper to enable such loyal people of the State of North Carolina to restore said State to its constitutional relations to the Federal Government and to present such a republican form of State government as will entitle the State to the guaranty of the United States therefor and its people to protection by the United States against invasion, insurrection, and domestic violence: *Provided*, That in any election that may be hereafter held for choosing delegates to any State convention as aforesaid no person shall be qualified as an elector or shall be eligible as a member of such convention unless he shall

have previously taken and subscribed the oath of amnesty as set forth in the President's proclamation of May 29, A. D. 1865, and is a voter qualified as prescribed by the constitution and laws of the State of North Carolina in force immediately before the 20th day of May, A. D. 1861, the date of the so-called ordinance of secession; and the said convention, when convened, or the legislature that may be thereafter assembled, will prescribe the qualification of electors and the eligibility of persons to hold office under the constitution and laws of the State—a power the people of the several States composing the Federal Union have rightfully exercised from the origin of the Government to the present time.

And I do hereby direct—

. . . That the military commander of the department and all officers and persons in the military and naval service aid and assist the said provisional governor in carrying into effect this proclamation; and they are enjoined to abstain from in any way hindering, impeding, or discouraging the loyal people from the organization of a State government as herein authorized. . . .

Questions

1. According to President Johnson, what was his authority for this proclamation? Who was to be in charge of the process?

2. What steps did Johnson prescribe for restoring civil government in North Carolina?

3. Under Johnson's plan, would freedmen be able to vote? (*Hint:* See the section starting "*Provided.*")

16-2   Report on Conditions in the South (1865)

Carl Schurz

By December 1865, when Congress was gathering in Washington for a new session, Johnson had declared that all the Confederate states but Texas had met his requirements for restoration. Newly elected senators and congressmen from the former Confederacy had arrived to take seats in Congress (see text pp. 488–489).

Johnson's efforts to restore the South stalled. Congress exercised its constitutional authority to deny seats to delegations from the South and launched an investigation into conditions there (see text pp. 488–492). In response to a Senate resolution requesting "information in relation to the States of the Union lately in rebellion," Johnson painted a rosy picture: "In 'that portion of the Union lately in rebellion' the aspect of affairs is more promising than, in view of all the circumstances, could well have been expected. The people throughout the entire south evince a laudable desire to renew their allegiance to the government, and to repair the devastations of war by a prompt and cheerful return to peaceful pursuits. An abiding faith is entertained that their actions will conform to their professions, and that, in acknowledging the supremacy of the Constitution and the laws of the United States, their loyalty will be unreservedly given to the government, whose leniency they cannot fail to appreciate, and whose fostering care will soon restore them to a condition of prosperity. It is true, that in some of the States the demoralizing effects of war are to be seen in occasional disorders, but these are local in character, not frequent in occurrence, and are rapidly disappearing as the authority of civil law is extended and sustained."

Johnson's message to the Senate was accompanied by a report from Major General Carl Schurz (see also Document 13-6). Among the subjects on which Schurz reported were whether southern whites had accepted defeat and emancipation, and whether ex-slaves and southern Unionists were safe in the South and were receiving fair treatment. Schurz's report was apparently largely ignored by President Johnson, who had assigned him to make the report but was not happy with what he said.

Schurz went to considerable lengths to get an accurate reading of attitudes in the South. He tried to get a representative sample of people to interview in his three-month tour of portions of South Carolina, Georgia, Alabama, Mississippi, and Louisiana and gathered documentary evidence as well as interviews. Then he tried to analyze his findings carefully and make recommendations on the basis of those findings. Clearly, he believed that Reconstruction in the South involved more than the restoration of civil government.

Source: U.S. Congress, Senate, 39th Cong., 1st sess., 1865, Ex. Doc. No. 2, pp. 1–5, 8, 36–39, 41–44.

SIR: . . . You informed me that your "policy of reconstruction" was merely experimental, and that you would change it if the experiment did not lead to satisfactory results. To aid you in forming your conclusions upon this point I understood to be the object of my mission, . . .

CONDITION OF THINGS IMMEDIATELY AFTER THE CLOSE OF THE WAR

In the development of the popular spirit in the south since the close of the war two well-marked periods can be distinguished. The first commences with the sudden collapse of the confederacy and the dispersion of its armies, and the second with the first proclamation indicating the "reconstruction policy" of the government. . . . When the news of Lee's and Johnston's surrenders burst upon the southern country the general consternation was extreme. People held their breath, indulging in the wildest apprehensions as to what was now to come. . . . Prominent Unionists told me that persons who for four years had scorned to recognize them on the street approached them with smiling faces and both hands extended. Men of standing in the political world expressed serious doubts as to whether the rebel States would ever again occupy their position as States in the Union, or be governed as conquered provinces. The public mind was so despondent that if readmission at some future time under whatever conditions had been promised, it would then have been looked upon as a favor. The most uncompromising rebels prepared for leaving the country. The masses remained in a state of fearful expectancy. . . .

Such was, according to the accounts I received, the

character of that first period. The worst apprehensions were gradually relieved as day after day went by without bringing the disasters and inflictions which had been vaguely anticipated, until at last the appearance of the North Carolina proclamation substituted new hopes for them. The development of this second period I was called upon to observe on the spot, and it forms the main subject of this report.

RETURNING LOYALTY

. . . [T]he white people at large being, under certain conditions, charged with taking the preliminaries of "reconstruction" into their hands, the success of the experiment depends upon the spirit and attitude of those who either attached themselves to the secession cause from the beginning, or, entertaining originally opposite views, at least followed its fortunes from the time that their States had declared their separation from the Union. . . .

I may group the southern people into four classes, each of which exercises an influence upon the development of things in that section:

1. Those who, although having yielded submission to the national government only when obliged to do so, have a clear perception of the irreversible changes produced by the war, and honestly endeavor to accommodate themselves to the new order of things. Many of them are not free from traditional prejudice but open to conviction, and may be expected to act in good faith whatever they do. This class is composed, in its majority, of persons of mature age—planters, merchants, and professional men; some

of them are active in the reconstruction movement, but boldness and energy are, with a few individual exceptions, not among their distinguishing qualities.

2. Those whose principal object is to have the States without delay restored to their position and influence in the Union and the people of the States to the absolute control of their home concerns. They are ready, in order to attain that object, to make any ostensible concession that will not prevent them from arranging things to suit their taste as soon as that object is attained. This class comprises a considerable number, probably a large majority, of the professional politicians who are extremely active in the reconstruction movement. They are loud in their praise of the President's reconstruction policy, and clamorous for the withdrawal of the federal troops and the abolition of the Freedmen's Bureau.

3. The incorrigibles, who still indulge in the swagger which was so customary before and during the war, and still hope for a time when the southern confederacy will achieve its independence. This class consists mostly of young men, and comprises the loiterers of the towns and the idlers of the country. They persecute Union men and negroes whenever they can do so with impunity, insist clamorously upon their "rights," and are extremely impatient of the presence of the federal soldiers. A good many of them have taken the oaths of allegiance and amnesty, and associated themselves with the second class in their political operations. This element is by no means unimportant; it is strong in numbers, deals in brave talk, addresses itself directly and incessantly to the passions and prejudices of the masses, and commands the admiration of the women.

4. The multitude of people who have no definite ideas about the circumstances under which they live and about the course they have to follow; whose intellects are weak, but whose prejudices and impulses are strong, and who are apt to be carried along by those who know how to appeal to the latter. . . .

FEELING TOWARDS THE SOLDIERS AND THE PEOPLE OF THE NORTH

. . . [U]pon the whole, the soldier of the Union is still looked upon as a stranger, an intruder—as the "Yankee," "the enemy." . . .

It is by no means surprising that prejudices and resentments, which for years were so assiduously cultivated and so violently inflamed, should not have been turned into affection by a defeat; nor are they likely to disappear as long as the southern people continue to brood over their losses and misfortunes. They will gradually subside when those who entertain them cut resolutely loose from the past and embark in a career of new activity on a common field with those whom they have so long considered their enemies. . . . [A]s long as these feelings exist in their present strength, they will hinder the growth of that reliable kind of loyalty which springs from the heart and clings to the country in good and evil fortune.

SITUATION OF UNIONISTS

. . . It struck me soon after my arrival in the south that the known Unionists—I mean those who during the war had been to a certain extent identified with the national cause—were not in communion with the leading social and political circles; and the further my observations extended the clearer it became to me that their existence in the south was of a rather precarious nature. . . . Even Governor [William L.] Sharkey, in the course of a conversation I had with him in the presence of Major General Osterhaus, admitted that, if our troops were then withdrawn, the lives of northern men in Mississippi would not be safe. . . . [General Osterhaus said]: "There is no doubt whatever that the state of affairs would be intolerable for all Union men, all recent immigrants from the north, and all negroes, the moment the protection of the United States troops were withdrawn." . . .

NEGRO INSURRECTIONS AND ANARCHY

. . . [I do] not deem a negro insurrection probable as long as the freedmen were assured of the direct protection of the national government. Whenever they are in trouble, they raise their eyes up to that power, and although they may suffer, yet, as long as that power is visibly present, they continue to hope. But when State authority in the south is fully restored, the federal forces withdrawn, and the Freedmen's Bureau abolished, the colored man will find himself turned over to the mercies of those whom he does not trust. If then an attempt is made to strip him again of those rights which he justly thought he possessed, he will be apt to feel that he can hope for no redress unless he procure it himself. If ever the negro is capable of rising, he will rise then. . . .

There is probably at the present moment no country in the civilized world which contains such an accumulation of anarchical elements as the south. The strife of the antagonistic tendencies here described is aggravated by the passions inflamed and the general impoverishment brought about by a long and exhaustive war, and the south will have to suffer the evils of anarchical disorder until means are found to effect a final settlement of the labor question in accordance with the logic of the great revolution.

THE TRUE PROBLEM—DIFFICULTIES AND REMEDIES

In seeking remedies for such disorders, we ought to keep in view, above all, the nature of the problem which is to be solved. As to what is commonly termed "reconstruction," it is not only the political machinery of the States and their constitutional relations to the general government, but the whole organism of southern society that must be reconstructed, or rather constructed anew, so as to bring it in harmony with the rest of American society. The difficulties of this task are not to be considered overcome when the people of the south take the oath of allegiance and elect governors and legislatures and members of Congress, and militia captains. That this would be done had become certain as soon as the surrenders of the southern armies had made further resistance impossible, and nothing in the world was left, even to the most uncompromising rebel, but to submit or to emigrate. It was also natural that they should avail themselves of every chance offered them to resume control of their home affairs and to regain their influence in the Union. But this can hardly be called the first step towards the solution of the true problem, and it is a fair question to ask, whether the hasty gratification of their desire to resume such control would not create new embarrassments.

The true nature of the difficulties of the situation is this: The general government of the republic has, by proclaiming the emancipation of the slaves, commenced a great social revolution in the south, but has, as yet, not completed it. Only the negative part of it is accomplished. The slaves are emancipated in point of form, but free labor has not yet been put in the place of slavery in point of fact. And now, in the midst of this critical period of transition, the power which originated the revolution is expected to turn over its whole future development to another power which from the beginning was hostile to it and has never yet entered into its spirit, leaving the class in whose favor it was made completely without power to protect itself and to take an influential part in that development. The history of the world will be searched in vain for a proceeding similar to this which did not lead either to a rapid and violent reaction, or to the most serious trouble and civil disorder. It cannot be said that the conduct of the southern people since the close of the war has exhibited such extraordinary wisdom and self-abnegation as to make them an exception to the rule.

In my despatches from the south I repeatedly expressed the opinion that the people were not yet in a frame of mind to legislate calmly and understandingly upon the subject of free negro labor. And this I reported to be the opinion of some of our most prominent military commanders and other observing men. It is, indeed, difficult to imagine circumstances more unfavorable for the development of a calm and unprejudiced public opinion than those under which the southern people are at present laboring. The war has not only defeated their political aspirations, but it has broken up their whole social organization. . . .

In which direction will these people be most apt to turn their eyes? Leaving the prejudice of race out of the question, from early youth they have been acquainted with but one system of labor, and with that one system they have been in the habit of identifying all their interests. They know of no way to help themselves but the one they are accustomed to. . . .

It is certain that every success of free negro labor will augment the number of its friends, and disarm some of the prejudices and assumptions of its opponents. I am convinced one good harvest made by unadulterated free labor in the south would have a far better effect than all the oaths that have been taken, and all the ordinances that have as yet been passed by southern conventions. But how can such a result be attained? The facts enumerated in this report, as well as the news we receive from the south from day to day, must make it evident to every unbiased observer that unadulterated free labor cannot be had at present, unless the national government holds its protective and controlling hand over it. . . . One reason why the southern people are so slow in accommodating themselves to the new order of things is, that they confidently expect soon to be permitted to regulate matters according to their own notions. Every concession made to them by the government has been taken as an encouragement to persevere in this hope, and, unfortunately for them, this hope is nourished by influences from other parts of the country. Hence their anxiety to have their State governments restored *at once*, to have the troops withdrawn, and the Freedmen's Bureau abolished, although a good many discerning men know well that, in view of the lawless spirit still prevailing, it would be far better for them to have the general order of society firmly maintained by the federal power until things have arrived at a final settlement. Had, from the beginning, the conviction been forced upon them that the adulteration of the new order of things by the admixture of elements belonging to the system of slavery would under no circumstances be permitted, a much larger number would have launched their energies into the new channel, and, seeing that they could do "no better," faithfully co-operated with the government. It is hope which fixes them in their perverse notions. That hope nourished or fully gratified, they will persevere in the same direction. That hope destroyed, a great many will, by the force of necessity, at once accommodate themselves to the logic of the change. If, therefore, the national government firmly and unequivocally announces its policy not to give up the control of the free-labor reform until it is finally accomplished, the progress of that reform will undoubtedly be far more rapid and far less difficult than it will be if the attitude of the government is such as to permit contrary hopes to be indulged in. . . .

IMMIGRATION [AND CAPITAL]

[The south would benefit] from immigration of northern people and Europeans. . . . The south needs capital. But capital is notoriously timid and averse to risk. . . . Capitalists will be apt to consider—and they are by no means wrong in doing so—that no safe investments can be made in the south as long as southern society is liable to be convulsed by anarchical disorders. No greater encouragement can, therefore, be given to capital to transfer itself to the south than the assurance that the government will continue to control the development of the new social system in the late rebel States until such dangers are averted by a final settlement of things upon a thorough free-labor basis.

How long the national government should continue that control depends upon contingencies. It ought to cease as soon as its objects are attained; and its objects will be attained sooner and with less difficulty if nobody is permitted to indulge in the delusion that it will cease *before* they are attained. This is one of the cases in which a determined policy can accomplish much, while a half-way policy is liable to spoil things already accomplished. . . .

NEGRO SUFFRAGE

It would seem that the interference of the national authority in the home concerns of the southern States would be rendered less necessary, and the whole problem of political and social reconstruction be much simplified, if, while the masses lately arrayed against the government are permitted to vote, the large majority of those who were always loyal, and are naturally anxious to see the free labor problem successfully solved, were not excluded from all influence upon legislation. In all questions concerning the Union, the national debt, and the future social organization of the south, the feelings of the colored man are naturally in sympathy with the views and aims of the national government. While the southern white fought against the Union, the negro did all he could to aid it; while the southern white sees in the national government his conqueror, the negro sees in it his protector; while the white owes to the national debt his defeat, the negro owes to it his deliverance; while the white considers himself robbed and ruined by the emancipation of the slaves, the negro finds in it the assurance of future prosperity and happiness. In all the important issues the negro would be led by natural impulse to forward the ends of the government, and by making his influence, as part of the voting body, tell upon the legislation of the States, render the interference of the national authority less necessary.

As the most difficult of the pending questions are intimately connected with the status of the negro in southern society, it is obvious that a correct solution can be more easily obtained if he has a voice in the matter. In the right to vote he would find the best permanent protection against oppressive class-legislation, as well as against individual persecution. The relations between the white and black races, even if improved by the gradual wearing off of the present animosities, are likely to remain long under the troubling influence of prejudice. It is a notorious fact that the rights of a man of some political power are far less exposed to violation than those of one who is, in matters of public interest, completely subject to the will of others. . . .

In discussing the matter of negro suffrage I deemed it my duty to confine myself strictly to the practical aspects of the subject. I have, therefore, not touched its moral merits nor discussed the question whether the national government is competent to enlarge the elective franchise in the States lately in rebellion by its own act; I deem it proper, however, to offer a few remarks on the assertion frequently put forth, that the franchise is likely to be extended to the colored man by the voluntary action of the southern whites themselves. My observation leads me to a contrary opinion. Aside from a very few enlightened men, I found but one class of people in favor of the enfranchisement of the blacks: it was the class of Unionists who found themselves politically ostracised and looked upon the enfranchisement of the loyal negroes as the salvation of the whole loyal element. But their numbers and influence are sadly insufficient to secure such a result. The masses are strongly opposed to colored suffrage; anybody that dares to advocate it is stigmatized as a dangerous fanatic; nor do I deem it probable that in the ordinary course of things prejudices will wear off to such an extent as to make it a popular measure. . . .

DEPORTATION OF THE FREEDMEN

. . . [T]he true problem remains, not how to remove the colored man from his present field of labor, but how to make him, where he is, a true freeman and an intelligent and useful citizen. The means are simple: protection by the government until his political and social status enables him to protect himself, offering to his legitimate ambition the stimulant of a perfectly fair chance in life, and granting to him the rights which in every just organization of society are coupled with corresponding duties.

CONCLUSION

I may sum up all I have said in a few words. If nothing were necessary but to restore the machinery of government in the States lately in rebellion in point of form, the movements made to that end by the people of the south might be considered satisfactory. But if it is required that the southern people should also accommodate themselves to the results of the war in point of spirit, those movements fall far short of what must be insisted upon. . . .

Questions

1. Why did Schurz recommend keeping the Freedmen's Bureau and the army in the South? How did that differ from what Johnson wanted?
2. Why did Schurz suggest that it might be wise to give African-Americans in the South the vote?
3. What does Schurz say about the Unionists in the South? About the emergence of a free labor system?

16-3   The Mississippi Black Codes (1865)

As Carl Schurz reported, after the Civil War whites in the South sought a system of race relations in which African-Americans would be clearly subordinate to whites and would constitute a readily accessible and controllable work force (see text p. 491).

Immediately after the Civil War southern whites wrote or revised vagrancy laws and the old slave codes as a means of establishing the system of race relations they wanted (see text p. 492). Below is one of their most famous attempts to codify race relations, the Black Codes passed by the Mississippi legislature.

The Mississippi codes gave blacks rights they had not had before and clearly acknowledged that chattel slavery had ended. The codes recognized the right of African-Americans to own property, though not in incorporated towns or cities. (Before the Civil War there were black property owners in Mississippi and even a few black slaveholders, but their legal standing was not clear.) The 1865 codes also recognized marriages among blacks as legal.

Not all the southern states passed comprehensive Black Codes, and some codes were much less stringent than those of Mississippi. South Carolina's codes differed in that they restricted blacks to buying property in cities or towns.

The creators of the codes drew their ideas from the world in which they lived. Slavery had just ended very abruptly, and the ravages of war were ever present. The men who drafted these codes used the old slave codes from the South, vagrancy laws from the North and the South, laws for ex-slaves in the British West Indies, and antebellum laws for free blacks. They were also aware that most northern states had laws that discriminated against African-Americans and that very few northern states allowed African-Americans to vote.

Most of these codes and similar measures were declared void by the Union army officials who were stationed in the former Confederate states. Subsequently, during Reconstruction, the rights of African-Americans were greatly expanded (see text pp. 492–493).

Source: Laws of Mississippi, 1865, pp. 82ff.

1. CIVIL RIGHTS OF FREEDMEN IN MISSISSIPPI

. . . That all freedmen, free negroes, and mulattoes may sue and be sued . . . may acquire personal property . . . and may dispose of the same in the same manner and to the same extent that white persons may: [but no] freedman, free negro, or mulatto . . . [shall] rent or lease any lands or tenements except in incorporated cities or towns, in which places the corporate authorities shall control the same. . . .

All freedmen, free negroes, or mulattoes who do now and have herefore lived and cohabited together as husband and wife shall be taken and held in law as legally married, and the issue shall be taken and held as legitimate for all purposes; that it shall not be lawful for any freedman, free negro, or mulatto to intermarry with any white person; nor for any white person to intermarry with any freedman, free negro, or mulatto; and any person who shall so intermarry, shall be deemed guilty of felony, and on conviction thereof shall be confined in the State penitentiary for life; and those shall be deemed freedmen, free negroes, and mulattoes who are of pure negro blood, and those descended from a negro to the third generation, inclusive, though one ancestor in each generation may have been a white person. . . .

[F]reedmen, free negroes, and mulattoes are now by law competent witnesses . . . in civil cases [and in criminal cases where they are the victims]. . . .

All contracts for labor made with freedmen, free negroes, and mulattoes for a longer period than one month shall be in writing, and in duplicate. . . . and said contracts shall be taken and held as entire contracts, and if the laborer shall quit the service of the employer before the expiration of his term of service, without good cause, he shall forfeit his wages for that year up to the time of quitting.

. . . Every civil officer shall, and every person may, arrest and carry back to his or her legal employer any freedman, free negro, or mulatto who shall have quit the service of his or her employer before the expiration of his or her term of service without good cause; and said officer and person shall be entitled to receive for arresting and carrying back every deserting employe aforesaid the sum of five dollars. . . .

. . . If any person shall persuade or attempt to persuade, entice, or cause any freedman, free negro, or mulatto to desert from the legal employment of any person before the expiration of his or her term of service, or shall knowingly employ any such deserting freedman, free negro, or mulatto, or shall knowingly give or sell to any such deserting freedman, free negro, or mulatto, any food, raiment, or other thing, he or she shall be guilty of a misdemeanor. . . .

2. MISSISSIPPI APPRENTICE LAW

. . . It shall be the duty of all sheriffs, justices of the peace, and other civil officers of the several counties in this State, to report to the probate courts of their respective counties semi-annually, at the January and July terms of said courts, all freedmen, free negroes, and mulattoes, under the age of eighteen, in their respective counties, beats or districts, who are orphans, or whose parent or parents have not the means or who refuse to provide for and support said minors; . . . the clerk of said court to apprentice said minors

to some competent and suitable person, on such terms as the court may direct, having a particular care to the interest of said minor: *Provided*, that the former owner of said minors shall have the preference when, in the opinion of the court, he or she shall be a suitable person for that purpose. . . .

. . . In the management and control of said apprentice, said master or mistress shall have the power to inflict such moderate corporal chastisement as a father or guardian is allowed to inflict on his or her child or ward at common law: *Provided*, that in no case shall cruel or inhuman punishment be inflicted. . . .

3. MISSISSIPPI VAGRANT LAW

. . . That all rogues and vagabonds, idle and dissipated persons, beggars, jugglers, or persons practicing unlawful games or plays, runaways, common drunkards, common night-walkers, pilferers, lewd, wanton, or lascivious persons, in speech or behavior, common railers and brawlers, persons who neglect their calling or employment, misspend what they earn, or do not provide for the support of themselves or their families, or dependents, and all other idle and disorderly persons, including all who neglect all lawful business, habitually misspend their time by frequenting houses of ill-fame, gaming-houses, or tippling shops, shall be deemed and considered vagrants, under the provisions of this act, and upon conviction thereof shall be fined not exceeding one hundred dollars . . . and be imprisoned at the discretion of the court, not exceeding ten days.

. . . All freedmen, free negroes and mulattoes in this State, over the age of eighteen years, found on the second Monday in January, 1866, or thereafter, with no lawful employment or business, or found unlawfully assembling themselves together, either in the day or night time, and all white persons so assembling themselves with freedmen, free negroes or mulattoes, or usually associating with freedmen, free negroes or mulattoes, on terms of equality, or living in adultery or fornication with a freed woman, free negro or mulatto, shall be deemed vagrants, and on conviction thereof shall be fined in a sum not exceeding, in the case of a freedman, free negro or mulatto, fifty dollars, and a white man two hundred dollars, and imprisoned at the discretion of the court, the free negro not exceeding ten days, and the white man not exceeding six months. . . .

4. PENAL LAWS OF MISSISSIPPI

. . . That no freedman, free negro or mulatto, not in the military service of the United States government, and not licensed so to do by the board of police of his or her county, shall keep or carry fire-arms of any kind, or any ammunition, dirk or bowie knife. . . .

. . . Any freedman, free negro, or mulatto committing

riots, routs, affrays, trespasses, malicious mischief, cruel treatment to animals, seditious speeches, insulting gestures, language, or acts, or assaults on any person, disturbance of the peace, exercising the function of a minister of the Gospel without a license from some regularly organized church, vending spirituous or intoxicating liquors, or committing any other misdemeanor, the punishment of which is not specifically provided for by law, shall, upon conviction thereof in the county court, be fined not less than ten dollars, and not more than one hundred dollars,

and may be imprisoned at the discretion of the court, not exceeding thirty days. . . .

. . . If any freedman, free negro, or mulatto, convicted of any of the misdemeanors provided against in this act, shall fail or refuse for the space of five days, after conviction, to pay the fine and costs imposed, such person shall be hired out by the sheriff or other officer, at public outcry, to any white person who will pay said fine and all costs, and take said convict for the shortest time.

Questions

1. What was the intent of these laws?
2. Who was charged with enforcing them? ("Every civil officer shall, and every person may, arrest and carry back to his or her legal employer. . . .") Who was considered a "person"? Who was not a "person"?
3. How were vagrants defined? Were these laws based on the assumption that the only vagrants were African-Americans? What restrictions were placed on the freedom of expression of African-Americans? What restrictions were placed on their freedom of association? On whites in Mississippi?

16-4   The Civil Rights Act of 1866

When Congress reconvened in December 1865, it blocked President Johnson's attempts to restore the South quickly. It extended the life of the Freedmen's Bureau over the president's veto and passed another landmark law, the Civil Rights Act of 1866, again over the president's veto (see text pp. 492–493). This act made African-Americans citizens and countered the *Dred Scott* decision of 1857, in which the Supreme Court had declared that no African-American who was descended from a slave was or could ever be a citizen.

Doubts about the constitutionality and permanence of the Civil Rights Act of 1866 prompted Congress to pass the Fourteenth Amendment (see text pp. 493 and D-13). Ratified in 1868, this amendment for the first time constitutionally defined citizenship and some of the basic rights of citizenship; it also embraced the Republican program for Reconstruction.

Source: United States, *Statutes at Large*, vol.14, pp. 27ff.

An Act to protect all Persons in the United States in their Civil Rights, and furnish the Means of their Vindication.

Be it enacted, That all persons born in the United States and not subject to any foreign power, excluding Indians not taxed, are hereby declared to be citizens of the United States; and such citizens, of every race and color, without regard to any previous condition of slavery or involuntary servitude, except as a punishment for crime whereof the party shall have been duly convicted, shall

have the same right, in every State and Territory in the United States, to make and enforce contracts, to sue, be parties, and give evidence, to inherit, purchase, lease, sell, hold, and convey real and personal property, and to full and equal benefit of all laws and proceedings for the security of person and property, as is enjoyed by white citizens, and shall be subject to like punishment, pains, and penalties, and to none other, any law, statute, ordinance, regulation, or custom, to the contrary notwithstanding.

SEC. 2. *And be it further enacted*, That any person who, under color of any law, statute, ordinance, regulation, or custom, shall subject, or cause to be subjected, any inhabitant of any State or Territory to the deprivation of any right secured or protected by this act, or to different punishment, pains, or penalties on account of such person having at any time been held in a condition of slavery or involuntary servitude, except as a punishment for crime whereof the party shall have been duly convicted, or by reason of his color or race, than is prescribed for the punishment of white persons, shall be deemed guilty of a misdemeanor, and, on conviction, shall be punished by fine not exceeding one thousand dollars, or imprisonment not exceeding one year, or both, in the discretion of the court.

SEC. 3. *And be it further enacted*, That the district courts of the United States, . . . shall have, exclusively of the courts of the several States, cognizance of all crimes and offences committed against the provisions of this act, and also, concurrently with the circuit courts of the United States, of all causes, civil and criminal, affecting persons who are denied or cannot enforce in the courts or judicial tribunals of the State or locality where they may be any of the rights secured to them by the first section of this act. . . .

SEC. 4. *And be it further enacted*, That the district attorneys, marshals, and deputy marshals of the United States, the commissioners appointed by the circuit and territorial courts of the United States, with powers of arresting, imprisoning, or bailing offenders against the laws of the United States, the officers and agents of the Freedmen's Bureau, and every other officer who may be specially em-

powered by the President of the United States, shall be, and they are hereby, specially authorized and required, at the expense of the United States, to institute proceedings against all and every person who shall violate the provisions of this act, and cause him or them to be arrested and imprisoned, or bailed, as the case may be, for trial before such court of the United States or territorial court as by this act has cognizance of the offence. . . .

SEC. 8. *And be it further enacted*, That whenever the President of the United States shall have reason to believe that offences have been or are likely to be committed against the provisions of this act within any judicial district, it shall be lawful for him, in his discretion, to direct the judge, marshal, and district attorney of such district to attend at such place within the district, and for such time as he may designate, for the purpose of the more speedy arrest and trial of persons charged with a violation of this act; and it shall be the duty of every judge or other officer, when any such requisition shall be received by him, to attend at the place and for the time therein designated.

SEC. 9. *And be it further enacted*, That it shall be lawful for the President of the United States, or such person as he may empower for that purpose, to employ such part of the land or naval forces of the United States, or of the militia, as shall be necessary to prevent the violation and enforce the due execution of this act.

SEC. 10. *And be it further enacted*, That upon all questions of law arising in any cause under the provisions of this act a final appeal may be taken to the Supreme Court of the United States.

Questions

1. What was the intent of the Civil Rights Act?
2. Who was responsible for enforcing this law, and what powers might they use? Was it necessary to wait until the law was violated before officers of the law could act?
3. According to the Fourteenth Amendment, who is a citizen of the United States? What rights does the amendment say citizens have? What does "equal protection of the laws" mean?

Questions for Further Thought

1. Compare and contrast President Johnson's description of conditions in the South (Document 16-1) with that of General Schurz (Document 16-2). Which do you find to be more accurate? Why?
2. What did Johnson and Schurz say about relations between blacks and whites?
3. Compare the Mississippi Black Codes (Document 16-3) with the Civil Rights Act of 1866 (Document 16-4). Why do you think Congress believed that it had to pass the Civil Rights Act and then adopt the Fourteenth Amendment?

Radical Reconstruction

When only Tennessee ratified the Fourteenth Amendment (and was readmitted to the Union), Congressional Republicans, strengthened by their victories in the 1866 Congressional elections, passed the Reconstruction Acts (see text p. 494). These laws forced unreconstructed Confederate states to meet Republican conditions for readmission, including granting African-American men the vote (Document 16-5). Although labeled as "radical," these measures actually fell short of what some in Congress called for (see text p. 496).

Northern support for Reconstruction fluctuated (Document 16-6). Forced to choose between presidential Reconstruction and the Reconstruction programs proposed by Congress, most northerners preferred the latter. However, northern support for Reconstruction faded after 1868 and virtually disappeared in the 1870s (see text p. 503).

Most southern whites had opposed Republican Reconstruction from the outset, though the intensity of the opposition fluctuated (see text pp. 497–498). The animosity of southern whites toward Reconstruction, Republicans, and African-Americans intensified during election campaigns and whenever a sensitive issue was put before the public (Document 16-6). The Ku Klux Klan was especially active during such times (Document 16-7), despite legislation enacted against it.

During Reconstruction African-Americans obtained a number of civil and political rights, most of which were lost in the years that followed Reconstruction (see text pp. 498–500 and American Voices, text p. 502). Blacks made other gains which they were able to keep even after Reconstruction: formalizing their marriages, stabilizing their families, distancing themselves from slavery, creating institutions such as the black church, pursuing educational opportunities, and acquiring property (Document 16-8). Over the years, increasing (though still small) numbers of African-Americans became property holders.

16-5   Thaddeus Stevens on Black Suffrage and Land Redistribution (1867)

The Radical Republicans, including Congressman Thaddeus Stevens of Pennsylvania, believed that besides the vote, freedmen would need an economic basis for controlling their lives (see text pp. 486–487). Below are excerpts from the remarks of Thaddeus Stevens and from a bill in which he proposed to alter the South drastically.

Source: Congressional Globe, January 3, 1867, p. 252; March 19, 1867, p. 203.

ON BLACK SUFFRAGE

Unless the rebel States, before admission, should be made republican in spirit, and placed under the guardianship of loyal men, all our blood and treasure will have been spent in vain. I waive now the question of punishment which, if we are wise, will still be inflicted by moderate confiscations. . . . Impartial suffrage, both in electing the delegates and ratifying their proceedings, is now the fixed rule. There is more reason why colored voters should be admit-

ted in the rebel States than in the Territories. In the States they form the great mass of the loyal men. Possibly with their aid loyal governments may be established in most of those States. Without it all are sure to be ruled by traitors; and loyal men, black and white, will be oppressed, exiled, or murdered. There are several good reasons for the passage of this bill. In the first place, it is just. I am now confining my argument to negro suffrage in the rebel States. Have not loyal blacks quite as good a right to choose rulers and make laws as rebel whites? In the second place, it is a necessity in order to protect the loyal white men in the seceded States. The white Union men are in a great minority in each of those States. With them the blacks would act in a body; and it is believed that in each of said States, except one, the two united would form a majority, control the States, and protect themselves. Now they are the victims of daily murder. . . .

Another good reason is, it would insure the ascendency of the Union party. . . . I believe . . . that on the continued ascendency of that party depends the safety of this great nation. If impartial suffrage is excluded in the rebel States, then every one of them is sure to send a solid rebel representative delegation to Congress, and cast a solid rebel electoral vote. They, with their kindred Copperheads of the North, would always elect the President and control Congress. While slavery sat upon her defiant throne, and insulted and intimidated the trembling North, the South frequently divided on questions of policy between Whigs and Democrats, and gave victory alternately to the sections. Now, you must divide them between loyalists, without regard to color, and disloyalists, or you will be the perpetual vassals of the free-trade, irritated, revengeful South. . . . I am for negro suffrage in every rebel State. If it be just, it should not be denied; if it be necessary, it should be adopted; if it be a punishment to traitors, they deserve it.

BILL ON LAND REDISTRIBUTION

Whereas it is due to justice, as an example to future times, that some proper punishment should be inflicted on the people who constituted the "confederate States of America," both because they, declaring an unjust war against the United States for the purpose of destroying republican liberty and permanently establishing slavery, as well as for the cruel and barbarous manner in which they conducted said war, in violation of all the laws of civilized warfare, and also to compel them to make some compensation for the damages and expenditures caused by said war: Therefore,

Be it enacted by the Senate and House of Representatives of the United States of America in Congress assembled, That all the public lands belonging to the ten States that formed the government of the so-called "confederate States of America" shall be forfeited by said States and become forthwith vested in the United States. . . .

That out of the lands thus seized and confiscated the slaves who have been liberated by the operations of the war and the amendment to the Constitution or otherwise, who resided in said "confederate States" on the 4th day of March, A.D. 1861, or since, shall have distributed to them as follows, namely: to each male person who is the head of a family, forty acres; to each adult male, whether the head of a family or not, forty acres; to each widow who is the head of a family, forty acres—to be held by them in fee-simple, but to be inalienable for the next ten years after they become seized thereof. . . .

That out of the balance of the property thus seized and confiscated there shall be raised, in the manner hereinafter provided, a sum equal to fifty dollars, for each homestead, to be applied by the trustees hereinafter mentioned toward the erection of buildings on the said homesteads for the use of said slaves; and the further sum of $500,000,000, which shall be appropriated as follows, to wit: $200,000,000 shall be invested in United States six per cent securities; and the interest thereof shall be semi-annually added to the pensions allowed by law to pensioners who have become so by reason of the late war; $300,000,000, or so much thereof as may be needed, shall be appropriated to pay damages done to loyal citizens by the civil or military operations of the government lately called the "confederate States of America." . . .

That in order that just discrimination may be made, the property of no one shall be seized whose whole estate on the 4th day of March, A.D. 1865, was not worth more than $5,000, to be valued by the said commission, unless he shall have voluntarily become an officer or employé in the military or civil service of the "confederate States of America," or in the civil or military service of some one of said States. . . .

Questions

1. On what grounds did Stevens justify granting African-American men the vote?
2. What did Stevens want to do with land confiscated in the South?
3. Why do you think Congress rejected Stevens's land confiscation and redistribution proposal? Do you think that if Congress had adopted the proposal, it would have made a difference in the history of the South or the United States? Why or why not?

16-6   The Rise and Fall of Northern Support for Reconstruction (1868, 1874)

Evidence of broad northern support for the Republican program could be found in many places other than the ballot box. Illustrations from *Harper's Weekly* such as the one in the text (p. 497) and the one from 1868 titled "This Is a White Man's Government" reflected popular attitudes in the North in the 1860s.

However, northern support for Reconstruction began to erode as early as 1868. For various reasons Republican state governments in the South got a very bad reputation in the North. Northern willingness to use force to keep Republican governments in office in the South, even when threatened by violence, intimidation, and fraud, was exhausted by 1874 (see text p. 503), the year the second *Harper's Weekly* illustration appeared. Both cartoons shown here are by Thomas Nast.

The first cartoon is packed with specific allusions. On the left is a caricature of an Irishman; note the cross and clay pipe in his hatband, which reads "5 POINTS." Five Points, in lower Manhattan, was reputed to be the most dangerous slum in the United States; even police officers did not go there except in groups. Note the liquor bottle in his pocket; his shillelagh reads "A VOTE." Just visible behind him are a black man who has been lynched from a lamppost and the burning Colored Orphan Asylum (references to the 1863 New York City draft riots; see text p. 456 and Document 15-3).

The center figure is Nathan Bedford Forrest (see text pp. 504–505), identifiable from the initials on his hatband. His upraised dagger reads "THE LOST CAUSE"; note also his whip and pistol. His belt buckle carries the initials CSA (for Confederate States of America). Forrest's lapel button—a skull with the words "FORT PILLOW"—recalls the 1864 massacre of African-American soldiers by Forrest's troops (see text p. 501). Behind Forrest a building labeled "SOUTHERN SCHOOL" is burning.

At right a figure representing Big Business holds aloft a bundle of money labeled "CAPITAL FOR VOTES." His lapel button reads "5TH AVENUE," home for many of the wealthy in New York City.

Together, the three figures are crushing an African-American Civil War veteran; note his Union jacket and cap, as well as the saber and the American flag.

Source: Thomas Nast, "This Is a White Man's Government," *Harper's Weekly*, September 5, 1868; Thomas Nast, "Colored Rule in a Reconstructed State," *Harper's Weekly*, March 14, 1874. Art courtesy the Research Libraries, New York Public Library.

Questions

1. Note the picture of African-Americans presented here and in the illustration on text p. 497. Contrast that with the portrayal of government by southern whites.
2. Compare the portrayal of African-Americans in the last illustration with that in the earlier illustrations.
3. What do you think accounts for the change?

COLORED RULE IN A RECONSTRUCTED (?) STATE.—[See Page 242.]

(THE MEMBERS CALL EACH OTHER THIEVES, LIARS, RASCALS, AND COWARDS.)

COLUMBIA. "You are Aping the lowest Whites. If you disgrace your Race in this way you had better take Back Seats."

16-7   *"A Fool's Errand. By One of the Fools"* (1879)

A native of Ohio, Albion Winegar Tourgee (1838–1905) was working as a school-teacher in New York when the Civil War began. In April 1861 he joined the 27th New York Regiment and was wounded at the first battle of Bull Run. He returned to the army in July 1862 as a lieutenant in the 105th Ohio Regiment. Captured in 1863 at Murfreesboro, he returned to Ohio through a prisoner exchange and then rejoined his regiment to fight at Chickamauga, Lookout Mountain, and Missionary Ridge. Twice charged with insubordination, Tourgee resigned his commission in December 1863 and returned to Ohio to study law. By the fall of 1865 he had relocated, as a "carpet-bagger" (see text p. 498), in Greensboro, North Carolina. In 1868, under the electoral rule imposed under radical Reconstruction (see text p. 494), Tourgee won election as a judge on the state superior court. He served there for six years, finding ample opportunity to defend the rights of freedmen and denounce the atrocities of the Ku Klux Klan. When his tenure on the court ended, President Grant appointed him pension agent at Raleigh, from which office he continued his battle with the Klan and with redeemer Democrats (see text pp. 501–503). By the summer of 1879 he had had enough and moved north with his family, making Mayville, New York, his home by 1881. In the novel *A Fool's Errand*, published in the year of his departure from North Carolina, Tourgee described his experiences during Reconstruction through the character Colonel Comfort Servosse, whom he depicted as "the Fool."

Source: [Albion W. Tourgee], *A Fool's Errand. By One of the Fools* (New York: Fords, Howard, & Hulbert, 1878), pp. 182–192.

It was in the winter of 1868-69 . . . when it was said that already Reconstruction had been an approved success, [and] the traces of the war been blotted out . . . a little company of colored men came to the Fool one day; and one of them, who acted as spokesman said,—

"What's dis we hear, Mars Kunnel [Master Colonel], bout de Klux?"

"The what?" he asked.

"De Klux—de Ku-Kluckers dey calls demselves."

"Oh! The Ku-Klux, Ku-Klux-Klan . . . you mean."

"Yes: dem folks what rides about at night a-pesterin' pore colored people, an' pretendin' tu be jes from hell, or some of de battle-fields ob ole Virginny."

"Oh, that's all gammon [humbug]! There is nothing in the world in it,—nothing at all. . . ."

"You don't think dey's ghostes, nor nothing' ob dat sort?" asked another.

"Think! I know they are not."

"So do I," growled one of their number who had not spoken before, in a tone . . . that . . . drew the eyes of the Fool upon him at once.

"So your mind's made up on that point too, is it Bob?" he asked laughingly.

"I know dey's not ghosts, Kunnel. I wish ter God dey was!" was the reply.

"Why, what do you mean, Bob?" asked the colonel in surprise.

"Will you jes help me take off my shirt, Jim?" said Bob . . . as he turned to one of those with him. . . .

"What d'ye tink ob dat, Kunnel?"

"My God!" exclaimed the Fool, starting back in surprise and horror. "What does this mean, Bob?"

"Seen de Kluckers, sah," was the grimly-laconic answer.

The sight which presented itself to the Fool's eyes was truly terrible. . . . The whole back was livid and swollen, bruised as if it had been brayed in a mortar. Apparently, after having cut the flesh with closely-laid welts and furrows, sloping downward from the left side towards the right, with the peculiar skill . . . which could only be obtained through the abundant opportunity for severe . . . flagellation which prevailed under . . . slavery, the operator had changed his position, and scientifically cross-checked the whole. . . . "Nobody but an ole oberseer ebber dun dat, Kunnel." . . . When his clothing had been resumed, he sat down and poured into the wondering ears of the Fool this story:—

BOB'S EXPERIENCE.

"Yer see, I'se a blacksmith at Burke's Cross-Roads. I've been thar ever since a few days arter I heer ob de surrender. I rented an ole house dar, an' put up a sort of shop . . . an' went to work. . . .

"Long a while back—p'raps five er six month—I refused ter du some work fer Michael Anson or his boy, 'cause they'd run up quite a score at de shop, an' allers put me off when I wanted pay. . . . Folks said I waz gettin' too smart fer a nigger, an' sech like; but I kep right on; tole em I waz a free man . . . an' I didn't propose ter do any man's work fer noffin'. Most everybody hed somefin' ter say about it; but it didn't seem ter hurt my trade very much. . . . When ther come an election, I sed my say, did my own votin', an' tole de other colored people dey waz free, an' hed a right ter du de same. Thet's bad doctrine up in our country. . . . Dey don't mind 'bout . . . our votin', so long ez we votes ez day tell us. Dat' dare idea uv liberty fer a nigger.

"Well, here a few weeks ago, I foun' a board stuck up on my shop one mornin', wid dese words on it:—

"'BOB MARTIN,—You're gettin' too dam smart! The white folks round Burke's Cross-Roads don't want any sech smart niggers round thar. You'd better git, er you'll hev a call from the

"'K.K.K.'

. . . [Y]esterday . . . my ole 'ooman . . . tuk part ob de chillen into bed wid her; an' de rest crawled in wid me. . . . I kinder remember hearin' de dog bark, but I didn't mind it; an', de fust ting I knew, de do' was bust in. . . . Dar was 'bout tirty of 'em standin' dar in de moonlight, all dressed in black gowns thet come down to ther boots, an' some sort of high hat on, dat come down ober der faces. . . . Den dey tied me tu a tree, an' done what you've seen. Dey tuk my wife an' oldes' gal out of de house, tore de close right about off 'em, an' abused 'em shockin' afore my eyes. After tarin' tings up a heap in de house, dey rode off, tellin' me dey reckoned I's larn to be 'spectful to white folks here-arter. . . .

"Why have you not complained of this outrage to the authorities?" . . . asked [the Fool] after a moment.

"I tole Squire Haskins an' Judge Thompson what I hev tole you," answered Bob.

"And what did they say?"

"Dat dey couldn't do noffin' unless I could sw'ar to the parties." . . .

There was a moment's silence. Then the colored man asked,—

"Isn't dere no one else, Kunnel, dat could do any ting? Can't de President or Congress do somefin'? De gov'ment sot us free, an' it 'pears like it oughtn't to let our old masters impose on us in no sech way now. . . . We ain't cowards. We showed dat in de wah. I'se seen darkeys go whar de white troops wa'n't anxious to foller 'em, mor'n once."

"Where was that, Bob?"

"Wal, at Fo't Wagner, for one."

"How did you know about that?"

"How did I know 'bout dat? Bress yer soul, Kunnel, I was dar!"

Questions

1. Tourgee, thinly disguised as Comfort Servosse in the novel, depicted himself as "the Fool." Why?
2. Could the president or Congress have acted in ways that they did not to suppress the Ku Klux Klan? Describe the measures you think would have been necessary.
3. Were equal rights for blacks and the restoration of civil government in the South compatible? Explain why or why not.

16-8 Black Farm Owners in the South (1870–1910); Black Homeowners in the South (1870–1910)

During Reconstruction the lives of African-Americans improved significantly, largely as a result of their own efforts. When Reconstruction ended, many of those gains were lost, particularly in the areas of civil and political rights (see text pp. 503, 506). Still, African-Americans continued to improve themselves. As the statistics below indicate, African-Americans after 1870 increasingly joined the ranks of farm owners and home-owners (see text pp. 506–507).

Source: Loren Schweninger, *Black Property Owners in the South, 1790–1915*, pp. 164, 170, 174, 180. Copyright 1990 by the Board of Trustees of the University of Illinois. Used with permission of the University of Illinois Press.

Black Farm Owners in the South, 1870–1910: Total Number and Percentage of Owners (Black and White)

State	1870		1890		Percentage of increase, 1870–1890	1900		Percentage of increase, 1890–1900	1910		Percentage of increase, 1900–1910
	Total	Percentage	Total	Percentage		Total	Percentage		Total	Percentage	
Alabama	1,152	1.3	8,847	13	668	14,110	15	59	17,047	15	21
Arkansas	1,203	5.2	8,004	24	565	11,941	25	49	14,660	23	23
Florida	596	3.5	4,940	38	729	6,551	48	33	7,286	50	11
Georgia	1,367	1.4	8,131	13	495	11,375	14	40	15,698	13	38
Louisiana	1,107	1.8	6,685	18	504	9,378	16	40	10,681	19	14
Mississippi	1,600	1.9	11,526	13	620	20,973	16	82	24,949	15	19
North Carolina	1,628	2.2	10,494	26	545	16,834	31	60	20,707	32	23
South Carolina	3,062	4.0	13,075	21	327	18,970	22	45	20,356	21	7
Tennessee	1,301	2.2	6,378	23	390	9,414	28	48	10,698	28	14
Texas	839	1.8	12,513	26	1,391	20,139	31	61	21,182	30	5
Virginia	860	1.0	13,678	43	1,490	26,527	59	94	32,168	67	21

Black Homeowners* in the South, 1870–1910: Total Number and Percentage of Owners (Black and White)

State	1870		1890		1910	
	Total	Percentage	Total	Percentage	Total	Percentage
Alabama	215	4.3	6,898	11	16,714	17
Arkansas	56	5.3	3,840	17	9,802	27
Florida	46	3.7	5,709	28	13,581	22
Georgia	232	2.9	11,874	12	22,544	16
Louisiana	639	5.7	7,917	11	16,160	16
Mississippi	138	4.5	5,430	11	13,783	20
North Carolina	199	5.6	9,516	15	19,627	26
South Carolina	312	4.8	8,026	11	12,730	15
Tennessee	187	3.0	8,285	16	16,070	23
Texas	27	1.0	8,367	22	20,443	26
Virginia	409	3.3	16,210	20	24,405	27

*Excludes farm homes

Questions

1. Which state(s) had the greatest increase in black farm owners? In black homeowners?
2. What do the tables reveal about African-Americans in the South in an era when they were systematically oppressed by whites?
3. How can you explain this evidence of the success of African-Americans in the South in the late nineteenth century?

Questions for Further Thought

1. What were the principal obstacles faced by radical Republicans as they passed the Civil Rights Acts of 1866 and 1875 as well as the Fourteenth and Fifteenth amendments? Did they successfully overcome those obstacles? Explain why or why not.
2. Do you agree with Tourgee (Document 16-7) that northern Reconstruction efforts were a "Fool's Errand"? Why do you think Tourgee came to that conclusion?
3. Clearly, emancipation and Reconstruction did not bring about equal rights for blacks. But what did change?

The North during Reconstruction

After the Civil War the Republican party remained firmly entrenched in power in the North and, with the implementation of radical Reconstruction, throughout the South as well. The war had offered Republicans an occasion to consolidate a great deal of power in the federal government (see text p. 508), a tendency that left many Americans ill at ease. The Democrats, traditionally the party of limited government, endeavored to free themselves of their proslavery past by presenting themselves as the party of reform. "Stalwart" Republicans remained solidly behind President Grant even as rumors of scandal in his first administration were proved to be true in his second (text pp. 509–511). But "Liberal" Republicans took a more critical look at their party and its leadership. Grant's efforts to push through the annexation of Santo Domingo precipitated a break with Senator Charles Sumner that provided a prominent example of a widening breach in Republican ranks (Document 16-9).

Northerners also grew increasingly uncertain about the future of federally directed Reconstruction in the southern states. Northerners did demand evidence that the South had accepted its defeat. Most northerners found that evidence in the ratification of the Fourteenth and Fifteenth amendments to the Constitution. The question then became a mater of what was to be accomplished by continued federal occupation of southern states. Democrats and Liberal Republicans argued that universal (manhood) suffrage should be accompanied by universal amnesty, that a republican form of government required the participation of all citizens, and that the perpetual disfranchisement of former rebels simply transformed them into an outlaw caste. The willingness of Liberal Republicans to join with Democrats to support Horace Greeley in 1872 (see text p. 510) marked the first significant break in Republican ranks and offered to the Democrats political issues that were free of association with the Civil War. The nomination of Samuel J. Tilden as the Democratic presidential candidate in 1876 changed the dynamics of party politics. Few doubted that Tilden had won the election, but there were enough disputed electoral votes to prevent his inauguration (see text pp. 511–512). Republican efforts to maintain control of the presidency led to the Compromise of 1877 (see text pp. 512–513) and to a new era of two-party politics (Document 16-10).

16-9　"Republicanism vs. Grantism" (1872)

Charles Sumner　　Charles Sumner had come to the U.S. Senate during the first wave of antislavery political insurgency across the North (see Document 14-7). Throughout the Civil War and Reconstruction he had been among the most vehement and politically powerful radical Republicans (see text p. 509). During the Grant administration, however, Sumner frequently opposed the president, most openly by denouncing Grant's efforts to acquire Santo Domingo (the present-day Dominican Republic) as a territory of the United States. Grant loyalists retaliated by deposing Sumner as chairman of the Foreign Relations Committee in 1872. With a remarkable number of former radical Republicans (George Washington Julian among them), Sumner cast his lot with the Liberal Republicans, strongly opposing Grant's reelection and supporting the candidacy of Horace Greeley (see text p. 510). This break in the ranks of the Republicans, specifically the defection of radical Republicans to the Liberal Republican platform of sectional reconciliation, marked the beginning of the end of Reconstruction. Here Sumner denounces "Grantism" (see text p. 510) on the Senate floor.

Source: Charles Sumner: His Complete Works (Lee and Shepard, 1900; reprint, New York: Negro Universities Press, 1969), vol. 20, pp. 83–171.

Mr. President,—I have no hesitation in declaring myself a member of the Republican Party, and one of the straitest of the sect. I doubt if any Senator can point to earlier or more constant service in its behalf. I began at the beginning, and from that early day have never failed to sustain its candidates and to advance its principles. . . .

Turning back to its birth, I recall a speech of my own at a State Convention in Massachusetts, as early as September 7, 1854, where I vindicated its principles and announced its name in these words: "as *Republicans* we go forth to encounter the *Oligarches* of Slavery." . . . The Republican Party was necessary and permanent, and always on an ascending plane. For such a party there was no death, but higher life and nobler aims; and this was the party to which I gave my vows. But, alas, how changed! Once country was the object, and not a man; once principle was inscribed on the victorious banners, and not a name only.

THE REPUBLICAN PARTY SEIZED BY THE PRESIDENT

It is not difficult to indicate when this disastrous change . . . became not merely manifest, but painfully conspicuous . . . suddenly and without any warning through the public press or any expression from public opinion, the President elected by the Republican Party precipitated upon the country an ill-considered and ill-omened scheme for the annexaton of a portion of the island of San Domingo. . . .

PRESIDENTIAL PRETENSIONS

. . . [t]he Presidential office has been used to advance his own family on a scale of nepotism dwarfing everything of

the kind in our history . . . and . . . all these assumptions have matured in a *personal government*, semi-military in character and breathing the military spirit,—being a species of Caesarism or *personalism*, abhorrent to republican institutions. . . . [T]he chosen head of the Republic is known chiefly for Presidential pretensions, utterly indefensible in character, derogatory to the country, and of evil influence, making personal objects a primary pursuit, so that . . . he is a bad example, through whom republican institutions suffer and the people learn to do wrong. . . .

PERSONAL GOVERNMENT UNREPUBLICAN

Personal Government is autocratic. It is the One-Man Power elevated above all else, and is therefore in direct conflict with republican government, whose consummate form is tripartite . . . each independent and coequal. . . .

A government of laws and not of men is the object of republican government; nay, more, it is the distinctive essence without which it becomes a tyranny. Therefore personal government in all its forms, and especially when it seeks to sway the action of any other branch or overturn its constitutional negative, is hostile to the first principles of republican institutions, and an unquestionable outrage. That our President has offended in this way is unhappily too apparent.

THE PRESIDENT AS CIVILIAN

To comprehend the personal government that has been installed over us we must know its author. His picture is the necessary frontispiece,—not as soldier, let it be borne in mind, but as civilian. . . .

To appreciate his peculiar character as a civilian it is

important to know his triumphs as a soldier, for the one is the natural complement of the other. The successful soldier is rarely changed to the successful civilian. There seems to be an incompatibility between the two. . . . One always a soldier cannot late in life become a statesman. . . . Washington and Jackson were civilians as well as soldiers. . . .

THE GREAT PRESIDENTIAL QUARRELER

Any presentment of the President would be imperfect which did not show how this ungovernable personality breaks forth in quarrel, making him the great Presidential quarreler of our history. . . . With the arrogance of arms he resents any impediment in his path,—as when, in the spring of 1870, without allusion to himself, I felt it my duty to oppose his San Domingo contrivance. . . .

DUTY OF THE REPUBLICAN PARTY

And now the question of Duty is distinctly presented to the Republican Party. . . . Do the Presidential pretensions merit the sanction of the party? Can Republicans, without departing from all obligations, whether of party or patriotism, recognize our ambitious Caesar as a proper representative? . . . Therefore with unspeakable interest will the country watch the National Convention at Philadelphia. It may be an assembly (and such is my hope) where ideas and principles are above all personal pretensions, and the unity of the party is symbolized in the candidate; or it may add another to Presidential rings, being an expansion of the military ring at the Executive Mansion, the senatorial ring in the [Senate] Chamber, and the political ring in the customhouses of New York and New Orleans. A National Convention which is a Republican ring cannot represent the Republican Party. . . . I wait the determination of the National Convention. . . . Not without anxiety do I wait, but with the earnest hope that the Convention will bring the Republican Party into ancient harmony, saving it especially from the suicidal folly of an issue on the personal pretensions of one man.

Questions

1. What does Sumner mean when he denounces "personal government"? Why is such a government "unrepublican"?
2. In Sumner's view, why did Grant's military career make him unsuitable for the presidency?
3. Sumner contrasts a party of "principle" with a party of "rings." What does he mean by making this distinction?

16-10　Montgomery Blair on the Compromise of 1877

Like his father, Andrew Jackson's close adviser Francis P. Blair, Montgomery Blair (1813–1883) left the Democratic party for the Republican party in the 1850s. Abraham Lincoln appointed the younger Blair postmaster general, and during the early years of the Civil War Montgomery Blair promoted conservative policies in the Lincoln administration to preserve the loyalties of border state slave owners like himself. After Lincoln settled on a policy of emancipation, Blair's vocal aversion to radical Republicans became a political liability, and Lincoln forced his resignation before the 1864 election. Blair returned to the Democratic party and urged its leaders to leave the "sham" proslavery democracy behind and present the Democratic party to the public as the party of reform. In the following correspondence with Gideon Welles, a fellow conservative (and former Democrat) in Lincoln's cabinet, Blair suggested a new course for the Democrats, reported on the electoral crisis of the 1850s, and analyzed its resolution in the Compromise of 1877 (see text pp. 512–513).

Source: Excerpted by permission from letters of Montgomery Blair to Gideon Welles about the Compromise of 1877, Frank and Montgomery Blair Papers, Missouri Historical Society, St. Louis.

M. Blair to G. Welles, 25 December 1875
Slave Democracy . . . Sham Democracy . . . sacrificed the peace of the country & the blood of [our] . . . countrymen. . . . [T]he Greeley movement got rid of the nasty sectional quarrel which blocked the way to the consideration of any other question. . . . The people see that they are in fact the victims of the monopolies created by the radicals['] abuses in possession of the Govt & that it is their great monied corporations that put Grant in power.

M. Blair to G. Welles, 8 June 1876
The [Democratic] party will have to return to its proper principles & to their proper leaders before we can ever hope to see it installed in power. . . . [I]t is absolutely necessary that the country should see that these followers have turned back to the men of the right school of Democracy. . . . Going to Greeley was not enough. It was not going as far as going to Tilden. . . . It will . . . end the dominance of Radicalism. . . .

M. Blair to G. Welles, 19 June 1876
I have great doubt I confess whether [Tilden] . . . can ever be elected President. But there is a chance now. The Govt. has become so corrupt in the hands of the Radicals that there is a deep & wide [mood] in favor of reform. . . . The time will come when Radicalism will become synonymous in the minds of the people with every thing detestable in Govt. Nothing but power makes our present rulers respectable. . . .

If we put up Tilden he can make an aggressive war upon the Rascality which is now the essence of Radicalism. Being sound in finance and having also sustained the war by contributions of money and speeches, he can fend off on the side issues the rads will try to make—and thus be able to focus on the reform issue & . . . the chaos of Govt. in the hands of the Rad party.

M. Blair to G. Welles, 15 January 1877
The situation here is very complicated, & it is not easy to predict the result. Every day . . . makes it plainer that Tilden is Elected & the enemy will find it difficult to prevent his inauguration. . . . But notwithstanding this there is a . . . class of politicians who are operating with great skill & industry to prevent the inauguration of Tilden. . . . Hayes['] . . . men turn to the southern leaders offering to reconstruct the old whig party at the South & to give up the negro and carpet bag govt. . . . I have no doubt . . . that the Rads are letting S.C. and La slide having already given up Fla.

M. Blair to G. Welles, 19 February 1877
The [electoral] commission is no mystery to me. It resulted from the demoralization of our forces. . . . Besides, I do not think the members of Congress really wanted Tilden here. His advent would put a stop to the system of expenditures which has made it profitable to be in congress. If the result is . . . to infuse a sterner policy on the Democracy we shall have lost nothing by defeat.

M. Blair to G. Welles, 3 March 1877
There never was any intention of inaugurating Tilden.

M. Blair to G. Welles, 20 July 1877
I am afraid the compromise bill will pass notwithstanding its objectionable character. I fear that some of our people do not want Tilden here. Reform after all is not exactly the thing some of them want. . . . But in making these men directly responsible for the defeat of Tilden[,] if he is defeated[,] we open the way for a better understanding of the real nature of the struggle in the future, & get rid of the treacherous leaders. . . .

Questions

1. In Blair's view, what aspects of the Democratic party had to change before it could elect a president?
2. Why does Blair think the "Radicals" are vulnerable in 1876?
3. How did the Republicans gain the support of southern Democrats to secure the inauguration of Hayes over Tilden

Questions for Further Thought

1. How did the Civil War reshape the two-party system?
2. As Grant began his second term, what were the great weaknesses of the Republican and Democratic parties?
3. The Compromise of 1877 achieved sectional reconciliation and ended Reconstruction. Do you view it as smart politics or as a corrupt bargain? Explain why.

CHAPTER 17

The American West

★   ★   ★

The Great Plains

Before the Civil War most Americans were likely to agree with Horace Greeley's assessment of the Great Plains as "a treeless desert" subject to wild temperature extremes (see text p. 520). However, a combination of factors made the plains attractive after the war, and from 1870 to 1890 the population west of the Mississippi grew from 7 million to almost 17 million.

Technology, coupled with the desire for a better life, opened up the Great West (see text pp. 522–523, 526–529). Railroads brought in settlers, sold them land, and shipped their crops to market. The flat farmland lent itself to mechanization: the combine and Kansas wheat seemed made for each other. Despite its sod huts and droughts, the plains offered a chance for land ownership and independence. However, not everyone wanted to spend a lifetime farming. Rather than farm the land, some newcomers extracted gold from it. Countless prospectors hoped to be among the lucky few to strike it rich in California or the Black Hills of South Dakota.

Newly arrived farmers and prospectors shared the land with native American tribes that had settled on the Great Plains long before or had been forced to relocate there by treaties with whites. Coexistence proved impossible (see text pp. 530–534). White settlers believed in individual property rights and social mobility, whereas the Indians they encountered agreed with the Sauk Chief Black Hawk: "Land cannot be sold, nothing can be sold but such things as can be carried away." The violence did not end until the Battle at Wounded Knee (see text pp. 533–534).

In Document 17-1 Charles Siringo recounts the challenge of roping wild steers in Texas during the 1870s. Documents 17-2 and 17-3 detail farm life on the plains. In Document 17-4 Helen Hunt Jackson notes the failure of the U.S. government to keep its promises to native Americans. Congress later attempted to remedy the Indians' plight through the Dawes Severalty Act (Document 17-5).

17-1   The Life of a Texas Cowboy

Charles A. Siringo

Charles A. Siringo (1855–1928) combined the careers of steer-roping cowboy (see text pp. 523, 526) and Western writer. This native of Matagorda County, Texas, also spent twenty-two years with Pinkerton's National Detective Agency. Siringo died in Hollywood, California, where the cowboy legend has taken on a life of its own.

Readers first encountered Siringo's *Texas Cowboy* in 1885.

Source: Charles A. Siringo, *A Texas Cowboy; or, Fifteen Years on the Hurricane Deck of a Spanish Pony, Taken from Real Life* (1885; reprint, Lincoln: University of Nebraska Press, 1966), pp. 45–50.

8. LEARNING TO ROPE WILD STEERS

About the middle of August we pulled out again with a fresh supply of horses, six to the man and a bran[d] new boss, Mr. Wiley Kuykendall.

Some of the boys hated to part with Mr. Nie, but I was glad of the change, for he wouldn't allow me to rope large steers nor fight when I got on the war-path. I remember one time he gave me fits for laying a negro out with a four-year old club; and another time he laid me out with his open hand for trying to carve one of the boys up with a butcher knife.

We commenced work about the first of September on "Big Sandy" in Lavaca county, a place noted for wild "brush" cattle. Very few people lived in that section, hence so many wild unbranded cattle.

To illustrate the class of people who lived on Big Sandy, [I] will relate a little picnic a negro and I had a few days after our arrival there.

While herding a bunch of cattle, gathered the day before, on a small prairie, we noticed a footman emerge from the thick timber on the opposite side from where we were and make straight for a spotted pony that was "hobbled" and grazing out in the open space.

He was indeed a rough looking customer, being half naked. He had nothing on his head but a thick mat of almost gray hair; and his feet and legs were bare.

We concluded to "rope" him and take him to camp, so taking down our ropes and putting spurs to our tired horses we struck out.

He saw us coming and only being about a hundred yards from the spotted pony, he ran to him and cutting the "hobbles," which held his two front legs together, jumped aboard of him and was off in the direction he had just come, like a flash. The pony must have been well trained for he had nothing to guide him with.

A four hundred yard race for dear life brought him to the "brush"—that is timber, thickly covered with an underbrush of live-oak "runners." He shot out of sight like an arrow. He was not a minute too soon, for we were right at his heels.

We gave up the chase after losing sight of him, for we couldn't handle our ropes in the "brush."

The next day the camp was located close to the spot where he disappeared at, and several of us followed up his trail. We found him and his three grown daughters, his wife having died a short while before, occupying a little one room log shanty in a lonely spot about two miles from the little prairie in which we first saw him. The whole outfit were tough looking citizens. The girls had never seen a town, so they said. They had about two acres in cultivation and from that they made their living. Their nearest neighbor was a Mr. Penny, who lived ten miles west and the nearest town was Columbus, on the Colorado river, fifty miles east.

As the cattle remained hidden out in the "brush" during the day-time, only venturing out on the small prairies at night, we had to do most of our work early in the morning, commencing an hour or two before daylight. As you might wish to know exactly how we did, will try and explain:—About two hours before daylight the cook would holloa "chuck," and then Mr. Wiley would go around and yell "breakfast, boys; d——n you get up!" two or three times in our ears.

Breakfast being over we would saddle up our ponies, which had been staked out the night before, and strike out for a certain prairie may be three or four miles off—that is all but two or three men, just enough to bring the herd, previously gathered, on as soon as it became light enough to see.

Arriving at the edge of the prairie we would dismount and wait for daylight.

At the first peep of day the cattle, which would be out in the prairie, quite a distance from the timber, would all turn their heads and commence grazing at a lively rate towards the nearest point of timber. Then we would ride around through the brush, so as not to be seen, until we got to the point of timber that they were steering for.

When it became light enough to see good, we would ride out, rope in hand, to meet them and apt as not one of the old-timers, may be a fifteen or twenty-year old steer, which were continuously on the lookout, would spy us before we got twenty yards from the timber. Then the fun would begin—the whole bunch, may be a thousand head, would stampede and come right towards us. They never were known to run in the opposite direction from the nearest point of timber. But with cattle raised on the prairies, it's the reverse, they will always leave the timber.

After coming in contact, every man would rope and tie down one of the finest animals in the bunch. Once in awhile some fellow would get more beef than he could manage; under those circumstances he would have to worry along until some other fellow got through with his job and came to his rescue.

If there was another prairie close by we would go to it and tie down a few more, but we would have to get there before sunup or they would all be in the brush. It was their habit to graze out into the little prairies at night-fall and go back to the brush by sunrise next morning.

Finally the herd which we had gathered before and which was already "broke in," would arrive from camp, where we had been night-herding them and then we would drive it around to each one of the tied-down animals, letting him up so he couldn't help from running right into the herd, where he would generally stay contented. Once in awhile though, we would strike an old steer that couldn't be made to stay in the herd. Just as soon as he was untied and let up he would go right through the herd and strike for the brush, fighting his way. Under those circumstances we would have to sew up their eyes with a needle and thread. That would bring them to their milk, as they couldn't see the timber.

I got into several scrapes on this trip, by being a new hand at the business. One time I was going at full speed and threw my rope onto a steer just as he got to the edge of the timber; I couldn't stop my horse in time, therefore the steer went on one side of a tree and my horse on the other and the consequence was, my rope being tied hard and fast to the saddle-horn, we all landed up against the tree in a heap.

At another time, on the same day, I roped a large animal and got my horse jerked over backwards on top of me and in the horse getting up he got me all wound up in the rope, so that I couldn't free myself until relieved by "Jack" a negro man who was near at hand. I was certainly in a ticklish predicament that time; the pony was wild and there I hung fast to his side with my head down while the steer, which was still fastened to the rope, was making every effort to gore us.

Just before Christmas Moore selected our outfit to do the shipping at Palacious Point, where a Morgan steamship landed twice a week to take on cattle for the New Orleans market.

We used to ship about five hundred head at each shipping. After getting rid of one bunch we would strike right back, to meet one of the gathering outfits, after another herd. There were three different outfits to do the gathering for us.

We kept that up all winter and had a tough time of it, too, as it happened to be an unusually cold and wet winter.

Towards spring the cattle began to get terribly poor, so that during the cold nights while night-herding them a great many would get down in the mud and freeze to death. Have seen as high as fifty head of dead ones scattered over the ground where the herd had drifted during the night. It's a pity if such nights as those didn't try our nerves.

Sometimes it would be twelve o'clock at night before we would get the cattle loaded aboard of the ship. But when we did get through we would surely have a picnic— filling up on Mr. Geo. Burkheart's red eye. Mr. Burkheart kept a store at the "Point" well filled with Cow Boys delight—in fact he made a specialty of the stuff.

Our camping ground was three miles from the Point, and some mornings the cook would get up and find several saddled horses standing around camp waiting for their corn—their riders having fallen by the wayside.

Questions

1. What were some of the problems and dangers cowboys faced in their work?
2. Using Siringo as an example, describe some characteristics of the typical cowboy of that era.
3. Hollywood has typically portrayed only one kind of cowboy: white. What evidence does Siringo offer of nonwhite cowboys?

17-2 "A Sod House Home"

Cass G. Barns

Cass G. Barns was a young Indiana doctor who decided to leave for Nebraska in 1881 despite a neighbor's warning "against all the ills he had ever heard of, Indians, cowboys, horse thieves, blizzards in winter and cyclones in summer, drouths [sic], hot winds, grasshoppers and rattlesnakes." Barns settled in Madison County, where he practiced medicine, started businesses, edited newspapers, and served as county commissioner and postmaster. In his memoirs, which were published in 1930, Barns describes the dugout and "soddies" that were part of that world (see text pp. 528–529).

Source: Reprinted from *The Sod House*, by Cass G. Barns, pp. 58–61, by permission of the University of Nebraska Press. Copyright 1930 by Cass G. Barns, renewed.

I have had the experience while making my rounds as a physician, to discover a stove pipe protruding from the ground surrounded by prairie grass. An inspection would reveal a door on the side of the ravine. I visited exactly such a dugout once when I hired the homesteader's wife to go home with me to do some work for our family. The excavation was about fourteen feet wide and sixteen feet dug into a hillside. A cook stove, bed, milk safe and a few other articles sufficed for the man and his wife and five children. The dirt floor had become uneven with depressions made by sweeping. The milk safe was blocked up one side to keep it from tipping over. . . .

This particular home had a pig pen near by. Its arrangement was born of necessity. Without fencing or hog house at his command, the homesteader had dug a hole in the ground so deep, and with such steep sides that a brood of pigs occupied it without being able to escape. This homesteader hauled water for household use in his wagon from an older place that possessed a well that was located a mile and a half away.

Another way of making a dugout was made mandatory where the hill was not high enough to leave a natural roof or the ravine was too shallow so an artificial roof had to be prepared. This was made by placing tree logs across the top of the cavity, then a layer of brush, then coarse hay and lastly sods and dirt completed the cover. Through this the stove pipe protruded. This roof had to be guarded to keep stray livestock from falling through it onto the family underneath.

The more pretentious sod houses followed a common plan of a building sixteen feet wide on outside and of variable length. A common house would be twenty feet long but some of them were longer, depending upon the resources of the builder.

The first step in making a new home would be to select the location and then choose the best low spot where the sod would be thickest and strongest. A breaking plow was used to turn over furrows on about half an acre of ground, using care to make the furrows of even width and

thickness so that the home wall would rise evenly. A spade was used to cut the furrow into sod bricks about three feet long. A float made of planks or the forks of a tree or even the wagon drawn by horses or oxen, was used to transport the sod bricks to the building place. The first layer in the wall was made by placing three foot-wide bricks side by side around the foundation except where the door would be located, carefully breaking joints. When the first row was placed, the cracks were filled with fine dirt and two more layers placed on top, all the time breaking joints as a brick layer breaks joints. Every third course was laid crosswise of the others to bind them together. This process was followed till the walls were high enough to take the roof. A door frame had been set on the ground and built around with sods and two window frames placed higher up in the wall, one by the door and the other opposite on the other side of the house. The wall was then carefully trimmed to symmetrical proportions by the use of a sharp spade.

The roof was the next to be considered. The most expensive soddies were made with a framed roof with a ridge peak in the middle, using 2×4 dimension stuff for rafters set on a 2×6 plate on the wall. Sheeting was nailed on the rafters and tar paper spread over the sheeting boards. This was again covered with sods somewhat thinner than the sods used for side walls. These were laid smoothly and the cracks filled with fine clay dirt. Such a roof would shed water very well but the dirt filling between cracks in the sods required renewing as the rains carried it away. The gable ends of the building might be boarded up, otherwise they were sodded up as the side walls had been.

A board floor might be laid and the inside side walls plastered up with the gray colored clay dug from below the black surface dirt, made a very presentable wall when finished. With doors and windows in place such a home with furniture brought from the old home in the east, with perhaps a carpet on the floor and an organ or piano and good furniture, a nice home would have been established that looked well inside even if it was very plain on the outside. But this is a roseate picture of the very few homes where the settler had brought some money with him. The house wall being three feet thick made a surprisingly comfortable home, being warm in winter and cool in summer.

But the settler might not have any money with which to buy boards yet must have a home to shelter his family. He followed the plan used in making the more pretentious sod house as far as he could and the walls were not much unlike the better ones. The roof was the difficult thing to provide and the most of the sod house homesteaders made the roof of crooked limbs, brush, coarse prairie hay and a thick covering of sod and dirt. To hold up such a load a forked tree was planted in each end of the house and a ridge pole log placed from one gable to the other resting in the forks. From the ridge pole to the walls, poles and limbs were laid. They were wonderfully crooked limbs but they covered a home for the homesteader and his family, and were comfortable, even if less prepossessing than the home of the neighbor who could afford a lumber roof to his "soddy."

Questions

1. Describe the construction of a sod house.
2. How would such living quarters affect family life?
3. Why do you think the settlers willingly endured these conditions?

17-3 "Our First Winter on the Prairie"

Hamlin Garland

During the first ten years of his life the novelist Hamlin Garland (1860–1940) lived in Wisconsin, Iowa, and the Dakota Territory. Garland's father was a farmer who seemed intent on proving the validity of Frederick Jackson Turner's frontier thesis (see text p. 248). But for a boy on the Great Plains historical forces mattered less than getting used to life in "this wide, sunny, windy country."

Source: Hamlin Garland, *A Son of the Middle Border* (New York: Macmillan, 1920), pp. 85–98.

For a few days my brother and I had little to do other than to keep the cattle from straying, and we used our leisure in becoming acquainted with the region round about.

It burned deep into our memories, this wide, sunny, windy country. The sky so big, and the horizon line so low and so far away, made this new world of the plain more majestic than the world of the Coulee.—The grasses and many of the flowers were also new to us. On the uplands the herbage was short and dry and the plants stiff and woody, but in the swales the wild oat shook its quivers of barbed and twisted arrows, and the crow's foot, tall and sere, bowed softly under the feet of the wind, while everywhere, in the lowlands as well as on the ridges, the bleaching white antlers of by-gone herbivora lay scattered, testifying to "the herds of deer and buffalo" which once fed there. We were just a few years too late to see them.

To the south the sections were nearly all settled upon, for in that direction lay the county town, but to the north and on into Minnesota rolled the unplowed sod, the feeding ground of the cattle, the home of foxes and wolves, and to the west, just beyond the highest ridges, we loved to think the bison might still be seen.

The cabin on this rented farm was a mere shanty, a shell of pine boards, which needed re-enforcing to make it habitable and one day my father said, "Well, Hamlin, I guess you'll have to run the plow-team this fall. I must help neighbor Button wall up the house and I can't afford to hire another man."

This seemed a fine commission for a lad of ten, and I drove my horses into the field that first morning with a manly pride which added an inch to my stature. I took my initial "round" at a "land" which stretched from one side of the quarter section to the other, in confident mood. I was grown up!

But alas! my sense of elation did not last long. To guide a team for a few minutes as an experiment was one thing—to plow all day like a hired hand was another. It was not a chore, it was a job. It meant moving to and fro hour after hour, day after day, with no one to talk to but the horses. It meant trudging eight or nine miles in the forenoon and as many more in the afternoon, with less than an hour off at noon. It meant dragging the heavy implement around the corners, and it meant also many ship-wrecks, for the thick, wet stubble matted with wild buckwheat often rolled up between the coulter and the standard and threw the share completely out of the ground, making it necessary for me to halt the team and jerk the heavy plow backward for a new start.

Although strong and active I was rather short, even for a ten-year-old, and to reach the plow handles I was obliged to lift my hands above my shoulders; and so with the guiding lines crossed over my back and my worn straw hat bobbing just above the cross-brace I must have made a comical figure. At any rate nothing like it had been seen in the neighborhood and the people on the road to town looking across the field, laughed and called to me, and neighbor Button said to my father in my hearing, "That chap's too young to run a plow," a judgment which pleased and flattered me greatly. . . .

The flies were savage, especially in the middle of the day, and the horses, tortured by their lances, drove badly, twisting and turning in their despairing rage. Their tails were continually getting over the lines, and in stopping to kick their tormentors from their bellies they often got astride the traces, and in other ways made trouble for me. Only in the early morning or when the sun sank low at night were they able to move quietly along their ways.

The soil was the kind my father had been seeking, a smooth dark sandy loam, which made it possible for a lad to do the work of a man. Often the share would go the entire "round" without striking a root or a pebble as big as a walnut, the steel running steadily with a crisp crunching ripping sound which I rather liked to hear. In truth work would have been quite tolerable had it not been so long drawn out. Ten hours of it even on a fine day made about twice too many for a boy.

Meanwhile I cheered myself in every imaginable way. I whistled. I sang. I studied the clouds. I gnawed the beautiful red skin from the seed vessels which hung upon the wild rose bushes, and I counted the prairie chickens as they began to come together in winter flocks running through the stubble in search of food. I stopped now and again to examine the lizards unhoused by the share, tormenting them to make them sweat their milky drops (they were curiously repulsive to me), and I measured the little granaries of wheat which the mice and gophers had deposited deep under the ground, storehouses which the plow had violated. My eyes dwelt enviously upon the sailing hawk, and on the passing of ducks. The occasional shadowy figure of a prairie wolf made me wish for Uncle David and his rifle.

On certain days nothing could cheer me. When the bitter wind blew from the north, and the sky was filled with wild geese racing southward, with swiftly-hurrying clouds, winter seemed about to spring upon me. The horses' tails streamed in the wind. Flurries of snow covered me with clinging flakes, and the mud "gummed" my boots and trouser legs, clogging my steps. At such times I suffered from cold and loneliness—all sense of being a man evaporated. I was just a little boy, longing for the leisure of boyhood.

Day after day, through the month of October and deep into November, I followed that team, turning over two acres of stubble each day. I would not believe this without proof, but it is true! At last it grew so cold that in the early morning everything was white with frost and I was obliged to put one hand in my pocket to keep it warm, while holding the plow with the other, but I didn't mind this so much, for it hinted at the close of autumn. I've no doubt facing the wind in this way was excellent discipline, but I didn't think it necessary then and my heart was sometimes bitter and rebellious.

The soldier did not intend to be severe. As he had always been an early riser and a busy toiler it seemed perfectly natural and good discipline, that his sons should also plow and husk corn at ten years of age. He often told of beginning life as a "bound boy" at nine, and these stories helped me to perform my own tasks without whining. I feared to voice my weakness.

At last there came a morning when by striking my heel upon the ground I convinced the boss that the soil was frozen too deep for the mold-board to break. "All right," he said, "you may lay off this afternoon."

Oh, those beautiful hours of respite! With time to play or read I usually read, devouring anything I could lay my hands upon. Newspapers, whether old or new, or pasted on the wall or piled up in the attic,—anything in print was wonderful to me. One enthralling book, borrowed from neighbor Button, was *The Female Spy*, a Tale of the Rebellion. Another treasure was a story called *Cast Ashore*, but this volume unfortunately was badly torn and fifty pages were missing so that I never knew, and do not know to this day, how those indomitable shipwrecked seamen reached their English homes. I dimly recall that one man carried a pet monkey on his back and that they all lived on "Bustards."

Finally the day came when the ground rang like iron under the feet of the horses, and a bitter wind, raw and gusty, swept out of the northwest, bearing gray veils of sleet. Winter had come! Work in the furrow had ended. The plow was brought in, cleaned and greased to prevent its rusting, and while the horses munched their hay in well-earned holiday, father and I helped farmer Button husk the last of his corn. . . .

The school-house which was to be the center of our social life stood on the bare prairie about a mile to the southwest and like thousands of other similar buildings in the west, had not a leaf to shade it in summer nor a branch to break the winds of savage winter. "There's been a good deal of talk about setting out a wind-break," neighbor Button explained to us, "but nothing has as yet been done." It was merely a square pine box painted a glaring white on the outside and a desolate drab within; at least drab was the original color, but the benches were mainly so greasy and hacked that original intentions were obscured. It had two doors on the eastern end and three windows on each side.

A long square stove (standing on slender legs in a puddle of bricks), a wooden chair, and a rude table in one corner, for the use of the teacher, completed the movable furniture. The walls were roughly plastered and the windows had no curtains.

It was a barren temple of the arts even to the residents of Dry Run, and Harriet and I, stealing across the prairie one Sunday morning to look in, came away vaguely depressed. We were fond of school and never missed a day if we could help it, but this neighborhood center seemed so small and bleak and poor.

With what fear, what excitement we approached the door on that first day, I can only faintly indicate. All the scholars were strange to me except Albert and Cyrus Button, and I was prepared for rough treatment. However, the experience was not so harsh as I had feared. True, Rangely Field did throw me down and wash my face in snow, and Jack Sweet tripped me up once or twice, but I bore these indignities with such grace and could command, and soon made a place for myself among the boys. . . .

I cannot recover much of that first winter of school. It was not an experience to remember for its charm. Not one line of grace, not one touch of color relieved the room's bare walls or softened its harsh windows. Perhaps this very barrenness gave to the poetry in our readers an appeal that seems magical. . . .

This winter was made memorable also by a "revival" which came over the district with sudden fury. It began late in the winter—fortunately, for it ended all dancing and merry-making for the time. It silenced Daddy Fairbanks' fiddle and subdued my mother's glorious voice to a wail. A cloud of puritanical gloom settled upon almost every household. Youth and love became furtive and hypocritic.

The evangelist, one of the old-fashioned shouting, hysterical, ungrammatical, gasping sort, took charge of the services, and in his exhortations phrases descriptive of lakes of burning brimstone and ages of endless torment abounded. Some of the figures of speech and violent gestures of the man still linger in my mind, but I will not set them down on paper. They are too dreadful to perpetuate. At times he roared with such power that he could have been heard for half a mile.

And yet we went, night by night, mother, father, Jessie, all of us. It was our theater. Some of the roughest characters in the neighborhood rose and professed repentance, for a season, even old Barton, the profanest man in the township, experienced a "change of heart."

We all enjoyed the singing, and joined most lustily in the tunes. Even little Jessie learned to sing *Heavenly Wings, There is a Fountain filled with Blood,* and *Old Hundred.*

As I peer back into that crowded little school-room, smothering hot and reeking with lamp smoke, and recall the half-lit, familiar faces of the congregation, it all has the quality of a vision, something experienced in another world. The preacher, leaping, sweating, roaring till the windows rattle, the mothers with sleeping babes in their arms, the sweet, strained faces of the girls, the immobile wondering men, are spectral shadows, figures encountered in the phantasmagoria of disordered sleep.

Questions

1. How did the weather shape life in the Dakota Territory?
2. What did Garland's life as a ten-year-old entail?
3. Was Garland's schooling adequate? Why or why not?

17-4 *A Century of Dishonor*

Helen Hunt Jackson   Born in Amherst, Massachusetts, Helen Hunt Jackson was raised in the New England moral climate that nurtured the abolitionist and women's movements of the mid-nineteenth century (see text pp. 367–379). However, this childhood friend of Emily Dickinson (see text p. 361) showed no interest in reform causes until her second marriage and a move to Colorado in 1875. Ironically, it was during a trip to Boston in 1879 that Jackson heard the Ponca chief Standing Bear speak on the plight of the Plains Indians.

The incident served as a conversion experience, and Jackson began making herself an expert on the history of government-Indian relations. Within two years she published *A Century of Dishonor* (see text p. 532). Not all readers were pleased with Jackson's condemnation of the government for its mistreatment of native Americans. Because the book was "written in good English" by an author "intensely in earnest," Theodore Roosevelt feared that it was "capable of doing great harm."

Source: Helen Hunt Jackson, *A Century of Dishonor* (New York: Harper & Brothers, 1881; reprint, New York: Harper & Row, 1965), pp. 338–342.

In 1869 President Grant appointed a commission of nine men, representing the influence and philanthropy of six leading States, to visit the different Indian reservations, and to "examine all matters appertaining to Indian affairs."

In the report of this commission are such paragraphs as the following: "To assert that 'the Indian will not work' is as true as it would be to say that the white man will not work.

"Why should the Indian be expected to plant corn, fence lands, build houses, or do anything but get food from day to day, when experience has taught him that the product of his labor will be seized by the white man to-morrow? The most industrious white man would become a drone under similar circumstances. Nevertheless, many of the Indians" (the commissioners might more forcibly have said 130,000 of the Indians) "are already at work, and furnish ample refutation of the assertion that 'the Indian will not work.' There is no escape from the inexorable logic of facts.

"The history of the Government connections with the Indians is a shameful record of broken treaties and unfulfilled promises. The history of the border white man's connection with the Indians is a sickening record of murder, outrage, robbery, and wrongs committed by the former, as the rule, and occasional savage outbreaks and unspeakably barbarous deeds of retaliation by the latter, as the exception.

"Taught by the Government that they had rights entitled to respect, when those rights have been assailed by the rapacity of the white man, the arm which should have been raised to protect them has ever been ready to sustain the aggressor.

"The testimony of some of the highest military officers of the United States is on record to the effect that, in our Indian wars, almost without exception, the first aggressions have been made by the white man; and the assertion is supported by every civilian of reputation who has studied the subject. In addition to the class of robbers and outlaws who find impunity in their nefarious pursuits on the frontiers, there is a large class of professedly reputable men who use every means in their power to bring on Indian wars for the sake of the profit to be realized from the presence of troops and the expenditure of Government funds in their midst. They proclaim death to the Indians at all times in words and publications, making no distinction between the innocent and the guilty. They irate the lowest class of men to the perpetration of the darkest deeds against their victims, and as judges and jurymen shield them from the justice due to their crimes. Every crime committed by a white man against an Indian is concealed or palliated. Every offence committed by an Indian against a white man is borne on the wings of the post or the telegraph to the remotest corner of the land, clothed with all the horrors which the reality or imagination can throw around it. Against such influences as these the people of the United States need to be warned."

To assume that it would be easy, or by any one sudden stroke of legislative policy possible, to undo the mischief and hurt of the long past, set the Indian policy of the country right for the future, and make the Indians at once safe and happy, is the blunder of a hasty and uninformed judgment. The notion which seems to be growing more prevalent, that simply to make all Indians at once citizens of the United States would be a sovereign and instantaneous panacea for all their ills and all the Government's perplexities, is a very inconsiderate one. To administer complete citizenship of a sudden, all round, to all Indians, barbarous and civilized alike, would be as grotesque a blunder as to dose them all round with any one medicine, irrespective of the symptoms and needs of their diseases. It would kill more than it would cure. Nevertheless, it is true, as was well stated by one of the superintendents of Indian Affairs in 1857, that, "so long as they are not citizens of the United States, their rights of property must remain insecure against invasion. The doors of the federal tribunals being barred against them while wards and dependents, they can only partially exercise the rights of free government, or give to those who make, execute, and construe the few laws they are allowed to enact, dignity sufficient to make them respectable. While they continue individually to gather the crumbs that fall from the table of the United States, idleness, improvidence, and indebtedness will be the rule, and industry, thrift, and freedom from debt the exception. The utter absence of individual title to particular lands deprives every one among them of the chief incentive to labor and exertion—the very mainspring on which the prosperity of a people depends."

All judicious plans and measures for their safety and salvation must embody provisions for their becoming citizens as fast as they are fit, and must protect them till then in every right and particular in which our laws protect other "persons" who are not citizens.

There is a disposition in a certain class of minds to be impatient with any protestation against wrong which is unaccompanied or unprepared with a quick and exact scheme of remedy. This is illogical. When pioneers in a new country find a tract of poisonous and swampy wilderness to be reclaimed, they do not withhold their hands from fire and axe till they see clearly which way roads should run, where good water will spring, and what crops will best grow on the redeemed land. They first clear the swamp. So with this poisonous and baffling part of the domain of our national affairs—let us first "clear the swamp."

However great perplexity and difficulty there may be in the details of any and every plan possible for doing at this late day anything like justice to the Indian, however hard it may be for good statesmen and good men to agree upon the things that ought to be done, there certainly is, or ought to be, no perplexity whatever, no difficulty whatever, in agreeing upon certain things that ought not to be done, and which must cease to be done before the first steps can be taken toward righting the wrongs, curing the ills, and wiping out the disgrace to us of the present condition of our Indians.

Cheating, robbing, breaking promises—these three are clearly things which must cease to be done. One more thing, also, and that is the refusal of the protection of the law to the Indian's rights of property, "of life, liberty, and the pursuit of happiness."

When these four things have ceased to be done, time, statesmanship, philanthropy, and Christianity can slowly and surely do the rest. Till these four things have ceased to be done, statesmanship and philanthropy alike must work in vain, and even Christianity can reap but small harvest.

Questions

1. Why did official reports critical of U.S. government policy toward native Americans not have a greater effect on the American public?
2. What was the importance of granting citizenship to Indians? What problems with granting citizenship does Jackson see?
3. What was Jackson's prescription for improved relations with native Americans?

17-5   The Dawes Severalty Act (1887)

Congress responded to Helen Hunt Jackson and other critics of its Indian policy with the Dawes Severalty Act of 1887 (see text pp. 532–533). The act attempted to "mainstream" Indians into American society: reservations were to be abolished, and Indians were to be transformed into land-owning individuals. The act accomplished little beyond reducing the amount of land under Indian control, and the reservation policy was revived in the 1930s.

Source: United States, *Statutes at Large*, vol. 24, pp. 388ff.

Be it enacted by the Senate and House of Representatives of the United States of America in Congress assembled, That in all cases where any tribe or band of Indians has been, or shall hereafter be, located upon any reservation created for their use, either by treaty stipulation or by virtue of an act of Congress or executive order setting apart the same for their use, the President of the United States be, and he hereby is, authorized, whenever in his opinion any reserva-tion or any part thereof of such Indians is advantageous for agricultural and grazing purposes, to cause said reservation, or any part thereof, to be surveyed, or resurveyed if necessary, and to allot the lands in said reservation in severalty to any Indian located thereon in quantities as follows:

To each head of a family, one-quarter of a section;

To each single person over eighteen years of age, one-eighth of a section;

To each orphan child under eighteen years of age, one-eighth of a section; and

To each other single person under eighteen years now living, or who may be born prior to the date of the order of the President directing an allotment of the lands embraced in any reservation, one-sixteenth of a section: *Provided*, That in case there is not sufficient land in any of said reservations to allot lands to each individual of the classes above named in quantities as above provided, the lands embraced in such reservation or reservations shall be allotted to each individual of each of said classes pro rata in accordance with the provisions of this act: *And provided further*, That where the treaty or act of Congress setting apart such reservation provides for the allotment of lands in severalty in quantities in excess of those herein provided, the President, in making allotments upon such reservation, shall allot the lands to each individual Indian belonging thereon in quantity as specified in such treaty or act: *And provided further*, That when the lands allotted are only valuable for grazing purposes, an additional allotment of such grazing lands, in quantities as above provided, shall be made to each individual. . . .

And provided further, That at any time after lands have been allotted to all the Indians of any tribe as herein provided, or sooner if in the opinion of the President it shall be for the best interests of said tribe, it shall be lawful for the Secretary of the Interior to negotiate with such Indian tribe for the purchase and release by said tribe, in conformity with the treaty or statute under which such reservation is held, of such portions of its reservation not allotted as such tribe shall, from time to time, consent to sell, on such terms and conditions as shall be considered just and equitable between the United States and said tribe of Indians, which purchase shall not be complete until ratified by Congress, and the form and manner of executing such release shall also be prescribed by Congress: *Provided however*, That all lands adapted to agriculture, with or without irrigation so sold or released to the United States by any Indian tribe shall be held by the United States for the sole purpose of securing homes to actual settlers and shall be disposed of by the United States to actual and bona fide settlers only in tracts not exceeding one hundred and sixty acres to any one person, on such terms as Congress shall prescribe, subject to grants which Congress may

make in aid of education: *And provided further*, That no patents shall issue therefor except to the person so taking the same as and for a homestead, or his heirs, and after the expiration of five years occupancy thereof as such homestead; and any conveyance of said lands so taken as a homestead, or any contract touching the same, or lien thereon, created prior to the date of such patent, shall be null and void. And the sums agreed to be paid by the United States as purchase money for any portion of any such reservation shall be held in the Treasury of the United States for the sole use of the tribe or tribes of Indians; to whom such reservations belonged; and the same, with interest thereon at three per cent per annum, shall be at all times subject to appropriation by Congress for the education and civilization of such tribe or tribes of Indians or the members thereof. . . . And hereafter in the employment of Indian police, or any other employes in the public service among any of the Indian tribes or bands affected by this act, and where Indians can perform the duties required, those Indians who have availed themselves of the provisions of this act and become citizens of the United States shall be preferred.

SEC. 6. That upon the completion of said allotments and the patenting of the lands to said allottees, each and every member of the respective bands or tribes of Indians to whom allotments have been made shall have the benefit of and be subject to the laws, both civil and criminal, of the State or Territory in which they may reside; and no Territory shall pass or enforce any law denying any such Indian within its jurisdiction the equal protection of the law. And every Indian born within the territorial limits of the United States to whom allotments shall have been made under the provisions of this act, or under any law or treaty, and every Indian born within the territorial limits of the United States who has voluntarily taken up, within said limits, his residence separate and apart from any tribe of Indians therein, and has adopted the habits of civilized life, is hereby declared to be a citizen of the United States, and is entitled to all the rights, privileges, and immunities of such citizens, whether said Indian has been or not, by birth or otherwise, a member of any tribe of Indians within the territorial limits of the United States without in any manner impairing or otherwise affecting the right of any such Indian to tribal or other property.

Questions

1. What was the stated purpose of this act?
2. Why did Congress offer citizenship to native Americans?
3. To what extent was the Dawes Act coercive?

Questions for Further Thought

1. Where is the romance in the kind of life Charles Siringo (Document 17-1) describes? What is it about modern life that makes the cowboy so appealing by comparison?
2. Using Documents 17-1 through 17-3 as background, consider how conditions on the Great Plains might have affected settlers' attitudes toward native Americans.
3. Note the way land was used by ranchers and farmers. Did the growth of those activities make it inevitable that the 1800s would be a century of dishonor in government-Indian relations (Documents 17-4)? Why or why not?

California and the Far West

Perhaps its distance from the rest of the country has made California the subject of so many dreams. Early prospectors in California could only imagine the riches awaiting them. However, California and the Far West were by no means empty when gold was discovered at Sutter's Mill in 1848: Spaniards and Mexicans had come long before (see text p. 535). When the region fell to the United States after the Mexican War, white America found itself in control of a decidedly Hispanic territory and culture (see text pp. 538–540).

Hispanics were not the only new group encountered in the Far West; there were also Navajos, Apaches, and Utes, along with Chinese immigrants. Like the forty-niners, the Chinese were first attracted by gold; they provided much of the labor for the construction of the Central Pacific Railroad (see text pp. 540–541). The Chinese formed their own ethnic enclaves and took low-paying jobs; other immigrant groups followed the same path in the slow climb up the ladder of class mobility. But the Chinese were perceived as different, and in 1882 Congress made them the first immigrant group to be excluded from this country (see text p. 541).

Documents 17-6 and 17-7 deal with the Chinese experience: the ordeal of railroad workers and white Americans' attempts to restrict immigration. In Document 17-8, John Muir describes some of the natural beauty that has drawn Americans to California for over 150 years.

17-6 Chinese Laborers on the Central Pacific Railroad

The famed meeting of the Union and Central Pacific railroads at Promontory Point, Utah, would have been impossible without immigrant labor (see text p. 540). Laying track was backbreaking work, and the mountainous terrain added to the danger. In deciding to use over 10,000 Chinese laborers, the Central Pacific had no problem discarding racial stereotypes of Asiatic weakness. As the railroad executive Charles Crocker explained (see text p. 540), "Wherever we put them, we found them good."

The following newspaper account gives a sense of the work involved and the respect the Chinese earned—albeit temporarily—for their efforts.

Source: Stuart Daggett, *Chapters on the History of the Southern Pacific* (New York: Ronald Press, 1922).

The Central Pacific Railroad—The Front—Wednesday, April 28. It is daybreak. The scene is in the Valley of Salt Lake. Around the edge of what at some remote period must have been the shore of that great inland sea, is to be performed a day's work for which no parallel can be found in the history of the world—the laying of ten miles of rail. Standing here upon the rising ground, a view of the whole field may be obtained. Yonder is the Lake, glistening in the morning sun. Along the line of the road may be seen the white camps of the Chinese laborers, and from every one of them squads of these people are advancing to the great battle with that old enemy of mankind—space. There is a jaunty air about the Oriental as he marches along; he has a woolen peaked cap, with ear flaps. He brings up rather the idea of an ancient crusader more than that of a coolie laborer. The enthusiasm of the occasion has evidently brought even him within its influence, and the Caucasian part of the force is worked up to the highest pitch of excitement.

HOW THE RAILS ARE CARRIED FORWARD AND LAID DOWN

The failure of the day before, caused by one of the engines attached to the train conveying the iron to the front running off the track just as two miles had been laid, nerved every man of them to such careful exertion that no accident could possibly occur. See that car loaded with iron coming up the track. It is wheeled along by a pair of horses, tandem fashion, after the manner of canal boats, the horses galloping at the side of the track. They are met by another car of a similar pattern coming down, after leaving its load at the front. This latter is bowled along (for the grade descends) by the men on each side, using their feet like oars. Surely this must be *contretemp* [*contretemps*, a mishap], for vehicles cannot pass on a single track—but stop—the down platform car stopped in an instant, it is lifted up, standing on the edge, and the loaded car passes on to the front without interruption. Arrived there, two men throw a wooden bar across the wheels to stop the motion, the horses are detached and gallop back to the rear. The two outer rails of the road on either side are seized, with iron nippers, hauled forward by four men, and laid on the ties over them; the car goes forward, and at it comes a gang of men, who half drive the spikes and screw on the fresh bolts. At a short interval behind them comes the first party of Chinamen, who drive home the spikes and add

others. Behind them again, advances a second squad of Chinamen, two deep, on either side of the track. The inner line with shovels, the outer with picks. The pickaxe men loosen a shovelful of earth; it is picked up by the inner line and thrown about the ends of the ties. An idea of the speed attained may be obtained from figures. I timed the movement twice, and found the speed to be as follows: First time, 240 feet of rail laid in one minute and twenty seconds; second time, 240 feet in one minute and fifteen seconds. This is about as fast as a leisurely walk—as fast as the early ox teams used to travel over the Plains. It may seem incredible, but it is nevertheless the fact, that the whole ten miles of rail were handled and laid down this day by eight white men.

But we have here only taken in a portion of the scene. Along the line are overseers galloping up and down, seeing that everything is properly done. Right at the front sits Mr. Charles Crocker, the General Superintendent. . . . The eye of Mr. Crocker takes in every detail of the operation, and his merry laugh when anything amusing takes place awakens the long-slumbering echoes.

By six o'clock two miles are laid, and a train containing two more miles of rail is pushed forward from the rear. It steams up to the last rail just laid; a squad of men rush at it; it took exactly ten minutes to unload it. There are one hundred tons of iron to the mile, so that two hundred tons of iron, together with ten tons of spikes were unloaded within the time stated. Then the iron cars are loaded, and are started off one after another, as already described. While this advance is made along the line, the ties are being hauled along by a parallel road on the right, while the water-carts and tool wagons move on the left.

By noon there is no longer any doubt that the great feat will be successfully accomplished. In six hours and forty-two minutes six miles of track were laid, but here are these 1,200 or 1,400 men to be fed. They have advanced six miles from a home from which they started. Look far to the rear and behold a strange phenomenon; it looks like a village of one street in motion. This is the boarding-house train, composed of a number of plain wooden-house cars with peaked roofs. Here are the bunks of the workmen, arranged after the manner of the steerage of a ship; and likewise their dining-rooms. I have seen the men at their meals and inspected their food. They are fed like fighting cocks. Their bread and meat are of the very best description, and as soon as the implements are thrown down the boarding-house train is at hand, and the white laborers retire to their dinner. The Chinamen bring their food with them and dine on the line of work.

So far as I have been able to observe there was not the slightest antagonism between the two races engaged on the works of the Central Pacific. Passing along this line of Chinamen, I hear the Caucasian commander of the gang singing out, "Hurry up there, ye devils, shure we have no time to lose," and the answer comes from the whole squad, in a laughing manner, "Tach I Yah," which I inferred meant, "Ready and begorra, we do that same," for a closing up of the ranks, a brisker gait and a livelier movement of shovels and pick-axes immediately followed.

Questions

1. What were some of the activities of a Chinese work gang?
2. What kinds of racial stereotypes were used in describing Chinese laborers?
3. How does the writer imply at the end of the document that other immigrant laborers were involved in railroad construction?

17-7   The Chinese Exclusion Act (1882)

Immigration has always made Americans uneasy, in part because of the fear that newcomers will not be assimilated. Chinese immigrants provoked extreme anxiety on the West Coast with their different language, customs, and dress. Congress responded to the pleas of nativists by passing the Chinese Exclusion Act in 1882 (see text p. 541).

Source: United States, *Statutes at Large*, vol. 22, pp. 58ff.

Whereas, in the opinion of the Government of the United States the coming of Chinese laborers to this country endangers the good order of certain localities within the territory thereof: Therefore,

Be it enacted by the Senate and House of Representatives of the United States of America in Congress assembled, That from and after the expiration of ninety days next after the passage of this act, and until the expiration of ten years next after the passage of this act, the coming of Chinese laborers to the United States be, and the same is hereby, suspended; and during such suspension it shall not be lawful for any Chinese laborer to come, or, having so come after the expiration of said ninety days, to remain within the United States. . . .

SEC. 4. That for the purpose of properly identifying Chinese laborers who were in the United States on the seventeenth day of November, eighteen hundred and eighty, or who shall have come into the same before the expiration of ninety days next after the passage of this act, and in order to furnish them with the proper evidence of their right to go from and come to the United States of their free will and accord, as provided by the treaty between the United States and China dated November seventeenth, eighteen hundred and eighty, the collector of customs of the district from which any such Chinese laborer shall depart from the United States shall, in person or by deputy, go on board each vessel having on board any such Chinese laborer and cleared or about to sail from his district for a foreign port, and on such vessel make a list of all such Chinese laborers, which shall be entered in registry-books to be kept for that purpose, in which shall be stated the name, age, occupation, last place of residence, physical marks or peculiarities, and all facts necessary for the identification of each of such Chinese laborers, which books shall be safely kept in the custom-house; and every such Chinese laborer so departing from the United States shall be entitled to, and shall receive, free of any charge or cost upon application therefor, from the collector or his deputy, at the time such list is taken, a certificate, signed by the collector or his deputy and attested by his seal of office, in such form as the Secretary of the Treasury shall prescribe, which certificate shall contain a statement of the name, age, occupation, last place of residence, personal description, and facts of identification of the Chinese laborer to whom the certificate is issued, corresponding with the said list and registry in all particulars. . . .

SEC. 14. That hereafter no State court or court of the United States shall admit Chinese to citizenship; and all laws in conflict with this act are hereby repealed.

Questions

1. What does the omission of specific reasons for barring the Chinese from this country indicate about the motivations of Congress?
2. How did sections 4 and 14 affect Chinese immigrants?
3. What does the act suggest about the attitude of Americans toward the Chinese?

17-8 "Hetch Hetchy Valley"

John Muir

In 1849 the eleven-year-old John Muir came to the United States with his family from Scotland. Muir's interest in nature was nurtured by the family's settling in rural Wisconsin. As a young man Muir made walking trips through the Midwest and Canada before embarking on a thousand-mile trek to the Gulf of Mexico.

Muir's passionate love of nature led to his founding of the Sierra Club in 1892 and his support for the creation of Yosemite National Park (see text pp. 542–543). Muir (1838–1914) was less a conservationist than a preservationist who wanted nature to be saved for its own sake. When San Francisco moved in 1913 to improve its water supply system, the plan called for damming the Hetch Hetchy Valley in Yosemite. Even Muir's eloquent defense of the valley could not save it.

Source: John Muir, *The Mountains of California* (Boston and New York: Houghton Mifflin Company, 1917), vol. 2, pp. 278–290.

Yosemite is so wonderful that we are apt to regard it as an exceptional creation, the only valley of its kind in the world; but Nature is not so poor as to have only one of anything. Several other yosemites have been discovered in the Sierra that occupy the same relative positions on the range and were formed by the same forces in the same kind of granite. One of these, the Hetch Hetchy Valley, is in the Yosemite National Park, about twenty miles from Yosemite, and is easily accessible to all sorts of travelers by a road and trail that leaves the Big Oak Flat road at Bronson Meadows a few miles below Crane Flat, and to mountaineers by way of Yosemite Creek basin and the head of the middle fork of the Tuolumne.

It is said to have been discovered by Joseph Screech, a hunter, in 1850, a year before the discovery of the great Yosemite. After my first visit to it in the autumn of 1871, I have always called it the "Tuolumne Yosemite," for it is a wonderfully exact counterpart of the Merced Yosemite, not only in its sublime rocks and waterfalls but in the gardens, groves and meadows of its flowery park-like floor. The floor of Yosemite is about four thousand feet above the sea; the Hetch Hetchy floor about thirty-seven hundred feet. And as the Merced River flows through Yosemite, so does the Tuolumne through Hetch Hetchy. The walls of both are of gray granite, rise abruptly from the floor, are sculptured in the same style and in both every rock is a glacier monument.

Standing boldly out from the south wall is a strikingly picturesque rock called by the Indians, Kolana, the outermost of a group twenty-three hundred feet high, corresponding with the Cathedral Rocks of Yosemite both in relative position and form. On the opposite side of the Valley, facing Kolana, there is a counterpart of El Capitan that rises sheer and plain to a height of eighteen hundred feet, and over its massive brow flows a stream which makes the most graceful fall I have ever seen. From the edge of the cliff to the top of an earthquake talus it is perfectly free in the air for a thousand feet before it is broken into cascades among talus boulders. It is in all its glory in June, when the snow is melting fast, but fades and vanishes toward the end of summer. The only fall I know with which it may fairly be compared is the Yosemite Bridal Veil; but it excels even that favorite fall both in height and airy-fairy beauty and behavior. Lowlanders are apt to suppose that mountain streams in their wild career over cliffs lose control of themselves and tumble in a noisy chaos of mist and spray.

On the contrary, on no part of their travels are they more harmonious and self-controlled. Imagine yourself in Hetch Hetchy on a sunny day in June, standing waist-deep in grass and flowers (as I have often stood), while the great pines sway dreamily with scarcely perceptible motion. . . .

It appears, therefore, that Hetch Hetchy Valley, far from being a plain, common, rock-bound meadow, as many who have not seen it seem to suppose, is a grand landscape garden, one of Nature's rarest and most precious mountain temples. As in Yosemite, the sublime rocks of its walls seem to glow with life, whether leaning back in repose or standing erect in thoughtful attitudes, giving welcome to storms and calms alike, their brows in the sky, their feet set in the groves and gay flowery meadows, while birds, bees, and butterflies help the river and waterfalls to stir all the air into music—things frail and fleeting and types of permanence meeting here and blending, just as they do in Yosemite, to draw her lovers into close and confiding communion with her.

Sad to say, this most precious and sublime feature of the Yosemite National Park, one of the greatest of all our natural resources for the uplifting joy and peace and health of the people, is in danger of being dammed and made into a reservoir to help supply San Francisco with water and light, thus flooding it from wall to wall and burying its gardens and groves one or two hundred feet deep. This grossly destructive commercial scheme has long been planned and urged (though water as pure and abundant can be got from sources outside of the people's park, in a dozen different places), because of the comparative cheapness of the dam and of the territory which it is sought to divert from the great uses to which it was dedicated in the Act of 1890 establishing the Yosemite National Park.

The making of gardens and parks goes on with civilization all over the world, and they increase both in size and number as their value is recognized. Everybody needs beauty as well as bread, places to play in and pray in, where Nature may heal and cheer and give strength to body and soul alike. This natural beauty-hunger is made manifest in the little windowsill gardens of the poor, though perhaps only a geranium slip in a broken cup, as well as in the carefully tended rose and lily gardens of the rich, the thousands of spacious city parks and botanical gardens, and in our magnificent national parks—the Yellowstone, Yosemite, Sequoia, etc.—Nature's sublime wonderlands, the admiration and joy of the world. Nevertheless, like anything else worth while, from the very beginning, however well guarded, they have always been subject to attack by despoiling gain-seekers and mischiefmakers of every degree from Satan to Senators, eagerly trying to make everything immediately and selfishly commercial, with schemes disguised in smug-smiling philanthropy, industriously, shampiously crying, "Conservation, conservation, panutilization," that man and beast may be fed and the dear Nation made great. Thus long ago a few enterprising merchants utilized the Jerusalem temple as a place of business instead of a place of prayer, changing money, buying and selling cattle and sheep and doves; and earlier still, the first forest reservation, including only one tree, was likewise despoiled. Ever since the establishment of the Yosemite National Park, strife has been going on around its borders and I suppose this will go on as part of the universal battle between right and wrong, however much its boundaries may be shorn, or its wild beauty destroyed. . . .

These temple destroyers, devotees of ravaging commercialism, seem to have a perfect contempt for Nature, and, instead of lifting their eyes to the God of the mountains, lift them to the Almighty Dollar.

Dam Hetch Hetchy! As well dam for watertanks the people's cathedrals and churches, for no holier temple has ever been consecrated by the heart of man.

Questions

1. What did Muir find important about Hetch Hetchy?
2. What is the connection between the Temple of Solomon (the "Jerusalem temple") and the valley?
3. How does Muir's failure to address the practical concerns of San Franciscans affect the thrust of his argument?

Questions for Further Thought

1. Using both the railroad account (Document 17-6) and the reaction to Chinese immigration (see also text pp. 540–541) as background, consider whether government has the right to restrict immigration. Why or why not?
2. What are the differing views of nature offered in the account of railroad construction and John Muir's defense of Hetch Hetchy (Document 17-8)?

3. If you were John Muir, how would you have appealed to the people of San Francisco in defending Hetch Hetchy?

The Agricultural Interest

Thomas Jefferson believed that farmers were "the chosen people of God," but Jefferson never had to contend with locusts and hail. Those were only two of the problems facing farmers on the Great Plains.

Weather extremes and physical isolation made farm life hard on all family members; something as simple as a mail-order catalogue formed a vital link to the less harsh, more familiar world back east. Innovations such as the railroad, barbed wire, and scientific cultivating methods allowed farmers to become part of the national economy, but not easily (see text pp. 543–547).

Despite their mythical standing as the moral backbone of the nation, farmers could not afford to ignore the business side of agriculture (see text pp. 543–545). They had to know which crops to grow and when to harvest, and they had to decide whether the new machinery was worth the cost. Too little or too much rain could reduce a farm to a bad debt. However, nature was not the only challenge. Farmers were particularly dependent on the railroads, which exploited their advantage by setting exorbitant rates for shipping crops to market (see text p. 546). Furthermore, no matter how good the growing season, farmers worried that their buying power was being eroded by the decisions of faceless bankers and politicians. The only solution appeared to be organized political protest (see text pp. 546–547).

Documents 17-9 and 17-10 show American farmers much as they saw themselves: naive, but still capable of defending their position in society.

17-9   "Farmer Green's Reaper" (1874)

Midwestern farmers believed in the virtues of hard work and perseverance, which had worked for their fathers and were supposed to work for everyone else. The changes wrought by commercial agriculture caught many farmers unprepared (see text pp. 543–545), as shown in this 1874 Granger story about Farmer Green's reaper.

Source: Edward Winslow Martin, *History of the Grange Movement; or, The Farmer's War against Monopolies* (Chicago: National Publishing Company, 1874), pp. 339–346.

The sad history of Farmer Green (a veritable character, although we introduce him here by a fictitious name) should be a lesson and a warning to all his brethren.

Farmer Green was a resident of Iowa, and was reputed to be a sensible and prosperous man. He was far on in life, and had cleared his farm of debt, had stocked it with many things needful to his business, and was generally counted a prosperous man. His snug farm was his pride and boast,

and he looked forward to the time when he should be able to add to it by the purchase of a desirable section of land adjoining it.

It was the early summer, and Farmer Green was rejoicing in the magnificent crop of wheat that was springing up on his land, and giving the promise of a handsome return for his care and labor. Day after day he watched the superb growth, and counted over in his mind the number of bushels of golden grain it would yield when the summer sun had warmed it into maturity. Many were the plans he laid for the use of the proceeds of that glorious crop. The goodwife's wants should be all supplied this year, and none of the children should be forced to put up with the deprivations that had fallen to their lot when he was still struggling to clear the farm from its encumbrance of debt.

One day, as he stood watching the bright field of green that spread out before him, and imagining what he would do when the grain was harvested and the money received for it, he was accosted by a stranger who came driving down the road from the village.

"A beautiful crop of wheat you've got there," said the stranger, as he drew rein before the farm gate.

"Yes," said Farmer Green, "I reckon it will turn out pretty well."

"A fine farm you have, too," said the stranger, glancing admiringly around him.

"Yes," said the farmer, pleased with the compliment to his place. "There's none better in the neighborhood."

"Paid for yet?" asked the stranger.

"Every dollar, thank God," said the owner, heartily. "It's clear at last, and I hope to keep it so."

"That's right," said the stranger. "Never contract a debt you're not sure of paying, and the farm will remain yours. That's a mighty nice crop of wheat," he added, as if speaking to himself. "I never saw anything look prettier. It will be ready for cutting soon. How do you cut it? By hand?"

"Yes," replied the farmer. "We've no reapers in this part of the country, and we farm in the oldfashioned way."

"That's a pity," said the stranger. "A reaper would work beautifully on this land. Why it would be no trouble at all to get your wheat in with a good reaper."

"That's true," said Farmer Green.

"You ought to have a reaper to cut it with," said the stranger.

"Can't afford it; haven't got the money to spare," said the farmer.

"See here, now," said the stranger, in a more confidential tone. "I'm selling a patent reaper—a first-class machine, and dirt-cheap at the money asked for it. You'd better let me sell you one."

"It's no use to talk about it, my friend. I haven't the money to spare."

"I don't want your money now," said the man, temptingly. "I'll sell you one at a bargain, and wait till it has paid for itself."

And with that the agent produced pencil and paper, and went into a calculation, showing the farmer how much it would cost him to cut his crop that year, and how much the reaper would save him, as well as a calculation of the amount of grain he could cut for other farmers in the vicinity.

"So you see," added the agent, persuasively, "before the time of payment comes around you will have saved and earned enough to pay for the reaper, and will still have a fine machine capable of doing more work, equally profitable, next season."

Farmer Green's better judgment bade him refuse the terms thus offered, liberal as they seemed. He knew the evil consequences of running into debt, and his conscience bade him put the temptation behind him. He wanted a reaper, however; he had always wanted one; and here was an opportunity of purchasing one upon terms which would enable him to pay for it out of its actual earnings. There was not a reaper in the county, and he felt confident that he would be able to keep it busy on his neighbors' farms, all through the season, after he had cut his own crop.

The agent was a smooth tongued, plausible fellow, and he plied the farmer with every argument he was master of. The result was that the farmer bought the reaper. He had not the money to pay for it, but he gave what is called in Iowa "an iron-clad note" for it. In plainer English, he gave his note accompanied with a statement of property. By the laws of Iowa such a note is equivalent to a mortgage. And so, in order to purchase the reaper, the farmer had imperilled his property, and had placed the safety of his home upon the turn of a chance.

The machine arrived in due time, and was found to be all the agent had claimed for it. It was a capital reaper, and a very handsome machine withal. Farmer Green could not help feeling a little downhearted as he remembered the risk he had incurred in order to obtain it; but he consoled himself with the hope that he would be able to make it pay for itself. When the harvest came around, the machine proved itself a good worker. Farmer Green soon had his crop cut and stacked, and then began to look about him for engagements for cutting his neighbors' grain. Some were willing to make the trial, and a few jobs of this kind enabled him to earn something with his reaper. But the work was less in amount than he had looked forward to, for the agent who had sold him the reaper had found other customers in the vicinity, and the demand for Farmer Green's machine was very much less than he had anticipated. The reaper stood idle under its shed during the better portion of the harvest season, and the farmer was doomed to a severe disappointment.

When the crop was sold there was another disappointment. There had been a heavy decline in the price of wheat, and the farmer did not receive as much as he had expected for his grain. All this while the day upon which the note must be paid was drawing near, and the farmer's chances of meeting it were rapidly diminishing. And still another blow fell upon him. Just after the harvest his wife fell sick, and her illness was long and expensive.

Upon the appointed day, the agent of the Reaper Company presented the note of Farmer Green, and demanded its payment. With a sad heart the farmer related his troubles to him, and told him he was unable to meet his note. He had not the money. The agent's face grew very long as he listened to the woful tale, and after considerable hesitation, he said he was very sorry; that Farmer Green should have made allowance for all these risks, in making the purchase. However, the mischief was done, and there was nothing but to accept the situation. If the farmer could not pay, he supposed the time would have to be extended, but it would be necessary to charge him a fair rate of interest. Farmer Green said that that was only just. He had done his best to meet the note, but failing to do so, he was willing to pay for his failure. What, he inquired, would be a fair rate of interest?

"Twenty per cent. per annum," replied the agent, gravely.

Farmer Green's heart sank, and he said in a despairing tone, that the rate was too high.

"For ordinary interest, perhaps," replied the agent; "but, you see, we assume a serious risk in this case. I'd rather have the money down than one hundred per cent. interest. But you haven't got it. We take the risk of your failing entirely to pay us, and it is only fair that we should be paid for this risk as well as for the delay we are put to."

There was no help for it, and Farmer Green was obliged to pay the extortionate demand. He had placed himself at the mercy of the Reaper Company, and he must do their bidding. He hoped that a succession of good crops would enable him to pay the interest and take up the note; but, alas for him, this hope was destined to disappointment also. He paid the interest once or twice, but the burden was too heavy for him, and at last, in sheer despair, he mortgaged the farm, paid the note, and got rid of the Reaper Company. But he had only shifted his burdens. The mortgage proved as troublesome as the note had been, and instead of being able to decrease it, he was obliged to increase it as time passed on. By the first false step he had

placed the farm of which he was so proud in danger. He had voluntarily incurred a useless debt, and the rest of his bad luck was simply the logical consequence of a reckless and foolish act. He ran behind steadily, and at length his difficulties increased to such an extent that in order to rid himself of the debts he had no hope of paying in any other way, he sold his farm, discharged the mortgage, and bidding adieu to his old home and friends, went farther West, to a section where lands were cheaper, and there began life anew at the time he had once hoped to enjoy some rest from his labors.

And yet, Farmer Green, with all his shrewdness, never attributed his misfortunes to their true cause. He never admitted, even to himself, that his great error had been in contracting a useless debt, and assuming an obligation he had no certainty of meeting. He never believed that it was the reaper that ruined him, yet such was the case. Had he put by the temptation held out to him by the Reaper agent, there would have been no burden resting upon him, and his short crop, and other misfortunes, would not have driven him to the expedients he was obliged to resort to. "Out of debt, out of danger" is a true maxim; the wisdom and force of which only those who have passed through the agony and humiliation of such a slavery can appreciate.

There are debts enough that the farmer cannot help assuming; burdens that fall upon him through no fault of his. They are heavy enough, God knows, and they should teach him to assume none from which he can possibly escape.

Improved machinery is useful where it is honestly made, but even the best is worth less than the farmer ordinarily pays for it. He is charged too high, and his hard earnings, instead of constituting a fund for the rearing of his children and the protection of his old age, go to make up the colossal fortunes of the manufacturers and dealers in such machinery. A reform is needed, and it is near at hand.

Questions

1. How does this story convey the defensiveness of midwestern farmers in the 1870s?
2. Who is the salesman made to resemble in his tempting offer to Farmer Green?
3. How sound was the Grange's advice about debt and the use of farm machinery?

17-10 "Auntie Monopoly's Greeting" (1873)

Stephe Smith

Even if they did not fully understand their economic problems, farmers remained passionate in their belief that something was terribly wrong, as this history of the Grange argues (see text pp. 546–547). The author's "Auntie Monopoly" is better understood as "antimonopoly."

Source: Stephe Smith, *Grains for the Grangers, Discussing All Points Bearing upon the Farmers' Movement for the Emancipation of White Slaves from the Slave-Power of Monopoly* (Chicago: Union Publishing Company, 1873), pp. 15–22.

AUNTIE MONOPOLY
TO
HER POOR RELATIONS,
GREETING.

. . . Having followed the standard of AUNTIE MONOPOLY from the time of her first great victory over the Corn Laws, I am happy in being assured of my revered relation's continued respect and confidence. As a tried and trusted Poor Relation, I am honored with a commission as envoy to other Poor Relations, and her adherents everywhere, bearing glad tidings of the progress of the cause, and her best wishes for its continued success. Doubt and uncertainty disappear day by day, and agriculturists approach a clearer and more intelligent understanding of the Economic Problem. A movement having for its object the emancipation of a people from the slave power of the Monopoly system, has already captivated public opinion and bids fair to become the most popular movement of the day. In your intelligent efforts to escape the evil consequences of the monopoly system, day by day, you are acquiring a more definite conception of the remedy to be applied. This steady advancement of thought is not limited to the State of Illinois, where my relative was first offered shelter from the sneers and gibes of bloated and protected Capital. The organization of "Granges" is proceeding with gratifying rapidity in all sections, and in all states. As they multiply, thought and inquiry are stimulated, and sophistry gives way to established truth. To help this on, my Aunt has directed me to compile and prepare from the best sources, all that has the slightest bearing upon the subject, and to send the result to you in a form convenient alike for study and preservation. Her fervent prayers go with *"Grains for the Grangers"* with the hope that they may yield an abundant harvest, when Elections call the producing classes to the field.

Auntie Monopoly would impress upon your mind that knowledge is power. Ignorance and poverty are the props of tyranny and oppression. Ignorant men are generally credulous, and readily influenced by positive assertions when uttered by men of property and position in the world. It often happens that the intellects of poor ignorant men are confused and blunted through the mere presence of those whom they regard to be great and good. Hence they are often the victims of well-tutored knaves, who have won enough of popular approbation to hold some office. They become the playthings and support of demagogues, who, while pretending to devote their time and labor for the common advantage of those who constituted them, are only attentive to their own selfish interests. The difference of mental efficiency between a child and a man, depends more upon the inexperience and want of knowledge of the child than upon the greater age of the man. Those who are inferior in experience and information are children, no matter about their age; in conflict with the highly cultivated minds of educated men, they must always be beaten, especially where they are also opposed by selfish, dishonest pretensions.

It is a duty and a privilege of every American citizen to express his views on all points affecting the common good or interests of all classes. While he is bound to bow in obedience to all laws in existence, he may attempt to point out their errors, that they may be corrected. Even when his opinions are wrong, they may be expressed advantageously to himself, because discussion will elucidate and bring out the truth and render it manifest to all, or at any rate, to the majority.

In presenting her compliments to Uncle Sam in these pages, Auntie Monopoly would not be so rude as to withhold a word in defence of Congress. It is its custom to rely on the reports of committees and the heads of bureaus in the executive departments, especially upon technical points. If the heads of bureaus be feeble, prejudiced, antiquated men, with personal interests in personal schemes, destitute of the spirit of progress which is characteristic of our age and country; or men who are only capable of imitation and of following the precedents of other nations; or men so conservative that they naturally oppose all change and improvement, it is to be anticipated that Congress and the Executive himself will be often led astray, in spite of the best intentions. It is time that the capabilities and qualifications of heads of bureaus should be scrutinized, and where they are found corrupt or incompetent, even in a moderate degree, more efficient men should be substituted. The dominant party has promised this scrutiny and fed your impatience with subterfuge. Rings of men seek to control and do control the party in many districts for plunder and only plunder. There are many great, good and brave men in the Republican party, who seem appalled at the corruption of the times—perfectly helpless in their protestations. The corruptionists long ago seized the forts and batteries,—the papers and party organs with a few exceptions—and the most of the offices. It is useless and dangerous to fight against such things inside of a corrupt party. Just as dangerous and hopeless as it was for Southern patriots to remain and resist treason in the bosom of the South during the rebellion. To speak out, is political degradation and inquisitorial proscription; to keep silent lest the party may suffer, is voluntary slavery. Hence true reformers assume an independent attitude in politics, applauding the right and condemning the wrong in men and in parties.

My Aunt trusts that you will be warned in time against the deluge of advice that will sweep upon you from all quarters. You will be tendered more of this porridge than was the negro before and since the war, or the monopolist Joseph, when he went into Egypt to secure a corner on grain. A monopolist governor thinks you should mind your own business and let politics alone. All present and prospective candidates for office within party lines, agree with the monopolist governor. Every big and little postmaster will urge you to let politics alone. Every courthouse ring, and cliques composed of little big men in villages, are sure that you should steer clear of politics. The organs too, the little penny whistles through which refuse party wind escapes, being but echos themselves, repeat the cry. My Auntie asks in her modest way, how you are to reform an abuse, if you let politics alone? How punish the Credit-Mobilier thieves, and back-pay grabbers? How reform the currency, revive commerce, open markets and force cheap transportation? How reach the Tariff and other monopolies? How accomplish any tangible or valuable result? It is not your aim, Auntie Monopoly adds, to parade griefs and outrages without doing something to remedy them.

A strong, able and well-directed opposition is almost as important to the success of a free government, as a worthy and competent administration. Government by one party, unrestrained by any apprehension of defeat, or nerved to new measures by a profound conviction that the very existence of the government depends upon the success of the dominant party, is always attended with danger. The people operating upon and controlling and directing their government through the working of the representative principle, organization among them becomes unavoidable and as indispensable in politics as it is found to be in war. This necessity is not confined to a free government, for it is evidently only through an organization of their followers and retainers, that the Privileged Few ruling the many, and striving to perpetuate their own power, can succeed in securing the passive obedience of the inert masses, or in overcoming the open, but unconcerted and ill-devised opposition of numbers in any state. Again, it is as clearly only through an organization of themselves, that a free populace, by their delegates and representatives, are enabled to meet together and deliberate upon their affairs, and to devise and concert such action as their welfare demands. A free people who only delegate defined and limited powers to their government, usually require discussion and deliberation on their affairs prior to decision and action. For in order to enable any portion of a people to have a single representative, it is necessary to agree upon some one as a common choice. Now this certainly can only be effected by an organization. This organization necessarily becomes in such a case the basis of a party.

The "Granges" are made up of men of both parties and the most significant feature of the movement is the clearness with which it demonstrates the fact, that party lines are weakening and fading out. You have adhered to existing political organizations until they have fallen behind the requirements of the times. You demand active results from the party in power. You would compel Legislatures to acknowledge an allegiance higher than that of mere party, that you may be in a position to treat on something like terms of equality with that overshadowing monopoly which is everywhere putting the masses on their mettle. So long as the old party organizations are maintained, old party leaders and traditions must be supported. They are kept up solely for that purpose. This you do not want. The spirit of Reform will never find a practical embodiment until the professional politicians on both sides, with their Salary-grab, and Credit-Mobilier attachments, are dropped out of sight. You must take the matter in your own hands, regardless alike of Democratic and Republican parties as they stand. The process of new formation is recognizable in the Farmer's organizations, Auntie Monopoly conventions, and independent municipal and local combinations all over the land.

Your appeal is based upon justice and right. The great producing classes—Farmers and Mechanics—find themselves at the absolute mercy of the money-changers. You are met by the money power at every turn. To the greedy it offers fortunes, to the ambitious, it tenders high office. Congressmen and even our chief magistrate grasp backward and forward to secure it, violating every trust that you have reposed in them. Unscrupulous "leaders" have long since sunk their love of country in their loyalty to party and the selfish gratification of their avarice or their ambition. The irrepressible conflict between capital and labor lies at the bottom of your movement—a conflict between the money interest and the producing interest.

Your Movement holds forth the only fair chance of

saving the public morals and the public liberty. The obstacles in the way of success are fallacious legislation, and concentrated power of capital in the hands of the few. All depends upon intelligent and united effort among yourselves, and the prompt application of the remedy at the polls. . . .

Questions

1. Who are the villains here?
2. What is the author's solution to the farmers' plight?
3. What are the advantages and dangers of basing a reform movement on the kind of emotion that seems to drive the author?

Questions for Further Thought

1. How do Documents 17-9 and 17-10 show the stress experienced by American farmers in modernizing their business and their beliefs?
2. How would you rewrite the story of Farmer Green (Documents 17-9) to offer more practical advice?

CHAPTER 18

Capital and Labor in the Age of Enterprise 1877–1900

★　　　★　　　★

Industrial Capitalism Triumphant

In one sense at least, Calvin Coolidge was right: the business of America has always been business. And in the late nineteenth century business was getting increasingly bigger.

The steel and railroad industries led the transformation of the nation's economy. The Bessemer converter (see New Technology, text p. 553) allowed Americans to replace iron with steel, a far stronger metal. Steel went into everything from battleships to railroads, and in the United States the Age of Steel became synonymous with the Industrial Revolution.

Steel rails allowed railroads to operate more efficiently and expand nationwide (see text pp. 555–557, 560). In 1890, sixty years after the first American railroads were built, the rail network totaled 167,000 miles. To keep trains running on time, the major railroads created four time zones in 1883; it was a good, if imperious, business decision, the kind railroads had to make to remain profitable. Other businesses soon learned that the railroad industry offered both transportation and a blueprint for functioning on a national scale.

Men like Andrew Carnegie and Gustavus Swift (see text pp. 561–562) saw the importance of an efficient chain of command and understood how a national rail system could enrich their businesses. Steel made in Pittsburgh could be shipped to and sold in Chicago, which then sent meat from the Union Stock Yards back east in refrigerated boxcars. Even the South, long an economic backwater, enjoyed a boom in railroad construction that led to a somewhat transformed regional economy.

Herbert N. Casson (Document 18-1) argues there was romance to the steel-mill blast furnace. In Document 18-2 Florence Leslie describes the pleasures of a cross-country train journey. In Document 18-3 Philip Danforth Armour inadvertently demonstrates why meat packers made unpopular millionaires.

18-1 "The Future of Steel" (1907)

Herbert N. Casson

If the railroads helped move the national economy along, the steel industry helped build it. Steel went into rails, bridges, and skyscrapers, each an important component in the new industrial order. Like other technological innovations, steel seemed to come out of nowhere and become an indispensable part of economic life. In 1850 there was no steel industry in the United States, but by 1900 the Bessemer converter and the open-hearth furnace had created an insatiable demand for the 2,500 tons of material an integrated steel mill could turn out daily (see text pp. 552–554).

The steel industry followed the lead of railroads as a big business. Controlling every aspect of production, from raw materials to marketing, required the use of the chain-of-command system pioneered by the railroads. It was brutal work, but to Herbert N. Casson the business of blast furnaces and slag heaps was touched with romance.

Source: Herbert N. Casson, *The Romance of Steel: The Story of a Thousand Millionaires* (1907; reprint, Freeport, N.Y.: Books for Libraries Press, 1971), pp. 340–345.

THE WONDERS OF STEEL

To sum up once more the wonders of American steel magic, let me give a few final illustrations. If all our five hundred and eighty seven rolling-mills were arranged in a circle around Pittsburgh, the circle would be a hundred miles in diameter. Inside this might be a circle three-quarters as large, composed of our five hundred and thirty-two smaller steel-mills and our three thousand one hundred and sixty-one puddling furnaces. The five hundred and seventy-seven open-hearth works would make a third circle, fifty miles across. The four hundred and ten furnaces would form a fourth, thirty-five miles in diameter. And in the centre would be a flaming hub of one hundred and three Bessemer converters, a mile in circumference, pouring out a fiery river of molten steel at the rate of two and a quarter million pounds every hour of the day and night.

Put the whole American nation on the scales and, at ninety pounds apiece, they will weigh no more than the iron that our furnaces are making every two months. In the last three years we have produced enough to outweigh all the men, women and children in the world.

King Steel has dethroned King Corn and King Cotton. There are men now living who can remember when the United States produced no steel at all and very little iron, yet to-day our furnaces make enough iron to put a belt around the earth, ten feet wide and an inch thick. This, the iron men say, is a fair year's work. As we have seen, we use six times our own weight of iron in one year—two thousand seven hundred and fifty pounds per family. We feed our furnaces every twelve months a mountain of ore that would tower a hundred feet above our highest skyscrapers.

Gather together all the families that depend directly upon the iron and steel trade for their living, and they will make a State more populous than Illinois, which is the third largest in the Union. This "iron and steel world," as it justly calls itself, has its own literature—technical books that are as mysterious as Sanskrit to the ordinary reader, and magazines whose advertising brings a small fortune with every issue. It has its own laws, its own perils, its own rewards. If we consider it with regard to these three factors—its numbers, its wealth and its organisation—there is no trade to equal it on the face of the earth.

How do we know it will grow? Because of the increasing number of new uses for iron and steel. It is only a matter of time until railroads will have to buy steel ties as well as steel rails. The heavier traffic and the increased cost of wooden ties will make the steel tie a necessity. Steel ties are not an experiment. The Carnegie company has been using them for six or seven years on one of its ore railways. The Erie, Baltimore and Ohio, Pennsylvania, New York Central, and Lake Shore railroads are already throwing out wooden ties and laying down steel ones. Such an improvement will enormously increase the steel bills of the railroads. They are to-day buying one-eighth of all the steel, and a ton of ties will not go half as far on a railway as a ton of rails. At the Homestead works there is already a steel-tie department—the germ of a new industry.

As for the pressed-steel car business, that has been an established success for half a dozen years. One company reports earnings of fourteen million dollars in that time. England has not yet started in this line. When Charles T. Yerkes was equipping his new underground London railway he was obliged to place an order for four hundred steel cars with an American firm, as no English manufacturer could make them. Steel trolley-cars are now running on the streets of American cities. Six months ago the first steel baggage-car was placed on the rails of the Erie Railroad. The frequent loss of life in wooden passenger-coaches, which are easily "telescoped" in the event of a collision, is compelling railroads to consider the steel-car proposition. It was noticed by railway men that among the cars exhibited at the St. Louis Exhibition, not one was made of wood.

THE NEW STEEL CITY

Then there are to be the new steel cities of the future. We have already built our cities twice—once of wood and once of brick. For nearly twenty years we have been building a few high city structures of steel, but steel-makers declare that the private houses of the coming generation will contain a surprising amount of steel in various forms.

"I'm building a new house at Pride's Crossing, Massachusetts, and I'm astonished to see how much steel it takes," said Mr. Frick.

"Expanded steel," which resembles a mesh made by steel ribbons, is replacing lath. Ornamental steel ceilings are replacing plaster. Corrugated iron in thin sheets is replacing wooden siding in the building of factories. In England and Germany many new uses are being found for steel in connection with cement—an absolutely fire-proof combination. As steel plants are now manufacturing cement from their slag, they will reap a double profit if this method of building is adopted in the United States.

Wood has had its day in the building of cities. The recent disastrous fires in Buffalo, Baltimore, and San Francisco have shown that the steel frame is not enough. As long as wooden floors, partitions, doors, window-frames, etc., remain, there is danger. Our total fire loss is between one and two hundred millions a year. In the last twenty-four years more than three billions have gone up in smoke. And experts announce that the timber supply of Minnesota will be exhausted in less than fifteen years. So it is not unlikely that the boys and girls now in the public schools will live to see the passing of the frame house, and the substitution of a structure made of cement and steel.

Several American cities can now boast steel-frame churches of the largest size. New York's magnificent Subway is practically a thirty-mile tube made of steel and cement, just as its elevated railway is a thirty-mile steel bridge. That collossal structure, the new twenty-million-dollar Williamsburg Bridge, between New York and Long Island, required forty-five thousand tons of steel. In a skyscraper of the first class, such as the new First National Bank Building, of Chicago, for instance, with its eighteen acres of floor space, ten thousand tons of steel are riveted together.

Take another item—wire. It is hard to realise, but true, that there are twice as many millions in wire as there are in structural steel. At its present rate of increase, wire will soon require more steel than rails. Out of every ten pounds of steel produced, one is manufactured into wire. Nothing else takes so many forms. It can be made into a Brooklyn Bridge cable, with six thousand four hundred strands, or into an almost invisible thread, one-tenth as thick as a hair

from your head. It may be woven into the cage-front of a tiger, or into a fine-spun gauze with forty thousand meshes to the square inch. You will find it in your piano, sustaining a tension of about twenty tons, and in your watch, made into the tiny hairspring. In fact, when we sum up the almost innumerable uses of wire, we can understand the enthusiasm of John W. Gates, when he exclaimed, "There's millions in it!" and forthwith made himself the wire king of the United States.

To-day, even in the most insignificant items, there are millions to be made. Last year former King Cotton paid about two and a half millions to King Steel for cotton-ties alone—thin strips of sheet-iron used to bind the bales of cotton. A carpet-tack is not an imposing article of commerce, yet a single factory in Chicago is producing three million pounds in a year. A wire nail looks unimportant enough, yet any one who owned the thirteen million kegs of wire nails that we produced last year would possess a fortune equal at least to that of Frick.

Many an order for a single steel article carries in itself a competency. To name a few, there are—the new steel dry-dock at New Orleans, five hundred and twenty-five feet in length and one hundred feet wide; the three hundred and ten foot steel chimney of the Nichols Chemical Company, Brooklyn; an engine in the United States Steel Corporation's plant at Youngstown that weighs nearly a million pounds; the Manhattan bridge; the three enormous steel flumes, eighteen feet in diameter and a mile in length, which have recently been laid at Niagara Falls; and J. J. Hill's group of steel elevators at Superior, Wisconsin, holding three million bushels of grain apiece.

There has been for several years a block of steel roadway in New York City, the necessary steel plates having been donated by Mr. Schwab. To equip a road with these steel plates would cost, it is said, not more than fifteen hundred dollars a mile, and it is being freely predicted that the road of the future will be of this kind. "I expect to see a road of this sort from New York to San Francisco, and around the suburbs of all our large American cities," said W. E. Scarritt, president of the American Automobile Association.

Almost every week the newspapers announce a new use for steel. Steel bathtubs are being stamped out at the rate of a hundred and fifty a day. Steel furniture is worrying the furniture makers of Michigan. Barrels, so one manufacturer says, are henceforth to come from the steel mill and not from the cooper-shop. As we use about three hundred million barrels a year just now, this one item may mean new plants, new multimillionaires.

Now that steel is being used in construction work, there is scarcely any limit upon the novelties that we may expect. We hear of an aërial ferry in Duluth, by means of which a car is swung in midair from shore to shore, and of an aërial hotel in Switzerland, above the Lake of the Four Cantons, hanging two thousand feet above the water.

Questions

1. How did the steel industry fit into Casson's view of progress?
2. According to Casson, in what ways did steel affect the growth of cities?
3. How good a prophet was Casson? Have any of his predictions come true?

18-2   From Gotham to the Golden Gate (1877)

Florence Leslie

The railroads had a social impact as Americans took to rail travel. Part of the attraction was the railroads' ability to shrink distances. In 1830 a person had to spend three fairly unpleasant weeks to make the trip overland from New York to Chicago; by 1857 the train had reduced this journey to two days. If time indeed was money, the railroads promised to save and make fortunes (see text pp. 555–557, 560).

But there was more to trains than convenience. A trip by train was something special. It introduced the idea of comfort into travel, at least for those who could afford first class. A far-flung rail network encouraged Americans to discover what their country looked like; long before television, railroads served as a unifying social force. With the train came some of this nation's most impressive architecture in the form of railroad stations.

Florence Leslie made a transcontinental trip by rail from New York ("Gotham") to San Francisco in 1877. The excerpt reprinted here describes the route from Chicago to Cheyenne in the Wyoming Territory. Her story shows the wonder and pleasure a train trip could inspire.

Source: Florence Leslie, *California: A Pleasure Trip from Gotham to the Golden Gate* (New York: G. W. Carleton & Company, 1877), pp. 35–49, 51.

On arriving at the station, we find that we have exchanged our beloved Wagner Home [sleeping car] for the famous Pullman Hotel Car, exhibited at the Centennial Exposition, and built at a cost of $35,000. We are greeted on entering, by two superb pyramids of flowers, one from Mr. Potter Palmer [a Chicago real estate magnate] and the other with compliments of the Pullman Car Co.; then new-found Chicago friends arrive in rapid succession, to wish us Godspeed, and, in the midst of a cheerful bustle and excitement, we are off, and able to look about us at our new home. First, we are impressed with the smooth and delightful motion, and are told it is owing to a new invention, in the shape of paper wheels [compressed paper at the center of the wheel] applied to this car, and incredible though the information sounds, meekly accept it, and proceed to explore the internal resources of our kingdom. We find everything closely resembling our late home, except that one end of the car is partitioned off and fitted up as a kitchen, storeroom, scullery—reminding one, in their compactness and variety, of the little Parisian *cuisines*

[kitchens], where every inch of space is utilized, and where such a modicum of wood and charcoal produces such marvelous results.

Our *chef*, of ebon color, and proportions suggesting a liberal sampling of the good things he prepares, wears the regulation snow-white apron and cap, and gives us cordial welcome and information; showing us, among other things, that his refrigerator and larder are boxes adroitly arranged beneath the car, secured by lock and key, and accessible at every station. At six the tables are laid for two each, with dainty linen, and the finest of glass and china, and we presently sit down to dinner. Our repast is Delmonican [after a famous New York restaurant] in its nature and style, consisting of soup, fish, *entrees*, roast meat and vegetables, followed by the conventional dessert and the essential spoonful of black coffee.

We are not a late party that night, retiring at ten, and in the morning are startled by an announcement from the "Sultana," a tall, willowy woman, with dark, almond-shaped eyes, who affects brilliant tints, and lounges among her cushions and wraps of crimson and gold, with grace peculiarly her own, and with a luxuriance so Eastern, as to have won for her the *sobriquet* [nickname] of Sultana. We are startled by the announcement that her rest had been disturbed by the howling of wolves! The young lady who does the romantic for our party turns pale with envy, especially when the brakeman, appealed to as authority, admits that there is a small coyote wolf about the prairies, even so far east, which might possibly have been heard. All day, until sunset, we sweep along over rolling prairie lands of a rich, tawny yellow, with here and there a tiny town, and here and there a lonely settler's cabin, with a little winding footpath stretching up to it.

At Dixon, the train stopped for the passengers' supper, and we stole away for a little exercise and solitude. A storm was imminent, the distant thunder muttered ominously, the lightening came in pulses, and from the far, dusky reaches of the prairie, blew a wind stronger and freer, yet softer, than other winds, with a fragrance sweeter than flowers on its breath. Some strange, wild influence in the scene sent a new sensation tingling through one's blood. All sorts of poetic fancies and inspirations seemed hovering close above one's head, when a dash of rain recalled the realism of life, and sent us hastening back to the car, where all the lamps were lighted and the tables laid for dinner. . . .

Arrived in Omaha, the true beginning, perhaps, of our California trip, we took a carriage, and set forth to view the town. We found it big, lazy, and apathetic; the streets dirty and ill-paved; the clocks without hands to point out the useless time. the shops, whose signs mostly bore German names, deserted of customers, while principals and clerks lounged together in the doorways, listless and idle. This depressing state of affairs is, presumably, temporary, for we are told that, two years ago, Omaha was one of the most thriving and busy cities of the West, claiming for itself, indeed, a place as first commercial emporium of that vast section; and, certainly, its position at the terminus of the three great Eastern roads, and the beginning of the one great Western one, would naturally entitle it to that preeminence, when aided by the enterprise and the dollars of such men as have, in twenty years, built a great city from a wayside settlement. Doubtless, when the hard times, which seem to affect everybody and everything, from the baby's Christmas toys to the statesman's visions of international commerce, are over, Omaha will shake off the lethargy depressing her at present, and rise to the position her citizens fondly claim for her. . . .

Returning to the station, we found the platform crowded with the strangest and most motley groups of people it has ever been our fortune to encounter. Men in alligator boots, and loose overcoats made of blankets and wagon rugs, with wild, unkempt hair and beards, and bright, resolute eyes, almost all well-looking, but wild and strange as denizens of another world.

The women looked tired and sad, almost all of them, and were queerly dressed, in gowns that must have been their grandmothers', and with handkerchiefs tied over their heads in place of hats; the children were bundled up anyhow, in garments of nondescript purpose and size, but were generally chubby, neat and gay, as they frolicked in and out among the boxes, baskets, bundles, bedding, babies'-chairs, etc., piled waist high on various parts of the platform. Mingling with them, and making some inquiries, we found that these were emigrants, bound for the Black Hills, by rail to Cheyenne and Sioux City, and after that by wagon trains. A family of French attracted attention by the air of innate refinement and fitness which seems to attach to every grade of society in *la belle France*, and we chatted with them for some moments. A great many families claimed German nationality, and Ireland, England, and Scotland were represented, as well as our own country. One bright little creature—perhaps three years of age—was quite insulted at being called a baby, and exclaimed, indignantly:

"No, no, me not baby!"

"What are you, then? A young lady?" we inquired.

"No, me 'ittle woman. Me helps mammy sweep," replied the mite; and apologizing for our blunder, we handed her some silver for candy, which she accepted with alacrity; and as we watched her setting off on her shopping expedition, a neat, pretty old lady, perched upon a big bundle, said, with much conscious pride.

"That's my grandchild, ma'am."

After passing North Bend, we came upon an Indian camp belonging to a portion of the Omahaw [sic] tribe. The lodges—five or six in number—were of white skin, and picturesque in shape: their occupants gathered around a small camp-fire—the men, tall, straight, dark, and dignified, wrapped in toga-like blankets; the women, dirty and degraded, with their pappooses bundled on their backs, the queer, little dark faces peeping out like prairie dogs from their burrows. Further on we met a second band—half a dozen men on horseback—carrying their lodges bundled up and driving a little herd of shaggy Indian ponies. It was a wonderfully new picture for us, the great plains rolling away on either side in apparently illimitable extent, clad in their richest shades of russet and tawny gold in the distance, and the tender grass and moist black earth close at hand, a wild mass of thunder-clouds crowding up from the south, and the low-hanging trail of smoke from our engine sweeping away northward, like a troop of spirits, and this little, lonely band of Omahaws riding slowly away into the storm, casting uneasy glances backward at the flying train. A second picture to place beside that of Niagara in memory's gallery, a second proof that the foremost of human artists is, after all, but the feeblest copyist of the Artist whose name is Wonderful.

The old emigrant trail here runs southward beside the track, and we had the luck to pass two real emigrant wagons: one, white-topped and rather neat-looking, had halted for the night, with the horses picketed out to graze, and the camp-fire lighted; while the other, dark, weather-beaten and forlorn, was doggedly making its way forward.

Our train stopped for supper at Grand Island, a considerable place, and, like most western places, confidently expecting to be larger when the time arrived. We dismounted to look at our first specimens of buffalo grass, a short, dry, tufted herbage, said to be the especial dainty of not only buffalo, but of all grazing creatures, who leave all other food for it, and unhesitatingly as a gourmand accepts fresh truffles. In front of the station was a little enclosure with a most spasmodic fountain, beside which we lingered for some moments and then returned with alacrity to our Pullman home. . . .

And now, not without some little excitement, we arrived at Cheyenne, as it is styled upon the maps, the Magic City of the Plains, the City on Wheels, the Town of a Day, as romanticists call it, or in yet more vigorous vernacular, H-ll on Wheels, which latter is, perhaps, its most popular name among its own inhabitants. In view of this reputation, our conductor strongly advised against any night ex-

ploration, at least by the ladies of the party, of the streets and shops at Cheyenne, stating that the town swarmed with miners *en route* for, or returning from, the Black Hills, many of them desperadoes, and all utterly reckless in the use of the bowie-knife and pistol; or, at the very least, in the practice of language quite unfit for ears polite, although well adapted to a place which they themselves had dubbed with so suggestive a name. This opposition, was, of course, decisive; and the three ladies, as one man, declared fear was a word unknown in their vocabulary, that purchases essential to their comfort were to be made, and that exercise was absolutely necessary to their health. Under such stress of argument the masculine mind gave way perforce, and not only the sworn beau of the party, but most of the other gentlemen, endorsed the movement and volunteered to act as escort, producing, loading, and flourishing such an arsenal of weapons as they did so that their valiant charges huddled together, far more affrighted at their friends than their enemies, and piteously imploring that the firearms should be safely hidden until needed; the order was obeyed, and at about half-past nine P.M. the exploring party set forth.

Questions

1. What aspects of train travel strike Leslie as unique and even romantic?
2. Why was it no accident that the chef was "of ebon color"? Why did railroads hire black service employees?
3. Compare the train with the interstate highway system. How is the car an improvement over train travel? At what cost?

18-3   Philip Danforth Armour Testifies before the U.S. Senate (1889)

As discussed in the textbook (pp. 561–562), meat packing was another giant industry that emerged in the late nineteenth century. The great Union Stock Yards in Chicago opened on Christmas Day 1865. Because of Chicago's position as a rail center and proximity to pork and cattle producers, the yards grew quickly. In 1910 they sprawled over 500 acres, with room for 13,000 holding pens. More than 10.2 million cattle and hogs were slaughtered in 1919, a year when the yards employed almost 46,000 people.

The men who founded the meat-packing business were much respected for their ability to make money but little loved for their unwillingness to share it. One of the leading packers was Philip Danforth Armour, a New England native and onetime gold prospector who moved his packing business to Chicago in 1875 (see text p. 562). Armour once claimed, "Through the wages I disburse and the provisions I supply, I give more people food than any man living." Armour was humbler in 1889, when he appeared before a Senate committee to testify about price-fixing. The following is an excerpt from Armour's testimony.

Source: Armour's testimony before the U.S. Senate, 1889. In Harper Leech and John Charles Carroll, *Armour and His Times* (New York: D. Appleton-Century, 1938), pp. 193–196.

The depression in prices and the present state of the cattle market are due to overproduction, especially of grass fed cattle, the marketing of immature animals, which are too thin for the block (this has affected all corn fed cattle except the choicest) and the enforced competition of farmers raising cattle on the higher priced and highly improved farms of Illinois, Iowa, Missouri, Kansas, and Nebraska with the ranchers of the west and southwest who had thousands of this character of inferior cattle upon public lands or lands of little value. The gradual absorption of the ranges by actual settlers and overproduction of range cattle have greatly overcrowded the remaining range country, and consequently lessened the quantity of range grass and impaired its nutritive quality. As a natural result grass fed range cattle have deteriorated in weight and value, and the southwestern steers now coming in weigh 10 to 20 pounds less than the steers of a similar character did six years ago. Grass fed southwestern steers are not as good as they were then and cannot be expected to command the same prices.

Many other causes have transpired since to depress this branch of the cattle business and to cause the over marketing of cattle, among which may be mentioned the thinning of large ranches; drought and short pasture, severe winters and a necessity on the part of the cattle corporations and owners for the realization of quick profits to meet the payments of guaranteed dividends or of interest or mortgages. I am fully convinced that the farmers of Illinois, Iowa, Missouri, Kansas, and Nebraska have suffered serious losses in cattle values because of the effect upon the cattle market of such over shipments.

It is but a question of time when the Argentine Republic will prove a formidable competitor to American beef in foreign countries and probably in this, and in this contingency the action of Congress and the states in discrediting American beef products abroad by agitation and legislation may prove to be of a most harmful character; for unless we can market our surplus products abroad, cattle men must expect low prices and poor markets. Another evidence of our overproduction, and one which shows that cattle raisers themselves recognize it as the true cause of depressed markets, is the large number of young cows and heifers which are being sent to the slaughter pens and the large number of young heifers that are annually being spayed. When ranches and farms are so thinned out as to make the supply of cattle nearer the demand, and when we can market our surplus abroad, we may expect to see steady and proper cattle values; for it is a well established rule of trade that a surplus of any commodity in a market will reduce the value of the whole production of that commodity.

The dressed beef men, as they are called, are in no way responsible for the fixing of the price which the consumer pays for his meat. They sell only at wholesale. They are jobbers, so to speak, of meats. They neither attempt nor desire to enter the retailers' field. The margin between the wholesale price which we sell at and the retail price which the consumer pays in the market can be very readily ascertained.

The dressed beef business is protected by no patent. The methods in slaughtering the animal and preparing its product for the market are well known, and open to any one who wishes to engage in it. Armour and Company have wholesale beef markets and agencies throughout the country. Through the press and otherwise we advertise the products we have for sale, and the prices, and keep our beef and products constantly before the public. To these markets everybody is invited. Our prices are quoted to every enquirer, and any person can readily see for himself whether we are charging or receiving exorbitant prices or not.

There has never been any combination or agreement of any kind between the firm of Armour and Company, of which I am a member, and any other party or parties, to fix the price which we should pay for live cattle, or to control this price which should be paid therefor; nor has there been any attempt on the part of this firm, in connection with others engaged in the dressed beef business, or with other purchasers of cattle, to control or depress the market for cattle.

The firm of Armour and Company is not in any combination with other parties in the dressed beef business, or the shippers of beef in the carcass, to fix the price at which beef carcasses shall be sold.

We do arrange price lists for cut meats and canned meats, from time to time, with others producing these commodities. This is done according to the state of the market, according to supply and demand, and is absolutely necessary to protect dealers in those articles from the sudden and violent declines in prices which otherwise would follow an oversupply. In no case are the prices quoted exorbitant, nor would it be possible to make them exorbitant and maintain them for any length of time. The almost unlimited supply of such cattle, and the limited demand which the market affords for these articles, make the exacting of large prices impossible.

Questions

1. According to Armour, what forces control the price of cattle?
2. Why does Armour portray meat packers simply as wholesalers?

3. The Senate committee later issued a report charging Armour and three other leading meat packers with price-fixing and other misdeeds. How could these excesses
   occur in a market economy that rewarded efficiency, not dishonesty?

Questions for Further Thought

1. Herbert Casson (Document 18-1) and Philip Armour (Document 18-3) offered a
   highly selective view of American industry. What was left out, and why?
2. In what ways did rail travel (see Document 18-2) homogenize American society?
3. Americans tend to view the late nineteenth century as a time of barbershop quartets and marching bands. How do Documents 18-1 through 18-3 alter that notion? Why has it persisted so long nonetheless?

The World of Work

The idea of free persons working as they see fit is deeply rooted in the American consciousness; in the nineteenth century both the tenets of Jacksonian democracy and the
ideology of the Republican party reflected this belief.

But the notion of a nation of independent artisans could not survive the industrialization of the nineteenth century. Just as the 1800s saw the evolution of the factory system and a national economy, they bore witness to the creation of a modern working
class. The first women workers in New England's textile mills might have regarded
their jobs as temporary, but by the end of the century women, together with men and
children, had become a permanent part of the industrial work force.

Factories got labor from various sources, both native and immigrant (see text pp.
566–568). Industrialists wanted a work force that was both docile and efficient. When
the pool of white men was exhausted, industrialists hired women, children, and
African-Americans (see text pp. 566–570). Factory owners soon found that the more
diversified the work force, the harder it was for unions to organize.

Frederick Winslow Taylor developed a new system to keep costs in line: scientific
management (see text p. 574). Taylor proposed a method to reduce the time and labor
power that went into production. Factory owners were intrigued by the idea, but employees worried that "Taylorism" would lead to overwork and unemployment. Soon
the stopwatch became a cultural metaphor for the unyielding discipline of industrial
America.

In Document 18-4 Rocco Corresca describes city life for an Italian immigrant. The
narrator of Document 18-5 describes being a black woman employed as a domestic for
a white family in the South. Document 18-6 is from Frederick W. Taylor, who is confident about the promise of scientific management.

18-4 "The Biography of a Bootblack" (1902)

Rocco Corresca

Not all immigrants came to the United States as part of families intent on becoming Americans. Many were like the young Rocco Corresca, whose 1902 account appears here. He came to New York with a companion who may or may not have been his brother. Corresca intended to save enough money to buy a farm in Italy, but his success as a bootblack convinced him that his future lay in the United States (see text pp. 567–568).

Source: Rocco Corresca, "The Biography of a Bootblack" (1902). In Leon Stein and Philip Taft, eds., *Workers Speak: Self Portraits* (1902–1906; reprint, New York: Arno and New York Times, 1971), pp. 83–87.

When I was a very small boy I lived in Italy in a large house with many other small boys, who were all dressed alike and were taken care of by some nuns. It was a good place, situated on the side of the mountain, where grapes were growing and melons and oranges and plums.

They taught us our letters and how to pray and say the catechism, and we worked in the fields during the middle of the day. We always had enough to eat and good beds to sleep in at night, and sometimes there were feast days, when we marched about wearing flowers.

Those were good times and they lasted till I was nearly eight years of age. Then an old man came and said he was my grandfather. He showed some papers and cried over me and said that the money had come at last and now he could take me to his beautiful home. He seemed very glad to see me and after they looked at his papers he took me away and we went to the big city—Naples. He kept talking about his beautiful house, but when we got there it was a dark cellar that he lived in and I did not like it at all. Very rich people were on the first floor. They had carriages and servants and music and plenty of good things to eat, but we were down below in the cellar and had nothing. There were four other boys in the cellar and the old man said they were all my brothers. All were larger than I and they beat me at first till one day Francisco said that they should not beat me any more, and then Paulo, who was the largest of all, fought him till Francisco drew a knife and gave him a cut. Then Paulo, too, got a knife and said that he would kill Francisco, but the old man knocked them both down with a stick and took their knives away and gave them beatings.

Each morning we boys all went out to beg and we begged all day near the churches and at night near the theatres, running to the carriages and opening the doors and then getting in the way of the people so that they had to give us money or walk over us. The old man often watched us and at night he took all the money, except when we could hide something. . . .

It was very hard in the winter time for we had no shoes and we shivered a great deal. The old man said that we were no good, that we were ruining him, that we did not bring in enough money. He told me that I was fat and that people would not give money to fat beggars. He beat me, too, because I didn't like to steal, as I had heard it was wrong.

"Ah!" said he, "that is what they taught you at that place, is it? To disobey your grandfather that fought with Garibaldi! That is a fine religion!"

The others all stole as well as begged, but I didn't like it and Francisco didn't like it either.

Then the old man said to me: "If you don't want to be a thief you can be a cripple. That is an easy life and they make a great deal of money."

I was frightened then, and that night I heard him talking to one of the men that came to see him. He asked how much he would charge to make me a good cripple like those that crawl about the church. They had a dispute, but at last they agreed and the man said that I should be made so that people would shudder and give me plenty of money.

I was much frightened, but I did not make a sound and in the morning I went out to beg with Francisco. I said to him: "I am going to run away. I don't believe Tony is my grandfather. I don't believe that he fought for Garibaldi, and I don't what to be a cripple, no matter how much money the people may give."

"Where will you go?" Francisco asked me.

"I don't know," I said; "somewhere."

He thought awhile and then he said: "I will go, too."

So we ran away out of the city and begged from the country people as we went along. We came to a village down by the sea and a long way from Naples and there we found some fishermen and they took us aboard their boat. We were with them five years, and tho it was a very hard life we liked it well because there was always plenty to eat. Fish do not keep long and those that we did not sell we ate.

The chief fisherman, whose name was Ciguciano, had a daughter, Teresa, who was very beautiful, and tho she was two years younger than I, she could cook and keep house quite well. She was a kind, good girl and he was a good man. . . .

Now and then I had heard things about America—that it was a far off country where everybody was rich and that Italians went there and made plenty of money, so that they could return to Italy and live in pleasure ever after. One day I met a young man who pulled out a handful of gold and told me he had made that in America in a few days.

I said I should like to go there, and he told me that if I went he would take care of me and see that I was safe. I told Francisco and he wanted to go, too. So we said good-by to our good friends. Teresa cried and kissed us both and the priest came and shook our hands and told us to be good men, and that no matter where we went God and his saints were always near us and that if we lived well we should all meet again in heaven. We cried, too, for it was our home, that place. Ciguciano gave us money and slapped us on the back and said that we should be great. But he felt bad, too, at seeing us go away after all that time.

The young man took us to a big ship and got us work away down where the fires are. We had to carry coal to the place where it could be thrown on the fires. Francisco and I were very sick from the great heat at first and lay on the coal for a long time, but they threw water on us and made us get up. We could not stand on our feet well, for everything was going around and we had no strength. We said that we wished we had stayed in Italy no matter how much gold there was in America. We could not eat for three days and could not do much work. Then we got better and sometimes we went up above and looked about. There was no land anywhere and we were much surprised. How could the people tell where to go when there was no land to steer by?

We were so long on the water that we began to think we should never get to America or that, perhaps, there was not any such place, but at last we saw land and came up to New York.

We were glad to get over without giving money, but I have heard since that we should have been paid for our work among the coal and that the young man who had sent us got money for it. We were all landed on an island and the bosses there said that Francisco and I must go back because we had not enough money, but a man named Bartolo came up and told them that we were brothers and he was our uncle and would take care of us. He brought two other men who swore that they knew us in Italy and that Bartolo was our uncle. I had never seen any of them before, but even then Bartolo might be my uncle, so I did not say anything. The bosses of the island let us go out with Bartolo after he had made the oath.

We came to Brooklyn to a wooden house in Adams Street that was full of Italians from Naples. Bartolo had a room on the floor and there were fifteen men in the room, all boarding with Bartolo. He did the cooking on a stove in the middle of the room and there were beds all around the sides, one bed above another. It was very hot in the room, but we were soon asleep, for we were very tired.

The next morning, early, Bartolo told us to go out and pick rags and get bottles. He gave us bags and hooks and showed us the ash barrels. On the streets where the fine houses are the people are very careless and put out good things, like mattresses and umbrellas, clothes, hats and boots. We brought all these to Bartolo and he made them new again and sold them on the sidewalk; but mostly we brought rags and bones. The rags we had to wash in the back yard and then we hung them to dry on lines under the ceiling in our room. The bones we kept under the beds till Bartolo could find a man to buy them.

Most of the men in our room worked at digging the sewer. Bartolo got them the work and they paid him about one quarter of their wages. Then he charged them for board and he bought the clothes for them, too. So they got little money after all.

Bartolo was always saying that the rent of the room was so high that he could not make anything, but he was really making plenty. He was what they call a padrone and is now a very rich man. The men that were living with him had just come to the country and could not speak English. They had all been sent by the young man we met in Italy. Bartolo told us all that we must work for him and that if we did not the police would come and put us in prison.

He gave us very little money, and our clothes were some of those that were found on the street. Still we had enough to eat and we had meat quite often, which we never had in Italy. Bartolo got it from the butcher—the meat that he could not sell to the other people—but it was quite good meat. Bartolo cooked it in the pan while we all sat on our beds in the evening. Then he cut it into small bits and passed the pan around, saying:

"See what I do for you and yet you are not glad. I am too kind a man, that is why I am so poor."

We were with Bartolo nearly a year, but some of our countrymen who had been in the place a long time said that Bartolo had no right to us and we could get work for a dollar and a half a day, which, when you make it *lire* (reckoned in the Italian currency) is very much. So we went away one day to Newark and got work on the street. Bartolo came after us and made a great noise, but the boss said that if he did not go away soon the police would have him. Then he went, saying that there was no justice in this country.

We paid a man five dollars each for getting us the work and we were with the boss for six months. He was Irish, but a good man and he gave us our money every Saturday night. We lived much better than with Bartolo, and when the work was done we each had nearly $200 saved. Plenty of the men spoke English and they taught us, and we taught them to read and write. That was at night, for we had a lamp in our room, and there were only five other men who lived in that room with us.

We got up at half-past five o'clock every morning and made coffee on the stove and had a breakfast of bread and cheese, onions, garlic and red herrings. We went to work at seven o'clock and in the middle of the day we had soup and bread in a place where we got it for two cents a plate. In the evenings we had a good dinner with meat of some kind and potatoes. We got from the butcher the meat that other people would not buy because they said it was old, but they don't know what is good. We paid four or five cents a pound for it and it was the best, tho I have heard of people paying sixteen cents a pound.

When the Newark boss told us that there was no more work Francisco and I talked about what we would do and we went back to Brooklyn to a saloon near Hamilton Ferry, where we got a job cleaning it out and slept in a little room upstairs. There was a bootblack named Michael on the corner and when I had time I helped him and learned the business. Francisco cooked the lunch in the saloon and he, too, worked for the bootblack and we were soon able to make the best polish.

Then we thought we would go into business and we got a basement on Hamilton avenue, near the Ferry, and put four chairs in it. We paid $75 for the chairs and all the other things. We had tables and looking glasses there and curtains. We took the papers that have the pictures in and made the place high toned. Outside we had a big sign that said:

THE BEST SHINE FOR TEN CENTS.

Men that did not want to pay ten cents could get a good shine for five cents, but it was not an oil shine. We had two boys helping us and paid each of them fifty cents a day. The rent of the place was $20 a month, so the expenses were very great, but we made money from the beginning. We slept in the basement, but got our meals in the saloon till we could put a stove in our place, and then Francisco cooked for us all. That would not do, tho, because some of our customers said that they did not like to smell garlic and onions and red herrings. I thought that was strange, but we had to do what the customers said. So we got the woman who lived upstairs to give us our meals and paid her $1.50 a week each. She gave the boys soup in the middle of the day—five cents for two plates.

We remembered the priest, the friend of Ciguciano, and what he had said to us about religion, and as soon as we came to the country we began to go to the Italian church. The priest we found here was a good man, but he asked the people for money for the church. The Italians did not like to give because they said it looked like buying religion. The priest says it is different here from Italy because all the churches there are what they call endowed, while here all they have is what the people give. Of course I and

Francisco understand that, but the Italians who cannot read and write shake their hands and say that it is wrong for a priest to want money.

We had said that when we saved $1,000 each we would go back to Italy and buy a farm, but now that the time is coming we are so busy and making so much money that we think we will stay. We have opened another parlor near South Ferry, in New York. We have to pay $30 a month rent, but the business is very good. The boys in this place charge sixty cents a day because there is so much work.

At first we did not know much of this country, but by and by we learned. There are here plenty of Protestants who are heretics, but they have a religion, too. Many of the finest churches are Protestant, but they have no saints and no altars, which seems strange.

These people are without a king such as ours in Italy. It is what they call a Republic, as Garibaldi wanted, and every year in the fall the people vote. They wanted us to vote last fall, but we did not. A man came and said that he would get us made Americans for fifty cents and then we could get two dollars for our votes. I talked to some of our people and they told me that we should have to put a paper in a box telling who we wanted to govern us.

I went with five men to the court and when they asked me how long I had been in the country I told them two years. Afterward my countrymen said I was a fool and would never learn politics. "You should have said you were five years here and then we would swear to it," was what they told me.

There are two kinds of people that vote here, Republicans and Democrats. I went to a Republican meeting and the man said that the Republicans want a Republic and the Democrats are against it. He said that Democrats are for a king whose name is Bryan and who is an Irishman. There are some good Irishmen, but many of them insult Italians. They call us Dagoes. So I will be a Republican.

I like this country now and I don't see why we should have a king. Garibaldi didn't want a king and he was the greatest man that ever lived.

I and Francisco are to be Americans in three years. The court gave us papers and said we must wait and we must be able to read some things and tell who the ruler of the country is.

There are plenty of rich Italians here, men who a few years ago had nothing and now have so much money that they could not count all their dollars in a week. The richest ones go away from the other Italians and live with the Americans.

We have joined a club and have much pleasure in the evenings. The club has rooms down in Sacket Street and we meet many people and are learning new things all the time. We were very ignorant when we came here, but now we have learned much. . . .

Questions

1. Under what conditions did Corresca live in Italy?
2. What arrangement did Bartolo make with the men he housed?
3. What were some of the similarities and differences between Corresca's old and new lives?

18-5 "More Slavery at the South"

Anonymous
(A Black Domestic)

As the textbook notes (see p. 568), more than one-fourth of the nonfarm work force in 1900 consisted of women, most of whom worked out of necessity. Outside of teaching, social work, and nursing, women did not expect to enjoy a professional career (or equal pay), and a majority worked in factories or as domestics. This reading details the work of an African-American woman (see text pp. 566–567). Although caring for white children gave her a degree of social status, she found her life "just as bad as, if not worse than, it was during the days of slavery."

Source: Anonymous (A Negro Nurse), "More Slavery at the South," *The Independent* 72 (January 25, 1912), pp. 196–200. In W. Elliot Brownlee and Mary M. Brownlee, *Women in the American Economy: A Documentary History, 1675 to 1929* (New Haven, Conn.: Yale University Press, 1976), pp. 244–249.

I am a negro woman, and I was born and reared in the South. I am now past forty years of age and am the mother of three children. My husband died nearly fifteen years ago, after we had been married about five years. For more than thirty years—or since I was ten years old—I have been a servant in one capacity or another in white families in a thriving Southern city, which has at present a population of more than 50,000. In my early years I was at first what might be called a "house-girl," or better, a "house-boy." I used to answer the doorbell, sweep the yard, go on errands, and do odd jobs. Later on I became a chambermaid. . . . Still later I was graduated into a cook, in which position I served at different times for nearly eight years in all. During the last ten years I have been a nurse. I have worked for only four different families during all these thirty years. But, belonging to the servant class, which is the majority class among my race at the South, and associating only with servants, I have been able to become intimately acquainted not only with the lives of hundreds of household servants, but also with the lives of their employers. I can, therefore, speak with authority on the so-called servant question; and what I say is said out of an experience which covers many years.

To begin with, then, I should say that more than two-thirds of the negroes of the town where I live are menial servants of one kind or another, and besides that more

than two-thirds of the negro women here, whether married or single, are compelled to work for a living,—as nurses, cooks, washerwomen, chambermaids, seamstresses, hucksters [peddlers], janitresses, and the like. I will say, also, that the condition of this vast host of poor colored people is just as bad as, if not worse than, it was during the days of slavery. Though today we are enjoying nominal freedom, we are literally slaves. And, not to generalize, I will give you a sketch of the work I have to do—and I'm only one of many.

I frequently work from fourteen to sixteen hours a day. I am compelled by my contract, which is oral only, to sleep in the house. I am allowed to go home to my own children, the oldest of whom is a girl of 18 years, only once in two weeks, every other Sunday afternoon—even then I'm not permitted to stay all night. I not only have to nurse a little white child, now eleven months old, but I have to act as playmate or "handy-andy," not say governess, to three other children in the home, the oldest of whom is only nine years of age. I wash and dress the baby two or three times each day; I give it its meals, mainly from a bottle; I have to put it to bed each night; and, in addition, I have to get up and attend to its every call between midnight and morning. If the baby falls to sleep during the day, as it has been trained to do every day about eleven o'clock, I am not permitted to rest. It's "Mammy, do this," or "Mammy, do that," or "Mammy, do the other," from my mistress, all the time. So it is not strange to see "Mammy" watering the lawn in front with the garden hose, sweeping the sidewalk, mopping the porch and halls, dusting around the house, helping the cook, or darning stockings. Not only so, but I have to put the other three children to bed each night as well as the baby, and I have to wash them and dress them each morning. I don't know what it is to go to church; I don't know what it is to go to a lecture or entertainment or anything of the kind; I live a treadmill life; and I see my own children only when they happen to see me on the streets when I am out with the children, or when my children come to the "yard" to see me, which isn't often, because my white folks don't like to see their servants' children hanging around their premises. You might as well say that I'm on duty all the time—from sunrise to sunrise, every day in the week. I am the slave, body and soul, of this family. And what do I get for this work—this lifetime bondage? The pitiful sum of ten dollars a month! And what am I expected to do with these ten dollars? With this money I'm expected to pay my house rent, which is four dollars per month, for a little house of two rooms, just big enough to turn round in; and I'm expected, also to feed and clothe myself and three children. For two years my oldest child, it is true, has helped a little toward our support by taking in a little washing at home. She does the washing and ironing of two white families, with a total of five persons; one of these families pays her $1.00 per week, and the other 75 cents per week, and my daughter has to furnish her own soap and starch and wood. For six months my youngest child, a girl about thirteen years old, has been nursing, and she receives $1.50 per week but has no night work. When I think of the low rate of wages we poor colored people receive, and when I hear so much said about our unreliability, our untrustworthiness, and even our vices, I recall the story of the private soldier in a certain army who, once upon a time, being upbraided by the commanding officer because the heels of his shoes were not polished, is said to have replied: "Captain, do you expect all the virtues for $13 per month?"

Of course, nothing is being done to increase our wages, and the way things are going at present it would seem that nothing could be done to cause an increase in wages. We have no labor unions or organizations of any kind that could demand for us a uniform scale of wages for cooks, washerwomen, nurses, and the like; and, for another thing, if some negroes did here and there refuse to work for seven and eight and ten dollars a month, there would be hundreds of other negroes right on the spot ready to take their places and do the same work, or more, for the low wages that had been refused. So that, the truth is, we have to work for little or nothing or become vagrants! And that, of course, in this State would mean that we would be arrested, tried, and despatched to the "State Farm," where we would surely have to work for nothing or be beaten with many stripes!

Nor does this low rate of pay tend to make us efficient

servants. The most that can be said of us negro household servants in the South—and I speak as one of them—is that we are to the extent of our ability willing and faithful slaves. We do not cook according to scientific principles because we do not know anything about scientific principles. Most of our cooking is done by guesswork or by memory. We cook well when our "hand" is in, as we say, and when anything about the dinner goes wrong, we simply say, "I lost my hand today!" We don't know anything about scientific food for babies, nor anything about what science says must be done for infants at certain periods of their growth or when certain symptoms of disease appear; but somehow we "raise" more of the children than we kill, and, for the most part, they are lusty chaps—all of them. But the point is, we do not go to cooking-schools nor to nurse-training schools, and so it cannot be expected that we should make as efficient servants without such training as we should make were such training provided. And yet with our cooking and nursing, such as it is, the white folks seem to be satisfied—perfectly satisfied. I sometimes wonder if this satisfaction is the outgrowth of the knowledge that more highly trained servants would be able to demand better pay! . . .

Another thing—it's a small indignity, it may be, but an indignity just the same. No white person, not even the little children just learning to talk, no white person at the South ever thinks of addressing any negro man or woman as Mr., or Mrs., or Miss. The women are called, "Cook," or "Nurse," or "Mammy," or "Mary Jane," or "Lou," or "Dilcey," as the case might be, and the men are called "Bob," or "Boy," or "Old Man," or "Uncle Bill," or "Pate." In many cases our white employers refer to us, and in our presence, too, as their "niggers." No matter what they call us—no matter what they teach their children to call us—we must tamely submit, and answer when we are called; we must enter no protest; if we did object, we should be driven out without the least ceremony, and, in applying for work at other places, we should find it very hard to procure another situation. In almost every case, when our intending employers would be looking up our record, the information would be given by telephone or otherwise that we were "impudent," "saucy," "dishonest," and "generally unreliable." In our town we have no such thing as an employment agency or intelligence bureau, and, therefore, when we want work, we have to get out on the street and go from place to place, always with hat in hand, hunting for it. . . .

You hear a good deal nowadays about the "service pan." The "service pan" is the general term applied to "leftover" food, which in many a Southern home is freely placed at the disposal of the cook, or, whether so placed or not, it is usually disposed of by the cook. In my town, I know, and I guess in many other towns also, every night when the cook starts for her home she takes with her a pan or a plate of cold victuals. The same thing is true on Sunday afternoon after dinner—and most cooks have nearly every Sunday afternoon off. Well, I'll be frank with you, if it were not for the service pan, I don't know what the majority of our Southern colored families would do. The service pan is the mainstay in many a home. Good cooks in the South receive on an average $8 per month. Porters, butlers, coachmen, janitors, "office boys" and the like, receive on an average $16 per month. Few and far between are the colored men in the South who receive $1 or more per day. Some mechanics do; as, for example, carpenters, brick masons, wheelwrights, blacksmiths, and the like. The vast majority of negroes in my town are serving in menial capacities in homes, stores and offices. Now taking it for granted, for the sake of illustration, that the husband receives $16 per month and the wife $8. That would be $24 between the two. The chances are that they will have anywhere from five to thirteen children between them. Now, how far will $24 go toward housing and feeding and clothing ten or twelve persons for thirty days? And, I tell you, with all of us poor people the service pan is a great institution; it is a great help to us, as we wag along the weary way of life. And then most of the white folks expect their cooks to avail themselves of these perquisites; they allow it; they expect it. I do not deny that the cooks find opportunity to hide away at times, along with the cold "grub," a little sugar, a little flour, a little meal, or a little piece of soap; but I indignantly deny that we are thieves. We don't steal; we just "take" things—they are a part of the oral contract, expressed or implied. We understand it, and most of the white folks understand it. Others may denounce the service pan, and say that it is used only to support idle negroes, but many a time, when I was a cook, and had the responsibility of rearing my three children upon my lone shoulders, many a time I have had occasion to bless the Lord for the service pan!. . .

Questions

1. How did domestic work humiliate women such as the narrator?
2. What is the paradox the narrator experiences in working for white families?
3. What was the service pan? What was its significance to African-American workers?

18-6 *The Principles of Scientific Management* (1911)

Frederick Winslow Taylor

Frederick Winslow Taylor (1856–1915) combined the American love of machines with a passion for improving production systems (see text p. 574). Taylor believed so deeply in the ideal of efficiency that he designed his own tennis racquet and golf putter. Trained as an engineer, he began to implement his notion of "scientific management" in the 1890s. Taylor argued that productivity could be improved through better-designed machines and work habits as well as a pay formula based on piecework. This selection is taken from *The Principles of Scientific Management* (1911).

There were skeptics, and in 1912 Taylor went before a special committee of the House of Representatives to defend what he called "this great mental revolution." However, critics persisted in charging that scientific management dehumanized work by emphasizing machines and productivity.

Source: Frederick Winslow Taylor, "The Principles of Scientific Management" (1911). In Frederick Winslow Taylor, *Scientific Management* (New York: Harper & Bros., 1947; reprint, Westport, Conn.: Greenwood Press, 1972), pp. 58–67.

To return now to our pig-iron handlers at the Bethlehem Steel Company. If Schmidt had been allowed to attack the pile of 47 tons of pig iron without the guidance or direction of a man who understood the art, or science, of handling pig iron, in his desire to earn his high wages he would probably have tired himself out by 11 or 12 o'clock in the day. He would have kept so steadily at work that his muscles would not have the proper periods of rest absolutely needed for recuperation, and he would have been completely exhausted early in the day. By having a man, however, who understood this law, stand over him and direct his work, day after day, until he acquired the habit of resting at proper intervals, he was able to work at an even gait all day long without unduly tiring himself.

Now one of the very first requirements for a man who is fit to handle pig iron as a regular occupation is that he shall be so stupid and so phlegmatic that he more nearly resembles in his mental make-up the ox than any other type. The man who is mentally alert and intelligent is for this very reason entirely unsuited to what would, for him, be the grinding monotony of work of this character. Therefore the workman who is best suited to handling pig iron is unable to understand the real science of doing this class of work. He is so stupid that the word "percentage" has no meaning to him, and he must consequently be trained by a man more intelligent than himself into the habit of working in accordance with the laws of this science before he can be successful.

The writer trusts that it is now clear that even in the case of the most elementary form of labor that is known, there is a science, and that when the man best suited to this class of work has been carefully selected, when the science of doing the work has been developed, and when the carefully selected man has been trained to work in accordance with this science, the results obtained must of necessity be overwhelmingly greater than those which are possible under the plan of "initiative and incentive."

Let us, however, again turn to the case of these pig-iron handlers, and see whether, under the ordinary type of management, it would not have been possible to obtain practically the same results.

The writer has put the problem before many good managers, and asked them whether, under premium work, piece work, or any of the ordinary plans of management, they would be likely even to approximate 47 tons per man per day, and not a man has suggested that an output of over 18 to 25 tons could be attained by any of the ordinary expedients. It will be remembered that the Bethlehem men were loading only $12\frac{1}{2}$ tons per man.

To go into the matter in more detail, however: As to the scientific selection of the men, it is a fact that in this gang of 75 pig-iron handlers only about one man in eight was physically capable of handling $47\frac{1}{2}$ tons per day. With the very best of intentions, the other seven out of eight men were physically unable to work at this pace. Now the one man in eight who was able to do this work was in no sense superior to the other men who were working on the gang. He merely happened to be a man of the type of the ox,—no rare specimen of humanity, difficult to find and therefore very highly prized. On the contrary, he was a man so stupid that he was unfitted to do most kinds of laboring work, even. The selection of the man, then, does not involve finding some extraordinary individual, but merely picking out from among very ordinary men the few who are especially suited to this type of work. Although in this particular gang only one man in eight was suited to doing the work, we had not the slightest difficulty in getting all the men who were needed—some of them from inside of the works and others from the neighboring country—who were exactly suited to the job.

Under the management of "initiative and incentive" the attitude of the management is that of "putting the work up to the workmen." What likelihood would there be, then, under the old type of management, of these men properly selecting themselves for pig-iron handling? Would they be likely to get rid of seven men out of eight from their own gang and retain only the eighth man? No! And no expedient could be devised which would make these men properly select themselves. Even if they fully realized the necessity of doing so in order to obtain high wages (and they are not sufficiently intelligent properly to grasp this necessity), the fact that their friends or their brothers who were working right alongside of them would temporarily be thrown out of a job because they were not suited to this kind of work would entirely prevent them from properly selecting themselves, that is, from removing the seven out of eight men on the gang who were unsuited to pig-iron handling.

As to the possibility, under the old type of management, of inducing these pig-iron handlers (after they had been properly selected) to work in accordance with the science of doing heavy laboring, namely, having proper scientifically determined periods of rest in close sequence to periods of work. As has been indicated before, the essential idea of the ordinary types of management is that each workman has become more skilled in his own trade than it is possible for any one in the management to be, and that, therefore, the details of how the work shall best be done must be left to him. The idea, then, of taking one man after another and training him under a competent teacher into new working habits until he continually and habitually works in accordance with scientific laws, which have been developed by some one else, is directly antagonistic to the old idea that each workman can best regulate his own way of doing the work. And besides this, the man suited to handling pig iron is too stupid properly to train himself. Thus it will be seen that with the ordinary types of management the development of scientific knowledge to replace rule of thumb, the scientific selection of the men, and inducing the men to work in accordance with these scientific principles are entirely out of the question. And this because the philosophy of the old management puts the entire responsibility upon the workmen, while the philosophy of the new places a great part of it upon the management.

With most readers great sympathy will be aroused because seven out of eight of these pig-iron handlers were thrown out of a job. This sympathy is entirely wasted, because almost all of them were immediately given other jobs with the Bethlehem Steel Company. And indeed it should be understood that the removal of these men from pig-iron handling, for which they were unfit, was really a kindness to themselves, because it was the first step toward finding them work for which they were peculiarly fitted, and at which, after receiving proper training, they could permanently and legitimately earn higher wages.

Although the reader may be convinced that there is a certain science back of the handling of pig iron, still it is more than likely that he is still skeptical as to the existence of a science for doing other kinds of laboring. One of the important objects of this paper is to convince its readers that every single act of every workman can be reduced to a science. With the hope of fully convincing the reader of this fact, therefore, the writer proposes to give several more simple illustrations from among the thousands which are at hand.

For example, the average man would question whether there is much of any science in the work of shoveling. Yet there is but little doubt, if any intelligent reader of this paper were deliberately to set out to find what may be called the foundation of the science of shoveling, that with perhaps 15 to 20 hours of thought and analysis he would be almost sure to have arrived at the essence of this science. On the other hand, so completely are the rule-of-thumb ideas still dominant that the writer has never met a single shovel contractor to whom it had ever even occurred that there was such a thing as the science of shoveling. This science is so elementary as to be almost self-evident.

For a first class shoveler there is a given shovel load at which he will do his biggest day's work. What is this shovel load? Will a first-class man do more work per day with a shovel load of 5 pounds, 10 pounds, 15 pounds, 20, 25, 30, or 40 pounds? Now this is a question which can be answered only through carefully made experiments. By first selecting two or three first-class shovelers, and paying them extra wages for doing trustworthy work, and then gradually varying the shovel load and having all the conditions accompanying the work carefully observed for several weeks by men who were used to experimenting, it was found that a first-class man would do his biggest day's work with a shovel load of about 21 pounds. For instance, that this man would shovel a larger tonnage per day with a 21-pound load than with a 24-pound load or than with an 18-pound load on his shovel. It is, of course, evident that no shoveler can always take a load of exactly 21 pounds on his shovel, but nevertheless, although his load may vary 3 or 4 pounds one way or the other, either below or above

the 21 pounds, he will do his biggest day's work when his average for the day is about 21 pounds.

The writer does not wish it to be understood that this is the whole of the art or science of shoveling. There are many other elements, which together go to make up this science. But he wishes to indicate the important effect which this one piece of scientific knowledge has upon the work of shoveling.

At the works of the Bethlehem Steel Company, for example, as a result of this law, instead of allowing each shoveler to select and own his own shovel, it became necessary to provide some 8 to 10 different kinds of shovels, etc., each one appropriate to handling a given type of material; not only so as to enable the men to handle an average load of 21 pounds, but also to adapt the shovel to several other requirements which become perfectly evident when this work is studied as a science. A large shovel tool room was built, in which were stored not only shovels but carefully designed and standardized labor implements of all kinds, such as picks, crowbars, etc. This made it possible to issue to each workman a shovel which would hold a load of 21 pounds of whatever class of material they were to handle: a small shovel for ore, say, or a large one for ashes. Iron ore is one of the heavy materials which are handled in a works of this kind, and rice coal, owing to the fact that it is so slippery on the shovel, is one of the lightest materials. And it found on studying the rule-of-thumb plan at the Bethlehem Steel Company, where each shoveler owned his own shovel, that he would frequently go from shoveling ore, with a load of about 30 pounds per shovel, to handling rice coal, with a load on the same shovel of less than 4 pounds. In the one case, he was so overloaded that it was impossible for him to do a full day's work, and in the other case he was so ridiculously underloaded that it was manifestly impossible to even approximate a day's work.

Briefly to illustrate some of the other elements which go to make up the science of shoveling, thousands of stopwatch observations were made to study just how quickly a laborer, provided in each case with the proper type of shovel, can push his shovel into the pile of materials and then draw it out properly loaded. These observations were made first when pushing the shovel into the body of the pile. Next when shoveling on a dirt bottom, that is, at the outside edge of the pile, and next with a wooden bottom, and finally with an iron bottom. Again a similar accurate time study was made of the time required to swing the shovel backward and then throw the load for a given horizontal distance, accompanied by a given height. This time study was made for various combinations of distance and height. With data of this sort before him, coupled with the law of endurance described in the case of the pig-iron handlers, it is evident that the man who is directing shovelers can first teach them the exact methods which should be employed. . . .

Questions

1. In what ways does Taylor exhibit a bias against workers? How does he cloak that bias in the mantle of objective science?
2. Who was likely to benefit from and who was likely to be hurt by scientific management?
3. Given business's need to make a profit, what, if any, alternative is there to scientific management?

Questions for Further Thought

1. Imagine that Frederick Winslow Taylor (Document 18-6) and Rocco Corresca (Document 18-4) have traded occupations. How might the experiences of each affect his approach to his new position?
2. Why do you think many African-Americans left domestic jobs in the South (Document 18-5) for jobs in the North like those described in Document 18-4?
3. Frederick Winslow Taylor (Document 18-6) sensed that Americans defer to the power of "science." Why does that happen? In what ways did scientific management discourage innovation on the work floor?

The Labor Movement

When Thomas B. McGuire, a wagon driver, told a Senate committee in 1883 that he had once wanted to "become something of a capitalist eventually," he gave voice to a hope held by many working-class Americans (see text p. 574). But McGuire found it impossible to climb the class ladder. The national economy had changed and did not provide easy mobility for those who saw themselves as the heirs of the artisans and mechanics of an earlier America.

Labor unrest grew throughout the 1870s and 1880s, with the Knights of Labor as the immediate beneficiary (see text pp. 574–576). Under the leadership of Terence Powderly, the Knights were an urban version of the Grange, combining social activities with group protest (Document 18-7). The Knights vowed to fight for "labor emancipation" but had little idea how to bring it about. The group was in a severe decline by the 1890s. In its place the American Federation of Labor arose as the nation's preeminent labor organization (see text pp. 576–578). Labor's frustrations led some workers to political radicalism and a few to violence. Among those making that journey was Albert Parsons, a veteran of the Confederate army. Parsons wrote a short autobiography (Document 18-8) as he awaited execution for his role in the Haymarket Square riot (see text pp. 576–577).

Trade unionism accepted capitalism; socialism did not. Although the Pullman boycott of 1894 constituted another labor defeat, it helped turn the union leader Eugene Debs into a socialist (see text pp. 580–581). An Indiana native, Debs put an American face on a largely European movement (Document 18-9). He ran for president five times on the Socialist ticket and got 920,000 votes in 1920.

The following three selections show that working-class America was of more than one mind and had more than one voice.

18-7   "The Army of Unemployed" (1887)

Terence V. Powderly

The growth of the factory system left the working class unsettled. Periodically, as with the Haymarket Square riot and the Pullman boycott (see text pp. 576–577, 579–580), discontent led to violence. But overall, workers were more concerned with finding a way to protect their interests.

The Knights of Labor, founded in 1869, offered some promise in that regard. The group's use of ritual and ceremony cloaked it in nineteenth-century respectability: the Knights could claim that they were little different from the Masons. The Knights were not a union in the modern sense; they focused on education rather than organization (see text pp. 575–576). Although membership reached 700,000 by 1885, the Knights did not win any significant victories.

In the following selection Terence V. Powderly, the Knights' Grand Master Workman, struggles to offer a solution to the labor problems of the 1880s.

Source: Terence V. Powderly, "The Army of Unemployed," in George E. McNeill, ed., *The Labor Movement: The Problem of Today* (Boston: A. M. Bridgeman & Company, and New York: M. W. Hazen Company, 1887; reprint, New York: Augustus M. Kelley Publishers, 1971), pp. 577–584.

The Cincinnati riots, that occurred less than one year ago, were not brought about through the agitation of the labor-leader. If the demand for "the removal of unjust technicalities, delays and discriminations in the administration of justice," had been listened to when first made by the Knights of Labor, Cincinnati would have been spared sorrow and disgrace, and her "prominent citizens" would not have had to lead a mob, in order to open the eyes of the country to the manner in which her courts were throttled, and virtue and truth were trampled upon in her temples of justice. That the army of the discontented is gathering fresh recruits day by day, is true; and if this army should become so large, that, driven to desperation, it should one day arise in its wrath, and grapple with its real or fancied enemy, the responsibility for that act must fall upon the heads of those who could have averted the blow, but who turned a deaf ear to the supplication of suffering humanity, and gave the screw of oppression an extra turn, because they had the power. Workingmen's organizations are doing all they can to avert the blow; but if that day dawns upon us, it will be chargeable directly to men who taunt others with unequal earnings, and distort the truth, as was done in an interview recently had with Mr. William H. Vanderbilt:—

One of the troubles in this country, just now, is the relation of wages to the cost of production. A skilled workman, in almost every branch of business, gets every day money enough to buy a barrel of flour. I don't refer to ordinary laborers, but to men skilled at their trades. The man who makes the article receives as much wages, in many instances, as the article is worth when it is finished. This is not exactly fair, in my opinion, and must be adjusted. Until wages bear a truer relation to production, there can be no real prosperity in the country.

I have seen no denial of the above, and take it for granted that it is a correct report. Mr. Vanderbilt starts out well enough; but he is in error when he says that "a skilled workman, in almost every branch of business, gets money enough every day to buy a barrel of flour." I know of no business in the United States, in which a skilled mechanic, working regularly at his trade day by day, gets money enough for his day's labor to buy a barrel of flour. That they earn the price of a barrel of flour, I do not deny; but that they get it, is not true. It may be that Mr. Vanderbilt refers to superintendents, foremen or contractors; for they are the only ones that receive such wages. The average wages paid to the skilled mechanic will not exceed $2.50 a day. I know of but few branches of business in which men can command that price. The wages of skilled mechanics are on the decline, while the price of flour remains unchanged, from $5.75 to $8.50 a barrel. If Mr. Vanderbilt will demonstrate how one can purchase a six-dollar barrel of flour for two dollars and a half, he will have solved a very difficult problem for the workingman. . . .

It may be said that many of the employees of the manufacturing establishments are minors, and consequently cannot perform as great an amount of labor as a corresponding number of adults. That argument might have had some weight years ago, but now it is fruitless. The age and strength of the workman are no longer regarded as factors in the field of production; it is the skill of the operator in managing a labor-saving machine that is held to be the most essential. It is true that a child can operate a machine as successfully as a man, and that muscle is no longer a requisite in accomplishing results. It is also true that less time is required to perform a given amount of labor than heretofore. This being the case, the plea for shorter hours is not unreasonable. Benjamin Franklin said, one hundred years ago, that "if the workers of the world would labor but four hours each day, they could produce enough in that length of time to supply the wants of mankind." While it is true that the means of supplying the wants of man have increased as if by magic, yet man has acquired no new wants; he is merely enabled to gratify his needs more fully. If it were true in Franklin's time that four hours of toil each day would prove sufficient to minister to the necessities of the world's inhabitants, the argument certainly has lost none of its force since then. At that time, it took the sailing-vessel three months to cross the ocean; the stage-coach made its thirty or forty miles a day; the electric wire was not dreamed of; and the letter that traveled but little faster than the stage-coach was the quickest medium of communication.

It required six days' labor at the hands of the machinist, with hammer, chisel and file to perfect a certain piece of machinery at the beginning of this century. The machinist of the present day can finish a better job in six hours, with the aid of a labor-saving machine. In a yarn-mill in Philadelphia, the proprietor says that improved machinery has caused a displacement of fifty per cent. of the former employees within five years, and that one person, with the aid of improved machinery, can perform the work that it took upward of one hundred carders and spinners to do with the tools and implements in use at the beginning of this century. In Massachusetts, it has been estimated that 318,768 men, women and children do, with improved machinery, the work that it would require 1,912,468 men to perform, if improved machinery were not in use. To insure safety on a passenger-train, it is no longer necessary to have a brakeman at each end of the car; the automatic air-brake does the work, while one brakeman can shout, "All right here!" for the whole train. The employee that has had a limb cut off in a collision, must beg for bread or turn the crank of a hand-organ, and gather his pennies under the legend, "Please assist a poor soldier, who lost his leg at Gettysburg." He is no longer stationed, flag in hand, at the switch; the automatic lever directs the course of the train, and renders the one-legged switchman unnecessary. It is said that the iron-moulder recently invented is capable of performing as much labor as three skilled workmen; while the following dispatch to a Philadelphia paper, from Mahanoy City, shows what is being done in the mines.—

For the past three years the reduction in wages has been systematic and steady. When one of the officials of one of the great companies was interviewed on the matter, he replied that the advance in labor-saving machinery had lightened the labor of the men. A miner at one of the Reading collieries says that some months ago he expended a large sum for a patent drill, which enabled him to do five times the usual amount of work. He was employed in driving a gangway, the price paid being $10 a yard; but at the end of the week, when the officials saw the amount of work he had done, the rate was reduced to $4.50 a yard. . . .

A great many remedies are recommended for the ills that I speak of. Let me deal with what seems to be the most unimportant,—the reduction of the hours of labor to eight a day. Men, women and children are working from ten to eighteen hours a day, and two million men have nothing to do. If four men, following a given occupation, at which they work ten hours a day, would rest from their labors two hours each day, the two hours taken from the labor of each, if added together, would give the tramp that stands looking on, an opportunity of stepping into a position at eight hours a day. It is said that a vast majority of those who are idle would not work, if they had work to do. That statement is untrue; but let us admit that five hundred thousand of the two million idle men would not work, and we still have a million and a half who are anxious and willing to work. If but six million of the seventeen million producers will abstain from working ten, fifteen, and eighteen hours a day, and work but eight, the one million and a half of idle men that are willing to work, can again take their places in the ranks of the world's producers. Need it be said, that a million and a half of new hats will be needed; that a corresponding number of pairs of shoes, suits of clothing, and a hundred other things will be required; that the wants of these men and their families will be supplied; that shelves will be emptied of their goods, and that the money expended will again go into circulation. It would entail hardship on some branches of business, to require men employed in them to work eight hours a day. Miners and those working by contract could not very well adopt the eight-hour plan, without lengthening their hours of labor. Before giving the matter a second thought, many of these men look upon the eight-hour agitation as of no consequence to them. If a mechanic is thrown out of employment, and cannot find anything to do at his trade, he turns toward the first place where an opportunity for work is presented. If he is re-enforced by two million idle men, the number that apply at the mouth of the mine, or seek to secure contracts at lower figures, becomes quite large; and the miner and contract-man grumble, because so many men are crowding in upon them in quest of work. Every new applicant for work in the mine makes it possible for the boss to let his contract to a lower bidder; therefore, it is clearly to the interest of the miner to assist in reducing the hours of labor in the shop, mill and factory, to the end that the idle millions may be gathered in from the streets to self-sustaining positions.

The eight-hour system, to be of value to the masses, must be put in operation all over the country; for the manufacturers of one State cannot successfully compete with those of other States, if they run their establishments but eight hours, while others operate theirs ten or twelve hours a day. The movement should be national, and should have the hearty co-operation of all men. . . .

When the President of the United States issued his Thanksgiving proclamation, in 1884, there were millions of men and women in want of bread, notwithstanding "the abundant harvests and continued prosperity which God hath vouchsafed to this nation;" and the cry, not of thanksgiving, went up from millions of farmers, of "Too much wheat!" Doubting as to the exact meaning of the

Creator in growing so much wheat, they invoked the aid of such institutions as the Chicago Board of Trade, in the hope of thwarting the will of God, by cornering wheat. These men invoked blessings on their Thanksgiving dinners, and thanked God for the turkey, while they hoarded the wheat away from those who asked for bread.

Give men shorter hours in which to labor, and you give them more time to study, and learn why bread is so scarce, while wheat is so plenty. You give them more time in which to learn that millions of acres of American soil are controlled by alien landlords, that have no interest in America but to draw a revenue from it. You give them time to learn that America belongs to Americans, native and naturalized, and that the landlord who drives his tenant from the Old World must not be permitted to exact tribute from him when he settles in our country.

Questions

1. How does Powderly's use of the term *mechanic* suggest that the Knights were a backward-looking movement?
2. What does Powderly suggest as a remedy for the workers' situation?
3. How does Powderly characterize businessmen?

18-8 The Autobiography of Albert Parsons (1887)

The Haymarket Square riot of of 1886 (see text pp. 576–577) left seven Chicago police officers dead and led to the conviction of eight men for criminal conspiracy; seven of the defendants were sentenced to death, and four were executed. The riot and the trial convinced political radicals of the injustice inherent in American society, while the middle class recoiled from the violence and talk of revolution that were associated with the incident. Workers found themselves caught in the middle between extremes that saw them as the pawns of either the revolutionaries or the capitalists. One of those condemned to death was Albert Parsons (1848–1887), a Confederate army veteran who eventually became a dedicated anarchist. This excerpt is from an autobiography Parsons composed while awaiting execution.

Source: "Autobiography of Albert R. Parsons," in Philip S. Foner, ed., *The Autobiographies of the Haymarket Martyrs*, AIMS Historical Series No. 5 (New York: Humanities Press, 1969), pp. 28–31, 42–45, 55–57.

My mother died when I was not yet two years old and my father died when I was five years of age. Shortly after this my eldest brother, William Henry Parsons, who had married and was then living at Tyler, Tex., became my

guardian. He was proprietor and editor of the Tyler *Telegraph*; that was in 1851, '52, '53. Two years later our family moved West to Johnston county, on the Texas frontier, while the buffalo, antelope and Indian were in that region.

Here we lived, on a ranch, for about three years, when we moved to Hill county and took up a farm in the valley of the Brazos river. My frontier life had accustomed me to the use of the rifle and the pistol, to hunting and riding, and in these matters I was considered quite an expert. At that time our neighbors did not live near enough to hear each other's dog bark, or the cocks crow. It was often five to ten or fifteen miles to the next house. In 1859, I went to Waco, Texas, where, after living with my sister (the wife of Maj. Boyd) and going to school, meantime, for about a year, I was indentured an apprentice to the Galveston *Daily News*, for seven years, to learn the printer's trade. Entering upon my duties as a "printer's devil," I also became a paper carrier for the *Daily News*, and in a year and a half was transformed from a frontier boy into a city civilian. When the slave-holder's rebellion broke out in 1861, though quite small and but thirteen years old, I joined a local volunteer company called the "Lone Star Greys." My first military exploit was on the passenger steamer Morgan, where we made a trip out into the Gulf of Mexico and intercepted and assisted in the capture of U.S. Gen. Twigg's army, which had evacuated the Texas frontier forts and came to the sea coast at Indianapolis to embark for Washington, D.C.

My first military exploit was a "run-away" trip on my part for which I received an ear pulled from my guardian when I returned. These were stirring "wartimes" and, as a matter of course, my young blood caught the infection. I wanted to enlist in the rebel army and join Gen. Lee in Virginia, but my guardian, Mr. Richardson, proprietor of the *News*, a man of 60 years, and the leader of the secession movement in Texas, ridiculed the idea, on account of my age and size, and ended by telling me that "it's all bluster anyway. It will be ended in the next sixty days and I'll hold in my hat all the blood that's shed in this war." This statement from one whom I thought knew all about it, only served to fix all the firmer my resolve to go and go at once, before too late. So I took "French leave" and joined an artillery company at an improvised fort at Sabine Pass, Texas, where Capt. Richard Parsons, an older brother, was in command of an infantry company. Here I exercised in infantry drill and served as "powder monkey" [a boy responsible for supplying powder] for the cannoneers. My military enlistment expired in twelve months, when I left Fort Sabine and joined Parson's Texas cavalry brigade, then on the Mississippi river. My brother, Maj. Gen. W.H. Parsons (who during the war was by his soldiers invested with the sobriquet "Wild Bill,") was at that time in command of the entire cavalry outposts on the west bank of the Mississippi river from Helena to the mouth of the Red river. His cavalrymen held the advance in every movement of the Trans-Mississippi army, from the defeat of the Federal General Curtis on White river to the defeat of Gen. Banks' army on Red river, which closed the fighting on the west side of the Mississippi. I was a mere boy of 15 when I joined my brother's

command at the front on White river, and was afterward a member of the renowned McInoly scouts under Gen. Parson's orders, which participated in all the battles of the Curtis, Canby and Banks campaign.

On my return to Waco, Texas, at the close of the war, I traded a good mule, all the property I possessed, for forty acres of corn in the field standing ready for harvest, to a refugee who desired to flee the country. I hired and paid wages (the first they had ever received) to a number of ex-slaves, and together we reaped the harvest. From the proceeds of its sales, I obtained a sum sufficient to pay for six months' tuition at the Waco university, under control of Rev. Dr. R. B. Burleson, where I received about all the technical education I ever had. Soon afterwards I took up the trade of type-setting, and went to work in a printing office in the town. In 1868 I founded and edited a weekly newspaper in Waco, named *The Spectator*. In it I advocated, with [ex-Confederate General James] General Longstreet, the acceptance, in good faith, of the terms of surrender, and supported the thirteenth, fourteenth and fifteenth constitutional amendments, and the reconstruction measures, securing the political rights of the colored people. (I was strongly influenced in taking this step out of respect and love for the memory of dear old "Aunt Ester," then dead, and formerly a slave and house servant of my brother's family, she having been my constant associate, and practically raised me, with great kindness and a mother's love.) I became a Republican, and, of course, had to go into politics. I incurred thereby the hate and contumely of many of my former army comrades, neighbors, and the Ku Klux Klan. My political career was full of excitement and danger. I took the stump to vindicate my convictions. The lately enfranchised slaves over a large section of the country came to know and idolize me as their friend and defender, while on the other hand I was regarded as a political heretic and traitor by many of my former associates. The *Spectator* could not long survive such an atmosphere. In 1869 I was appointed traveling correspondent and agent for the Houston *Daily Telegraph*, and started out on horseback (our principal mode of travel at that time) for a long tour through northwestern Texas. It was during this trip through Johnson county that I first met the charming young Spanish Indian maiden who, three years later, became my wife. She lived in a most beautiful region of country, on her uncle's ranch, near Buffalo Creek. I lingered in this neighborhood as long as I could, and then pursued my journey with fair success. In 1870, at 21 years of age, I was appointed Assistant Assessor of United States Internal Revenues, under General Grant's administration. About a year later I was elected one of the secretaries of the Texas State Senate, and was soon after appointed Chief Deputy Collector of United States Internal Revenue, at Austin, Texas, which position I held, accounting satisfactorily for large sums of money, until 1873, when I resigned the position. In August, 1873, I accompanied an editorial excursion, as the representative of the Texas *Agriculturist* at Austin, Texas, and in company with a large delegation of Texas editors, made an extended tour through Texas, Indian Nation, Missouri, Iowa, Illinois, Ohio, and Pennsylvania, as guests of the Missouri, Kansas & Texas railway, I decided to settle in Chicago. I had married in Austin, Texas, in the fall of 1872, and my wife joining me at Philadelphia we came to Chicago together, where we have lived till the present time. I at once became a member of Typographical Union No. 16, and "subbed" for a time on the *Inter-Ocean*, when I went to work under "permit" on the *Times*. Here I worked over four years holding a situation at "the case." In 1874 I became interested in the "Labor question," growing out of the effort made by Chicago working people at that time to compel the "Relief and Aid Society," to render to the suffering poor of the city an account of the vast sums of money (several millions of dollars) held by that society and contributed by the whole world to relieve the distress occasioned by the great Chicago fire of 1871. It was claimed by the working people that the money was being used for purposes foreign to the intention of its donors; that rings of speculators were corruptly using the money, while the distressed and impoverished people for whom it was contributed, were denied its use. This raised a great sensation and scandal among all the city newspapers, which defended the "Relief and Aid Society," and denounced the dissatisfied workingmen as "communists, robbers, loafers," etc. I began to examine into this subject, and I found that the complaints of the working people against the society were just and proper. I also discovered a great similarity between the abuse heaped upon these poor people by the organs of the rich and the actions of the late Southern slave holders in Texas toward the newly enfranchised slaves, whom they accused of wanting to make their former masters "divide" by giving them "forty acres and a mule," and it satisfied me there was a great fundamental wrong at work in society, and in existing social and industrial arrangements.

From this time dated my interest and activity in the labor movement. The desire to know more about this subject led me in contact with socialists and their writings, they being the only people who at that time had made any protest against or offered any remedy for, the enforced poverty of the wealth producers and its collateral evils of ignorance, intemperance, crime and misery. There were very few socialists or "communists" as the daily papers were fond of calling them, in Chicago at that time. The result was, the more I investigated and studied the relations of poverty to wealth, its causes and cure, the more interested I became in the subject. In 1876, a workingmen's congress of organized labor met in Pittsburgh, Pa. I watched its proceedings. A split occurred between the conservatives and radicals, the latter of whom withdrew and organized the "Workingmen's Party of the United States." The year previous I had become a member of the "Social

Democratic Party of America." This latter was now merged into the former. The organization was at once pounced upon by the monopolist class, who, through the capitalist press everywhere, denounced us as "socialists, communists, robbers, loafers," etc.

This was very surprising to me, and also had an exasperating effect upon me, and a powerful impulse possessed me to place myself right before the people by defining and explaining the objects and principles of the workingmen's party, which I was thoroughly convinced were founded both in justice and on necessity. I therefore entered heartily into the work of enlightening my fellow men. First, the ignorant and blinded wage-workers who misunderstood us, and secondly, the educated labor exploiters who misrepresented us. I soon unconsciously became a "labor agitator," and this brought down upon me a large amount of capitalist odium. But this capitalist abuse and slander only served to renew my zeal all the more in the great work of social redemption. . . .

In 1880 I withdrew from all active participation in the political Labor party, having been convinced that the number of hours per day that the wage-workers are compelled to work, together with the low wages they received, amounted to their practical disfranchisement as voters. I saw that long hours and low wages deprived the wage-workers, as a class, of the necessary time and means, and consequently left them but little inclination to organize for political action to abolish class legislation. My experience in the Labor party had also taught me that bribery, intimidation, duplicity, corruption, and bulldozing grew out of the conditions which made the working people poor and the idlers rich, and that consequently the ballot-box could not be made an index to record the popular will until the existing debasing, impoverishing, and enslaving industrial conditions were first altered. For these reasons I turned my activities mainly toward an effort to reduce the hours of labor to at least a normal working day, so that the wage-workers might thereby secure more leisure from mere drudge work, and obtain better pay to minister to their higher aspirations. . . .

What, then, is our offense, being anarchists? The word *anarche* is derived from two Greek words *an*, signifying no, or without, and *arche*, government; hence anarchy means no government. Consequently anarchy meant a condition of society which has no king, emperor, president or ruler of any kind. In other words anarchy is the social administration of all affairs by the people themselves; that is to say, self government, individual liberty. Such a condition of society denies the right of majorities to rule over or dictate to minorities. Though every person in the world agree upon a certain plan and only one objected thereto, the objector would, under anarchy, be respected in his natural right to go his own way. And when such person is thus held responsible by all the rest for the violation of the inherent right of any one how then, can injustice flourish or wrong triumph? For the greatest good to the greatest number anarchy substitutes the equal right of each and every one. The natural law is all sufficient for every purpose, every desire and every human being. The scientist then becomes the natural leader, and is accepted as the only authority among men. Whatever can be demonstrated will by self interest be accepted, otherwise rejected. The great natural law of power derived alone from association and cooperation will of necessity and from selfishness be applied by the people in the production and distribution of wealth, and what the trades unions and labor organizations seek now to do, but are prevented from doing because of obstruction and coercion, will under perfect liberty—anarchy—come easiest to hand. Anarchy is the extension of the boundaries of liberty until it covers the whole range of the wants and aspirations of man—*not* men, but *Man*.

Power is might, and might always makes its own right. Thus in the very nature of things, might makes itself right whether or no. Government, therefore, is the agency or power by which some person or persons govern or rule other persons, and the inherent right to govern is found wherever the power or might to do so is manifest. In a natural state, intelligence of necessity controls ignorance, the strong the weak, the good the bad, etc. Only when the natural law operates is this true, however. On the other hand when the statute is substituted for the natural law, and government holds sway, then, and then only, power centers itself in the hands of a few, who dominate, dictate, rule, degrade and enslave the many. The broad distinction and irreconcilable conflict between wage laborers and capitalists, between those who buy labor or sell its products, and the wage worker who sells his labor (himself) in order to live, arises from the social institution called government; and the conflicting interests, the total abolition of warring classes, and the end of domination and exploitation of man by man is to be found only in a free society, where all and each are equally free to unite or disunite, as interest or inclination may incline. . . .

This Haymarket affair has exposed to public view the hideous enormities of capitalism and the barbarous despotism of government. The tragedy and the effects of it have demonstrated first: That government is power, and statute law is license, because it is privilege. It has shown the people, the poor, the wage-slaves, that law, statute law is a privilege, and that privileges are for sale to those who can buy them. Government enacts law; the police, the soldier and the jailor at the behest of the rich enforce it. Law is license, the whole earth and all it contains has been sold to a few who are thus authorized by statute law, licensed to rob the many of their natural inheritance. Law is license. The few are licensed by law to own the land, the machinery, the houses, food, clothes and shelter of the people, whose industry, whose labor created them. Law is license; law, statute law, is the coward's weapon, the tool of the thief. By it humanity has ever been degraded and enslaved. By law mankind is robbed of its birthright, liberty transformed into slavery; life into death; the fair earth into a den of thieves and murderers. The untold millions, the men, women and children of toil, the *proletariat*, are by law deprived of their lives, their liberties and their happiness. Law is license; Government—authority—is despotism.

Anarchy, natural law, is liberty. Liberty is the natural right to do what one pleases, bounded and limited only by the equal right of every one else to the same liberty. Privileges are none; equal rights of all. Liberty, Fraternity, Equality.

Questions

1. What changed Parsons's political and racial views after the Civil War?
2. How does he define anarchism?
3. To what extent are Parsons's views grounded in reality? In theory? Why should the distinction matter to working-class Americans?

18-9 "How I Became a Socialist" (1902)

Eugene V. Debs

For some people the goals of organized labor were too limited. Even if the AFL won some victories, the economy would remain firmly under the control of a capitalist elite. Rather than accept that prospect, some workers turned to socialism.

The movement had a deep if limited appeal. Socialism promised to address inequality in industrial America by giving workers—the great majority of the population—control over the economy and the government. This was not Jeffersonian or

Jacksonian democracy, and socialism remained a marginal idea as long as it appeared to be a Marxist import from Europe.

Eugene V. Debs (1855–1926) helped make socialism respectable, even mainstream, in the first decades of the twentieth century (see text pp. 580–581). Debs came from a middle-class family in Terre Haute, Indiana, and at one time had been a conventional Democrat and trade unionist. In this essay Debs explains the reasons for his change of philosophy. The "anarchists" he mentions were the four Chicago labor figures who were hanged for their role in the Haymarket Square riot of 1886 (see text pp. 576–577).

Source: Eugene V. Debs, "How I Became a Socialist," *The Comrade,* April 1902.

As I have some doubt about the readers of *The Comrade* having any curiosity as to "how I became a socialist" it may be in order to say that the subject is the editor's, not my own; and that what is here offered is at his bidding— my only concern being that he shall not have cause to wish that I had remained what I was instead of becoming a socialist.

On the evening of February 27, 1875, the local lodge of the Brotherhood of Locomotive Firemen was organized at Terre Haute, Indiana, by Joshua A. Leach, then grand master, and I was admitted as a charter member and at once chosen secretary. "Old Josh Leach," as he was affectionately called, a typical locomotive fireman of his day, was the founder of the brotherhood, and I was instantly attracted by his rugged honesty, simple manner and homely speech. How well I remember feeling his large, rough hand on my shoulder, the kindly eye of an elder brother searching my own as he gently said: "My boy, you're a little young, but I believe you're in earnest and will make your mark in the brotherhood." Of course, I assured him that I would do my best. What he really thought at the time flattered my boyish vanity not a little when I heard of it. He was attending a meeting at St. Louis some months later, and in the course of his remarks said: "I put a tow-headed boy in the brotherhood at Terre Haute not long ago, and some day he will be at the head of it." . . .

My first step was thus taken in organized labor and a new influence fired my ambition and changed the whole current of my career. I was filled with enthusiasm and my blood fairly leaped in my veins. Day and night I worked for the brotherhood. To see its watchfires glow and observe the increase of its sturdy members were the sunshine and shower of my life. To attend the "meeting" was my supreme joy, and for ten years I was not once absent when the faithful assembled.

At the convention held in Buffalo in 1878 I was chosen associate editor of the magazine, and in 1880 I became grand secretary and treasurer. With all the fire of youth I entered upon the crusade which seemed to fairly glitter with possibilities. For eighteen hours at a stretch I was glued to my desk reeling off the answers to my many correspondents. Day and night were one. Sleep was time wasted and often, when all oblivious of her presence in the still small hours my mother's hand turned off the light, I went to bed under protest. Oh, what days! And what quenchless zeal and consuming vanity! . . .

My grip was always packed; and I was darting in all directions. To tramp through a railroad yard in the rain, snow or sleet half the night, or till daybreak, to be ordered out of the roundhouse for being an "agitator," or put off a train, sometimes passenger, more often freight, while attempting to deadhead over the division, were all in the program, and served to whet the appetite to conquer. One night in midwinter at Elmira, New York, a conductor on the Erie kindly dropped me off in a snowbank, and as I clambered to the top I ran into the arms of a policeman, who heard my story and on the spot became my friend.

I rode on the engines over mountain and plain, slept in the cabooses and bunks, and was fed from their pails by the swarthy stokers who still nestle close to my heart, and will until it is cold and still.

Through all these years I was nourished at Fountain Proletaire. I drank deeply of its waters and every particle of my tissue became saturated with the spirit of the working class. I had fired an engine and been stung by the exposure and hardship of the rail. I was with the boys in their weary watches, at the broken engine's side and often helped to bear their bruised and bleeding bodies back to wife and child again. How could I but feel the burden of their wrongs? How could the seed of agitation fail to take deep root in my heart?

And so I was spurred on in the work of organizing, not the firemen merely, but the brakemen, switchmen, telegraphers, shopmen, trackhands, all of them in fact, and as I had now become known as an organizer, the calls came from all sides and there are but few trades I have not helped to organize and less still in whose strikes I have not at some time had a hand.

In 1894 the American Railway Union was organized and a braver body of men never fought the battle of the working class.

Up to this time I had heard but little of socialism, knew practically nothing about the movement, and what little I did know was not calculated to impress me in its favor. I was bent on thorough and complete organization of the railroad men and ultimately the whole working class, and all my time and energy were given to that end. My supreme conviction was that if they were only organized in every branch of the service and all acted together in concert they could redress their wrongs and regulate the conditions of their employment. The stockholders of the corporation acted as one, why not the men? It was such a plain proposition—simply to follow the example set before their eyes by their masters—surely they could not fail to see it, act as one, and solve the problem.

It is useless to say that I had yet to learn the working of the capitalist system, the resources of its masters and the weakness of its slaves. Indeed, no shadow of a "system" fell athwart my pathway; no thought of ending wage misery marred my plans. I was too deeply absorbed in perfecting wage servitude and making it a "thing of beauty and a joy forever."

It all seems very strange to me now, taking a backward look, that my vision was so focalized on a single objective point that I utterly failed to see what now appears as clear as the noonday sun—so clear that I marvel that any workingman, however dull, uncomprehending, can resist it.

But perhaps it was better so. I was to be baptized in socialism in the road of conflict and I thank the gods for reserving to this fitful occasion the fiat, "Let there be light!"—the light that streams in steady radiance upon the broad way to the socialist republic.

The skirmish lines of the A.R.U. were well advanced. A series of small battles was fought and won without the loss of a man. A number of concessions was made by the corporations rather than risk an encounter. Then came the fight on the Great Northern, short, sharp, and decisive. The victory was complete—the only railroad strike of magnitude ever won by an organization in America.

Next followed the final shock—the Pullman strike—and the American Railway Union again won, clear and complete. The combined corporations were paralyzed and helpless. At this juncture there was delivered, from wholly unexpected quarters, a swift succession of blows that blinded me for an instant and then opened wide my eyes—and in the gleam of every bayonet and the flash of every rifle *the class struggle was revealed.* This was my first practical lesson in socialism, though wholly unaware that it was called by that name.

An army of detectives, thugs and murderers was equipped with badge and beer and bludgeon and turned loose; old hulks of cars were fired; the alarm bells tolled; the people were terrified; the most startling rumors were set afloat; the press volleyed and thundered, and over all the wires sped the news that Chicago's white throat was in the clutch of a red mob; injunctions flew thick and fast, arrests followed, and our office and headquarters, the heart of the strike, was sacked, torn out and nailed up by the "lawful" authorities of the federal government; and when in company with my loyal comrades I found myself in Cook County Jail at Chicago, with the whole press screaming conspiracy, treason and murder, and by some fateful coincidence I was given the cell occupied just previous to his execution by the assassin of Mayor Carter Harrison, Sr., overlooking the spot, a few feet distant, where the anarchists were hanged a few years before, I had another exceedingly practical and impressive lesson in socialism.

Acting upon the advice of friends we sought to employ John Harlan, son of the Supreme Justice, to assist in our defense—a defense memorable to me chiefly because of the skill and fidelity of our lawyers, among whom were the brilliant Clarence Darrow and the venerable Judge Lyman Trumbull, author of the thirteenth amendment to the Constitution, abolishing slavery in the United States.

Mr. Harlan wanted to think of the matter overnight; and the next morning gravely informed us that he could not afford to be identified with the case, "for," said he, "you will be tried upon the same theory as were the anarchists, with probably the same result." That day, I remember, the jailer, by way of consolation, I suppose, showed us the bloodstained rope used at the last execution and explained in minutest detail, as he exhibited the gruesome relic, just how the monstrous crime of lawful murder is committed.

But the tempest gradually subsided and with it the bloodthirstiness of the press and "public sentiment." We were not sentenced to the gallows, nor even to the penitentiary—though put on trial for conspiracy—for reasons that will make another story.

The Chicago jail sentences were followed by six months at Woodstock and it was here that socialism gradually laid hold of me in its own irresistible fashion. Books and pamphlets and letters from socialists came by every mail and I began to read and think and dissect the anatomy of the system in which workingmen, however organized, could be shattered and battered and splintered at a single stroke. . . .

It was at this time, when the first glimmerings of socialism were beginning to penetrate, that Victor L. Berger—and I have loved him ever since—came to Woodstock, as if a providential instrument, and delivered the first impassioned message of socialism I had ever heard—the very first to set the "wires humming in my system." As a souvenir of that visit there is in my library a volume of *Capital*, by Karl Marx, inscribed with the compliments of Victor L. Berger, which I cherish as a token of priceless value.

The American Railway Union was defeated but not conquered—overwhelmed but not destroyed. It lives and pulsates in the socialist movement, and its defeat but blazed the way to economic freedom and hastened the dawn of human brotherhood.

Questions

1. What makes Debs's story persuasive?
2. To what extent was Debs a romantic?
3. How did the Pullman boycott affect Debs's thinking?

Questions for Further Thought

1. Compare the arguments presented by Powderly, Parsons, and Debs (Documents 18-7 through 18-9). What was the premise in each case?
2. Of the three, who do you think best understood labor's situation? Who offered the most attractive solution? Explain.
3. Considering that all three men shared many of the same experiences in fighting for the working class, why did Powderly remain a moderate while Parsons and Debs became radicals?

CHAPTER 19

The Politics of Late Nineteenth-Century America

★   ★   ★

The Politics of the Status Quo, 1877–1893

The Civil War and Reconstruction commanded Americans' attention for sixteen years, but with the election of Rutherford B. Hayes in 1876, voters signaled that they were tired of the South's problems. The plight of former slaves no longer elicited concern as people tried to go back to the everyday life they remembered. However, the Gilded Age would not allow that. Too much had changed since 1860, as Americans slowly came to realize. The time of the merchant, the yeoman, and the mechanic had passed.

Still, people fought to make the new conform to the old. In politics the presidency reverted to its passive, antebellum form (see text pp. 587–588), but a figurehead in the White House, even a war hero, could not solve the problems that accompanied industrialization. On the local and state levels the parties campaigned feverishly for the spoils of office rather than the chance to modernize government.

Americans embraced various ideas to rationalize their conditions. Some took heart in the way Horatio Alger championed the ideology of individualism in his rags-to-riches stories, while others applied the theories of Charles Darwin to society (see text pp. 588–590). Still others hoped that American cultural values would solve the nation's mounting social problems; the trick was to make everyone act and speak like a white Anglo-Saxon Protestant. In each case middle-class Americans were encouraged to think that no fundamental change was necessary in society, at least on their part.

In Document 19-1 Horatio Alger (see text pp. 589–590) delivers a sermon on the role of character in success. In Document 19-2 William Graham Sumner (see text p. 589) defends Social Darwinism. Thomas Nast's cartoon (Document 19-3) reflects the anxiety of Protestant Americans over the growing presence of immigrants. Frances Willard (Document 19-4) shows that there was more to temperance than hatchets.

19-1 *Ragged Dick*

Horatio Alger

Horatio Alger (1832–1899) offered his readers Social Darwinism with a happy face (see text p. 589). Whereas William Graham Sumner emphasized intelligence and cunning as the key factors in achieving success (see text pp. 589–590), Alger wrote novels that extolled the role of character in a person's life. Adolescent readers found that no matter how poor they were, Alger's protagonists learned that virtue invariably was translated into material success. Alger had little reason to vary the formula in the 130 books he wrote: they sold 20 million copies in his lifetime. Following is one variation on the Horatio Alger success story.

Source: Horatio Alger, Jr., *Ragged Dick* (1868). In Horatio Alger, Jr., *Struggling Upward and Other Works* (New York: Bonanza Books, 1945), pp. 273–277.

An Exciting Adventure

Dick now began to look about for a position in a store or counting-room. Until he should obtain one he determined to devote half the day to blacking boots, not being willing to break in upon his small capital. He found that he could earn enough in half a day to pay all his necessary expenses, including the entire rent of the room. Fosdick desired to pay his half; but Dick steadily refused, insisting upon paying so much as compensation for his friend's services as instructor.

It should be added that Dick's peculiar way of speaking and use of slang terms had been somewhat modified by his education and his intimacy with Henry Fosdick. Still he continued to indulge in them to some extent, especially when he felt like joking, and it was natural to Dick to joke, as my readers have probably found out by this time. Still his manners were considerably improved, so that he was more likely to obtain a situation than when first introduced to our notice.

Just now, however, business was very dull, and merchants, instead of hiring new assistants, were disposed to part with those already in their employ. After making several ineffectual applications, Dick began to think he should be obliged to stick to his profession until the next season. But about this time something occurred which considerably improved his chances of preferment.

This is the way it happened.

As Dick, with a balance of more than a hundred dollars in the savings bank, might fairly consider himself a young man of property, he thought himself justified in occasionally taking a half holiday from business, and going on an excursion. On Wednesday afternoon Henry Fosdick was sent by his employer on an errand to that part of Brooklyn near Greenwood Cemetery. Dick hastily dressed himself in his best, and determined to accompany him.

The two boys walked down to the South Ferry, and, paying their two cents each, entered the ferry-boat. They remained at the stern, and stood by the railing, watching the great city, with its crowded wharves, receding from view. Beside them was a gentleman with two children,—a girl of eight and a little boy of six. The children were talking gayly to their father. While he was pointing out some object of interest to the little girl, the boy managed to creep, unobserved, beneath the chain that extends across the boat, for the protection of passengers, and, stepping incautiously to the edge of the boat, fell over into the foaming water.

At the child's scream, the father looked up, and, with a cry of horror, sprang to the edge of the boat. He would have plunged in, but, being unable to swim, would only have endangered his own life, without being able to save his child.

"My child!" he exclaimed in anguish,—"who will save my child? A thousand—ten thousand dollars to any one who will save him!"

There chanced to be but few passengers on board at the time, and nearly all these were either in the cabins or standing forward. Among the few who saw the child fall was our hero.

Now Dick was an expert swimmer. It was an accomplishment which he had possessed for years, and he no sooner saw the boy fall than he resolved to rescue him. His determination was formed before he heard the liberal offer made by the boy's father. Indeed, I must do Dick the justice to say that, in the excitement of the moment, he did not hear it at all, nor would it have stimulated the alacrity with which he sprang to the rescue of the little boy.

Little Johnny had already risen once, and gone under for the second time, when our hero plunged in. He was obliged to strike out for the boy, and this took time. He reached him none too soon. Just as he was sinking for the third and last time, he caught him by the jacket. Dick was stout and strong, but Johnny clung to him so tightly, that it was with great difficulty he was able to sustain himself.

"Put your arms round my neck," said Dick.

The little boy mechanically obeyed, and clung with a grasp strengthened by his terror. In this position Dick could bear his weight better. But the ferry-boat was receding fast. It was quite impossible to reach it. The father, his face pale with terror and anguish, and his hands clasped in suspense, saw the brave boy's struggles, and prayed with agonizing fervor that he might be successful. But it is probable, for they were now midway of the river, that both Dick and the little boy whom he had bravely undertaken to rescue would have been drowned, had not a row-boat been fortunately near. The two men who were in it witnessed the accident, and hastened to the rescue of our hero.

"Keep up a little longer," they shouted, bending to their oars, "and we will save you."

Dick heard the shout, and it put fresh strength into him. He battled manfully with the treacherous sea, his eyes fixed longingly upon the approaching boat.

"Hold on tight, little boy," he said. "There's a boat coming."

The little boy did not see the boat. His eyes were closed to shut out the fearful water, but he clung the closer to his young preserver. Six long, steady strokes, and the boat dashed along side. Strong hands seized Dick and his youthful burden, and drew them into the boat, both dripping with water.

"God be thanked!" exclaimed the father, as from the steamer he saw the child's rescue. "That brave boy shall be rewarded, if I sacrifice my whole fortune to compass it."

"You've had a pretty narrow escape, young chap," said one of the boatmen to Dick. "It was a pretty tough job you undertook."

"Yes," said Dick. "That's what I thought when I was in the water. If it hadn't been for you, I don't know what would have 'come of us."

"Anyhow you're a plucky boy, or you wouldn't have dared to jump into the water after this little chap. It was a risky thing to do."

"I'm used to the water," said Dick, modestly. "I didn't stop to think of the danger, but I wasn't going to see that little fellow drown without tryin' to save him."

The boat at once headed for the ferry wharf on the Brooklyn side. The captain of the ferry-boat, seeing the rescue, did not think it necessary to stop his boat, but kept on his way. The whole occurrence took place in less time than I have occupied in telling it.

The father was waiting on the wharf to receive his little boy, with what feeling of gratitude and joy can be easily understood. With a burst of happy tears he clasped him to his arms. Dick was about to withdraw modestly, but the gentleman perceived the movement, and, putting down the child, came forward, and, clasping his hand, said with emotion, "My brave boy, I owe you a debt I can never repay. But for your timely service I should now be plunged into an anguish which I cannot think of without a shudder."

Our hero was ready enough to speak on most occasions, but always felt awkward when he was praised.

"It wasn't any trouble," he said, modestly. "I can swim like a top."

"But not many boys would have risked their lives for a stranger," said the gentleman. "But," he added with a sudden thought, as his glance rested on Dick's dripping garments, "both you and my little boy will take old in wet clothes. Fortunately I have a friend living close at hand, at whose house you will have an opportunity of taking off your clothes, and having them dried."

Dick protested that he never took cold; but Fosdick, who had now joined them, and who, it is needless to say, had been greatly alarmed at Dick's danger, joined in urging compliance with the gentleman's proposal, and in the end our hero had to yield. His new friend secured a hack, the driver of which agreed for extra recompense to receive the dripping boys into his carriage, and they were whirled rapidly to a pleasant house in a side street, where matters were quickly explained, and both boys were put to bed.

"I aint used to going' to bed quite so early," thought Dick. "This is the queerest excursion I ever took."

Like most active boys Dick did not enjoy the prospect of spending half a day in bed; but his confinement did not last as long as he anticipated.

In about an hour the door of his chamber was opened, and a servant appeared, bringing a new and handsome suit of clothes throughout.

"You are to put on these," said the servant to Dick; "but you needn't get up till you feel like it."

"Whose clothes are they?" asked Dick.

"They are yours."

"Mine! Where did they come from?"

"Mr. Rockwell sent out and bought them for you. They are the same size as your wet ones."

"Is he here now?"

"No. He bought another suit for the little boy, and has gone back to New York. Here's a note he asked me to give you."

Dick opened the paper, and read as follows,—

"Please accept this outfit of clothes as the first instalment of a debt which I can never repay. I have asked to have your wet suit dried, when you can reclaim it. Will you oblige me by calling to-morrow at my counting room, No.—, Pearl Street.

"Your friend,

"JAMES ROCKWELL."

Questions

1. What qualities does the hero demonstrate?
2. How does the role of chance serve both as a plot device and an unintended flaw in Alger's view?
3. Why would this kind of book be so popular?

19-2 "The Forgotten Man" (1883)

William Graham Sumner

Social Darwinism invoked science to argue that society should not go out of its way to help the poor or check the abuses of robber barons. Its proponents tried to apply Charles Darwin's theory of natural selection to society, not just to plants and animals (see text pp. 589–590). The most prominent American Social Darwinist was the Yale professor William Graham Sumner (1840–1910), who warned, "if we do not like the survival of the fittest, we have only one possible alternative, and that is the survival of the unfittest" (see text p. 589). The lecture on which this essay is based was an 1883 address by Sumner to the Brooklyn Historical Society.

Source: William Graham Sumner, "The Forgotten Man," an address to the Brooklyn Historical Society in 1883. In Albert Galloway Keller, ed., *The Forgotten Man and Other Essays* (New Haven, Conn.: Yale University Press, 1919).

Now you know that "the poor and the weak" are continually put forward as objects of public interest and public obligation. In the appeals which are made, the terms "the poor" and "the weak" are used as if they were terms of exact definition. Except the pauper, that is to say, the man who cannot earn his living or pay his way, there is no possible definition of a poor man. Except a man who is incapacitated by vice or by physical infirmity, there is no definition of a weak man. The paupers and the physically incapacitated are an inevitable charge on society. About them no more need be said. But the weak who constantly arouse the pity of humanitarians and philanthropists are the shiftless, the imprudent, the negligent, the impractical, and the inefficient, or they are the idle, the intemperate, the extravagant, and the vicious. Now the troubles of these persons are constantly forced upon public attention, as if they and their interests deserved especial consideration, and a great portion of all organized and unorganized effort for the common welfare consists in attempts to relieve these classes of people. I do not wish to be understood now as saying that nothing ought to be done for these people by those who are stronger and wiser. That is not my point. What I want to do is to point out the thing which is overlooked and the error which is made in all these charitable efforts. The notion is accepted as if it were not open to any question that if you help the inefficient and vicious you may gain something for society or you may not, but that

you lose nothing. This is a complete mistake. Whatever capital you divert to the support of a shiftless and good-for-nothing person is so much diverted from some other employment, and that means from somebody else. I would spend any conceivable amount of zeal and eloquence if I possessed it to try to make people grasp this idea. Capital is force. If it goes one way it cannot go another. If you give a loaf to a pauper you cannot give the same loaf to a laborer. Now this other man who would have got it but for the charitable sentiment which bestowed it on a worthless member of society is the Forgotten Man. The philanthropists and humanitarians have their minds all full of the wretched and miserable whose case appeals to compassion, attacks the sympathies, takes possession of the imagination, and excites the emotions. They push on towards the quickest and easiest remedies and they forget the real victim.

Now who is the Forgotten Man? He is the simple, honest laborer, ready to earn his living by productive work. We pass him by because he is independent, self-supporting, and asks no favors. He does not appeal to the emotions or excite the sentiments. He only wants to make a contract and fulfill it, with respect on both sides and favor on neither side. He must get his living out of the capital of the country. The larger the capital is, the better living he can get. Every particle of capital which is wasted on the vicious, the idle, and the shiftless is so much taken from the capital available to reward the independent and productive laborer. But we stand with our backs to the independent and productive laborer all the time. We do not remember him because he makes no clamor; but I appeal to you whether he is not the man who ought to be remembered first of all, and whether, on any sound social theory, we ought not to protect him against the burdens of the good-for-nothing. In these last years I have read hundreds of articles and heard scores of sermons and speeches which were really glorifications of the good-for-nothing, as if these were the charge of society, recommended by right reason to its care and protection. We are addressed all the time as if those who are respectable were to blame because some are not so, and as if there were an obligation on the part of those who have done their duty towards those who have not done their duty. Every man is bound to take care of himself and his family and to do his share in the work of society. It is totally false that one who has done so is bound to bear the care and charge of those who are wretched because they have not done so. The silly popular notion is that the beggars live at the expense of the rich, but the truth is that those who eat and produce not, live at the expense of those who labor and produce. The next time that you are tempted to subscribe a dollar to a charity, I do not tell you not to do it, because after you have fairly considered the matter, you may think it right to do it, but I ask you to stop and remember the Forgotten Man and understand that if you put your dollar in the savings bank it will go to swell the capital of the country which is available for division amongst those who, while they earn it, will reproduce it with increase.

Let us now go on to another class of cases. There are a great many schemes brought forward for "improving the condition of the working classes." I have shown already that a free man cannot take a favor. One who takes a favor or submits to patronage demeans himself. He falls under obligation. He cannot be free and he cannot assert a station of equality with the man who confers the favor on him. The only exception is where there are exceptional bonds of affection or friendship, that is, where the sentimental relation supersedes the free relation. Therefore, in a country which is a free democracy, all propositions to do something for the working classes have an air of patronage and superiority which is impertinent and out of place. No one can do anything for anybody else unless he has a surplus of energy to dispose of after taking care of himself. In the United States, the working classes, technically so called, are the strongest classes. It is they who have a surplus to dispose of if anybody has. Why should anybody else offer to take care of them or to serve them? They can get whatever they think worth having and, at any rate, if they are free men in a free state, it is ignominious and unbecoming to introduce fashions of patronage and favoritism here. A man who, by superior education and ex-

perience of business, is in a position to advise a struggling man of the wages class, is certainly held to do so and will, I believe, always be willing and glad to do so; but this sort of activity lies in the range of private and personal relations.

I now, however, desire to direct attention to the public, general, and impersonal schemes, and I point out the fact that, if you undertake to lift anybody, you must have a fulcrum or point of resistance. All the elevation you give to one must be gained by an equivalent depression on someone else. The question of gain to society depends upon the balance of the account, as regards the position of the persons who undergo the respective operations. But nearly all the schemes for "improving the condition of the working man" involve an elevation of some working men at the expense of other working men. When you expend capital or labor to elevate some persons who come within the sphere of your influence, you interfere in the conditions of competition. The advantage of some is won by an equivalent loss of others. The difference is not brought about by the energy and effort of the persons themselves. If it were, there would be nothing to be said about it, for we constantly see people surpass others in the rivalry of life and carry off the prizes which the others must do without. In the cases I am discussing, the difference is brought about by an interference which must be partial, arbitrary, accidental, controlled by favoritism and personal preference. I do not say, in this case, either, that we ought to do no work of this kind. On the contrary, I believe that the arguments for it quite outweigh, in many cases, the arguments against it. What I desire, again, is to bring out the forgotten element which we always need to remember in order to make a wise decision as to any scheme of this kind. I want to call to mind the Forgotten Man, because, in this case also, if we recall him and go to look for him, we shall find him patiently and perseveringly, manfully and independently struggling against adverse circumstances without complaining or begging. If, then, we are led to heed the groaning and complaining of others and to take measures for helping these others, we shall, before we know it, push down this man who is trying to help himself.

Let us take another class of cases. So far we have said nothing about the abuse of legislation. We all seem to be under the delusion that the rich pay the taxes. Taxes are not thrown upon the consumers with any such directness and completeness as is sometimes assumed; but that, in ordinary states of the market, taxes on houses fall, for the most part, on the tenants and that taxes on commodities fall, for the most part, on the consumers, is beyond question. Now the state and municipality go to great expense to support policemen and sheriffs and judicial officers, to protect people against themselves, that is, against the results of their own folly, vice, and recklessness. Who pays for it? Undoubtedly the people who have not been guilty of folly, vice, or recklessness. Out of nothing comes nothing.

We cannot collect taxes from people who produce nothing and save nothing. The people who have something to tax must be those who have produced and saved.

When you see a drunkard in the gutter, you are disgusted, but you pity him. When a policeman comes and picks him up you are satisfied. You say that "society" has interfered to save the drunkard from perishing. Society is a fine word, and it saves us the trouble of thinking to say that society acts. The truth is that the policeman is paid by somebody, and when we talk about society we forget who it is that pays. It is the Forgotten Man again. It is the industrious workman going home from a hard day's work, whom you pass without noticing, who is mulcted of a percentage of his day's earnings to hire a policeman to save the drunkard from himself. All the public expenditure to prevent vice has the same effect. Vice is its own curse. If we let nature alone, she cures vice by the most frightful penalties. It may shock you to hear me say it, but when you get over the shock, it will do you good to think of it: a drunkard in the gutter is just where he ought to be. Nature is working away at him to get him out of the way, just as she sets up her processes of dissolution to remove whatever is a failure in its line. Gambling and less mentionable vices all cure themselves by the ruin and dissolution of their vic-

tims. Nine-tenths of our measures for preventing vice are really protective towards it, because they ward off the penalty. "Ward off," I say, and that is the usual way of looking at it; but is the penalty really annihilated? By no means. It is turned into police and court expenses and spread over those who have resisted vice. It is the Forgotten Man again who has been subjected to the penalty while our minds were full of the drunkards, spendthrifts, gamblers, and other victims of dissipation. Who is, then, the Forgotten Man? He is the clean, quiet, virtuous, domestic citizen, who pays his debts and his taxes and is never heard of out of his little circle. Yet who is there in the society of a civilized state who deserves to be remembered and considered by the legislator and statesman before this man?

Another class of cases is closely connected with this last. There is an apparently invincible prejudice in people's minds in favor of state regulation. All experience is against state regulation and in favor of liberty. The freer the civil institutions are, the more weak or mischievous state regulation is. The Prussian bureaucracy can do a score of things for the citizen which no governmental organ in the United States can do; and, conversely, if we want to be taken care of as Prussians and Frenchmen are, we must give up something of our personal liberty.

Questions

1. Why does Sumner oppose all attempts to help the weak?
2. To what extent was Sumner a true friend of the "Forgotten Man," especially if that man found himself unemployed in the Panic of 1893?
3. What would be the ultimate cost to a society that allowed nature to eliminate vice through people's destruction, as Sumner proposes?
4. How might Social Darwinism have affected organized religion at that time?

19-3 "The Economical Council, Albany, New York" (1869)

Thomas Nast

Thomas Nast (1840–1902) was a talented cartoonist (see text p. 588 and Document 16-6) whose images of Santa Claus, the Democratic donkey, and the Republican elephant have become part of our cultural landscape. Nast's political cartoons were so effective that they helped topple New York's Tweed Ring in the early 1870s (see text pp. 592–594, 627, 630). "I don't care so much what the papers write about me, my constituents can't read," Boss Tweed complained, "but damn it, they can see pictures!" However, some of those cartoons revealed as much about Thomas Nast as about William Marcy Tweed.

Source: Thomas Nast, "The Economical Council, Albany, New York," *Harper's Weekly,* December 25, 1869. In Albert Bigelow Paine, *Th. Nast: His Period and His Pictures* (Pearson Publishing, 1904; reprint, Gloucester, Mass.: Peter Smith, 1967), p. 139.

Questions

1. Why do you think Nast depicted members of the Tweed Ring as Roman Catholic bishops?
2. Which ethnic group was stereotyped in the apelike guard to the right of Boss Tweed?
3. How does the cartoon suggest the kind of politics that predominated in large American cities in the late nineteenth and early twentieth centuries?

19-4 *Woman and Temperance* (1876)

Frances E. Willard

The reform movements of the late 1800s brought women out of the home and into the larger community. Abolition and temperance touched on politics, which in turn led to the call for suffrage and women's right to shape responses to the issues that affected them (see text pp. 594–596). Frances E. Willard (1839–1898), the founder of the Woman's Christian Temperance Union (see text p. 596), emerged as a symbol of the change in status women experienced after the Civil War. The following selection is excerpted from Willard's first major temperance speech, delivered in 1876. Willard likens the alcohol interests to Chimborazo, the highest peak in Ecuador.

Source: Frances E. Willard, "Woman and Temperance," a speech delivered in 1876. In Frances E. Willard, *Woman and Temperance or, The Work and Workers of the Woman's Christian Temperance Union* (1883; reprint, New York: Arno Press, 1972), pp. 452–457.

The rum power looms like a Chimborazo among the mountains of difficulty over which our native land must climb to reach the future of our dreams. The problem of the rum power's overthrow may well engage our thoughts as women and as patriots. To-night I ask you to consider it in the light of a truth which Frederick Douglass has embodied in these words: "We can in the long run trust all the knowledge in the community to take care of all the ignorance of the community, and all of its virtue to take care of all of its vice." The difficulty in the application of this principle lies in the fact that vice is always in the active, virtue often in the passive. Vice is aggressive. It deals swift, sure blows, delights in keen-edged weapons, and prefers a hand-to-hand conflict, while virtue instinctively fights its unsavory antagonist at arm's length; its great guns are unwieldy and slow to swing into range.

Vice is the tiger, with keen eyes, alert ears, and cat-like tread, while virtue is the slow-paced, complacent, easy-going elephant, whose greatest danger lies in its ponderous weight and consciousness of power. So the great question narrows down to one of two(?) methods. It is not, when we look carefully into the conditions of the problem, How shall we develop more virtue in the community to offset the tropical growth of vice by which we find ourselves en-

vironed ? but rather, How the tremendous force we have may best be brought to bear, how we may unlimber the huge cannon now pointing into vacancy, and direct their full charge at short range upon our nimble, wily, vigilant foe?

As bearing upon a consideration of that question, I lay down this proposition: All pure and Christian sentiment concerning any line of conduct which vitally affects humanity will, sooner or later, crystallize into law. But the keystone of law can only be firm and secure when it is held in place by the arch of that keystone, which is public sentiment. . . .

There is a class whose instinct of self-preservation must forever be opposed to a stimulant which nerves, with dangerous strength, arms already so much stronger than their own, and so maddens the brain God meant to guide those arms, that they strike down the wives men love, and the little children for whom, when sober, they would die. The wife, largely dependent for the support of herself and little ones upon the brain which strong drink paralyzes, the arm it masters, and the skill it renders futile, will, in the nature of the case, prove herself unfriendly to the actual or potential source of so much misery. But besides this primal instinct of self-preservation, we have, in the same class of which I speak, another far more high and sacred—I mean the instinct of a mother's love, a wife's devotion, a sister's faithfulness, a daughter's loyalty. And now I ask you to consider earnestly the fact that none of these blessed rays of light and power from woman's heart, are as yet brought to bear upon the rum-shop at the focus of power. They are, I know, the sweet and pleasant sunshine of our homes; they are the beams which light the larger home of social life and send their gentle radiance out even into the great and busy world. But I know, and as the knowledge has grown clearer, my heart was thrilled with gratitude and hope too deep for words, that in a republic all these now divergent beams of light can, through that magic lens, that powerful sun-glass which we name the ballot, be made to converge upon the rum-shop in a blaze of light that shall reveal its full abominations, and a white flame of heat which, . . . shall burn this cancerous excrescence from America's fair form. Yes, for there is nothing in the universe so sure, so strong, as love; and love shall do all this—the love of maid for sweetheart, wife for husband, of a sister for her brother, of a mother for her son. And I call upon you who are here to-day, good men and brave—you who have welcomed us to other fields in the great fight of the angel against the dragon in society—I call upon you thus to match force with force, to set over against the liquor-dealer's avarice our instinct of self-preservation; and to match the drinker's love of liquor with our love of him! When you can centre all this power in that small bit of paper which falls

"As silently as snow-flakes fall upon the sod,
  But executes a freeman's will as lightnings do the will of
  God,"

the rum power will be as much doomed as was the slave power when you gave the ballot to the slaves.

In our argument it has been claimed that by the changeless instincts of her nature and through the most sacred relationships of which that nature has been rendered capable, God has indicated woman, who is the born conservator of home, to be the Nemesis of home's arch enemy, King Alcohol. And further, that in a republic, this power of hers may be most effectively exercised by giving her a voice in the decision by which the rum-shop door shall be opened or closed beside her home.

This position is strongly supported by evidence. About the year 1850 petitions were extensively circulated in Cincinnati (later the fiercest battle ground of the woman's crusade), asking that the liquor traffic be put under the ban of law. Bishop Simpson—one of the noblest and most discerning minds of his century—was deeply interested in this movement. It was decided to ask for the names of women as well as those of men, and it was found that the former signed the petition more readily and in much larger numbers than the latter. Another fact was ascertained which rebuts the hackneyed assertion that women of the lower class

will not be on the temperance side in this great war. For it was found—as might, indeed, have been most reasonably predicted—that the ignorant, the poor (many of them wives, mothers, and daughters of intemperate men), were among the most eager to sign the petition.

MANY A HAND WAS TAKEN FROM THE WASH-TUB to hold the pencil and affix the signature of women of this class, and many another, which could only make the sign of the cross, did that with tears, and a hearty "God bless you." "That was a wonderful lesson to me," said the good Bishop, and he has always believed since then that God will give our enemy into our hands by giving to us an ally still more powerful, woman with the ballot against rum-shops in our land. It has been said so often that the very frequency of reiteration has in some minds induced belief that women of the better class will never consent to declare themselves at the polls. But tens of thousands from the most tenderly-sheltered homes have gone day after day to the saloons, and have spent hour after hour upon their sanded floors, and in their reeking air—places in which not the worst politician would dare to locate the ballot box of freemen—though they but stay a moment at the window, slip in their votes, and go their way.

Nothing worse can ever happen to women at the polls than has been endured by the hour on the part of conservative women of the churches in this land, as they, in scores of towns, have plead with rough, half-drunken men to vote the temperance tickets they have handed them, and which, with vastly more of propriety and fitness they might have dropped into the box themselves. They could have done this in a moment, and returned to their homes, instead of spending the whole day in the often futile endeavor to beg from men like these the votes which should preserve their homes from the whisky serpent's breath for one uncertain year. I spent last May in Ohio, traveling constantly, and seeking on every side to learn the views of the noble women of the Crusade. They put their opinions in words like these: "We believe that as God led us into this work by way of the saloons,

HE WILL LEAD US OUT BY WAY OF THE BALLOT. We have never prayed more earnestly over the one than we will over the other. One was the Wilderness, the other is the Promised Land."

A Presbyterian lady, rigidly conservative, said: "For my part, I never wanted to vote until our gentlemen passed a prohibition ordinance so as to get us to stop visiting saloons, and a month later repealed it and chose a saloon-keeper for mayor."

Said a grand-daughter of Jonathan Edwards, a woman with no toleration toward the Suffrage Movement, a woman crowned with the glory of gray hairs—a central figure in her native town—

AND AS SHE SPOKE THE COURAGE AND FAITH OF THE
PURITANS THRILLED HER VOICE—

"If, with the ballot in our hands, we can, as I firmly believe, put down this awful traffic, I am ready to lead the
women of my town to the polls, as I have often led them to
the rum shops."

We must not forget that for every woman who joins
the Temperance Unions now springing up all through the
land, there are at least a score who sympathize but do not
join. Home influence and cares prevent them, ignorance of
our aims and methods, lack of consecration to Christian
work—a thousand reasons, sufficient in their estimation,
though not in ours, hold them away from us. And yet they
have this Temperance cause warmly at heart; the logic of
events has shown them that there is but one side on which
a woman may safely stand in this great battle, and on that
side they would indubitably range themselves in the quick,
decisive battle of election day, nor would they give their
voice a second time in favor of the man who had once betrayed his pledge to enforce the most stringent law for the
protection of their homes. There are many noble women,
too, who, though they do not think as do the Temperance
Unions about the deep things of religion, and are not as yet
decided in their total abstinence sentiments, nor ready for
the blessed work of prayer, are nevertheless decided in
their views of Woman Suffrage, and ready to vote a Temperance ticket side by side with us. And there are the
drunkard's wife and daughters, who from very shame will
not come with us, or who dare not, yet who could freely
vote with us upon this question; for the folded ballot tells
no tales.

Among other cumulative proofs in this argument from
experience, let us consider, briefly, the attitude of the
Catholic Church toward the Temperance Reform. It is
friendly, at least. Father Matthew's spirit lives to-day in
many a faithful parish priest. In our procession on the Centennial Fourth of July, the banners of Catholic Total Abstinence Societies were often the only reminders that the Republic has any temperance people within its borders, as
they were the only offset to brewers' wagons and distillers'
casks, while among the monuments of our cause, by which
this memorable year is signalized, their fountain in Fair-
mount Park—standing in the midst of eighty drinking
places licensed by our Government—is chief. Catholic
women would vote with Protestant women upon this issue
for the protection of their homes.

Again, among the sixty thousand churches of America, with their eight million members, two-thirds are
women. Thus, only one-third of this trustworthy and

thoughtful class has any voice in the laws by which, between the church and the public school, the rum shop nes-
tles in this Christian land. Surely all this must change before the Government shall be upon His shoulders "Who
shall one day reign King of nations as He now reigns King
of saints."

Furthermore, four-fifths of the teachers in this land are
women, whose thoughtful judgment, expressed with the
authority of which I speak, would greatly help forward the
victory of our cause. And, finally, by those who fear the effect of the foreign element in our country, let it be remembered that we have sixty native for every one woman who
is foreign born, for it is men who emigrate in largest number to our shores.

When all these facts (and many more that might be
added) are marshaled into line, how illogical it seems for
good men to harangue us as they do about our "duty to
educate public sentiment to the level of better law," and
their exhortations to American mothers to "train their
sons to vote aright." As said Mrs. Governor Wallace, of Indiana—until the Crusade an opponent of the franchise—
"What a bitter sarcasm you utter, gentlemen, to us who
have the public sentiment of which you speak, all burning
in our hearts, and yet are not permitted to turn it to account."

Let us, then, each one of us, offer our earnest prayer to
God, and speak our honest word to man in favor of this
added weapon in woman's hands, remembering that every
petition in the ear of God, and every utterance in the ears
of men, swells the dimensions of that resistless tide of influence which shall yet float within our reach all that we
ask or need. Dear Christian women who have crusaded in
the rum shops, I urge that you begin crusading in halls of
legislation, in primary meetings, and the offices of excise
commissioners. Roll in your petitions, burnish your arguments, multiply your prayers. Go to the voters in your
town—procure the official list and see them one by one—
and get them pledged to a local ordinance requiring the
votes of men and women before a license can be issued to
open rum-shop doors beside your homes; go to the Legislature with the same; remember this may be just as really
Christian work as praying in saloons was in those other
glorious days. Let us not limit God, whose modes of operation are so infinitely varied in nature and in grace. I believe in the correlation of spiritual forces, and that the heat
which melted hearts to tenderness in the Crusade is soon to
be the light which shall reveal our opportunity and duty as
the Republic's daughters.

Questions

1. Why does Willard invoke the name of the abolitionist Frederick Douglass in a speech on temperance?
2. To what extent is her argument based on a kind of political feminism?
3. How do Catholics—not normally sympathetic to the temperance movement—fare with Willard as opposed to Thomas Nast (Document 19-3)?

Questions for Further Thought

1. Frances Willard (Document 19-4) and William Graham Sumner (Document 19-2) were contemporaries, and both would have considered themselves good Protestants. Why did they differ so widely on society's proper response to the dangers of alcohol?
2. Where are the arguments of Horatio Alger (Document 19-1), William Graham Sumner, and Frances Willard heard today?
3. To what extent do Nast (Document 19-3), Sumner, and Willard seem to be aware of and tolerant toward cultural difference among Americans?

The Crisis of American Politics: The 1890s

The 1890s of popular legend are filled with images of barbershop quartets and bicycles built for two. However, reality must include less pleasant events, such as the Panic of 1893 and the Pullman boycott a year later.

There was also the divisive issue of the money supply, which came to a head after being debated for decades (see text pp. 600–602). Few Americans fully understood the relationship between the economy and the amount of money in circulation. By the late nineteenth century the national economy was undervalued; in other words, factories and railroads were enriching the nation faster than the money supply could expand. The monetary system needed to modernize (in part, by expanding) as the economy had, but most politicians and businessmen treated such an idea as heresy. They insisted on tying the money supply to a precious metal as if nothing had changed since the days of Egypt and Rome.

Farmers knew better. Their crops were not earning enough to pay off loans for land and machinery. As debtors they advocated moderate inflation: their crops would earn more, and the inflated profits could be used to retire debts that remained largely fixed. For a time paper money was popular as an inflationary device, but it lacked the appeal of a precious metal. The use of silver, however, could be traced back to the ancient world, and silver was far more abundant than gold. The cry for greenbacks eventually gave way to the farmers' call for the unlimited coinage of silver (see text pp. 599–600).

The farmers of the South and the Great Plains wanted more than inflation. As discussed in the textbook (pp. 597–600), by 1890 they had developed a sophisticated critique of American capitalism and a third-party movement to challenge the political status quo. Populists such as Luna Kellie (Document 19-5) hoped to restructure the political and economic system. The Populist ally Jacob Coxey proposed a way (Document 19-6) to combat unemployment in the 1890s. One of the Populist's central ideas catapulted the Democrat William Jennings Bryan to fame in 1896 (Document 19-7).

19-5   "Stand Up for Nebraska" (1894)

Luna Kellie

The Populist movement (see text pp. 597–600) helped disprove the stereotype of the American farmer as a rural reactionary. The party's 1892 platform—with its call for farm relief, an income tax, and greater government control of the economy—would not be fully realized until the advent of the New Deal forty years later. As Eleanor Roosevelt and Frances Perkins furthered reform in the 1930s, so had women Populists a generation earlier. The following selection is a speech by the Nebraska Populist Luna Kellie.

Source: Luna Kellie, "Stand Up for Nebraska," *Alliance Independent*, January 11, 1894. In Jane Taylor Nelsen, ed., *A Prairie Populist: The Memoirs of Luna Kellie* (Iowa City: University of Iowa Press, 1992), pp. 127–132.

There are those who think the work of the Nebraska Farmers' Alliance is ended; that while the bankers of the state keep up their organization with the avowed purpose of "better influencing legislation" in their behalf, while the merchants, manufacturers, lawyers, doctors, men of every trade or profession, find it to their interest to keep up organizations to aid each other and look after their political welfare, the agriculturalists of the state and nation have no interest in common sufficient for the existence of an organization, but should leave their financial and political business for office seeking politicians to look after. It grieves us to think how little has been accomplished by the Alliance compared with all that is necessary to be done before the farmers of the state obtain anything like justice. At times we grow weary and discouraged when we realize that the work of the Alliance is hardly begun, and that after the weary years of toil of the best men and women of the state we have hardly taken a step on the road to industrial freedom. We know that although we may not arrive there *our children* will enter into the promised land, and we can make their trials fewer and lighter, even if we live not to see the full light of freedom for mankind. We work in the knowledge that our labor of education is not in vain, some one, sometime, will arise and call the Alliance blessed. Meanwhile to us who have learned "to labor and to wait" there come sometimes sweet glimpses of the land beyond, and it seems so near, the road so short, that we can not have long to wait to enter and possess the land.

There's a land where the toiler is free,
   Where no robber of labor can come,
Where wealth gives not power to oppress,
   Nor another man's labor to own.

In that sweet by and by
   Which has been for long ages foretold,
In that sweet by and by
   Moral worth will rank higher than gold.

We can dwell in that land of the free,
   If we will, in the near by and by;
We can soon wrest the scepter from gold.
   We can make labor free if we try.

Vote no interest whatever to gold,
   Vote for naught which will favor a class,
Make an injury offered to one
   The most vital concern of the mass.

It does not seem as if that would be hard to do, nor that the road to the promised land of freedom need be long; yet there is a shorter one given by a noted guide hundreds of years ago. But they say, he was visionary, and his way impracticable. It was simply "Do unto others as ye would they should do unto you." The Christian way closely followed at the ballot box would soon right every legalized injustice, and yet the majority of the voters pretend to be his followers. Had they been so in deed and in truth how different would be the condition of our country. We have annually seen the greater part of the wealth produced in the state legislated out of the hands of the rightful owners and into the pockets of those who are allowed to eat, although they *will not* work.

The condition of the farmers of the state has changed greatly in the last three years.

Then the abolishment of high rates of interest on money and reduction of freight rates was all the average Alliance member desired. Thousands of farmers who would have preserved their homes if they could have obtained that relief at that time have now had the mortgage cleared off their farms by the sheriff and are today without a home, and they now demand that *occupancy and use shall be the sole title of land*.

So with the transportation question. While a slight reduction would have satisfied three years ago, the people now know that they have the constitutional right to take the railroads, under right of eminent domain and run them at cost in the interest of *all the people*; and never again will any party arouse any enthusiasm among them who advocate less.

Of course the renter does not care greatly for anything which does not free him from the servitude of giving one third or one half his labor for the *chance* to work on the earth. The farmers comprising this organization are the wealthier class of the farmers of the state, and doubtless most of them own land and a home; but if we do unto others as we would they should do unto us we must look out for the interest of our neighbors, who are mostly renters. This is now a state of renters, and the politicians will find they have a new factor to deal with, and that the rapidly increasing number of renters is proportioned very like that of the stay at home vote. And it is reasonable that any man should stay at home unless he sees some hope of benefiting himself by going to the polls. A renter does not care greatly for transportation charges. He who owns the land owns the man who works it, and as soon as freight rates go down the prices rise [and] the renter is raised in proportion. So also he regards the money question. If the value of his products is increased by increasing money volume the rent is raised in proportion so as barely to allow him to exist to produce more. He has no hope of education for his children, or of giving them a better chance in life than he has until he is permitted to go upon the unoccupied land of the state and make for himself a home while adding yearly to the state's productive capacity and wealth. It will soon be necessary for any organization political or social that wishes the renters' allegiance, to advocate occupancy and use as the sole title to land. And if they desire the allegiance of those who, owing to an insufficient money volume, have become debtors, they must advocate a sufficient medium of exchange so that no usury interest will be exacted for its use. The Alliance must not ask if an idea is popular, but

rather is it right? If right advocate it, agitate it, write it, speak it, vote it. We can make it popular. If we wish the farmers to join and keep up this society we must convince them each and every one that it will benefit him individually. We should take a decided step forward in co-operative work. We can compel the building of a co-operative road to the Gulf. We can get an agent to contract the crops of the state at foreign markets for better prices. We can by ordering machinery, flour, coal, etc., in large quantities get greatly reduced prices, and we ought to place ourselves on a level with the Grange . . . in these respects, then each member can soon receive a benefit and a new impetus be given.

Some think the People's party has taken the place of the Alliance. It has to some extent, but cannot entirely.

Leaving our business co-operation which a political organization will not touch, the Alliance has an educational work to perform which no political party can do. Politicians are notoriously cowardly, and not over truthful, especially the law-interpreting class which make speeches for them, and the people will not put faith in them or be taught by them.

A farmer can teach his brother farmers much better the principles of political economy and what he needs to better his condition than the most silvery-tongued office-seeking lawyer that ever lived in any party. There is a large class (yearly becoming larger) who put no faith in political organizations of any class, as regards benefiting the toilers. They think as soon as the party attains power politicians will crowd to the front who care only for the "spoils of office," and the wishes of the voters will be ignored. The Alliance must make it its future work to educate this class to demand the Referendum and direct legislation. It is an excellent time to show the folly of placing one-sixth of the legislative power in the hands of a corrupt governor and president.

If this is to become a government by the people, they must have the right to initiate new laws and not have important questions tabled by a committee appointed by some scoundrel in the shape of a speaker. No power higher than the vote or veto of the people can exist in a free country. The Nebraska farmers and toilers whose productive labor has made the state all it is, whose labor will make it all it ever will become, should stand up for Nebraska by showing what wealth has been produced from her fertile soil and the vast amount paid by her each year to foreigners for the privilege of using the highways of our own state, and as interest money borrowed to replace that legislated from the pockets of our farmers.

Had the farmers of Nebraska obtained justice ten years ago not a dollar of foreign capital would now be drawing interest in the state. That is the sole reason why the loan agents oppose every effort to increase the price of Nebraska's products.

Stand up for Nebraska! from the hand of her God
She came forth, bright and pure as her own golden rod.
Sweet peas and wild roses perfumed all the air.
Her maker pronounced her both fertile and fair.
Not a boodler or pauper disgraced the state then;
Stand up for Nebraska and cleanse her again.

Stand up for Nebraska! and shame upon those
Who fear the extent of their steals to disclose.
Who say that she cannot grow wealth or create;
But must coax foreign capital into the state.
Such insults each friend of the state deeply grieves:—
Stand up for Nebraska and banish her thieves.

Stand up for Nebraska! and ope' her jails wide
To receive all who force us our crops to divide;
For when we've divided our hard worked for grain,
Next year we're compelled to divide up again
With others whose labor no wealth doth create.
Stand up for Nebraska; drive them from the state.

Stand up for Nebraska, so fertile and fair,
'Tis no fault of hers that her granaries are bare;
For the wealth that her farmers each year do create
Is more than at present is owned in the state.
Stop the thieving and quickly her wealth will enhance;
Stand up for Nebraska and give her a chance.

Stand up for Nebraska. Clear up the disgrace
Of giving the vile, lowest thieves highest place.
That our children may honor the good and the true
We must set an example, and honor them too.
None but men of high honor in power we must place
Stand up for Nebraska, clear up her disgrace.

Stand up for Nebraska, and, like Governor W———te[?],
Let her say what shall pay off the debts of the state.
Let the vile baseborn traitors who enslaved her beware;
Their scheme is unfolded, we know why and where
They made our crops worthless, to be England's gain,
Stand up for Nebraska, raise the price of her grain.

Stand up for Nebraska. In the center she lies.
The most valuable jewel 'neath the fairest of skies.
So favored by nature, her vile man-made laws
We find of her poverty are the sole cause.
Let her own her own highways and a road to the south:
Stand up for Nebraska by your votes, not your mouth.

Stand up for Nebraska! Let no foot of her soil
Be held by the idlers to tax rent from toil.
Bid the hard-working tenants of other states come,
And build on each wild quarter section a home.
And soon the world over the watchword will be,
Stand up for Nebraska, the home of the free.

Questions

1. What successes of the Nebraska Populists does Kellie cite?
2. What other reforms does Kellie call for?
3. What does the speech reveal about Kellie's and her audience's attachment to their state?

19-6 "Coxey's Bills" (1894)

Jacob S. Coxey (1854–1951) was a successful Ohio businessman who sympathized with the Populist cause. As the Panic of 1893 became a depression, Coxey led a protest march from his home in Massillon to Washington, D.C. (see text p. 601). Coxey told his followers, "We will send a petition to Washington with boots on." However, the 5,000 or so members of "Coxey's Army" met defeat on May Day 1894 when Coxey and others were arrested for trespassing on Capitol Hill. Here are the two Congressional bills Coxey hoped would end or at least alleviate the depression. Neither of the bills was passed.

Source: Jacob S. Coxey, "Coxey's Bills." In Donald L. McMurry, *Coxey's Army: A Study of the Industrial Army Movement of 1894* (Boston: Little, Brown, 1929), pp. 301–303.

I. The Good Roads Bill.—53rd Congress, 2d Session, H. R. 7438, June 12, 1894.

A BILL to provide for the improvement of public roads, and for other purposes.

Be it enacted by the Senate and the House of Representatives of the United States of America in Congress assembled, That the Secretary of the Treasury of the United States is hereby authorized and instructed to have engraved and have printed, immediately after the passage of this bill, five hundred millions of dollars of Treasury notes, a legal tender for all debts, public and private, said notes to be in denominations of one, two, five, and ten dollars, and to be placed in a fund to be known as the "general country-road fund system of the United States," and to be expended solely for said purpose.

Sec. 2. That it shall be the duty of the Secretary of War to take charge of the construction of said general county-road system of the United States, and said construction to commence as soon as the Secretary of the Treasury shall inform the Secretary of War that the said fund is available, which shall not be later than sixty days from and after the passage of this bill, when it shall be the duty of the Secretary of War to inaugurate the work and expend the sum of twenty millions of dollars per month pro rata with the number of miles of road in each State and Territory in the United States.

Sec. 3. That all labor other than that of the office of the Secretary of War, "whose compensations are already fixed by law," shall be paid by the day, and that the rate be not less than one dollar and fifty cents per day for common labor and three dollars and fifty cents for team and labor, and that eight hours per day shall constitute a day's labor under the provisions of this bill, and that all citizens of the United States making application to labor shall be employed.

2. The Non-Interest-Bearing Bond Bill.—53rd Congress, 2d Session, H. R. 7463, June 15, 1894.

A BILL to provide for public improvements and employment of the citizens of the United States.

Be it enacted by the Senate and House of Representatives of the United States of America in Congress assembled, That whenever any State, Territory, county, township, municipality, or incorporated town or village deem it necessary to make any public improvements they shall deposit with the Secretary of the Treasury of the United States a non-interest-bearing twenty-five-year bond, not to exceed one-half of the assessed valuation of the property in said State, Territory, county, township, municipality, or incorporated town or village, and said bond to be retired at the rate of four per centum per annum.

Sec. 2. That whenever the foregoing section of this act has been complied with it shall be mandatory upon the Secretary of the Treasury of the United States to have engraved and printed Treasury notes in the denominations of one, two, five and ten dollars each, which shall be a full legal tender for all debts, public and private, to the face value of said bond and deliver to said State, Territory, county, township, municipality, or incorporated town or village ninety-nine per centum of said notes, and retain one per centum for expense of engraving and printing same.

Sec. 3. That after the passage of this act it shall be compulsory upon every incorporated town or village, municipality, township, county, State or Territory to give employment to any idle man applying for work, and that the rate be not less than one dollar and fifty cents per day for common labor and three dollars and fifty cents per day for team and labor, and that eight hours per day shall constitute a day's labor under the provisions of this act.

Questions

1. What are the main points of the two bills?
2. Why was it politically expedient to cast the bills as public improvements?
3. Given the level of unemployment at that time, why were these proposals so controversial?

19-7 The "Cross of Gold" Speech (1896)

William Jennings Bryan

Voters saw William Jennings Bryan (1860–1925) either as a prophet or as a heretic; that impassioned politician did not allow a middle ground (see text pp. 601–602). A former two-term congressman from Nebraska, Bryan won the Democratic presidential nomination in 1896 with one of the most brilliant speeches in American politics, which is reprinted here. His effect on the Democratic convention was electrifying. The speech overwhelmed conservative, business-oriented Democrats who had hoped to nominate a backer of the gold standard. However, on the national scale Bryan sounded too much like an agrarian radical, and voters rejected him for president three times.

Source: William Jennings Bryan, *The First Battle: A Story of the Campaign of 1896* (Chicago: W. B. Conkey Company, 1896), pp. 199–206.

Mr. Chairman and Gentlemen of the Convention: I would be presumptuous, indeed, to present myself against the distinguished gentlemen to whom you have listened if this were a mere measuring of abilities; but this is not a contest between persons. The humblest citizen in all the land, when clad in the armor of a righteous cause, is stronger than all the hosts of error. I come to speak to you in defense of a cause as holy as the cause of liberty—the cause of humanity.

When this debate is concluded, a motion will be made to lay upon the table the resolution offered in commendation of the administration. We object to bringing this question down to the level of persons. The individual is but an atom; he is born, he acts, he dies; but principles are eternal; and this has been a contest over a principle.

Never before in the history of this country has there been witnessed such a contest as that through which we have just passed. Never before in the history of American politics has a great issue been fought out as this issue has been, by the voters of a great party. On the fourth of March, 1895, a few Democrats, most of them members of Congress, issued an address to the Democrats of the nation, asserting that the money question was the paramount issue of the hour; declaring that a majority of the Democratic party had the right to control the action of the party on this paramount issue; and concluding with the request that the believers in the free coinage of silver in the Democratic party should organize, take charge of, and control the policy of the Democratic party. Three months later, at Memphis, an organization was perfected, and the silver Democrats went forth openly and courageously proclaiming their belief, and declaring that, if successful, they would crystallize into a platform the declaration which they had made. Then began the conflict. With a zeal approaching the zeal which inspired the crusaders . . . our silver Democrats went forth from victory unto victory until they are now assembled, not to discuss, not to debate, but to enter up the judgment already rendered by the plain people of this country. In this contest brother has been arrayed against brother, father against son. The warmest ties of love, acquaintance and association have been disregarded; old leaders have been cast aside when they have refused to give expression to the sentiments of those whom they would lead, and new leaders have sprung up to give direction to this cause of truth. Thus has the contest been waged, and we have assembled here under as binding and

solemn instructions as were ever imposed upon representatives of the people. . . .

When you (turning to the gold delegates) come before us and tell us that we are about to disturb your business interests, we reply that you have disturbed our business interests by your course.

We say to you that you have made the definition of a business man too limited in its application. The man who is employed for wages is as much a business man as his employer; the attorney in a country town is as much a business man as the corporation counsel in a great metropolis; the merchant at the cross-roads store is as much a business man as the merchant of New York; the farmer who goes forth in the morning and toils all day—who begins in the spring and toils all summer—and who by the application of brain and muscle to the natural resources of the country creates wealth, is as much a business man as the man who goes upon the board of trade and bets upon the price of grain; the miners who go down a thousand feet into the earth, or climb two thousand feet upon the cliffs, and bring forth from their hiding places the precious metals to be poured into the channels of trade are as much business men as the few financial magnates who, in a back room, corner the money of the world. We come to speak for this broader class of business men.

Ah, my friends, we say not one word against those who live upon the Atlantic coast, but the hardy pioneers who have braved all the dangers of the wilderness, who have made the desert to blossom as the rose—the pioneers out there (pointing to the West), who rear their children near to Nature's heart, where they can mingle their voices with the voices of the birds—out there where they have erected schoolhouses for the education of their young, churches where they praise their Creator, and cemeteries where rest the ashes of their dead—these people, we say, are as deserving of the consideration of our party as any people in this country. It is for these that we speak. We do not come as aggressors. Our war is not a war of conquest; we are fighting in the defense of our homes, our families, and posterity. We have petitioned, and our petitions have been scorned; we have entreated, and our entreaties have been disregarded; we have begged, and they have mocked when our calamity came. We beg no longer; we entreat no more; we petition no more. We defy them.

The gentleman from Wisconsin has said that he fears a Robespierre. My friends, in this land of the free you need not fear that a tyrant will spring up from among the people. What we need is an Andrew Jackson to stand, as Jackson stood, against the encroachments of organized wealth.

They tell us that this platform was made to catch votes. We reply to them that changing conditions make new issues; that the principles upon which Democracy rests are as everlasting as the hills, but that they must be applied to new conditions as they arise. Conditions have arisen, and we are here to meet those conditions. They tell us that the income tax ought not to be brought in here; that it is a new idea. They criticise us for our criticism of the Supreme Court of the United States. My friends, we have not criticised; we have simply called attention to what you already know. If you want criticisms, read the dissenting opinions of the court. There you will find criticisms. They say that we passed an unconstitutional law; we deny it. The income tax law was not unconstitutional when it was passed; it was not unconstitutional when it went before the Supreme Court for the first time; it did not become unconstitutional until one of the judges changed his mind, and we cannot be expected to know when a judge will change his mind. The income tax is just. It simply intends to put the burdens of government justly upon the backs of the people. I am in favor of an income tax. When I find a man who is not willing to bear his share of the burdens of the government which protects him, I find a man who is unworthy to enjoy the blessings of a government like ours.

They say that we are opposing national bank currency; it is true. . . . We say in our platform that we believe that the right to coin and issue money is a function of government. We believe it. We believe that it is a part of sovereignty, and can no more with safety be delegated to private individuals than we could afford to delegate to private individuals the power to make penal statutes or levy taxes. Mr. [Thomas] Jefferson, who was once regarded as good Democratic authority, seems to have differed in opinion from the gentleman who has addressed us on the part of the minority. Those who are opposed to this proposition tell us that the issue of paper money is a function of the bank, and that the Government ought to go out of the banking business. I stand with Jefferson rather than with them, and tell them, as he did, that the issue of money is a function of government, and that the banks ought to go out of the governing business.

They complain about the plank which declares against life tenure in office. They have tried to strain it to mean that which it does not mean. What we oppose by that plank is the life tenure which is being built up in Washington, and which excludes from participation in official benefits the humbler members of society.

Let me call your attention to two or three important things. The gentleman from New York says that he will propose an amendment to the platform providing that the proposed change in our monetary system shall not affect contracts already made. Let me remind you that there is no intention of affecting those contracts which according to present laws are made payable in gold; but if he means to say that we cannot change our monetary system without protecting those who have loaned money before the change was made, I desire to ask him where, in law or in morals, he can find justification for not protecting the debtors when the act of 1873 [dropping silver as a medium of exchange] was passed, if he now insists that we must protect the creditors.

He says he will also propose an amendment which will provide for the suspension of free coinage if we fail to maintain the parity within a year. We reply that when we advocate a policy which we believe will be successful, we are not compelled to raise a doubt as to our own sincerity by suggesting what we shall do if we fail. I ask him, if he would apply his logic to us, why he does not apply it to himself. He says he wants this country to try to secure an international agreement. Why does he not tell us what he is going to do if he fails to secure an international agreement? There is more reason for him to do that than there is for us to provide against the failure to maintain the parity. Our opponents have tried for twenty years to secure an international agreement, and those are waiting for it most patiently who do not want it at all.

And now, my friends, let me come to the paramount issue. If they ask us why it is that we say more on the money question than we say upon the tariff question, I reply that, if protection has slain its thousands, the gold standard has slain its tens of thousands. If they ask us why we do not employ in our platform all the things that we believe in, we reply that when we have restored the money of the Constitution all other necessary reforms will be possible; but that until this is done there is no other reform that can be accomplished.

Why is it that within three months such a change has come over the country? Three months ago, when it was confidently asserted that those who believe in the gold standard would frame our platform and nominate our candidates, even the advocates of the gold standard did not think that we could elect a president. And they had good reason for their doubt, because there is scarcely a State here today asking for the gold standard which is not in the absolute control of the Republican party. But note the change. Mr. McKinley was nominated at St. Louis upon a platform which declared for the maintenance of the gold standard until it can be changed into bimetallism by international agreement. Mr. McKinley was the most popular man among the Republicans, and three months ago everybody in the Republican party prophesied his election. How is today? Why, the man who was once pleased to think that he looked like Napoleon—that man shudders today when he remembers that he was nominated on the anniversary of the battle of Waterloo. Not only that, but as he listens he can hear with ever-increasing distinctness the sound of the waves as they beat upon the lonely shores of St. Helena.

Why this change? Ah, my friends, is not the reason for the change evident to any one who will look at the matter? No private character, however pure, no personal popularity, however great, can protect from the avenging wrath of an indignant people a man who will declare that he is in favor of fastening the gold standard upon this country, or who is willing to surrender the right of self-government and place the legislative control of our affairs in the hands of foreign potentates and powers.

We go forth confident that we shall win. Why? Because upon the paramount issue of this campaign there is not a spot of ground upon which the enemy will dare to challenge battle. If they tell us that the gold standard is a good thing, we shall point to their platform and tell them that their platform pledges the party to get rid of the gold standard and substitute bimetallism. If the gold standard is a good thing, why try to get rid of it? I call your attention to the fact that some of the very people who are in this convention today and who tell us that we ought to declare in favor of international bimetallism—thereby declaring that the gold standard is wrong and the principle of bimetallism is better—these very people four months ago were open and avowed advocates of the gold standard, and were then telling us that we could not legislate two metals together, even with the aid of all the world. If the gold standard is a good thing, we ought to declare in favor of its retention and not in favor of abandoning it; and if the gold standard is a bad thing why should we wait until other nations are willing to help us to let go? Here is the line of battle, and we care not upon which issue they force the fight; we are prepared to meet them on either issue or on both. If they tell us that the gold standard is the standard of civilization, we reply to them that this, the most enlightened of all the nations of the earth, has never declared for a gold standard and that both the great parties this year are declaring against it. If the gold standard is the standard of civilization, why, my friends, should we not have it? If they come to meet us on that issue we can present the history of our nation. More than that; we can tell them that they will search the pages of history in vain to find a single instance where the common people of any land have ever declared themselves in favor of the gold standard. They can find where the holders of fixed investments have declared for a gold standard, but not where the masses have.

Mr. Carlisle said in 1878 that this was a struggle between "the idle holders of idle capital" and "the struggling masses, who produce the wealth and pay the taxes of the country;" and, my friends, the question we are to decide is: Upon which side will the Democratic party fight; upon the side of "the idle holders of idle capital" or upon the side of "the struggling masses?" That is the question which the party must answer first, and then it must be answered by each individual hereafter. The sympathies of the Democratic party, as shown by the platform, are on the side of the struggling masses who have ever been the foundation of the Democratic party. There are two ideas of government. There are those who believe that, if you will only legislate to make the well-to-do prosperous, their prosperity will leak through on those below. The Democratic idea, however, has been that if you legislate to make the masses prosperous, their prosperity will find its way up through every class which rests upon them.

You come to us and tell us that the great cities are in favor of the gold standard; we reply that the great cities rest upon our broad and fertile prairies. Burn down your cities and leave our farms, and your cities will spring up again as if by magic; but destroy our farms and the grass will grow in the streets of every city in the country.

My friends, we declare that this nation is able to legislate for its own people on every question, without waiting for the aid or consent of any other nation on earth; and upon that issue we expect to carry every State in the Union. . . . It is the issue of 1776 over again. Our ancestors, when but three millions in number, had the courage to declare their political independence of every other nation; shall we, their descendants, when we have grown to seventy millions, declare that we are less independent than our forefathers? No, my friends, that will never be the verdict of our people. Therefore, we care not upon what lines the battle is fought. If they say bimetallism is good, but that we cannot have it until other nations help us, we reply that, instead of having a gold standard because England has, we will restore bimetallism, and then let England have bimetallism because the United States has it. If they dare to come out in the open field and defend the gold standard as a good thing, we will fight them to the uttermost. Having behind us the producing masses of this nation and the world, supported by the commercial interests, the laboring interests, and the toilers everywhere, we will answer their demand for a gold standard by saying to them: You shall not press down upon the brow of labor this crown of thorns, you shall not crucify mankind upon a cross of gold.

Questions

1. What reforms does Bryan propose?
2. Cite some of the more powerful examples of Bryan's use of imagery.
3. How might that imagery have alienated the urban residents whose votes Bryan needed to be elected president?

Questions for Further Thought

1. What aspects of the frontier experience might have led Nebraska farmers (Document 19-5) to accept a woman speaker (see text Chapter 17)?
2. How do Kellie and Bryan (Document 19-7) use imagery to make their points? Give one or two examples of how politicians today use imagery.
3. How would William Graham Sumner (Document 19-2) have reacted to the ideas in these speeches?
4. How do Coxey's ideas (Document 19-6) compare to those of Powderly, Parsons, and Debs (see Documents 18-7 through 18-9)?

Race and Politics in the South

The defeat of the Populists was doubly tragic in the South. If that coalition of black and white farmers had won, it no doubt would have governed the region far differently than did the Redeemers and their successors. In coming close to victory, the Populists only hastened the creation of a Jim Crow world (see text p. 607).

The idea of racial supremacy had been a key element in antebellum society. Without it the planter class would have had little to offer the vast majority of whites, who were only marginally better off than slaves. The Redeemers (conservative Democrats) followed the same strategy (see text p. 605). As an Alabamian observed in 1886, "The white laboring classes here are separated from the Negroes, working all day side by side with them, by an innate consciousness of race superiority."

The threat posed by interracial coalitions was handled in number of ways. The former Populist leader Tom Watson (see text p. 605) learned that political success depended on accepting segregation. His onetime followers, black as well as white, discovered that protest could lead to disfranchisement (Document 19-8). In Document 19-9, Ida B. Wells describes the violence blacks faced in the South.

Whereas poor whites could embrace the concept of their own racial supremacy, blacks faced a more difficult choice between the arguments of Booker T. Washington and those of W. E. B. Du Bois (see text pp. 608–609). Washington won fame as the ex-slave who founded the Tuskegee Institute. He counseled the acceptance of segregation to give blacks a chance to build a self-sufficient community. In contrast, the Harvard-trained Du Bois demanded social equality. For African-Americans in the age of Jim Crow survival depended on blending Washington's Atlanta Compromise (Document 19-10) with Du Bois's passion for civil rights (Document 19-11).

19-8 The 1890 Mississippi Constitution

Long before George Orwell conceived of doublespeak, there was the 1890 Mississippi constitution. It had the veneer of a liberal document, complete with a lengthy bill of rights, but the text also included a section that detailed how voting rights could be denied (see text p. 606). Such disfranchisement schemes persisted in the South into the 1960s.

Source: In Francis N. Thorpe, ed., *The Federal and State Constitutions . . . of the United States* (Washington, D.C.: U.S. Government Printing Office, 1909), vol. 4, pp. 2091–2093, 2120–2121.

We, the people of Mississippi, in Convention assembled, grateful to Almighty God, and invoking His blessing on our work, do ordain and establish this Constitution. . . .

ARTICLE 3

Bill of Rights

SEC. 5. All political power is vested in, and derived from, the people; all government of right originates with the people, is founded upon their will only, and is instituted solely for the good of the whole.

SEC. 6. The people of this State have the inherent, sole and exclusive right to regulate the internal government and police thereof, and to alter and abolish their constitution and form of government whenever they deem it necessary to their safety and happiness; provided, such change be not repugnant to the constitution of the United States.

SEC. 7. The right to withdraw from the Federal Union on account of any real or supposed grievance, shall never be assumed by this State, nor shall any law be passed in derogation of the paramount allegiance of the citizens of this State to the government of the United States.

SEC. 8. All persons resident in this State, citizens of the United States, are hereby declared citizens of the State of Mississippi.

SEC. 9. The military shall be in strict subordination to the civil power.

SEC. 10. Treason against the State shall consist only in levying war against the same or in adhering to its enemies, giving them aid and comfort. No person shall be convicted of treason unless on the testimony of two witnesses to the same overt act, or on confession in open court.

SEC. 11. The right of the people peaceably to assemble and petition the government on any subject shall never be impaired.

SEC. 12. The right of every citizen to keep and bear arms in defense of his home, person or property, or in aid of the civil power when thereto legally summoned, shall not be called in question, but the legislature may regulate or forbid carrying concealed weapons.

SEC. 13. The freedom of speech and of the press shall be held sacred, and in all prosecutions for libel the truth may be given in evidence, and the jury shall determine the law and the facts under the direction of the court; and if it shall appear to the jury that the matter charged as libelous is true, and was published with good motives and for justifiable ends, the party shall be acquitted.

SEC. 14. No person shall be deprived of life, liberty or property, except by due process of law.

SEC. 15. There shall be neither slavery nor involuntary servitude in this State, otherwise than in the punishment of crime, whereof the party shall have been duly convicted.

SEC. 16. Ex post facto laws, or laws impairing the obligation of contracts, shall not be passed.

SEC. 17. Private property shall not be taken or damaged for public use except on due compensation being first made to the owner or owners thereof, in a manner to be prescribed by law; and whenever an attempt is made to take private property for a use alleged to be public, the question whether the contemplated use be public shall be a judicial question, and as such determined without regard to legislative assertion that the use is public.

SEC. 18. No religious test as a qualification for office shall be required; and no preference shall be given by law to any religious sect, or mode of worship; but the free enjoyment of all religious sentiments and the different modes of worship shall be held sacred. The rights hereby secured shall not be construed to justify acts of licentiousness injurious to morals or dangerous to the peace and safety of the State, or to exclude the Holy Bible from use in any public school of this State.

SEC. 19. Human life shall not be imperiled by the practice of dueling; and any citizen of this State who shall hereafter fight a duel, or assist in the same as second, or send, accept, or knowingly carry a challenge therefor, whether such act be done in the State, or out of it, or who shall go out of the State to fight a duel, or to assist in the same as second, or to send, accept or carry a challenge, shall be disqualified from holding any office under this constitution and shall be disfranchised.

SEC. 20. No person shall be elected or appointed to office in this State for life or during good behavior, but the term of all offices shall be for some specified period.

SEC. 21. The privilege of the writ of habeas corpus shall not be suspended, unless when in case of rebellion or invasion, the public safety may require it, nor ever without the authority of the legislature.

SEC. 22. No person's life or liberty shall be twice placed in jeopardy for the same offense; but there must be an actual acquittal or conviction on the merits to bar another prosecution.

SEC. 23. The people shall be secure in their persons, houses and possessions, from unreasonable seizure or search; and no warrant shall be issued without probable cause, supported by oath or affirmation, specially designating the place to be searched and the person or thing to be seized.

SEC. 24. All courts shall be open; and every person for an injury done him in his lands, goods, person or reputation, shall have remedy by due course of law, and right and justice shall be administered without sale, denial or delay.

SEC. 25. No person shall be debarred from prosecuting or defending any civil cause, for or against him or herself before any tribunal in this State, by him or herself, or counsel, or both.

SEC. 26. In all criminal prosecutions the accused shall have a right to be heard by himself or counsel, or both, to demand the nature and cause of the accusation, to be confronted by the witnesses against him, to have compulsory process for obtaining witnesses in his favor, and in all prosecutions by indictment or information, a speedy and public trial by an impartial jury of the county where the offense was committed; and he shall not be compelled to give evidence against himself; but in prosecutions for rape, adultery, fornication, sodomy or the crime against nature, the court may in its discretion exclude from the court room all persons except such as are necessary in the conduct of the trial.

SEC. 27. No person shall for any indictable offense, be proceeded against criminally by information, except in cases arising in the land or naval forces, or the militia when in actual service, or by leave of the court for misdemeanor in office; but the legislature in cases not punishable by death or by imprisonment in the penitentiary, may dispense with the inquest of the grand jury, and may authorize prosecutions before justices of the peace, or such other inferior court or courts as may be established, and the proceedings in such cases shall be regulated by law.

SEC. 28. Cruel or unusual punishment shall not be inflicted, nor excessive fines be imposed.

SEC. 29. Excessive bail shall not be required; and all persons shall, before conviction, be bailable by sufficient sureties, except for capital offenses when the proof is evident or presumption great.

SEC. 30. There shall be no imprisonment for debt.

SEC. 31. The right of trial by jury shall remain inviolate.

SEC. 32. The enumeration of rights in this constitution shall not be construed to deny or impair others retained by, and inherent in, the people.

ARTICLE 12

Franchise

SEC. 240. All elections by the people shall be by ballot.

SEC. 241. Every male inhabitant of this State, except idiots, insane persons and Indians not taxed, who is a citizen of the United States, twenty-one years old and upwards, who has resided in this State two years, and one year in the election district, or in the incorporated city or town, in which he offers to vote, and who is duly registered as provided in this article, and who has never been convicted of bribery, burglary, theft, arson, obtaining money or goods under false pretenses, perjury, forgery, imbezzlement or bigamy, and who has paid, on or before the first day of February of the year in which he shall offer to vote, all taxes which may have been legally required of him, and which he has had an opportunity of paying according to law, for the two preceding years, and who shall produce to the officers holding the election satisfactory evidence that he has paid said taxes, is declared to be a qualified elector; but any minister of the gospel in charge of an organized church shall be entitled to vote after six months residence in the election district, if otherwise qualified.

SEC. 242. The legislature shall provide by law for the registration of all persons entitled to vote at any election, and all persons offering to register shall take the following oath or affirmation: "I ——— ———, do solemnly swear (or affirm) that I am twenty-one years old, (or I will be before the next election in this county) and that I will have resided in this State two years, and ———election district of ——— county one year next preceding the ensuing election [or if it be stated in the oath that the person proposing to register is a minister of the gospel in charge of an organized church, then it will be sufficient to aver therein, two years residence in the State and six months in said election district], and am now in good faith a resident of the same, and that I am not disqualified from voting by reason of having been convicted of any crime named in the constitution of this State as a disqualification to be an elector; that I will truly answer all questions propounded to me concerning my antecedents so far as they relate to my right to vote, and also as to my residence before my citizenship in this district; that I will faithfully support the constitution of the United States and of the State of Mississippi, and will bear true faith and allegiance to the same. So help me God." In registering voters in cities and towns, not wholly in one election district, the name of such city or town may be substituted in the oath for the election district. Any willful and corrupt false statement in said affidavit, or in answer to any material question propounded as herein authorized, shall be perjury.

SEC. 243. A uniform poll tax of two dollars, to be used in aid of the common schools, and for no other purpose, is hereby imposed on every male inhabitant of this State between the ages of twenty-one and sixty years, except persons who are deaf and dumb or blind, or who are maimed by loss of hand or foot; said tax to be a lien only upon taxable property. The board of supervisors of any county may, for the purpose of aiding the common schools in that county, increase the poll tax in said county, but in no case shall the entire poll tax exceed in any one year three dollars on each poll. No criminal proceedings shall be allowed to enforce the collection of the poll tax.

SEC. 244. On and after the first day of January, A. D., 1892, every elector shall, in addition to the foregoing qualifications, be able to read any section of the constitution of this State; or he shall be able to understand the same when read to him, or give a reasonable interpretation thereof. A new registration shall be made before the next ensuing election after January the first, A. D., 1892.

Questions

1. What methods of disfranchisement does this constitution allow?
2. Given the obvious intent of the constitution's authors, why do you think they bothered with a bill of rights?
3. How does Mississippi's bill of rights compare with that in the U.S. Constitution (see text pp. D-12–D-13)?

19-9 "Lynching at the Curve"

Ida B. Wells

Violence was not an abstract concept for an African-American like Ida B. Wells, who was born a slave in 1862. She worked as a teacher before becoming the part owner of a Memphis newspaper in 1889 (see text p. 608). The lynching Wells describes here persuaded her to leave Memphis. Wells eventually settled in Chicago, where she took part in suffrage and other reform activities until her death in 1931.

Source: Ida B. Wells, *Crusade for Justice: The Autobiography of Ida B. Wells*, ed. Alfreda M. Duster, pp. 47–51. Copyright 1970 by the University of Chicago Press. Reprinted by permission.

While I was thus carrying on the work of my newspaper, happy in the thought that our influence was helpful and that I was doing the work I loved and had proved that I could make a living out of it, there came the lynching in Memphis which changed the whole course of my life. I was on one of my trips away from home. I was busily engaged in Natchez when word came of the lynching of three men in Memphis. It came just as I had demonstrated that I could make a living by my newspaper and need never tie myself down to school teaching.

Thomas Moss, Calvin McDowell, and Henry Stewart owned and operated a grocery story in a thickly populated suburb. Moss was a letter carrier and could only be at the store at night. Everybody in town knew and loved Tommie. An exemplary young man, he was married and the father of one little girl, Maurine, whose godmother I was. He and his wife Betty were the best friends I had in town. And he believed, with me, that we should defend the cause of right and fight wrong wherever we saw it.

He delivered mail at the office of the *Free Speech*, and whatever Tommie knew in the way of news we got first. He owned his little home, and having saved his money he went into the grocery business with the same ambition that a young white man would have had. He was the president of the company. His partners ran the business in the daytime.

They had located their grocery in the district known as the "Curve" because the streetcar line curved sharply at that point. There was already a grocery owned and operated by a white man who hitherto had had a monopoly on the trade of this thickly populated colored suburb. Thomas's grocery changed all that, and he and his associates were made to feel that they were not welcome by the white grocer. The district being mostly colored and many of the residents belonging either to Thomas's church or to his lodge, he was not worried by the white grocer's hostility.

One day some colored and white boys quarreled over a game of marbles and the colored boys got the better of the fight which followed. The father of the white boys whipped the victorious colored boy, whose father and friends pitched in to avenge the grown white man's flogging of a colored boy. The colored men won the fight, whereupon the white father and grocery keeper swore out a warrant for the arrest of the colored victors. Of course the colored grocery keepers had been drawn into the dispute. But the case was dismissed with nominal fines. Then the challenge was issued that the vanquished whites were coming on Saturday night to clean out the People's Grocery Company.

Knowing this, the owners of the company consulted a lawyer and were told that as they were outside the city limits and beyond police protection, they would be justified in protecting themselves if attacked. Accordingly the grocery company armed several men and stationed them in the rear of the story on that fatal Saturday night, not to attack but to repel a threatened attack. And Saturday night was the time when men of both races congregated in their respective groceries.

About ten o'clock that night, when Thomas was posting his books for the week and Calvin McDowell and his clerk were waiting on customers preparatory to closing, shots rang out in the back room of the store. The men stationed there had seen several white men stealing through the rear door and fired on them without a moment's pause. Three of these men were wounded, and others fled and gave the alarm.

Sunday morning's paper came out with lurid headlines telling how officers of the law had been wounded while in the discharge of their duties, hunting up criminals whom they had been told were harbored in the People's Grocery Company, this being "a low dive in which drinking and gambling were carried on: a resort of thieves and thugs." So ran the description in the leading white journals of Memphis of this successful effort of decent black men to carry on a legitimate business. The same newspaper told of the arrest and jailing of the proprietor of the store and many of the colored people. They predicted that it would go hard with the ringleaders if these "officers" should die. The tale of how the peaceful homes of that suburb were raided on that quiet Sunday morning by police pretending to be looking for others who were implicated in what the papers had called a conspiracy, has been often told. Over a hundred colored men were dragged from their homes and put in jail on suspicion.

All day long on that fateful Sunday white men were permitted in the jail to look over the imprisoned black men. Frenzied descriptions and hearsays were detailed in the papers, which fed the fires of sensationalism. Groups of white men gathered on the street corners and meeting places to discuss the awful crime of Negroes shooting white men.

There had been no lynchings in Memphis since the Civil War, but the colored people felt that anything might happen during the excitement. Many of them were in business there. Several times they had elected a member of their race to represent them in the legislature in Nashville. And a Negro, Lymus Wallace, had been elected several times as a member of the city council and we had had representation on the school board several times. Mr. Fred Savage was then our representative on the board of education.

The manhood which these Negroes represented went to the county jail and kept watch Sunday night. This they did also on Monday night, guarding the jail to see that nothing happened to the colored men during this time of race prejudice, while it was thought that the wounded white men would die. On Tuesday following, the newspapers which had fanned the flame of race prejudice announced that the wounded men were out of danger and would recover. The colored men who had guarded the jail for two nights felt that the crisis was past and that they need not guard the jail the third night.

While they slept a body of picked men was admitted to the jail, which was a modern Bastille. This mob took out of their cells Thomas Moss, Calvin McDowell, and Henry Stewart, the three officials of the People's Grocery Company. They were loaded on a switch engine of the railroad which ran back of the jail, carried a mile north of the city limits, and horribly shot to death. One of the morning papers held back its edition in order to supply its readers with the details of that lynching.

From its columns was gleaned the above information, together with details which told that "It is said that Tom Moss begged for his life for the sake of his wife and child and his unborn baby"; that when asked if he had anything to say, told them to "tell my people to go West—there is no justice for them here"; that Calvin McDowell got hold of one of the guns of the lynchers and because they could not loosen his grip a shot was fired into his closed fist. When the three bodies were found, the fingers of McDowell's right hand had been shot to pieces and his eyes were gouged out. This proved that the one who wrote that news report was either an eyewitness or got the facts from someone who was.

Questions

1. How and why did the lynching take place?
2. Why would public officials allow a lynching, which by its very nature represents a challenge to authority?
3. For the supporters of Jim Crow in Memphis, the lynching served one purpose. How did it affect the black community?

19-10   The Atlanta Exposition Address (1895)

Booker T. Washington

During his lifetime Booker T. Washington (1856–1915) was hailed as an African-American hero: he was an ex-slave who went on to found the Tuskegee Institute (see text pp. 608–609). His accommodationist approach did not win support for long. Washington's reputation suffered after his death, especially during the civil rights movement of the 1960s, when he was criticized as an apologist for segregation. More recently, however, some black leaders have revived his concept of self-help. Both ideas—segregation and group autonomy—appear in Washington's Atlanta Exposition Address of 1895.

Source: Booker T. Washington, *Up from Slavery: An Autobiography* (1900; reprint, Williamstown, Mass.: Corner House Publishers, 1978), pp. 218–225.

Mr. President and Gentlemen of the Board of Directors and Citizens.

One-third of the population of the South is of the Negro race. No enterprise seeking the material, civil, or moral welfare of this section can disregard this element of our population and reach the highest success. I but convey to you, Mr. President and Directors, the sentiment of the masses of my race when I say that in no way have the value and manhood of the American Negro been more fittingly and generously recognized than by the managers of this magnificent Exposition at every stage of its progress. It is a recognition that will do more to cement the friendship of the two races than any occurrence since the dawn of our freedom.

Not only this, but the opportunity here afforded will awaken among us a new era of industrial progress. Ignorant and inexperienced, it is not strange that in the first years of our new life we began at the top instead of at the bottom; that a seat in Congress or the state legislature was more sought than real estate or industrial skill; that the political convention of stump speaking had more attractions than starting a dairy farm or truck garden.

A ship lost at sea for many days suddenly sighted a friendly vessel. From the mast of the unfortunate vessel was seen a signal, "Water, water; we die of thirst!" The answer from the friendly vessel at once came back, "Cast down your bucket where you are." A second time the signal, "Water, water; send us water!" ran up from the distressed vessel, and was answered, "Cast down your bucket where you are." The captain of the distressed vessel, at last heeding the injunction, cast down his bucket, and it came up full of fresh, sparkling water from the mouth of the Amazon River. To those of my race who depend on bettering their condition in a foreign land or who underestimate the importance of cultivating friendly relations with the Southern white man, who is their next-door neighbour, I would say: "Cast down your bucket where you are"—cast it down in making friends in every manly way of the people of all races by whom we are surrounded.

Cast it down in agriculture, mechanics, in commerce, in domestic service, and in the professions. And in this connection it is well to bear in mind that whatever other sins the South may be called to bear, when it comes to business, pure and simple, it is in the South that the Negro is given a man's chance in the commercial world, and in nothing is this Exposition more eloquent than in emphasizing this chance. Our greatest danger is that in the great leap of slavery to freedom we may overlook the fact that the masses of us are to live by the productions of our hands, and fail to keep in mind that we shall prosper in proportion as we learn to dignify and glorify common labour and put brains and skill into the common occupations of life; shall prosper in proportion as we learn to draw the line between the superficial and the substantial, the ornamental gewgaws of life and the useful. No race can prosper till it learns that there is as much dignity in tilling a field as in writing a poem. It is at the bottom of life we must begin, and not at the top. Nor should we permit our grievances to overshadow our opportunities.

To those of the white race who look to the incoming of those of foreign birth and strange tongue and habits for the prosperity of the South, were I permitted I would repeat what I say to my own race, "Cast down your bucket where you are." Cast it down among the eight millions of Negroes whose habits you know, whose fidelity and love you have tested in days when to have proved treacherous meant the ruin of your firesides. Cast down your bucket among these people who have, without strikes and labour wars, tilled your fields, cleared your forests, builded your railroads and cities, and brought forth treasures from the bowels of the earth, and helped make possible this magnificent representation of the progress of the South. Casting down your bucket among my people, helping and encouraging them as you are doing on these grounds, and to education of head, hand, and heart, you will find that they will buy your surplus land, make blossom the waste places in your fields, and run your factories. While doing this, you can be sure in the future, as in the past, that you and your families will be surrounded by the most patient, faithful, law-abiding, and unresentful people that the world has seen. As we have proved our loyalty to you in the past, in nursing your children, watching by the sick-bed of your mothers and fathers, and often following them with tear-dimmed eyes to their graves, so in the future, in our humble way, we shall stand by you with a devotion that no foreigner can approach, ready to lay down our lives, if need be, in defence of yours, interlacing our industrial, commercial, civil, and religious life with yours in a way that shall make the interests of both races one. In all things that are purely social we can be as separate as the fingers, yet one as the hand in all things essential to mutual progress.

There is no defence or security for any of us except in the highest intelligence and development of all. If anywhere there are efforts tending to curtail the fullest growth of the Negro, let these efforts be turned into stimulating, encouraging, and making him the most useful and intelligent citizen. Effort or means so invested will pay a thousand per cent. interest. These efforts will be twice blessed—"blessing him that gives and him that takes."

There is no escape through law of man or God from the inevitable:—

The laws of changeless justice bind
    Oppressor with oppressed;
And close as sin and suffering joined
    We march to fate abreast.

Nearly sixteen millions of hands will aid you in pulling the load upward, or they will pull against you the load downward. We shall constitute one-third and more of the ignorance and crime of the South, or one-third its intelligence and progress; we shall contribute one-third to the business and industrial prosperity of the South, or we shall prove a veritable body of death, stagnating, depressing, retarding every effort to advance the body politic.

Gentlemen of the Exposition, as we present to you our humble effort at an exhibition of our progress, you must not expect overmuch. Starting thirty years ago with ownership here and there in a few quilts and pumpkins and chickens (gathered from miscellaneous sources), remember the path that has led from these to the inventions and production of agricultural implements, buggies, steam-engines, newspapers, books, statuary, carving, paintings, the management of drug-stores and banks, has not been trodden without contact with thorns and thistles. While we take pride in what we exhibit as a result of our independent efforts, we do not for a moment forget that our part in this exhibition would fall far short of your expectations but for the constant help that has come to our educational life, not only from the Southern states, but especially from Northern philanthropists, who have made their gifts a constant stream of blessing and encouragement.

The wisest among my race understand that the agitation of questions of social equality is the extremest folly, and that progress in the enjoyment of all the privileges that will come to us must be the result of severe and constant struggle rather than of artificial forcing. No race that has anything to contribute to the markets of the world is long in any degree ostracized. It is important and right that all privileges of the law be ours, but it is vastly more important that we be prepared for the exercises of these privileges. The opportunity to earn a dollar in a factory just now is worth infinitely more than the opportunity to spend a dollar in an opera-house.

In conclusion, may I repeat that nothing in thirty years has given us more hope and encouragement, and drawn us so near to you of the white race, as this opportunity offered by the Exposition; and here bending, as it were, over the altar that represents the results of the struggles of your race and mine, both starting practically empty-handed three decades ago, I pledge that in your effort to work out the great and intricate problem which God had laid at the doors of the South, you shall have at all times the patient, sympathetic help of my race; only let this be constantly in mind, that, while from representations in these buildings of the product of field, of forest, of mine, of factory, letters, and art, much good will come, yet far above and beyond material benefits will be that higher good, that, let us pray God, will come, in a blotting out of sectional differences and racial animosities and suspicions, in a determination to administer absolute justice, in a willing obedience among all classes to the mandates of law. This, this, coupled with our material prosperity, will bring into our beloved South a new heaven and a new earth.

Questions

1. What is Washington's message to blacks? To whites?
2. Why does Washington mention immigrants?
3. What does he mean in saying, "In all things that are purely social we can be as separate as the fingers, yet one as the hand in all things essential to mutual progress"?

19-11   "Of Mr. Booker T. Washington and Others" (1903)

W. E. B. Du Bois

Unlike Booker T. Washington, W. E. B. Du Bois (see photo on text p. 663) never experienced slavery. Du Bois was born in Barrington, Massachusetts, in 1868 and was educated at Fisk and Harvard, where he earned a Ph.D. As the selection here indicates, Du Bois could not accept Washington's toleration of segregation (see text p. 609). His call for social equality led him to participate in the founding of the NAACP. Du Bois spent his last years in Ghana, where he died in 1963.

Du Bois's critique of Washington appears in *The Souls of Black Folk*, first published in 1903.

Source: W. E. B. Du Bois, *The Souls of Black Folk* (A. C. McClurg, 1903; reprint, New York: Penguin Books, 1989), pp. 36–50.

Easily the most striking thing in the history of the American Negro since 1876 is the ascendancy of Mr. Booker T. Washington. It began at the time when war memories and ideals were rapidly passing; a day of astonishing commercial development was dawning; a sense of doubt and hesitation overtook the freedmen's sons,—then it was that his leading began. Mr. Washington came, with a simple definite programme, at the psychological moment when the nation was a little ashamed of having bestowed so much sentiment on Negroes, and was concentrating its energies on Dollars. His programme of industrial education, conciliation of the South, and submission and silence as to civil and political rights, was not wholly original; the Free Negroes from 1830 up to wartime had striven to build industrial schools, and the American Missionary Association had from the first taught various trades; and Price and others had sought a way of honorable alliance with the best of the Southerners. But Mr. Washington first indissolubly linked these things; he put enthusiasm, unlimited energy, and perfect faith into this programme, and changed it from a by-path into a veritable Way of Life. And the tale of the methods by which he did this is a fascinating study of human life.

It startled the nation to hear a Negro advocating such a programme after many decades of bitter complaint; it startled and won the applause of the South, it interested and won the admiration of the North; and after a confused murmur of protest, it silenced if it did not convert the Negroes themselves.

To gain the sympathy and coöperation of the various elements comprising the white South was Mr. Washington's first task; and this, at the time Tuskegee was founded, seemed, for a black man, well-nigh impossible. And yet ten years later it was done in the word spoken at Atlanta: "In all things purely social we can be as separate as the five fingers, and yet one as the hand in all things essential to mutual progress." This "Atlanta Compromise" is by all odds the most notable thing in Mr. Washington's career. The South interpreted it in different ways: The radicals received it as a complete surrender of the demand for civil and political equality; the conservatives, as a generously conceived working basis for mutual understanding. So both approved it, and to-day its author is certainly the most distinguished Southerner since Jefferson Davis, and the one with the largest personal following.

Next to this achievement comes Mr. Washington's work in gaining place and consideration in the North. Others less shrewd and tactful had formerly essayed to sit on these two stools and had fallen between them; but as Mr. Washington knew the heart of the South from birth and training, so by singular insight he intuitively grasped the spirit of the age which was dominating the North. And so thoroughly did he learn the speech and thought of triumphant commercialism, and the ideals of material prosperity, that the picture of a lone black boy poring over a French grammar amid the weeds and dirt of a neglected home soon seemed to him the acme of absurdities. One wonders what Socrates and St. Francis of Assisi would say to this.

And yet this very singleness of vision and thorough oneness with his age is a mark of the successful man. It is as though Nature must needs make men narrow in order to give them force. So Mr. Washington's cult has gained unquestioning followers, his work has wonderfully prospered, his friends are legion, and his enemies are confounded. To-day he stands as the one recognized spokesman of his ten million fellows, and one of the most notable figures in a nation of seventy millions. One hesitates, therefore, to criticise a life which, beginning with so little, has done so much. And yet the time is come when one may speak in all sincerity and utter courtesy of the mistakes and shortcomings of Mr. Washington's career, as well as of his triumphs, without being thought captious or envious, and without forgetting that it is easier to do ill than well in the world.

The criticism that has hitherto met Mr. Washington

has not always been of this broad character. In the South especially has he had to walk warily to avoid the harshest judgments,—and naturally so, for he is dealing with the one subject of deepest sensitiveness to that section. Twice—once when at the Chicago celebration of the Spanish-American War he alluded to the color-prejudice that is "eating away the vitals of the South," and once when he dined with President Roosevelt—has the resulting Southern criticism been violent enough to threaten seriously his popularity. In the North the feeling has several times forced itself into words, that Mr. Washington's counsels of submission overlooked certain elements of true manhood, and that his educational programme was unnecessarily narrow. Usually, however, such criticism has not found open expression, although, too, the spiritual sons of the Abolitionists have not been prepared to acknowledge that the schools founded before Tuskegee, by men of broad ideals and self-sacrificing spirit, were wholly failures or worthy of ridicule. While, then, criticism has not failed to follow Mr. Washington, yet the prevailing public opinion of the land has been but too willing to deliver the solution of a wearisome problem into his hands, and say, "If that is all you and your race ask, take it."

Among his own people, however, Mr. Washington has encountered the strongest and most lasting opposition, amounting at times to bitterness, and even to-day continuing strong and insistent even though largely silenced in outward expression by the public opinion of the nation. Some of this opposition is, of course, mere envy; the disappointment of displaced demagogues and the spite of narrow minds. But aside from this, there is among educated and thoughtful colored men in all parts of the land a feeling of deep regret, sorrow, and apprehension at the wide currency and ascendancy which some of Mr Washington's theories have gained. These same men admire his sincerity of purpose, and are willing to forgive much to honest endeavor which is doing something worth the doing. They coöperate with Mr. Washington as far as they conscientiously can; and, indeed, it is no ordinary tribute to this man's tact and power that, steering as he must between so many diverse interests and opinions, he so largely retains the respect of all.

But the hushing of the criticism of honest opponents is a dangerous thing. It leads some of the best of the critics to unfortunate silence and paralysis of effort, and others to burst into speech so passionately and intemperately as to lose listeners. Honest and earnest criticism from those whose interests are most nearly touched,—criticism of writers by readers, of government by those governed, of leaders by those led,—this is the soul of democracy and the safeguard of modern society. If the best of the American Negroes receive by outer pressure a leader whom they had not recognized before, manifestly there is here a certain palpable gain. Yet there is also irreparable loss,—a loss of that peculiarly valuable education which a group receives

when by search and criticism it finds and commissions its own leaders. The way in which this is done is at once the most elementary and the nicest problem of social growth. History is but the record of such group-leadership; and yet how infinitely changeful is its type and character! And of all types and kinds, what can be more instructive than the leadership of a group within a group?—that curious double movement where real progress may be negative and actual advance be relative retrogression. All this is the social student's inspiration and despair. . . .

Mr. Washington represents in Negro thought the old attitude of adjustment and submission; but adjustment at such a peculiar time as to make his programme unique. This is an age of unusual economic development, and Mr Washington's programme naturally takes an economic cast, becoming a gospel of Work and Money to such an extent as apparently almost completely to overshadow the higher aims of life. Moreover, this is an age when the more advanced races are coming in closer contact with the less developed races, and the race-feeling is therefore intensified; and Mr. Washington's programme practically accepts the alleged inferiority of the Negro races. Again, in our own land, the reaction from the sentiment of war time has given impetus to race-prejudice against Negroes, and Mr. Washington withdraws many of the high demands of Negroes as men and American citizens. In other periods of intensified prejudice all the Negro's tendency to self-assertion has been called forth; at this period a policy of submission is advocated. In the history of nearly all other races and peoples the doctrine preached at such crises has been that manly self-respect is worth more than lands and houses, and that a people who voluntarily surrender such respect, or cease striving for it, are not worth civilizing.

In answer to this, it has been claimed that the Negro can survive only through submission. Mr. Washington distinctly asks that black people give up, at least for the present, three things,—

First, political power,

Second, insistence on civil rights,

Third, higher education of Negro youth,—

and concentrate all their energies on industrial education, the accumulation of wealth, and the conciliation of the South. This policy has been courageously and insistently advocated for over fifteen years, and has been triumphant for perhaps ten years. As a result of this tender of the palm-branch, what has been the return? In these years there have occurred:

1. The disfranchisement of the Negro.

2. The legal creation of a distinct status of civil inferiority for the Negro.

3. The steady withdrawal of aid from institutions for the higher training of the Negro.

These movements are not, to be sure, direct results of Mr. Washington's teachings; but his propaganda has, without a shadow of doubt, helped their speedier accomplish-

ment. The question then comes: Is it possible, and probable, that nine millions of men can make effective progress
in economic lines if they are deprived of political rights,
made a servile caste, and allowed only the most meagre
chance for developing their exceptional men? If history
and reason give any distinct answer to these questions, it is
an emphatic *No.* And Mr. Washington thus faces the triple
paradox of his career:

1. He is striving nobly to make Negro artisans business men and property-owners; but it is utterly impossible,
under modern competitive methods, for workingmen and
property-owners to defend their rights and exist without
the right of suffrage.

2. He insists on thrift and self-respect, but at the same
time counsels a silent submission to civic inferiority such as
is bound to sap the manhood of any race in the long run.

3. He advocates common-school and industrial training, and depreciates institutions of higher learning; but neither the Negro common-schools, nor Tuskegee itself, could
remain open a day were it not for teachers trained in
Negro colleges, or trained by their graduates.

This triple paradox in Mr. Washington's position is the
object of criticism by two classes of colored Americans.
One class is spiritually descended from Toussaint the Savior, through Gabriel, Vesey, and Turner, and they represent
the attitude of revolt and revenge; they hate the white
South blindly and distrust the white race generally, and so
far as they agree on definite action, think that the Negro's
only hope lies in emigration beyond the borders of the
United States. An yet, by the irony of fate, nothing has
more effectually made this programme seem hopeless than
the recent course of the United States toward weaker and
darker peoples in the West Indies, Hawaii, and the Philippines,—for where in the world may we go and be safe
from lying and brute force?

The other class of Negroes who cannot agree with Mr.
Washington has hitherto said little aloud. They deprecate
the sight of scattered counsels, of internal disagreement;
and especially they dislike making their just criticism of a
useful and earnest man an excuse for a general discharge of
venom from small-minded opponents. Nevertheless, the
questions involved are so fundamental and serious that it is
difficult to see how men like the Grimkes, Kelly Miller,
J. W. E. Bowen, and other representatives of this group,
can much longer be silent. Such men feel in conscience
bound to ask of this nation three things:

1. The right to vote.

2. Civic equality.

3. The education of youth according to ability.

They acknowledge Mr. Washington's invaluable service in counselling patience and courtesy in such demands;
they do not ask that ignorant black men vote when ignorant whites are debarred, or that any reasonable restrictions in the suffrage should not be applied; they know that
the low social level of the mass of the race is responsible

for much discrimination against it, but they also know, and
the nation knows, that relentless color-prejudice is more
often a cause than a result of the Negro's degradation; they
seek the abatement of this relic of barbarism, and not its
systematic encouragement and pampering by all agencies
of social power from the Associated Press to the Church of
Christ. They advocate, with Mr. Washington, a broad system of Negro common schools supplemented by thorough
industrial training; but they are surprised that a man of
Mr. Washington's insight cannot see that no such educational system ever has rested or can rest on any other basis
than that of the well-equipped college and university, and
they insist that there is a demand for a few such institutions throughout the South to train the best of the Negro
youth as teachers, professional men, and leaders.

This group of men honor Mr. Washington for his attitude of conciliation toward the white South; they accept
the "Atlanta Compromise" in its broadest interpretation;
they recognize, with him, many signs of promise, many
men of high purpose and fair judgment, in this section;
they know that no easy task has been laid upon a region already tottering under heavy burdens. But, nevertheless,
they insist that the way to truth and right lies in straight-
forward honesty, not in indiscriminate flattery; in praising
those of the South who do well and criticising uncompro-
misingly those who do ill; in taking advantage of the opportunities at hand and urging their fellows to do the
same, but at the same time in remembering that only a firm
adherence to their higher ideals and aspirations will ever
keep those ideals within the realm of possibility. They do
not expect that the free right to vote, to enjoy civic rights,
and to be educated, will come in a moment; they do not
expect to see the bias and prejudices of years disappear at
the blast of a trumpet; but they are absolutely certain that
the way for a people to gain their reasonable rights is not
by voluntarily throwing them away and insisting that they
do not want them; that the way for a people to gain respect
is not by continually belittling and ridiculing themselves;
that, on the contrary, Negroes must insist continually, in
season and out of season, that voting is necessary to modern manhood, that color discrimination is barbarism, and
that black boys need education as well as white boys.

In failing thus to state plainly and unequivocally the
legitimate demands of their people, even at the cost of opposing an honored leader, the thinking classes of American
Negroes would shirk a heavy responsibility,—a responsibility to themselves, a responsibility to the struggling
masses, a responsibility to the darker races of men whose
future depends so largely on this American experiment, but
especially a responsibility to this nation,—this common
Fatherland. It is wrong to aid and abet a national crime
simply because it is unpopular not to do so. The growing
spirit of kindliness and reconciliation between the North
and South after the frightful differences of a generation
ago ought to be a source of deep congratulation to all, and

especially to those whose mistreatment caused the war; but if that reconciliation is to be marked by the industrial slavery and civic death of those same black men, with permanent legislation into a position of inferiority, then those black men, if they are really men, are called upon by every consideration of patriotism and loyalty to oppose such a course by all civilized methods, even though such opposition involves disagreement with Mr. Booker T. Washington. We have no right to sit silently by while the inevitable seeds are sown for a harvest of disaster to our children, black and white. . . .

The South ought to be led, by candid and honest criticism, to assert her better self and do her full duty to the race she has cruelly wronged and is still wronging. The North—her co-partner is guilt—cannot salve her conscience by plastering it with gold. We cannot settle this problem by diplomacy and suaveness, by "policy" alone. If worse come to worst, can the moral fibre of this country survive the slow throttling and murder of nine millions of men?

The black men of America have a duty to perform, a duty stern and delicate,—a forward movement to oppose a part of the work of their greatest leader. So far as Mr. Washington preaches Thrift, Patience, and Industrial Training for the masses, we must hold up his hands and strive with him, rejoicing in his honors and glorying in the strength of this Joshua called of God and of man to lead the headless host. But so far as Mr. Washington apologizes for injustice, North or South, does not rightly value the privilege and duty of voting, belittles the emasculating effects of caste distinctions, and opposes the higher training and ambition of our brighter minds,—so far as he, the South, or the Nation, does this,—we must unceasingly and firmly oppose them. By every civilized and peaceful method we must strive for the rights which the world accords to men, clinging unwaveringly to those great words which the sons of the Fathers would fain forget: "We hold these truths to be self-evident: That all men are created equal; that they are endowed by their Creator with certain unalienable rights; that among these are life, liberty, and the pursuit of happiness."

Questions

1. Which aspects of Washington's philosophy does Du Bois criticize?
2. Who does Du Bois expect to lead in the criticism of Washington?
3. What role does Du Bois envision for blacks in American society?
4. In this essay does Du Bois appear to consider himself an American or an African-American? Why would that matter in regard to his view of Washington?

Questions for Further Thought

1. Which philosophy was better suited to the Jim Crow world of Mississippi, Booker T. Washington's (Document 19-10) or W. E. B. Du Bois's (Document 19-11)? Why?
2. How did the Mississippi constitution (Document 19-8) encourage the kind of violence described by Ida B. Wells?
3. Which aspects of Washington's speech have enjoyed a resurgence in popularity? Why?

CHAPTER 20

The Rise of the City

★   ★   ★

Urbanization

In a sense Americans have never been comfortable with or in cities. "The yellow fever will discourage the growth of great cities in our nation, and I view great cities as pestilential to the morals, the health, and the liberties of man," Thomas Jefferson wrote to Benjamin Rush in 1800. "True, they nourish some of the elegant arts, but the useful ones can thrive elsewhere, and less perfection in the others, with more health, virtue and freedom, would be my choice." Rush responded: "I consider them [cities] in the same light that I do abscesses on the human body, viz., as reservoirs of all the impurities of a community."

Jefferson envisioned a nation of yeomen farmers, but the Industrial Revolution impelled those farmers to leave the countryside for urban factory work. With the advent of steam power, factories increasingly were located in cities during the nineteenth century (see text pp. 616–618). The labor, transportation, and markets needed for success were tied in with ever-growing cities. There was unimagined wealth in urban America, together with problems that could not be solved by individuals working alone (see text pp. 618–621).

In Document 20-1 the progressive reformer Frederic Howe offers a strong defense of the city, or at least of its potential. The Italian visitor Giuseppe Giacosa (Document 20-2) provides an eyewitness account of an industrial city and one of its by-products, smoke (see text p. 622). Although the citizens of Chicago could not do much about the air, they were diligent about the water supply (see text p. 623). Document 20-3 describes the construction of the Chicago Sanitary and Ship Canal, which kept sewage away from the drinking supply and served as practice for the construction of the Panama Canal.

20-1 The "City Beautiful" (1905)

Frederic C. Howe   Like many other Americans, Frederic C. Howe (1867–1940) moved from a small town to a city. Howe was born in Meadville, Pennsylvania. He attended Johns Hopkins University and eventually (and, he says in his autobiography, reluctantly) became a lawyer. Rather than practice in a small town, Howe moved to Cleveland, where he served as an adviser to Mayor Tom Johnson (1901–1909). That experience helped convince Howe that city life was filled with promise. In the following selection from *The City: The Hope of Democracy* (1905), Howe considers the importance of the "City Beautiful" movement (see text p. 622).

Source: Frederic C. Howe, *The City: The Hope of Democracy* (New York: Charles Scribner's Sons, 1905; reprint, Seattle: University of Washington Press, 1967), pp. 239–245.

One of the most significant evidences of the gain we are making appears in the beautification of our cities. This interest is general. In Washington, New York, Boston, Cleveland, San Francisco, and Chicago public and private movements have been organized for the unified treatment of the city's architecture, while hundreds of other communities are aiming to make their cities more presentable through parks, cleaner streets and higher ideas of municipal art.

This indicates that the public is learning to act in an organized way. Heretofore we have lacked a city sense. In consequence, collective action has been impossible. It also indicates a new attitude towards the city, a belief in its life, outward form and appearance, its architectural expression, its parks, schools, and playgrounds. A determination has come to make the city a more beautiful as well as a more wholesome place of living. All this is foreign to the business man's ideal of merely getting his money's worth out of government. The belief in the city as a home, as an object of public-spirited endeavor, has superseded the earlier commercial ideals that characterized our thought.

The great cities of every age have probably passed through a similar evolution. First business, commerce, and wealth, then culture, beauty, and civic activity. It was so with Athens, which became great as a commercial centre before it was adorned by the hands of Pericles and Phidias. Rome became mistress of the Mediterranean before she enriched her streets and public places with the spoils of foreign conquest. The mediæval Italian cities of Florence, Venice, and Milan were the creations of organized democracy, as well as the centres of the world's trade with the East. In these cities it was freedom that gave birth to a local patriotism that inspired democracy to its highest achievements in the realm of art, literature, and architecture. And it is probable that, next to religion, democracy and the sense of a free city have been the greatest inspirations to art in the history of mankind. . . .

The splendid projects now on foot in America are an evidence that modern democracy is not satisfied with the commonplace. Just as the monumental cathedrals which everywhere dot Europe are the expression of the ideals and aspirations of mankind, so in America, democracy is coming to demand and appreciate fitting monuments for the realization of its life, and splendid parks and structures as the embodiment of its ideals. The twentieth century offers high promise of the ultimate possibilities of democracy in generous expenditure for public purposes. . . .

Probably no other city in America has projected as well as assured the carrying out of the systematic beautification of the city on so splendid a scale as has the city of Cleveland. This is the more remarkable inasmuch as no American city, with the possible exception of Chicago, is so essentially democratic in its instincts. Nowhere have the movements centring about municipal ownership, taxation, and the great industrial issues found more ready response at the hands of the voters than in this great industrial centre on the southern shore of Lake Erie. Cleveland is a commercial city *par excellence*. It has been termed the Sheffield of America. It is a centre second only to Pittsburg[h] in the iron, steel, coal, and coke trade. One-third of its population is foreign-born. But despite this fact, as well as the newness of its life, it has shown a willingness to expend many millions of dollars in the development of the artistic side of its existence.

The city is fortunate in the fact that all its public buildings are to be constructed at the same time. A uniform plan of procedure was thus possible. The Federal Building, County Courthouse, City Hall, and Public Library, as well as several other semi-public structures, are all to be built. Under ordinary circumstances and with the subterranean political and commercial forces at work in a city, isolated construction would doubtless have been the result. But public-spirited men have brought about a harmony of action among the many political agencies which had to be satisfied, and achieved a result not far from ideal in its possibilities. Through the aid of state legislation a Board of Supervising Architects was appointed, endowed with a final veto upon the location, plans, and style of architecture of all the public buildings. Despite some local jealousies, the city called to its aid Daniel H. Burnham, of Chicago, the supervising architect of the Chicago Exposition; John M. Carrere, supervising architect of the Pan-American Exposition of Buffalo, and Arnold W. Brunner, of New York, the architect of the new Federal Building in Cleveland. The members of this commission were employed by the city at generous salaries and given absolute freedom in the working out of a ground plan for the arrangement and development of the scheme. The commission is also entrusted with the problem of improving the public square, the approaches to the sites of the public buildings, and the development of the lake front.

This is the most significant forward step taken in America in the matter of municipal art. It is comparable to the designs of Napoleon III., who remade Paris, with the aid of Baron Haussmann, or to the prescience of Jefferson, who called a distinguished architect to the aid of the new government in the laying out of the national capital on its present scale.

The commission thus appointed was at work for more than two years, and has presented the results of its labors in a completed plan for the arrangement of the public buildings. The design has met with such enthusiastic approval that its consummation is now assured. The total expenditure involved approximates $14,000,000 for public purposes, with from three to five millions more for a terminal railway station, music-hall, museum, and the like. It involves the clearing of a large area of land laying between the business portion of the city and Lake Erie, and the utilization of this space as a site for the public buildings, parkage, a splendid mall, and the development of a lakefront park sixty acres in extent into a splendid terminal railway station, which is to be the gateway to the city. . . .

Questions

1. For Howe, the city has a symbolic function "foreign to the business man's ideal of merely getting his money's worth out of government." What is that function?
2. How did the people of Cleveland create a city beautiful?
3. Why should museums and lakefront parks matter to the urban poor and working classes?

20-2   A Visitor in Chicago (1892)

Giuseppe Giacosa

Rudyard Kipling said of Chicago, "Having seen it, I urgently desire never to see it again. It is inhabited by savages." Kipling might have added that the residents were smoke-eating savages, at that (see text pp. 622–623). Coal used for residential heating and industrial power led to what now would be recognized as a serious air pollution problem. Giuseppe Giacosa (1847–1906) encountered that problem during a visit from Italy in 1892.

Source: Giuseppe Giacosa, "Chicago and Her Italian Colony," *Nuova Antologia*, March 1893, pp. 16–28, trans. L. B. Davis. In Bessie Louise Pierce, ed., *As Others See Chicago: Impressions of Visitors, 1673–1933*, pp. 276–278. Copyright © 1933 by the University of Chicago Press. Reprinted by permission.

I had two different impressions of Chicago, one sensual and immediate, which comes from seeing persons and things. The other, intellectual and gradual, born from intelligence, induction and comparisons. To the eye, the city appears abominable. . . . I would not want to live there for anything in the world. I think that whoever ignores it is not entirely acquainted with our century and of what is is the ultimate expression.

During my stay of one week, I did not see in Chicago anything but darkness: smoke, clouds, dirt and an extraordinary number of sad and grieved persons. Certain remote quarters are the exception, in which there breathes from little houses and tiny gardens a tranquil air of rustic habitation where a curious architecture with diverting and immature whims makes a pleasant appearance, where the houses seem to be toys for the use of the hilarious people who live there in complete repose, eating candy, swinging in their faithful little rocking chairs, and contemplating oleographs.

But with the exception of these rare cases, the rich metropolis gave me a sense of oppression so grave that I still doubt whether, beyond their factories, there exist celestial spaces. Was it a storm-cloud? I cannot say, because the covered sky spreads a light equal and diffused, which makes no shade; while here, depending on the time of day, a few thick shadows line the houses. And I can not even say that a ghost of the sun shines, because the appearance of things close up makes me always uncertain and confused. I am inclined to believe that that spacious plain, *café au lait* in colour, which stretches along the edge of the city, which appears to the eye three hundred paces wide, and which disappears in gray space, might be the lake; but I could not press close to it with security. Certainly the ships plow through a dense atmosphere rather than a watery plain.

I recall one morning when I happened to be on a high railroad viaduct. From it the city seemed to smolder a vast unyielding conflagration, so much was it wrapped in smoke. . . . Perhaps, in Chicago, I was influenced by bad weather, by which incentive I do not affirm how things may be, but that I saw them thus, and hence was born the ill-tempered, pouting expression which I read on almost every face. It made me feel, in noting it, how I interpose in such a crowd; a few might show a little courtesy, I do not mean with hats off, but by a nod or glance of recognition. They all were running about desperately. In New York there are more people than in Chicago, and none idle; nevertheless I observe on their streets our same quick friendliness. Here, it seems to me, all might be lost, as I, without company in the formidable tumult. Or if two persons should discourse together, their speech would be in a whining tone, low and nasal, without the least variance of accent. . . . They say that all Americans have nasal voices. That does not seem to me true of New Yorkers, or only

slightly; but it could be said of Chicagoans that their voices come out of their nostrils, and that articulation is made in the pharynx. It is a positive fact that a great many noses in Chicago are in a continuous pathological condition. I have seen in many shop windows certain apparatus for covering the nose, a kind of nasal protector, or false nostrils—but without intent to deceive. I did not see any in operation, however; October, as it seems, still yields to the most delicate the use of the natural nose, but the kingdom of the artificial must be nearby, and I cannot forgive myself for having missed seeing it.

Furthermore, the mass of factories is overpowering without being imposing. That immense building, the Auditorium, where there is a hotel for more than 1,000 guests, an abundance of seats and writing desks of every kind, a conservatory of music, and on the sixth or seventh floor, I don't recall which, a theatre seating 8,000 persons; is this not marvelous to think upon? Its vastness lacks ostentation; it is a vastness of the whole, ostentation means a coordination of parts. All the immense factories of Chicago have low, squatty doors and suffocating stories which the menacing building crushes ridiculously. The two floors of the Tolomei Palace at Siena would be, in Chicago, divided into eight compartments. Certain important houses of twenty stories do not measure one and half voltas, the height of the Stozzi Palace. Surely they take care to mask the frequency of compartments by means of openings which reach from the first floor to the fourth, but to see this from the street, in the height of a single window, three men seated at three writing desks, people and furniture almost suspended in the air, and leaning against a transparent wall, gives one a feeling of irritating unrest. . . .

The dominant characteristic of the exterior life of Chicago is violence. Everything leads you to extreme expressions: dimensions, movements, noises, rumors, window displays, spectacles, ostentation, misery, activity, and alcoholic degradation.

Questions

1. How bad was the pollution Giacosa experienced?
2. No doubt familiar with the history of cities such as Rome and Venice, Giacosa might have had set notions about what a city should be. Does he betray any prejudices in describing Chicago?
3. At the time of Giacosa's visit many Americans viewed smoke not as a nuisance but as a sign of prosperity. Why?

20-3   Building the Chicago Sanitary and Ship Canal (1895)

As Chicago expanded in the nineteenth century, pollution flowed into Lake Michigan from the Chicago River. The lake provided the city with water, and the presence of raw sewage led to periodic outbreaks of typhoid fever. In 1889 Chicago responded by creating a metropolitan sanitary district, which began work on the Chicago Sanitary and Ship Canal (see text p. 623). Completed in just over seven years, the $28\frac{1}{2}$-mile canal was opened in 1900 and reversed the flow of the Chicago River away from Lake Michigan.

Despite the canal's importance, little public attention was paid to the men who constructed it. The following report gives a sense of the difficulties and hardships involved in their work.

Source: Proceedings of the Board of Trustees of the Sanitary District of Chicago, January 1, 1895–December 31, 1895 (Chicago: John F. Higgins, 1896), pp. 2805–2807.

LABOR, WAGES AND COST OF LIVING ON THE DRAINAGE CHANNEL

The influences that have established and sustained the rate of wages on the Drainage Canal are largely attributable to the continued efforts of the Drainage Trustees that laborers should not get less than $1.50 for a day's work. When work commenced on the channel the general stagnation in business had caused a fall in wages in all industries, with reductions in the number of men employed, and the contractors by concerted action could have fixed the rate for common labor at 10 to $12\frac{1}{2}$ cents per hour; but the Board of Trustees upheld the minimum rate of 15 cents per hour for common labor, which is higher than is paid in Chicago, and thereby also influenced the wages paid in stone quarries at Lemont and other places, acting as a regulator where a trade union of laborers could not be organized to maintain the rights of labor.

Powerful machinery for digging and hoisting, steam shovels, excavators, inclines, conveyors, derricks, cantilevers, cableways, channellers, steam drills, pumps, etc., multiplied the effective productiveness of human labor, so that the contractors were encouraged to pay fair wages to their laborers, mechanics and artisans. The men work by the hour and are not rushed or hurried; there are always great numbers of laborers resting and others take the vacant places in a sort of rotation, which requires as much as threefold number of men from whom to fill the needed average working force for each day. A large proportion of laborers do not intend to work full time and many do not work more than they must work to pay their living expenses. This class, who come and go when it suits their convenience, is estimated by thousands, and is nicknamed as "hobos." They are mostly native born, of nomadic habits, but the immigrants attempt to get as much work as they can do in this climate, and stick to it except on their church holidays, which are their days of rest and recreation. Machinery does the hardest work of digging and shoveling, and horse-power is used in removing the top soil, more than 1,000 horses and mules being thus employed. The work done by hand in the rock sections is hard on men who are not used to it. The rock is blasted and then broken so that it can be thrown into iron buckets or loaded on trucks for removal. It requires strength, endurance and some skill to handle the shattered rock of all sizes so as to avoid being hurt or hurting somebody else through carelessness or lack of skill in moving the stuff. The work lasts ten hours during the day and eleven hours at night, but it is not as continuous and hurried as building operations in Chicago are conducted. The eight-hour law is nullified by the Supreme Court; the contractors could not arrange for three shifts, nor do the laborers ask for short work. The masses on the channel do not average fifty hours a week in the hard work of digging and loading the rock and earth, and only a small proportion of the whole number of the laborers keep at work every day of the week or month. They are not obliged to do so and it is not their habit to work without interruption. Men may stop work at any time, get their wages and after spending them go to work again on some one of the twenty-nine sections of the Drainage Channel, and the number of those who work but part of the time is so large that especially after pay day it is difficult to wake up a full working force in the channel. This sort of transient workers [*sic*] corresponds with the floating population of some lodging house localities in Chicago. Laborers of different nationalities work together in the same squad and live peaceably in the same camp. There have been no race fights among them and wages of laborers are the same American standard for each and all. . . .

There are many saloons near the sections of the Channel, but a large proportion of the laborers are not habitual frequenters of saloons, preferring to buy the beer by the keg or half barrel and drinking the beer in their cabins, paying in company, as they call it. The Austrians, Italians and Polanders on some sections board, and drink in partnership at an individual expense of about $15.00 per month, and they consider it good living under the circumstances. . . .

Trade unions are impracticable along thirty miles of a channel in an almost uninhabited stretch of territory along the Illinois and Michigan Canal, and the tracks of two trunk railroads. It would not be practicable to picket the route against new comers, and this explains the constant stream of laborers to fill vacancies in the working forces. There has been from the beginning absolute free trade in labor on this public work, and the contractors on the whole have not reduced wages by attempting to import low-priced working people, and the few hundred colored teamsters and laborers earn the same wages as the white laborers. The Italians are paid for the same work the same wages as the native born laborers. This is a great achievement in the necessary amalgamation of the working forces in a mixed population by raising all laborers to the high American standard of earning a living.

The work on the Drainage Channel, including the commissary and boarding houses, employs about 8,700 breadwinners, at fair wages, which are mostly spent for a good living, not much of it being hoarded. A very large proportion of the laborers and mechanics are unmarried and spend most of their money soon after pay-day.

The contractors furnish boarding and lodging for many thousand men, thereby securing a working force which otherwise could not be kept up. The greater part of the Drainage Channel is too far distant from settlements which could afford sufficient living accommodations, so that most sections were supplied by the contractors with frame buildings for the workingmen. They are scattered in great numbers along the Illinois and Michigan Canal, the railroad track and the Drainage Channel.

On a few sections colored men (only a few hundred) are employed as laborers and teamsters; they board in small numbers together and in boarding houses at $3.50 per week. They earn the same wages as white men, but they do not work so many consecutive days. They live in overcrowded cabins and shanties, with hardly any furniture and scanty bedding. It is said that some of them work steady and manage to save a part of their earnings. Colored laborers work on Sections, 6, 8, 11, 12, 14 and 15, in small proportion to the Austrians, Italians, Irish and Swedes; very few work on the earth sections. They are not employed in separate gangs, but work on the channel mixed among the mass of white laborers, and there is no discord of races among the hard workers in the pit. . . .

The health of the workers on the Drainage Channel is very good; bad accidents happen to men working in the pit, in inclines, cableways, steam shovels and other excavations. The employes each pay 50 cents a month to a hospital fund, for which they receive medical attendance in case of sickness and accidents. There are two hospitals in Mount Forest, and certain contractors utilize hospitals in Chicago and Joliet. The dry weather has been very favorable to the general health.

Board in the camps is from $4 to $4.50 per week. About two thirds of all employed men, mostly single men, board in the camps so as not to waste time in walking great distances. The married men live with their families in huts, cabins, tents and cottages along the channel, paying a mere nominal rent to the contractors who erected these frame houses for their working forces and collect about $5 a month rent from a family cottage and 50 cents to $1 a month form each occupant of a dwelling used by men who board together in company so called, chiefly living on canned goods and buying vegetables, milk, bread, fresh meats, etc., from the pedlers' wagons which run into all settlements. The beer wagons follow regular routes and bottled beer is a favorite drink, especially in the Austrian settlements near Willow Springs and Lockport.

Counting men, women and children, the population in the camps and dwellings near them in the neighboring villages, there are over 10,000 inhabitants in temporary frame dwellings, which will represent no commercial value after the completion of the Drainage Channel, and the builder will not have collected as rent more than a fractional part of the cost. . . .

Questions

1. What were some of the dangers faced by these construction workers?
2. What was the status of African-American workers on the project?
3. Considering that the workers were willing to endure these conditions, what kind of lives must they have left behind in Europe or the rural South?

Questions for Further Thought

1. Why have Americans tended to view cities from the perspective of Giuseppe Giacosa (Document 20-2), not that of Frederic Howe (Document 20-1)?

2. Using Giacosa as an example, discuss the advantages and problems facing a historian who uses eyewitness accounts.

3. Technology allowed city dwellers to build skyscrapers, design reliable mass-transit systems, and safeguard water supplies. In light of those successes, how do you explain the persistence of problems such as inadequate education and housing?

City People

Unlike most Europeans, who tend to think of themselves as part of a national community, Americans have always celebrated their individuality. The man or woman alone on the frontier became a powerful myth, but city life did not make for individualism. Success in business was a product of chain of command and interdependence. Even going from one end of a city to the other meant depending on strangers such as streetcar conductors and bridge tenders, and directions could come in Polish, Yiddish, or Italian (see Table 20-2 on text p. 624). To their credit, Americans adapted, some more quickly than others.

For Mark Twain, New York was "too large," an inconvenience (see text p. 618); for immigrants, it was dangerously crowded. The journalist Jacob Riis, a Danish immigrant, noted that New York's Thirteenth Ward had a population density of 274,432 people *per square mile* in 1890. In that setting, diseases such as cholera and tuberculosis became all too familiar to the residents.

When it became obvious by the turn of the century that change was necessary, the urban middle class formed numerous reform groups for public health, decent housing, and better schools and playgrounds. Some reformers argued the cause of good government, whereas others demanded change in the name of Christianity (see text p. 633). However, large segments of the urban population were not interested in reform. Their needs were satisfied by machine politics (see text pp. 627, 630), with perhaps a little baseball and vaudeville on the side (see text pp. 633–636).

The Reverend Josiah Strong (Document 20-4) plays on the fears and prejudices of middle-class city dwellers. The problem of the American city, Strong argues, lay with non-Protestant immigrants and the conditions they confronted (see text p. 616).

The letters that make up Document 20-5 show how a Polish family dealt with the uncertainties of the immigration experience. In Document 20-6 Mayor James Michael Curley of Boston reflects on his exceptional career in American urban politics.

20-4   The Dangers of Cities (1886)

Josiah Strong

Americans accepted the city, among other reasons, because it generated prosperity. By the second half of the nineteenth century there was a large urban middle class, confident in its success but worried about the future of city life. The Reverend Josiah Strong

(1847–1916) addressed some of those concerns (see text p. 618) in *Our Country*, first printed in 1886. Strong did not want simply to sit by as nature ran its course in the American city, as Social Darwinists recommended (see text pp. 589–590 and Document 19-2). However, Strong's call to action reflected the prejudices of his day.

Source: Josiah Strong, *Our Country* (1886; reprint, edited by Jurgen Herbst, Cambridge, Mass.: Harvard University Press, 1963), pp. 171–174, 176, 183–185.

The city is the nerve center of our civilization. It is also the storm center. The fact, therefore, that it is growing much more rapidly than the whole population is full of significance. . . .

The city has become a serious menace to our civilization, because in it, excepting Mormonism, each of the dangers we have discussed is enhanced, and all are focalized. It has a peculiar attraction for the immigrant. Our fifty principal cities in 1880 contained 39.3 per cent of our entire German population, and 45.8 per cent of the Irish. Our ten larger cities at that time contained only nine per cent of the entire population, but 23 per cent of the foreign. While a little less than one-third of the population of the United States was foreign by birth or parentage, sixty-two per cent of the population of Cincinnati was foreign, eighty-three per cent of Cleveland, sixty-three per cent of Boston, eighty per cent of New York, and ninety-one per cent of Chicago. A census of Massachusetts, taken in 1885, showed that in 65 towns and cities of the state 65.1 per cent of the population was foreign by birth or parentage.

Because our cities are so largely foreign, Romanism finds in them its chief strength.

For the same reason the saloon, together with the intemperance and the liquor power which it represents, is multiplied in the city. East of the Mississippi there was, in 1880, one saloon to every 438 of the population; in Boston, one to every 329; in Cleveland, one to every 192; in Chicago, one to every 179; in New York, one to every 171; in Cincinnati, one to every 124. Of course the demoralizing and pauperizing power of the saloons and their debauching influence in politics increase with their numerical strength.

It is the city where wealth is massed; and here are the tangible evidences of it piled many stories high. Here the sway of Mammon is widest, and his worship the most constant and eager. Here are luxuries gathered—everything that dazzles the eye, or tempts the appetite; here is the most extravagant expenditure. Here, also, is the *congestion* of wealth the severest. Dives and Lazarus are brought face to face; here, in sharp contrast, are the *ennui* of surfeit and the desperation of starvation. The rich are richer, and the poor are poorer, in the city than elsewhere; and, as a rule, the greater the city, the greater are the riches of the rich and the poverty of the poor. Not only does the proportion of the poor increase with the growth of the city, but their condition becomes more wretched. The poor of a city of 8,000 inhabitants are well off compared with many in New York; and there are hardly such depths of woe, such utter and heart-wringing wretchedness in New York as in London. . . .

Socialism centers in the city, and the materials of its growth are multiplied with the growth of the city. Here is heaped the social dynamite; here roughs, gamblers, thieves, robbers, lawless and desperate men of all sorts, congregate; men who are ready on any pretext to raise riots for the purpose of destruction and plunder; here gather foreigners and wage-workers who are especially susceptible to social arguments; here skepticism and irreligion abound; here inequality is the greatest and most obvious, and the contrast between opulence and penury the most striking; here is suffering the sorest. As the greatest wickedness in the world is to be found not among the cannibals of some far-off coast, but in Christian lands where the light of truth is diffused and rejected, so the utmost depth of wretchedness exists not among savages who have few wants, but in great cities, where, in the presence of plenty and of every luxury men starve. Let a man become the owner of a home, and he is much less susceptible to socialistic propagandism. But real estate is so high in the city that it is almost impossible for a wage-worker to become a householder. . . .

1. In gathering up the results of the foregoing discussion of these several perils, it should be remarked that to preserve republican institutions requires a *higher average* intelligence and virtue among large populations than among small. The government of 5,000,000 people was a simple thing compared with the government of 50,000,000; and the government of 50,000,000 is a simple thing compared with that of 500,000,000. There are many men who can conduct a small business successfully, who are utterly incapable of managing large interests. In the latter there are multiplied relations whose harmony must be preserved. A mistake is farther reaching. It has, as it were, a longer leverage. This is equally true of the business of government. The man of only average ability and intelligence discharges creditably the duties of mayor in his little town; but he would fail utterly at the head of the state or the nation. If the people are to govern, they must grow more intelligent as the population and the complications of government increase. And a higher morality is even more essential. As civilization increases, as society becomes more

complex, as labor-saving machinery is multiplied and the division of labor becomes more minute, the individual becomes more fractional and dependent. Every savage possesses all the knowledge of the tribe. Throw him upon his own resources, and he is self-sufficient. A civilized man in like circumstances would perish. The savage is independent. Civilize him, and he becomes dependent; the more civilized, the more dependent. And, as men become more dependent on each other, they should be able to rely more implicitly on each other. More complicated and multiplied relations require a more delicate conscience and a stronger sense of justice. And any failure in character or conduct under such conditions is farther reaching and more disastrous in its results.

Is our progress in morals and intelligence at all comparable to the growth of population? The nation's illiteracy has not been discussed, because it is not one of the perils which peculiarly threaten the West; but any one who would calculate our political horoscope must allow it great influence in connection with the baleful stars which are in the ascendant. But the danger which arises from the corruption of popular morals is much greater. The republics of Greece and Rome, and if I mistake not, all the republics that have ever lived and died, were more intelligent at the end than at the beginning; but growing intelligence could not compensate decaying morals. What, then, is our moral progress? Are popular morals as sound as they were twenty years ago? There is, perhaps, no better index of general morality than Sabbath observance; and everybody knows there has been a great increase of Sabbath desecration in twenty years. We have seen that we are now using as a beverage 29 per cent more of alcohol per caput [per head] than we were fifty years ago. Says Dr. S. W. Dike: "It is safe to say that divorce has been doubled, in proportion to marriages or population, in most of the Northern States within thirty years. Present figures indicate a still greater increase." And President Woolsey, speaking of the United States, said in 1883: "On the whole, there can be little, if any, question that the ratio of divorces to marriages or to population exceeds that of any country in the Christian world." While the population increased thirty per cent from 1870 to 1880, the number of criminals in the United States increased 82.33 per cent. It looks very much as if existing tendencies were in the direction of the deadline of vice. Excepting Mormonism, all the perils which have been discussed seem to be increasing more rapidly than the population. *Are popular morals likely to improve under their increasing influence?*

2. The fundamental idea of popular government is the distribution of power. It has been the struggle of liberty for ages to wrest power from the hands of one or the few, and lodge it in the hands of the many. We have seen, in the foregoing discussion, that centralized power is rapidly growing. The "boss" makes his bargain, and sells his ten thousand or fifty thousand voters as if they were so many cattle. Centralized wealth is centralized power; and the capitalist and corporation find many ways to control votes. The liquor power controls thousands of votes in every considerable city. The president of the Mormon Church casts, say, sixty thousand votes. The Jesuits, it is said, are all under the command of one man in Washington. The Roman Catholic vote is more or less perfectly controlled by the priests. That means that the Pope can dictate some hundreds of thousands of votes in the United States. Is there anything unrepublican in all this? And we must remember that, if present tendencies continue, these figures will be greatly multiplied in the future. And not only is this immense power lodged in the hand of one man, which in itself is perilous, but it is wielded without the slightest reference to any policy or principle of government, solely in the interests of a church or a business, or for personal ends.

The result of a national election may depend on a single state; the vote of that state may depend on a single city; the vote of that city may depend on a "boss," or a capitalist, or a corporation; or the election may be decided, and the policy of the government may be reversed, by the socialist, or liquor, or Roman Catholic or immigrant vote.

It matters not by what name we call the man who wields this centralized power—whether king, czar, pope, president, capitalist, or boss. Just so far as it is absolute and irresponsible, it is dangerous.

3. These several dangerous elements are singularly netted together, and serve to strengthen each other. It is not necessary to prove that any *one* of them is likely to destroy our national life, in order to show that it is imperiled. A man may die of wounds no one of which is fatal. No sober-minded man can look fairly at the facts, and doubt that *together* these perils constitute an array which will seriously endanger our free institutions, if the tendencies which have been pointed out continue; and especially is this true in view of the fact that these perils peculiarly confront the West, where our defense is weakest.

Questions

1. What problems did Strong associate with immigrants and "the liquor power"?
2. Why did he fear the growth of socialism in the cities?
3. How did Strong stereotype Mormon and Catholic voters? Why did he assume that Protestant voters would act differently?

20-5   The Immigrant Experience: Letters Home (1901–1903)

The American city could be a forbidding place for newcomers. To gauge the extent of immigrants' experiences, the sociologists William I. Thomas (1863–1947) and Florian Znaniecki (1882–1958) undertook a massive research project that led to the publication of *The Polish Peasant in Europe and America* (1918). Their work focused on letters exchanged between immigrants in the United States and their families and friends in the old country. Thomas and Znaniecki hoped to demonstrate how city life overwhelmed rural immigrants and led to their "social disorganization" (see text pp. 624–626).

Source: Letters from Konstanty and Antoni Butkowski to their parents, December 6, 1901–April 21, 1903, in William I. Thomas and Florian Ananiecki, *The Polish Peasant in Europe and America*, 2d ed. (New York: Knopf, 1927; reprint, New York: Dover, 1958), pp. 782–789.

SOUTH CHICAGO, December 6, 1901

DEAR PARENTS: I send you my lowest bow, as to a father and mother, and I greet you and my brothers with these words: "Praised be Jesus Christus," and I hope in God that you will answer me, "For centuries of centuries. Amen."

And now I wish you, dearest parents, and you also, dearest brother, to meet the Christmas eve and merry holidays in good health and happiness. May God help you in your intentions. Be merry, all of you together. [Health and success; letter received.] I could not answer you at once, for you know that when one comes from work he has no wish to occupy himself with writing [particularly] as I work always at night. . . . I sent you money, 100 roubles, on November 30. I could not send more now, for you know that winter is coming and I must buy clothes. I inform you that Marta has no work yet. She will get work after the holidays, and it may happen that she will marry. . . . I inform you about Jasiek, my brother, that he wrote me a letter from Prussia asking me to take him to America, but he is still too young. Inform me about Antoni, how his health is, for in the spring I will bring him to me. I will send him a ship-ticket, if God grants me health. [Greetings for family and relatives.]

[KONSTANTY BUTKOWSKI]

February 17, 1902

DEAREST PARENTS: . . . I inform you that I have sent a ship-ticket for Antoni. . . . Expect to receive it soon. . . . And remember, Antoni, don't show your papers to anybody, except in places where you must show them. . . . And if you receive the ticket soon, don't wait, but come at once. And if you receive it a week or so before Easter, then don't leave until after the holidays. But after the holidays don't wait; come at once. . . . And send me a telegram from the Castle Garden. You won't pay much and I shall know and will go to the railway-station. Take 15 roubles with you, it will be enough, and change them at once for Prussian

money. As to the clothes, take the worst which you have, some three old shirts, that you may have a change on the water. And when you come across the water happily, then throw away all these rags. Bring nothing with you except what you have upon yourself. And don't bring any good shoes either, but everything the worst. As to living, take some dry bread and much sugar, and about half a quart of spirits, and some dry meat. You may take some onions, but don't take any cheese. . . . And be careful in every place about money. Don't talk to any girls on the water. . . . Learn in Bzory when Wojtek will come, for he comes to the same place where I am, so you would have a companion. And about Jan Plonka, if he wants to come, he is not to complain about [reproach] me for in America there are neither Sundays nor holidays; he must go and work. I inform [him] that I shall receive him as my brother. If he wishes he may come. . . .

[KONSTANTY BUTKOWSKI]

November 11 [1902]

DEAREST PARENTS: . . . Now I inform you about Antoni, that he is working in Chicago; it costs 15 cents to go to him. He is boarding, as well as Marta, with acquaintances, with Malewski. He has an easy and clean work, but he earns only enough to live, for he is unable to do heavy work. I see them almost every evening. I go to them. And Marta works in a tailor-shop, but she refuses to listen to me, else she would have been married long ago. So I inform you that I loved her as my own sister, but now I won't talk to her any more, for she refuses to listen. Family remains family only in the first time after coming from home, and later they forget and don't wish any more to acknowledge the familial relations; the American meat inflates them.

I have nothing more to write, except that we are all in good health. Moreover, I declare about your letters, give them to somebody else to write, for neither wise nor fool can read such writing. If such writers are to write you may as well not send letters, for I won't read them, only I will throw them into the fire, for I cannot understand. I beg you, describe to me about our country, how things are going on there. And please don't be angry with me for this which I shall write. I write you that it is hard to live alone, so please find some girl for me, but an orderly [honest] one, for in America there is not even one single orderly girl. . . .

KONSTANTY BUTKOWSKI

December 21[1902]

I, your son, Konstanty Butkowski, inform you, dear parents, about my health. . . . I thank you kindly for your letter, for it was happy. As to the girl, although I don't know her, my companion, who knows her, says that she is stately and pretty. I believe him, as well as you, my parents. For although I don't know her, I ask you, my dear parents, and as you will write me so it will be well. Shall I send her a ship-ticket, or how else shall I do? Ask Mr. and Mrs. Sadowski [her parents], what they will say. And I beg you, dear parents, give them my address and let them write a letter to me, then I shall know with certainty. And write me, please, about her age and about everything which concerns her. I don't need to enumerate; you know yourselves, dear parents. For to send a ship-ticket it is not the same as to send a letter which costs a nickel; what is done cannot be undone. So I beg you once more, as my loving parents, go into this matter and do it well, that there may be no cheating. . . . I shall wait for your letter with great impatience, that I may know what to do. . . .

KONSTANTY BUTKOWSKI

Please inform me, which one is to come, whether the older or the younger one, whether Aleksandra or Stanislawa. Inform me exactly.

June 13 [1902]

DEAREST PARENTS: . . . Konstanty works in the same factory as before and earns $2 a day. I have yet no work, but don't be anxious about me, dear parents . . . for I came to a brother and uncle, not to strangers. If our Lord God gives me health, I shall work enough in America. [News about friends and relatives.] Now I inform you, dear parents, about Wladyslawa Butkowska [cousin]. She lives near us, we see each other every day. She is a doctor's servant. And this doctor has left his wife in Chicago and came [sic] to South Chicago. She cooks for him, and she is alone in his house, so people talk about her, that she does not behave well. He pays her $5 a week. I don't know whether it is true or not, but people talk thus because he has left his wife. . . .

[ANTONI BUTKOWSKI[

CHICAGO, December 31, 1902

DEAR PARENTS: . . . If Konstanty wrote you to send him a girl answer him that he may send a ship-ticket either to the one from Popów or to the one from Grajewo. Let the one come which is smarter, for he does not know either of them, so send the one which pleases you better. For in America it is so: Let her only know how to prepare for the table, and be beautiful. For in America there is no need of a girl who knows how to spin and to weave. If she knows how to sew, it is well. For if he does not marry he will never make a fortune and will never have anything; he wastes his work and has nothing. And if he marries he will sooner put something aside. For he won't come back any more. In America it is so: Whoever does not intend to return to his country, it is best for him to marry young; then he will sooner have something, for a bachelor in America will never have anything, unless he is particularly self-controlled. [Greetings, wishes, etc.]

ANTONI BUTKOWSKI

SOUTH CHICAGO, April 21, 1903

Now I, Antoni, your son, my dearest parents, and my uncle and the whole family, we inform you that your son Konstanty is no longer alive. He was killed in the foundry [steel-mills]. Now I inform you, dear parents, that he was insured in an association for $1,000. His funeral will cost $300. And the rest which remains, we have the right to receive this money. So now I beg you, dear parents, send an authorization and his birth-certificate to my uncle, Piotr Z., for I am still a minor and cannot appear in an American lawsuit. When he joined his association he insured himself for $1,000 . . . . and made a will in your favor, dear parents. But you cannot get it unless you send an authorization to our uncle, for the lawsuit will be here, and it would be difficult for you to get the money [while remaining] in our country, while we shall get it soon and we will send it to you, dear parents. So now, when you receive this letter, send us the papers soon. Only don't listen to stupid people, but ask wise people. . . .

Now I inform you, dear parents, that strange people will write to you letters. Answer each letter, and answer thus, that you commit everything to Piotr Z. For they will try to deceive you, asking to send the authorization to them. But don't listen to anybody . . . only listen to me, as your son; then you will receive money paid for your son and my brother. [Repeats the advice; wishes from the whole family.]

Now I beg you, dear parents, don't grieve. For he is no more, and you won't raise him, and I cannot either. For if you had looked at him, I think your heart would have burst open with sorrow [he was so mutilated]. But in this letter I won't describe anything, how it was with him. It killed him on April 20. In the next letter I shall describe to you everything about the funeral. . . . Well, it is God's will; God has wished thus, and has done it. Only I beg you, dear parents, give for a holy mass, for the sake of his soul. And he will be buried beautifully, on April 22.

[ANTONI BUTKOWSKI]

Questions

1. What were the everyday concerns of Konstanty and his brother Antoni?
2. How did the relationship between Konstanty Butkowski and his parents change over time? How do his letters show this?
3. Does the correspondence reveal more than the sociologists intended? If so, what?

20-6 *I'd Do It Again*

James Michael Curley

The son of Irish immigrants, James Michael Curley (1874–1958) served as the model for Boss Skeffington in Edwin O'Connor's novel *The Last Hurrah.* Curley was an unabashed Democrat and a machine politician (see text pp. 627, 630). As four-time mayor of Boston, Curley depended on public works. Every new school and park benefited his Irish Catholic working-class constituency and guaranteed its vote in the next election. And every vote for Curley infuriated Boston's Brahmins, the wealthy descendants of its seventeenth-century (Protestant) founders. As his autobiography shows, Curley was not above the grand gesture and self-promotion: they were good politics.

Source: Reprinted with the permission of Simon & Schuster from *I'd Do It Again: A Record of All My Uproarious Years* by James Michael Curley, pp. 36, 125–127. Copyright © 1957 by Samuel Nesson, renewed 1985 by Samuel Nesson.

My father was earning less than two dollars a day in the city's paving division when he died three days after one of the other members of the construction gang challenged him to lift onto a wagon an edgestone that weighed over four hundred pounds. Father lifted it, all right, but then dropped it and collapsed, and was never to recover from the strain. Since he left no insurance money, my mother was obliged to work as a cleaning-woman, and as a scrub-woman toiling nights in office buildings downtown. I thought of her one night while leaving City Hall during my first term as Mayor. I told the scrubwomen cleaning the corridors to get up: "The only time a woman should go down on her knees is when she is praying to Almighty God," I said. Next morning I ordered long-handled mops and issued an order that scrubwomen were never again to get down on their knees in City Hall. . . .

My long-range program for civic beautification, which was to encompass my four terms as mayor, would have been effected far sooner but for the Machiavellian tactics of the very persons who had been swindling the city, while blubbering about the high cost of government.

As Al Smith used to say, let's look at the record. In 1890, the Boston tax rate was $12.60. During my first mayoralty term (1914–17) the average rate was $17.75. The increase during that administration was a mere $1.15. It was when I was out of office that the Boston tax rate

shot up. Maladministration is intolerable when there are no civic improvements to show for a drained treasury.

From the moment I assumed office, my enemies campaigned against me day and night. Bankers, editors and empire-builders attacked me in language no less colorful than had been used by some of the tin-pot ward boss Achilles whom I had sent to their tents to sulk. These unfortunate persons of limited perspective changed their tune later. In 1930, John F. Fitzgerald called me "the greatest fighter known in Boston politics," and also late in 1915 he had assured everyone what a splendid gentleman I was; but only a short time before he had spoken of me as a despised enemy. One of my worst critics at this time was Robert Washburn, the most vitriolic writer on the *Boston Transcript*, that "Sturdy Old Lady of Milk Street" as she was known to her Brahmin readers. In a 1933 editorial, Washburn mentioned the changed attitude toward me:

"Some who have been the first to berate him now assert that Boston is the best governed city in the country. They endorse him, from Alpha to Omega, without limitation of qualification." He was referring to the purified Beaconese who gather at shrines like the Odd Volume Club and the Boston Athenauem. He went on to say that I had made myself "a master of literature and of diction, on whom Harvard has 'nuthin.' He has a modulation of voice unsurpassed. He can purr like a pussycat, fight like a tiger-

cat. He touches his hat to some obscure and too much forgotten woman with a gallantry which would discount even
the South. He dynamites an adversary so that the frag-
ments cannot be gathered together in as few as twelve baskets."

It was an agonizing reappraisal, indeed, for the
burghers of Louisburg Square and their brethren and
sistren, although there is still remained the incorrigible
who loathed me because I did not subscribe to the doctrine, "to him that hath shall be given." One Brahmin,
commenting on the legislation that succored the poor,
said, "God help the rich now that Curley's Mayor. The
poor, after all, can beg."

My enemies screamed that Curley was out to ruin
Boston, and the *Boston Herald* and its sister sheet, the
Boston Evening Traveler, bitterly assailed my program of
reform and civic improvement, but when they saw the results, they also saw the light.

In August of 1930, I received the Mayor of Waltham,
England. After listening while I read to the press a list of
awards of contracts for building and road construction, he
remarked:

"You are spending a lot of money on building and
roads."

"I think it is better to spend public money in improvements of this kind," I answered, "than to spend it on the
dole system that obtains in England."

He agreed.

There was a dole system in Boston, so to speak, when
I became Mayor in 1914. I took people off welfare rolls
and restored their self-respect by providing them with jobs,
and while reducing the ranks of the unemployed, launched
a program of public works that had so shamefully been neglected by my predecessors in office. I extended tunnel and
transit systems, expanded hospital facilities, replaced slum
sections with parks and playgrounds and filled in swampy
lowlands to provide beaches for the poor who had previously had little if any opportunity to enjoy bathing or
swimming in the ocean, even though they lived on the Atlantic seaboard. Even a Republican legislature honored my
request for funds to assist with these projects. I persuaded
Boston businessmen to donate $82,000 to develop the Port
of Boston. Meanwhile, I saw that there was no unnecessary hardship when the impact of World War I was felt in
Boston. I arranged for food and shelter for thousands of
people thrown out of work, housing them in schoolhouses
and other city-owned buildings.

Boston survived the depression occasioned by that
war, and even the sharpest critics will concede that before
my first term as Mayor had ended, fewer persons were out
of work or on welfare rolls than at any other time during
the history of Boston. . . .

Questions

1. What is the political significance of symbolic gestures such as issuing long-
   handled mops to the scrubwomen at City Hall?
2. What was Curley's alternative to welfare?
3. Curley tended to blame his failures on his Protestant critics. How might this us-
   versus-them stance have both helped and hurt him politically?
4. What do the careers of Curley and New York's Big Tim Sullivan (see American
   Lives, text pp. 628–629) suggest about urban conditions early in the twentieth
   century?

Questions for Further Thought

1. Consider immigrant life as it is described in Documents 20-5 and 18-4. Were the
   Polish and Italian experiences similar or different? How do these experiences suggest the difficulty of creating a political coalition between groups?
2. How did James Curley (Document 20-6) help his constituents? In what ways
   might his style of politics have complicated their lives?
3. Josiah Strong and Frederic Howe spoke out about the need for a common or civic
   culture in the American city. How did the idea of the "private city" (see text pp.
   621–623) frustrate such hopes? What challenge did the presence of so many im-

Upper Class/Middle Class

"To clear, cultivate and transform the huge uninhabited continent which is their domain, the Americans need the everyday support of an energetic passion; that passion can only be the love of wealth," Alexis de Tocqueville wrote. That same passion carried over into urban life.

The wealthy were the most obvious beneficiaries of urbanism, although daily newspapers gave millions the vicarious thrill of reading about the Astors and the Vanderbilts. Some members of the elite collected art, others collected European nobility (as in-laws), and nearly every rich person seemed to build an incredibly expensive mansion or summer home (see the illustration on text p. 637). However, not all millionaires spent their money exclusively on themselves. John Rockefeller and Andrew Carnegie, among others, took seriously the Christian obligation of stewardship. Rockefeller financed the University of Chicago, and Carnegie took a particular interest in funding public libraries (see text p. 642).

The Industrial Revolution produced wealth for more than the fortunate few. The manufacturing economy also created a sizable, largely urban middle class (see text pp. 638–639). Its members fought to reform the cities and, when that failed, began to move to the suburbs. With husbands out of the house, middle-class housewives took charge of family and household matters (see text pp. 639–642). In the process they grew interested in political issues and women's rights. The middle class also provided an audience for both high and popular culture.

The following selections give a sense of the emotional and intellectual ferment of American cities. In Document 20-7 the social critic Thorstein Veblen argues that "conspicuous consumption" by the wealthy had a definite purpose. Catharine Beecher (Document 20-8) offers her view on how women could create the ideal middle-class household. Theodore Dreiser's *Sister Carrie* (Document 20-9) succeeds both as fiction and as social history, while Henry Adams (Document 20-10) broods over the meaning of the Machine Age.

20-7 Conspicuous Consumption (1899)

Thorstein Veblen

Thorstein Veblen (1857–1929) published *The Theory of the Leisure Class* in 1899. Veblen's thesis centered on the idea of conspicuous consumption. In his view, the purchases and interests of the wealthy were intended to demonstrate their superiority (see text pp. 636–638). The theory proved more popular than its author. Something of an iconoclast, Veblen failed to capitalize on the critical success his work had. He held a series of teaching jobs before his death.

Source: Thorstein Veblen, *The Theory of the Leisure Class: An Economic Study of Institutions* (1899; reprint, New York: Modern Library, 1934), pp. 73–75, 140–143.

During the earlier stages of economic development, consumption of goods without stint, especially consumption of the better grades of goods—ideally all consumption in excess of the subsistence minimum,—pertains normally to the leisure class. This restriction tends to disappear, at least formally, after the later peaceable stage has been reached, with private ownership of goods and an industrial system based on wage labour or on the petty household economy. But during the earlier quasi-peaceable stage, when so many of the traditions through which the institution of a leisure class has affected the economic life of later times were taking form and consistency, this principle has had the force of a conventional law. It has served as the norm to which consumption has tended to conform, and any appreciable departure from it is to be regarded as an aberrant form, sure to be eliminated sooner or later in the further course of development.

The quasi-peaceable gentleman of leisure, then, not only consumes of the staff of life beyond the minimum required for subsistence and physical efficiency, but his consumption also undergoes a specialisation as regards the quality of the goods consumed. He consumes freely and of the best, in food, drink, narcotics, shelter, services, ornaments, apparel, weapons and accoutrements, amusements, amulets, and idols or divinities. In the process of gradual amelioration which takes place in the articles of his consumption, the motive principle and the proximate aim of innovation is no doubt the higher efficiency of the improved and more elaborate products for personal comfort and well-being. But that does not remain the sole purpose of their consumption. The canon of reputability is at hand and seizes upon such innovations as are, according to its standard, fit to survive. Since the consumption of these more excellent goods is an evidence of wealth, it becomes honorific; and conversely, the failure to consume in due quantity and quality becomes a mark of inferiority and demerit.

This growth of punctilious discrimination as to qualitative excellence in eating, drinking, etc., presently affects not only the manner of life, but also the training and intellectual activity of the gentleman of leisure. He is no longer simply the successful, aggressive male,—the man of strength, resource, and intrepidity. In order to avoid stultification he must also cultivate his tastes, for it now becomes incumbent on him to discriminate with some nicety between the noble and the ignoble in consumable goods. He becomes a connoisseur in creditable viands of various degrees of merit, in manly beverages and trinkets, in seemly apparel and architecture, in weapons, games, dancers, and the narcotics. This cultivation of the æsthetic faculty requires time and application, and the demands made upon the gentleman in this direction therefore tend to change his life of leisure into a more or less arduous application to the business of learning how to live a life of ostensible leisure in a becoming way. Closely related to the requirement that the gentleman must consume freely and of the right kind of goods, there is the requirement that he must know how to consume them in a seemly manner. His life of leisure must be conducted in due form. Hence arise good manners in the way pointed out in an earlier chapter. High-bred manners and ways of living are items of conformity to the norm of conspicuous leisure and conspicuous consumption.

Conspicuous consumption of valuable goods is a means of reputability to the gentleman of leisure. As wealth accumulates on his hands, his own unaided effort will not avail to sufficiently put his opulence in evidence by this method. The aid of friends and competitors is therefore brought in by resorting to the giving of valuable presents and expensive feasts and entertainments. Presents and feasts had probably another origin than that of naïve ostentation, but they acquired their utility for this purpose very early, and they have retained that character to the present; so that their utility in this respect has now long been the substantial ground on which these usages rest. Costly entertainments, such as the potlatch or the ball, are peculiarly adapted to serve this end. The competitor with whom the entertainer wishes to institute a comparison is, by this method, made to serve as a means to the end. He consumes vicariously for his host at the same time that he is a witness to the consumption of that excess of good things which his host is unable to dispose of single-handed, and he is also made to witness his host's facility in etiquette. . . .

In the case of those domestic animals which are honorific and are reputed beautiful, there is a subsidiary basis of merit that should be spoken of. Apart from the birds which belong in the honorific class of domestic animals, and which owe their place in this class to their non-lucrative character alone, the animals which merit particular attention are cats, dogs, and fast horses. The cat is less reputable than the other two just named, because she is less wasteful; she may even serve a useful end. At the same time the cat's temperament does not fit her for the honorific purpose. She lives with man on terms of equality, knows nothing of that relation of status which is the ancient basis of all distinctions of worth, honour, and repute, and she does not lend herself with facility to an invidious comparison between her owner and his neighbours. The exception to this last rule occurs in the case of such scarce and fanciful products as the Angora cat, which have some slight honorific value on the ground of expensiveness, and have, therefore, some special claim to beauty on pecuniary grounds.

The dog has advantages in the way of uselessness as well as in special gifts of temperament. He is often spoken of, in an eminent sense, as the friend of man, and his intelligence and fidelity are praised. The meaning of this is that the dog is man's servant and that he has the gift of an unquestioning subservience and a slave's quickness in guessing his master's mood. Coupled with these traits, which fit him well for the relation of status—and which must for the present purpose be set down as serviceable traits—the dog has some characteristics which are of a more equivocal æsthetic value. He is the filthiest of the domestic animals in his person and the nastiest in his habits. For this he makes up in a servile, fawning attitude towards his master, and a readiness to inflict damage and discomfort on all else. The dog, then, commends himself to our favour by affording play to our propensity for mastery, and as he is also an item of expense, and commonly serves no industrial purpose, he holds a well-assured place in men's regard as a thing of good repute. The dog is at the same time associated in our imaginations with the chase—a meritorious employment and an expression of the honourable predatory impulse.

Standing on this vantage ground, whatever beauty of form and motion and whatever commendable mental traits he may possess are conventionally acknowledged and magnified. And even those varieties of the dog which have been bred into grotesque deformity by the dog-fancier are in good faith accounted beautiful by many. These varieties of dogs—and the like is true of other fancy-bred animals—are rated and graded in æsthetic value somewhat in proportion to the degree of grotesqueness and instability of the particular fashion which the deformity takes in the given case. For the purpose in hand, this differential utility on the ground of grotesqueness and instability of structure is reducible to terms of a great scarcity and consequent expense. The commercial value of canine monstrosities, such as the prevailing styles of pet dogs both for men's and women's use, rests on their high cost of production, and their value to their owners lies chiefly in their utility as items of conspicuous consumption. Indirectly, through reflection upon their honorific expensiveness, a social worth is imputed to them; and so, by an easy substitution of words and ideas, they come to be admired and reputed beautiful. Since any attention bestowed upon these animals is in no sense gainful or useful, it is also reputable; and since the habit of giving them attention is consequently not deprecated, it may grow into an habitual attachment of great tenacity and of a most benevolent character. So that in the affection bestowed on pet animals the canon of expensiveness is present more or less remotely as a norm which guides and shapes the sentiment and the selection of its object. The like is true, as will be noticed presently, with respect to affection for persons also; although the manner in which the norm acts in that case is somewhat different.

The case of the fast horse is much like that of the dog. He is on the whole expensive, or wasteful and useless—for the industrial purpose. What productive use he may possess, in the way of enhancing the well-being of the community or making the way of life easier for men, takes the form of exhibitions of force and facility of motion that gratify the popular æsthetic sense. This is of course a substantial serviceability. The horse is not endowed with the spiritual aptitude for servile dependence in the same measure as the dog; but he ministers effectually to his master's impulse to convert the "animate' forces of the environment to his own use and discretion and so express his own dominating individuality through them. The fast horse is at least potentially a race-horse, of high or low degree; and it is as such that he is peculiarly serviceable to his owner. The utility of the fast horse lies largely in his efficiency as a means of emulation; it gratifies the owner's sense of aggression and dominance to have his own horse outstrip his neighbour's. This use being not lucrative, but on the whole pretty consistently wasteful, and quite conspicuously so, it is honorific, and therefore gives the fast horse a strong presumptive position of reputability. Beyond this, the race horse proper has also a similarly non-industrial but honorific use as a gambling instrument. . . .

Questions

1. How does conspicuous consumption work?
2. Where do dogs and racehorses fit into Veblen's thesis?
3. Was Veblen's theory applicable only to the rich in the twentieth century? How could he have broadened his critique?

20-8　"The Christian Family"

Catharine E. Beecher

Like her sister, Harriet Beecher Stowe, the author of *Uncle Tom's Cabin*, Catharine E. Beecher (1800–1878) hoped to reach a wide audience through her writings. *The American Woman's Home* was subtitled in part "a guide to the formation and maintenance of economical, healthful, beautiful and Christian homes" (see text pp. 639–642) and was dedicated "to THE WOMEN OF AMERICA, in whose hands rest the real destinies of the republic, as moulded by the early training and preserved amid the maturer influences of home. . . ." Beecher's more famous sister was listed as a coauthor to increase the book's popularity; Catharine did most of the writing.

Source: Catharine E. Beecher, "The Christian Family," in Catharine E. Beecher and Harriet Beecher Stowe, *The American Woman's Home or, Principles of Domestic Science* (J. B. Ford & Company, 1869; reprint, Watkins Glen, N.Y.: Library of Victorian Culture, American Life Foundation, 1979), pp. 17–22.

It is the aim of this volume to elevate the honor and the remuneration of all employments that sustain the many difficult and varied duties of the family state, and thus to render each department of woman's profession as much desired and respected as are the most honored professions of men.

What, then, is the end designed by the family state which Jesus Christ came into this world to secure?

It is to provide for the training of our race to the highest possible intelligence, virtue, and happiness, by means of the self-sacrificing labors of the wise and good, and this with chief reference to a future immortal existence.

The distinctive feature of the family is self-sacrificing labor of the stronger and wiser members to raise the weaker and more ignorant to equal advantages. The father undergoes toil and self-denial to provide a home, and then the mother becomes a self-sacrificing laborer to train its inmates. The useless, troublesome infant is served in the humblest offices; while both parents unite in training it to an equality with themselves in every advantage. Soon the older children become helpers to raise the younger to a level with their own. When any are sick, those who are well become self-sacrificing ministers. When the parents are old and useless, the children become their self-sacrificing servants.

Thus the discipline of the family state is one of daily self-devotion of the stronger and wiser to elevate and support the weaker members. Nothing could be more contrary to its first principles than for the older and more capable children to combine to secure to themselves the highest advantages, enforcing the drudgeries on the younger, at the sacrifice of their equal culture.

Jesus Christ came to teach the fatherhood of God and consequent brotherhood of man. He came as the "first-born Son" of God and the Elder Brother of man, to teach by example the self-sacrifice by which the great family of man is to be raised to equality of advantages as children of God. For this end, he "humbled himself" from the highest to the lowest place. He chose for his birthplace the most despised village; for his parents the lowest in rank; for his trade, to labor with his hands as a carpenter, being "subject to his parents" thirty years. And, what is very significant, his trade was that which prepares the family home, as if he would teach that the great duty of man is labor—to provide for and train weak and ignorant creatures. Jesus Christ worked with his hands nearly thirty years, and preached less than three. And he taught that his kingdom is exactly opposite to that of the world, where all are striving for the highest positions. "Whoso will be great shall be your minister, and whoso will be chiefest shall be servant of all."

The family state then, is the aptest earthly illustration of the heavenly kingdom, and in it woman is its chief minister. Her great mission is self-denial, in training its members to self-sacrificing labors for the ignorant and weak: if not her own children, then the neglected children of her Father in heaven. She is to rear all under her care to lay up treasures, not on earth, but in heaven. All the pleasures of this life end here; but those who train immortal minds are to reap the fruit of their labor through eternal ages.

To man is appointed the out-door labor—to till the earth, dig the mines, toil in the foundries, traverse the ocean, transport merchandise, labor in manufactories, construct houses, conduct civil, municipal, and state affairs, and all the heavy work, which, most of the day, excludes him from the comforts of a home. But the great stimulus to all these toils, implanted in the heart of every true man, is the desire for a home of his own, and the hopes of paternity. Every man who truly lives for immortality responds to the beatitude, "Children are a heritage from the Lord: blessed is the man that hath his quiver full of them!" The more a father and mother live under the influence of that "immortality which Christ hath brought to light," the more is the blessedness of rearing a family understood and appreciated. Every child trained aright is to dwell forever in exalted bliss with those that gave it life and trained it for heaven.

The blessed privileges of the family state are not confined to those who rear children of their own. Any woman who can earn a livelihood, as every woman should be trained to do, can take a properly qualified female associate, and institute a family of her own, receiving to its heavenly influences the orphan, the sick, the homeless, and the sinful, and by motherly devotion train them to follow the self-denying example of Christ, in educating his earthly children for true happiness in this life and for his eternal home.

And such is the blessedness of aiding to sustain a truly Christian home, that no one comes so near the pattern of the All-perfect One as those who might hold what men call a higher place, and yet humble themselves to the lowest in order to aid in training the young, "not as men-pleasers, but as servants to Christ, with good-will doing service as to the Lord, and not to men." Such are preparing for high places in the kingdom of heaven. "Whosoever will be chiefest among you, let him be your servant."

It is often the case that the true humility of Christ is not understood. It was not in having a low opinion of his own character and claims, but it was in taking a low place in order to raise others to a higher. The worldling seeks to raise himself and family to an equality with others, or, if possible, a superiority to them. The true follower of Christ comes down in order to elevate others.

The maxims and institutions of this world have ever been antagonistic to the teachings and example of Jesus Christ. Men toil for wealth, honor, and power, not as means for raising others to an equality with themselves, but mainly for earthly, selfish advantages. Although the experience of this life shows that children brought up to labor have the fairest chance for a virtuous and prosperous life, and for hope of future eternal blessedness, yet it is the aim of most parents who can do so, to lay up wealth that their children need not labor with the hands as Christ did. And although exhorted by our Lord not to lay up treasure on earth, but rather the imperishable riches which are gained in toiling to train the ignorant and reform the sinful, as yet a large portion of the professed followers of Christ, like his first disciples, are "slow of heart to believe."

Not less have the sacred ministries of the family state been undervalued and warred upon in other directions; for example, the Romish Church has made celibacy a prime virtue, and given its highest honors to those who forsake the family state as ordained by God. Thus came great communities of monks and nuns, shut out from the love and labors of a Christian home; thus, also, came the monkish systems of education, collecting the young in great establishments away from the watch and care of parents, and the healthful and self-sacrificing labors of a home. Thus both religion and education have conspired to degrade the family state.

Still more have civil laws and social customs been opposed to the principles of Jesus Christ. It has ever been assumed that the learned, the rich, and the powerful are not to labor with the hands, as Christ did, and as Paul did when he would "not eat any man's bread for naught, but wrought with labor, not because we have not power" [to live without hand-work,] "but to make ourselves an example." (2 Thess. 3.)

Instead of this, manual labor has been made dishonorable and unrefined by being forced on the ignorant and poor. Especially has the most important of all hand-labor, that which sustains the family, been thus disgraced; so that to nurse young children, and provide the food of a family by labor, is deemed the lowest of all positions in honor and profit, and the last resort of poverty. And so our Lord, who himself took the form of a servant, teaches, "How hardly shall they that have riches enter the kingdom of heaven!" —that kingdom in which all are toiling to raise the weak, ignorant, and sinful to such equality with themselves as the children of a loving family enjoy. One mode in which riches have led to antagonism with the true end of the family state is in the style of living, by which the hand-labor, most important to health, comfort, and beauty, is confined to the most ignorant and neglected members of society, without any effort being made to raise them to equal advantages with the wise and cultivated.

And, the higher civilization has advanced, the more have children been trained to feel that to labor, as did Christ and Paul, is disgraceful, and to be made the portion of a degraded class. Children of the rich grow up with the feeling that servants are to work for them, and they themselves are not to work. To the minds of most children and servants, "to be a lady," is almost synonymous with "to be waited on, and do no work." It is the earnest desire of the authors of this volume to make plain the falsity of this growing popular feeling, and to show how much happier and more efficient family life will become when it is strengthened, sustained, and adorned by family work.

Questions

1. To what extent does Beecher offer a traditional view of women?
2. Where does she broaden or modernize women's role in society?
3. What prejudice does she reveal?

20-9 *Sister Carrie*

Theodore Dreiser

In 1900 Theodore Dreiser (1871–1945) published *Sister Carrie*, the story of a small-town Wisconsin girl. Carrie Meeber leaves Columbia City for a factory job in Chicago. She hates the work and eventually becomes a successful (though unhappy) actress in New York. The story of an independent woman—and one who lived out of wedlock with men—shocked its turn-of-the-century audience (see text p. 643). Worried that the public would reject such a non-Victorian work, the publisher printed only a thousand copies of *Sister Carrie* and virtually ignored it. The book finally received greater acceptance when it was reissued in 1912.

Source: Theodore Dreiser, *Sister Carrie* (New York: Doubleday, Page & Company, 1900; reprint, New York: Bantam Books, 1958), pp. 28–33.

It was with weak knees and a slight catch in her breathing that she came up to the great shoe company at Adams and Fifth Avenue and entered the elevator. When she stepped out on the fourth floor there was no one at hand, only great aisles of boxes piled to the ceiling. She stood, very much frightened, awaiting some one.

Presently Mr. Brown came up. He did not seem to recognise her.

"What is it you want?" he inquired.

Carrie's heart sank.

"You said I should come this morning to see about work—"

"Oh," he interrupted. "Um—yes. What is your name?"

"Carrie Meeber."

"Yes," said he. "You come with me."

He led the way through dark, box-lined aisles which had the smell of new shoes, until they came to an iron door which opened into the factory proper. There was a large, low-ceiled room, with clacking, rattling machines at which men in white shirt sleeves and blue gingham aprons were working. She followed him diffidently through the clattering automatons, keeping her eyes straight before her, and flushing slightly. They crossed to a far corner and took an elevator to the sixth floor. Out of the array of machines and benches, Mr. Brown signalled a foreman.

"This is the girl," he said, and turning to Carrie[,] "You go with him." He then returned, and Carrie followed her new superior to a little desk in a corner, which he used as a kind of official centre.

"You've never worked at anything like this before, have you?" he questioned, rather sternly.

"No, sir," she answered.

He seemed rather annoyed at having to bother with such help, but put down her name and then led her across to where a line of girls occupied stools in front of clacking machines. On the shoulder of one of the girls who was punching eye-holes in one piece of the upper, by the aid of the machine, he put his hand.

"You," he said, "show this girl how to do what you're doing. When you get through, come to me."

The girl so addressed rose promptly and gave Carrie her place.

"It isn't hard to do," she said, bending over. "You just take this so, fasten it with this clamp, and start the machine."

She suited action to word, fastened the piece of leather, which was eventually to form the right half of the upper of a man's shoe, by little adjustable clamps, and pushed a small steel rod at the side of the machine. The latter jumped to the task of punching, with sharp, snapping clicks, cutting circular bits of leather out of the side of the upper, leaving the holes which were to hold the laces. After observing a few times, the girl let her work at it alone. Seeing that it was fairly well done, she went away.

The pieces of leather came from the girl at the machine to her right, and were passed to the girl at her left. Carrie saw at once that an average speed was necessary or the work would pile up on her and all those below would be delayed. She had no time to look about, and bent anxiously to her task. The girls at her left and right realised her predicament and feelings, and, in a way, tried to aid her, as much as they dared, by working slower.

At this task she laboured incessantly for some time, finding relief from her own nervous fears and imaginings in the humdrum, mechanical movement of the machine. She felt, as the minutes passed, that the room was not very light. It had a thick odour of fresh leather, but that did not worry her. She felt the eyes of the other help upon her, and troubled lest she was not working fast enough.

Once, when she was fumbling at the little clamp, having made a slight error in setting in the leather, a great hand appeared before her eyes and fastened the clamp for her. It was the foreman. Her heart thumped so that she could scarcely see to go on.

"Start your machine," he said, "start your machine. Don't keep the line waiting."

This recovered her sufficiently and she went excitedly on, hardly breathing until the shadow moved away from behind her. Then she heaved a great breath.

As the morning wore on the room became hotter. She felt the need of a breath of fresh air and a drink of water but did not venture to stir. The stool she sat on was without a back or foot-rest, and she began to feel uncomfortable. She found, after a time, that her back was beginning to ache. She twisted and turned from one position to another slightly different, but it did not ease her for long. She was beginning to weary.

"Stand up, why don't you?" said the girl at her right, without any form of introduction. "They won't care."

Carrie looked at her gratefully. "I guess I will," she said.

She stood up from her stool and worked that way for a while, but it was a more difficult position. Her neck and shoulders ached in bending over.

The spirit of the place impressed itself on her in a rough way. She did not venture to look around, but above the clack of the machine she could hear an occasional remark. She could also note a thing or two out of the side of her eye.

"Did you see Harry last night?" said the girl at her left, addressing her neighbour.

"No."

"You ought to have seen the tie he had on. Gee, but was a mark."

"S-s-t," said the other girl, bending over her work. The first, silenced, instantly assumed a solemn face. The foreman passed slowly along, eyeing each worker distinctly. The moment he was gone, the conversation was resumed again.

"Say," began the girl at her left, "what jeh think he said?"

"I don't know."

"He said he saw us with Eddie Harris at Martin's last night."

"No!" They both giggled.

A youth with tan-coloured hair, that needed clipping very badly, came shuffling along between the machines, bearing a basket of leather findings under his left arm, and pressed against his stomach. When near Carrie, he stretched out his right hand and gripped one girl under the arm.

"Aw, let me go," she exclaimed angrily. "Duffer."

He only grinned broadly in return.

"Rubber!" he called back as she looked after him. There was nothing of the gallant in him.

Carrie at last could scarcely sit still. Her legs began to tire and she wanted to get up and stretch. Would noon never come? It seemed as if she had worked an entire day. She was not hungry at all, but weak, and her eyes were tired, straining at the one point where the eye-punch came down. The girl at the right noticed her squirmings and felt sorry for her. She was concentrating herself too thoroughly—what she did really required less mental and physical strain. There was nothing to be done, however. The halves of the uppers came piling steadily down. Her hands began to ache at the wrists and then in the fingers, and towards the last she seemed one mass of dull, complaining muscles, fixed in an eternal position and performing a single mechanical movement which became more and more distasteful, until at last it was absolutely nauseating. When she was wondering whether the strain would ever cease, a dull-sounding bell clanged somewhere down an elevator shaft, and the end came. In an instant there was a buzz of action and conversation. All the girls instantly left their stools and hurried away in an adjoining room, men passed through, coming from some department which opened on the right. The whirling wheels began to sing in a steadily modifying key, until at last they died away in a low buzz. There was an audible stillness, in which the common voice sounded strange.

Carrie got up and sought her lunch box. She was stiff, a little dizzy, and very thirsty. On the way to the small space portioned off by wood, where all the wraps and lunches were kept, she encountered the foreman, who stared at her hard.

"Well," he said, "did you get along all right?"

"I think so," she replied, very respectfully.

"Um," he replied, for want of something better, and walked on.

Under better material conditions, this kind of work would not have been so bad, but the new socialism which involves pleasant working conditions for employees had not then taken hold upon manufacturing companies.

The place smelled of the oil of the machines and the new leather—a combination which, added to the stale odours of the building, was not pleasant even in cold weather. The floor, though regularly swept every evening, presented a littered surface. Not the slightest provision had been made for the comfort of the employees, the idea being that something was gained by giving them as little and making the work as hard and unremunerative as possible. What we know of foot-rests, swivel-back chairs, dining-rooms for the girls, clean aprons and curling irons supplied free, and a decent cloak room, were unthought of. The washrooms were disagreeable, crude, if not foul places, and the whole atmosphere was sordid.

Carried looked about her, after she had drunk a tinful of water from a bucket in one corner, for a place to sit and eat. The other girls had ranged themselves about the windows or the work-benches of those of the men who had gone out. She saw no place which did not hold a couple or a group of girls, and being too timid to think of introducing herself, she sought out her machine and, seated upon her stool, opened her lunch on her lap. There she sat listening to the chatter and comment about her. It, was the most party, silly and graced by the current slang. Several of the men in the room exchanged compliments with the girls at long range.

"Say, Kitty," called one to a girl who was doing a waltz step in a few feet of space near one of the windows, "are you going to the ball with me?"

"Look out, Kitty," called another, "you'll jar your back hair."

"Go on, Rubber," was her only comment.

As Carrie listened to this and much more of similar familiar badinage among the men and girls, she instinctively withdrew into herself. She was not used to this type, and felt that there was something hard and low about it all. She feared that the young boys about would address such remarks to her—boys who . . . seemed uncouth and ridiculous. She made the average feminine distinction between clothes, putting worth, goodness, and distinction in a dress suit, and leaving all the unlovely qualities and those beneath notice in overalls and jumper.

She was glad when the short half hour was over and the wheels began to whirr again. Though wearied, she would be inconspicuous. This illusion ended when another young man passed along the aisle and poked her indifferently in the ribs with his thumb. She turned about, indignation leaping to her eyes, but he had gone on and only once turned to grin. She found it difficult to conquer an inclination to cry.

The girl next to her noticed her state of mind. "Don't you mind," she said. "He's too fresh."

Carrie said nothing, but bent over her work. She felt as though she could hardly endure such a life. Her idea of work had been so entirely different. All during the long afternoon she thought of the city outside and its imposing show, crowds, and fine buildings. Columbia City and the better side of her home life came back. By three o'clock she was sure it must be six, and by four it seemed as if they had forgotten to note the hour and were letting all work overtime. The foreman became a true ogre, prowling constantly about, keeping her tied down to her miserable task. What she heard of the conversation about her only made her feel sure that she did not want to make friends with any of these. When six o'clock came she hurried eagerly away, her arms aching and her limbs stiff from sitting in one position.

As she passed out along the hall after getting her hat, a young machine hand, attracted by her looks, made bold to jest with her.

"Say, Maggie," he called, "if you wait, I'll walk with you."

It was thrown so straight in her direction that she knew who was meant, but never turned to look.

In the crowded elevator, another dusty, toil-stained youth tried to make an impression on her by leering in her face.

One young man, waiting on the walk outside for the appearance of another, grinned at her as she passed.

"Ain't going my way, are you?" he called jocosely.

Carrie turned her face to the west with a subdued heart. As she turned the corner, she saw through the great shiny window the small desk at which she had applied. There were the crowds, hurrying with the same buzz and energy-yielding enthusiasm. She felt a slight relief, but it was only at her escape. She felt ashamed in the face of better dressed girls who went by. She felt as though she should be better served, and her heart revolted.

Questions

1. According to Dreiser, why did so many women work in such difficult conditions?
2. What did the banter between workers accomplish?
3. How does *Sister Carrie* succeed as social history in ways that a factory-inspection report from that era could not?

20-10   Henry Adams at the Columbian Exposition of 1893

Henry Adams (1838–1918) could be forgiven for his air of self-importance. He was, after all, the great-grandson and grandson of presidents. A historian and social critic (see text p. 642), Adams dissented from the popular view that progress and the Industrial Age were one. In this passage from his autobiography, *The Education of Henry Adams* (1918), Adams relates his experience (like the rest of the book, written in the third person) with modern technology at the Columbian Exposition of 1893.

Source: Henry Adams, *The Education of Henry Adams* (Boston: Massachusetts Historical Society, 1918; reprint, New York: Modern Library, 1931), pp. 340–343.

The first astonishment became greater every day. That the Exposition should be a natural growth and product of the Northwest offered a step in evolution to startle Darwin; but that it should be anything else seemed an idea more startling still; and even granting it were not—admitting it to be a sort of industrial, speculative growth and product of the Beaux Arts artistically induced to pass the summer on the shore of Lake Michigan—could it be made to seem at home there? Was the American made to seem at home in it? Honestly, he had the air of enjoying it as though it were

all his own; he felt it was good; he was proud of it; for the most part, he acted as though he had passed his life in landscape gardening and architectural decoration. If he had not done it himself, he had known how to get it done to suit him, as he knew how to get his wives and daughters dressed at Worth's or Paquin's [designers of the finest women's clothes]. Perhaps he could not do it again; the next time he would want to do it himself and would show his own faults; but for the moment he seemed to have leaped directly from Corinth and Syracuse and Venice, over the heads of London and New York, to impose classical standards on plastic Chicago. Critics had no trouble in criticising the classicism, but all trading cities had always shown traders' taste, and, to the stern purist of religious faith, no art was thinner than Venetian Gothic. All trader's taste smelt of bric-à-brac; Chicago tried at least to give her taste a look of unity.

One sat down to ponder on the steps beneath Richard Hunt's dome almost as deeply as on the steps of Ara Cœli, and much to the same purpose. Here was a breach of continuity—a rupture in historical sequence! Was it real, or only apparent? One's personal universe hung on the answer, for, if the rupture was real and the new American world could take this sharp and conscious twist towards ideals, one's personal friends would come in, at last, as winners in the great American chariot-race for fame. If the people of the Northwest actually knew what was good when they saw it, they would some day talk about Hunt and Richardson [architects], La Farge and St. Gaudens [sculptors], Burnham and McKim, and Stanford White [architects] when their politicians and millionaires were otherwise forgotten. The artists and architects who had done the work offered little encouragement to hope it; they talked freely enough, but not in terms that one cared to quote; and to them the Northwest refused to look artistic. They talked as though they worked only for themselves; as though art, to the Western people, was a stage decoration; a diamond shirt-stud; a paper collar; but possibly the architects of Pæstum and Girgenti [ancient Italian cities] had talked in the same way, and the Greek had said the same thing of Semitic Carthage two thousand years ago.

Jostled by these hopes and doubts, one turned to the exhibits for help, and found it. The industrial schools tried to teach so much and so quickly that the instruction ran to waste. Some millions of other people felt the same helplessness, but few of them were seeking education, and to them helplessness seemed natural and normal, for they had grown up in the habit of thinking a steam-engine or a dynamo as natural as the sun, and expected to understand one as little as the other. For the historian alone the Exposition made a serious effort. Historical exhibits were common, but they never went far enough; none were thoroughly worked out. One of the best was that of the Cunard steamers, but still a student hungry for results found himself obliged to waste a pencil and several sheets of paper trying to calculate exactly when, according to the given increase of power, tonnage, and speed, the growth of the ocean steamer would reach its limits. His figures brought him, he thought, to the year 1927; another generation to spare before force, space, and time should meet. The ocean steamer ran the surest line of triangulation into the future, because it was the nearest of man's products to

a unity; railroads taught less because they seemed already finished except for mere increase in number; explosives taught most, but needed a tribe of chemists, physicists, and mathematicians to explain; the dynamo taught least because it had barely reached infancy, and, if its progress was to be constant at the rate of the last ten years, it would result in infinite costly energy within a generation. One lingered long among the dynamos, for they were new, and they gave to history a new phase. Men of science could never understand the ignorance and naïveté of the historian, who, when he came suddenly on a new power, asked naturally what it was; did it pull or did it push? Was it a screw or thrust? Did it flow or vibrate? Was it a wire or a mathematical line? And a score of such questions to which he expected answers and was astonished to get none.

Education ran riot at Chicago, at least for retarded minds which had never faced in concrete form so many matters of which they were ignorant. Men who knew nothing whatever—who had never run a steam-engine, the simplest of forces—who had never put their hands on a lever—had never touched an electric battery—never talked through a telephone, and had not the shadow of a notion what amount of force was meant by a *watt* or an *ampère* or an *erg*, or any other term of measurement introduced within a hundred years—had no choice but to sit down on the steps and brood as they had never brooded on the benches of Harvard College, either as student or professor, aghast at what they had said and done in all these years, and still more ashamed of the childlike ignorance and babbling futility of the society that let them say and do it. The historical mind can think only in historical processes, and probably this was the first time since historians existed, that any of them had sat down helpless before a mechanical sequence. Before a metaphysical or a theological or a political sequence, most historians had felt helpless, but the single clue to which they had hitherto trusted was the unity of natural force.

Did he himself quite know what he meant? Certainly not! If he had known enough to state his problem, his education would have been complete at once. Chicago asked in 1893 for the first time the question whether the American people knew where they were driving. Adams answered, for one, that he did not know, but would try to find out. On reflecting sufficiently deeply, under the shadow of Richard Hunt's architecture, he decided that the American people probably knew no more than he did; but that they might still be driving or drifting unconsciously to some point in thought, as their solar system was said to be drifting towards some point in space; and that, possibly, if relations enough could be observed, this point might be fixed. Chicago was the first expression of American thought as a unity; one must start there. . . .

Questions

1. Why did the fair's architecture confuse Adams?
2. In what ways did the technology on display overwhelm him?
3. Has this kind of unsettling encounter with modernity been repeated by subsequent generations? In what ways?

Questions for Further Thought

1. Thorstein Veblen (Document 20-7) thought he could expose the vanity and purposeful extravagance of the rich. *Conspicuous consumption* has become part of our vocabulary, but our fascination with the rich and famous has not abated. Why?
2. Which is a more important gauge of American society in 1900, that Theodore Dreiser could publish *Sister Carrie* (Document 20-9) or that his publisher abandoned the novel in fear of protests? Why?
3. Henry Adams (Document 20-10) wanted to find out "whether the American people knew where they were driving." Where has technology taken us in the last century?
4. Compare the ways in which Catharine Beecher (Document 20-8) and Theodore Dreiser portray American women. Is one portrait more realistic than the other? Why or why not?

CHAPTER 21

The Progressive Era
1900–1914

★   ★   ★

The Course of Reform

Progressivism might have been the most diverse and contradictory reform movement in American history. Such varied measures as the direct election of senators, a government controlled by experts, women's rights, immigration restriction, prohibition, and voter disfranchisement were all labeled as "progressive." Given this array of interests, virtually everyone could claim to be progressive (see text p. 648).

Many Americans were drawn to structural and moral reform. Structural reform stressed efficiency in government (see text pp. 648, 651–652); the idea was to apply Frederick W. Taylor's theories (see Chapter 18) to city government. Theoretically at least, more efficient government would lead to lower taxes. While some groups advocated civil service and modern accounting practices, others wanted government (particularly at the local and state levels) to enforce standards of morality (see text pp. 649–650). Moral reformers focused on urban vice districts, where gambling and prostitution flourished with an assist from alcohol. The proffered solution was prohibition across the board—no cards, madams, or whiskey.

Social reform was the smallest but most important element of the progressive movement. Structural and moral reformers tended to be middle-class activists who expected others to change; social reformers, though coming from the same background, realized that the middle class was part of the problem. They were influenced by a number of sources, including crusading journalists (nicknamed muckrakers by Theodore Roosevelt) such as Lincoln Steffens and Ida Tarbell; Supreme Court Justice Oliver Wendell Holmes and the philosopher William James, both of whom championed the idea of pragmatism, or judging an idea by its consequences (see text p. 649); and the educational reformer John Dewey. Social reformers wanted to expand the role of government into the areas of social welfare and economic regulation. That fight ranged from city councils and state houses to Capitol Hill and the White House.

All the elements of the progressive movement welcomed women into their ranks. Long active in charity and reform work, middle-class women contributed organizational expertise to the reform drive and became increasingly committed to women's rights. Social reformers took up the cause, as they did that of greater acceptance of immigrants and African-Americans. In terms of race, however, the era was hardly "progressive": between 1900 and 1914 over a thousand blacks were lynched.

In Document 21-1 the journalist Walter Lippmann discusses the sense of drift produced by modern life. The Reverend Walter Rauschenbusch (Document 21-2) explains the Social Gospel, which revitalized American Protestantism and fueled the progressive movement (see text pp. 649–650). In Document 21-3 Ida M. Tarbell shows that investigative journalism existed long before the Watergate scandal. Robert La Follette (Document 21-4) recalls the difficulties his reform measures faced in the Wisconsin legislature. Jane Addams's experience with garbage (Document 21-5) illustrates the monumental challenges that confronted urban social reformers. The working class not only lived but worked in miserable conditions, as Document 21-6 indicates. Document 21-7 is a Progressive Era statute from Indiana that might seem more appropriate to Germany in the 1930s.

21-1   *Drift and Mastery* (1914)

Walter Lippmann

Walter Lippmann's career spanned much of the twentieth century, from the Progressive Era to the Great Society of the 1960s. Both a gifted critic and a journalist, Lippmann (1889–1974) was fascinated by the workings of American society. In the introduction to *Drift and Mastery* (1914) (see text p. 648), Lippmann discusses how the success of American democracy led to a new set of problems.

Source: Walter Lippmann, *Drift and Mastery: An Attempt to Diagnose the Current Unrest* (Mitchell Kennerley, 1914; reprint, Madison: University of Wisconsin Press, 1985), pp. 15–19.

In the early months of 1914 widespread unemployment gave the anarchists in New York City an unusual opportunity for agitation. The newspapers and the police became hysterical, men were clubbed and arrested on the slightest provocation, meetings were dispersed. The issue was shifted, of course, from unemployment to the elementary rights of free speech and assemblage. Then suddenly, the city administration, acting through a new police commissioner, took the matter in hand, suppressed official lawlessness, and guaranteed the men who were conducting the agitation their full rights. This had a most disconcerting effect on the anarchists. They were suddenly stripped of all the dramatic effect that belongs to a clash with the police. They had to go back to the real issue of unemployment, and give some message to the men who had been following them. But they had no message to give: they knew what they were against but not what they were for, and their intellectual situation was as uncomfortable as one of those bad dreams in which you find yourself half-clothed in a public place.

Without a tyrant to attack an immature democracy is always somewhat bewildered. Yet we have to face the fact in America that what thwarts the growth of our civilization is not the uncanny, malicious contrivance of the plutocracy, but the faltering method, the distracted soul, and the murky vision of what we call grandiloquently the will of the people. If we flounder, it is not because the old order is strong, but because the new one is weak. Democracy is more than the absence of czars, more than freedom, more than equal opportunity. It is a way of life, a use of freedom, an embrace of opportunity. For republics do not come in when kings go out, the defeat of a propertied class is not followed by a coöperative commonwealth, the emancipation of woman is more than a struggle for rights. A servile community will have a master, if not a monarch, then a landlord or a boss, and no legal device will save it. A nation of uncritical drifters can change only the form of tyranny, for like Christian's sword, democracy is a weapon in the hands of those who have the courage and the skill to wield it; in all others it is a rusty piece of junk.

The issues that we face are very different from those of the last century and a half. The difference, I think, might be summed up roughly this way: those who went before inherited a conservatism and overthrew it; we inherit freedom, and have to use it. The sanctity of property, the patriarchal family, hereditary caste, the dogma of sin, obedience to authority,—the rock of ages, in brief, has been blasted for us. Those who are young to-day are born into a world in which the foundations of the older order survive only as habits or by default. So Americans can carry through their purposes when they have them. If the standpatter is still powerful amongst us is because we have not learned to use our power, and direct it to fruitful ends. The American conservative, it seems to me, fills the vacuum where democratic purpose should be.

So far as we are concerned, then, the case is made against absolutism, commercial oligarchy, and unquestioned creeds. *The rebel program is stated.* Scientific invention and blind social currents have made the old authority impossible in fact, the artillery fire of the iconoclasts has shattered its prestige. We inherit a rebel tradition. The dominant forces in our world are not the sacredness of property, nor the intellectual leadership of the priest; they are not the divinity of the constitution, the glory of industrial push, Victorian sentiment, New England respectability, the Republican Party, or John D. Rockefeller. Our time, of course, believes in change. The adjective "progressive" is what we like, and the word "new," be it the New Nationalism of Roosevelt, the New Freedom of Wilson, or the New Socialism of the syndicalists. The conservatives are more lonely than the pioneers, for almost any prophet to-day can have disciples. The leading thought of our world has ceased to regard commercialism either as permanent or desirable, and the only real question among intelligent people is how business methods are to be altered, not whether they are to be altered. For no one, unafflicted with invincible ignorance, desires to preserve our economic system in its existing form.

The business man has stepped down from his shrine; he is no longer an oracle whose opinion on religion, science, and education is listened to dumbly as the valuable by-product of a paying business. We have scotched the romance of success. In the emerging morality the husband is not regarded as the proprietor of his wife, nor the parents as autocrats over the children. We are met by women who are "emancipated"; for what we hardly know. We are not stifled by a classical tradition in art: in fact artists to-day are somewhat stunned by the rarefied atmosphere of their freedom. There is a wide agreement among thinking people that the body is not a filthy thing, and that to implant in a child the sense of sin is a poor preparation for a temperate life.

The battle for us, in short, does not lie against crusted prejudice, but against the chaos of a new freedom.

This chaos is our real problem. So if the younger critics are to meet the issues of their generation they must give their attention, not so much to the evils of authority, as to the weaknesses of democracy. But how is a man to go about doing such a task? He faces an enormously complicated world, full of stirring and confusion and ferment. He hears of movements and agitations, criticisms and reforms, knows people who are devoted to "causes," feels angry or hopeful at different times, goes to meetings, reads radical books, and accumulates a sense of uneasiness and pending change.

He can't, however, live with any meaning unless he formulates for himself a vision of what is to come out of the unrest. I have tried in this book to sketch such a vision for myself. At first thought it must seem an absurdly presumptuous task. But it is a task that everyone has to attempt if he is to take part in the work of his time. For in so far as we can direct the future at all, we shall do it by laying what we see against what other people see.

This doesn't mean the constructing of utopias. The kind of vision which will be fruitful to democratic life is one that is made out of latent promise in the actual world. There is a future contained in the trust and the union, the new status of women, and the moral texture of democracy. It is a future that can in a measure be foreseen and bent somewhat nearer to our hopes. A knowledge of it gives a sanction to our efforts, a part in a larger career, and an invaluable sense of our direction. We make our vision, and hold it ready for any amendment that experience suggests. It is not a fixed picture, a row of shiny ideals which we can exhibit to mankind, and say: Achieve these or be damned. All we can do is to search the world as we find it, extricate the forces that seem to move it, and surround them with criticism and suggestion. Such a vision will inevitably reveal the bias of its author; that is to say it will be a human hypothesis, not an oracular revelation. But if the hypothesis is honest and alive it should cast a little light upon our chaos. It should help us to cease revolving in the mere routine of the present or floating in a private utopia. For a vision of latent hope would be woven of vigorous strands; it would be concentrated on the crucial points of contemporary life, on that living zone where the present is passing into the future. It is the region where thought and action count. Too far ahead there is nothing but your dream; just behind, there is nothing but your memory. But in the unfolding present, man can be creative if his vision is gathered from the promise of actual things.

The day is past, I believe, when anybody can pretend to have laid down an inclusive or a final analysis of the democratic problem. Everyone is compelled to omit infinitely more than he can deal with; everyone is compelled to meet the fact that a democratic vision must be made by the progressive collaboration of many people. Thus I have touched upon the industrial problem at certain points that seem to me of outstanding importance, but there are vast sections and phases of industrial enterprise that pass unnoticed. The points I have raised are big in the world I happen to live in, but obviously they are not the whole world.

It is necessary, also, to inquire how "practical" you can be in a book of generalizations. That amounts to asking how detailed you can be. Well, it is impossible when you mention a minimum wage law, for example, to append a draft of the bill and a concrete set of rules for its administration. In human problems especially there is a vagueness which no one can escape entirely. Even the most voluminous study in three volumes of some legal question does not meet at every point the actual difficulties of the lawyer in a particular case. But it can be useful if it is made with a sense of responsibility to action. I have tried, therefore, to avoid gratuitously fine sentiments; I have tried to suggest nothing that with the information at my command doesn't seem at least probable.

This book, then, is an attempt to diagnose the current unrest and to arrive at some sense of what democracy implies. It begins with the obvious drift of our time and

gropes for the conditions of mastery. I have tried in the essays that follow to enter the American problem at a few significant points in order to trace a little of the immense suggestion that radiates from them. I hope the book will leave the reader, as it does me, with a sense of the varied talents and opportunities, powers and organizations that may contribute to a conscious revolution. I have not been able to convince myself that one policy, one party, one class, or one set of tactics, is as fertile as human need.

It would be very easy if such a belief were possible. It would save time and energy and no end of grubbing: just to keep on repeating what you've learnt, eloquent, supremely confident, with the issues clean, a good fight and an inevitable triumph: Marx, or Lincoln, or Jefferson with you always as guide, counsellor and friend. All the thinking done by troubled dead men for the cocksure living; no class to consider but your own; no work that counts but yours; every party but your party composed of fools and rascals; only a formula to accept and a specific fight to win,—it would be easy. It might work on the moon.

Questions

1. What does Lippmann think is threatening American civilization?
2. How does he distinguish between his proposals and a utopia?
3. Why does Lippmann not offer a single comprehensive answer to the social conditions he has studied?

21-2   "The Church and the Social Movement" (1907)

Walter Rauschenbusch

While serving as the pastor of a Baptist church in New York's Hell's Kitchen, Walter Rauschenbusch learned firsthand that the poor could not be satisfied merely by exhortations to faith. Rauschenbusch set out to apply the teachings of the Gospels to contemporary urban life (see text pp. 649–650). His writings on the Social Gospel, such as the following selections from *Christianity and the Social Crisis* (1907), were those of a Christian socialist. Rauschenbusch shocked the Protestant middle class no less than James Curley did (see Document 20-6).

Source: Walter Rauschenbusch, *Christianity and the Social Crisis* (New York: Macmillan, 1912), pp. 304–305, 328–331. Courtesy of Carl Raushenbush, age 95 (Walter's last surviving child).

Other organizations may conceivably be indifferent when confronted with the chronic or acute poverty of our cities. The Christian Church cannot. The very name of "Christian" would turn into an indictment if it did not concern itself in the situation in some way.

One answer to the challenge of the Christian spirit has been the organization of institutional church work. A church perhaps organizes a day-nursery or kindergarten; a playground for the children; a meeting-place for young people, or educational facilities for those who are ambitious. It tries to do for people who are living under abnormal conditions what these people under normal conditions ought to do for themselves. This saving helpfulness toward the poor must be distinguished sharply from the money-making efforts of some churches called institutional, which simply run a continuous sacred variety performance.

Confront the Church of Christ with a homeless, playless, joyless, proletarian population, and that is the kind of work to which some Christian spirits will inevitably feel impelled. All honor to me! But it puts a terrible burden on the Church. Institutional work is hard work and costly work. It requires a large plant and an expensive staff. It puts such a strain on the organizing ability and the sympathies of the workers that few can stand it long. The Church by the voluntary gifts and labors of a few here tries to furnish what the entire coöperative community ought to furnish.

Few churches have the resources and leadership to undertake institutional work on a large scale, but most churches in large cities have some institutional features, and all pastors who are at all willing to do it, have institutional work thrust on them. They have to care for the poor. Those of us who passed through the last great industrial depression will never forget the procession of men out of work, out of clothes, out of shoes, and out of hope. They wore down our threshold, and they wore away our hearts. This is the stake of the churches in modern poverty. They are buried at times under a stream of human wreckage. They are turned aside constantly from their more spiritual functions to "serve tables." They have a right, therefore, to inquire who is unloading this burden of poverty and suffering upon them by underpaying, exhausting, and maiming the people. The good Samaritan did not go after the robbers with a shot-gun, but looked after the wounded and helpless man by the wayside. But if hundreds of good Samaritans travelling the same road should find thousands of bruised men groaning to them, they would not be such very good Samaritans if they did not organize a vigilance committee to stop the manufacturing of wounded men. If they did not, presumably the asses who had to lug the wounded to the tavern would have the wisdom to inquire into the causes of their extra work. . . .

In its struggle the working class becomes keenly conscious of the obstacles put in its way by the great institutions of society, the courts, the press, or the Church. It demands not only impartiality, but the kind of sympathy which will condone its mistakes and discern the justice of its cause in spite of the excesses of its followers. When our sympathies are enlisted, we develop a vast faculty for making excuses. If two dogs fight, our own dog is rarely the aggressor. Stealing peaches is a boyish prank when our boy does it, but petty larceny when that dratted boy of our neighbor does it. If the other political party grafts, it is a flagrant shame; if our own party does it, we regret it politely or deny the fact. If Germany annexes a part of Africa,

it is brutal aggression; if England does it, she "fulfils her mission of civilization." If the business interests exclude the competition of foreign merchants by a protective tariff, it is a grand national policy; if the trades-unions try to exclude the competition of non-union labor, it is a denial of the right to work and an outrage.

The working class likes to get that kind of sympathy which will take a favorable view of its efforts and its mistakes, and a comprehension of the wrongs under which it suffers. Instead of that the pulpit of late has given its most vigorous interest to the wrongs of those whom militant labor regards as traitors to its cause. It has been more concerned with the fact that some individuals were barred from a job by the unions, than with the fact that the entire wage-working class is debarred from the land, from the tools of production, and from their fair share in the proceeds of production.

It cannot well be denied that there is an increasing alienation between the working class and the churches. That alienation is most complete wherever our industrial development has advanced farthest and has created a distinct class of wage-workers. Several causes have contributed. Many have dropped away because they cannot afford to take their share in the expensive maintenance of a church in a large city. Others because the tone, the spirit, the point of view in the churches, is that of another social class. The commercial and professional classes dominate the spiritual atmosphere in the large city churches. As the workingmen grow more class-conscious, they come to regard the business men as their antagonists and the possessing classes as exploiters who live on their labor, and they resent it when persons belonging to these classes address them with the tone of moral superiority. When ministers handle the labor question, they often seem to the working class partial against them even when the ministers think they are most impartial. Foreign workingmen bring with them the long-standing distrust for the clergy and the Church as tools of oppression which they have learned abroad, and they perpetuate that attitude here. The churches of America suffer for the sins of the churches abroad. The "scientific socialism" imported from older countries through its literature and its advocates is saturated with materialistic philosophy and is apt to create dislike and antagonism for the ideas and institutions of religion.

Thus in spite of the favorable equipment of the Church in America there is imminent danger that the working people will pass from indifference to hostility, from religious enthusiasm to anti-religious bitterness. That would be one of the most unspeakable calamities that could come upon the Church. If we would only take warning by the fate of the churches in Europe, we might avert the desolation that threatens us. We may well be glad that in nearly every city there are a few ministers who are known as the outspoken friends of labor. Their fellow-ministers may regard them as radicals, lacking in balance, and very likely they are; but in the present situation they are among the most valuable servants of the Church. The workingmen see that there is at least a minority in the Church that champions their cause, and that fact helps to keep their judgment in hopeful suspense about the Church at large. Men who are just as one-sided in favor of capitalism pass as sane and conservative men. If the capitalist class have their court-chaplains, it is only fair that the army of labor should have its army-chaplains who administer the consolations of religion to militant labor.

Thus the Church has a tremendous stake in the social crisis. It may try to maintain an attitude of neutrality, but neither side will permit it. If it is quiescent, it thereby throws its influence on the side of things as they are, and the class which aspires to a fitter place in the organization of society will feel the great spiritual force of the Church as a dead weight against it. If it loses the loyalty and trust of the working class, it loses the very class in which it originated, to which its founders belonged, and which has lifted it to power. If it becomes a religion of the upper classes, it condemns itself to a slow and comfortable death. Protestantism from the outset entered into an intimate alliance with the intelligence and wealth of the city population. As the cities grew in importance since the Reformation, as commerce overshadowed agriculture, and as the business class crowded the feudal aristocracy out of its leading position since the French Revolution, Protestantism throve with the class which had espoused it. It lifted its class, and its class lifted it. . . .

Questions

1. In Rauschenbusch's opinion, why are churches supposed to help the poor?
2. What consequences does Rauschenbusch fear if churches fail to act?
3. Would (and should) the First Amendment interfere with Rauschenbusch's call for an activist faith? Why or why not?
4. How did the religious faith of the Butkowski family (see Document 20-5) and that of Rauschenbusch differ?

21-3   The Rise of the Standard Oil Company

Ida M. Tarbell

The world of John D. Rockefeller was of great interest to Ida M. Tarbell (1857–1944), whose father joined the oil business in its infancy. Tarbell was one of the investigative journalists Theodore Roosevelt condemned as muckrakers (see text pp. 650–651). Although Tarbell hoped her book would be taken "as a legitimate historical study," Rockefeller was not impressed. Encouraged to answer Tarbell's charges, he reportedly said, "Not a word. Not a word about that misguided woman." This selection deals with the creation of Rockefeller's oil company.

Source: Ida M. Tarbell, *The History of The Standard Oil Company* (S. S. McClure Company, 1902, 1903, 1904; reprint, New York: Macmillan, 1933), pp. 41–49.

When young Rockefeller was thirteen years old, his father moved from the farm in Central New York, where the boy had been born (July 8, 1839), to a farm near Cleveland, Ohio. He went to school in Cleveland for three years. In 1855 it became necessary for him to earn his own living. It was a hard year in the West and the boy walked the streets for days looking for work. He was about to give it up and go to the country when, to quote the story as Mr. Rockefeller once told it to his Cleveland Sunday-school, "As good fortune would have it I went down to the dock and made one more application, and I was told that if I would come in after dinner—our noon-day meal was dinner in those days—they would see if I could come to work for them. I went down after dinner and I got the position, and I was permitted to remain in the city." The position, that of a clerk and bookkeeper, was not lucrative. According to a small ledger which has figured frequently in Mr. Rockefeller's religious instructions, he earned from September 26, 1855, to January, 1856, fifty dollars. "Out of that," Mr. Rockefeller told the young men of his Sunday-school class, "I paid my washerwoman and the lady I boarded with, and I saved a little money to put away."

He proved an admirable accountant—one of the early-and-late sort, who saw everything, forgot nothing and never talked. In 1856 his salary was raised to twenty-five dollars a month, and he went on always "saving a little money to put away." In 1858 came a chance to invest his savings. Among his acquaintances was a young Englishman, M. B. Clark. Older by twelve years than Rockefeller he had left a hard life in England when he was twenty to seek fortune in America. He had landed in Boston in 1847, without a penny or a friend, and it had taken three months for him to earn money to get to Ohio. Here he had taken the first job at hand, as man-of-all-work, wood-chopper, teamster. He had found his way to Cleveland, had become a valuable man in the houses where he was employed, had gone to school at nights, had saved money. They were two of a kind, Clark and Rockefeller, and in 1858 they pooled their earnings and started a produce commission business on the Cleveland docks. The venture succeeded. Local historians credit Clark and Rockefeller with doing a business of $450,000 the first year. The war came on, and as neither partner went to the front, they had full chance to take advantage of the opportunity for produce business a great army gives. A greater chance than furnishing army supplies, lucrative as most people found that, was in the oil business (so Clark and Rockefeller began to think), and in 1862, when an Englishman of ability and energy, one Samuel Andrews, asked them to back him in starting a refinery, they put in $4,000 and promised to give more if necessary. Now Andrews was a mechanical genius. He devised new processes, made a better and better quality of oil, got larger and larger percentages of refined from his crude. The little refinery grew big, and Clark and Rockefeller soon had $100,000 or more in it. In the meantime Cleveland was growing as a refining centre. The business which in 1860 had been a gamble was by 1865 one of the most promising industries of the town. It was but the beginning—so Mr. Rockefeller thought—and in that year he sold out his share of the commission business and put his money into the oil firm of Rockefeller and Andrews.

In the new firm Andrews attended to the manufacturing. The pushing of the business, the buying and the selling, fell to Rockefeller. From the start his effect was tremendous. He had the frugal man's hatred of waste and disorder, of middlemen and unnecessary manipulation, and he began a vigorous elimination of these from his business. The residuum that other refineries let run into the ground, he sold. Old iron found its way to the junk shop. He bought his oil directly from the wells. He made his own barrels. He watched and saved and contrived. The ability with which he made the smallest bargain furnishes topics to Cleveland story-tellers to-day. Low-voiced, soft-footed, humble, knowing every point in every man's business, he never tired until he got his wares at the lowest possible fig-

ure. "John always got the best of the bargain," old men tell you in Cleveland to-day, and they wince though they laugh in telling it. "Smooth," "a *savy* fellow," is their description of him. To drive a good bargain was the joy of his life. "The only time I ever saw John Rockefeller enthusiastic," a man told the writer once, "was when a report came in from the creek that his buyer had secured a cargo of oil at a figure much below the market price. He bounded from his chair with a shout of joy, danced up and down, hugged me, threw up his hat, acted so like a madman that I have never forgotten it."

He could borrow as well as bargain. The firm's capital was limited; growing as they were, they often needed money, and had none. Borrow they must. Rarely if ever did Mr. Rockefeller fail. There is a story handed down in Cleveland from the days of Clark and Rockefeller, produce merchants, which is illustrative of his methods. One day a well-known and rich business man stepped into the office and asked for Mr. Rockefeller. He was out, and Clark met the visitor. "Mr. Clark," he said, "you may tell Mr. Rockefeller, when he comes in, that I think I can use the $10,000 he wants to invest with me for your firm. I have thought it all over."

"Good God!" cried Clark, "we don't want to invest $10,000. John is out right now trying to borrow $5,000 for us."

It turned out that to prepare him for a proposition to borrow $5,000 Mr. Rockefeller had told the gentleman that he and Clark wanted to invest $10,000!

"And the joke of it is," said Clark, who used to tell the story, "John got the $5,000 even after I had let the cat out of the bag. Oh, he was the greatest borrower you ever saw!"

These qualities told. The firm grew as rapidly as the oil business of the town, and started a second refinery—William A. Rockefeller and Company. They took in a partner, H. M. Flagler, and opened a house in New York for selling oil. Of all these concerns John D. Rockefeller was the head. Finally, in June, 1870, five years after he became an active partner in the refining business, Mr. Rockefeller combined all his companies into one—the Standard Oil Company. The capital of the new concern was $1,000,000. The parties interested in it were John D. Rockefeller, Henry M. Flagler, Samuel Andrews, Stephen V. Harkness, and William Rockefeller.

The strides the firm of Rockefeller and Andrews made after the former went into it were attributed for three or four years mainly to his extraordinary capacity for bargaining and borrowing. Then its chief competitors began to suspect something. John Rockefeller might get his oil cheaper now and then, they said, but he could not do it often. He might make close contracts for which they had neither the patience nor the stomach. He might have an unusual mechanical and practical genius in his partner. But these things could not explain all. They believed they bought, on the whole, almost as cheaply as he, and they knew they made as good oil and with as great, or nearly as great, economy. He could sell at no better price than they. Where was his advantage? There was but one place where it could be, and that was in transportation. He must be getting better rates from the railroads than they were. In 1868 or 1869 a member of a rival firm long in the business, which had been prosperous from the start, and which prided itself on its methods, its economy and its energy, Alexander, Scofield and Company, went to the Atlantic and Great Western road, then under the Erie management, and complained. "You are giving others better rates than you are us," said Mr. Alexander, the representative of the firm. "We cannot compete if you do that." The railroad agent did not attempt to deny it—he simply agreed to give Mr. Alexander a rebate also. The arrangement was interesting. Mr. Alexander was to pay the open, or regular, rate on oil from the Oil Regions to Cleveland, which was then forty cents a barrel. At the end of each month he was to send to the railroad vouchers for the amount of oil shipped and paid for at forty cents, and was to get back from the railroad, in money, fifteen cents on each barrel. This concession applied only to oil brought from the wells. He was never able to get a rebate on oil shipped eastward. According to Mr. Alexander, the Atlantic and Great Western gave the rebates on oil from the Oil Regions to Cleveland up to 1871 and the system was then discontinued. Late in 1871, however, the firm for the first time got a rebate on the Lake Shore road on oil brought from the field. . . .

A still more important bit of testimony as to the time when rebates first began to be given to the Cleveland refiners and as to who first got them and why, is contained in an affidavit made in 1880 by the very man who made the discrimination. This man was General J. H. Devereux, who in 1868 succeeded Amasa Stone as vice-president of the Lake Shore Railroad. General Devereux said that his experience with the oil traffic had begun with his connection with the Lake Shore; that the only written memoranda concerning oil which he found in his office on entering his new position was a book in which it was stated that the representatives of the twenty-five oil-refining firms in Cleveland had agreed to pay a cent a gallon on crude oil removed from the Oil Regions. General Devereux says that he soon found there was a deal of trouble in store for him over oil freight. The competition between the twenty-five firms was close, the Pennsylvania was "claiming a patent right" on the transportation of oil and was putting forth every effort to make Pittsburg[h] and Philadelphia the chief refining centres. Oil Creek was boasting that it was going to be the future refining point for the world. All of this looked bad for what General Devereux speaks of as the "then very limited refining capacity of Cleveland." This remark shows how new he was to the business, for, as we have already seen, Cleveland in 1868 had anything but a limited refining capacity. Between three and four million

dollars were invested in oil refineries, and the town was receiving within 35,000 barrels of as much oil as New York City, and within 300,000 as much as Pittsburg[h], and it was boasting that the next year it would outstrip these competitors, which, as a matter of fact, it did.

The natural point for General Devereux to consider, of course, was whether he could meet the rates the Pennsylvania were giving and increase the oil freight for the Lake Shore. The road had a branch running to Franklin, Pennsylvania, within a few miles of Oil City. This he completed, and then, as he says in his affidavit, "a sharper contest than ever was produced growing out of the opposition of the Pennsylvania Railroad in competition. Such rates and arrangements were made by the Pennsylvania Railroad that it was publicly proclaimed in the public print in Oil City, Titusville and other places that Cleveland was to be wiped out as a refining centre as with a sponge." General Devereux goes on to say that all the refiners of the town, without exception, came to him in alarm, and expressed their fears that they would have either to abandon their business there or move to Titusville or other points in the Oil Regions; that the only exception to this decision was that offered by Rockefeller, Andrews and Flagler, who, on his assurance that the Lake Shore Railroad could and would handle oil as cheaply as the Pennsylvania Company, proposed to stand their ground at Cleveland and fight it out on that line. And so General Devereux gave the Standard the rebate on the rate which Amasa Stone had made with all the refiners. Why he should not have quieted the fears of the twenty-four or twenty-five other refiners by lowering their rate, too, does not appear in the affidavit. At all events the rebate had come, and, as we have seen, it soon was suspected and others went after it, and in some cases got it. But the rebate seems to have been granted generally only on oil brought from the Oil Regions. Mr. Alexander claims he was never able to get his rate lowered on his Eastern shipments. The railroad took the position with him that if he could ship as much oil as the Standard he could have as low a rate, but not otherwise. Now in 1870 the Standard Oil Company had a daily capacity of about 1,500 barrels of crude. The refinery was the largest in the town, though it had some close competitors. Nevertheless on the strength of its large capacity it received the special favour. It was a plausible way to get around the theory generally held then, as now, though not so definitely crystallised into law, that the railroad being a common carrier had no right to discriminate between its patrons. It remained to be seen whether the practice would be accepted by Mr. Rockefeller's competitors without a contest, or, if contested, would be supported by the law.

What the Standard's rebate on Eastern shipments was in 1870 it is impossible to say. Mr. Alexander says he was never able to get a rate lower than $1.33 a barrel by rail, and that it was commonly believed in Cleveland that the Standard had a rate of ninety cents. Mr. Flagler, however, the only member of the firm who has been examined under oath on that point, showed, by presenting the contract of the Standard Oil Company with the Lake Shore road in 1870, that the rates varied during the year from $1.40 to

$1.20 and $1.60, according to the season. When Mr. Flagler as asked if there was no drawback or rebate on this rate he answered, "None whatever."

Questions

1. What is Tarbell's opinion of Rockefeller?
2. How did Standard Oil gain an advantage over its competitors?
3. Why would Rockefeller's business practices be likely to infuriate Tarbell's middle-class readers?

21-4 From *La Follette's Autobiography*

Although he spent some thirty years in public office, Robert M. La Follette (1855–1925) was anything but a professional politician in the conventional sense. As a Wisconsin congressman, governor, and senator, La Follette left no doubt that he stood on the side of reform. His emphasis on social reform and expert administration during his governorship (1901–1905) became known nationally as the Wisconsin Idea (see text p. 652). In this excerpt from his autobiography, La Follette recalls his attempts to pass legislation involving direct primary elections and railroad taxation. Although both measures were defeated in the 1901 legislative session, La Follette ultimately succeeded in having them passed.

Source: Robert M. La Follette, *La Follette's Autobiography: A Personal Narrative of Political Experiences* (Madison, Wis.: Robert M. La Follette Company, 1913; reprint, Madison: University of Wisconsin Press, 1960), pp. 105–108, 111.

All the governors before me, so far as I know, had sent in their messages to the legislature to be mumbled over by a reading clerk. I know that I could make a very much stronger impression with my recommendations if I could present my message in person to the legislature in joint session. I felt that it would invest the whole matter with a new seriousness and dignity that would not only affect the legislators themselves, but react upon the public mind. This I did: and in consequence awakened a wide interest in my recommendations throughout the state.

The predominant notes in the message were direct primaries and railroad taxation—one political and one economic reform.

The railroads at that time paid taxes in the form of a license fee upon their gross earnings. The report of the Tax Commission showed that while real property in Wisconsin paid 1.19 per cent. of its market value in taxes, the railroads paid only .53 per cent. of their market value (based on the average value of stocks and bonds) or less than one half the rate paid by farmers, manufacturers, home owners and others. Upon this showing we contended that the railroads were not bearing their fair share of the burdens of

the state. The Tax Commission suggested two measures of reform. One of their bills provided for a simple increase in the license tax, the other provided for a physical valuation of the railroads and a wholly new system of taxation upon an ad valorem basis, measures which I had earnestly advocated in my campaign speeches, and recommended in my message. I regarded this latter as the more scientific method of taxation. The Commission stated that while they had so framed the bills as to err on the side of injustice to the people rather than to the railroads, the passage of either of them would mean an increase of taxes paid by railroads and other public service corporations of more than three quarters of a million dollars annually.

No sooner had the taxation and direct primary bills been introduced than the lobby gathered in Madison in full force. Lobbyists had been there before, but never in such numbers or with such an organization. I never saw anything like it. The railroads, threatened with the taxation bills, and the bosses, threatened by the direct primary, evidently regarded it as the death struggle. Not only were the regular lobbyists in attendance but they made a practice during the entire winter of bringing in delegations of more or less influential men from all parts of the state, some of whom often remained two or three weeks and brought every sort of pressure to bear on the members of the legislature. The whole fight was centred upon me personally. They thought that if they could crush me, that would stop the movement. How little they understood! Even if they had succeeded in eliminating me, the movement, which is fundamental, would still have swept on! They sought to build up in the minds of the people the fear that the executive was controlling the legislative branch of the government. They deliberately organized a campaign of abuse and misrepresentation. Their stories were minutely detailed and spread about among the hotels and on railroad trains. They said that I had completely lost my head. They endeavored to give me a reputation for discourtesy and browbeating; stories were told of my shameless treatment of members, of my backing them up against the wall of the executive office, shaking my fist in their faces and warning them if they did not pass our bills I would use all my power to crush them. In so far as anything was said in disparagement of the administration members of the legislature it was that they were sycophants who took their orders every morning from the executive office. The newspapers, controlled by the machine interests, began to print these abusive statements and sent them broadcast. At first we took no notice of their campaign of misrepresentation, but it grew and grew until it got on the nerves of all of us. It came to be a common thing to have one after another of my friends drop in and say: "Governor, is it true that you have had a row with——? Is it true that you ordered—— out of the executive office?"

It seems incredible, as I look back upon it now, that it could be humanly possible to create such an atmosphere of distrust. We felt that we were fighting something in the dark all the while; there was nothing we could get hold of.

In spite of it all, however, we drove straight ahead. After the bills prepared by the Tax Commission were in, the primary election bill was drafted and redrafted and introduced by E. Ray Stevens of Madison, one of the ablest men ever in public life in Wisconsin, and now a judge of the circuit court of the state. The committee having it in charge at once began a series of open meetings, and the lobby brought to Madison people from every part of the state to attend the hearings and to protest. Extended speeches were made against it, and these were promptly printed and sent broadcast. The most preposterous arguments were advanced. They argued that the proposed law was unconstitutional because it interfered with the "right of the people to assemble!" They tried to rouse the country people by arguing that it favored the cities; they said that city people could get out more readily to primaries than country people. It did not seem to occur to them that practically every argument they made against the direct primary applied far more strongly to the old caucus and convention system.

But we fought as vigorously as they, and presently it began to appear that we might get some of our measures through. It evidently made an impression on the lobby. One night, after the legislature had been in session about two months, Emanuel Phillipp came to my office. He moved his chair up close to mine.

"Now, look here," he said, "you want to pass the primary election bill, don't you? I will help you put it through."

"Phillipp," I said, "there is no use in you and me trying to mislead each other. I understand and you understand that the senate is organized against both the direct primary and taxation bills. You know that better than I do."

"Well," he said, "now look here. This railroad taxation matter—wouldn't you be willing to let that go if you could get your primary bill through? What good will it do you, anyhow, to increase railroad taxation? We can meet that all right just by raising rates or by changing a classification here and there. No one will know it and we can take back every cent of increased taxes in rates from the people."

"Phillipp," I said, "you have just driven in and clinched the argument for regulating your rates. And that is the next thing we are going to do. No," I said, "these pledges are straight promises."

"But," he argued, "if you can get this primary election bill through you will have done a great thing. And I will pass it for you, if you will let up on railroad taxation."

"Just how will you pass it?" I asked.

"How will I pass it?" he repeated. "How will I pass it? Why, I'll take those fellows over to a room in the Park Hotel, close the door and stand them up against the wall. And I'll say to them, 'You vote for the primary election bill!' And they'll vote for it, because I own them, they're mine!" And this was Phillipp's last interview with me. . . .

When we continued to make progress in spite of all this opposition the lobby made another move against us. It brought to bear all the great influence of the federal office-holders who were especially disturbed over the possible effect of a direct primary upon their control of the state. United States District Attorney Wheeler, an appointee of Spooner, and the United States District Attorney of the Eastern District, an appointee of Quarles, were much on the ground; so were United States Marshal Monahan and Collector of Internal Revenue Fink.

Finally, before the vote on the direct primary was taken in the senate, Senator Spooner, who rarely came to Wisconsin while Congress was in session, appeared in Madison. He was there only a few days, but he was visited by members of the senate, and we felt his influence strongly against us.

All the efforts of the lobby, combined with the opposition of the newspapers and the federal office-holders, was not without its effect upon our forces. Every moment from the time the senate convened down to the final vote on the railroad taxation bills they were weakening us, wearing us down, getting some men one way, some another, until finally before the close of the session they had not only the senate but a majority of the Republicans in the assembly. It was a pathetic and tragic thing to see honest men falling before these insidious forces. For many of them it meant plain ruin from which they never afterward recovered.

In order to make very clear the methods employed I shall here relate in detail the stories of several of the cases which came directly under my own observation. I shall withhold the real names of the Senators and Assemblymen concerned, because many of them were the victims of forces and temptations far greater than they could resist. If I could also give the names of the men really responsible for the corruption, bribery and debauchery—the men higher up, the men behind the lobbyists—I would do it without hesitation.

Questions

1. How does La Follette signal that he is different from previous governors?
2. What were the elements of his railroad tax proposal?
3. According to La Follette, how did the opposition counterattack?

21-5 *Twenty Years at Hull-House* (1910)

Jane Addams

Social reformers found that American cities were filled with problems, not the least of which was garbage. It seemed to accumulate without end in overcrowded working-class and immigrant neighborhoods, and the propensity of horses to produce manure on city streets made matters worse. The leader of the settlement house movement (see text pp. 653, 656), Jane Addams (1860–1935), declared war against garbage in her Hull House neighborhood on Chicago's West Side. The undertaking was not the most important of Addams's illustrious career, but it illustrates the commitment to social justice that helped her win a share of the Nobel Peace Prize in 1931.

Source: Jane Addams, *Twenty Years at Hull-House: With Autobiographical Notes* (Phillips Publishing Company, 1910; reprint, New York: New American Library, n.d.), pp. 200–204.

One of the striking features of our neighborhood twenty years ago, and one to which we never became reconciled, was the presence of huge wooden garbage boxes fastened to the street pavement in which the undisturbed refuse accumulated day by day. The system of garbage collecting was inadequate throughout the city but it became the greatest menace in a ward such as ours, where the normal amount of waste was much increased by the decayed fruit and vegetables discarded by the Italian and Greek fruit peddlers, and by the residuum left over from the piles of filthy rags which were fished out of the city dumps and brought to the homes of the rag pickers for further sorting and washing.

The children of our neighborhood twenty years ago played their games in and around these huge garbage boxes. They were the first objects that the toddling child learned to climb; their bulk afforded a barricade and their contents provided missiles in all the battles of the older boys; and finally they became the seats upon which absorbed lovers held enchanted converse. We are obliged to remember that all children eat everything which they find and that odors have a curious and intimate power of entwining themselves into our tenderest memories, before even the residents of Hull-House can understand their own early enthusiasm for the removal of these boxes and the establishment of a better system of refuse collection.

It is easy for even the most conscientious citizen of Chicago to forget the foul smells of the stockyards and the garbage dumps, when he is living so far from them that he is only occasionally made conscious of their existence, but the residents of a Settlement are perforce constantly surrounded by them. During our first three years on Halsted Street, we had established a small incinerator at Hull-House and we had many times reported the untoward conditions of the ward to the city hall. We had also arranged many talks for the immigrants, pointing out that although a woman may sweep her own doorway in her native village and allow the refuse to innocently decay in the open air and sunshine, in a crowed city quarter, if the garbage is not properly collected and destroyed, a tenement-house mother may see her children sicken and die, and that the immigrants must therefore not only keep their own houses clean, but must also help the authorities to keep the city clean.

Possibly our efforts slightly modified the worst conditions, but they still remained intolerable, and the fourth summer the situation became for me absolutely desperate when I realized in a moment of panic that my delicate little nephew for whom I was guardian could not be with me at Hull-House at all unless the sickening odors were reduced. I may well be ashamed that other delicate children who were torn from their families, not into boarding school but into eternity, had not long before driven me into effective action. Under the direction of the first man who came as a resident to Hull-House we began a systematic investigation of the city system of garbage collection, both as to its efficiency in other wards and its possible connection with the death rate in the various wards of the city.

The Hull-House Woman's Club had been organized the year before by the resident kindergartner who had first inaugurated a mothers' meeting. The members came together, however, in quite a new way that summer when we discussed with them the high death rate so persistent in our ward. After several club meetings devoted to the subject, despite the fact that the death rate rose highest in the congested foreign colonies and not in the streets in which most of the Irish American club women lived, twelve of their number undertook in connection with the residents, to carefully investigate the condition of the alleys. During August and September the substantiated reports of violations of the law sent in from Hull-House to the health department were one thousand and thirty-seven. For the club woman who had finished a long day's work of washing or ironing followed by the cooking of a hot supper, it would have been much easier to sit on her doorstep during a summer evening than to go up and down ill-kept alleys and get into trouble with her neighbors over the condition of their garbage boxes. It required both civic enterprise and moral conviction to be willing to do this three evenings a week during the hottest and most uncomfortable months of the year. Nevertheless, a certain number of women persisted, as did the residents, and three city inspectors in succession were transferred from the ward because of unsatisfactory services. Still the death rate remained high and the condition seemed little improved throughout the next winter. In

sheer desperation, the following spring when the city contracts were awarded for the removal of garbage, with the backing of two well-known business men, I put in a bid for the garbage removal of the nineteenth ward. My paper was thrown out on a technicality but the incident induced the mayor to appoint me the garbage inspector of the ward.

The salary was a thousand dollars a year, and the loss of that political "plum" made a great stir among the politicians. The position was no sinecure whether regarded from the point of view of getting up at six in the morning to see that the men were early at work; or of following the loaded wagons, uneasily dropping their contents at intervals, to their dreary destination at the dump; or of insisting that the contractor must increase the number of his wagons from nine to thirteen and from thirteen to seventeen, although he assured me that he lost money on every one and that the former inspector had let him off with seven; or of taking careless landlords into court because they would not provide the proper garbage receptacles; or of arresting the tenant who tried to make the garbage wagons carry away the contents of his stable.

With the two or three residents who nobly stood by, we set up six of those doleful incinerators which are supposed to burn garbage with the fuel collected in the alley itself. The one factory in town which could utilize old tin cans was a window weight factory, and we deluged that with ten times as many tin cans as it could use—much less would pay for. We made desperate attempts to have the dead animals removed by the contractor who was paid most liberally by the city for that purpose but who, we slowly discovered, always made the police ambulances do the work, delivering the carcasses upon freight cars for shipment to a soap factory in Indiana where they were sold for a good price although the contractor himself was the largest stockholder in the concern. Perhaps our greatest achievement was the discovery of a pavement eighteen inches under the surface in a narrow street, although after it was found we triumphantly discovered a record of its existence in the city archives. The Italians living on the street were much interested but displayed little astonishment, perhaps because they were accustomed to see buried cities exhumed. This pavement became the *casus belli* [cause of war] between myself and the street commissioner when I insisted that its restoration belonged to him, after I had removed the first eight inches of garbage. The matter was finally settled by the mayor himself, who permitted me to drive him to the entrance of the street in what the children called my "garbage phaëton" and who took my side of the controversy.

Questions

1. How was garbage collected in Chicago?
2. Why were conditions so bad in the area around Hull House?
3. What did Jane Addams accomplish as a garbage collector?

21-6 The Lawrence, Massachusetts, Strike (1912)

Middle-class social reformers in the Progressive Era finally learned what workers had known for generations: factory employment could be both miserable and dangerous (see text pp. 659–661). Conditions were so bad in the textile mill town of Lawrence, Massachusetts, that the workers there cooperated with the radical Industrial Workers of the World (see text p. 581), which led a successful strike in 1912. Samuel Lipson's testimony before the Socialist congressman Victor L. Berger demonstrates why the textile workers took action.

Source: U.S. Congress, House Committee on Rules, *Hearings on H. Res. 409 and 433, The Strike at Lawrence, Mass.*, 62nd Cong., 2d sess., 1912, H. Doc. 671, pp. 32–36.

MR. BERGER. Why did you go on a strike?

MR. LIPSON. I went out on strike because I was unable to make a living for my family.

MR. BERGER. How much wages were you receiving?

MR. LIPSON. My average wage, or the average wage of my trade, is from $9 to $10 a week.

MR. BERGER. What kind of work do you do?

MR. LIPSON. I am a weaver.

MR. BERGER. You are a skilled workman?

MR. LIPSON. Yes, sir; for years.

MR. BERGER. You have been a skilled workman for years and your wages average from $9 to $10 per week?

MR. LIPSON. Yes, sir; that was the average.

MR. BERGER. How many children do you have?

MR. LIPSON. I have four children and a wife.

MR. BERGER. You support a wife and four children from a weekly wage averaging from $9 to $10 per week and you are a skilled workman. Did you have steady work?

MR. LIPSON. Usually the work was steady, but there was times when I used to make from $3 to $4 and $5 per week. We have had to live on $3 per week. We lived on bread and water. . . .

MR. BERGER. How much rent do you pay?

MR. LIPSON. I pay $2.50.

MR. BERGER. Per week?

MR. LIPSON. Yes, sir.

MR. BERGER. You pay $2.50 per week for rent out of $10 weekly wages?

MR. LIPSON. Yes, sir. You asked me whether I supported my family out of $10 per week. Of course we do not use butter at the present time; we use a kind of molasses; we are trying to fool our stomachs with it.

MR. BERGER. It is a bad thing to fool your stomach.

MR. LIPSON. We know that, but we can not help it. When we go to the store without any money, the storekeeper tells us that he can not sell us anything without the money.

MR. BERGER. How much were you reduced by reason of the recent cut in the wages?

MR. LIPSON. From 50 to 65 to 75 cents per week.

MR. BERGER. How much does a loaf of bread cost in Lawrence?

MR. LIPSON. Twelve cents; that is what I pay.

MR. BERGER. The reduction in your wages, according to this, took away five loaves of bread from you every week?

MR. LIPSON. Yes, sir. When we go into the store now with a dollar and get a peck of potatoes and a few other things, we have no change left out of that dollar. Of course we are living according to what we get. . . .

MR. BERGER. How many months in the year were you employed?

MR. LIPSON. I was employed the year through. The company keeps us in the mills no matter whether there is work or not, and sometimes we only go home with $3 or $4 in our envelopes.

MR. BERGER. Do you do piecework?

MR. LIPSON. Yes, sir.

MR. BERGER. What can you tell us about the speeding-up system . . . ?

MR. LIPSON. The speeding-up system is according to the premium.

MR. BERGER. They have premiums, also? That is interesting. Kindly give the committee a description of the premium system at Lawrence, Mass.

MR. LIPSON. The premiums are not alike in all the mills. In some mills they start with $35 and some small change. They get 5 per cent more; and if they come up to it they get 5 per cent more in the month. In other mills, where the machinery runs faster, they are started, say, at $39 per month, and they add 5 per cent per month. When it happens to the weaver to make $44 per month, that means he is getting 10 per cent. It is a heavy month when they get 10 per cent. The loom operatives also get premiums. When a section makes up a certain amount of cloth, they get a certain premium. Therefore they have us to speed up the machinery. If a man can not come up to it he gets fired out. Sometimes one is sick, and sometimes our stomach is empty, because our pay does not always last to the end of the month. When we come to that, we wish it was Saturday, because we usually get our pay on Saturday, but we stay in the mills just the same. They stay there, sick at the loom.

MR. BERGER. What is the effect, then, of the premium system on the weaker workingman—on the man who can not work as fast as the others?

MR. LIPSON.   The effect upon him is that he is working less. There is no work for him. He has no work; they do not employ him.

MR. BERGER.   The general tendency, then, is to push the skilled workers harder, so as to compel the rest also to work so much more?

MR. LIPSON.   Yes, sir; there are always some people who are healthier. Those who have come recently from the old country are healthier, and they are still fresh from the old country. They have red cheeks, and so on. They are apt to find it pretty hard for the first few weeks, because they are not used to such machinery. They call them "devils" and not machinery. After working for a while they are getting used to it, but they say that in England and France they did not do as much in a week as they do in three days in this country. Experienced weavers, who have been weavers for years, are trying to get used to it, and if they are healthy and fresh people from the old country, they are able to make the 10 per cent premium; that is, of course, by whipping up themselves. If the others do not make it, the boss says, "Why not try to make the 10 per cent?" Maybe they will say, "We will try," and the boss says, "If you do not make it, you can find another place."

MR. BERGER.   You are a member of the strike committee, are you not?"

MR. LIPSON.   Yes, sir.

MR. BERGER.   Tell us the immediate cause of the strike.

MR. LIPSON.   The workers in the American Woolen Co.'s mills had meetings and discussed the question of what can we do to make a living. It was unbearable. In one of our meetings we decided to see the agent of the mill, and one committee went up to see the agent of the mill, and he told them to go back to their machines; he did not want to give them any answer at all. At another one of the mills they were absolutely turned down, and in the Washington mill they were told to go to Boston and see the president of the American Woolen Co., Mr. Wood. When they told us to do that, we sent a special delivery letter to Mr. Wood, telling him about how it is in Lawrence. We expected to get an answer, because it was a special-delivery letter, and we are waiting for that answer still. Well, they were trying to make up two hours, and they tried to

speed up the machinery in order to make us do 56 hours work in 54 hours time, and try to cut off the pay at the same time. The question was whether we could make a living. Well, they cut down the wages after they speeded up the machinery, and as they were trying still to speed up the machinery and trying to cut down the wages, we thought we would have to starve.

MR. BERGER. Do you mean to convey by your statement that you were required to do 56 hours work in 54 hours time, because a law was recently passed in Massachusetts cutting down the hours of labor to 54 per week?

MR. LIPSON.   Yes, sir.

MR. BERGER. Were you working 56 hours before that new act was passed?

MR. LIPSON.   Yes, sir.

MR. BERGER. What effect did this have on the strike?

MR. LIPSON. The people were complaining that it was impossible for them to bear their sufferings any longer, in so many ways.

MR. BERGER. Do you mean that they were required to furnish as much product in 54 hours as in 56 hours?

MR. LIPSON.   Yes, sir.

MR. BERGER.   And then suffer a cut in wages besides?

MR. LIPSON.   Yes, sir.

MR. BERGER.   How many nationalities are there represented among the workers at Lawrence?

MR. LIPSON.   Sixteen nationalities.

MR. BERGER.   Mention some of them.

MR. LIPSON.   There are Germans, Polish, English, Italians, Armenians, Turks, Syrians, Greeks, Belgians, some from France, Jewish, Lithuanians—there are 16 in all.

MR. BERGER.   Are there any Bulgarians?

MR. LIPSON.   That is so, and Austrians. I can not name them all now; I am not familiar with geography.

MR. BERGER.   Are there any Portuguese?

MR. LIPSON.   Yes, sir; Portuguese and Armenians. . . .

MR. BERGER.   How many nationalities are represented on the strike committee?

MR. LIPSON.   Every nationality is represented by four delegates, and also on the subcommittee of that committee by about three or four.

MR. BERGER.   How many of the workers of Lawrence are women and children? How many are men?

MR. LIPSON.   I can not tell you about how many, but I can tell you that the majority of them are women and children, and as we are speeding up, these children are doing more work. If they can not do the work, they are fired out. They must do the work that goes from one machine to another, and they must prepare the work for us. If they do not speed up, they are fired out.

MR. BERGER.   Do you mean that the children are discharged?

MR. LIPSON.   Yes, sir.

MR. BERGER.   If the children do not speed up, they lose their places in the mills?

MR. LIPSON.   Yes, sir; and the women who are used in the same place are pushed out sometimes and the children take their places.

MR. BERGER.   Do they have any accidents in the factory?

MR. LIPSON.   Yes, sir.

MR. BERGER.   Give a few instances of accidents.

MR. LIPSON.   There is a girl over there, Camella Teoli, and everyone present can see her. She is an Italian girl, but also speaks English. She started to work in the spinning department, on a machine that is a long one, with three or four different sides. The machine was speeded up and was running with such speed that her hair was caught and her scalp was cut by the machine. Her scalp was torn down, as you see. She was there working for the American Woolen Co. two years ago, and she is still under the treatment of a physician and at work at the same time, because the family consists of seven and she is the oldest. She is 16 years old; her father works in the mill and gets $7 per week. Of course, her parents have no money to have a trial with the company.

MR. BERGER.   She has not sued the company?

MR. LIPSON.   No, sir. That happened two years ago, and she is working to keep up the family. They are poor and she and the father are working to keep up the family. The youngest is a little older than a year.

MR. BERGER.   She would not stand much chance in a lawsuit against the American Woolen Co. The American Woolen Co. is a powerful concern.

MR. LIPSON.   Yes, sir; that is true.

MR. BERGER.   What are the demands of the strikers now?

MR. LIPSON.   The demands are 15 per cent increase in wages, based on 54 hours work per week, and double pay for overtime. The reason I wish to call your attention to the demand for 15 per cent increase is this: These people work sometimes only two or three days in a week. Her father works only three days in a week, and has $2.88 per week for the family, and they absolutely live on bread and water. If you would look at the other children, you would see that they look like skeletons. . . .

MR. BERGER.   What reception did the strikers get from the mill owners?

MR. LIPSON.   I told you before.

MR. BERGER.   I want to know whether you got any other answer. You said Mr. Wood did not answer your letter, and that the foreman simply told the committee to go back to your machines.

MR. LIPSON.   Yes, sir. They said if we did not like it to get out.

MR. BERGER.   Well, you failed to tell us that before, and it is important.

MR. LIPSON.   We are so used to it that I did not mention it. To you these things are new, but to us it is an old story. . . .

Questions

1. How did Samuel Lipson try to extend his family's budget?
2. Explain the speeding-up system. What were its effects on factory workers?
3. What were the immediate causes of the strike in Lawrence?

21-7 The Dark Side of Progressivism (1907)

The Ben Ishmael tribe in the Midwest consisted of African-Americans, whites, and native Americans who lived together as gypsies; they were 10,000 strong at the turn of the century. The members of the tribe had long been accused of and jailed for prostitution, begging, and vagrancy, among other minor crimes. The state of Indiana found the Ishmaelites troubling enough that in 1907 the legislature passed a law calling for the sterilization of certain prison inmates. The act was the first of its kind in the nation and represents progressivism at its worst, demonstrating a willingness to invoke science (in this case eugenics, the study of improving human heredity) for reactionary, racist ends (see text p. 662). The threat of such extreme action helped persuade the tribe to assimilate into mainstream society.

Source: Laws of the State of Indiana, 1907, pp. 377–378.

PREAMBLE.

Whereas, Heredity plays a most important part in the transmission of crime, idiocy and imbecility;

PENAL INSTITUTIONS—SURGICAL OPERATIONS.

Therefore, *Be it enacted by the general assembly of the State of Indiana,* That on and after the passage of this act it shall be compulsory for each and every institution in the state, entrusted with the care of confirmed criminals, idiots, rapists and imbeciles, to appoint upon its staff, in addition to the regular institutional physician, two (2) skilled surgeons of recognized ability, whose duty it shall be, in conjunction with the chief physician of the institution, to examine the mental and physical condition of such inmates as are recommended by the institutional physician and board of managers. If, in the judgment of this committee of experts and the board of managers, procreation is inadvisable and there is no probability of improvement of the mental condition of the inmate, it shall be lawful for the surgeons to perform such operation for the prevention of procreation as shall be decided safest and most effective. But this operation shall not be performed except in cases that have been pronounced unimprovable: *Provided,* That in no case shall the consultation fee be more than three ($3.00) dollars to each expert, to be paid out of the funds appropriated for the maintenance of such institution.

Questions

1. What assumption is made in the statute's preamble?
2. Which types of inmates were considered eligible for sterilization?
3. Did the screening process respect an inmate's human rights?
4. Besides procreation, what does the legislation seem to be intended to control?

Questions for Further Thought

1. Describe the urban living and working conditions indicated in Documents 21-5 and 21-6. Why were these problems so difficult to solve?
2. Who would be more offended by the Indiana sterilization act, Walter Rauschenbusch (Document 21-2) or Walter Lippmann (Document 21-1)? Why?
3. What intellectual and emotional traits do Rauschenbusch, Tarbell, La Follette, and Addams share?

Progressivism and National Politics

Politics in the Progressive Era never lacked excitement. Tom Johnson, the mayor of Cleveland from 1901 to 1909, used circus tents to house his political rallies; an advocate of the single tax (on real estate, especially land held for speculation) and municipal ownership of public utilities, Johnson raced from rally to rally in his car, the Red Devil. The Wisconsin governor and U.S. senator Robert La Follette was so combative that he earned the nickname "Fighting Bob." And then there was Theodore Roosevelt....

Roosevelt drove conservative Republicans to despair. "Don't any of you realize there's only one life between this madman and the White House?" the Republican boss Mark Hanna (see text p. 665) asked after Roosevelt's nomination as vice-president in 1900. Hanna's fears were realized when William McKinley was assassinated in 1901. Roosevelt virtually redefined the presidency and in so doing modernized the office. His progressivism drew heavily on the ideas of Alexander Hamilton and the leadership qualities of Abraham Lincoln (see text pp. 439–445). Roosevelt believed that government should foster social and economic progress, as outlined in Hamilton's "Report on Manufactures" (1791) (see text p. 217). In this view, government was best run by men who could demonstrate a combination of energy and wisdom, as Lincoln had during the Civil War and Teddy Roosevelt thought he would in the first decade of the new century. As president, Roosevelt put his ideas to work in his Square Deal with legislation aimed at the conservation of natural resources, railroad regulation, and consumer protection (see text pp. 664–668).

In keeping with his reputation as a trustbuster (see text pp. 666–667), Roosevelt thought that a modern economy could thrive under a system of regulation, not laissez-faire competition. That belief, coupled with a commitment to social justice, formed the basis of Roosevelt's New Nationalism in 1912 (see text p. 670). Woodrow Wilson disagreed with Roosevelt's theories, offering in their place an updated version of Jacksonian democracy (see text pp. 670–673). "What this country needs above all else," Wilson said during the 1912 presidential campaign, "is a body of laws which will look after the men who are on the make rather than the men who are already made." The Democrat and his New Freedom triumphed, but in his presidency Wilson borrowed much from the New Nationalism.

Document 21-8 offers a taste of Roosevelt's third-party rhetoric. The Progressive party platform (Document 21-9) is exceptionally comprehensive in its social welfare proposals. The progressive lawyer Louis Brandeis's faith in competition, as shown in Document 21-10, greatly influenced Woodrow Wilson.

21-8   "The Struggle for Social Justice" (1912)

Theodore Roosevelt

When Theodore Roosevelt (1858–1919) left the White House in 1908 and went on safari in Africa, a wag commented, "I hope some lion will do his duty." Roosevelt returned home safely only to be disappointed by the conservative politics of his successor, William Howard Taft (see text pp. 668–669). Roosevelt challenged Taft for the Republican presidential nomination in 1912 and, when that failed, formed his own Progressive party (see text pp. 669–670). During the campaign Roosevelt often spoke about issues of social justice.

Source: Theodore Roosevelt, *Progressive Principles: Selections from Addresses Made during the Presidential Campaign of 1912,* ed. Elmer H. Youngman (New York: Progressive National Service, 1913), pp. 199–207.

Lincoln made his fight on the two great fundamental issues of the right of the people to rule themselves, and not to be ruled by any mere part of the people, and of the vital need that this rule of the people should be exercised for social and industrial justice in a spirit of broad charity and kindliness to all, but with stern insistence that privilege should be eliminated from our industrial life and should be shorn of its power in our political life.

In describing his actions I am using the words which we use at the present day; but they exactly and precisely set forth his position fifty years ago. This position is ours at the present day.

The very rich men whom we mean when we speak of Wall Street have at this crisis shown that they are not loyal to the cause of human rights, human justice, human liberty. The rich man who is a good citizen first of all and a rich man only next, stands on a level with all other good citizens, and the rich man of this type is with us in this contest just as other good citizens, who happen to be wage-workers or retail traders or professional men, are with us. But the rich man who trusts in his riches, the rich man who feels that his wealth entitles him to more than his share of political, social and industrial power, is naturally against us. So likewise the men of little faith, the timid men who fear the people and do not dare trust them, the men who at the bottom of their hearts disbelieve in our whole principle of democratic governmental rule, are also against us. . . .

The representatives of privilege, the men who stand for the special interests and against the rule of the plain people and who distrust the people, care very little for party names.

They oppose us who stand for the cause of progress and of justice. They were accurately described by Lincoln . . . when he said that there had been nothing in politics since the Revolution so congenial to their nature as the position taken taken by his opponents.

The same thing is true now. Those people are against me because they are against the cause I represent.

These men against whom we stand include the men who desire to exploit the people for their own purposes and to profit financially by the wicked alliance between crooked business and crooked politics. Of course, they include also a large number of worthy and respectable men, who have no improper purpose to serve but who either do not see far into the future, or who are misled as to the facts of the case. Finally, they include those who at this moment represent what Lincoln described as the "old exclusive silk-stocking Whigs—nearly all the Whigs of the nice exclusive sort.". . .

The boss system is based on and thrives by injustice. Wherever you get the boss, wherever you get a Legislature controlled by mercenary politicians, there you will always find that privilege flourishes; there you will always find the great special interests striking hands with the crooked politicians and helping them plunder the people in the interest of both wings of the corrupt alliance.

It is to the interest of every honest man, and perhaps most especially to the interest of the honest big business man, that this alliance shall be broken up, and that we shall have a genuine rule of the people in a spirit of honesty and fair play toward all.

There is far more in this contest than is involved in the momentary victory of any man or any faction.

We are now fighting one phase of the eternal struggle for right and for justice. . . .

As far as we are concerned, the battle is just begun, and we shall go on with it to the end. We hail as our brothers all who contend in any way for the great cause of human rights, for the realization in measurable degree of the doctrines of the brotherhood of man.

We do not for a moment believe that any system of laws, no matter how good, or that any governmental action, can ever take the place of the individual character of the average man and the average woman, which must always in the last analysis be the chief factor in that man's or that woman's success.

But we insist that without just laws and just governmental action the high standard of character of the average American will not suffice to get all that as a Nation we are entitled to.

We must, through the law, make conditions of life more fair, make equality of opportunity more real. We must strive for industrial as well as political democracy.

Every man who fights for the protection of children from excessive toil, for the protection of women from working in factories for too long hours, for the protection, in short, of the workingman and his family so that he may live decently and bring up his children honorably and well—every man who works for any such cause is our fellow worker and we hail him as such.

Remember, that when we work to make this country a better place to live in for those who have been harshly treated by fate, we are also at the same time making it a better place to live in for those who have been well treated by fate.

The great representatives and beneficiaries of privilege, nineteen-twentieths of whom are opposing us with intense animosity, are acting with the utmost short-sightedness from the standpoint of the welfare of their children and their children's children.

We who stand for justice wish to make this country a better place to live in for the man who actually toils, for the wage-worker, for the farmer, for the small business man; and in so striving, we are really defending the cause of the children of those beneficiaries of privilege against what would be fatal action by their fathers. . . .

None of us can really prosper permanently if there are masses among us who are debased and degraded.

The sons of the millionaires will find this a very poor country to live in if men and women who make up the bulk of our ordinary citizenship do not have conditions so shaped that they can lead self-respecting lives on a basis which will permit them to retain their own sense of dignity, to treat their children aright, and to take their part in the life of the community as good citizens.

Exactly as each of us in his private life must stand up for his own rights and yet must respect the rights of others and acknowledge in practical fashion that he is indeed his brother's keeper, so all of us taken collectively, the people as a whole, must feel our obligation to work by governmental action, and in all other ways possible, to make the conditions better for those who are unfairly pressed down in the fierce competition of modern industrial life.

I ask justice for those who in actual life meet with most injustice—and I ask this not only for their sakes but for our own sakes, for the sake of the children and the children's children who are to come after us.

The children of all of us will pay in the future if we do not do justice in the present.

This country will not be a good place for any of us to live in if we do not strive with zeal and efficiency to make it a reasonably good place for all of us to live in.

Nor can our object be obtained save through the genuine control of the people themselves. The people must rule or gradually they will lose all power of being good citizens. The people must control their own destinies or the power of such control will atrophy.

Our cause is the cause of the plain people. It is the cause of social and industrial justice to be achieved by the plain people through the resolute and conscientious use of all the machinery, public and private, State and National, governmental and individual, which is at their command.

This is a great fight in which we are engaged, for it is a fight for human rights, and we who are making it are really making it for every good citizen of this Republic, no matter to what party he may belong.

Questions

1. By Roosevelt's standards, what constitutes a moral rich man?
2. Why does Roosevelt invoke Abraham Lincoln in this speech?
3. How does Roosevelt define social justice?

21-9 The Progressive Party Platform of 1912

There was nothing ordinary about the Progressive party's presidential convention held in Chicago in August 1912 (see text pp. 669–670). The delegates sang "Onward Christian Soldiers" from the convention floor, Jane Addams seconded the nomination of the candidate, and Theodore Roosevelt delivered an acceptance speech titled "A Confession of Faith." The party platform was no less remarkable as it blended Roosevelt's view of the future with a deeply ingrained religious passion.

Source: In Kirk H. Porter and Donald Bruce Johnson, comps., *National Party Platforms 1840–1964* (Urbana: University of Illinois Press, 1966), pp. 175–178.

The conscience of the people, in a time of grave national problems, has called into being a new party, born of the nation's sense of justice. We of the Progressive party here dedicate ourselves to the fulfillment of the duty laid upon us by our fathers to maintain the government of the people, by the people and for the people whose foundations they laid.

We hold with Thomas Jefferson and Abraham Lincoln that the people are the masters of their Constitution, to ful-

fill its purposes and to safeguard it from those who, by perversion of its intent, would convert it into an instrument of injustice. In accordance with the needs of each generation the people must use their sovereign powers to establish and maintain equal opportunity and industrial justice, to secure which this Government was founded and without which no republic can endure.

This country belongs to the people who inhabit it. Its resources, its business, its institutions and its laws should be utilized, maintained or altered in whatever manner will best promote the general interest.

It is time to set the public welfare in the first place.

THE OLD PARTIES

Political parties exist to secure responsible government and to execute the will of the people.

From these great tasks both of the old parties have turned aside. Instead of instruments to promote the general welfare, they have become the tools of corrupt interests which use them impartially to serve their selfish purposes. Behind the ostensible government sits enthroned an invisible government owing no allegiance and acknowledging no responsibility to the people.

To destroy this invisible government, to dissolve the unholy alliance between corrupt business and corrupt politics is the first task of the statesmanship of the day.

The deliberate betrayal of its trust by the Republican party, the fatal incapacity of the Democratic party to deal with the new issues of the new time, have compelled the people to forge a new instrument of government through which to give effect to their will in laws and institutions.

Unhampered by tradition, uncorrupted by power, undismayed by the magnitude of the task, the new party offers itself as the instrument of the people to sweep away old abuses, to build a new and nobler commonwealth.

A COVENANT WITH THE PEOPLE

This declaration is our covenant with the people, and we hereby bind the party and its candidates in State and Nation to the pledges made herein.

THE RULE OF THE PEOPLE

The National Progressive party, committed to the principles of government by a self-controlled democracy expressing its will through representatives of the people, pledges itself to secure such alterations in the fundamental law of the several States and the United States as shall insure the representative character of the government.

In particular, the party declares for direct primaries for the nomination of State and National officers, for nationwide preferential primaries for candidates for the presidency; for the direct election of United States Senators by the people; and we urge on the States the policy of the short ballot, with responsibility to the people secured by the initiative, referendum and recall.

AMENDMENT OF CONSTITUTION

The Progressive party, believing that a free people should have the power from time to time to amend their fundamental law so as to adapt it progressively to the changing needs of the people, pledges itself to provide a more easy and expeditious method of amending the Federal Constitution.

NATION AND STATE

Up to the limit of the Constitution, and later by amendment of the Constitution, if found necessary, we advocate bringing under effective national jurisdiction those problems which have expanded beyond reach of the individual States.

It is as grotesque as it is intolerable that the several States should by unequal laws in matter of common concern become competing commercial agencies, barter the lives of their children, the health of their women and the safety and well being of their working people for the benefit of their financial interests.

The extreme insistence on States' rights by the Democratic party in the Baltimore platform demonstrates anew its inability to understand the world into which it has survived or to administer the affairs of a union of States which have in all essential respects become one people.

EQUAL SUFFRAGE

The Progressive party, believing that no people can justly claim to be a true democracy which denies political rights on account of sex, pledges itself to the task of securing equal suffrage to men and women alike.

CORRUPT PRACTICES

We pledge our party to legislation that will compel strict limitation of all campaign contributions and expenditures, and detailed publicity of both before as well as after primaries and elections.

PUBLICITY AND PUBLIC SERVICE

We pledge our party to legislation compelling the registration of lobbyists; publicity of committee hearings except on foreign affairs, and recording of all votes in committee; and forbidding federal appointees from holding office in State or National political organizations, or taking part as officers or delegates in political conventions for the nomination of elective State or National officials.

THE COURTS

The Progressive party demands such restriction of the power of the courts as shall leave to the people the ultimate authority to determine fundamental questions of social welfare and public policy. To secure this end, it pledges itself to provide:

1. That when an Act, passed under the police power of the State, is held unconstitutional under the State Constitution, by the courts, the people, after an ample interval for

deliberation, shall have an opportunity to vote on the question whether they desire the Act to become law, notwithstanding such decision.

2. That every decision of the highest appellate court of a State declaring an Act of the Legislature unconstitutional on the ground of its violation of the Federal Constitution shall be subject to the same review by the Supreme Court of the United States as is now accorded to decisions sustaining such legislation.

ADMINISTRATION OF JUSTICE

The Progressive party, in order to secure to the people a better administration of justice and by that means to bring about a more general respect for the law and the courts, pledges itself to work unceasingly for the reform of legal procedures and judicial methods.

We believe that the issuance of injunctions in cases arising out of labor disputes should be prohibited when such injunctions would not apply when no labor disputes existed.

We also believe that a person cited for contempt in labor disputes, except when such contempt was committed in the actual presence of the court or so near thereto as to interfere with the proper administration of justice, should have a right to trial by jury.

SOCIAL AND INDUSTRIAL JUSTICE

The supreme duty of the Nation is the conservation of human resources through an enlightened measure of social and industrial justice. We pledge ourselves to work unceasingly in State and Nation for:

Effective legislation looking to the prevention of industrial accidents, occupational diseases, overwork, involuntary unemployment, and other injurious effects incident to modern industry;

The fixing of minimum safety and health standards for the various occupations, and the exercise of the public authority of State and Nation, including the Federal Control over interstate commerce, and the taxing power, to maintain such standards;

The prohibition of child labor;

Minimum wage standards for working women, to provide a "living wage" in all industrial occupations;

The general prohibition of night work for women and the establishment of an eight hour day for women and young persons;

One day's rest in seven for all wage workers;

The eight hour day in continuous twenty-four-hour industries;

The abolition of the convict contract labor system; substituting a system of prison production for governmental consumption only; and the application of prisoners' earnings to the support of their dependent families;

Publicity as to wages, hours and conditions of labor;

full reports upon industrial accidents and diseases, and the opening to public inspection of all tallies, weights, measures and check systems on labor products;

Standards of compensation for death by industrial accident and injury and trade disease which will transfer the burden of lost earnings from the families of working people to the industry, and thus to the community;

The protection of home life against the hazards of sickness, irregular employment and old age through the adoption of a system of social insurance adapted to American use;

The development of the creative labor power of America by lifting the last load of illiteracy from American youth and establishing continuation schools for industrial education under public control and encouraging agricultural education and demonstration in rural schools;

The establishment of industrial research laboratories to put the methods and discoveries of science at the service of American producers;

We favor the organization of the workers, men and women, as a means of protecting their interests and of promoting their progress. . . .

BUSINESS

We believe that true popular government, justice and prosperity go hand in hand, and, so believing, it is our purpose to secure that large measure of general prosperity which is the fruit of legitimate and honest business, fostered by equal justice and by sound progressive laws.

We demand that the test of true prosperity shall be the benefits conferred thereby on all the citizens, not confined to individuals or classes, and that the test of corporate efficiency shall be the ability better to serve the public; that those who profit by control of business affairs shall justify that profit and that control by sharing with the public the fruits thereof.

We therefore demand a strong National regulation of inter-State corporations. The corporation is an essential part of modern business. The concentration of modern business, in some degree, is both inevitable and necessary for national and international business efficiency. But the existing concentration of vast wealth under a corporate system, unguarded and uncontrolled by the Nation, has placed in the hands of a few men enormous, secret, irresponsible power over the daily life of the citizen—a power insufferable in a free Government and certain of abuse.

This power has been abused, in monopoly of National resources, in stock watering, in unfair competition and unfair privileges, and finally in sinister influences on the public agencies of State and Nation. We do not fear commercial power, but we insist that it shall be exercised openly, under publicity, supervision and regulation of the most efficient sort, which will preserve its good while eradicating and preventing its ill.

To that end we urge the establishment of a strong Federal administrative commission of high standing, which shall maintain permanent active supervision over industrial corporations engaged in inter-State commerce, or such of them as are of public importance, doing for them what the Government now does for the National banks, and what is now done for the railroads by the Inter-State Commerce Commission.

Such a commission must enforce the complete publicity of those corporation transactions which are of public interest; must attack unfair competition, false capitalization and special privilege, and by continuous trained watchfulness guard and keep open equally all the highways of American commerce.

Thus the business man will have certain knowledge of the law, and will be able to conduct his business easily in conformity therewith; the investor will find security for his capital; dividends will be rendered more certain, and the savings of the people will be drawn naturally and safely into the channels of trade.

Under such a system of constructive regulation, legitimate business, freed from confusion, uncertainty and fruitless litigation, will develop normally in response to the energy and enterprise of the American business man.

We favor strengthening the Sherman Law by prohibiting agreement to divide territory or limit output; refusing to sell to customers who buy from business rivals; to sell below cost in certain areas while maintaining higher prices in other places; using the power of transportation to aid or injure special business concerns; and other unfair trade practices.

Questions

1. Why would a political party insist on making a covenant with voters? What does this "covenant" suggest about the way progressives viewed themselves and politics?
2. How does this platform propose to change the courts?
3. What does the section on social and industrial justice indicate about the United States in 1912?

21-10 Louis D. Brandeis in Defense of Competition (1912)

Born in Virginia and raised in the South, Woodrow Wilson came naturally to a Democratic ideology that stressed the virtues of the common people and the free market (see text pp. 670–673). Both ideas thrived below the Mason-Dixon Line. Those beliefs were reinforced by Louis D. Brandeis (1856–1941), a famous lawyer and reformer who served as a Wilson campaign adviser (see text p. 671). Brandeis authored his defense of competition in 1912.

His comment on the "crimes of trade-union leaders" refers to a 1911 bombing of the offices of the *Los Angeles Times* that left twenty dead. Two labor activists, the brothers James and John McNamara, were convicted for their roles in the explosion.

Source: "Shall We Abandon the Policy of Competition?" from *The Curse of Bigness: Miscellaneous Papers* by Louis D. Brandeis; Osmond K. Fraenkel, editor. Copyright 1934 by Louis D. Brandeis; renewed © 1962 by Susan Brandeis Gilbert and Elizabeth Brandeis Raushenbush. Used by permission of Viking Penguin, a division of Penguin Books USA Inc. (In reprint edition, Port Washington, N.Y.: Kennikat Press, 1965, pp. 104–108.)

Shall we abandon as obsolete the long-cherished policy of competition, and accept in its place the long-detested policy of monopoly? The issue is not (as it is usually stated by advocates of monopoly), "Shall we have unrestricted competition or regulated monopoly?" It is, "Shall we have regulated competition or regulated monopoly?"

Regulation is essential to the preservation and development of competition, just as it is necessary to the preservation and best development of liberty. We have long curbed physically the strong, to protect those physically weaker. More recently we have extended such prohibitions to business. We have restricted theoretical freedom of contract by factory laws. The liberty of the merchant and manufacturer to lie in trade, expressed in the fine phrase of *caveat emptor* [let the buyer beware], is yielding to the better conceptions of business ethics, before pure-food laws and postal-fraud prosecutions. Similarly, the right to competition must be limited in order to preserve it. For excesses of competition lead to monopoly, as excesses of liberty lead to absolutism. The extremes meet.

The issue, therefore, is: Regulated competition *versus* regulated monopoly. The policy of regulated competition is distinctly a constructive policy. It is the policy of development as distinguished from the destructive policy of private monopoly.

It is asserted that to persist in the disintegration of existing unlawful trusts is to pursue a policy of destruction. No statement could be more misleading. Progress demands that we remove the obstacles in the path of progress; and private monopoly is the most serious obstacle.

One has heard of late the phrases: "You can't make people compete by law." "Artificial competition is undesirable."

These are truisms, but their implication is false. The suggestion is not that traders be compelled to compete, but that they be prevented from killing competition. Equally misleading is the phrase, "Natural monopolies should not be interfered with." There are no natural monopolies today in the industrial world. The Oil Trust and the Steel Trust have been referred to as natural monopolies, but they are both most unnatural. The Oil Trust acquired its control of the market by conduct which involved flagrant violations of law. Without the aid of criminal rebating, of bribery and corruption, the Standard Oil would never have acquired the vast wealth and power which enabled it to destroy its small competitors by price-cutting and similar practices.

The Steel Trust acquired control not through greater efficiency, but by buying up existing plants and ore supplies at fabulous prices. It is believed that not a single industrial monopoly exists today which is the result of natural growth. Competition has been suppressed either by ruthless practices or by an improper use of inordinate wealth and power. . . .

The only argument that has been seriously advanced in favor of private monopoly is that competition involves waste, while the monopoly prevents waste and leads to efficiency. This argument is essentially unsound. The wastes of competition are negligible. The economies of monopoly are superficial and delusive. The efficiency of monopoly is at the best temporary.

Undoubtedly competition involves waste. What human activity does not? The wastes of democracy are among the greatest obvious wastes, but we have compensations in democracy which far outweigh that waste and make it more efficient than absolutism. So it is with competition. The waste is relatively insignificant. There are wastes of competition which do not develop, but kill. These the law can and should eliminate, by regulating competition.

It is true that the unit in business may be too small to be efficient. It is also true that the unit may be too large to be efficient, and this is no uncommon incident of monopoly.

Whenever trusts have developed efficiency, their fruits have been absorbed almost wholly by the trusts themselves. From such efficiency as they have developed, the community has gained substantially nothing.

The proposed Government commission to fix prices would not greatly relieve the evils attendant upon monopoly. It might reduce a trust's profits, but it would fail to reduce the trust's prices; because the limitation of the monopoly's profits would, by lessening this incentive, surely reduce the monopoly's efficiency.

To secure successful management of any private business, reward must be proportionate to success. The establishment of any rule fixing a maximum return on capital would, by placing a limit upon the fruits of achievement, tend to lessen efficiency.

No selling price for monopoly products could be set constitutionally at a point lower than that which would allow a reasonable return on capital. And in the absence of comparative data from any competing businesses producing the same article at less cost, it would be virtually impossible to determine that the cost should be lower.

The success of the Interstate Commerce Commission has been invoked as an argument in favor of licensing and regulating monopoly.

But the Interstate Commerce Commission has been effective principally in preventing rate increases and in stopping discrimination. In those instances where the Commission has reduced rates (as distinguished from preventing increases) the Commission rested its decisions largely on the ground that existing rates amount to discriminations against particular places or articles, or the lower rates were justified by a comparison with other rates of the same or other companies. Price-fixing of that nature applied to industrial thrusts would afford little protection to the public.

In the second place, there is a radical difference between attempts to fix rates for transportation and similar public services, and fixing prices in industrial businesses. Problems of transportation, while varying infinitely in detail, are largely the same throughout the whole country, and they are largely the same yesterday, today, and tomorrow. In industry we have, instead of uniformity, infinite variety; instead of stability, constant change.

In the third place, the problems of the Interstate Commerce Commission, relatively simple as they are, already far exceed the capacity of that or any single board. Think of the infinite questions which would come before an industrial commission seeking to fix rates, and the suffering of the community from the inability of that body promptly and efficiently to dispose of them.

Every business requires for its business health the *memento mori* [reminder of mortality] of competition from without. It requires likewise a certain competition from within, which can exist only where the ownership and management, on the one hand, and the employees, on the other, shall each be alert, hopeful, self-respecting, and free to work out for themselves the best conceivable conditions.

The successful, the powerful trusts, have created conditions absolutely inconsistent with these—America's—industrial and social needs. It may be true that as a legal proposition mere size is not a crime, but mere size may become an industrial and social menace, because it frequently creates as against possible competitors and as against the employees conditions of such gross inequality, as to imperil the welfare of the employees and of the industry.

In the midst of our indignation over the unpardonable crimes of trade-union leaders, disclosed at Los Angeles, would not our statesmen and thinkers seek to ascertain the underlying cause of this widespread, deliberate outburst of crimes of violence? What was it that led men like the McNamaras to believe really that the only recourse they had for improving the condition of the wage-earner was to use dynamite against property and life?

Certainly it was not individual depravity. Was it not because they, and men like them, believed that the wage-earner, acting singly, or collectively, is not strong enough to secure substantial justice? Is there not a causal connection between the development of these huge indomitable trusts and the horrible crimes now under investigation? Are not these irresistible trusts important contributing causes of these crimes—these unintelligent expressions of despairing social unrest? Is it not irony to speak of the equality of opportunity, in a country cursed with their bigness?

The right of labor to organize and to deal collectively with its employers should not be curtailed.

There is not the slightest danger that labor will assume control of industry. It has become exceedingly difficult for the unions to maintain themselves because of the constant inflow of foreign labor and the great number of non-union men. This maintains a state of competition, which, did it exist in the industrial and financial business of the country, would make unnecessary any change in existing laws.

The only right claimed by the labor unions is that of collective bargaining, and this right employers also should have and exercise. It would be perfectly proper for independent competing employers to form employers' organizations, and to deal with the labor unions upon exactly the same footing as is the case with unions—that is, collectively.

Nothing has been done to improve the conditions under which men labor, that has not increased their efficiency. Shorter hours often lead to greater production; and there is economy in high wages.

Questions

1. How does Brandeis counter the argument that some monopolies are inevitable or natural?
2. Why does he support competition instead of monopoly?
3. What are his views on organized labor?

Questions for Further Thought

1. What would Jane Addams (Document 21-5) find appealing in Theodore Roosevelt's speech on social justice (Document 21-8) and in the Progressive party's platform (Document 21-9)?
2. How do Progressive Era politicians such as Robert La Follette (Document 21-4) and Theodore Roosevelt differ from their counterparts today?
3. Where was the argument about regulation versus competition stronger, in the Progressive platform or in Louis Brandeis's statement (Document 21-10)? Why?

CHAPTER 22

An Emerging World Power 1877–1914

★　　　★　　　★

The Roots of Expansionism

Many aspects of nineteenth-century American foreign policy were isolationist (see text p. 678). Between 1814 and 1898, the United States avoided war with European nations and American secretaries of state heeded George Washington's warning against entangling alliances (see Document 7-10). However, an active foreign policy did exist: the Louisiana and Alaska purchases, relations with Mexico, and the status of native American tribes were important issues.

By the 1890s a far more ambitious American foreign policy was evolving. The change reflected the status of the United States as an emerging economic power. By the turn of the century American factory, oil, and steel products were competing for a share of the world market. The republic whose citizens had once made clothes at home was selling sewing machines worldwide (see illustration on text p. 680). The republic that under Thomas Jefferson had all but abandoned its navy had begun an ambitious naval buildup by the century's end.

However, economic strength brought its own set of problems. Americans soon discovered that the modern world did not respond well to the counsel of eighteenth-century leaders, especially if the United States wanted to be a world power. Stepping onto the world stage meant answering a series of difficult questions: How was a democracy to act as a world power? What was the proper mix of self-interest and principle in foreign policy? Should the United States control overseas possessions, especially if the native peoples resisted? Both the American public and its leaders struggled over the answers as applied to Latin America, the Philippines, Cuba, Puerto Rico, and Hawaii (see text pp. 682–684).

Document 22-1, a letter from Secretary of State James G. Blaine to President Benjamin Harrison, suggests the awakening of American diplomacy in 1890. In Document 22-2 Grace Service recounts her life as an American missionary in China. Alfred

Thayer Mahan's treatise on sea power (Document 22-3) challenges the assumptions of a society long suspicious of the military. Document 22-4 presents the Reverend Josiah Strong's argument for the justness—and inevitability—of an American empire.

22-1 American Diplomacy Revitalized (1890)

James G. Blaine

History is as much a product of the mundane as of the exceptional. The letter reprinted here does not involve critical treaty negotiations or an attempt to avoid war; it is simply a note about posting another diplomat to certain small Central American countries. However, to a historian it provides evidence that the United States was revitalizing its diplomatic corps in the 1880s and 1890s. Secretary of State James G. Blaine served under Presidents James Garfield and Benjamin Harrison and championed Pan-Americanism, or closer relations among the nations of the Americas (see text p. 679).

Source: Secretary of State James G. Blaine to President Benjamin Harrison, August 16, 1890, in Albert T. Volwiler, ed., *The Correspondence between Benjamin Harrison and James G. Blaine, 1882–1893* (Philadelphia: American Philosophical Society, 1940), pp. 116–117.

Bar Harbor, Me. August 16, 1890.

Confidential

Mr President:

I respectfully submit the following note of explanation and of recommendation.

Formerly, this Government sent a Minister to each of the five States of Central America—and this at a period when our relations with those States were far less intimate and important than they have become of late years.

It was finally considered extravagant to send so many Ministers to so small an area, and the number was reduced to one for the five States. It has been found, of late years, almost impossible for one Minister to properly represent the interests of the United States in that region. Guatemala being the largest State and the most considerable in population and wealth, is naturally the headquarters of the Minister. From that point he can readily attend to all matters in Honduras and in San Salvador; but it is next to impossible that he can properly represent this Government's interests in Nicaragua and Costa Rica. Central America is naturally divided in its political relations, into the two groups—three in the northern section and two in the southern. Our relations in connection with the Inter-Oceanic Canal, growing daily more important, are wholly confined to Nicaragua and to Costa Rica. A Minister for those two countries is imperatively needed. Without his presence our interests constantly suffer, with the possibility of great embarrassments suddenly arising.

I respectfully recommend, therefore, that you nominate to the Senate a Minister for Nicaragua and Costa Rica—renominating Mr Mizner for Guatemala, Honduras and San Salvador. They should be of equal rank and pay—Ministers Plenipotentiary, with the salary each of $7,500 per annum. This conclusion has been in my mind for more than a year, but the disturbed and critical condition of the northern States of Central America has strikingly enforced it within the last month.

If this recommendation shall meet with your favor, I will at once submit to you the names of several persons from whom a proper selection may be made within your discretion; or very probably you may have a proper man in your mind, without suggestion from me.

I am, with great respect

Your obedient servant

Questions

1. What had been the diplomatic arrangement for the region?
2. Why were there so few American diplomats in the countries discussed?
3. How did Blaine argue for an expanded diplomatic presence?

22-2 "Open House Days" for a China Missionary (1905)

Grace Service

China has long fascinated Americans as a market for either souls or products (see text pp. 681–682); Grace (1879–1954) and Robert (1879–1935) Service devoted themselves to the former. The Services were a college-educated couple who in 1905 volunteered to work in China for the Young Men's Christian Association. They spent the rest of their lives in China. It would be the land that welcomed their three sons just as it claimed the life of their infant daughter.

Grace Service's memoirs were edited by her son John, whose career as a China specialist for the State Department became a victim of the witch-hunts of Senator Joseph McCarthy (see Document 28-8).

Source: John S. Service, ed., *Golden Inches: The China Memoir of Grace Service*, pp. 67–75. Copyright © 1989 by the Regents of the University of California. Reprinted by permission of the University of California Press.

When we left Kiating that September we hired a cargo boat with a high *peng* (a rounded mat roof) and a good wooden floor. The Boy had gone with us as cook to Golden Summit and did so well that we now discharged the dirty cook at Kiating, giving him travel money. The hold of our boat was loaded with loose dried beans which looked to be a clean and non-odorous cargo. We put all our things on the floor level, and the boat was large enough to give plenty of room and, best of all, good head space. Our teacher was with us on the boat and we studied as we traveled. We could even sit at our new desk to study and write. The trip to Chengtu was expected to take about a week.

The floods that summer had caused damage along the river and we saw signs on every hand. Once, walking on the bank, we noticed tangled vines above our heads in tree branches. These were peanut vines that had been washed out of the fields and lodged in the trees. Even at Chengtu the river had covered the big stone bridge outside the South Gate. Close to this place, a big section of the city wall had been undermined (and took many months to repair). But, despite the summer flood, the river was now rather low for that time of the year—and our boat was large.

Life was very pleasant for the first two or three days, and we congratulated ourselves on the size and comfort of our craft. Then trouble began. At first we found only a few tiny white worms. In a few hours they had multiplied and were into everything: food boxes, beds, clothing, even into our ears when we took refuge tucked tightly inside a bed net. The little worms were everywhere. Complaints to the captain were useless; worms meant nothing to him. We then tried to hurry the boat, but its draft was considerable and the river seemed to be falling. We could only proceed by the main channel and frequently had to wait for other boats to negotiate narrow spots. After a couple of days of worms, we began to have a pest of little white moths. The

worms were busying themselves in their life cycle under our very eyes. These tiny blundering creatures flew everywhere, and our tempers were decidedly on edge.

I began to feel that we would never reach Chengtu, and the eternal singsong of Bob repeating Chinese phrases after his teacher's intoned speech made me weary beyond words. To be honest, I was probably as much of a trial to live with as the worms and moths! Bob suggested that from a village about a hundred *li* from Chengtu, I could reach the city in a day in my chair, the Boy escorting me. But when we reached the village that evening, it was impossible to find chair men. Next morning it was raining, which ruled out the possibility of making the trip in one day even if bearers could be found. So I settled down to sticking it out on the bean boat. We had still more trouble, having to lighten cargo at one place where the channel was shallow and the current swift. We did not reach Chengtu until the next Tuesday. Then there was a joyous farewell to that nice, clean boat full of its worms and moths with whom we had spent eleven unforgettable days.

We were delighted to reach our Chinese home again. A quick check showed that the robbers had taken practically all my table linen as well as some other things. Otherwise all was in good order. A few days of scrubbing, washing windows, hanging clean curtains, and changing shelf and drawer papers made us as clean and fresh as could be. I liked the new desk very much and had it set up in our living room, where it became my special possession and delight. Bob had a large Chinese desk of red bean wood in his study, so he did not need it. My new desk was of what was called "buried nanmu." It had a large flat top. On each side above the table top were six small drawers. Between these stacks an open space was just right for a row of books. Below on either side were tiers of large drawers. Many and many a letter I wrote on that desk, and many that I received were stowed inside.

That fall we studied, and continued to widen our acquaintances among Chinese. Bob spent much time and thought making plans and establishing contacts with people. An advisory committee was formed as a preliminary step toward the organization of a full-fledged YMCA. Sunday afternoon meetings were held, sometimes at our house, sometimes at the Hodgkins'.

I was still miserable with my severe pain and suffered exceedingly with backaches which wore me out. My cook could not make good bread, and there were no bakeries whatsoever. The bread, rolls, cakes, and cookies all had to come from my hands. For ourselves alone, this was not much; but we entertained Chinese constantly, and they were all pleased to have foreign-style refreshments. Late that year I finally got our new cook, who had been our Boy at Omei, trained to make acceptable cookies and cupcakes. This was a great help. Tea had always to be served to our guests. If they did not eat the cakes served with it, these were gladly pocketed to be taken home to a small brother or sister, to children, or even to a mother interested in sampling the odd things served by the Westerners.

About that time we rented a piece of land at the rear of the Methodist school adjacent to us on the west. It belonged to the mission but was then not needed. It gave us space for two tennis courts with a tea pavilion west of them in the shadow of a high wall. There was also some ground left over for raising vegetables. Eventually we enjoyed many products of our own garden.

Our young friends among Chinese students began to ask if I would call on their families or be at home to receive calls from them. Doors thus opened in both directions, and we became deeply involved in our surroundings. I began to teach English to a few young men. At first my work was individual instruction in conversation and composition. Our careful attention was given to the young man who was later to become the first Chinese YMCA secretary in Chengtu. In 1907 I did not keep a careful record of the guests at special teas we had for Chinese students, but I know the total ran into 600 or 700. For 1908 I did keep a weekly record. It gives a total of 967 as counted. However, on numerous occasions we were not able to count late comers, so our figures would read "42 plus" and so on. Also these records showed only those who came to our regular, announced teas. Bob had many individual callers in both those years; in 1908 he doubtless entertained well over 1,200. These contacts were valuable to him and gave me considerable to oversee and manage.

When Chinese women called, I had to drop everything. They often came at inopportune times for us, as Chinese meal hours were not the same as ours, and they would stay and stay and stay. To come at ten in the forenoon, or even around noon, and then sit until three in the afternoon was asking a good deal of a hostess, but we had to conform to the habits of the country. A lady often brought a whole train of attendants: perhaps a sister or two, several grown daughters or younger children, and often four or five amahs. The guests sat down to visit, and the servants stood around gazing at everything and being what one might call movable fixtures in the room. It took me a long time to accustom myself to these calls. Gradually I learned the technique, and despite my lack of adequate language could carry them off with some sort of aplomb. I learned the polite phrases, and could fall back on the children and stock questions. Eventually, some of the women became my real friends, so that barriers no longer made such a chasm between us.

All women guests wanted to see our entire house. Most of them, if they expressed any opinion, thought we wasted too much time trying to be clean: clean kitchens and clean floors were no necessity to them. When I visited their homes, I was impressed by the dirty kitchens and their lack of any adequate attention to the floors. Their kitchens were in what we would call sheds. Most of their floors were dingy brick or grimy wood. Frequent expectoration, together with the habit of allowing babies to urinate freely on the floor anywhere and everywhere, made for unhygienic conditions and offensive odors. Cobwebs never seemed to bother Chinese; to this day I have to call servants' attention to them. Upper walls and ceiling spaces seem never to come within range of the Chinese eye; special orders must be given if you want to be sure that high corners will be cleaned. On the other hand, Chinese take great care in polishing the flat top and side surfaces of furniture such as cupboards and sideboards; and a Boy will carefully dust framed pictures every day, sometimes even dusting behind them.

Another of my household duties at this time was my husband's collars. Men were still wearing stiff collars every day. It seemed impossible for the Chinese to get them stiff enough, or to keep from scorching them during the ironing. And there were no tailors in these early years who knew anything about "foreign-style" sewing. So what sewing I needed, I also did myself, by hand and machine. I sent for American patterns and made clothes as I could, studying the illustrations of magazines and inspecting the clothes of new arrivals from home. It was my boast that I could cut out a man's shirt one evening and have it finished, save buttonholes, by the next afternoon. I learned to stitch such pieces without any basting and thus could save time. I taught my amah to do buttonholes. Her first attempts were what my New England grandmother would have called "pigs' eyes," but Amah improved and became a fine buttonholer.

I was busy during these early Chengtu days. Often I rose at 6:30 in the morning to work down my bread. Then there was study, sewing, and general housekeeping. This could include a lot of mold prevention, and packing away all woolens and winter things at the approach of hot weather. Dry cleaners were unheard of, and laundry work demanded much attention and training of servants. It is quite a task to do up men's white summer suits, be they duck, silk, serge, or flannel. I found the Szechwanese to be good washers but poor rinsers. It was my rule to demand ample water for that use. By this means I kept our clothes from taking on that dull, muddy tinge which many housewives regard as one of the prices of living in the Orient.

Late in 1907 the West China Missionary Conference was impending, and I was determined to find a Boy who could be wide-awake and efficient. I interviewed several prospects without success. At last a young fellow named Liu Pei-yun appeared. I had never wanted a country boy, because it seemed to me that some education, however little, would hold more potential for training. This boy was the son of a buyer of silk yarn. He could read and write and was an apt pupil in learning the work expected from him. On arrival he knew nothing whatsoever of any foreign furnishings or usages. When I first showed him how to set the table, he asked what the forks were and how they were used! He became a trusted servant, was married in our home, and worked for us from the fall of 1907 until that of 1920. Bob then helped him set up a business for himself in Chengtu. In later years he visited us several times in Shanghai and has always kept up connection with our family. . . .

The American community grew slowly. Late in 1907 another young Californian, C. W. Batdorf [UC 1906], had come to teach in the government university near us. He and Mr. Bullock [also UC 1906] kept bachelor's hall together. We were always glad to help them when we could; I made curtains, sheets, and such items for them. Early in 1908, Chee Soo Lowe, a California-born Chinese who had graduated in mining from the University of California [still another member of 1906], came to investigate the mineral resources of Szechwan under employment by the viceroy. He was often in our home and we greatly enjoyed him.

As the Chinese ladies became less bashful I began to have more callers. Many of them besought me to start some sort of classes for them. They wanted to "learn foreign ways," to knit, crochet, and even to bake the light cakes which they ate in our homes. We were constantly invited to Chinese feasts. Here the procedure is the reverse of our custom. Chinese socializing is done before the meal, and the guests leave directly from the table. This meant that we often sat talking while the very food we were to eat was in preparation. We might hear the fowls squawking as they were chased and killed to be served to us later. The men and women always ate in separate rooms: the men in the main hall or some such public apartment, while we women were relegated to women's bedrooms. I was teaching a few pupils and kept busy in spite of not being well. I still had my attacks of severe pain now and then and was forced to spend a good many days in bed.

Questions

1. What conditions did the Services encounter?
2. How does Grace Service characterize the Chinese people?
3. Why would a Westerner tend to feel superior to the Chinese people in 1907–1908? Do the Services?

22-3 *The Influence of Sea Power upon History* (1890)

Alfred Thayer Mahan

Except in times of war, Americans have never favored the establishment of a large, standing military force. The navy, for example, was greatly expanded during the Civil War, only to deteriorate over the next twenty-five years. To the naval officer Alfred T. Mahan (1840–1914), the situation had to be reversed if the United States was to become a true world power. Mahan's *The Influence of Sea Power upon History, 1660–1783* appeared in 1890 and had an enormous influence on U.S. foreign policy (see text pp. 682–683). Before the end of the decade the U.S. navy had modernized to the point where it easily defeated its Spanish counterpart.

Source: Alfred Thayer Mahan, *The Influence of Sea Power upon History, 1660–1783* (Boston: Little, Brown, 1890), pp. 83–89.

As the practical object of this inquiry is to draw from the lessons of history inferences applicable to one's own country and service, it is proper now to ask how far the conditions of the United States involve serious danger, and call for action on the part of the government, in order to build again her sea power. It will not be too much to say that the action of the government since the Civil War, and up to this day, has been effectively directed solely to what has been called the first link in the chain which makes sea power. Internal development, great production, with the accompanying aim and boast of self-sufficingness, such has been the object, such to some extent the result. In this the government has faithfully reflected the bent of the controlling elements of the country, though it is not always easy to feel that such controlling elements are truly representative, even in a free country. However that may be, there is no doubt that, besides having no colonies, the intermediate link of a peaceful shipping, and the interests involved in it, are now likewise lacking. In short, the United States has only one link of the three.

The circumstances of naval war have changed so much within the last hundred years, that it may be doubted whether such disastrous effects on the one hand, or such brilliant prosperity on the other, as were seen in the wars between England and France, could now recur. In her secure and haughty sway of the seas England imposed a yoke on neutrals which will never again be borne; and the principle that the flag covers the goods is forever secured. The commerce of a belligerent can therefore now be safely carried on in neutral ships, except when contraband of war or to blockaded ports; and as regards the latter, it is also certain that there will be no more paper blockades. Putting aside therefore the question of defending her seaports from capture or contribution, as to which there is practical unanimity in theory and entire indifference in practice, what need has the United States of sea power? Her commerce is even now carried on by others; why should her people desire that which, if possessed, must be defended at great cost? So far as this question is economical, it is outside the scope of this work; but conditions which may entail suffering and loss on the country by war are directly pertinent to it. Granting therefore that the foreign trade of the United States, going and coming, is on board ships which an enemy cannot touch except when bound to a blockaded port, what will constitute an efficient blockade? The present definition is, that it is such as to constitute a manifest danger to a vessel seeking to enter or leave the port. This is evidently very elastic. Many can remember that during the Civil War, after a night attack on the United States fleet off Charleston, the Confederates next morning sent out a steamer with some foreign consuls on board, who so far satisfied themselves that no blockading vessel was in sight that they issued a declaration to that effect. On the strength of this declaration some Southern authorities

claimed that the blockade was technically broken, and could not be technically re-established without a new notification. Is it necessary, to constitute a real danger to blockade runners, that the blockading fleet should be in sight? Half a dozen fast steamers, cruising twenty miles off-shore between the New Jersey and Long Island coast, would be a very real danger to ships seeking to go in or out by the principal entrance to New York; and similar positions might effectively blockade Boston, the Delaware, and the Chesapeake. The main body of the blockading fleet, prepared not only to capture merchant-ships but to resist military attempts to break the blockade, need not be within sight, nor in a position known to the shore. The bulk of Nelson's fleet was fifty miles from Cadiz two days before Trafalgar, with a small detachment watching close to the harbor. The allied fleet began to get under way at 7 A.M., and Nelson, even under the conditions of those days, knew it by 9.30. The English fleet at that distance was a very real danger to its enemy. It seems possible, in these days of submarine telegraphs, that the blockading forces in-shore and off-shore, and from one port to another, might be in telegraphic communication with one another along the whole coast of the United States, readily giving mutual support; and if, by some fortunate military combination, one detachment were attacked in force, it could warn the others and retreat upon them. Granting that such a blockade off one port were broken on one day, by fairly driving away the ships maintaining it, the notification of its being re-established could be cabled all over the world the next. To avoid such blockades there must be a military force afloat that will at all times so endanger a blockading fleet that it can by no means keep its place. Then neutral ships, except those laden with contraband of war, can come and go freely, and maintain the commercial relations of the country with the world outside.

It may be urged that, with the extensive sea-coast of the United States, a blockade of the whole line cannot be effectively kept up. No one will more readily concede this than officers who remember how the blockade of the Southern coast alone was maintained. But in the present condition of the navy, and, it may be added, with any additions not exceeding those so far proposed by the government, the attempt to blockade Boston, New York, the Delaware, the Chesapeake, and the Mississippi, in other words, the great centres of export and import, would not entail upon one of the large maritime nations efforts greater than have been made before. England has at the same time blockaded Brest, the Biscay coast, Toulon, and Cadiz, when there were powerful squadrons lying within the harbors. It is true that commerce in neutral ships can then enter other ports of the United States than those named; but what a dislocation of the carrying traffic of the country, what failure of supplies at times, what inadequate means of transport by rail or water, of dockage, of lighterage, of warehousing, will be involved in such an enforced change of the ports of entry! Will there be no money loss, no suffering, consequent upon this? And when with much pain and expense these evils have been partially remedied, the enemy may be led to stop the new inlets as he did the old. The people of the United States will certainly not starve, but they may suffer grievously. As for supplies which are contraband of war, is there not reason to fear that the United States is not now able to go alone if an emergency should arise?

The question is eminently one in which the influence of the government should make itself felt, to build up for the nation a navy which, if not capable of reaching distant countries, shall at least be able to keep clear the chief approaches to its own. The eyes of the country have for a quarter of a century been turned from the sea; the results of such a policy and of its opposite will be shown in the instance of France and of England. Without asserting a narrow parallelism between the case of the United States and either of these, it may safely be said that it is essential to the welfare of the whole country that the conditions of trade and commerce should remain, as far as possible, unaffected by an external war. In order to do this, the enemy must be kept not only out of our ports, but far away from our coasts.[1]

Can this navy be had without restoring the merchant shipping? It is doubtful. History has proved that such a purely military sea power can be built up by a despot, as was done by Louis XIV.; but though so fair seeming, experience showed that his navy was like a growth which

having no root soon withers away. But in a representative government any military expenditure must have a strongly represented interest behind it, convinced of its necessity. Such an interest in sea power does not exist, cannot exist here without action by the government. How such a merchant shipping should be built up, whether by subsidies or by free trade, by constant administration of tonics or by free movement in the open air, is not a military but an economical question. Even had the United States a great national shipping, it may be doubted whether a sufficient navy would follow; the distance which separates her from other great powers, in one way a protection, is also a snare. The motive, if any there be, which will give the United States a navy, is probably now quickening in the Central American Isthmus. Let us hope it will not come to the birth too late.

Here concludes the general discussion of the principal elements which affect, favorably or unfavorably, the growth of sea power in nations. The aim has been, first to consider those elements in their natural tendency for or against, and then to illustrate by particular examples and by the experience of the past. Such discussions, while undoubtedly embracing a wider field, yet fall mainly within the province of strategy, as distinguished from tactics. The considerations and principles which enter into them belong to the unchangeable, or unchanging, order of things, remaining the same, in cause and effect, from age to age. They belong, as it were, to the Order of Nature, of whose stability so much is heard in our day; whereas tactics, using as its instruments the weapons made by man, shares in the change and progress of the race from generation to generation. From time to time the superstructure of tactics has to be altered or wholly torn down; but the old foundations of strategy so far remain, as though laid upon a rock. There will next be examined the general history of Europe and America, with particular reference to the effect exercised upon that history, and upon the welfare of the people, by sea power in its broad sense. From time to time, as occasion offers, the aim will be to recall and reinforce the general teaching, already elicited, by particular illustrations. The general tenor of the study will therefore be strategical, in that broad definition of naval strategy which has before been quoted and accepted: "Naval strategy has for its end to found , support, and increase, as well in peace as in war, the sea power of a country." In the matter of particular battles, while freely admitting that the change of details has made obsolete much of their teaching, the attempt will be made to point out where the application or neglect of true general principles has produced decisive effects; and, other things being equal, those actions will be preferred which, from their association with the names of the most distinguished officers, may be presumed to show how far just tactical ideas obtained in a particular age or a particular service. It will also be desirable, where analogies between ancient and modern weapons appear on the surface,

---

[1] The word "defence" in war involves two ideas, which for the sake of precision in thought should be kept separated in the mind. There is defence pure and simple, which strengthens itself and awaits attack. This may be called passive defence. On the other hand, there is a view of defence which asserts that safety for one's self, the real object of defensive preparation, is best secured by attacking the enemy. In the matter of sea-coast defence, the former method is exemplified by stationary fortifications, submarine mines, and generally all immobile works destined simply to stop an enemy if he tries to enter. The second method comprises all those means and weapons which do not wait for attack, but go to meet the enemy's fleet, whether it be but for a few miles, or whether to his own shores. Such a defence may seem to be really offensive war, but it is not; it becomes offensive only when its object of attack is changed from the enemy's fleet to the enemy's country. England defended her own coasts and colonies by stationing her fleets off the French ports, to fight the French fleet if it came out. The United States in the Civil War stationed her fleets off the Southern ports, not because she feared for her own, but to break down the Confederacy by isolation from the rest of the world, and ultimately by attacking the ports. The methods were the same; but the purpose in one case was defensive, in the other offensive.

The confusion of the two ideas leads to much unnecessary wrangling as to the proper sphere of army and navy in coast-defence. Passive defences belong to the army; everything that moves in the water to the navy, which has the prerogative of the offensive defence. If seamen are used to garrison forts, they become part of the land forces, as surely as troops, when embarked as part of the complement, become part of the sea forces.

to derive such probable lessons as they offer, without laying undue stress upon the points of resemblance. Finally, it must be remembered that, among all changes, the nature of man remains much the same; the personal equation, though uncertain in quantity and quality in the particular instance, is sure always to be found.

Questions

1. According to Mahan, how could an enemy cripple American trade and commerce?
2. Why does he see this country's geographical isolation from other powerful nations as both a strength and a weakness?
3. In general, what is Mahan's view of history?

22-4 America in the World's Future (1886)

Josiah Strong

The interests of the Reverend Josiah Strong ranged from the cities (see Document 20-4) to foreign policy. In this excerpt from *Our Country*, Strong blends religion with a sense of Anglo-Saxon superiority to portray America's coming greatness. Like other observers of his time, Strong invoked Social Darwinism (see text pp. 589–590 and Document 19-2). He was not alone in arguing that nations, too, evolve through a process of natural selection. Others making that case included Brooks Adams and John Fiske (see text p. 684).

Source: Josiah Strong, *Our Country* (1886; reprint, edited by Jurgen Herbst, Cambridge, Mass.: Harvard University Press, 1963), pp. 210, 212–216.

Mr. Darwin is not only disposed to see, in the superior vigor of our people, an illustration of his favorite theory of natural selection, but even intimates that the world's history thus far has been simply preparatory for our future, and tributary to it. He says: "There is apparently much truth in the belief that the wonderful progress of the United States, as well as the character of the people, are the results of natural selection; for the most energetic, restless, and courageous men from all parts of Europe have emigrated during the last ten or twelve generations to that great country, and have there succeeded best. Looking at the distant future, I do not think that the Rev. Mr. Zincke takes an exaggerated view when he says: 'All other series of events—as that which resulted in the culture of mind in Greece, and that which resulted in the Empire of Rome—only appear to have purpose and value when viewed in connection with, or rather as subsidiary to, the great stream of Anglo-Saxon emigration to the West.'" . . .

Again, another marked characteristic of the Anglo-Saxon is what may be called an instinct or genius for colonizing. His unequaled energy, his indomitable persever-

ance, and his personal independence, made him a pioneer. He excels all others in pushing his way into new countries. It was those in whom this tendency was strongest that came to America, and this inherited tendency has been further developed by the westward sweep of successive generations across the continent. So noticeable has this characteristic become that English visitors remark it. Charles Dickens once said that the typical American would hesitate to enter heaven unless assured that he could go farther west.

Again, nothing more manifestly distinguished the Anglo-Saxon than his intense and persistent energy, and he is developing in the United States an energy which, in eager activity and effectiveness, is peculiarly American.

This is due partly to the fact that Americans are much better fed than Europeans, and partly to the undeveloped resources of a new country, but more largely to our climate, which acts as a constant stimulus. Ten years after the landing of the Pilgrims, the Rev. Francis Higginson, a good observer, wrote: "A sup of New England air is better than a whole flagon of English ale." Thus early had the stimulating effect of our climate been noted. Moreover, our social institutions are stimulating. In Europe the various ranks of society are, like the strata of the earth, fixed and fossilized. There can be no great change without a terrible upheaval, a social earthquake. Here society is like the waters of the sea, mobile . . . that which is at the bottom to-day may one day flash on the crest of the highest wave. Every one is free to become whatever he can make of himself; free to transform himself from a rail-splitter or a tanner or a canal-boy, into the nation's President. Our aristocracy, unlike that of Europe, is open to all comers. Wealth, position, influence, are prizes offered for energy; and every farmer's boy, every apprentice and clerk, every friendless and penniless immigrant, is free to enter the list. Thus many causes co-operate to produce here the most forceful and tremendous energy in the world.

What is the significance of such facts? These tendencies infold the future; they are the mighty alphabet with which God writes his prophecies. May we not, by a careful laying together of the letters, spell out something of his meaning? It seems to me that God, with infinite wisdom and skill, is training the Anglo-Saxon race for an hour sure to come in the world's future. Heretofore there has always been in the history of the world a comparatively unoccupied land westward, into which the crowded countries of the East have poured their surplus populations. But the widening waves of migration, which millenniums ago rolled east and west from the valley of the Euphrates, meet to-day on our Pacific coast. There are no more new worlds. The unoccupied arable lands of the earth are limited, and will soon be taken. The time is coming when the pressure of population on the means of subsistence will be felt here as it is now felt in Europe and Asia. Then will the world enter upon a new stage of its history—*the final competition of races, for which the Anglo-Saxon is being schooled.* Long before the thousand millions are here, the mighty *centrifugal* tendency, inherent in this stock and strengthened in the United States, will assert itself. Then the race of unequaled energy, with all the majesty of numbers and the might of wealth behind it—the representative, let us hope, of the largest liberty, the purest Christianity, the highest civilization—having developed peculiarly aggressive traits calculated to impress its institutions upon mankind, will spread itself over the earth. If I read not amiss, this powerful race will move down upon Mexico, down upon Central and South America, out upon the islands of the sea, over upon Africa and beyond. And can any one doubt that the result of this competition of races will be the "survival of the fittest"? "Any people," says Dr. Bushnell, "that is physiologically advanced in culture, though it be only in a degree beyond another which is mingled with it on strictly equal terms, is sure to live down and finally live out its inferior. Nothing can save the inferior race but a ready and pliant assimilation. Whether the feebler and more abject races are going to be regenerated and

raised up, is already very much of a question. What if it should be God's plan to people the world with better and finer material?

"Certain it is, whatever expectations we may indulge, that there is a tremendous overbearing surge of power in the Christian nations, which, if the others are not speedily raised to some vastly higher capacity, will inevitably submerge and bury them forever. These great populations of Christendom—what are they doing, but throwing out their colonies on every side, and populating themselves, if I may so speak, into the possession of all countries and climes?" To this result no war of extermination is needful; the contest is not one of arms, but of vitality and of civilization. "At the present day," says Mr. Darwin, "civilized nations are everywhere supplanting barbarous nations, excepting where the climate opposes a deadly barrier; and they succeed mainly, though not exclusively, through their arts, which are the products of the intellect." Thus the Finns were supplanted by the Aryan races in Europe and Asia, the Tartars by the Russians, and thus the aborigines of North America, Australia and New Zealand are now disappearing before the all-conquering Anglo-Saxons. It seems as if these inferior tribes were only precursors of a superior race, voices in the wilderness crying: "Prepare ye the way of the Lord!" The savage is a hunter; by the incoming of civilization the game is driven away and disappears before the hunter becomes a herder or an agriculturist. The savage is ignorant of many diseases of civilization which, when he is exposed to them, attack him before he learns how to treat them. Civilization also has its vices, of which the uninitiated savage is innocent. He proves an apt learner of vice, but dull enough in the school of morals.

Every civilization has its destructive and preservative elements. The Anglo-Saxon race would speedily decay but for the salt of Christianity. Bring savages into contact with our civilization, and its destructive forces become operative at once, while years are necessary to render effective the saving influences of Christian instruction. Moreover, the pioneer wave of our civilization carries with it more scum than salt. Where there is one missionary, there are hundreds of miners or traders or adventurers ready to debauch the native.

Whether the extinction of inferior races before the advancing Anglo-Saxon seems to the reader sad or otherwise, it certainly appears probable. I know of nothing except climatic conditions to prevent this race from populating Africa as it has peopled North America. And those portions of Africa which are unfavorable to Anglo-Saxon life are less extensive than was once supposed. The Dutch Boers, after two centuries of life there, are as hardy as any race on earth. The Anglo-Saxon has established himself in climates totally diverse—Canada, South Africa, and India—and, through several generations, has preserved his essential race characteristics. He is not, of course, superior to climatic influences; but even in warm climates, he is likely to retain his aggressive vigor long enough to supplant races already enfeebled. Thus, in what Dr. Bushnell calls "the out-populating power of the Christian stock," may be found God's final and complete solution of the dark problem of heathenism among many inferior peoples.

Some of the stronger races, doubtless, may be able to preserve their integrity; but, in order to compete with the Anglo-Saxon, they will probably be forced to adopt his methods and instruments, his civilization and his religion. Significant movements are now in progress among them. While the Christian religion was never more vital, or its hold upon the Anglo-Saxon mind stronger, there is taking place among the nations a widespread intellectual revolt against traditional beliefs. "In every corner of the world," says Mr. Froude, "there is the same phenomenon of the decay of established religions. . . . Among the Mohammedans, Jews, Buddhists, Brahmins, traditionary

creeds are losing their hold. An intellectual revolution is sweeping over the world, breaking down established opinions, dissolving foundations on which historical faiths have been built up." The contact of Christian with heathen nations is awakening the latter to new life. Old superstitions are loosening their grasp. The dead crust of fossil faiths is being shattered by the movements of life underneath. In Catholic countries, Catholicism is losing its influence over educated minds, and in some cases the masses have already lost all faith in it. Thus, while on this continent God is training the Anglo-Saxon race for its mission, a complemental work has been in progress in the great world beyond. God has two hands. Not only is he preparing in our civilization the die with which to stamp the nations, but, by what Southey called the "timing of Providence," he is preparing mankind to receive our impress.

Questions

1. How would you characterize Strong's version of Social Darwinism (see text p. 684)?
2. What kind of Christianity is he talking about?
3. What does Strong predict about the fate of peoples that encounter the United States as it expands?

Questions for Further Thought

1. Is there a direct connection between James G. Blaine's effort to modernize the State Department (Document 22-1) and Josiah Strong's call for an American empire (Document 22-4)? Why or why not?
2. How do the attitudes and experiences of Grace Service in China (Document 22-2) compare to those of Jane Addams in Chicago (Document 21-5)? Would they have considered themselves partners doing the same kind of work?
3. What might people in the Caribbean or Pacific find threatening in the arguments of Strong (Document 22-4)? Might they feel threatened by Service (Document 22-2)?
4. What do the writings of Alfred Mahan (Document 22-3) and Josiah Strong offer if taken together? Explain.

An American Empire

Throughout the nineteenth century Americans argued about the direction of foreign policy. Some people thought it should be guided by Manifest Destiny, or the belief that the United States was destined for greatness in an imperial sense (see text p. 684). Others insisted on a foreign policy based on mission, with the United States leading the rest of the world by setting a selfless example. Presidential administrations over the past century have occasionally embraced one of these extremes, but for the most part American foreign policy has been a not always successful mixture of the two.

Both tendencies were apparent with regard to Cuba in the 1890s. As described in the textbook (pp. 685, 688–689), Spain, once the greatest European power, had seen its empire reduced to a few islands, none of which were governed well. When Cuban nationalists demanded independence, Spanish officials responded with repression, and the United States took notice. The destruction of the battleship *Maine* in Havana's harbor made war inevitable (see text p. 688), but the United States seemed uncertain whether to free Cuba or annex it.

Along with the war resolution against Spain, Congress passed the Teller Amendment (see text p. 689), which announced the American intention to "leave the government and control of the Island to its people." Yet three years later the Cuban constitution included the American-authored Platt Amendment, which granted the United States the power to intervene in Cuban affairs. Also, in peace negotiations with Spain, the United States took control of the Philippines, another Spanish colony that was seeking independence. Americans who took their own revolution seriously were disturbed to see the U.S. government acting like Spain's. "We earnestly condemn the policy of the present national administration in the Philippines," read the platform of the American Anti-Imperialist League. "It seeks to extinguish the spirit of 1776 in those islands." But other Americans saw the islands as a stepping-stone to the great China market (see text pp. 692–694).

In Document 22-5 the Spanish ambassador, Enrique Dupuy de Lôme, acts indiscreetly, a cardinal sin for a diplomat. Albert J. Beveridge (Document 22-6) attempts to present a reasoned defense of imperialism. Mark Twain dismisses any such talk in Document 22-7.

22-5   The de Lôme Letter (1897)

Diplomacy often fails when diplomats are indiscreet, as Enrique Dupuy de Lôme found out (see text p. 688). The Spanish ambassador to the United States, de Lôme wrote what he thought was a private letter to a friend in Cuba. Somehow the correspondence was stolen and leaked to the American press; de Lôme resigned immediately. This incident strained already tenuous relations between an old empire and an emerging world power.

Source: Letter written by Señor Don Enrique Dupuy de Lôme to Señor Don José Canalejas, probably about the middle of December 1897, in *Relating to the Foreign Relations of the United States, with the Annual Message of the President, Transmitted to Congress December 5, 1898* (Washington, D.C.: Government Printing Office, 1901), pp. 1007–1008.

LEGATION OF SPAIN, *Washington.*
His Excellency Don JOSÉ CANALEJAS.
MY DISTINGUISHED AND DEAR FRIEND: You have no reason to ask my excuses for not having written to me. I ought also to have written to you, but I have put off doing so because overwhelmed with work and nous sommes quittes.

The situation here remains the same. Everything depends on the political and military outcome in Cuba. The prologue of all this, in this second stage [phase] of the war, will end the day when the colonial cabinet shall be ap-

pointed and we shall be relieved in the eyes of this country of a part of the responsibility for what is happening in Cuba, while the Cubans, whom these people think so immaculate, will have to assume it.

Until then, nothing can be clearly seen, and I regard it as a waste of time and progress, by a wrong road, to be sending emissaries to the rebel camp, or to negotiate with the autonomists who have as yet no legal standing, or to try to ascertain the intentions and plans of this Government. The [Cuban] refugees will keep on returning one by one, and as they do so will make their way into the sheepfold, while the leaders in the field will gradually come back. Neither the one nor the other class had the courage to leave in a body and they will not be brave enough to return in a body.

The message has been a disillusion to the insurgents, who expected something different; but I regard it as bad [for us].

Besides the ingrained and inevitable bluntness [groseria] with which is repeated all that the press and public opinion in Spain have said about Weyler, it once more shows what McKinley is, weak and a bidder for the admiration of the crowd, besides being a would-be politician [politicastro] who tries to leave a door open behind himself while keeping on good terms with the jingoes of his party.

Nevertheless, whether the practical results of it [the message] are to be injurious and adverse depends only upon ourselves.

I am entirely of your opinions; without a military end of the matter nothing will be accomplished in Cuba, and without a military and political settlement there will always be the danger of encouragement being given to the insurgents by a part of the public opinion if not by the Government.

I do not think sufficient attention has been paid to the part England is playing.

Nearly all the newspaper rabble that swarms in your hotels are Englishmen, and while writing for the Journal they are also correspondents of the most influential journals and reviews of London. It has been so ever since this thing began. As I look at it, England's only object is that the Americans should amuse themselves with us and leave her alone, and if there should be a war, that would the better stave off the conflict which she dreads but which will never come about.

It would be very advantageous to take up, even if only for effect, the question of commercial relations, and to have a man of some prominence sent hither in order that I may make use of him here to carry on a propaganda among the Senators and others in opposition to the junta and to try to win over the refugees.

So, Amblard is coming. I think he devotes himself too much to petty politics, and we have got to do something very big or we shall fail.

Adela returns your greeting, and we all trust that next year you may be a messenger of peace and take it as a Christmas gift to poor Spain.

Ever your attached friend and servant,

ENRIQUE DUPUY DE LÔME.

Questions

1. What are de Lôme's views of the British press and of President McKinley?
2. How does he show himself to be unfamiliar with American politics and the formation of public opinion in the United States?
3. Was de Lôme entitled to believe that his correspondence was private? Why or why not?

22-6 American Imperialism in the Pacific (1902)

Albert Beveridge

Albert J. Beveridge (1862–1927) was both a politician and a historian. Thus, he was more polished than Josiah Strong (Document 22-4) in offering a comprehensive argument for American imperialism, as he does here concerning the Pacific. The Indiana senator gave the speech excerpted below to a San Francisco audience in 1902.

Source: Albert J. Beveridge, "The Command of the Pacific," in *The Meaning of the Times and Other Speeches* (Indianapolis: Bobbs-Merrill, 1908; reprint, Freeport, N.Y.: Books for Libraries Press, 1968), pp. 188, 190–197.

Fellow Americans of California and the Pacific Slope:
The Pacific is the ocean of the future; and the Pacific is yours. The markets of the Orient are the Republic's future commercial salvation; and the Orient's commercial future

is yours. Important as other questions are, the one great question that covers seas, and islands, and continents; that will last when other questions have been answered and forgotten; that will determine your present prosperity and the greatness of your children's children in their day, is the mastery of the Pacific and the commercial conquest of the eastern world.

That question is peculiarly your question, people of the Pacific slope. If your wealth is to increase you must produce a surplus; and if you produce a surplus, you must sell it. And where will you sell it, people of the Pacific slope, save over the seas of sunset? If your laboring-men are to be employed, you must have commerce; and where will commerce great enough for your ever increasing population be found, save in your supply of the ever increasing demands of the millions of the Orient? . . .

Mark now the historic conjunction of the elements of national growth, national duty and national necessity. First, the time had come when the Republic was prepared to do its part in governing peoples and lands not ready to govern themselves. Second, at this hour of our preparation for this duty, war gave us the Philippines and our possessions in the Gulf [of Mexico]. And, third, at that very time our commerce was crying aloud for new markets where we might sell the surplus products of our factories and farms—and the only remaining markets on the globe were those surrounding the lands which war had given us. American duty, American preparedness, American commercial necessity came in the same great hour of fate.

Let us consider the argument of advantage to ourselves, flowing from the Philippines, the Orient and from American mastery of the Pacific. What is the great commercial necessity of the Republic? It is markets—foreign markets. At one time we needed to build up our industries here and for that purpose to save for them our home markets. Protection did that; and to-day our home market is supplied. Now we have invaded the markets of Europe and filled them almost to their capacity with American goods. Our great combinations of capital devoted to manufacturing and transportation compete successfully with foreign manufacturers in their own countries.

But still we have a surplus; and an unsold surplus is commercial peril. Every unsold bushel of wheat reduces the pride of every other one of the millions of bushels of wheat produced. If our manufacturers produce more than they can sell, that surplus product causes the mills to shut down until they produce no more than they can sell. And after we supply our own market, after we sell all we can to the markets of Europe, we still have an unsold surplus. If our prosperity continues this must be sold.

Where shall the Republic sell its surplus? Where shall the Pacific coast sell its surplus? And your surplus unsold means your commerce paralyzed, your laboring-men starving. Expansion answers that question. . . .

If it is not true that her possessions help England's commerce, why does not England give them up? Why does not Germany give up her possession in Northern China? Why is she spending tens of millions of dollars there, building German railways, German docks and vast plants for future German commerce? Why does Russia spend a hundred million dollars of Russian gold building Russian railways through Manchuria and binding that territory, vast in extent as all the states of the Pacific slope combined, to the Russian empire with bands of steel? Why is Japan now preparing to take Manchuria from Russia as she has already taken Formosa from China?

The Philippines do not help us in Oriental commerce! They have helped us even now by making the American name known throughout the East, and our commerce with the islands and countries influenced by the Philippines has in two short years leaped from $43,000,000 to $120,000,000.

If an American manufacturer established a great storehouse in London believing that it would help his business and then found his sales in London increasing 300 per cent. in less than three years, would he give away that branch establishment because some theorist told him that branch houses did not help trade and that he could sell as much and more if he shipped direct from his factory to the English purchaser?

And yet this practically is what the Opposition asks the American people to believe about and do with the Philippines. From every English and German possession in the East English and German goods are shipped in bulk and then reshipped as quick orders near at hand call for them. And these possessions influence the entire population of the countries where they are located.

If this is true of English and German possessions, will it not be true of America's possessions at the very door of this mighty market? If it is not true, it will be because American energy, American sagacity, American enterprise are not equal to the commercial opportunity which the Philippines give us in the Orient. Americans never yet found an obstacle which they did not overcome, an opportunity they did not make their own.

Has the decay of American energy begun with you, men of the West? Who says so is infidel to American character. Answer these slanders of your energy and power, people of the Pacific states—answer them with our ballots! Tell the world that, of all this masterful Nation, none more vital than the men and women who hold aloft the Republic's flag on our Pacific shores!

If we need this Oriental market—and we can not dispose of our surplus without it—what American farmer is willing for us to give the Philippines to America's competitors? What American manufacturer is willing to surrender this permanent commercial advantage to the nations who are striving for those very markets? Yet, that is what the Opposition asks you to do. For if we quit them certainly Germany or England or Japan will take them.

And these markets, great as they are, are hardly yet opened to the modern world. They are like a gold mine worked by ancient methods and yielding only a fraction of its wealth. Apply to that gold mine modern machinery, modern science, modern methods and its stream of gold swells in volume. This illustration applies to Oriental markets. For example, China buys from all the world at the present time $250,000,000 worth of foreign products. These are consumed by less than 75,000,000 of the Chinese people. The reason of this is that foreign goods can not penetrate the interior. There are no railways, no roads; merchandise must be transported on human backs, and corrupt officials lay heavy transportation taxes at every stage. But now all this begins to change. All over China railroads are projected, surveyed and even now are building.

And wherever they have gone Chinese commerce has increased, just as our own commerce increases here wherever a railroad goes. And wherever railways go wagon roads branch from them. Thus the methods of modern civilization are weaving a network of modern conditions among this most ancient of peoples. And if China now buys $250,000,000 worth of products from the rest of the world, what will she buy when all this change that is now taking place brings her 400,000,000 as purchasers to the markets of the world? The most conservative experts estimate that China alone will buy at least one thousand million dollars worth of the products of other countries every year. . . .

The Philippines and the Orient are your commercial opportunity. Does our duty as a Nation forbid you to accept it? Does our fitness for the work prevent us from doing it? Or does the Nation's preparedness, the Republic's duty and the commercial necessity of the American people unite in demanding of American statesmanship the holding of the Philippines and the commercial conquest of the Oriental world?

Do they say that it is a wrong to any people to govern them without their consent? Consider Hayti [sic] and read in her awful decline since French government there was overthrown the answer to that theory. Remember that English administration in Egypt has in less than twenty years made fertile her fields and redeemed her people, debased by a thousand years of decline, and read in that miracle the answer to that theory.

Examine every example of administration of government in the Orient or Africa by a superior power and find the answer to that theory. Come nearer home. Analyze the three years of American administration in Porto [sic] Rico—American schools for the humblest, just laws, honest government, prosperous commerce. Now sail for less than a day to the sister island of San [sic] Domingo and behold commerce extinguished, justice unknown, government and law a whim, religion degenerated to voodoo rites, and answer whether American administration in Porto Rico, even if it had been without the consent of the governed, is not better for that people than San Domingo's independent savagery.

Let us trust the American people! The most fervent belief in their purity, their power and their destiny is feeble, after all, compared with the reality on which that faith is founded. Great as our fathers were, the citizens of this Republic, on the whole, are greater still to-day, with broader education, loftier outlook. And if this were not so, we should not be worthy of our fathers; for, to do as well as they we must do better. Over the entire Republic the people's common schools increase, churches multiply, culture spreads, the poorest have privileges impossible to the wealthiest fifty years ago.

When any man fears the decay of American institutions, he ignores the elemental forces around him which are building future generations of Americans, stronger, nobler than ourselves. And those who ask you to believe that administration of orderly government in the Philippines will poison the fountain of Americanism here at home, ask you to believe that your children are a mockery, your schools a myth, your churches a dream.

American soldiers, American teachers, American administrators—all are the instruments of the Nation in discharging the Nation's high duty to the ancient and yet infant people which circumstance has placed in our keeping. If it is said that our duty is to teach the world by example, I ask if our duty ends with that? Does any man's duty to his children end with mere example? Does organized society owe no duty to the orphan and the abandoned save that of example? Why, then, are our schools, our asylums, our benevolent institutions, which force physical and mental training upon the neglected youth of the Republic? And does the parent or does organized society refrain from discharging this duty if the child resists?

And just so nations can not escape the larger duties to senile or infant peoples. Nations can not escape the charge laid upon them to develop the world's neglected resources, to make the wilderness, the fields, the mines and countries inhabited by barbarous peoples useful to civilized man. No nation lives to itself alone. It can not if it would. Even the great powers influence one another, not only by example, but by tariffs, by trade arrangements, by armies, by navies. How much greater should be this influence when circumstance gives to the keeping of a great power the destiny of an undeveloped race and the fortunes of an undeveloped country?

Questions

1. What are some of Beveridge's justifications for American imperialism in the Pacific?

2. What assumption does he make concerning Asian markets and the American surplus?

3. How does Beveridge believe that Puerto Rico—and, by implication, the Philippines—will benefit from American control?

22-7 "To the Person Sitting in Darkness" (1901)

Mark Twain

Although Secretary of State John Hay called the fight with Spain "a splendid little war," not everyone viewed it that way. A group of prominent Americans who opposed the acquisition of colonies founded the American Anti-Imperialist League (see text p. 692). Among their number was the famed author Mark Twain. He ostensibly addressed part of the following essay "To the Person Sitting in Darkness," that is, to what today would be called a person in the Third World.

Twain refers to Joseph Chamberlain, who as colonial secretary for the British government refused to consider South African independence. Chamberlain's policies helped cause the Boer War, which was being fought when Twain wrote this essay.

Source: Excerpted from Mark Twain, "To the Person Sitting in Darkness" (1901). In *Mark Twain: Collected Tales, Sketches, Speeches, and Essays, 1891–1910* (New York: Library of America, 1992), pp. 465–473.

And by and by comes America, and our Master of the Game plays it badly—plays it as Mr. Chamberlain was playing it in South Africa. It was a mistake to do that; also, it was one which was quite unlooked for in a Master who was playing it so well in Cuba. In Cuba, he was playing the usual and regular *American* game, and it was winning, for there is no way to beat it. The Master, contemplating Cuba, said: "Here is an oppressed and friendless little nation which is willing to fight to be free; we go partners, and put up the strength of seventy million sympathizers and the resources of the United States: play!" Nothing but Europe combined could call that hand: and Europe cannot combine on anything. There, in Cuba, he was following our great tradition in a way which made us very proud of him, and proud of the deep dissatisfaction which his play was provoking in continental Europe. Moved by a high inspiration, he threw out those stirring words which proclaimed that forcible annexation would be "criminal aggression"; and in that utterance fired another "shot heard round the world." The memory of that fine saying will be outlived by the remembrance of no act of his but one—that he forgot it within the twelvemonth, and its honorable gospel along with it.

For, presently, came the Philippine temptation. It was strong; it was too strong, and he made that bad mistake: he played the European game, the Chamberlain game. It was a pity; it was a great pity, that error; that one grievous error, that irrevocable error. For it was the very place and time to play the American game again. And at no cost. Rich winnings to be gathered in, too; rich and permanent; indestructible; a fortune transmissible forever to the children of the flag. Not land, not money, not dominion—no, something worth many times more than that dross: our share, the spectacle of a nation of long harrassed and persecuted slaves set free through our influence; our posterity's share, the golden memory of that fair deed. The game was in our hands. If it had been played according to the American rules, Dewey would have sailed away from Manila as soon as he had destroyed the Spanish fleet—after putting up a sign on shore guaranteeing foreign property and life against damage by the Filipinos, and warning the Powers that interference with the emancipated patriots would be regarded as an act unfriendly to the United States. The Powers cannot combine, in even a bad cause, and the sign would not have been molested.

Dewey could have gone about his affairs elsewhere, and left the competent Filipino army to starve out the little Spanish garrison and send it home, and the Filipino citizens to set up the form of government they might prefer, and deal with the friars and their doubtful acquisitions according to Filipino ideas of fairness and justice—ideas which have since been tested and found to be as high an order as any that prevail in Europe or America.

But we played the Chamberlain game, and lost the chance to add another Cuba and another honorable deed to our good record.

The more we examine the mistake, the more clearly we perceive that it is going to be bad for the Business. The Person Sitting in Darkness is almost sure to say: "There is something curious about this—curious and unaccountable.

There must be two Americans; one that sets the captive free, and one that takes a once-captive's new freedom away from him, and picks a quarrel with him with nothing to found it on; then kills him to get his land."

The truth is, the Person Sitting in Darkness *is* saying things like that; and for the sake of the Business we must persuade him to look at the Philippine matter in another and healthier way. We must arrange his opinions for him. I believe it can be done; for Mr. Chamberlain has arranged England's opinion of the South African matter, and done it most cleverly and successfully. He presented the facts—some of the facts—and showed those confiding people what the facts meant. He did it statistically, which is a good way. He used the formula: "Twice 2 are 14, and 2 from 9 leaves 35." Figures are effective; figures will convince the elect.

Now, my plan is a still bolder one than Mr. Chamberlain's, though apparently a copy of it. Let us be franker than Mr. Chamberlain; let us audaciously present the whole of the facts, shirking none, then explain them according to Mr. Chamberlain's formula. This daring truthfulness will astonish and dazzle the Person Sitting in the Darkness, and he will take the Explanation down before his mental vision has had time to get back into focus. Let us say to him:

"Our case is simple. On the 1st of May, Dewey destroyed the Spanish fleet. This left the Archipelago in the hands of its proper and rightful owners, the Filipino nation. Their army numbered 30,000 men, and they were competent to whip out or starve out the little Spanish garrison; then the people could set up a government of their own devising. Our traditions required that Dewey should now set up his warning sign, and go away. But the Master of the Game happened to think of another plan—the European plan. He acted upon it. This was, to send out an army—ostensibly to help the native patriots put the finishing touch upon their long and plucky struggle for independence, but really to take their land away from them and keep it. That is, in the interest of Progress and Civilization. The plan developed, stage by stage, and quite satisfactorily. We entered into a military alliance with the trusting Filipinos, and they hemmed in Manila on the land side, and by their valuable help the place, with its garrison of 8,000 or 10,000 Spaniards, was captured—a thing which we could not have accomplished unaided at that time. We got their help by—by ingenuity. We knew they were fighting for their independence, and that they had been at it for two years. We knew they supposed that we also were fighting in their worthy cause—just as we had helped the Cubans fight for Cuban independence—and we allowed them to go on thinking so. *Until Manila was ours and we could get along without them.* Then we showed our hand. Of course, they were surprised—that was natural; surprised and disappointed; disappointed and grieved. To them it looked un-American; uncharacteristic; foreign to our es-

tablished traditions. And this was natural, too; for we were only playing the American Game in public—in private it was the European. It was neatly done, very neatly, and it bewildered them. They could not understand it; for we had been so friendly—so affectionate, even—with those simple-minded patriots! We, our own selves, had brought back out of exile their leader, their hero, their hope, their Washington—Aguinaldo; brought him in a warship, in high honor, under the sacred shelter and hospitality of the flag; brought him back and restored him to his people, and got their moving and eloquent gratitude for it. Yes, we had been so friendly to them, and had heartened them up in so many ways! We had lent them guns and ammunition; advised with them; exchanged pleasant courtesies with them; placed our sick and wounded in their kindly care; intrusted our Spanish prisoners to their humane and honest hands; fought shoulder to shoulder with them against "the common enemy" (our own phrase); praised their mercifulness, praised their fine and honorable conduct; borrowed their trenches, borrowed strong positions which they had previously captured from the Spaniards; petted them, lied to them—officially proclaiming that our land and naval forces came to give them their freedom and displace the bad Spanish Government—fooled them, used them until we needed them no longer; then derided the sucked orange and threw it away. We kept the positions which we had beguiled them of; by and by, we moved a force forward and overlapped patriot ground—a clever thought, for we needed trouble, and this would produce it. A Filipino soldier, crossing the ground, where no one had a right to forbid him, was shot by our sentry. The badgered patriots resented this with arms, without waiting to know whether Aguinaldo, who was absent, would approve or not. Aguinaldo did not approve; but that availed nothing. What we wanted, in the interest of Progress and Civilization, was the Archipelago, unencumbered by patriots struggling for independence; and War was what we needed. We clinched our opportunity. It is Mr. Chamberlain's case over again—at least in its motive and intention; and we played the game as adroitly as he played it himself."

At this point in our frank statement of fact to the Person Sitting in Darkness, we should throw in a little trade taffy about the Blessings of Civilization—for a change and for the refreshment of his spirit—then go on with our tale:

We and the patriots having captured Manila, Spain's ownership of the Archipelago and her sovereignty over it were at an end—obliterated—annihilated—not a rag or shred of either remaining behind. It was then that we conceived the divinely humorous idea of *buying* both of these specters from Spain! [It is quite safe to confess this to the Person Sitting in Darkness, since neither he nor any other sane person will believe it.] In buying those ghosts for twenty millions, we also contracted to take care of the friars and their accumulations. [I think we also agreed to propagate leprosy and smallpox, but as to this there is doubt. But it is not important; persons afflicted with the friars do not mind other diseases.]

"With our Treaty ratified, Manila subdued, and our Ghosts secured, we had no further use for Aguinaldo and the owners of the Archipelago. We forced a war, and we have been hunting America's guest and ally through the woods and swamps ever since."

At this point in the tale, it will be well to boast a little of our war work and our heroisms in the field, so as to make our performance look as fine as England's in South Africa; but I believe it will not be best to emphasize this too much. We must be cautious. Of course, we must read the war telegrams to the Person, in order to keep up our frankness; but we can throw an air of humorousness over them, and that will modify their grim eloquence a little, and their rather indiscret [*sic*] exhibitions of gory exultation. Before reading to him the following display heads of the dispatches of November 18, 1900, it will be well to practice on them in private first, so as to get the right tang of lightness and gayety into them:

"ADMINISTRATION WEARY OF
PROTRACTED HOSTILITIES!"

"REAL WAR AHEAD FOR FILIPINO
REBELS"[1]

"WILL SHOW NO MERCY!" . . .

Of course, we must not venture to ignore our General MacArthur's reports—oh, why do they keep on printing those embarrassing things?—we must drop them trippingly from the tongue and take the chances:

During the last ten months our losses have been 268 killed and 750 wounded; Filipino loss, *three thousand two hundred and twenty-seven killed,* and 694 wounded.

We must stand ready to grab the Person Sitting in Darkness, for he will swoon away at this confession, saying: "Good God! those 'niggers' spare their wounded, and the Americans massacre theirs!"

We must bring him to, and coax him and coddle him, and assure him that the ways of Providence are best, and that it would not become us to find fault with them; and then, to show him that we are only imitators, not originators, we must read the following passage from the letter of an American soldier lad in the Philippines to his mother, published in *Public Opinion,* of Decorah, Iowa, describing the finish of a victorious battle:

"WE NEVER LEFT ONE ALIVE. IF ONE WAS WOUNDED, WE WOULD RUN OUR BAYONETS THROUGH HIM.

Having now laid all the historical facts before the Person Sitting in Darkness, we should bring him to again, and explain them to him. We should say to him:

"They look doubtful, but in reality they are not. There have been lies; yes, but they were told in a good cause. We have been treacherous; but that was only in order that real good might come out of apparent evil. True, we have crushed a deceived and confiding people; we have turned against the weak and the friendless who trusted us; we have stamped out a just and intelligent and well-ordered republic; we have stabbed an ally in the back and slapped the face of a guest; we have bought a Shadow from an enemy that hadn't it to sell; we have robbed a trusting friend of his land and his liberty; we have invited our clean young men to shoulder a discredited musket and do bandits' work under a flag which bandits have been accustomed to fear, not to follow; we have debauched America's honor and blackened her face before the world; but each detail was for the best. We know this. The Head of every State and Sovereignty in Christendom and 90 per cent. of every legislative body in Christendom, including our Congress and our fifty state legislatures, are members not only of the church, but also of the Blessings-of-Civilization Trust. This world-girdling accumulation of trained morals, high principles, and justice cannot do an unright thing, an unfair thing, an ungenerous thing, an unclean thing. It knows what it is about. Give yourself no uneasiness; it is all right."

Now then, that will convince the Person. You will see. It will restore the Business. Also, it will elect the Master of the Game to the vacant place in the Trinity of our national gods; and there on their high thrones the Three will sit, age after age, in the people's sight, each bearing the Emblem of his service: Washington, the Sword of the Liberator; Lincoln, the Slave's Broken Chains; the Master, the Chains Repaired.

It will give the Business a splendid new start. You will see.

Everything is prosperous, now; everything is just as we should wish it. We have got the Archipelago, and we shall never give it up. also, we have every reason to hope that we shall have an opportunity before very long to slip out of our congressional contract with Cuba and give her something better in the place of it. It is a rich country, and many of us are already beginning to see that the contract was a sentimental mistake. But now—right now—is the best time to do some profitable rehabilitating work—work that will set us up and make us comfortable, and discourage gossip. We cannot conceal from ourselves that, privately, we are a little troubled about our uniform. It is one of our prides; it is acquainted with honor; it is familiar with great deeds and noble; we love it, we revere it; and so this errand it is

---

[1] "Rebels!" Mumble that funny word—don't let the Person catch it distinctly.—M.T.

on makes us uneasy. And our flag—another pride of ours, our chiefest! We have worshipped it so; and when we have seen it in far lands—glimpsing it unexpectedly in that strange sky, waving its welcome and benediction to us—we have caught our breaths, and uncovered our heads, and couldn't speak, for a moment, for the thought of what it was to us and the great ideals it stood for. Indeed, we *must* do something about these things; it is easily managed. We can have a special one—our states do it: we can have just our usual flag, with the white stripes painted black and the stars replaced by the skull and crossbones.

And we do not need that Civil Commission out there. Having no powers, it has to invent them, and that kind of work cannot be effectively done by just anybody; an expert is required. Mr. Croker can be spared. We do not want the United States represented there, but only the Game.

By help of these suggested amendments, Progress and Civilization in that country can have a boom, and it will take in the Persons who are Sitting in Darkness, and we can resume Business at the old stand.

Questions

1. How does Twain say he will argue the cause of empire?
2. What is his real purpose in recounting recent events?
3. Why is Twain so cynical?

Questions for Further Thought

1. Discuss the portrayals of Third World peoples by Josiah Strong (Document 22-4) and Albert Beveridge (Document 22-6). Over time, how would this attitude affect both an American audience and the people depicted?
2. How does the tone of Twain's essay (Document 22-7) differ from that of Josiah Strong and Albert Beveridge?

Onto the World Stage

American foreign policy focused on two areas: the Caribbean and the Pacific. Beginning in the 1890s, European nations exhibited what the United States feared was an imperial interest in the Caribbean. For example, in 1895 Great Britain pressed a border claim for British Guiana against Venezuela. Grover Cleveland responded by invoking the Monroe Doctrine (see text pp. 683–684).

Seven years after the Venezuela crisis Venezuela defaulted on some loans (see text pp. 698–699). Great Britain, Germany, and Italy then sent a naval force that fired on Venezuelan installations. This time Theodore Roosevelt mounted a diplomatic counteroffensive with the so-called Roosevelt Corollary to the Monroe Doctrine (see text p. 699). Roosevelt warned that governmental incompetence by Caribbean nations would "force the United States, however reluctantly, in flagrant cases . . . of wrong doing or impotence, to the exercise of an international police power."

Although Europe heeded the warning, the United States was only partially successful as the dominant Caribbean power. Policy makers found that it was easier to build the Panama Canal (see text pp. 697–698) than to avoid invoking the Roosevelt Corollary. By 1917 American troops had landed at various times in Cuba, the Dominican

Republic, Haiti, Mexico, and Nicaragua. Although the intent was to create order out of chaos, the policy resulted in anti-Americanism throughout the region.

In Asia the United States spent two years breaking the insurrection of Philippine nationalists; these military operations cost some 4,300 American and as many as 300,000 Filipino lives (see text pp. 692–694). Once pacified, the islands were supposed to serve as a springboard for American business interests in China. However, China proved a difficult market to enter. Europeans were long established there, and in 1900 the Chinese attempted to end all foreign domination. Although the Boxer Rebellion (see text p. 700) failed, it allowed Secretary of State John Hay to insist that all the powers recognize the independence of China, along with the legitimacy of American interests there.

John Hay's Open Door Notes are reprinted in Document 22-8; they should be read as a contrast to Document 22-9, the Roosevelt Corollary. In Document 22-10 Woodrow Wilson reveals a foreign policy perspective that promised intervention in the affairs of Latin America.

22-8   Open Door Notes (1899, 1900)

John Hay

Unwilling to make a military commitment to China, the United States pressed its interests through diplomacy (see text pp. 700–701). The following notes from Secretary of State John Hay (1838–1905) made up the Open Door Policy, which remained in force until the triumph of Mao Zedong (Mao Tse-tung) in 1949. Hay's first communication is to Andrew D. White, the American ambassador to Germany. His second is a telegram sent to the American embassies and missions in all the countries that wanted to trade with China.

Source: John Hay to Andrew D. White, September 6, 1899; and John Hay's circular letter to the powers cooperating in China, July 3, 1900. In Henry Steele Commager and Milton Cantor, eds., *Documents of American History*, 10th ed. (Englewood Cliffs, N.J.: Prentice Hall, 1988), vol. 2, pp. 9–11.

JOHN HAY TO ANDREW D. WHITE

Department of State, Washington, September 6, 1899

At the time when the Government of the United States was informed by that of Germany that it had leased from His Majesty the Emperor of China the port of Kiao-chao and the adjacent territory in the province of Shantung, assurance were given to the ambassador of the United States at Berlin by the Imperial German minister for foreign affairs that the rights and privileges insured by treaties with China to citizens of the United States would not thereby suffer or be in anywise impaired within the area over which Germany had thus obtained control.

More recently, however, the British Government recognized by a formal agreement with Germany the exclusive right of the latter country to enjoy in said leased area and the contiguous "sphere of influence or interest" certain privileges, more especially those relating to railroads and mining enterprises; but as the exact nature and extent of the rights thus recognized have not been clearly defined, it is possible that serious conflicts of interest may at any time arise not only between British and German subjects within said area, but that the interests of our citizens may also be jeopardized thereby.

Earnestly desirous to remove any cause of irritation and to insure at the same time to the commerce of all nations in China the undoubted benefits which should accrue from a formal recognition by the various powers claiming "spheres of interest" that they shall enjoy perfect equality of treatment for their commerce and navigation within such "spheres," the Government of the United States would be pleased to see His German Majesty's Government give formal assurance, and lend its cooperation in securing like assurances from the other interested powers, that each, within its respective sphere of whatever influence—

First. Will in no way interfere with any treaty port or any vested interest within any so-called "sphere of interest" or leased territory it may have in China.

Second. That the Chinese treaty tariff of the time being shall apply to all merchandise landed or shipped to all such ports as are within said "sphere of interest" (unless they be "free ports"), no matter to what nationality it may belong, and that duties so leviable shall be collected by the Chinese Government.

Third. That it will levy no higher harbor dues on vessels of another nationality frequenting any port in such "sphere" than shall be levied on vessels of its own nationality, and no higher railroad charges over lines built, controlled, or operated within its "sphere" on merchandise belonging to citizens or subjects of other nationality transported through such "sphere" than shall be levied on similar merchandise belonging to its own nationals transported over equal distances.

The liberal policy pursued by His Imperial German Majesty in declaring Kiao-chao a free port and in aiding the Chinese Government in the establishment there of a customhouse are so clearly in line with the proposition which this Government is anxious to see recognized that it entertains the strongest hope that Germany will give its acceptance and hearty support.

The recent ukase of His Majesty the Emperor of Russia declaring the port of Ta-lien-wan open during the whole of the lease under which it is held from China to the merchant ships of all nations, coupled with the categorical assurances made to this Government by His Imperial Majesty's representative at this capital at the same time and since repeated to me by the present Russian ambassador, seem to insure the support of the Emperor to the proposed measure. Our ambassador at the Court of St. Petersburg has in consequence, been instructed to submit it to the Russian Government and to request their early consideration of it. A copy of my instruction on the subject to Mr. Tower is herewith inclosed for your confidential information.

The commercial interests of Great Britain and Japan will be so clearly served by the desired declaration of intentions, and the views of the Governments of these countries as to the desirability of the adopting of measures insuring the benefits of equality of treatment of all foreign trade throughout China are so similar to those entertained by the United States, that their acceptance of the propositions herein outlined and their cooperation in advocating their adoption by the other powers can be confidently expected. I enclosed herewith copy of the instruction which I have sent to Mr. Choate on the subject.

In view of the present favorable conditions, you are instructed to submit the above considerations to His Imperial German Majesty's Minister for Foreign Affairs, and to request his early consideration of the subject.

CIRCULAR TELEGRAM TO THE POWERS COOPERATING IN CHINA

Department of State, Washington, July 3, 1900

In this critical posture of affairs in China it is deemed appropriate to define the attitude of the United States as far as present circumstances permit this to be done. We adhere to the policy initiated by us in 1857 of peace with the Chinese nation, of furtherance of lawful commerce, and of protection of lives and property of our citizens by all means guaranteed under extraterritorial treaty rights and by the law of nations. If wrong be done to our citizens we propose to hold the responsible authors to the uttermost accountability. We regard the condition at Pekin as one of virtual anarchy, whereby power and responsibility are practically devolved upon the local provincial authorities. So long as they are not in overt collusion with rebellion and use their power to protect foreign life and property, we regard them as representing the Chinese people, with whom we seek to remain in peace and friendship. The purpose of the President is, as it has been heretofore, to act concurrently with the other powers; first, in opening up communication with Pekin and rescuing the American officials, missionaries, and other Americans who are in danger; secondly, in affording all possible protection everywhere in China to American life and property; thirdly, in guarding and protecting all legitimate American interests; and fourthly, in aiding to prevent a spread of the disorders to the other provinces of the Empire and a recurrence of such disasters. It is of course too early to forecast the means of attaining this last result; but the policy of the Government of the United States is to seek a solution which may bring about permanent safety and peace to China, preserve Chinese territorial and administrative entity, protect all rights guaranteed to friendly powers by treaty and international law, and safeguard for the world the principle of equal and impartial trade with all parts of the Chinese Empire. . . .

Questions

1. What was the purpose of Hay's first Open Door Note?
2. In what ways does the second note differ from the first?
3. Taken together, what do the notes say about the American attitude toward China?

22-9   The Roosevelt Corollary to the Monroe Doctrine (1904, 1905)

On domestic issues Theodore Roosevelt pursued a Square Deal for the American public, but in foreign policy he preferred a big stick. This could take the form of the Great White Fleet, the muscle-flexing voyage of U.S. battleships around the world in 1907–1908 (see text pp. 700–701), or an addition to the Monroe Doctrine. These two statements from Roosevelt in 1904 and 1905 constitute the Roosevelt Corollary. The United States thus became the "policeman" of the Caribbean, a role it continued to play down to the 1980s in Grenada (see text p. 1022) and Panama.

Source: Theodore Roosevelt, fourth annual message to Congress, December 6, 1904; and Theodore Roosevelt, fifth annual message to Congress, December 5, 1905. In James D. Richardson, ed., *A Compilation of the Messages and Papers of the Presidents* (Washington, D.C.: U.S. Printing Office, n.d.), vol. 10, pp. 831–832; vol. 14, pp. 6944ff.

ROOSEVELT'S ANNUAL MESSAGE TO CONGRESS, DECEMBER 6, 1904

. . . It is not true that the United States feels any land hunger or entertains any project as regards the other nations of the Western Hemisphere save such as are for their welfare. All that this country desires is to see the neighboring countries stable, orderly, and prosperous. Any country whose people conduct themselves well can count upon our hearty friendship. If a nation shows that it knows how to act with reasonable efficiency and decency in social and political matters, if it keeps order and pays its obligations, it need fear no interference from the United States. Chronic wrong doing, or an impotence which results in a general loosening of the ties of civilized society, may in America, as elsewhere, ultimately require intervention by some civilized nation, and in the Western Hemisphere the adherence of the United States to the Monroe Doctrine may force the United States, however reluctantly, in flagrant cases of such wrong doing or impotence, to the exercise of an international police power. If every country washed by the Caribbean Sea would show the progress in stable and just civilization which with the aid of the Platt amendment Cuba has shown since our troops left the island, and which so many of the republics in both Americas are constantly and brilliantly showing, all question of interference by this Nation with their affairs would be at an end. Our interests and those of our southern neighbors are in reality identical. They have great natural riches, and if within their borders the reign of law and justice obtains, prosperity is sure to come to them. While they thus obey the primary laws of civilized society they may rest assured that they will be treated by us in a spirit of cordial and helpful sympathy. We would interfere with them only in the last resort, and then only if it became evident that their inability or unwillingness to do justice at home and abroad had violated the rights of the United States or had invited foreign aggression to the detriment of the entire body of American nations. It is a mere truism to say that every nation . . . which desires to maintain its freedom, its independence, must ultimately realize that the right of such independence can not be separated from the responsibility of making good use of it.

ROOSEVELT'S ANNUAL MESSAGE TO CONGRESS, DECEMBER 5, 1905

. . . It must be understood that under no circumstances will the United States use the Monroe Doctrine as a cloak for territorial aggression. We desire peace with all the world, but perhaps most of all with the other peoples of the American Continent. There are, of course, limits to the wrongs which any self-respecting nation can endure. It is always possible that wrong actions toward this Nation, or toward citizens of this Nation, in some State unable to keep order among its own people, unable to secure justice from outsiders, and unwilling to do justice to those outsiders who treat it well, may result in our having to take action to protect our rights; but such action will not be taken with a view to territorial aggression, and it will be taken at all only with extreme reluctance and when it has become evident that every other resource has been exhausted.

Moreover, we must make it evident that we do not intend to permit the Monroe Doctrine to be used by any nation on this Continent as a shield to protect it from the consequences of its own misdeeds against foreign nations. If a republic to the south of us commits a tort against a foreign nation, such as an outrage against a citizen of that nation, then the Monroe Doctrine does not force us to interfere to prevent punishment of the tort, save to see that the punishment does not assume the form of territorial occupation. . . . The case is more difficult when it refers to a contractual obligation. Our own Government has always refused to enforce such contractual obligations on behalf of its citizens by an appeal to arms. It is much to be wished that all foreign governments would take the same view. But they do not; and in consequence we are liable at any time to be brought face to face with disagreeable alternatives. On the one hand, this country would certainly decline to go to war to prevent a foreign government from collecting a just debt; on the other hand, it is very inadvisable to permit any foreign power to take possession, even temporarily, of the custom houses of an American Republic in order to enforce the payment of its obligations; for such temporary occupation might turn into a permanent occupation. The only escape from these alternatives may at any time be that we must ourselves undertake to bring about some

arrangement by which so much as possible of a just obligation shall be paid. It is far better that this country should put though such an arrangement, rather than allow any foreign country to undertake it. To do so insures the defaulting republic from having to pay debt of an improper character under duress, while it also insures honest creditors of the republic from being passed by in the interest of dishonest or grasping creditors. Moreover, for the United States to take such a position offers the only possible way of insuring us against a clash with some foreign power. The position is, therefore, in the interest of peace as well as in the interest of justice. It is of benefit to our people; it is of benefit to foreign peoples; and most of all it is really of benefit to the people of the country concerned. . . .

Questions

1. Under what circumstances does Roosevelt propose to intervene in the affairs of Caribbean nations?
2. Why would he abstain from intervention?
3. What kind of precedent was set with this announcement of "an international police power"?

22-10 Woodrow Wilson on Relations with Latin America (1913)

The contrast between the foreign policies of Theodore Roosevelt and Woodrow Wilson (see text pp. 701–702) was one between Manifest Destiny and mission. Wilson hoped the United States could lead by the force of example, but this statement on relations with Latin America shows that Wilson, like Roosevelt, expected other nations to adhere to American standards of conduct.

Source: Woodrow Wilson, statement on relations with Latin America, March 12, 1913. In Woodrow Wilson, *The Papers of Woodrow Wilson*, ed. Arthur S. Link (Princeton, N.J.: Princeton University Press, 1978), vol. 27, pp. 172–173.

One of the chief objects of my administration will be to cultivate the friendship and deserve the confidence of our sister republics of Central and South America, and to promote in every proper and honorable way the interests which are common to the peoples of the two continents. I earnestly desire the most cordial understanding and cooperation between the peoples and leaders of America and, therefore, deem it my duty to make this brief statement.

Cooperation is possible only when supported at every turn by the orderly processes of just government based upon law, not upon arbitrary or irregular force. We hold, as I am sure all thoughtful leaders of republican government everywhere hold, that just government rests always

upon the consent of the governed, and that there can be no freedom without order based upon law and upon the public conscience and approval. We shall look to make these principles the basis of mutual intercourse, respect, and helpfulness between our sister republics and ourselves. We shall lend our influence of every kind to the realization of these principles in fact and practice, knowing that disorder, personal intrigue and defiance of constitutional rights weaken and discredit government and injure none so much as the people who are unfortunate enough to have their common life and their common affairs so tainted and disturbed. We can have no sympathy with those who seek to seize the power of government to advance their own personal interests or ambition. We are the friends of peace, but we know that there can no no lasting or stable peace in such circumstances. As friends, therefore, we shall prefer those who act in the interest of peace and honor, who protect private rights and respect the restraints of constitutional provision. Mutual respect seems to us the indispensable foundation of friendship between states, as between individuals.

The United States has nothing to seek in Central and South America except the lasting interests of the peoples of the two continents, the security of governments intended for the people and for no special group or interest, and the development of personal and trade relationships between the two continents which shall redound to the profit and advantage of both and interfere with the rights and liberties of neither.

From these principles may be read so much of the future policy of this government as it is necessary now to forecast; and in the spirit of these principles I may, I hope, be permitted with as much confidence as earnestness to extend to the governments of all the republics of America the hand of genuine disinterested friendship and to pledge my own honor and the honor of my colleagues to every enterprise of peace and amity that a fortunate future may disclose.

Questions

1. What does Wilson believe the United States can offer Latin America?
2. How does he define the basis of cooperation?
3. What kind of friendship is Wilson offering to other countries?

Questions for Further Thought

1. In what ways could the Open Door Notes (Document 22-8) and the Roosevelt Corollary (Document 22-9) antagonize the peoples they were meant to protect? In light of European and Japanese competition for foreign markets, could the United States have fashioned alternative policies? What kind?
2. How might repeated American interventions have affected the development of nationalism in the Caribbean?
3. To what extent does Woodrow Wilson's policy statement (Document 22-10) differ from the Open Door Notes and especially the Roosevelt Corollary?

CHAPTER 23

War and the American State 1914–1920

★   ★   ★

The Great War, 1914–1918

When the Great War began in August 1914, both the Allies and the Central Powers expected victory within a matter of weeks. No one anticipated a war that would last four years and take 14.5 million lives.

In the Napoleonic Wars a century before opposing armies had fired at one another with muskets across an open field. In 1914 the tactics remained largely the same, but the weapons had changed profoundly. With the use of machine guns and high-powered rifles, frontal assaults caused ruinous casualties. Combat on the Western Front quickly evolved into trench warfare (see text p. 711). Opposing armies again faced one another, but this time it was from the confines of a 25,000-mile network of trenches running from Belgium into France. Periodically, an army would mount an offensive, with soldiers pouring into the disputed "no-man's-land" in an attempt to break through the enemy's lines. Casualties in a single battle often numbered in the hundreds of thousands on each side. Poison gas and artillery barrages added to the horror of a soldier's existence.

The war did not directly affect the United States at first, as President Wilson tried to maintain a policy of neutrality (see text pp. 712–714). Although cultural ties and aggressive British propaganda generated sympathy for the Allies, it was not completely successful. German-Americans tended to support the old country, and Irish-Americans were cool to the English, who appeared to be more interested in liberating Belgium than in freeing Ireland. Leading progressives, socialists, and pacifists all argued against war, and Henry Ford financed the voyage of a "peace ship," the passengers on which hoped to negotiate an end to the conflict (see text p. 712). But circumstances conspired against Wilson. When the British navy swept the German merchant marine from the Atlantic, American business favored the Allies at the expense of the Central Powers.

The Germans attempted to neutralize this trade advantage through U-boat, or sub-marine, warfare, and American lives were lost in unannounced attacks, such as that on the *Lusitania* (see text pp. 712–713). On different occasions in 1915 and 1916 President Wilson forced the Germans to abandon unrestricted submarine warfare, but in January 1917 Germany resumed its attacks. A month later Americans learned that Germany had offered Mexico a chance to recover Texas, New Mexico, and Arizona if it declared war on the United States (see text pp. 713–714). In April Congress voted for war, and American doughboys soon learned firsthand about the Western Front (see text pp. 717, 720–721).

Document 23-1 is a chilling war poem by Alan Seeger. The virtual impossibility of neutrality is the subject of Document 23-2. In Document 23-3 Hervey Allen describes life at the front. Document 23-4 is a product of the army's desire to classify its personnel.

23-1 "I Have a Rendezvous with Death" (1916)

Alan Seeger

Alan Seeger did not wait for the United States to declare war. A Harvard graduate, Seeger (1888–1916) was living in France when war broke out; he soon joined the French Foreign Legion. The poem reprinted here was prophetic: Seeger was killed in action on the Fourth of July, 1916, one of the 1.26 million soldiers killed or wounded in the Battle of the Somme (see text p. 711).

Source: Alan Seeger, "I Have a Rendezvous with Death," in *Poems of Alan Seeger* (New York: Charles Scribner's Sons, 1916).

I have a rendezvous with Death
At some disputed barricade,
When Spring comes back with rustling shade
And apple-blossoms fill the air—
I have a rendezvous with Death
When Spring brings back blue days and fair.

It may be he shall take my hand
And lead me into his dark land
And close my eyes and quench my breath—
It may be I shall pass him still.
I have a rendezvous with Death
On some scarred slope of battered hill,

When Spring comes round again this year
And the first meadow-flowers appear.

God knows 'twere better to be deep
Pillowed in silk and scented down,
Where love throbs out in blissful sleep,
Pulse nigh to pulse, and breath to breath,
Where hushed awakenings are dear . . .
But I've a rendezvous with Death
At midnight in some flaming town,
When Spring trips north again this year,
And I to my pledged word am true,
I shall not fail that rendezvous.

Questions

1. To what extent can Seeger be considered a romantic?
2. What enabled him to consider the future so calmly?
3. What does this war poem indicate about the soldiers and the kind of war they fought in 1916?

23-2   The Impossibility of Neutrality (1915)

William Jennings Bryan

At the war's outset Americans assumed that neutrality would come without risk, but German submarines quickly taught them otherwise. In May 1915 the British liner *Lusitania* sank after being struck by a torpedo (see text pp. 712–713). Among the 1,198 dead were 128 Americans. In this letter to Woodrow Wilson written shortly after the sinking, Secretary of State William Jennings Bryan outlines some of the difficulties inherent in a policy of neutrality. Bryan resigned in June 1915 to protest what he thought was an inconsistent policy on neutrality: critical of German infractions but silent about British violations.

Source: William Jennings Bryan to Woodrow Wilson (1915). In *Papers Relating to the Foreign Relations of the United States: The Lansing Papers (1914–1920)* (Washington, D.C.: U.S. Government Printing Office, 1939), vol. 1, pp. 392–393.

Washington [, *undated*].

My Dear Mr. President: Your more than generous note received with draft of protest to Germany. I have gone over it very carefully and will give it to Mr. Lansing at once, for I agree with you that it is well to act without delay in order to give direction to public opinion. I do not see that you could have stated your position more clearly or more forcibly. In one sentence I suggest "as the last few weeks have shown" so that it will read: "Submarines, we respectfully submit, cannot be used against Merchantmen, as the last few weeks have shown, without an inevitable violation of many sacred principles of justice and humanity." The only other amendment that occurs to me relates to the *Cushing* and *Gulflight*. Would it not be wise to make some reference to the rules sent us and the offer to apologize and make reparation in case a neutral ship was sunk by mistake? I suggest something like this: "Apology and reparation for destruction of neutral ships, sunk by mistake, while they may satisfy international obligation, if no loss of life results, can not justify or excuse a practice, the natural and almost necessary effect of which is to subject neutral nations to new and innumerable risks, for it must be remembered that peace, not war, is the normal state and that nations that resort to war for a settlement of international disputes are not at liberty to subordinate the rights of neutrals to the supposed or even actual needs of belligerents." I am in doubt of the propriety of referring to the note published by [German ambassador] Bernstorff.

But, my dear Mr. President, I join in this document with a heavy heart. I am as sure of your patriotic purpose as I am of my own, but after long consideration both careful and prayerful, I cannot bring myself to the belief that it is wise to relinquish the hope of playing the part of a friend to both sides in the role of peace maker and this note will, I fear, result in such relinquishment—a hope which requires for its realization the retention of the confidence of both sides. It will be popular in this country for a time at least, and possibly permanently, because public sentiment, already favorable to the Allies, has been perceptibly increased by the *Lusitania* tragedy, but there is peril in this very fact. Your position being the position of the government will be approved—that approval varying in emphasis in proportion to the intensity of the feeling against Germany. There being no intimation that the final accounting will be postponed until the war is over, the jingo element will not only predict but demand war (see enclosed editorial from *Washington Post* of this morning), and the line will be more distinctly drawn between those who sympathize with Germany and the rest of the people. Outside of the country the demand will be applauded by the Allies and the more they applaud the more Germany will be embittered, because we unsparingly denounce the retaliatory methods employed by her, without condemning the announced purpose of the Allies to starve the non-combatants of Germany and without complaining of the conduct of Great Britain in relying on passengers including men, women and children of the United States to give immunity to vessels carrying munitions of war—without even suggesting that she should convoy passenger ships as carefully as she does ships carrying horses and gasoline. This enumeration does not include a reference to Great Britain's indifference to the increased dangers thrown upon us by the misuse of our flag or to her unwarranted interference with our trade with neutral nations. Germany cannot but construe the strong statement of the case against her, coupled with silence as to the unjustifiable action of the Allies as evidence of partiality toward the latter—an impression which will be deepened in proportion to the loudness of the praise which the Allies bestow upon the statement of this government's position. The only way, as I see it, to prevent irreparable injury being done by the statement is to issue simultaneously a protest against the objectionable conduct of the Allies which will keep them from rejoicing and show Germany that we are defending our rights against aggression from both sides.

I am only giving you, my dear Mr. President, the situa-

tion as it appears to me—and praying all the while that I may be wholly mistaken and that your judgement may be vindicated by events. . . .

Questions

1. Why is Bryan concerned about the president's note of protest on the *Lusitania* incident?
2. What are his criticisms of Great Britain?
3. How does Bryan propose to handle the official protest so that the United States will be able to maintain neutrality?

23-3 "German Dugouts" (1918)

Hervey Allen

The poet and novelist Hervey Allen (1888–1949) joined the National Guard after his graduation from the University of Pittsburgh in 1915. Before going to France, Allen served with the expeditionary force that pursued Pancho Villa in Mexico (see text p. 714). The following is an excerpt from Allen's wartime diary, *Toward the Flame.*

Source: Excerpted from Hervey Allen, "German Dugouts" (1918), in *Toward the Flame: A War Diary* by Hervey Allen. Copyright 1926, 1934 by Hervey Allen. Copyright 1954, © 1962 by Ann Andrews Allen. Reprinted by permission of Henry Holt and Co., Inc. (In reprint edition, Pittsburgh: University of Pittsburgh Press, 1968, pp. 111–119.)

I awoke to hear the pleasant clinking of mess pans. The rain had stopped, but the forest was still dripping, and the mud was deep and peculiarly slippery. The captain and I crawled out, both about the same time, and made our way to the kitchen where a savory mess was being dished out, smoking hot gobs of bread and canned sweet potato, a favorite and frequent delicacy at the front. Paul and some of the other French soldiers were helping. By this time the men were happy again. A little rest and something to eat were doing wonders. The captain and I were not much behind the rest of the company as trenchermen, although I avoided eating much meat at the front.

We were issued beef in immense quantities, sometimes having to bury a whole quarter of it. It became tainted very easily, where of course there was no possible means of refrigeration. This meat ration came wrapped in burlap, generally reasonably fresh; but once open, it had to be carried around in the ration carts, and unless quickly cooked, it spoiled very rapidly, especially in those summer days along the Marne when the sun was hot.

Another thing which hastened the destruction of perishable food was the immense amount of decay all along the front. All those rotten woods were filled with dead horses, dead men, the refuse, excrement and the garbage of armies. The ground must have been literally alive with pus

and decay germs. Scratch your hand, cut yourself in shaving, or get a little abrasion on your foot, and almost anything could happen. Bichloride tablets were invaluable; I always threw one into my canvas basin for good luck.

During the meal, Lieutenant Scott, who had been assistant division gas officer for a while, but who had now returned to the company, joined us, and mentioned that he was making all arrangements for a new gas alarm, having found some empty brass shells used for that purpose "over there"—and he pointed to a cape of trees that ran out from a wood-island into the surrounding fields.

That part of the world consisted of a great level plateau, prairie-like fields interspersed with woods, the "bois" of the French maps, like islands of all sizes and shapes. We were then camped in one of these wood "islands," and across "there," where the lieutenant had pointed, was another "island" in which were the remnants of a German battery. The captain and I strolled across after dinner, letting the warm sun dry us off.

The guns were still in their pits, as "Fritz" had left very suddenly here. The guns pointed their noses up at a high angle like hounds baying the moon, but they were silent now. The wood was full of little dugouts, walks, and houses. The Germans had evidently stayed here a long time. Out in the field were a large number of big shell craters in a line, *one, two, three* . . . where our 220's had evidently been ranging on the battery. They had come quite near, within fifty yards or so.

Along the edge of these thickets were a number of graves. I was greatly impressed by them. The crosses were well carved out of new wood, and the grave mounds carefully spaded. Here were wreaths of wax flowers, evidently sent from home, and a board giving the epitaph of the deceased, with his rank and honors: "He was a good Christian and fell in France fighting for the Fatherland, *Hier ruht in Gott* [Here he rests in God]." Verily, these seemed to be the same Goths and Vandals who left their graves even in Egypt; unchanged since the days of Rome, and still fighting her civilization, the woods-people against the Latins. Only the illuminating literary curiosity of a Tacitus was lacking to make the inward state of man visible by the delineation of the images of outer things.

We entered some of the dugouts, small, mound-like structures with straw inside. Some of the officers' were larger. There was a little beer garden in the middle of the wood with a chapel and a wreathed cross near by, white stones and twisting "rustic" paths. The railings and booths along these paths were made from roots and branches cleverly bent and woven, and sometimes carved. It reminded me of American "porch furniture" of a certain type. All quite German. Cast-off boots, shell-timers, one or two coats, and shrapnel-bitten helmets lay about with round Boche [an insulting nickname for "German"] hats, "the little round button on top." Picture post-cards and magazines, pistol holsters, and one or two broken rifles completed this cartoon of invasion.

All the litter of material thus left behind was useless. I noticed the pictures of some fat, and rather jolly-looking German girls, and piles of a vast quantity of shells. We looked around thoroughly, but were very wary of traps. I remember making up my mind to make for one of these dugouts in case we were shelled. One always kept a weather eye open.

About all this stuff there was at that time the dire taint of danger. Somehow everything German gave one the creeps. It was connected so intimately with all that was unpleasant, and associated so inevitably with organized fear, that one scarce regarded its owners as men. It seemed *then* as if we were fighting some strange, ruthless, insect-beings from another planet; that we had stumbled upon their nests after smoking them out. One had the same feeling as when waking up at night and realizing that there are rats under the bed.

The captain and I walked along the edge of the wood, encountering our French contingent on the way. They were "at home" in an old German dugout, happily squatted around several small fires, preparing their meal as *they* liked it. After a good deal of difficulty, they had prevailed on our mess sergeant to issue them their rations in bulk so that they could do their own cooking. Such little differences of customs are in reality most profound. Our physical habits were more like the Germans'!

The non-commissioned gas officer picked us up here. He was carrying back the big brass shell for a gas alarm. It gave forth a mellow musical note when touched with a bar of iron or a bayonet. The Germans had used this one themselves for that purpose, so it already had the holes and wire for suspending it. . . .

We moved before it was light, which is very early in summer time in France. The dim columns of men coming out of the woods, the lines of carts and kitchens assembling in the early, gray dawn, all without a light, and generally pretty silently, was always impressive.

In a few minutes we were headed back in the direction from which we had come. There was a full moon, or one nearly so, hanging low in the west. As I jolted along, on legs that seemed more like stilts than limbs with knees, the heavy equipment sagged at every step, and seemed to clink one's teeth together weakly. At last the weariness and the jangle took on a fagged rhythm that for me fell into the comfort of rhyme.

We were beginning to be pretty tired by now and even here needed relief. One no longer got up in the morning full of energy. Hunger, dirt, and strain were telling, and we felt more or less "all in" that day in particular. One was consciously weak.

Nevertheless the country was beautiful; the full moon just sinking in the west looked across the smoking, misty valleys at the rising sun. There was a gorgeous bloody-gold color in the sky, and the woods and fields sparkled deliciously green, looking at a little distance fresh and untouched. But that was only a distant appearance, for this was the country over which two days before the Americans had driven the Germans from one machine gun nest to another, and on from crest to crest. A nearer approach showed the snapped tree-trunks, the tossed branches and shell-pitted ground, and at one halt that we made, Nick called me down a little slope to see something.

There was a small spring in a draw beside the road, where two Germans were lying. One was a bit, brawny fellow with a brown beard, and the other a mere lad. He looked to be about 14 or 15 with a pathetically childish chin, but he carried potatomasher bombs. They had evidently stopped here to try to fill their canteens, probably both desperate with thirst, when they were overtaken by our men. The young boy must have sheltered himself behind the man while the latter held our fellows back a little. There was a scorched place up the side of the ravine where a hand grenade had exploded, but the big German had been surrounded, and killed by the bayonet right through his chest. His hands were still clutching at the place where the steel had gone through. He was one of the few I ever saw who had been killed by the bayonet. The boy was lying just behind him. His back appeared to have been broken, probably by a blow with the butt of a rifle, and he was contorted into a kind of arch, only his feet and shoulders resting on the ground. It was he who had probably thrown the grenade that had exploded near by. The little spring had evidently been visited by the wounded, as there were blood and first-aid wrappings about. I refused to have the company water tank filled there. . . .

Questions

1. Describe conditions at the front.
2. How does Allen regard the enemy?
3. What did he find at the small spring? What does that scene indicate about the unpredictability of combat?

23-4 Army Mental Tests

War presented the U.S. Army with the immense challenge of classifying millions of men for military service. Intelligence testing appeared to be the key to that undertaking (see text p. 720). The tests excerpted below were reprinted in book form in 1920, and for some Americans measuring intelligence became more than a tool: xenophobes and racists now had a "scientific" argument to back their views.

Source: Tests 2 and 3 in Clarence S. Yoakum and Robert M. Yerkes, comps. and eds., *Army Mental Tests*, published with the authorization of the War Department (New York: Henry Holt, 1920), pp. 206–209.

TEST 2
Get the answers to these examples as quickly as you can.
Use the side of this page to figure on if you need to.

SAMPLES
{
1 How many are 5 men and 10 men? ....Answer (**15**)
2 If you walk 4 miles an hour for 3 hours, how far do you walk? ....Answer (**12**)
}

1 How many are 30 men and 7 men?...Answer (   )

2 If you save $7 a month for 4 months, how much will you save? ....Answer (   )

3 If 24 men are divided into squads of 8, how many squads will there be?....................Answer (   )

4 Mike had 12 cigars. He bought 3 more, and then smoked 6. How many cigars did he have left? ....Answer (   )

5 A company advanced 5 miles and retreated 3 miles. How far was it then from its first position? ....Answer (   )

6 How many hours will it take a truck to go 66 miles at the rate of 6 miles an hour? ....Answer (   )

7 How many cigars can you buy for 50 cents at the rate of 2 for 5 cents?....................Answer (   )

8 A regiment marched 40 miles in five days. The first day they marched 9 miles, the second day 6 miles, the third 10 miles, the fourth 8 miles. How many miles did they march the last day?...Answer (   )

9 If you buy two packages of tobacco at 7 cents each and a pipe for 65 cents, how much change should you get from a two-dollar bill?..Answer (   )

10 If it takes 6 men 3 days to dig a 180-foot drain, how many men are needed to dig it in half a day? ....Answer (   )

11   A dealer bought some mules for $800. He sold them for $1,000, making $40 on
     each mule. How many mules were there?..Answer (   )
12   A rectangular bin holds 400 cubic feet of lime. If the bin is 10 feet long and
     5 feet wide, how deep is it?..Answer (   )
13   A recruit spent one-eighth of his spare change for post cards and four times as much for a
     box of letter paper, and then had 90 cents left. How much money did he have at first?............Answer (   )
14   If 3^1/$_2$ tons of coal cost $21, what will 5^1/$_2$ tons cost? ....Answer (   )
15   A ship has provisions to last her crew of 500 men 6 months. How long would it last
     1,200 men?...Answer (   )
16   If a man runs a hundred yards in 10 seconds, how many feet does he run in
     a fifth of a second?..Answer (   )
17   A U-boat makes 8 miles an hour under water and 15 miles on the surface. How long
     will it take to cross a 100-mile channel, if it has to go two-fifths of the way under water?........Answer (   )
18   If 241 squads of men are to dig 4,097 yards of trench, how many yards must be dug
     by each squad?...Answer (   )
19   A certain division contains 3,000 artillery, 15,000 infantry and 1,000 cavalry. If
     each branch is expanded proportionately until there are in all 20,900 men, how
     many will be added to the artillery? ....Answer (   )
20   A commission house which had already supplied 1,897 barrels of apples to a
     cantonment delivered the remainder of its stock to 29 mess halls. Of this remainder
     each mess hall received 54 barrels. What was the total number of barrels supplied? ....Answer (   )

TEST 3

This is a test of common sense. Below are sixteen questions.
Three answers are given to each question. You are to look at
the answers carefully; then make a cross in the square before
the best answer to each question, as in the sample:

SAMPLE {
Why do we use stoves? Because
☐ they look well
☒ they keep us warm
☐ they are black
}

Here the second answer is the best one and is marked with
a cross. Begin with No. 1 and keep on until time is called.

1 Cats are useful animals, because
   ☐ they catch mice
   ☐ they are gentle
   ☐ they are afraid of dogs
2 Why are pencils more commonly carried than fountain pens? Because
   ☐ they are brightly colored
   ☐ they are cheaper
   ☐ they are not so heavy
3 Why is leather used for shoes? Because
   ☐ it is produced in all countries
   ☐ it wears well
   ☐ it is an animal product
4 Why judge a man by what he does rather than what he
   says? Because
   ☐ what a man does shows what he really is
   ☐ it is wrong to tell a lie
   ☐ a deaf man cannot hear what is said

5 If you were asked what you thought of a person whom
   you didn't know, what should you say?
   ☐ I will go and get acquainted
   ☐ I think he is all right
   ☐ I don't know him and can't say
6 Streets are sprinkled in summer
   ☐ to make the air cooler
   ☐ to keep automobiles from skidding
   ☐ to keep down dust
7 Why is wheat better for food than corn? Because
   ☐ it is more nutritious
   ☐ it is more expensive
   ☐ it can be ground finer
8 If a man made a million dollars, he ought to
   ☐ pay off the national debt
   ☐ contribute to various worthy charities
   ☐ give it all to some poor man

9 Why do many persons prefer automobiles to street cars? Because
☐ an auto is made of higher grade materials
☐ an automobile is more convenient
☐ street cars are not as safe

10 The feathers on a bird's wings help him to fly because they
☐ make a wide, light surface
☐ keep the air off his body
☐ keep the wings from cooling off too fast

11 All traffic going one way keeps to the same side of the street because
☐ most people are right handed
☐ the traffic policeman insists on it
☐ it avoids confusion and collisions

12 Why do inventors patent their inventions? Because
☐ it gives them control of their inventions
☐ it creates a greater demand
☐ it is the custom to get patents

13 Freezing water bursts pipes because
☐ cold makes the pipes weaker
☐ water expands when it freezes
☐ the ice stops the flow of water

14 Why are high mountains covered with snow? Because
☐ they are near the clouds
☐ the sun seldom shines on them
☐ the air is cold there

15 If the earth were nearer the sun
☐ the stars would disappear
☐ our months would be longer
☐ the earth would be warmer

16 Why is it colder nearer the poles than nearer the equator? Because
☐ the poles are always farther from the sun
☐ the sunshine falls obliquely at the poles
☐ there is more ice at the poles

Questions

1. What factors might affect test performance?
2. Who was most likely to test well? Poorly?
3. Is it possible that the tests, while not accurate indicators of intelligence, say something about the state of American education at that time? How so?

Questions for Further Thought

1. What compelled both sides to fight on for four years even though Woodrow Wilson offered to mediate a peace settlement?
2. What made American neutrality unworkable?
3. How did Alan Seeger (Document 23-1) and Hervey Allen (Document 23-3) react to the conditions they encountered? How were their responses similar, and how were they different?
4. To what extent would the "intelligence" the army sought to measure (Document 23-4) have mattered at the front, as detailed by Hervey Allen?

Mobilizing the Home Front

Woodrow Wilson did not share the public's excitement over the declaration of war; he knew what was coming. "Once lead this country into war, and they'll forget there ever was such a thing as tolerance," Wilson observed (see text p. 727). "To fight you must be ruthless and brutal, and the spirit of ruthless brutality will enter into the very fiber of our national life."

The war did transform American society (see text pp. 722–723), and government grew as it never had before. The War Industries Board (WIB) coordinated production, the Railroad Administration operated the national rail lines, and the Food Administration made it possible to feed the people of Europe. Business did not mind this change. Washington focused on results, not on the means of obtaining them, and so antitrust prosecutions were suspended. Not only was business allowed to grow, it was encouraged to send representatives for government service. The WIB was headed by Bernard Baruch, a veteran of Wall Street.

The war affected the home front in other ways. Organized labor benefited from the arbitration decisions of the National War Labor Board, and the labor shortage brought new groups into factory work (see text pp. 723–724). For African-Americans there was now an alternative to southern sharecropping; by the war's end, hundreds of thousands had migrated to find factory work in the North. Mexican-Americans also took advantage of the opportunity to get higher-paying jobs in industry. The options were greater for women: war industry jobs and—at least for those who were white and middle class—a choice of government service or volunteer work for organizations such as the Red Cross and the YWCA (see text pp. 724–726). The United States failed to make the world safe for democracy, but American women built on their wartime contributions to win the right to vote.

Wilson was right about the change in spirit, much of it caused by government propaganda. Most, though not all, Americans supported the war. They bought Liberty bonds (see text p. 722), listened to speeches by "four-minute men" (see text p. 727), and learned new names for sauerkraut and hamburgers (see text p. 727). Meanwhile, the Committee on Public Information played on wartime fears and anxieties. The dreaded Hun could be anywhere, and so dissent, whether the product of ethnicity or of ideology, carried a risk. Wartime civil liberties were greatly diminished under the Espionage and Sedition Acts, as Eugene Debs found when he was given a ten-year prison sentence for condemning the war (see text p. 728). More than a thousand people were convicted for speech that Supreme Court Justice Oliver Wendell Holmes said would "create a clear and present danger to the safety of the country" (see text p. 728).

Document 23-5 is an example of wartime patriotism taken to the extreme. Document 23-6 shows how the war changed the social roles of American women. The story of the "four-minute men" is told by George Creel in Document 23-7.

23-5   "The Kaiser in the Making"

In the summer of 1917 the Chicago Board of Education discovered that multicultural instruction could have a direct relationship with world affairs. In an effort to make spelling and grammar relevant to immigrant students, the board included the following exercise in its eighth-grade speller. But with the declaration of war in April 1917, the board looked like an agent of disloyalty (see text pp. 727–728). With people already acting on their own to remove the offensive exercise, the board voted to do the same thing.

Source: "The Kaiser in the Making," in *The Chicago Public School Spelling Book for Grades Four, Five, Six, Seven, Eight* (Chicago: Board of Education, 1914), p. 154.

SPELLING—Eighth Grade

December 19, 1910

Note: Dictate to the pupils the following text. . . .
The pupils will be marked on the words in italics. . . .

THE KAISER IN THE MAKING

In the *gymnasium* at Cassel the German *Kaiser* spent three years of his boyhood, a *diligent* but not a *brilliant* pupil, ranking tenth among *seventeen candidates* for the *university*.

Many tales are told of this *period* of his life, and one of them, at least, is *illuminating*.

A *professor*, it is said, wishing to curry favor with his royal pupil, informed him *overnight* of the chapter in Greek that was to be made the *subject* of the next day's lesson.

The young *prince* did what many boys would not have done. As soon as the class room was *opened* on the following morning, he entered and wrote *conspicuously* on the blackboard the *information* that had been given him.

One may say *unhesitatingly* that a boy capable of such an action has the root of a fine *character* in him, *possesses* that *chivalrous* sense of fair play which is the nearest thing to a *religion* that may be looked for at that age, hates *meanness* and *favoritism*, and will *wherever possible*, expose them. There is in him a *fundamental* bent toward what is clean, manly and aboveboard.

Questions

1. What lessons in character was the exercise intended to convey?
2. Which groups would have found this exercise offensive?
3. What does the reaction to the exercise suggest about the wartime atmosphere in Chicago?

23-6   The Home Front: Women Fund-Raisers

As Chapter 23 in the textbook notes, "Women were the largest group that took advantage of new opportunities in wartime" (p. 724). Jobs opened up in industry and government service, and women who wanted to serve overseas volunteered for the Red Cross and the Young Women's Christian Association. YWCA fund-raising provided a different kind of challenge, as shown in this 1920 state history of wartime welfare campaigns in Iowa.

Source: Excerpted from Marcus L. Hansen, "The Campaign of the Young Women's Christian Association," in *Welfare Campaigns in Iowa* (Iowa City: State Historical Society of Iowa, 1920), pp. 100–103, 105–106, 108, 111–112.

In the recent struggle there were many active participants who did not shoulder a rifle. A year after the declaration of a state of war a million and a half men were in military service: at that time a million and a half women were engaged in the manufacture of war materials: and as the number in the one class increased, the other force expanded correspondingly. Most of these women were living a life just as novel, just as separated from their previous existence as were the soldiers: and the woman worker was as prone to homesickness and loneliness as was the recruit in the camp. If he needed welfare work and the people furnished it, should she not also be remembered?

The inspector general of the Iowa militia had reported in 1901, on the presence of women in the militia camps, that they were "a nuisance, underfoot, and a detriment to the good work and benefits expected of camp". But, whether a nuisance or not, women were bound to come to the places where the soldiers were—to enjoy a family picnic, to visit the sick in the hospital, or to say a final good-bye before the departure over-seas. Cast alone into a city of barracks, the mother, the sister, or the friend was just as be-wildered as was the recruit on his first visit to the neigh-boring city. If the War Camp Community Service provided for him, should not someone think of her?

Welfare work among soldiers had as one object the preservation of their efficiency by removing the incentives to immorality. But who would guide past temptation in the vicinity of the military camp the girl now suddenly brought into contact with thousands of fighting men?

It was to the Young Women's Christian Association that the welfare of the industrial workers, the women in the camps, and the girls in the cantonment cities was en-trusted. The Women's Branch of the Industrial Service Sec-tion of the Ordnance Department invited the Association to supervise the recreational activities in these industries. Upon the request of a camp commander the Association was ready to construct a Hostess House for the conve-nience of women visitors, and safeguards were thrown around the girls by the organization of Patriotic Leagues—an outgrowth of work which had already been done under the Social Morality Committee of this society.

The Young Women's Christian Association was not without experience in tasks of this nature. For fifty years there had existed local groups of young women, some as-sociated with the International Board of Women's and Young Women's Christian Associations and some with the American committee. In December, 1906, a National Board of the Young Women's Christian Association was created by these local groups, and by the constitution adopted in 1909 general supervision over all the work was delegated to this board which consisted of fifty-six mem-bers and fifteen auxiliary members. The country was di-vided into eleven fields, each of which was represented on the National Board by one delegate. The North Central Field included Iowa, Minnesota, Nebraska, North Dakota, and South Dakota, and had its headquarters at Minneapo-lis, Minnesota. Each field had an executive secretary who was aided by industrial, extension, county, student, and of-fice secretaries.

Following the precedent of the Young Men's Christian Association, the women organized a special War Work Council to which was delegated all activities which arose in connection with the war. The first problem was the fi-nancing of these various tasks, and it was with this subject that the War Work Council dealt at their first meeting held in New York City on June 7, 1917. It was there resolved that the country should be appealed to for $1,000,000 of which $50,000 would be expended in work abroad.

Although an active campaign was started to obtain $1,000,000, it did not remain the goal. So great was the demand for hostess houses, so insistent the appeal from abroad, that on October 9th decision was made to place the sum at $4,000,000 of which $1,000,000 would be ex-pended in France and Russia. . . .

How a rural county was organized is illustrated in a report written by Miss Caroline W. Daniels of Indepen-dence. "On Nov. 20, 1917, District Y. W. workers from Dubuque called a meeting in the High School Auditorium to organize Buchanan Co. About two dozen women were present. Miss Doris Campbell was chosen Sec-Treas. and I chairman. That afternoon Miss Campbell and I in her car began a tour of the newspaper offices of the county and that evening we had an organization meeting of prospec-tive war leaders for Independence, the county seat. With the consent of the Red Cross officers we used their organi-zation as a fulcrum throughout the county outside the Co. seat. Our method was to drive to every Red Cross group of workers; get permission to explain the need to them while they worked; arrange for some one of their number to take charge of a canvass in their town or township, or region; tell them of their share of the sum asked for from the county (basing this on population); and depart. The same method was used with any other groups we could get ac-cess to:—clubs, societies, etc. These groups received us with good will, and took our request as one of the war ne-cessities that must be met, however weary and already over worked they felt. These visits were supplemented by let-ters, literature, posters, newspaper notices, announcements by townships of returns, etc., etc."

In the cities where there was a local branch of the As-sociation the task was left to this organization. Accord-ingly, Dubuque was omitted from the plans made by the chairman of that district. The organization of Burlington became the center of the campaign in that city and its members were active workers in many Iowa cities. The scheme of the local campaigns was practically the same as that used by the men in their efforts—that is, competitive teams organized on military lines. Women served as cap-tains, lieutenants, and privates; and at Fort Dodge they acted as "four minute men" presenting the merits of their cause in the theaters. In other places, however, women did not bear the entire responsibility. Sioux City had as its campaign manager, John O. Knutson, president of the Ro-tary Club; and on the executive and advisory committees appeared both men and women. Likewise, though the cap-tains of the eighteen soliciting teams were women, many men served in the ranks. . . .

Just as the high school boys were an effective factor in the raising of the fund of the Young Men's Christian Asso-ciation, so the high school girls contributed to the success of the women's endeavor. Indeed, at Fort Dodge the system was much the same. High school girls were organized on military lines, with a major and two captains. Each captain chose a lieutenant and a corporal from each class. A meet-ing was held at which time pledge cards, stating the will-ingness of the girls to give fifty cents a month for ten months, were passed out with instructions to take them home and have them countersigned by their parents. When the cards were returned it was found that $635 had been pledged. More than forty girls of the East High School in

Waterloo pledged five dollars each toward the cause. In Washington the high school girls conducted the local campaign and received pledges of more than eight hundred dollars. . . .

Besides apathy and indifference there were in this campaign distinct objections to be overcome. Such was the "dancing girls story". A special article in a Chicago Sunday paper stated that the Young Women's Christian Association planned to bring several hundred girls to Camp Lewis, Washington, and pay them fifteen dollars weekly to dance with the soldiers of the cantonment who were to pay fifteen cents for each dance. In varying forms this story was widely copied and caused some people to hesitate in their giving, although it was immediately declared by campaign officials to be "absolutely false in every detail."

Even in remote rural districts rumors arose. The nature of the reports against which workers had to contend is illustrated by an incident occurring in one Iowa community. After considerable trouble a chairman was found for a township; but "later it was reported to us", states the narrative of the county chairman, "that she changed her mind and telephoned all around the neighborhood warning the women to have nothing to do with the movement as she had discovered (?) that it was all a scheme to collect money for building houses of ill fame for the soldiers of Camp Dodge!!! We bombarded her with publicity material, but got no returns from that township. In less virulent form we ran into this notion a number of times. The work for Red Cross nurses made instant appeal everywhere; but 'Hostess Houses' were either suspected or openly disapproved of. Work to keep safe young girls who flocked to Des Moines met with much criticism from country women who thought 'mothers should look after their own girls' 'that was what they were doing.'"

Questions

1. What kind of general prejudice faced women who became involved with the military?
2. What kind of work did women fund-raisers do?
3. How were the skills women learned in 1917–1918 applicable in the 1920s and later?

23-7 The Home Front: The "Four-Minute Men" (1920)

George Creel

Washington fought the propaganda war through the Committee on Public Information, which was headed by the journalist George Creel (1876–1953). As described in the textbook (pp. 726–728), the CPI used speakers, movies, posters, and pamphlets to spread its not always accurate message. This excerpt on the "four-minute men" comes from Creel's history of the CPI, *How We Advertised America* (1920).

Source: George Creel, *How We Advertised America: The First Telling of the Amazing Story of the Committee on Public Information That Carried the Gospel of Americanism to Every Corner of the Globe* (New York: Harper & Bros., 1920), pp. 84–88, 90–92.

There was nothing more time-wasting than the flood of people that poured into Washington during the war, each burdened with some wonderful suggestions that could be imparted only to an executive head. Even so, all of them had to be seen, for not only was it their right as citizens, but it was equally the case that the idea might have real value. Many of our best suggestions came from the most unlikely sources.

In the very first hours of the Committee, when we were still penned in the navy library, fighting for breath, a handsome, rosy-cheeked youth burst through the crowd and caught my lapel in a death-grip. His name was Donald Ryerson. He confessed to Chicago as his home, and the plan that he presented was the organization of volunteer speakers for the purpose of making patriotic talks in motion-picture theaters. He had tried out the scheme in Chicago, and the success of the venture had catapulted him on the train to Washington and to me.

Being driven to the breaking-point has certain compensations, after all. It forces one to think quickly and confines thought largely to the positive values of a suggestion rather than future difficulties. Had I had the time to weigh the proposition from every angle, it may be that I would have decided against it, for it was delicate and dangerous business to turn loose on the country an army of speakers impossible of exact control and yet vested in large degree with the authority of the government. In ten minutes we had decided upon a national organization to be called the "Four Minute Men," and Mr. Ryerson rushed out with my appointment as its director.

When the armistice brought activities to a conclusion the Four Minute Men numbered 75,000 speakers, more than 7,555,190 speeches had been made, and a fair estimate of audiences makes it certain that a total of 134,454,514 people had been addressed. Notwithstanding the nature of the work, the infinite chances of blunder and bungle, this unique and effective agency functioned from first to last with only one voice ever raised to attack its faith and efficiency. As this voice was that of Senator Sherman of Illinois, this attack is justly to be set down as part of the general praise.

The form of presentation decided upon was a glass slide to be thrown on the theater-curtain, and worded as follows:

4   MINUTE MEN   4
(Copyright, 1917. Trade-mark.)

....

(Insert name of speaker)

will speak four minutes on a subject
of national importance. He speaks
under the authority of
THE COMMITTEE ON PUBLIC INFORMATION
GEORGE CREEL, CHAIRMAN
WASHINGTON, D. C.

A more difficult decision was as to the preparation of the matter to be sent out to speakers. We did not want stereotyped oratory, and yet it was imperative to guard against the dangers of unrestraint. It was finally agreed that regular bulletins should be issued, each containing a budget of material covering every phase of the question to be discussed, and also including two or three illustrative four-minute speeches. Mr. Waldo P. Warren of Chicago was chosen to write the first bulletin, and when he was called away his duties fell upon E. T. Gundlach, also of Chicago, the patriotic head of an advertising agency. These bulletins, however, prepared in close and continued consultation with the proper officials of each government department responsible for them, were also gone over carefully by Professor Ford and his scholars.

The idea, from the very first, had the sweep of a prairie fire. Speakers volunteered by the thousand in every state, the owners of the motion-picture houses, after a first natural hesitancy, gave exclusive privileges to the organization, and the various government departments fairly clamored for the services of the Four Minute Men. The following list of bulletins will show the wide range of topics:

Topic	Period
Universal Service by Selective Draft	May 12–21, 1917
First Liberty Loan	May 22–June 15, 1917
Red Cross	June 18–25, 1917
Organization	
Food Conservation	July 1–14, 1917
Why We Are Fighting	July 23–Aug. 5, 1917
The Nation in Arms	Aug. 6–26, 1917
The Importance of Speed	Aug. 19–26, 1917
What Our Enemy Really Is	Aug. 27–Sept. 23, 1917
Unmasking German Propaganda	Aug. 27–Sept. 23, 1917 (supplementary topic)
Onward to Victory	Sept. 24–Oct. 27, 1917
Second Liberty Loan	Oct. 8–28, 1917
Food Pledge	Oct. 29–Nov. 4, 1917
Maintaining Morals and Morale	Nov. 12–25, 1917
Carrying the Message	Nov. 26–Dec. 22, 1917
War Savings Stamps	Jan. 2–19, 1918
The Shipbuilder	Jan. 28–Feb. 9, 1918
Eyes for the Navy	Feb. 11–16, 1918
The Danger to Democracy	Feb. 18–Mar. 10, 1918
Lincoln's Gettysburg Address	Feb. 12, 1918
The Income Tax	Mar. 11–16, 1918
Farm and Garden	Mar. 25–30, 1918
President Wilson's Letter to Theaters	Mar. 31–Apr. 5, 1918
Third Liberty Loan	Apr. 6–May 4, 1918
Organization	(Republished Apr. 23, 1918)
Second Red Cross Campaign	May 13–25, 1918
Danger to America	May 27–June 12, 1918
Second War Savings Campaign	June 24–28, 1918
The Meaning of America	June 29–July 27, 1918
Mobilizing America's Man Power	July 29–Aug. 17, 1918
Where Did You Get Your Facts?	Aug. 26–Sept. 7, 1918
Certificates to Theater Members	Sept. 9–14, 1918
Register	Sept. 5–12, 1918
Four Minute Singing	For general use
Fourth Liberty Loan	Sept. 28–Oct. 19, 1918
Food Program for 1919	Changed to Dec. 1–7; finally cancelled
Fire Prevention	Oct. 27–Nov. 2, 1918
United War Work Campaign	Nov. 3–18, 1918
Red Cross Home Service	Dec. 7, 1918
What Have We Won?	Dec. 8–14, 1918
Red Cross Christmas Roll Call	Dec. 15–23, 1918
A Tribute to the Allies	Dec. 24, 1918

Almost from the first the organization has the projectile force of a French "75," [a French artillery piece] and it was increasingly the case that government department heads turned to the Four Minute Men when they wished to arouse the nation swiftly and effectively. At a time when the Third Liberty Loan was lagging, President Wilson bought a fifty-dollar bond and challenged the men and women of the nation to "match" it. The Treasury Department asked the Committee to broadcast the message, and paid for the telegrams that went out to the state and county chairmen. Within a few days fifty thousand Four Minute Men were delivering the challenge to the people of every community in the United States, and the loan took a leap that carried it over the top. General Crowder followed the same plan in his registration campaign, putting up the money for the telegrams that went to the state and county chairmen, and like Secretary McAdoo, he obtained the same swift service and instant results. . . .

National arrangements were made to have Four Minute Men appear at the meetings of lodges, fraternal organizations, and labor unions, and this work progressed swiftly. In most cases these speakers were selected from the membership of the organizations to whom they spoke.

Under the authority of state lecturers of granges, four minute messages, based upon the official bulletins, were given also at all meetings of the granges in many states. The work was next extended to reach the lumber-camps of the country, some five hundred organizations being formed in such communities. Indian reservations were also taken in, and furnished some of the largest and most enthusiastic audiences.

The New York branch organized a church department to present four-minute speeches in churches, synagogues, and Sunday-schools. The idea spread from city to city, from state to state, and proved of particular value in rural communities. Some of the states, acting under authority from headquarters, organized women's divisions to bring the messages of the government to audiences at matinée performances in the motion-picture theaters, and to the members of women's clubs and other similar organizations.

College Four Minute Men were organized, under instructors acting as chairmen, to study the regular Four Minute Men bulletins, and practise speaking upon the subjects thereof, each student being required to deliver at least

one four-minute speech to the student body during the semester, in addition to securing satisfactory credits, in order to qualify as a Four Minute Man. This work was organized in 153 colleges. . . .

The Junior Four Minute Men was an expansion that proved to be almost as important as the original idea, for the youngsters of the country rallied with a whoop, and, what was more to the point, gave results as well as enthusiasm. Like so many other activities of the Committee, the Junior movement was more accidental than planned. At the request of the state of Minnesota the Washington office prepared a special War Savings Stamps bulletin. Results were so instant and remarkable that the idea had to be carried to other states, more than a million and a half copies of the bulletin being distributed to school-children during the campaign. Out of it all came the Junior Four Minute Men as a vital and integral part of the Committee on Public Information.

It was our cautious fear, at first, that regular school-work might be interrupted, but it soon developed that the idea had real educational value, helping teachers in their task instead of hindering. The general plan was for the teacher to explain the subject, using the bulletin as a text-book, and the children then wrote their speeches and submitted them to the teacher or principal. The best were selected and delivered as speeches or were read. In a few cases extemporaneous talks were given.

Details of the contests were left largely to the discretion of the teachers. In small schools there was generally one contest for the whole school. In schools of more than five or six classes it was usual to have separate contests for the higher and lower classes, and sometimes for each grade. There were many different ways of conducting these contents. Sometimes they were considered as a regular part of the school-work and were held in the class-room with no outsiders present, but more often they were made special events, the entire school, together with parents and other visitors, being present. Both boys and girls were eligible and the winners were given an official certificate from the government, commissioning them as four-minute speakers upon the specified topic of the contest. . . .

Questions

1. How did the "four-minute men" program work?
2. Where was the potential for abuse in this program?
3. Was there anything about the "four-minute men" that might have attracted the attention of George Orwell?

Questions for Further Thought

1. Drawing on the documents in this section, consider the ways in which war transforms society.

2. How did each of the wartime activities discussed in this section gain public cooperation?

3. How might the kind of wartime patriotism generated by the Committee on Public Information (Document 23-7) have affected the objectivity of the army mental tests (Document 23-4)?

An Unsettled Peace, 1919–1920

Americans fought alongside the British and the French, but in many ways the doughboys experienced a different war. U.S. casualties were far lower (about 111,000 dead) than what the British or French suffered in any of their major battles before the Americans went "over there" (see text p. 717).

Because his war had differed from that of British Prime Minister David Lloyd George and French Premier Georges Clemenceau, Woodrow Wilson envisioned a different peace, one based on his Fourteen Points address to Congress in January 1918. Wilson wanted a postwar world that rested on national self-determination, arms reduction, and free trade. Most important was the fourteenth point: "A general association of nations must be formed under specific covenants for the purpose of affording mutual guarantees of political independence and territorial integrity to great and small States alike." This was to be the foundation of the League of Nations (see text p. 729).

The plan made for excellent wartime propaganda, but the British and the French did not want to use it for much else. "God gave us the Ten Commandments, and we broke them," Clemenceau said. "Wilson gives us the Fourteen Points. We shall see." Outmaneuvered at the Versailles peace conference, Wilson had to accept a peace treaty that saddled Germany with a "war guilt" clause and reparations set at $33 billion in 1921. For what it was worth, Wilson did get his League of Nations (see text pp. 730–731).

Treaty negotiations preoccupied the president for close to a year, but the United States never ratified the treaty or joined the League. Concentrating on foreign policy, Wilson largely ignored domestic issues, with disastrous consequences. Labor and racial strife (see text pp. 731–733) left the public on edge and ready to believe that a radical conspiracy was afoot. In November 1919 Attorney General A. Mitchell Palmer began the notorious Palmer raids. Thousands of radicals were arrested, and those unfortunate enough to be aliens had their civil liberties denied (see text pp. 734–735). The government eventually deported 294 radicals to the Soviet Union. Wilson fought for the League against that backdrop. Wilson's speaking tour on its behalf in late September led to his having an incapacitating stroke (see text p. 731). By May 1920 the League of Nations and the Red Scare had both become passé as Americans turned their attention elsewhere.

Senator Henry Cabot Lodge argues against the League of Nations in Document 23-8. The Chicago race riot is the subject of Document 23-9. In Document 23-10 Calvin Coolidge demonstrates a politician's ability to know when to speak out.

23-8   Opposition to the League of Nations (1919)

Henry Cabot Lodge

Woodrow Wilson did not realize that domestic politics would play a critical role in the campaign for his peace plan. The president erred badly in not appointing any prominent Republicans as delegates to the Paris Conference (see text p. 731). Henry Cabot Lodge (1850–1924), the chairman of the Senate Foreign Relations Committee, would have been a likely choice. Instead, Lodge led the opposition with attacks such as the following. His mention of George Washington's Farewell Address (Document 7-10) was intended to suggest that League supporters were unpatriotic.

Source: Henry Cabot Lodge, speech to the U.S. Senate, February 28, 1919. In Henry Cabot Lodge, *The Senate and the League of Nations* (New York: Charles Scribner's Sons, 1925), pp. 227–233.

Mr. President, all people, men and women alike, who are capable of connected thought abhor war and desire nothing so much as to make secure the future peace of the world. Everybody hates war. Everyone longs to make it impossible. We ought to lay aside once and for all the unfounded and really evil suggestion that because men differ as to the best method of securing the world's peace in the future, anyone is against permanent peace, if it can be obtained, among all the nations of mankind. . . . We all earnestly desire to advance toward the preservation of the world's peace, and difference in method makes no distinction in purpose. It is almost needless to say that the question now before us is so momentous that it transcends all party lines. . . . No question has ever confronted the United States Senate which equals in importance that which is involved in the league of nations intended to secure the future peace of the world. There should be no undue haste in considering it. My one desire is that not only the Senate, which is charged with responsibility, but that the press and the people of the country should investigate every proposal with the utmost thoroughness and weigh them all carefully before they make up their minds. If there is any proposition or any plan which will not bear, which will not court the most thorough and most public discussion, that fact makes it an object of suspicion at the very outset. . . .

In the first place, the terms of the league—the agreements which we make,—must be so plain and so explicit that no man can misunderstand them. . . . The Senate can take no action upon it, but it lies open before us for criticism and discussion. What is said in the Senate ought to be placed before the peace conference and published in Paris, so that the foreign Governments may be informed as to the various views expressed here.

In this draft prepared for a constitution of a league of nations, which is now before the world, there is hardly a clause about the interpretation of which men do not already differ. As it stands there is serious danger that the very nations which sign the constitution of the league will quarrel about the meaning of the various articles before a twelvemonth has passed. It seems to have been very hastily drafted, and the result is crudeness and looseness of expression, unintentional, I hope. There are certainly many doubtful passages and open questions obvious in the articles which can not be settled by individual inference, but which must be made so clear and so distinct that we may all understand the exact meaning of the instrument to which we are asked to set our hands. The language of these articles does not appear to me to have the precision and unmistakable character which a constitution, a treaty, or a law ought to present. The language only too frequently is not the language of laws or statutes. The article concerning mandatories, for example, contains an argument and a statement of existing conditions. Arguments and historical facts have no place in a statute or a treaty. Statutory and legal language must assert and command, not argue and describe. I press this point because there is nothing so vital to the peace of the world as the sanctity of treaties. The suggestion that we can safely sign because we can always violate or abrogate is fatal not only to any league but to peace itself. You can not found world peace upon the cynical "scrap of paper" doctrine so dear to Germany. To whatever instrument the United States sets its hand it must carry out the provisions of that instrument to the last jot and tittle, and observe it absolutely both in letter and in spirit. If this is not done the instrument will become a source of controversy instead of agreement, of dissension instead of harmony. This is all the more essential because it is evident, although not expressly stated, that this league is intended to be indissoluble, for there is no provision for its termination or for the withdrawal of any signatory. We are left to infer that any nation withdrawing from the league exposes itself to penalties and probably to war. Therefore, before we ratify, the terms and language in which the terms are stated must be exact and as precise, as free from any possibility of conflicting interpretations, as it is possible to make them,

The explanation or interpretation of any of these doubtful passages is not sufficient if made by one man, whether that man be the President of the United States, or a Senator, or anyone else. These questions and doubts must be answered and removed by the instrument itself.

It is to be remembered that if there is any dispute about the terms of this constitution there is no court provided that I can find to pass upon differences of opinion as to the terms of the constitution itself. There is no court to fulfill the function which our Supreme Court fulfills. There is provision for tribunals to decide questions submitted for arbitration, but there is no authority to decide differing interpretations as to the terms of the instrument itself.

What I have just said indicates the vast importance of the form and the manner in which the agreements which we are to sign shall be stated. I now come to questions of substance, which seem to me to demand the most careful thought of the entire American people, and particularly of those charged with the responsibility of ratification. We abandon entirely by the proposed constitution the policy laid down by Washington in his Farewell Address and the Monroe doctrine. It is worse than idle, it is not honest, to evade or deny this fact, and every fairminded supporter of this draft plan for a league admits it. I know that some of the ardent advocates of the plan submitted to us regard any suggestion of the importance of the Washington policy as foolish and irrelevant. Perhaps it is. Perhaps the time has come when the policies of Washington should be abandoned; but if we are to cast them aside I think that at least it should be done respectfully and with a sense of gratitude to the great man who formulated them. For nearly a century and a quarter the policies laid down in the Farewell Address have been followed and adhered to by the Government of the United States and by the American people. I doubt if any purely political declaration has ever been observed by any people for so long a time. The principles of the Farewell Address in regard to our foreign relations have been sustained and acted upon by the American people down to the present moment. Washington declared against permanent alliances. He did not close the door on temporary alliances. He did not close the door on temporary alliances for particular purposes. Our entry in the great war just closed was entirely in accord with and violated in no respect the policy laid down by Washington. When we went to war with Germany we made no treaties with the nations engaged in the war against the German Government. The President was so careful in this direction that he did not permit himself ever to refer to the nations by whose side we fought as "allies," but always as "nations associated with us in the war." The attitude recommended by Washington was scrupulously maintained even under the pressure of the great conflict. Now, in the twinkling of an eye, while passion and emotion reign, the Washington policy is to be entirely laid aside and we are to enter upon a permanent and indissoluble alliance. That

which we refuse to do in war we are to do in peace, deliberately, coolly, and with no war exigency. Let us not overlook the profound gravity of this step.

Washington was not only a very great man but he was also a very wise man. He looked far into the future and he never omitted human nature from his calculations. He knew well that human nature had not changed fundamentally since mankind had a history. Moreover, he was destitute of any personal ambitions to a degree never equaled by any other very great man known to us. In all the vital questions with which he dealt it was not merely that he thought of his country first and never thought of himself at all. He was so great a man that the fact that this country had produced him was enough of itself to justify the Revolution and our existence as a Nation. Do not think that I overstate this in the fondness of patriotism and with the partiality of one of his countrymen. The opinion I have expressed is the opinion of the world. . . .

That was the opinion of mankind then, and it is the opinion of mankind to-day, when his statue has been erected in Paris and is about to be erected in London. If we throw aside the political testament of such a man, which has been of living force down to the present instant, because altered circumstances demand it, it is a subject for deep regret and not for rejoicing. . . .

But if we put aside forever the Washington policy in regard to our foreign relations we must always remember that it carries with it the corollary known as the Monroe doctrine. Under the terms of this league draft reported by the committee to the peace conference the Monroe doctrine disappears. It has been our cherished guide and guard for nearly a century. The Monroe doctrine is based on the principle of self-preservation. To say that it is a question of protecting the boundaries, the political integrity, or the American States, is not to state the Monroe doctrine. . . . The real essence of that doctrine is that American questions shall be settled by Americans alone; that the Americas shall be separated from Europe and from the interference of Europe in purely American questions. That is the vital principle of the doctrine.

I have seen it said that the Monroe doctrine is preserved under article 10 [calling for a collective security agreement among League members]; that we do not abandon the Monroe doctrine, we merely extend it to all the world. How anyone can say this passes my comprehension. The Monroe doctrine exists solely for the protection of the American Hemisphere, and to that hemisphere it was limited. If you extend it to all the world, it ceases to exist, because it rests on nothing but the differentiation of the American Hemisphere from the rest of the world. Under this draft of the constitution of the league of nations, American questions and European questions and Asian and African questions are all alike put within the control and jurisdiction of the league. Europe will have the right to take part in the settlement of all American questions, and we, of course, shall have the right to share in the settlement of all questions in Europe and Asia and Africa. Europe and Asia are to take part in policing the American continent and the Panama Canal, and in return we are to have, by way of compensation, the right to police the Balkans and Asia Minor when we are asked to do so. Perhaps the time has come when it is necessary to do this, but it is a very grave step, and I wish now merely to point out that the American people ought never to abandon the Washington policy and the Monroe doctrine without being perfectly certain that they earnestly wish to do so. Standing always firmly by these great policies, w have thriven and prospered and have done more to preserve the world's peace than any nation, league, or alliance which ever existed. For this reason I ask the press and the pubic and, of course, the Senate to consider well the gravity of this proposition before it takes the heavy responsibility of finally casting aside these policies which we have adhered to for a century and more and under which we have greatly served the cause of peace both at home and abroad. . . .

Questions

1. What aspect of the draft of the constitution for the League of Nations disturbs Lodge?
2. Why does he mention George Washington and the other Founders?
3. What was the supposed threat to the Monroe Doctrine (see text p. 261 and the special documents module on American foreign policy)?

23-9 Report on the Chicago Riot (1919)

Focusing his attention on the peace treaty, President Wilson left unattended several festering domestic issues, including race relations. During the war African-Americans moved to the North to take industrial jobs in cities such as Chicago (see text p. 724). Racial friction led to a riot in the summer of 1919 in which thirty-eight Chicagoans were killed in five days of violence (see text pp. 731–732). This official riot report describes the details better than it conveys the emotions involved.

Source: Excerpted from *The Negro in Chicago: A Study of Race Relations and a Race Riot in 1919.* Copyright © 1922 by The University of Chicago Press. Reprinted by permission. (In reprint edition, New York: Arno Press and New York Times, 1968, pp. 17–21.)

. . . Racial outbreaks are often characterized by hangings, burnings, and mutilations, and frequently the cause given for them is a reported Negro attack upon a white woman. None of these features appeared in the Chicago riot. An attempted hanging was reported by a white detective but was unsubstantiated. A report that Joseph Lovings, one of the Negroes killed in the riot, was burned, was heralded abroad and even carried to the United States Senate, but it was false. The coroner's physicians found no burns on his body.

Reports of assaults upon women were at no time mentioned or even hinted at as a cause of the Chicago riot, but after the disorder started reports of such crimes were published in the white and Negro press, but they had no foundation in fact.

Of the ten women wounded in the Chicago riot, seven were white, two were Negroes, and the race of one is unknown. All but one of these ten injuries appears to have been accidental. The exception was the case of Roxy Pratt, a Negro woman who, with her brother, was chased down Wells Street from Forty-seventh by gangsters and was seriously wounded by a bullet. No cases of direct attacks upon white women by Negro men were reported.

The Commission has the record of numerous instances, principally during the first twenty-four hours, where individuals of opposing races met, knives or guns were drawn, and injury was inflicted without the element of mob stimulus.

On Monday mobs operated in sudden, excited assaults, and attacks on street cars provided outstanding cases, five persons being killed and many injured. Nicholas Kleinmark, a white assailant, was stabbed to death by a Negro named Scott, acting in self-defense. Negroes killed were Henry Goodman at Thirtieth and Union streets; John

Mills, on Forty-seventy Street near Union; Louis Taylor at Root Street and Wentworth Avenue; and B. F. Hardy at Forty-sixth Street and Cottage Grove Avenue. All died from beatings.

Crowds armed themselves with stones, bricks, and baseball bats and scanned passing street cars for Negroes. Finding them, trolleys were pulled off wires and entrance to the cars forced. Negroes were dragged from under car seats and beaten. Once off the car the chase began. If possible, the vanguard of the mob caught the fleeing Negroes and beat them with clubs. If the Negro outran the pursuers, stones and bricks brought him down. Sometimes the chase led through back yards and over fences, but it was always short.

Another type of race warfare was the automobile raids carried on by young men crowded in cars, speeding across the dead line at Wentworth Avenue and the "Black Belt," and firing at random. Crowded colored districts, with people sitting on front steps and in open windows, were subjected to this menace. Strangely enough, only one person was killed in these raids, Henry Baker, Negro.

Automobile raids were reported wherever colored people had established themselves, in the "Black Belt," both on the main business streets and in the residence sections, and in the small community near Ada and Loomis streets in the vicinity of Ogden Park.

These raids began Monday night, continued spasmodically all day Tuesday, and were again prevalent that night. In spite of the long period, reports of motorcycle policeman show no white raiders arrested. One suspected raiding automobile was caught on State Street Tuesday night, after collision with a patrol wagon. One of the occupants, a white man, had on his person the badge and identification card of a policeman assigned to the Twenty-fourth Precinct. No case was worked up against him, and the other men in the machine were not heard of again in connection with the raid.

Most of the police motorcycle squad was assigned to the Stanton Avenue station, which was used as police headquarters in the "Black Belt." Several automobile loads of Negroes were arrested, and firearms were found either upon their persons or in the automobile.

In only two cases were Negroes aggressively rioting found outside of the "Black Belt." One of these was the case of the saloon-keeper already mentioned, and the other was that of a deputy sheriff, who, with a party of other men, said they were on the way to the Stock Yards to rescue some beleaguered members of their race. It is reported that they wounded five white people en route. Sheriff Peters said he understood that the deputy sheriff was attacked by white mobs and fired to clear the crowd. He was not convicted.

"Sniping" was a form of retaliation by Negroes which grew out of the automobile raids. These raiding automobiles were fired upon from yards, porches, and windows throughout the "Black Belt." One of the most serious cases reported was at Thirty-first and State streets, where Negroes barricaded the streets with rubbish boxes. Motorcycle Policeman Cheney rammed through and was hit by a bullet. His companion officer following was knocked from his machine and the machine punctured with bullets.

After the wounding of Policeman Cheney and Sergeant Murray, of the Sixth Precinct, policemen made a thorough search of all Negro homes near the scene of the "sniping." Thirty-four Negroes were arrested. of these, ten were discharged, ten were found not guilty, one was given one day in jail, one was given five days in jail, one was fined and put on probation, two were fined $10 and costs, one was fined $25; six were given thirty days each in the House of Correction, and one, who admitted firing twice but said he was firing at one of the automobiles, was sentenced to six months in the House of Correction. His case was taken to the appellate court.

Concerted retaliatory race action showed itself in the Italian district around Taylor and Loomis streets when rumor said that a little Italian girl had been killed or wounded by a shot fired by a Negro. Joseph Lovings, an innocent Negro, came upon the excited crowd of Italians. There was a short chase through back yards. Finally Lovings was dragged from his hiding-place in a basement and brutally murdered by the crowd. The coroner reported fourteen bullet wounds on his body, eight still having bullets in them; also various stab wounds, contusions of the head, and fractures of the skull. Rumor made the tale more hideous, saying that Lovings was burned after gasoline had been poured over the dead body. This was not true.

This same massing of race against race was shown in a similar clash between Italians and Negroes on the North Side. The results here, however, were not serious. It was reported in this last case that immediately after the fracas the Negroes and Italians were again on good terms. This was not true in the neighborhood of the Lovings outrage. Miss Jane Addams, of Hull-House, which is near the scene of Lovings' death, testified before the Commission that before the riot the Italians held no particular animosity toward Negroes, for those in the neighborhood were mostly from South Italy and accustomed to the dark-skinned races, but that they were developing antipathy. In the September following the riot, she said the neighborhood was still full of wild stories so stereotyped in character that they appeared to indicate propaganda spread for a purpose.

The gang which operated in the "Loop" was composed partly of soldiers and sailors in uniform; they were boys of from seventeen to twenty-two, out for a "rough" time and using race prejudice as a shield for robbery. At times this crowd numbered 100. Its depredations began shortly after 2:00 A.M. Tuesday. The La Salle Street railroad station was entered twice, and Negro men were beaten and robbed. About 3:00 A.M. activities were transferred to Wabash Avenue. In the hunt for Negroes one restaurant was wrecked and the vandalism was continued in another restaurant where two Negroes were found. One was severely injured and the other was shot down. The gangsters rolled the body into the gutter and turned the pockets inside out; they stood on the corner of Wabash Avenue and Adams Street and divided the spoils, openly boasting later of having secured $52, a diamond ring, a watch, and a brooch.

Attacks in the "Loop" continued as late as ten o'clock Tuesday morning, Negroes being chased through the streets and beaten. Warned by the Pinkerton Detective Agency, business men with stores on Wabash Avenue came to protect their property. The rioting was reported to the police by the restaurant men. Policemen rescued two Negroes that morning, but so many policemen had been concentrated in and near the "Black Belt" that there were only a few patrolmen in the whole "Loop" district, and these did not actively endeavor to cope with the mob. In the meantime two Negroes were killed and others injured, while property was seriously damaged.

Tuesday's raids marked the peak of daring during the riot, and their subsidence was as gradual as their rise. For the next two days the gangs roamed the streets, intermittently attacking Negro homes. After Tuesday midnight their operations were not so open or so concerted. The riot gradually decreased in feeling and scope till the last event of a serious nature occurred, the incendiary fires back of the Stock Yards.

While there is general agreement that these fires were incendiary, no clue could be found to the perpetrators. Negroes were suspected, as all the houses burned belonged to whites. In spite of this fact, and the testimony of thirteen people who said they saw Negroes in the vicinity before or during the fires, a rumor persisted that the fires were set by white people with blackened faces. One of the men living in the burned district who testified to seeing a motor truck filled with Negroes said, when asked about the color of the men, "Sure, I know they were colored. Of course I don't know whether they were painted." An early milk-wagon driver said that he saw Negroes come out of a barn on Forty-third Street and Hermitage Avenue. Immediately afterward the barn burst into flames. He ran to a policeman and reported it. The policeman said he was "too busy" and "it is all right anyway." One of the colonels commanding a regiment of militia said he thought white people with blackened faces had set fire to the houses; he got this opinion from talking to the police in charge of that district.

Miss Mary McDowell, of the University of Chicago Settlement, which is located back of the Yards, said in testimony before the Commission:

I don't think the Negroes did burn the houses. I think the white hoodlums burned them. The Negroes weren't back there, they stayed at home after that Monday. When we got hold of the firemen confidentially, they said no Negroes set fire to them at all, but the newspapers said so and the people were full of fear. All kinds of mythical stories were afloat from some time.

The general superintendent of Armour & Company was asked, when testifying before the Commission, if he knew of any substantial reason why Negroes were accused of setting fires back of the Yards. He answered:

That statement was originated in the minds of a few individuals, radicals. It does not exist in the minds of the conservative and thinking people of the community, even those living in back of the Yards. They know better. I believe it goes without saying that there isn't a colored man, regardless of how little brains he'd have, who would attempt to go over into the Polish district and set fire to anybody's house over there. He wouldn't get that far.

The controlling superintendent of Swift & Company said he could not say it from his own experience, but he understood there was as much friction between the Poles and Lithuanians who worked together in the Yards as between the Negroes and the whites. The homes burned belonged to Lithuanians. The grand jury stated in its report: "The jury believes that these fires were started for the purpose of inciting race feeling by blaming same on the blacks."

The methods of attack used by Negroes and whites during the riot differed; the Negroes usually clung to individual attack and the whites to mob action. Negroes used chiefly firearms and knives, and the whites used their fists, bricks, stones, baseball bats, pieces of iron, hammers. Among the white men, 69 per cent were shot or stabbed and 31 per cent were beaten; among the Negroes almost the reverse was true, 35 per cent being shot and stabbed and 65 per cent beaten. A colonel in charge of a regiment of militia on riot duty says they found few whites but many Negroes armed. . . .

Questions

1. In general, how were people attacked during the riot?
2. What role did the automobile play in the rioting?

3. Consider the impact of the riot on participants, the city government, and the middle class. How might the incident have affected the city a decade or more later?

23-10   The Boston Police Strike (1919)

Calvin Coolidge

In 1919 Americans were preoccupied with more than race. There was also the labor question: everybody seemed to be on strike as 4 million workers walked off the job that year. Among the strikers were Boston police officers, who had been denied a raise to compensate for wartime inflation. Quite unintentionally, the officers furthered the career of Massachusetts Governor Calvin Coolidge (see text p. 733), who made this proclamation on the strike.

Source: In Calvin Coolidge, *Have Faith in Massachusetts: A Collection of Speeches and Messages*, 2d ed. (Boston and New York: Houghton Mifflin, 1919), pp. 225–227.

The Commonwealth of Massachusetts
By His Excellency Calvin Coolidge, Governor

A PROCLAMATION

There appears to be a misapprehension as to the position of the police of Boston. In the deliberate intention to intimidate and coerce the Government of this Commonwealth a large body of policemen, urging all others to join them, deserted their posts of duty, letting in the enemy. This act of their was voluntary, against the advice of their well wishers, long discussed and premeditated, and with the purpose of obstructing the power of the Government to protect its citizens or even to maintain its own existence. Its success meant anarchy. By this act through the operation of the law they dispossessed themselves. They went out of office. They stand as though they had never been appointed.

Other police remained on duty. They are the real heroes of this crisis. The State Guard responded most efficiently. Thousands have volunteered for the Guard and the Militia. Money has been contributed from every walk of life by the hundreds of thousands for the encouragement and relief of these loyal men. These acts have been spontaneous, significant, and decisive. I proposed to support all those who are supporting their own Government with every power which the people have entrusted to me.

There is an obligation, inescapable, no less solemn, to resist all those who do not support the Government. The authority of the Commonwealth cannot be intimidated or coerced. It cannot be compromised. To place the maintenance of the public security in the hands of a body of men who have attempted to destroy it would be to flout the sovereignty of the laws the people have made. It is my duty to resist any such proposal. Those who would counsel it join hands with those whose acts have threatened to destroy the Government. There is no middle ground. Every attempt to prevent the formation of a new police force is a blow at the Government. That way treason lies. No man has a right to place his own ease or convenience or the opportunity of making money above his duty to the State.

This is the cause of all the people. I call on every citizen to stand by me in executing the oath of my office by supporting the authority of the Government and resisting all assaults upon it.

Given at the Executive Chamber, in Boston, this twenty-fourth day of September, in the year of our Lord one thousand nine hundred and nineteen, and of the Independence of the United States of America the one hundred and forty-fourth.

CALVIN COOLIDGE.

By His Excellency the Governor,
   HERBERT H. BOYNTON
   Deputy, Acting Secretary of the Commonwealth

God save the Commonwealth of Massachusetts.

Questions

1. According to Coolidge, did the police have a right to strike? Why or why not?
2. How could Coolidge have found a "middle ground"?
3. How does he transform a labor dispute into a question of patriotism?

Questions for Further Thought

1. What do the documents in this section suggest about the relationship between domestic and foreign events?
2. How might the Chicago riot (Document 23-9) suggest why Boston police officers went on strike?
3. How is the style of argument similar in the speeches by Lodge (Document 23-8) and Coolidge (Document 23-10)?

CHAPTER 24

Modern Times
The 1920s

★　　　　　★　　　　　★

The Business-Government Partnership of the 1920s

In the 1920s middle-class Americans might have wondered what the progressive movement had been about (see text p. 740). New Nationalism or New Freedom, Roosevelt's confession of faith or Wilson's man on the make—none of it seemed to have any bearing on the prosperous 1920s.

Although prosperity was uneven (about 70 percent of the population lived in subsistence conditions), few critics challenged the New Era. The Democrats spent the decade converting themselves from a rural- to an urban-based party. For organized labor, the 1920s constituted what the historian Irving Bernstein called the lean years. Management weakened the American Federation of Labor through a combination of intimidation and welfare capitalism (see text p. 745). Rather than joining a union, workers contented themselves with the company picnic and the promise of an old-age pension.

It was as if King Midas had touched an entire decade. The gross national product increased by 40 percent, per capita income rose significantly, and after 1922 unemployment did not rise above 4 percent. Even the severe recession of 1920–1921 had a positive side effect in that wartime inflation was rolled back. Farmers, though, did not share in the prosperity as wartime expansion created a special set of problems. Europe was again able to feed itself, and the resulting American surplus, which persisted throughout the decade, drove crop prices downward. Reduced income also made it difficult for farmers to pay off loans for land and machinery that had been purchased in boom times.

The Republican party was happy to take credit for prosperity. The successive administrations of Warren G. Harding, Calvin Coolidge, and Herbert Hoover pursued an aggressive probusiness agenda: government expenditures and taxes were kept low, and the Sherman Antitrust Act was largely ignored (see text pp. 741–743). Not only did big business increasingly dominate the domestic economy, U.S. corporations expanded throughout the world (see text pp. 745–746).

Republican foreign policy in this period tended to be less aggressive than it had been in the era of Theodore Roosevelt (see text pp. 746–747). The Washington Naval Arms Conference and the Kellogg-Briand Pact (see text p. 747) signaled the government's willingness to disengage itself from world affairs.

Frederick Lewis Allen offers a critical portrait of Warren G. Harding in Document 24-1. The tone of Document 24-2, from the advertising executive Bruce Barton's life of Christ, differs markedly in tone. The Washington Naval Arms Conference, which produced this century's first serious attempt at arms reduction, is the subject of Document 24-3.

24-1 *Only Yesterday* (1931)

Frederick Lewis Allen

Frederick Lewis Allen (1890–1954) wrote *Only Yesterday* in 1931. Yet the 1920s, just two years past, was part of a time that no longer existed for Allen and the rest of the nation. From the vantage point of the early depression years, the complacency that had produced a Warren G. Harding (see text pp. 741–742) had died on Wall Street in October 1929.

Source: Excerpted from *Only Yesterday: An Informal History of the Nineteen-Twenties* by Frederick Lewis Allen. Copyright 1931 by Frederick Lewis Allen. Copyright renewed 1959 by Agnes Rogers Allen. In reprint edition, New York: Perennial Library, 1964, pp. 33–35, 102–107.

Back in the early spring of 1919, while Wilson was still at Paris, Samuel G. Blythe, an experienced observer of the political scene, had written in the *Saturday Evening Post* of the temper of the leaders of the Republican Party as they faced the issues of peace:

"You cannot teach an Old Guard new tricks. . . . The Old Guard surrenders but it never dies. Right at this minute, the ancient and archaic Republicans who think they control the destinies of the Republican Party—think they do!—are operating after the manner and style of 1896. The war hasn't made a dent in them. . . . The only way they look is backward."

The analysis was sound; but the Republican bosses, however open to criticism they may have been as statesmen, were at least good politicians. They had their ears where a good politician's should be—to the ground—and what they heard there was a rumble of discontent with Wilson and all that he represented. They determined that at the election of 1920 they would choose as the Republican standard-bearer somebody who would present, both to themselves and to the country, a complete contrast with the idealist whom they detested. As the year rolled round and the date for the Republican Convention approached, they surveyed the field. The leading candidate was General Leonard Wood, a blunt soldier, an inheritor of Theodore Roosevelt's creed of fearing God and keeping your powder dry; he made a fairly good contrast with Wilson, but he promised to be almost as unmanageable. Then there was Governor Lowden of Illinois—but he, too, did not quite fulfill the ideal. Herbert Hoover, the reliever of Belgium and war-time Food Administrator, was conducting a highly amateur campaign for the nomination; the politicians dismissed him with a sour laugh. Why, this man Hoover hadn't known whether he was a Republican or Democrat until the campaign began! Hiram Johnson was in the field, but he also might prove stiff-necked, although it was to his advantage that he was a Senator. The bosses' inspired choice was none of these men: it was Warren Gamaliel Harding, a commonplace and unpretentious Senator from Ohio.

Consider how perfectly Harding met the requirements. Wilson was a visionary who liked to identify himself with "forward-looking men"; Harding, as Mr. Lowry put it, was as old-fashioned as those wooden Indians which used to stand in front of cigar stores, "a flower of the period before safety razors." Harding believed that statesmanship had come to its apogee in the days of McKinley and Foraker. Wilson was cold; Harding was an affable small-town man, at ease with "folks"; an ideal companion, as one of his friends expressed it, "to play poker with all Saturday night." Wilson had always been difficult of access; Harding was accessible to the last degree. Wilson favored labor, distrusted business men as a class, and talked of "industrial democracy"; Harding looked back with longing eyes to the good old days when the government didn't bother business men with unnecessary regulations, but provided them with fat tariffs and instructed the Department of Justice not to have them on its mind. Wilson was at loggerheads with Congress, and particularly with the Senate; Harding was not only a Senator, but a highly amenable Senator. Wilson had been adept at making enemies; Harding hadn't an enemy in the world. He was genuinely genial. "He had no knobs, he was the same size and smoothness all the way round," wrote Charles Willis Thompson. Wilson thought in terms of the whole world; Harding was for America first. And finally, whereas Wilson wanted America to exert itself nobly, Harding wanted to give it a rest. At Boston, a few weeks before the Convention, he had correctly expressed the growing desire of the people of the country and at the same time had unwittingly added a new word to the language, when he said, "America's present need is not heroics but healing; not nostrums but normalcy; not revolution but restoration; . . . not surgery but serenity." Here was a man whom a country wearied of moral obligations and the hope of the world could take to its heart.

It is credibly reported that the decision in favor of Harding was made by the Republican bosses as early as February, 1920, four months before the Convention. But it was not until four ballots had been taken at the Convention itself—with Wood leading, Lowden second, and Harding fifth—and the wilted delegates had dispersed for the night, that the leaders finally concluded to put Harding over. Harding's political manager, an Ohio boss named Harry M. Daugherty, had predicted that the Convention would be deadlocked and that the nomination would be decided upon by twelve or thirteen men "at two o'clock in the morning in a smoke-filled room." He was precisely right. . . .

On the morning of March 4, 1921—a brilliant morning with a frosty air and a wind which whipped the flags of Washington—Woodrow Wilson, broken and bent and ill, limped from the White House door to a waiting automobile, rode down Pennsylvania Avenue to the Capitol with the stalwart President-elect at his side, and returned to the bitter seclusion of his private house in S Street. Warren Gamaliel Harding was sworn in as President of the United States. The reign of normalcy had begun. . . .

The nation was spiritually tired. Wearied by the excitements of the war and the nervous tension of the Big Red Scare, they hoped for quiet and healing. Sick of Wilson and his talk of America's duty to humanity, callous to political idealism, they hoped for a chance to pursue their private affairs without governmental interference and to

forget about public affairs. There might be no such word in the dictionary as normalcy, but normalcy was what they wanted. . . .

Warren Harding had two great assets, and these were already apparent. First, he looked as a President of the United States should. He was superbly handsome. His face and carriage had a Washingtonian nobility and dignity, his eyes were benign; he photographed well and the pictures of him in the rotogravure sections won him affection and respect. And he was the friendliest man who ever had entered the White House. He seemed to like everybody, he wanted to do favors for everybody, he wanted to make everybody happy. His affability was not merely the forced affability of the cold-blooded politician; it was transparently and touchingly genuine. "Neighbor," he had said to Herbert Hoover at their first meeting, during the war, "I want to be helpful." He meant it; and now that he was President, he wanted to be helpful to neighbors from Marion and neighbors from campaign headquarters and to the whole neighborly American public.

His liabilities were not at first so apparent, yet they were disastrously real. Beyond the limited scope of his political experience he was "almost unbelievably ill-informed," as William Allen White put it. His mind was vague and fuzzy. Its quality was revealed in the clogged style of his public addresses, in his choice of turgid and maladroit language ("noninvolvement" in European affairs, "adhesion" to a treaty), and in his frequent attacks of suffix trouble ("normalcy" for normality, "betrothment" for betrothal). It was revealed even more clearly in his helplessness when confronted by questions of policy to which mere good nature could not find the answer. White tells of Harding's coming into the office of one of his secretaries after a day of listening to his advisers wrangling over a tax problem, and crying out: "John, I can't make a damn thing out of this tax problem. I listen to one side and they seem right, and then—God!—I talk to the other side and they seem just as right, and here I am where I started. I know somewhere there is a book that will give me the truth, but, hell, I couldn't read the book. I know somewhere there is an economist who knows the truth, but I don't know where to find him and haven't the sense to know him and trust him when I find him. God! what a job!" His inability to discover for himself the essential facts of a problem and to think it through made him utterly dependent upon subordinates and friends whose mental processes were sharper than his own.

If he had been discriminating in the choice of his friends and advisers, all might have been well. But discrimination had been left out of his equipment. He appointed Charles Evans Hughes and Herbert Hoover and Andrew Mellon to Cabinet positions out of a vague sense that they would provide his administration with the necessary amount of statesmanship, but he was as ready to follow the lead of Daugherty or Fall or Forbes. He had little notion of technical fitness for technical jobs. Offices were plums to him, and he handed them out like a benevolent Santa Claus—beginning with the boys from Marion. He made his brother-in-law Superintendent of Prisons; he not only kept the insignificant Doctor Sawyer, of Sawyer's Sanitarium at Marion, as his personal physician, but bestowed upon him what a White House announcement called a "brigadier-generalcy' (suffix trouble again) and deputed him to study the possible coordination of the health agencies of the government; and for Comptroller of the Currency he selected D. R. Crissinger, a Marion lawyer whose executive banking experience was limited to a few months as president of the National City Bank and Trust Company—of Marion.

Nor did Harding appear to be able to distinguish between honesty and rascality. He had been trained in the sordid school of practical Ohio politics. He had served for years as the majestic Doric false front behind which Ohio lobbyists and fixers and purchasers of privilege had discussed their "business propositions" and put over their "little deals"—and they, too, followed him to Washington, along with the boys from Marion. Some of them he put into positions of power, others he saw assuming positions of power; knowing them intimately, he must have known—if he was capable of a minute's clear and unprejudiced thought—how they would inevitably use those positions; but he was too fond of his old cronies, too anxious to have them share his good fortune, and too muddle-minded to face the issue until it was too late. He liked to slip away from the White House to the house in H Street where the Ohio gang and their intimates reveled and liquor flowed freely without undue regard for prohibition, and a man could take his pleasure at the poker table and forget the cares of state; and the easiest course to take was not to inquire too closely into what the boys were doing, to hope that if they were grafting a little on the side they'd be reasonable about it and not do anything to let old Warren down.

And why did he choose such company? The truth was that under his imposing exterior he was just a common small-town man, an "average sensual man," the sort of man who likes nothing better in the world than to be with the old bunch when they gather at Joe's place for an all-Saturday-night session, with waistcoats unbuttoned and cigars between their teeth and an ample supply of bottles and cracked ice at hand. His private life was one of cheap sex episodes; as one reads the confessions of his mistress, who claims that as President he was supporting an illegitimate baby born hardly a year before his election, one is struck by the shabbiness of the whole affair: the clandestine meetings in disreputable hotels, in the Senate Office Building (where Nan Britton believed her child to have been conceived), and even in a coat-closet in the executive offices of the White House itself. (Doubts have been cast upon the truth of the story told in *The President's Daughter*, but is it easy to imagine any one making up out of whole cloth a supposedly autobiographical story compounded of such ignoble adventures?) Even making due allowance for the refracting of Harding's personality through that of Nan Britton, one sees with deadly clarity the essential ordinariness of the man, the commonness of his "Gee, dearie" and "Say, you darling," his being swindled out of a hundred dollars by card sharpers on a train ride, his naïve assurance to Nan, when detectives broke in upon them in a Broadway hotel, that they could not be arrested because it was illegal to detain a Senator while "en route to Washington to serve the people." Warren Harding's ambitious wife had tailored and groomed him into outward respectability and made a man of substance of him; yet even now, after he had reached the White House, the rowdies of the Ohio gang were fundamentally his sort. He had risen above them, he could mingle urbanely with their superiors, but it was in the smoke-filled rooms of the house in H Street that he was really most at home. . . .

Questions

1. What was the popular mood that led Republican leaders to nominate Warren G. Harding?
2. How did Harding win the presidential nomination at the Republican convention?
3. As described in this account, what were Harding's attributes as president? His weaknesses?
4. How reliable is a history written so soon after an event or time? What might make such a work suspect?

24-2 *The Man Nobody Knows* (1924)

Bruce Barton

In the 1920s Americans defined the national character in terms of confident problem solving. The advertising executive Bruce Barton (1886–1967) applied that definition to an unexpected source—religion. Barton reworked the New Testament into *The Man Nobody Knows* (1924), in which the author promised to "tell the story of the founder of modern business"—Jesus Christ (see text pp. 744–745).

Source: Reprinted with the permission of Simon & Schuster from the introduction to *The Man Nobody Knows: A Discovery of the Real Jesus* by Bruce Barton. Copyright © 1925 by The Bobbs-Merrill Company, Inc. Copyright renewed 1952 by Bruce Barton.

HOW IT CAME TO BE WRITTEN

The little boy's body sat bolt upright in the rough wooden chair, but his mind was very busy.

This was his weekly hour of revolt.

The kindly lady who could never seem to find her glasses would have been terribly shocked if she had known what was going on inside the little boy's mind.

"You must love Jesus," she said every Sunday, "and God."

The little boy did not say anything. He was afraid to say anything; he was almost afraid that something would happen to him because of the things he thought.

Love God! Who was always picking on people for having a good time, and sending little boys to hell because they couldn't do better in a world which he had made so hard! Why didn't God take some one his own size?

Love Jesus! The little boy looked up at the picture which hung on the Sunday-school wall. It showed a pale young man with flabby forearms and a sad expression. The young man had red whiskers.

Then the little boy looked across to the other wall. There was Daniel, good old Daniel, standing off the lions. The little boy liked Daniel. He liked David, too, with the trusty sling that landed a stone square on the forehead of Goliath. And Moses, with his rod and his big brass snake. They were winners—those three. He wondered if David could whip Jeffries. Samson could! Say, that would have been a fight!

But Jesus! Jesus was the "lamb of God." The little boy did not know what that meant, but it sounded like Mary's little lamb. Something for girls—sissified. Jesus was also "meek and lowly," a "man of sorrows and acquainted with grief." He went around for three years telling people not to do things.

Sunday was Jesus' day; it was wrong to feel comfortable or laugh on Sunday.

The little boy was glad when the superintendent thumped the bell and announced: "We will now sing the closing hymn." One more bad hour was over. For one more week the little boy had got rid of Jesus.

Years went by and the boy grew up and became a business man.

He began to wonder about Jesus.

He said to himself: "Only strong magnetic men inspire great enthusiasm and build great organizations. Yet Jesus built the greatest organization of all. It is extraordinary."

The more sermons the man heard and the more books he read the more mystified he became.

One day he decided to wipe his mind clean of books and sermons.

He said, "I will read what the men who knew Jesus personally said about him. I will read about him as though he were a new historical character, about whom I had never heard anything at all."

The man was amazed.

A physical weakling! Where did they get that idea? Jesus pushed a plane and swung an adze; he was a successful carpenter. He slept outdoors and spent his days walking around his favorite lake. His muscles were so strong that when he drove the money-changers out, nobody dared to oppose him!

A kill-joy! He was the most popular dinner guest in Jerusalem! The criticism which proper people made was that he spent too much time with publicans and sinners (very good fellows, on the whole, the man thought) and enjoyed society too much. They called him a "wine bibber and a gluttonous man."

A failure! He picked up twelve men from the bottom ranks of business and forged them into an organization that conquered the world.

When the man had finished his reading he exclaimed, "This is a man nobody knows.

"Some day," said he, "some one will write a book about Jesus. Every business man will read it and send it to his partners and his salesmen. For it will tell the story of the founder of modern business."

So the man waited for some one to write the book, but no one did. Instead, more books were published about the "lamb of God" who was weak and unhappy and glad to die.

The man became impatient. One day he said, "I believe I will try to write that book, myself."

And he did.

Questions

1. Which view of Christ does Barton reject?
2. How does he portray Jesus instead?
3. Why did readers accept Barton's depiction of Christ?

24-3 The Washington Naval Treaty of 1922

The Washington Naval Arms Conference of 1921–1922 was intended to control the growth of naval armaments. The resulting treaty placed a ten-year moratorium on the construction of large battleships (referred to as *capital ships* in the treaty) and set a tonnage ratio of 5:5:3:1.75:1.75 for building other ships: for every 5 tons constructed by the United States or Great Britain, Japan was permitted to build 3, and Italy and France 1.75 (see text p. 747).

Source: United States, *Statutes at Large*, vol. 43, part 2, pp. 1655ff.

CHAPTER I

General Provisions Relating to the Limitation of Naval Armament

ART. I. The Contracting Powers agree to limit their respective naval armament as provided in the present Treaty.

ART. II. The Contracting Powers may retain respectively the capital ships which are specified in Chapter II, Part 1. On the coming into force of the present Treaty, but subject to the following provisions of this Article, all other capital ships, built or building, of the United States, the British Empire and Japan shall be disposed of as prescribed in Chapter II, Part 2.

In addition to the capital ships specified in Chapter II, Part 1, the United States may complete and retain two ships of the *West Virginia* class now under construction. On the completion of these two ships the *North Dakota* and *Delaware* shall be disposed of as prescribed in Chapter II, Part 2.

The British Empire may, in accordance with the replacement table in Chapter II, Part 3, contract two new capital ships not exceeding 35,000 tons (35,560 metric tons) standard displacement each. On the completion of the said two ships the *Thunderer, King George V, Ajax* and *Centurion* shall be disposed of as prescribed in Chapter II, Part 2.

ART. III. Subject to the provisions of Article II, the Contracting Powers shall abandon their respective capital ship building programs, and no new capital ships shall be constructed or acquired by any of the Contracting Powers except replacement tonnage which may be constructed or acquired as specified in Chapter II, Part 3.

Ships which are replaced in accordance with Chapter

II, Part 3, shall be disposed of as prescribed in Part 2 of that Chapter.

ART. IV. The total capital ship replacement tonnage of each of the Contracting Powers shall not exceed in standard displacement, for the United States 525,000 tons (533,400 metric tons); for the British Empire 525,000 tons (533,400 metric tons); for France 175,000 tons (177,800 metric tons); for Italy 175,000 tons (177,800 metric tons); for Japan 315,000 tons (320,040 metric tons).

ART. V. No capital ship exceeding 35,000 tons (35,560 metric tons) standard displacement shall be acquired by, or constructed by, for, or within the jurisdiction of, any of the Contracting Powers.

ART. VI. No capital ship of any of the Contracting Powers shall carry a gun with a calibre in excess of 16 inches (406 millimetres).

ART. VII. The total tonnage for aircraft carriers of each of the Contracting Powers shall not exceed in standard displacement, for the United States 135,000 tons (137,160 metric tons); for the British Empire 135,000 tons (137,160 metric tons); for France 60,000 tons (60,960 metric tons); for Italy 60,000 tons (60,960 metric tons); for Japan 81,000 tons (82,296 metric tons).

ART. VIII. The replacement of aircraft carriers shall be effected only as prescribed in Chapter II, Part 3, provided, however, that all aircraft carrier tonnage in existence or building on November 12, 1921, shall be considered experimental, and may be replaced, within the total tonnage limit prescribed in Article VII, without regard to its age.

ART. IX. No aircraft carrier exceeding 27,000 tons (27,432 metric tons) standard displacement shall be acquired by, or constructed by, for or within the jurisdiction of any of the Contracting Powers.

However, any of the Contracting Powers may, provided that its total tonnage allowance of aircraft carriers is not thereby exceeded, build not more than two aircraft carriers, each of a tonnage of not more than 33,000 tons (33,528 metric tons) standard displacement, and in order to effect economy any of the Contracting Powers may use for this purpose any two of their ships, whether constructed or in course of construction, which would otherwise be scrapped under the provisions of Article II. The armament of any aircraft carriers exceeding 27,000 tons (27,432 metric tons) standard displacement shall be in accordance with the requirements of Article X, except that the total number of guns to be carried in case any of such guns be of a calibre exceeding 6 inches (152 millimetres), except anti-aircraft guns and guns not exceeding 5 inches (127 millimetres), shall not exceed eight.

ART. X. No aircraft carrier of any of the Contracting Powers shall carry a gun with a calibre in excess of 8 inches (203 millimetres). Without prejudice to the provisions of Article IX, if the armament carried includes guns exceeding 6 inches (152 millimetres) in calibre the total number of guns carried, except anti-aircraft guns and guns not exceeding 5 inches (127 millimitres), shall not exceed ten. If alternatively the armament contains no guns exceeding 6 inches (152 millimetres) in calibre, the number of guns is not limited. In either case the number of anti-aircraft guns and of guns not exceeding 5 inches (127 millimetres) is not limited.

ART. XI. No vessel of war exceeding 10,000 tons (10,160 metric tons) standard displacement, other than a capital ship or aircraft carrier, shall be acquired by, or constructed by, for, or within the jurisdiction of, any of the Contracting Powers. Vessels not specifically built as fighting ships nor taken in time of peace under government control for fighting purposes, which are employed on fleet duties or as troop transports or in some other way for the purpose of assisting in the prosecution of hostilities otherwise than as fighting ships, shall not be within the limitations of this Article.

No vessel of war of any of the Contracting Powers, hereafter laid down, other than a capital ship, shall carry a gun with a calibre in excess of 8 inches (203 millimetres).

ART. XIII. Except as provided in Article IX, no ship designated in the present Treaty to be scrapped may be reconverted into a vessel of war.

ART. XIV. No preparations shall be made in merchant ships in time of peace for the installation of warlike armaments for the purpose of converting such ships into vessels of war, other than the necessary stiffening of decks for the mounting of guns not exceeding 6 inch (152 millimetres) calibre.

ART. XV. No vessel of war constructed within the jurisdiction of any of the Contracting Powers for a non-Contracting Power shall exceed the limitations as to displacement and armament prescribed by the present Treaty for vessels of a similar type which may be constructed by or

for any of the Contracting Powers; provided, however, that the displacement for aircraft carriers constructed for a non-Contracting Power shall in no case exceed 27,000 tons (27,432 metric tons) standard displacement.

ART. XVI. If the construction of any vessel of war for a non-Contracting Power is undertaken within the jurisdiction of any of the Contracting Powers, such Power shall promptly inform the other Contracting Powers of the date of the signing of the contract and the date on which the keel of the ship is laid; and shall also communicate to them the particulars relating to the ship prescribed in Chapter II, Part 3, Section I (b), (4) and (5).

ART. XVII. In the event of a Contracting Power being engaged in war, such Power shall not use as a vessel of war any vessel of war which may be under construction within its jurisdiction for any other Power, or which may have been constructed within its jurisdiction for another Power and not delivered.

ART. XVIII. Each of the Contracting Powers undertakes not to dispose by gift, sale or any mode of transfer of any vessel of war in such a manner that such vessel may become a vessel of war in the Navy of any foreign Power.

ART. XIX. The United States, the British Empire and Japan agree that the status quo at the time of the signing of the present Treaty, with regard to fortifications and naval bases, shall be maintained in their respective territories and possessions specified hereunder:

(1) The insular possessions which the United States now holds or may hereafter acquire in the Pacific Ocean, except (a) those adjacent to the coast of the United States, Alaska and the Panama Canal Zone, not including the Aleutian Islands, and (b) the Hawaiian Islands;

(2) Hongkong [sic] and the insular possessions which the British Empire now holds or may hereafter acquire in the Pacific Ocean, east of the meridian of 110°east longitude, except (a) those adjacent to the coast of Canada, (b) the Commonwealth of Australia and its Territories, and (c) New Zealand;

(3) The following insular territories and possessions of Japan in the Pacific Ocean, to wit: the Kurile Islands, the Bonin Islands, Amami-Oshima, the Loochoo Islands, Formosa [Taiwan] and the Pescadores, and any insular territories or possessions in the Pacific Ocean which Japan may hereafter acquire.

The maintenance of the status quo under the foregoing provisions implies that no new fortifications or naval bases shall be established in the territories and possessions specified; that no measures shall be taken to increase the existing naval facilities for the repair and maintenance of naval forces, and that no increase shall be made in the coast defences of the territories and possessions above specified. This restriction, however, does not preclude such repair and replacement of worn-out weapons and equipment as is customary in naval and military establishments in time of peace. . . .

CHAPTER III

Miscellaneous Provisions

ART. XXI. If during the term of the present Treaty the requirements of the national security of any Contracting Power in respect of naval defence are, in the opinion of that Power, materially affected by any change of circumstances, the Contracting Powers will, at the request of such Power, meet in conference with a view to the reconsideration of the provisions of the Treaty and its amendment by mutual agreement.

In view of possible technical and scientific developments, the United States, after consultation with the other Contracting Powers, shall arrange for a conference of all the Contracting Powers which shall convene as soon as possible after the expiration of eight years from the coming into force of the present Treaty to consider what changes, if any, in the Treaty may be necessary to meet such developments.

ART. XXII. Whenever any Contracting Power shall become engaged in a war which in its opinion affects the naval defence of its national security, such Power may after notice to the other Contracting Powers suspend for the period of hostilities its obligations under the present Treaty other than those under Articles XIII and XVII, provided that such Power shall notify the other Contracting Powers that the emergency is of such a character as to require such suspension.

The remaining Contracting Powers shall in such case consult together with a view to agreement as to what temporary modifications if any should be made in the Treaty as between themselves. Should such consultation not produce agreement, duly made in accordance with the constitutional methods of the respective Powers, any one of said Contracting Powers may, by giving notice to the other Contracting Powers, suspend for the period of hostilities its obligations under the Present Treaty, other than those under Articles XIII and XVII.

On the cessation of hostilities the Contracting Powers will meet in conference to consider what modifications, if any, should be made in the provisions of the present Treaty.

ART. XXIII. The present Treaty shall remain in force until December 31st, 1936, and in case none of the Contracting Powers shall have given notice two years before that date of its intention to terminate the Treaty, it shall continue in force until the expiration of two years from the date on which notice of termination shall be given by one of the Contracting Powers, whereupon the Treaty shall terminate as regards all the Contracting Powers. Such notice shall be communicated in writing to the Government of the United States, which shall immediately transmit a certified copy of the notification to the other Powers and inform them of the date on which it was received. The notice shall be deemed to have been given and shall take effect on that date. In the event of notice of termination being given by the Government of the United States, such notice shall be given to the diplomatic representatives at Washington of the other Contracting Powers, and the notice shall be deemed to have been given and shall take effect on the date of the communication made to the said diplomatic representatives.

Within one year of the date on which a notice of termination by any Power has taken effect, all the Contracting Powers shall meet in conference.

ART. XXIV. The present Treaty shall be ratified by the Contracting Powers in accordance with their respective constitutional methods and shall take effect on the date of the deposit of all the ratifications, which shall take place at Washington as soon as possible. The Government of the United States will transmit to the other Contracting Powers a certified copy of the procès-verbal of the deposit of ratifications.

The present Treaty, of which the French and English texts are both authentic, shall remain deposited in the archives of the Government of the United States, and duly certified copies thereof shall be transmitted by that Government to the other Contracting Powers.

In faith whereof the above-named Plenipotentiaries have signed the present Treaty.

Done at the City of Washington, the sixth day of February, One Thousand Nine Hundred and Twenty-Two.

CHARLES EVANS HUGHES
HENRY CABOT LODGE
OSCAR W. UNDERWOOD
ELIHU ROOT
ARTHUR JAMES BALFOUR
LEE OF FAREHAM
A. C. GEDDES
R. L. BORDEN
G. F. PEARCE
JOHN W. SALMOND
ARTHUR JAMES BALFOUR
V. S. SRINIVASA SASTRI
A. SARRAUT
JUSSERAND
CARLO SCHANZER
V. ROLANDI RICCI
LUIGI ALBERTINI
T. KATO
K. SHIDEHARA
M. HANIHARA

Questions

1. Why do you think the treaty is so detailed?
2. How is Article XIX meant to satisfy the Japanese?
3. What kind of enforcement provisions exist in the treaty?

Questions for Further Thought

1. To what extent is today's electronic politics similar to the smoke-filled backroom politics of Warren G. Harding's day (Document 24-1)?
2. Why do Frederick Lewis Allen and Bruce Barton (Document 24-2) differ so widely in tone?
3. Can anything in Allen's depiction of the early 1920s explain Americans' acceptance of the naval arms treaty (Document 24-3)?

A New National Culture

Modernity took hold in the 1920s and created a new national culture. Regardless of class, race, or ethnicity, Americans shared a world shaped by the automobile, radio, and movie house (see text p. 747). The North and the South finally came together, if only through the Model T.

American society stressed consumption and leisure time. Never before had there been so many consumer goods to choose from: cars, refrigerators, vacuum cleaners, and toasters, all waiting to be bought. Thanks to advertising, they were (see text pp. 747–749). The Liberty Loan campaigns of World War I had shown the power of mass marketing (see Chapter 23). Just as the only way to "beat back the Hun" was to buy a bond, a few years later the new enemy was halitosis, and the only way to beat it was. . . . . When the desire to own outstripped the ability to pay, consumers discovered credit, or, as one critic suggested, "a dollar down and a dollar forever."

With the workweek dipping below fifty hours, Americans found themselves with an increasing amount of leisure time. People tended to go places by automobile (see text pp. 749–750), perhaps on vacation or to the movies or the ballpark. The Chicago theater architect George Rapp described the movie palace as a "shrine to democracy where there are no privileged patrons. The wealthy rub elbows with the poor." However, the actors on screen were treated like royalty; wherever Valentino or Clara Bow went, reporters were sure to follow (see text pp. 750–754).

Athletes also were revered as sportswriters turned them into heroes. Leisure time, disposable income, and publicity transformed baseball into this nation's civic religion. Babe Ruth was the first god among equals, or perhaps it was Lou Gehrig.

Documents 24-4 and 24-5 are advertisements for mouthwash and a Hollywood movie, respectively. In Document 24-6 the sportswriter Grantland Rice lends an apocalyptic touch to a Notre Dame–Army football game. The people of Middletown grapple with the changes ushered in by the automobile in Document 24-7.

24-4   Listerine Advertisement (1923)

The success of a consumer society depends on advertising (see text pp. 747–749). This mouthwash advertisement from 1923 uses elements that later became standard in selling everything from beer to blue jeans.

Source: Listerine ad by Lambert Pharmacal Company, St. Louis, in *Literary Digest*, November 17, 1923. Courtesy of Warner-Lambert Company, the copyright and trademark owner.

Questions

1. What is the role of the dentist in this ad?
2. What are the various reasons given for buying the product?
3. What kind of gender stereotyping is involved in both the artwork and the ad copy?

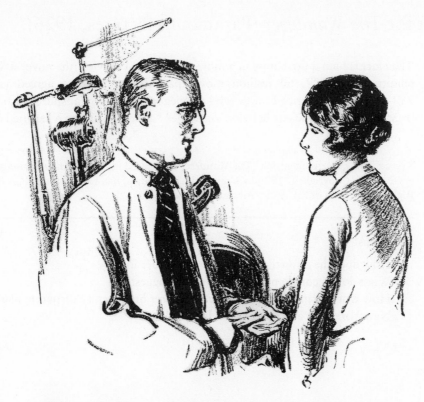

In his discreet way
he told her

IT had never occurred to her before. But in his discreet, professional way he was able to tell her. And she was sensible enough to be grateful instead of resentful.

In fact, the suggestion he made came to mean a great deal to her.

It brought her greater poise—that feeling of self-assurance that adds to a woman's charm—and, moreover, a new sense of daintiness that she had never been quite so sure of in the past.

* * * * * * * *

Many people suffer in the same way. Halitosis (the scientific term for unpleasant breath) creeps upon you unawares. Usually you are not able to detect it yourself. And, naturally enough, even your best friends will not tell you.

Fortunately, however, halitosis is usually due to some local condition—often food fermentation in the mouth; something you have eaten; too much smoking. And it may be corrected by the systematic use of Listerine as a mouth wash and gargle.

Dentists know that this well-known antiseptic they have used for half a century, possesses these remarkable properties as a breath deodorant.

Your druggist will supply you. He sells lots of Listerine. It has dozens of other uses as a safe antiseptic. It is particularly valuable, too, at this time of year in combating sore throat. Read the circular that comes with each bottle.—*Lambert Pharmacal Company, Saint Louis, U. S. A.*

For **HALITOSIS**   *use* **LISTERINE**

24-5   Advertisement for *The Wanderer* (Paramount Pictures, 1926)

"The fact is I am quite happy in a movie, even a bad movie," the novelist Walker Percy admitted. In 1927, 60 million movie patrons would have agreed (see text pp. 750–754). For the price of a ticket a moviegoer could be transported from the Bronx or Mason City to ancient Babylon via scenes "as convincing as a certified check."

Source: This advertisement for "The Wanderer" appeared in the *Saturday Evening Post*, January 2, 1926. Copyright © 1926 by Universal City Studios, Inc. Courtesy of MCA Publishing Rights, a Division of MCA Inc. All rights reserved.

Questions

1. How does the advertisement draw the reader in?
2. What do the couple pictured at the top suggest?
3. How would a movie such as *The Wanderer* homogenize disparate places such as New York City and small-town Iowa?

Personalities of Paramount and their Paramount Pictures

Ernest Torrence

—whose performance in The Covered Wagon as a Western Bad Man is excelled only by his Eastern Bad Man in The Wanderer, has a rare talent for rôles of sardonic villainy. Other Paramount Pictures showing his art are: Night Life of New York and The Pony Express.

Raoul Walsh

—is the director of The Wanderer. He also made The Thief of Bagdad. These two pictures are a story of marvellous art in themselves, spectacles literally unique of their kind. Mr. Walsh's next Paramount Picture will be: The Lucky Lady.

Greta Nissen

—is a new star of extraordinary charm. See her as Tisha the siren, in The Wanderer, and you will realise that this enchantress has an art all her own. Her other Paramount Pictures are: Lost—A Wife, The King on Main Street, and The Lucky Lady.

Wm. Collier Jr.

—is The Wanderer. He shows you the innocent and his money and their early parting. Many a mother's heart will beat quicker for her son because of the way this character is played. See William Collier, Jr., in: The Devil's Cargo, Eve's Secret and The Lucky Lady.

Esther Ralston

—is a rising favorite. She made a great impression as Wendy's mother in Peter Pan, and as the innocent cause of family dissension in The Trouble with Wives. Her other Paramount Pictures are: The Lucky Devil, Womanhandled, and The American Venus.

Bebe Daniels

—is admired by a host of fans for the sunny happiness she brings to the screen, seeming not to act but simply to live the stories. Paramount Pictures starring her are: Wild, Wild Susan, Lovers in Quarantine, and Miss Brewster's Millions.

Produced by
FAMOUS PLAYERS-LASKY CORP.
ADOLPH ZUKOR, President
New York City

The Wanderer

The Eternal Story of the Wandering Son

You see him leave home. You spend a fortune with him. Beautiful Greta Nissen, and Ernest Torrence as a shark of ancient days, take him, and you, to Babylon, and open the town with his fortune like an oyster.

Temptations no human being could resist, you see him fall for, and you hardly know whether to blame or envy, so nearly is the game worth the candle—until the dreadful bill of reckoning is presented, and then anyone can be wise—and you relax the dramatic spell thrown over you by the play, and tell yourself it is only a motion picture! But it is not, it is more, *and there are wanderers of 1926 who will see this* and have their eyes opened!

The scenes of life in ancient Babylon are as convincing as a certified check, and when the storm and the earthquake and the wrath of God flash upon the city you realize that none but an organization with resources as great as Paramount's could construct and destroy a city before your eyes for the simple betterment of one part of one plot of one Paramount Picture.

Great as this picture is in its spectacular sweep across your vision and imagination, and great as The Vanishing American, The Ten Commandments, A Kiss for Cinderella, and other Paramount Pictures are, not one of them, nor all of them together, are as great as the name that stands behind them, which is the sign of the organization steadily blazing the way to better and better pictures.

Paramount Pictures

"If it's a Paramount Picture it's the best show in town"

24-6 The "Four Horsemen" (1924)

Grantland Rice

Once they captured the public's imagination, the sports heroes of the 1920s never let go (see text pp. 755–756). The names Jack Dempsey, Red Grange, and Babe Ruth still convey powerful images seventy years later. Part of that success is due to the work of sportswriters. When Grantland Rice wrote about a college football game, as he did here in 1924, the story concerned far more than the final score. This kind of writing made legends out of the Notre Dame coach, Knute Rockne, and his backfield.

Source: Grantland Rice, "Notre Dame's Cyclone Beats Army," *New York Herald Tribune,* October 19, 1924. In Grantland Rice and Harford Powel, eds., *The Omnibus of Sport* (New York: Harper & Bros., 1932), pp. 31–36.

Outlined against a blue-gray October sky, the Four Horsemen rode again. In dramatic lore they are known as Famine, Pestilence, Destruction and Death. These are only aliases. Their real names are Stuhldreher, Miller, Crowley and Layden. They formed the crest of the South Bend cyclone before which another fighting Army football team was swept over the precipice at the Polo Grounds yesterday afternoon as 55,000 spectators peered down on the bewildering panorama spread on the green plain below.

A cyclone can't be snared. It may be surrounded, but somewhere it breaks through to keep on going. When the cyclone starts from South Bend, where the candle lights still gleam through the Indiana sycamores, those in the way must take to storm cellars at top speed. Yesterday the cyclone struck again as Notre Dame beat the Army, 13 to 7, with a set of backfield stars that ripped and crashed through a strong Army defense with more speed and power than the warring cadets could meet.

MARVELOUS BACKFIELD

Notre Dame won its ninth game in twelve Army starts through the driving power of one of the greatest backfields that ever churned up the turf of any gridiron in any football age. Brilliant backfields may come and go, but in Stuhldreher, Miller, Crowley and Layden, covered by a fast and charging line, Notre Dame can take its place in front of the field.

Coach McEwan sent one of his finest teams into action, an aggressive organization that fought to the last play around the first rim of darkness, but when Rockne rushed his Four Horsemen to the track they rode down everything in sight. It was in vain that 1,400 gray-clad cadets pleaded for the Army line to hold. The Army line was giving all it had, but when a tank tears in with the speed of a motorcycle, what chances has flesh and blood to hold? The Army had its share of stars in action, such stars as Garbisch, Farwick, Wilson, Wood, Ellinger and many others, but they were up against four whirlwind backs who picked up top speed from the first step as they swept through scant openings to slip on by the secondary defense. The Army had great backs in Wilson and Wood, but the Army had no such quartet, who seemed to carry the mixed blood of the tiger and the antelope.

CYCLONE STARTS LIKE ZEPHYR

Rockne's light and tottering line was just as tottering as the Rock of Gibraltar. It was something more than a match for the Army's great set of forwards, who had earned their fame before. Yet it was not until the second period that the first big thrill of the afternoon set the great crowd into a cheering whirl and brought about the wild flutter of flags that are thrown to the wind in exciting moments. At the game's start Rockne sent in almost entirely a second string cast. The Army got the jump and began to play most of the football. It was the Army attack that made three first downs before Notre Dame had caught its stride. The South Bend cyclone opened like a zephyr.

And then, in the wake of a sudden cheer, out rushed Stuhldreher, Miller, Crowley and Layden, the four star backs who had helped to beat the Army a year ago. Things were to be a trifle different now. After a short opening flurry in the second period, Wood, of the Army, kicked out of bounds on Notre Dame's 20-yard line. The cloud in the west at this point was no larger than a football. There was no sign of a tornado starting. But it happened to be at just this spot that Stuhldreher decided to put on his attack and begin the long and dusty hike.

DYNAMITE GOES OFF

On the first play the fleet Crowley peeled off fifteen yards and the cloud from the west was now beginning to show signs of lightning and thunder. The fleet, powerful Layden got six yards more and then Don Miller added ten. A forward pass from Stuhldreher to Crowley added twelve yards, and a moment later Don Miller ran twenty yards around Army's right wing. He was on his way to glory when Wilson, hurtling across the right of way, nailed him on the 10-yard line and threw him out of bounds. Crowley, Miller and Layden—Miller, Layden and Crowley—one or another, ripping and crashing through, as the Army defense threw everything it had in the way to stop this wild charge that had now come seventy yards. Crowley and Layden added five yards more and then, on a split play, Layden went ten yards across the line as if he had just been fired from the black mouth of a howitzer.

In that second period Notre Dame made eight first downs to the Army's none, which shows the unwavering power of the Western attack that hammered relentlessly and remorselessly without easing up for a second's breath. The Western line was going its full share, led by the crippled Walsh with a broken hand.

But always there was Miller or Crowley or Layden, directed through the right spot by the cool and crafty judgment of Stuhldreher, who picked his plays with the finest possible generalship. The South Bend cyclone had now roared eighty-five yards to a touchdown through one of the strongest defensive teams in the game. The cyclone had struck with too much speed and power to be stopped. It was the preponderance of Western speed that swept the Army back.

The next period was much like the second. The trouble began when the alert Layden intercepted an Army pass on the 48-yard line. Stuhldreher was ready for another march.

Once again the cheering cadets began to call for a rallying stand. They are never overwhelmed by any shadow of defeat as long as there is a minute of fighting left. But silence fell over the cadet sector for just a second as Crowley ran around the Army's right wing for 15 yards, where Wilson hauled him down on the 33-yard line. Walsh, the Western captain, was hurt in the play but soon resumed. Miller got 7 and Layden got 8 and then, with the ball on the Army's 20-yard line, the cadet defense rallied and threw Miller in his tracks. But the halt was only for the moment. On the next play Crowley swung out around the Army's left wing, cut in and then crashed over the line for Notre Dame's second touchdown.

On two other occasions the Notre Dame attack almost scored. Yeomans saving one touchdown by intercepting a pass on his 5-yard line as he ran back thirty-five yards before he was nailed by two tacklers. It was a great play in the nick of time. On the next drive Miller and Layden in two hurricane dashes took the ball forty-two yards to the Army's 14-yard line, where the still game Army defense stopped four plunges on the 9-yard line and took the ball.

ARMY LINE OUTPLAYED

Up to this point the Army had been outplayed by a crushing margin. Notre Dame had put under way four long marches and two of these had yield touchdowns. Even the stout and experienced Army line was meeting more than it could hold. Notre Dame's brilliant backs had been provided with the finest possible interference, usually led by Stuhldreher, who cut down tackler after tackler by diving at some rival's flying knees. Against this each Army attack had been smothered almost before it got under way. Even the great Wilson, the star from Penn State, one of the great backfield runners of his day and time, rarely had a chance to make any headway through a massed wall of tacklers who were blocking every open route.

The sudden change came late in the third quarter, when Wilson, raging like a wild man, suddenly shot through a tackle opening to run thirty-four yards before he was finally collared and thrown with a jolt. A few minutes later Wood, one of the best of all the punters, kicked out of bounds on Notre Dame's 5-yard line. Here was the chance. Layden was forced to kick from behind his own goal. The punt soared up the field as Yeomans called for a free kick on the 35-yard line. As he caught the ball he was nailed and spilled by a Western tackler, and the penalty gave the Army fifteen yards, with the ball at Notre Dame's 20-yard line.

At this point Harding was rushed to quarter in place of Yeomans, who had been one of the leading Army stars. On the first three plays the Army reached the 12-yard line, but it was now fourth down, with two yards left to go. Harding's next play was the feature of the game.

As the ball was passed, he faked a play to Wood, diving through the line, held the oval for just a half breath, then, tucking the same under his arm, swung out around Notre Dame's right end. The brilliant fake worked to perfection. The entire Notre Dame defense had charged forward in a surging mass to check the line attack and Harding, with open territory, sailed on for a touchdown. He traveled those last twelve yards after the manner of food shot from guns. He was over the line before the Westerners knew what had taken place. It was a fine bit of strategy, brilliantly carried out by every member of the cast.

The cadet sector had a chance to rip open the chilly atmosphere at last, and most of the 55,000 present joined in the tribute to football art. But that was Army's last chance to score. From that point on it was seesaw, up and down, back and fourth, with the rivals fighting bitterly for every inch of ground. It was harder now to make a foot than it had been to make ten yards. Even the all-star South Bend cast could no longer continue to romp for any set distances, as Army tacklers, inspired by the touchdown, charged harder and faster than they had charged before.

The Army brought a fine football team into action, but it was beaten by a faster and smoother team. Rockne's supposedly light, green line was about as heavy as Army's, and every whit as aggressive. What is even more important, it was faster on its feet, faster in getting around.

It was Western speed and perfect interference that once more brought about Army doom. The Army line couldn't get through fast enough to break up the attacking plays; and once started the bewildering speed and power of the Western backs slashed along for eight, ten and fifteen yards on play after play. And always in front of these offensive drives could be found the whirling form of Stuhldreher, taking the first man out of the play as cleanly as though he had used a hand grenade at close range. This Notre Dame interference was a marvelous thing to look upon.

It formed quickly and came along in unbroken order, always at terrific speed, carried by backs who were as hard to drag down as African buffaloes. On receiving the kick-off, Notre Dame's interference formed something after the manner of the ancient flying wedge, and they drove back up the field with the runner covered for twenty-five and thirty yards at almost every chance. And when a back such as Harry Wilson finds few chances to get started, you can

figure upon the defensive strength that is barricading the road. Wilson is one of the hardest backs in the game to suppress, but he found few chances yesterday to show his broken field ability. You can't run through a broken field until you get there.

One strong feature of the Army play was its headlong battle against heavy odds. Even when Notre Dame had scored two touchdowns and was well on its way to a third, the Army fought on with fine spirit until the touchdown chance came at last. And when the chance came Coach McEwan had the play ready for the final march across the line. The Army has a better team than it had last year. So has Notre Dame. We doubt that any team in the country could have beaten Rockne's array yesterday afternoon, East or West. It was a great football team brilliantly directed, a team of speed, power and team play. The Army has no cause for gloom over its showing. It played first class football against more speed than it could match.

Those who have tackled a cyclone can understand.

Questions

1. How does Rice transform a football game into an epic struggle?
2. In the process, what does he do to the athletes?
3. How might the sportswriting of this era have succeeded as a form of adult education?

24-7 "Re-Making Leisure" in Middletown (1929)

The sociologists Robert S. (1892–1970) and Helen Merrell (1896–1982) Lynd wanted to study the effects of modernization on an urban community "in that common denominator of America, the Middle West." They chose Muncie, Indiana, which they referred to as Middletown (see text p. 739). The Lynds' work, first published in 1929, has become a classic in American sociology.

This selection consider the automobile (see text pp. 749–750), a new but already troubling phenomenon in Middletown.

Source: Excerpts from *Middletown: A Study in American Culture* by Robert S. Lynd and Helen Merrell Lynd, pp. 253–260. Copyright 1929 by Harcourt Brace & Company and renewed 1957 by Robert S. and Helen M. Lynd. Reprinted by permission of the publisher.

The first real automobile appeared in Middletown in 1900. About 1906 it was estimated that "there are probably 200 in the city and county." At the close of 1923 there were 6,221 passenger cars in the city, one for every 6.1 persons, or roughly two for every three families. Of these 6,221 cars, 41 per cent. were Fords; 54 per cent. of the total were cars of models of 1920 or later, and 17 per cent. models earlier than 1917. These cars average a bit over 5,000 miles a year. For some of the workers and some of the business class, use of the automobile is a seasonal matter, but the increase in surfaced roads and in closed cars is rapidly making the car a year-round tool for leisure-time as well as getting-a-living activities. As, at the turn of the century, business class people began to feel apologetic if they did not have a telephone, so ownership of an automobile has now reached the point of being an accepted essential of normal living.

Into the equilibrium of habits which constitutes for each individual some integration in living has come this new habit, upsetting old adjustmets, and blasting its way through such accustomed and unquestioned dicta as "Rain or shine, I never miss a Sunday morning at church"; "A high school boy does not need much spending money"; "I don't need exercise, walking to the office keeps me fit"; "I wouldn't think of moving out of town and being so far from my friends"; "Parents ought always to know where their children are." The newcomer is most quickly and amicably incorporated into those regions of behavior in which men are engaged in dong impersonal, matter-of-fact things; much more contested is its advent where emotionally charged sanctions and taboos are concerned. No one questions the use of the auto for transporting groceries, getting to one's place of work or to the golf course, or in place of the porch for "cooling off after supper" on a hot summer evening; however much the activities concerned with getting a living may be altered by the fact that a factory can draw from workmen within a radius of forty-five miles, or however much old labor union men resent the intrusion of this new alternate way of spending an evening, these things are hardly major issues. But when auto riding tends to replace the traditional call in the family parlor as a way of approach between the unmarried, "the home is endangered," and all-day Sunday motor trips are a "threat against the church"; it is in the activities concerned with the home and religion that the automobile occasions the greatest emotional conflicts.

Group-sanctioned values are disturbed by the inroads of the automobile upon the family budget. A case in point is the not uncommon practice of mortgaging a home to buy an automobile. . . . That the automobile does represent a real choice in the minds of some at least is suggested by the acid retort of one citizen to the question about car ownership: "No, sir, we've *not* got a car. *That's* why we've got a home." According to an officer of a Middletown automobile financing company, 75 to 90 perc cent. of the cars purchased locally are bought on time payment, and a working man earning $35.00 a week frequently plans to use one week's pay each month as payment for his car.

The automobile has apparently unsettled the habit of careful saving for some families. "Part of the money we spend on the car would go to the bank, I suppose," said more than one working class wife. A business man explained his recent inviting of social oblivion by selling his car by saying: "My car, counting depreciation and everything, was costing mighty nearly $100.00 a month, and my wife and I sat down together the other night and just figured that we're getting along, and if we're to have anything

later on, we've just got to begin to save." The "moral" aspect of the competition between the automobile and certain accepted expenditures appears in the remark of another business man, "An automobile is a luxury, and no one has a right to one if he can't afford it. I haven't the slightest sympathy for any one who is out of work if he owns a car."

Men in the clothing industry are convinced that automobiles are bought at the expense of clothing, and the statements of a number of the working class wives bear this out:

> "We'd rather do without clothes than give up the car," said one mother of nine children. "We used to go to his sister's to visit, but by the time we'd get the children shoed and dressed there wasn't any money left for carfare. Now no matter how they look, we just poke 'em in the car and take 'em along."

> "We don't have no fancy clothes when we have the car to pay for," said another. "The car is the only pleaure we have."

Even food may suffer:

> "I'll go without food before I'll see us give up the car," said one woman emphatically, and several who were out of work were apparently making precisely this adjustment. . . .

Many families feel that an automobile is justified as an agency holding the family group together. "I never feel as close to my family as when we are all together in the car," said one business class mother, and one or two spoke of giving up Country Club membership or other recreations to get a car for this reason. "We don't spend anything on recreation except for the car. We save every place we can and put the money into the car. It keeps the family together," was an opinion voiced more than once. Sixty-one per cent. of 337 boys and 60 per cent. of 423 girls in the three upper years of the high school say that they motor more often with their parents than without them.

But this centralizing tendency of the automobile may be only a passing phase; sets in the other direction are almost equally prominent. "Our daughters [eighteen and fifteen] don't use our car much because they are always with somebody else in their car when we go out motoring," lamented one business class mother. . . . "What on earth *do* you want me to do? Just sit around home all evening!" retorted a popular high school girl of today when her father discouraged her going out motoring for the evening with a young blade in a rakish car waiting at the curb. The fact that 348 boys and 382 girls in the three upper years of the high school placed "use of the automobile" fifth and fourth respectively in a list of twelve possible sources of disagreement between them and their parents suggests that this may be an increasing decentralizing agent.

An earnest teacher in a Sunday School class of working class boys and girls in their late teens was winding up the lesson on the temptations of Jesus: "These three temptations summarize all the temptations we encounter today: physical comfort, fame, and wealth. Can you think of any temptation we have today that Jesus didn't have?" "Speed!" rejoined one boy. . . . The boys who have cars "step on the gas," and those who haven't cars sometimes steal them: "The desire of youth to step on the gas when it has no machine of its own," said the local press, "is considered responsible for the theft of the greater part of the [154] automobiles stolen from [Middletown] during the past year."

The threat which the automobile presents to some anxious parents is suggested by the fact that of thirty girls brought before the juvenile court in the twelve months preceding September 1, 1924, charged with "sex crimes," for whom the place where the offense occurred was given in the records, nineteen were listed as having committed the offense in an automobile. Here again the automobile appears to some as an "enemy" of the home and society.

Sharp, also, is the resentment aroused by this elbowing new device when it interferes with old-established religious habits. The minister trying to change people's behavior in desired directions through the spoken word must compete against the strong pull of the open road strengthened by endless printed "copy" inciting to travel. Preaching to 200 people on a hot, sunny Sunday in midsummer on "The Supreme Need of Today," a leading Middletown minister denounced "automobilitis—the thing those people have who go off motoring on Sunday instead of going to church". . . .

"We had a fine day yesterday," exclaimed an elderly pillar of a prominent church, by way of Monday morning greeting. "We left home at five in the morning. By seven we swept into —. At eight we had breakfast at —, eighty miles from home. From there we went on to Lake —, the longest in the state. I had never seen it before, and I've lived here all my life, but I sure do want to go again. Then we went to — [the Y.M.C.A. camp] and had our chicken dinner. It's a fine thing for people to get out that way on Sundays. No question about it. They see different things and get a larger outlook."

"Did you miss church?" he was asked.

"Yes, I did, but you can't do both. I never missed church or Sunday school for thirteen years and I kind of feel as if I'd done my share. The ministers ought not to rail against people's driving on Sunday. They ought just to realize that they won't be there every Sunday during the summer, and make church interesting enough so they'll want to come."

But if the automobile touches the rest of Middletown's living at many points, it has revolutionized its leisure; more, perhaps, than the movies or any other intrusion new to Middletown since the nineties, it is making leisure-time enjoyment a regularly expected part of every day and week rather than an occasional event. The readily available leisure-time options of even the working class have been multiplied many-fold. As one working class housewife remarked, "We just go to lots of things we couldn't go to if we didn't have a car." Beefsteak and watermelon picnics in a park or a near-by wood can be a matter of a moment's decision on a hot afternoon.

Not only has walking for pleasure become practically extinct, but the occasional event such as a parade on a holiday attracts far less attention now.

Questions

1. Why did the people of Middletown worry about the automobile's effect on religious worship?
2. What habits did the car seem to alter?
3. How did adolescents adapt to the automobile culture?

Questions for Further Thought

1. In what ways did advertising and popular entertainment affect civic culture in the 1920s?
2. Are the ads reprinted as Documents 24-4 and 24-5 different in degree or kind from current advertising? In what ways?

3. How did sports (Document 24-6) and movies succeed as unifying agents in American society?

4. Cars, movies, and advertising—were the residents of Middletown (Document 24-7) right to feel uneasy about the changes they saw occurring in their community? Why or why not?

Dissenting Values and Cultural Conflict

The 1920s were anything but staid. Some people delighted in the changes; others did not.

Since the beginning of the republic Americans had debated the question of immigration. Despite their eloquence, the words of Emma Lazarus inscribed on the Statue of Liberty ("Give me your tired, your poor, / Your huddled masses yearning to breathe free, / The wretched refuse of your teeming shore") did not reflect the popular mood. The Chinese were excluded in 1882, and the Japanese twenty-six years later. In 1921 Congress passed a quota system aimed at central, southern, and Eastern Europeans (see text p. 757). The law was further tightened in 1924, and xenophobes such as Maryland Senator William Bruce no longer had to be concerned about the entry of "indigestible lumps" into the "national stomach."

Many Americans worried about the presence of new immigrants. In the first half of the decade the Ku Klux Klan attracted recruits with the motto "Native, white, Protestant supremacy" (see text pp. 759–760). The Klan spread beyond the South by playing on anti-Catholic and anti-Semitic prejudices. The 1928 presidential campaign between the Protestant Herbert Hoover and the Irish Catholic Al Smith was contested against this backdrop of prejudice. But by the decade's end the Klan was in decline, and ethnic Americans were enjoying sweet revenge as they rose to power in the cities: soon they would play a crucial role in Democratic national politics.

Cultural upheaval was also manifested in other ways. Rural and small-town Americans felt their prestige slip away in what the Census Bureau identified as the first urban decade (see text p. 756). In those areas religious fundamentalism helped cushion the decline, and Prohibition preserved a vestige of political strength (see text pp. 760–761). A different kind of alienation led urban African-Americans to the teachings of Marcus Garvey (see text pp. 763–764). The leader of the back-to-Africa movement achieved a short-lived popularity among the black populations in northern cities.

American letters underwent change along with the rest of society in the 1920s. Young writers such as Ernest Hemingway, F. Scott Fitzgerald, and John Dos Passos voiced the discontent of a "lost generation," while Sinclair Lewis emerged as perhaps the most influential writer of the decade (see text pp. 761–763) by introducing readers to two quintessential American hypocrites: Elmer Gantry and George F. Babbit. In Harlem, African-Americans experienced an artistic renaissance in keeping with the emergence of the New Negro (see text pp. 762–763). Claude McKay, Countee Cullen, and Langston Hughes were among the writers who attempted to show, as W. E. B. Du Bois explained, how "to be a Negro and an American."

In Document 24-8, Madison Grant displays a nativist's dislike of immigrants. Document 24-9 is an editorial by Marcus Garvey that explains his ideas on black nationalism. Finally, Jane Addams (see Document 21-5) returns in Document 24-10 to defend Prohibition.

24-8   Nativism in the Twenties (1930)

Madison Grant

In his work on American nativism the historian John Higham has written about the "Tribal Twenties." Indeed, relations between racial and ethnic groups probably reached a nadir during that decade (see text pp. 757–760). One of the leading nativists of the time was Madison Grant, a charter member of the Society of Colonial Wars. Grant, however, proved to be a poor student of the American Revolution. His essay on "the alien in our midst," excerpted here, appeared in 1930, though it had a 1920s mind-set.

Source: Madison Grant, "Closing the Flood-Gates," in Madison Grant and Charles Steward Davison, eds., *The Alien in Our Midst or, Selling Our Birthright for a Mess of Pottage: The Written Views of a Number of Americans (Present and Former) on Immigration and Its Results* (New York: Galton Publishing Company, 1930), pp. 13–21.

Our Federal Republic has been more fortunate than other modern nations in the exceptional character of its founders. The end of the colonial period was marked by the appearance on the scene of action of an extraordinary group of statesmen. These men were deeply versed in the lessons taught by classical history as well as in the practical application of representative government, which had been slowly evolving in England. Thus equipped, they formulated a written constitution which has been sound enough and elastic enough to stand the strain of 150 years. During this period the nation, organized under its provisions, expanded across the continent and emerged from the scanty resources of the backwoods into one of the great powers of the world.

The group of men who formulated that constitution was drawn from a population scattered along the Eastern seaboard and numbering from three to four millions. It is doubtful whether our present one hundred millions could produce an equal number of statesmen—even if we admit that the best brains of the present are not devoted to the service of the state and have not been so devoted for the last fifty years.

The work of the founders was so well done that our chief concern today is to maintain the original spirit of the Constitution rather than to change or improve it. The last six or seven amendments have weakened rather than strengthened that instrument and certainly do not indicate any great degree of statesmanship.

The Revolution brought about by these Founders was political rather than social or religious. But ruling power was not taken from one class and given to another, though the governing classes of Colonial times were greatly weakened by the loss of many thousands of Loyalists who were driven from the country.

The Colonists were overwhelmingly Anglo-Saxon and were still more Nordic. Over ninety percent were British, including 82.1 per cent pure English and the balance Scotch and "Scotch-Irish." Over ninety-eight per cent were Nordic, including two and a half per cent Dutch and five and a half per cent German. This does not include the small Huguenot element, which was to a very great extent Nordic. Some, however, if not a majority, of the Pennsylvania Germans were Alpine. The only discordant elements were the Germans in Pennsylvania and small colonies of Portuguese at points on the New England coast, but the last were of little importance. The Founders, however, realized clearly that even these small minorities embodied a potential menace to the unity of the Republic. They realized also that the growth of the Colonial population was so rapid that there was no need of immigration.

Subsequent events have justified these opinions, and it is now known to the well-informed that the population of the United States would be as large as that of the present day, if there had been no immigration whatever. The originally large birth-rate of the native American falls wherever immigrants push in. Immigration means that for each new arrival from across the sea, one American is not born.

The introduction of serf labor to do rough work causes the withdrawal from such manual labor of the native Americans. One hears on every side, as an excuse for bringing in immigrants, that native Americans will not work in the field or in railroad gangs. It is true that they will not work alongside of Negroes or Slovaks or Mexicans, because a mean man makes the job a mean one. In the mountains of the South where there are no Negroes, and in those portions of the Northwest where there are few foreigners, native Americans can be seen today doing all the manual work, as was universally the case two generations ago.

A race that refuses to do manual work and seeks "white collar" jobs, is doomed through its falling birth-rate to replacement by the lower races or classes. In other words, the introduction of immigrants as lowly laborers means a replacement of race. These immigrants drive out the native; they do not mix with him. The Myth of the Melting Pot was the great fallacy of the last generation—fortunately it is utterly discredited today.

If the considered and recorded views of the Founders had prevailed and the nation after the Civil War had not made frantic efforts to "develop a continent" in a single generation and had not imported cheap serf labor for this purpose, the United States would have had today not only a population as large as its present one, but a population that was Nordic and Anglo-Saxon and homogeneous throughout.

Instead of a population homogeneous in race, religion, traditions and aspirations, as was the American nation down to 1840, we have—inserted into the body politic—an immense mass of foreigners, congregated for the most part in the large cities and in the industrial centers. The greater part of these foreigners, even if naturalized, are not in sympathy with American ideals, nor do they either understand or exercise the self-restraint necessary to govern a Republic. Many of these aliens, especially those from Eastern and Southern Europe were drawn from the lowest social strata of their homeland and mistake the liberty they find in America, and the easy-going tolerance of the native American, for an invitation to license and crime.

The closing years of the decade between 1840 and 1850 brought in the first of these foreigners. Germans, fleeing from their fatherland after the collapse of the revolutionary movements, for the most part took up unoccupied lands in the West, although some of them settled in the large cities, notably in St. Louis and Cincinnati. While it cannot be said that they improved the American population either physically or intellectually yet they accepted our form of government and made effort to maintain its traditions.

The Irish, on the other hand, who arrived a few years earlier, settled in the large cities and industrial centers of the North. These Irish were drawn from the submerged and primitive peasantry of South and West Ireland. In race they were partly Mediterranean and partly Nordic mixed with remnants of an aboriginal population. They were, for the most part, day laborers and domestic servants and Catholics. They came into conflict with the native Americans by trying to introduce their church institutions and parochial schools, which were and are regarded as hostile to the public school system of the United States.

When concentrated in large cities these Irish were responsive to the leadership of bosses and were organized in the solid blocs which demoralize our municipal politics. Our republican representative system, coupled with universal suffrage, does not work any too well even in rural districts, but it breaks down utterly in our cities. In recent decades the Irish have advanced somewhat in the social scale, because newcomers, the Poles, Slovaks, and Italians have in turn replaced them in the more menial tasks.

It must be noted that these later Irish differ racially, religiously and spiritually from the so-called "Scotch-Irish" immigrants of a century before. The name "Scotch-Irish" is a misnomer, for they were racially pure Scotch-English and had nothing in common with the native Irish of South Ireland. Being staunch Protestants, mostly Presbyterians, they were in antagonism to the Catholics from the South. The fathers or grandfathers of the so-called "Scotch-Irish" who migrated in the early part of the eighteenth century to America, were born in Scotland and England and had migrated to North Ireland. The descendants of these Scotch-English again migrated to these (then) colonies, mostly through Philadelphia, also to the Carolinas. From there they found their way into the backwoods beyond the old English settlements and southwest along the valleys of the Alleghenies. They formed a class of frontiersmen who settled Kentucky, Tennessee and the States beyond and were the chief Indian fighters of the later Colonial times. These facts were important at the time when the question of the quotas of Northern Ireland and Southern Ireland were being adjusted.

There were few Roman Catholics in the colonies. The Colonial laws were everywhere drastic against Catholics and even in Maryland, which is constantly referred to as a "Catholic colony", the Catholics were in such a great minority that in 1715, they were actually deprived of the franchise by the Protestant majority. John Fiske estimates the number of Roman Catholics at only one-twelfth of the population of Maryland in 1661–1689. The alleged tolerance said to have been exhibited by the Catholics of Maryland cannot be claimed as voluntary on their part for Lord Baltimore received his charter from a Protestant King on the express condition that no religious restrictions against Protestants were to be enacted.

Of their numbers in the United States the Official Catholic Year Book for the year 1928 says: "In 1775 there were only about 23,000 white Catholics in the country, administered to by thirty-four priests, the larger portion living in Maryland and Pennsylvania". In a book published in 1925, under the sanction of M. J. Curley, the Catholic Archbishop of Baltimore, in attempting to estimate the strength of the Catholic population in colonial times, it is stated that in 1790 the total Catholic population of the United States was 35,000 of which about 25,000 were Irish. From this it is obvious that a large proportion of the immigration even from Southern Ireland, and nearly all the immigration from Ulster in colonial times, was Protestant.

Undesirable as was substantially the whole of the immigration of the nineteenth century, it might have been partially Americanized, but, just when that transformation was beginning, two events of great portent happened. One was the exhaustion of free public land open to settlement, and the other was the extension of manufacturing with its call for cheap labor. America entered on a career of industrial development, which, while producing great wealth for a few, transformed whole countrysides and farming villages into factory towns.

The New England employer utilized the Irish who were at hand and imported French-Canadians. The mine owners in Pennsylvania imported Polish and Slovak miners. The industries of Ohio and of the adjoining states employed in large numbers members of nondescript races.

We may note, in passing, that the French-Canadians had nothing in common with the Colonial French Huguenots. The "habitant" from Quebec was and is a docile, sturdy undersized Breton peasant, speaking an archaic Norman dialect, while the early French Protestants, who escaped to America from persecution at home, were, to a very large extent, Nordic and were drawn from the skilled artisan and merchant classes and the lesser gentry.

In all the industrialized states, the replacement of the native American went on rapidly, but silently and unnoticed, except by a few patriotic men, until the drafts during the World War revealed that Vermont was full of French-Canadians; that farming lands along the Connecticut River Valley had been taken up by Poles; that Boston was overrun by the Irish; that New Haven had become almost an Italian city; that Rhode Island was swamped by aliens, and that Detroit and Chicago were to all intent foreign cities.

The native American element in New York City had been hopelessly submerged for half a century, but it came as a shock to the country to read the names in the draft lists, and to realize how complete was the transformation of some of the States. Massachusetts, Rhode Island, Connecticut and New Jersey are regarded by politicians as sub-

merged areas and the effort, which was made in the 1928 election, was practically an effort to unite politically all these nonassimilated foreign and urban elements and to take over the control of the Federal government.

This new grouping has been for some time foreshadowed by the singular political alliance in Boston, and later in New York City, between the Jews and the Catholics but the alien elements in the North are still too weak to gain control of the Federal government without the support of the Southern states.

Americans were shocked to find what an utterly subordinate place was occupied by the American stock in the opinions of some aliens. An example of this was a poster issued by some thoughtless enthusiast in the Treasury Department in one of the appeals for Liberty Loans. It showed a Howard Chandler Christy girl of pure Nordic type, pointing with pride to a list of names and saying "AMERICANS ALL". Then followed the list:

DuBois	Villotto
Smith	Levy
O'Brien	Turovich
Cejka	Kowalski
Jaucke	Chriczanevicz
Pappandrikopolous	Knutson
Andrassi	Gonzales

The one "American" in that list, so far as he figures at all, is hidden under the sobriquet of "Smith", and there is, we must presume, an implied suggestion that the very beautiful lady is the product of this remarkable melting pot. . . .

Questions

1. How do Grant's ideas differ from those of Social Darwinists (see text pp. 589–590, 684 and Document 22-4)?
2. What constitutes Grant's definition of race? How does he define "native Americans"?
3. What groups in the 1920s would have embraced Grant's argument (see text pp. 757–760)?

24-9   Editorial in the *Negro World* (1924)

Marcus Garvey

The Ku Klux Klan presented one view of African-Americans (see text pp. 759–760), and Marcus Garvey offered another. The Jamaican-born Garvey (1887–1940) simply reversed the Klan's argument: the United States, not the African-American community, was the problem (see text pp. 763–764). The solution appeared in this editorial, which Garvey wrote in 1924 after the Fourth International Convention of the Negro Peoples of the World.

Source: Marcus Garvey, editorial in *Negro World* (New York), September 2, 1924. In Robert A. Hill, ed., *The Marcus Garvey and Universal Negro Improvement Association Papers*, vol. 6, pp. 8–11. Copyright © 1989 by the Regents of the University of California. Reprinted by permission of the University of California Press and of the Marcus Garvey and UNIA Papers Project.

THE ENEMIES AT WORK

During the whole of the convention and a little prior thereto, the enemies of our cause tried to provoke and confuse our deliberation by the many unpleasant things they systematically published against the Universal Negro Improvement Association. Our enemies in America, especially the Negro Republican politicians of New York, used the general time fuse to explode on our tranquility and thereby destroy the purpose for which we were met, but as is customary, the Universal Negro Improvement Association is always ready for the enemy. They had arranged among themselves to get certain individuals of the Liberian government along with Ernest Lyons, the Liberian Consul-General, in Baltimore, himself a reactionary Negro politician of the old school, to circulate through the Negro press and other agencies such unpleasant news purported to be from Liberia as to create consternation in our ranks and bring about the demoralization that they hoped and calculated for, but as usual, the idiots counted without their hosts. They Universal Negro Improvement Association cannot be destroyed that way, in that it is not only an organization, but is the expression of the spiritual desires of the four hundred million black peoples of the world.

OUR COLONIZATION PROGRAM

As everybody knows, we are preparing to carry out our Liberian colonization program during this and succeeding months. Every arrangement was practically made toward this end. . . . Unfortunately, after all arrangements had been made in this direction, our steamship secured to carry the colonists and all plans laid, these enemies of progress worked in every way to block the carrying out of the plan. For the purpose of deceiving the public and carrying out their obstruction, they tried to make out by the protest that was filed by Ernest Lyons of Baltimore, with the government of Washington, that our Association was of an incendiary character and that it was the intention of the organization to disturb the good relationship that existed between Liberia and other friendly powers. A greater nonsense could not have been advanced by any idiot. What could an organization like the Universal Negro Improvement Association do to destroy the peace of countries that are already established and recognized? It is supposed that England and France are the countries referred to when, in fact, the authors of that statement know that England and France are only waiting an opportunity to seize more land in Liberia and to keep Liberia in a state of stagnation, so as to justify their argument that the blacks are not competent of self-government in Africa as well as elsewhere. If Edwin Barclay had any sense, he would know that the Universal Negro Improvement Association is more friendly to Liberia, because it is made up of Negroes, than England and France could be in a thousand years. Lyons' protest was camouflage.

NEGROES DOUBLE-CROSSING

Everybody knows that the hitch in the colonization plan of the Universal Negro Improvement Association in Liberia came about because of double-crossing. The Firestone Rubber and Tire Company, of Ohio, has been spending large sums of money among certain people. The offer, no doubt, was so attractive as to cause certain persons to found the argument to destroy the Universal Negro Improvement Association, so as to favor the Firestone Rubber and Tire Company who, subsequently, got one million acres of Liberian land for actually nothing, to be exploited for rubber and minerals, and in the face of the fact that Liberia is one of the richest rubber countries in the world, an asset that should have been retained for the Liberian people and members of the black race, but now wantonly given over to a white company to be exploited in the interest of white capital, and to create another international complication, as evidenced in the subsequent subjugation of Haiti and the Haitians, after the New York City Bank established itself in Haiti in a similar way as the Firestone Rubber and Tire Company will establish itself in Liberia. Why, every Negro who is doing a little thinking, knows that after the Firestone Rubber and Tire Company gets into Liberia to exploit the one million acres of land, it is only a question of time when the government will be taken out of the hands of the Negroes who rule it, and Liberia will become a white man's country in violation of the constitution of that government as guaranteeing its soil as a home for all Negroes of all climes and nationalities who desire to return to their native land. The thing is so disgraceful that we, ourselves, are ashamed to give full publicity to it, but we do hope that the people of Liberia, who control the government of Liberia, will be speedily informed so that they, through the Senate and House of Representatives, will repudiate the concessions granted to the Firestone Rubber and Tire Company, so as to save their country from eternal spoilation. If the Firestone Rubber and Tire Company should get the concessions in Liberia of one million acres of land, which should have been granted to the Universal Negro Improvement Association for development by Negroes for the good of Negroes, it simply means that in another short while thousands of white men will be sent away from America by the Firestone Rubber and Tire Company to exploit their concessions. These white men going out to colonize, as they generally regard tropical countries, will carry with them the spirit of all other white colonists, superiority over and subjugation of native peoples; hence it will only be a question of time when these gentlemen will change the black population of Liberia into a mongrel race, as they have done in America, [the] West Indies and other tropical countries, and there create another race problem such as is confusing us now in these United States of America. These white gentlemen are not going to allow black men to rule and govern them, so, like China and other places, there will be such complications as to ultimately lead to the abrogation of all native control and government and the setting up of new authority in a country that once belonged to the natives.

THE RAPE OF LIBERIA

It is the duty of every Negro in the world to protest against this rape of Liberia encouraged by those who are responsible for giving the concessions to the Firestone Rubber and Tire Company. Why, nearly one-half of the country has been given away and, when it is considered that out of the twelve million square miles of Africa, only Liberia is left as a free and independent black country, it becomes a shame and disgrace to see that men should be capable of giving away all this amount of land to the same people who have possession of over nine-tenths of the country's [continent's] area.

BRIGHT FUTURE FOR RACE

We beg to advise, however, the members and friends of the Universal Negro Improvement Association all over the world, that what has happened has not obstructed much the program of the Universal Negro Improvement Association as far as our colonization plans are concerned. All that we want is that everybody get behind the Black Cross Navigation and Trading Company and send us the necessary amount of money to pay for our first ship and secure other ships so as to carry out our trade contract with the Negroes of Africa, West Indies, South and Central America and these United States. The Association is devoting its time and energy now to building up an international commerce and trade so as to stabilize Negro industry. There is

much for us to do. In taking the raw materials from our people in Africa to America, as well as materials [from] the West Indies, South and Central America to the United States[,] and taking back to them our finished and manufactured products in exchange, we have a whole world of industrial conquest to make and it can be done splendidly if each Negro will give us the support that is necessary. We want not only one, two or three ships, but we want dozens of ships, so that every week our ships can be going out of the ports of New York, Philadelphia, Boston, Baltimore, New Orleans, Savannah or Mobile for Liberia, Sierre [*sic*] Leone, Gold Coast, Lagos, Abyssinia, Brazil, Argentina, Costa Rica, Guatemala, Nicaragua, Honduras, Jamaica, Barbados, Trinidad, British Guiana and British Honduras. Let our ships be on the seven seas, taking our commerce to England, France, Germany, Italy, Japan, China and India. The chance of making good in commerce and trade is as much ours as it is other races and so we call upon you everywhere to get behind the industrial program of the Universal Negro Improvement Association. If we can control the field of industry we can control the sentiment of the world and that is what the Universal Negro Improvement Association seeks for the four hundred millions of our race.

MOVE THE LITTLE BARRIERS

So, the little barriers that have been placed in the way by the envious and wicked of our own race can easily be removed if we will get together and work together. Now that the convention has risen, let us redouble our energy everywhere to put the program over. Let us work with our hearts, soul and minds to see that everything is accomplished for the good of the race. We must have our ship in action by next month. At least, we are calculating to have our ship sail out of New York by the 29th of October, laden with the first cargo for the tropics, and to bring back to us tropical fruits and produce, and from thence to sail for Africa, the land of our fathers. Help us make this possible. . . .

With very best wishes for your success, I have the honor to be, Your obedient servant,

MARCUS GARVEY
President-General
Universal Negro Improvement Association

Questions

1. What does Garvey propose?
2. Why does he consider black Republicans the enemy? What is his purpose in attacking the Firestone Company?
3. How do Garvey's views differ from those of Booker T. Washington (see Document 19-10) and W. E. B. Du Bois (see Document 19-11)? Does Garvey echo any of the points made by the others?

24-10 "A Decade of Prohibition" (1930)

Jane Addams

Support for Prohibition was strongest in rural areas but did not end once a person stepped inside city limits. Many urban social reformers welcomed the Eighteenth Amendment (see text p. 761). Among them was Jane Addams (see Chapter 21), who discusses her views in the second installment of her autobiography, which was published in 1930.

Source: Reprinted with the permission of Simon & Schuster from *The Second Twenty Years at Hull-House* by Jane Addams, pp. 223–229. Copyright 1930 by Macmillan Pubishing Company. Copyright renewed © 1958 by John A. Brittain.

In the winter of 1911 the Juvenile Protective Association of Chicago made a very careful investigation of three hundred and twenty-eight public dance halls, and found that 86,000 people frequent them on a Saturday evening, of whom the majority were boys between the ages of sixteen and eighteen and girls between fourteen and sixteen—the very ages at which pleasure is most eagerly demanded as the prerogative of youth. One condition they found to be general; most of the dance halls existed for the sale of liquor and dancing was of secondary importance. One hundred and ninety halls had saloons opening into them, liquor was sold in two hundred and forty out of three hundred and twenty-eight, and in the others, except in rare instances, return checks were given to facilitate the use of the neighboring saloons. At the halls where liquor was sold, by twelve o'clock practically all the boys, who in many halls outnumbered the girls, showed signs of intoxication.

Peculiar dangers were to be found in connection with masquerade and fancy dress balls where the masks encouraged undue license, and where the prizes awarded for the best costumes were usually a barrel of beer to the best group of men, a dozen bottles of wine to the best group of girls, and a quart of whiskey for a single character. At one hall it was found that a cash prize of one hundred dollars had been offered to the girl who at the end of the month had the largest number of drinks placed to her credit. As the owner of the hall lived and thrived by the sale of liquor, the dances were short—four to five minutes; the intermissions were long—fifteen to thirty minutes; thus giving ample opportunity for drinking. There was but little ventilation; apparently on the theory that the hotter it was, the more thirst would be superinduced and the more liquor would be sold. In dance halls which did not have a connecting saloon the method of selling liquor was as follows: the dance-hall keeper procured a government license for which he paid twenty-five dollars a year; when an organization applied for permission to rent the hall the dance-hall keeper went with the officers of the association to the federal bureau or loaned them his government license, and with this they secured a special bar permit for which they paid six dollars each. This special bar permit allowed the

sale of liquor from three o'clock in the afternoon until three o'clock the next morning, while under the city ordinances saloons were obliged to close at one o'clock. Because of this regulation, the patrons of the local saloons swarmed into the dance halls at midnight, paying of course an entrance fee and freely buying drinks. Many club dances came to depend upon the money thus brought in by late comers although they deprecated the "toughs" thus introduced. It was of course between these hours that the conduct became most obnoxious and that the dangers for young people were most apparent.

The carelessness of the city toward such social conditions was the more astounding in that we all know that public dance halls offered then as now the only opportunity open to thousands of young men for meeting the girls whom they will later marry. Nature, always anxious that human beings shall reveal themselves to each other, at no time makes the impulse so imperative as at that period when youth is dreaming of love and marriage. The imaginative powers, the sense that life possesses variety and color, are realized most easily in moments of pleasure and comradeship, and it is then that individual differences and variations are disclosed. All day long the young people work in factories where every effort is made that they shall conform to a common standard; as they walk upon the street they make painful exertions to appear in the prevailing mode of dress and to keep conventions. Only in moments of recreation does their sense of individuality expand; they are then able to reveal, as at no other time, that hidden self which is so important to each of us.

The owners of the dance halls were themselves sometimes touched by the helplessness of these young people who came to them in such numbers. They asked for help from the Juvenile Protective Association which at the request of individual dance halls, appointed social workers who with the aid of specially designated policemen endeavored to watch conditions in the halls. Not until after Prohibition was established in 1919, however, was it possible to do this for all the public dance halls within the city-wide Association of Dance Halls. The proprietors have come to pay the chaperon or investigator through the treasury of the J.P.A. The Association has also designated the person to be employed. Thus under Prohibition the large commercial dance halls in Chicago have come to be well chaperoned with a standard of conduct enforced by the dance-hall managers themselves. Every boy and man who pays an entrance fee is examined by an officer for a flask; if a flask is found, it is taken away from him and in his presence the contents are poured down the sewer. At one of the large dance halls a few months ago, in one evening, out of forty-five hundred persons examined, only three were found carrying flasks. Such a regulation of course would have been impossible unless the entire liquor business had been made illegal.

The entire dance-hall situation has been affected by it. Since there is no profit to be made from selling liquor, most of the public dances conducted by private organizations have been discontinued; therefore public dancing is more and more conducted in large halls by professional dance-hall promoters. This change has affected also the tactics of the politicians; some of them, since the abolition of the saloon, have hired vacant stores or other spaces, especially at election time, and established therein political clubs, paying the rent and in many ways putting the club members under obligations. They have even established such clubs for boys under voting age, in order to keep them in line. These organizations, however, since the abolition of the saloons, are not too successful, and political favors are gradually assuming other forms. One of the worst features of the pre-prohibition dance halls was drunkenness among the patrons, men and girls, who left the festivities late at night and whose condition was utilized by "runners" for houses of assignation. In many cases the men on the dance floor itself were procurers who had as far as possible placed their intended victims under the influence of liquor.

Drink was of course a leading lure and a necessary element in houses of prostitution, both from a financial and a social standpoint. Many students of the subject believed that professional houses of prostitution could not sustain themselves without the "vehicle of alcohol." Although the red light district of Chicago has been abolished, there are still of course many well-known houses, and it would be interesting to know how far their existence even now is dependent upon the liquor sold and consumed in them.

But if alcohol was associated intensively with these gross evils, it was also associated with homely and wholesome things. A certain type of treating had a social value which has disappeared, and doubtless large family parties have been less frequent, with the lure of drink and the consequent element of hilarity removed. Callers were then regaled with beer brought from the corner saloon, often illegally sold to a child who was hurriedly sent to get it for the visitor. Impecunious neighbors it was said sometimes called for the sake of the beer hospitality, and neighborliness has doubtless declined in those houses in which drink has disappeared. The Italians consider a wedding at which there is no wine for drinking the health of the bride to be an absolutely unnatural affair, and the substitute of "soft drinks" to be most unsatisfactory. Nevertheless, Bowen Hall, belonging to Hull-House, is used almost every weekend for a large Italian wedding party, although no alcoholic drinks are allowed there.

It is hard to exaggerate what excessive drinking did in the way of disturbing domestic relations and orderly family life. I knew for years a very charming Irish woman who with her three children led a dog's life because her recurrently deserting husband, when he returned from prolonged absences, always sold the accumulated household goods and clothing and reduced the family to absolute destitution and terror so long as he remained at home. Not until after his death, which occurred in a seizure of delirium tremens, was the capable mother able to establish a stable family life and to free her children from a fear which actually stunted their growth. But sometimes the mother of a family was not able to carry alone the burden of respectability and sobriety. I remember a wife and daughter who fell into drinking habits with the husband and father, and all three came to a disgraceful end. The father died in the so-called delirium tremens ward of the Cook County Hospital and the daughter in the venereal disease ward, the poor old mother surviving the loss of her family but a few months. This is a striking example of many similar family tragedies, not so often among the immigrants from southern Europe as among the families representing an older immigration.

Questions

1. What progress does Addams see with the coming of Prohibition?
2. What effect does she assume Prohibition will have on the drinking habits of immigrants?
3. Given the problems and corruption associated with alcohol, why do you think Prohibition failed in the long run?

Questions for Further Thought

1. To what extent, if any, do Madison Grant (Document 24-8) and Marcus Garvey (Document 24-9) offer variations on the same argument?
2. Did the success of advertising (Documents 24-4 and 24-5) in the 1920s doom Jane Addams's hopes for Prohibition (Document 24-10)? Why or why not?
3. How do the arguments of Madison Grant, Marcus Garvey, and Jane Addams suggest that the 1920s was a decade of cultural transition?

The Great Depression

★   ★   ★

The Coming of the Great Depression

The Great Depression of the 1930s was the worst economic crisis the United States had ever experienced. Few Americans were not touched by its consequences. Millions lost their jobs, their savings, and their homes, and even those fortunate enough to remain employed often faced wage cuts and a sense of economic insecurity. The impact of the decadelong depression was all the more severe because it followed one of the most prosperous decades in American history. American factories turned out a flood of consumer goods in the 1920s, from radios to Model-T Fords (see text Chapter 24). Soaring prices on the stock market were widely regarded as a symbol of the strength of the an economy (see text pp. 770–771). The Republican presidential candidate Herbert Hoover, in accepting his party's nomination in 1928, announced his belief that the United States had entered a permanent era of prosperity and that poverty would soon be eliminated from the land (see text p. 787).

But America's prosperity in the 1920s was based on shaky foundations. Lax regulation and easy credit created a speculative frenzy on Wall Street (see text pp. 770–771). Whole regions of the nation and sectors of the economy did not share the fruits of the decade's economic bounty, as the popular economist Stuart Chase warned in a prophetic book published shortly before the stock market crash (Document 25-1). Textiles, mining, and railroads were among the "sick" industries of the 1920s. And in the countryside, farmers were receiving low prices for their crops (see text p. 771). But most Americans wanted to believe, as John J. Raskob did, that everybody could be rich (Document 25-2).

Ultimately, consumer and investor confidence was destroyed by the stock market crash in October 1929, as the economy entered a seemingly endless downward spiral. The effects of the Great Depression were not restricted to the United States. Hard times spread to other countries in Europe and elsewhere (see text pp. 771–772). International trade was jeopardized as many countries adopted policies of economic nationalism, abandoning the gold standard in an attempt to protect the value of their currencies. In the early days of the crisis America's political and economic leaders attempted to convince their fellow Americans that their financial trouble would be short-lived. But as unemployment rose in the early 1930s, until one in four American workers was without a job, it became apparent that the return of prosperity was not just around the corner or even just down the block. As that reality set in, Americans began to ask themselves what had happened and what they could do next (Document 25-3).

25-1   "Balancing the Books" (1929)

Stuart Chase

Stuart Chase handed in the manuscript for his provocatively titled *Prosperity: Fact or Myth* in October 1929, just days before the stock market crash; it was rushed into print and distributed to bookstores by December. Chase (1888–1985) suggested that much of the surface prosperity of the 1920s was illusory (see text pp. 770–771). In the concluding chapter he argued that a secure and lasting prosperity awaited the "liberation of the engineer," by which he meant the application of scientific principles of planning to economic growth and development (see text p. 574 and Document 18-6).

Source: Stuart Chase, *Prosperity: Fact or Myth* (New York: C. Boni, 1929), pp. 173–177, 186–188.

BALANCING THE BOOKS

We have let us say an onion. The onion represents the total economic life of the United States at the present time. The heart of the onion is prosperity. How large does it bulk?

First, we must strip off all the states not included in the Middle Atlantic, East North Central, and Pacific states. The National Bureau of Economics finds that by and large these states have not prospered.

Second, in the prosperous belt, we strip off most of the farmers; they have not prospered.

Third, we strip off a large section of the middle class. The small business man, the independent storekeeper, the wholesaler, many professional men and women, have failed to keep income on a par with the new standard of living.

Fourth, we strip off the unemployed. Machinery appears to be displacing factory, railroad, and mining workers—and recently mergers are displacing executives, salesmen and clerks—faster than they can find employment in other fields. The net increase in "technological unemployment" since 1920 exceeds 650,000 men and women.

Fifth, we strip off the coal industry which has been in the doldrums throughout the period.

Sixth, we strip off the textile industry which has been seriously depressed.

Seventh, the boot and shoe industry. Ditto.

Eighth, the leather industry.

Ninth, the shipbuilding industry.

Tenth, the railroad equipment industry.

Eleventh, we strip off the excessive number of businesses which have gone bankrupt during the era.

Twelfth, we strip off those millions of unskilled workers who were teetering on the edge of a bare subsistence in 1922, and by no stretch of the imagination can be called prosperous to-day. The best that can be said is that their position is a little less precarious than it was.

In short only a part of the country has been prosperous, and even in that part are at least 11 soft spots—some of them very unpleasantly soft.

What then remains? . . .

The onion has shrunk, but it has not disappeared. We shall not list all the surviving leaves, but among the significant are:

1. A 20 per cent increase in the national income per capita from 1922 to 1928.

2. A 30 per cent increase in physical production.

3. A 100 per cent increase in the profits of the larger corporations.

4. A housing program expanding faster than population.

5. An increase in average health and longevity.

6. An increase in educational facilities greatly surpassing the growth of population.

7. A per capita increase in saving and insurance.

8. A booming stock market up to October 1929.

9. A 5-hour decline in the average working week.

10. A slowly rising wage scale against a fairly stationary price level.

11. An increasingly fecund, alert and intelligent science of management, resulting primarily in an ever growing productivity per worker. . . .

The trouble with nearly every item on this second list is that while it indicates that we are more prosperous than we were, nothing whatever is said about the *extent of prosperity* from which we started. The base line is missing. If we were barely comfortable in 1922, we ought to be reasonably comfortable to-day. But of course the fact is that some 80 per cent of all American families lived below the budget of health and decency in 1922, and the 20 per cent increase in per capita income since that date, while it has helped to be sure, still leaves probably two-thirds of all families below the line. Unfortunately, too, the 20 per cent cannot all go into intrinsically better food, housing and clothing, but must be applied to appease the clamoring salesmen of the new standard of living with their motor cars, radios, tootsie-rolls, silk stockings, moving pictures, near-fur coats and beauty shoppes. . . .

We have added a little real income and considerable fluff to the totally inadequate distribution of goods and services obtaining in 1922. Is this prosperity in the deeper sense? No. The most that can be said is that the last 7 or 8 years have registered a rate of advance in the direction of a prosperity which may some day be achieved. . . .

A beautiful technique this new science of management; the crowning achievement of prosperity. Given a free hand it might remake American industry humanly as well as technically. Given a free hand, it might abolish poverty, immeasurably diminish the stresses and strains which have dogged every step of the industrial revolution since the days of [James] Watt. It might flood the nation with essential and even beautiful goods at a fraction of their present cost, raise the curse of Adam, and lay the basis for, if not positively usher in, one of the noblest civilizations which the world has ever seen.

But the hands of management are not free. The technician is constantly undone by the sales department, which floundering in a pecuniary economy, sees no other way—and indeed there is no other way—to maintain capacity than by style changes, annual models, advertising misrepresentation, and high pressure merchandising. He is undone by the vested interests of the owners who demand their pound of flesh in rent, interest and dividends *now*, with no thought for the rounded perfection of engineering principles, and the time which they—and the physical laws which sanction them—demand. Foresters have worked out the technique for a perpetual lumber supply, with annual growth beautifully balanced against annual needs. But private enterprise cannot wait. Tear me down this grove tomorrow—and let the slash burn, and the soil run into the sea—I have a note maturing. So we cut our priceless heritage of forest four times as fast as it grows. In 30 years, at the present rate of exhaustion, it will be all but gone.

Above all, the technician is undone by failure to inaugurate a national system of super-management, whereby production might be articulated to consumptive needs, and the fabulous wastes of excess plants, excess machines, excess overhead costs, uneconomically located industries, cross hauling, jam, tangle and bottlenecks, brought under rational control. That such supermanagement is not beyond human capacity to operate, the experiences of the Supreme Economic Council during the War, and of the Russian Gosplan [the Soviet State Planning Committee] today, amply demonstrate. What a lordly science of engineering we might have, and to what great human benefit, if industrial anarchy gave way to industrial coördination and socialization in those fields where it logically belongs.

Prosperity in any deeper sense awaits the liberation of the engineer. If the owners will not get off his back—and why should they; they pay him little enough and he fills their safe deposit boxes?—I, for one, would not be sorry to see him combine with the wayfaring man to lift them off. A complicated technical structure should be run by engineers, not hucksters. But the technician is the modern Prometheus in chains.

Questions

1. Why does Stuart Chase compare the American economy in the 1920s to an onion?

2. What economic danger signs does Chase point to that suggest that prosperity will not last much longer?

3. What does Chase mean when he argues that securing future prosperity depends on the "liberation of the engineer"?

25-2 "Everybody Ought to Be Rich" (1929)

John J. Raskob

John J. Raskob (see text p. 770) enjoyed greater success in business than in some of his other ventures. Raskob (1879–1950) managed Al Smith's unsuccessful presidential campaign in 1928. A year later he gave investment tips to readers of the *Ladies' Home Journal*; two months after "Everybody Ought to Be Rich" appeared, Wall Street collapsed (see text pp. 770–771). In 1934 Raskob helped found the American Liberty League, a conservative group that tried to curb the New Deal's popularity. Judging by the 1936 election results, Raskob and the Liberty League failed.

Source: From Samuel Crowther, "Everybody Ought to Be Rich: An Interview with John J. Raskob," *Ladies' Home Journal*, August 1929.

Being rich is, of course, a comparative status. A man with a million dollars used to be considered rich, but so many people have at least that much in these days, or are earning incomes in excess of a normal return from a million dollars, that a millionaire does not cause any comment.

Fixing a bulk line to define riches is a pointless performance. Let us rather say that a man is rich when he has an income from invested capital which is sufficient to support him and his family in a decent and comfortable manner— to give as much support, let us say, as has ever been given by his earnings. That amount of prosperity ought to be attainable by anyone. A greater share will come to those who have greater ability. . . .

It is quite true that wealth is not so evenly distributed as it ought to be and as it can be. And part of the reason for the unequal distribution is the lack of systematic investment and also the lack of even moderately sensible investment.

One class of investors saves money and puts it into savings banks or other mediums that pay only a fixed interest. Such funds are valuable, but they do not lead to wealth. A second class tries to get rich all at once, and buys any wildcat security that comes along with the promise of immense returns. A third class holds that the return from interest is not enough to justify savings, but at the same time has too much sense to buy fake stocks—and so saves nothing at all. Yet all the while wealth has been here for the asking.

The common stocks of this country have in the past ten years increased enormously in value because the business of the country has increased. Ten thousand dollars invested ten years ago in the common stock of General Motors would now be worth more than a million and a half dollars. And General Motors is only one of many first-class industrial corporations.

It may be sad that this is a phenomenal increase and that conditions are going to be different in the next ten years. That prophecy may be true, but it is not founded on experience. In my opinion the wealth of the country is bound to increase at a very rapid rate. The rapidity of the rate will be determined by the increase in consumption, and under wise investment plans the consumption will steadily increase.

We Have Scarcely Started

Now anyone may regret that he or she did not have ten thousand dollars ten years ago and did not put it into General Motors or some other good company—and sigh over a lost opportunity. Anyone who firmly believes that the opportunities are all closed and that from now on the country will get worse instead of better is welcome to the opinion—and to whatever increment it will bring. I think that we have scarcely started, and I have thought so for many years.

In conjunction with others I have been interested in creating and directing at least a dozen trusts for investment in equity securities. This plan of equity investments is no mere theory with me. The first of these trusts was started in 1907 and the others in the years immediately following. Under all of these the plan provided for the saving of fifteen dollars per month for investment in equity securities only. There were no stocks bought on margin, no money borrowed, nor any stocks bought for a quick turn or resale. All stocks with few exceptions have been bought and held as permanent investments. The fifteen dollars was saved every month and the dividends from the stocks purchased were kept in the trust and reinvested. Three of these trusts are now twenty years old. Fifteen dollars per month equals one hundred and eighty dollars a year. In twenty years, therefore, the total savings amounted to thirty-six hundred dollars. Each of these three trusts is now worth well in excess of eighty thousand dollars. Invested at 6 per cent interest, this eighty thousand dollars would give the trust beneficiary an annual income of four hundred dollars per month, which ordinarily would represent more than the earning power of the beneficiary, because had he been able to earn as much as four hundred dollars per month he could have saved more than fifteen dollars.

Suppose a man marries at the age of twenty-three and begins a regular saving of fifteen dollars a month—and almost anyone who is employed can do that if he tries. If he invests in good common stocks and allows the dividends and rights to accumulate, he will at the end of twenty years have at least eighty thousand dollars and an income from investments of around four hundred dollars a month. He will be rich. And because anyone can do that I am firm in my belief that anyone not only can be rich but ought to be rich.

The obstacles to being rich are two: The trouble of saving, and the trouble of finding a medium for investment.

If Tom is known to have two hundred dollars in the savings bank then everyone is out to get it for some absolutely necessary purpose. More than likely his wife's sister will eventually find the emergency to draw it forth. But if he does withstand all attacks, what good will the money do him? The interest he receives is so small that he has no incentive to save, and since the whole is under his jurisdiction he can depend only upon his own will to save. To save in any such fashion requires a stronger will than the normal.

If he thinks of investing in some stock he has nowhere to turn for advice. He is not big enough to get much attention from his banker, and he has not enough money to go to a broker—or at least he thinks that he has not.

Suppose he has a thousand dollars; the bank can only advise him to buy a bond, for the officer will not take the risk of advising a stock and probably has not the experience anyway to give such advice. Tom can get really adequate attention only from some man who has a worthless security to sell, for then all of Tom's money will be profit.

The plan that I have had in mind for several years grows out of the success of the plans that we have followed for the executives in the General Motors and the Du Pont companies. In 1923, in order to give the executives of General Motors a greater interest in their work, we organized the Managers Securities Company, made up of eighty senior and junior executives. This company bought General Motors common stock to the then market value of thirty-three million dollars. The executives paid five million dollars in cash and borrowed twenty-eight million dollars. The stockholders of the Managers Securities Company are not stockholders of General Motors. They own stock in a company which owns stock in General Motors, so that, as far as General Motors is concerned, the stock is voted as a block according to the instructions of the directors of the Managers Securities Company. This supplies an important interest which can exercise a large influence in shaping the policies of General Motors.

From $25,000 to a Million

The holdings of the members in the securities company are adjusted in cases of men leaving the employ of the com-

pany. The plan of the Managers Securities Company contemplates no dissolution of that company, so that its holdings of General Motors stock will always be *en bloc*. The plan has been enormously successful, and much of the success of the General Motors Corporation has been due to the executives' having full responsibility and receiving financial rewards commensurate with that responsibility.

The participation in the Managers Securities Company was arranged in accordance with the position and salary of the executive. Minimum participation required a cash payment of twenty-five thousand dollars when the Managers Securities Company was organized. That minimum participation is now worth more than one million dollars.

Recently I have been advocating the formation of an equity securities corporation; that is, a corporation that will invest in common stocks only under proper and careful supervision. This company will buy the common stocks of first-class industrial corporations and issue its own stock certificates against them. This stock will be offered from time to time at a price to correspond exactly with the value of the assets of the corporation and all profit will go to the stockholders. The directors will be men of outstanding character, reputation and integrity. At regular intervals—say quarterly—the whole financial record of the corporation will be published together with all of its holdings and the cost thereof. The corporation will be owned by the public and with every transaction public. I am not at all interested in a private investment trust. The company would not be permitted to borrow money or go into any debt.

In addition to this company, there should be organized a discount company on the same lines as the finance companies of the motor concerns to be used to sell stock of the investing corporation on the installment plan. If Tom had two hundred dollars, this discount company would lend him three hundred dollars and thus enable him to buy five hundred dollars of the equity securities investment company stock, and Tom could arrange to pay off his loan just as he pays off his motor-car loan. When finished he would own outright five hundred dollars of equity stock. That would take his savings out of the free-will class and put them into the compulsory-payment class and his savings would no longer be fair game for relatives, for swindlers or for himself.

People pay for their motor car loans. They will also pay their loans contracted to secure their share in the nation's business. And in the kind of company suggested every increase in value and every right would go to the benefit of the stockholders and be reflected in the price and earning power of their stock. They would share absolutely in the nation's prosperity.

Constructive Saving

The effect of all this would, to my mind, be very far-reaching. If Tom bought five hundred dollars' worth of stock he would be helping some manufacturer to buy a new lathe or a new machine of some kind, which would add to the wealth of the country, and Tom, by participating in the profits of this machine, would be in a position to buy more goods and cause a demand for more machines. Prosperity is in the nature of an endless chain and we can break it only by our own refusal to see what it is.

Everyone ought to be rich, but it is out of the question to make people rich in spite of themselves.

The millennium is not at hand. One cannot have all play and no work. But it has been sufficiently demonstrated that many of the old and supposedly conservative maxims are as untrue as the radical notions. We can appraise things as they are.

Everyone by this time ought to know that nothing can be gained by stopping the progress of the world and dividing up everything—there would not be enough to divide, in the first place, and, in the second place, most of the world's wealth is not in such form it can be divided.

The socialistic theory of division is, however, no more irrational than some of the more hidebound theories of thrift or of getting rich by saving.

No one can become rich merely by saving. Putting aside a sum each week or month in a sock at no interest, or in a savings bank at ordinary interest, will not provide enough for old age unless life in the meantime be rigorously skimped down to the level of mere existence. And if everyone skimped in any such fashion then the country would be so poor that living at all would hardly be worth while.

Unless we have consumption we shall not have production. Production and consumption go together and a rigid national program of saving would, if carried beyond a point, make for general poverty, for there would be no consumption to call new wealth into being.

Therefore, savings must be looked at not as a present deprivation in order to enjoy more in the future, but as a constructive method of increasing not only one's future but also one's present income.

Saving may be a virtue if undertaken as a kind of mental and moral discipline, but such a course of saving is not to be regarded as a financial plan. Constructive saving in order to increase one's income is a financial operation and to be governed by financial rules; disciplinary saving is another matter entirely. The two have been confused.

Most of the old precepts contrasting the immorality of speculation with the morality of sound investment have no basis in fact. They have just been so often repeated as true that they are taken as true. If one buys a debt—that is, takes a secured bond or mortgage at a fixed rate of interest—then that is supposed to be an investment. In the case of the debt, the principal sum as well as the interest is fixed and the investor cannot get more than he contracts for. The law guards against getting more and also it regulates the procedure by which the lender can take the property of the

borrower in case of default. But the law cannot say that the property of the debtor will be worth the principal sum of the debt when it falls due; the creditor must take that chance.

The investor in a debt strictly limits his possible gain, but he does not limit his loss. He speculates in only one direction in so far as the actual return in dollars and cents is concerned. But in addition he speculates against the interest rate. If his security pays 4 per cent and money is worth 6 or 7 per cent then he is lending at less than the current rate; if money is worth 3 per cent, then he is lending at more than he could otherwise get.

The buyer of a common share in an enterprise limits neither his gains nor his losses. However, he excludes one element of speculation—the change in the value of money. For whatever earnings he gets will be in current money values. If he buys shares in a wholly new and untried enterprise, then his hazards are great, but if he buys into established enterprises, then he takes no more chance than does the investor who buys a debt.

It is difficult to see why a bond or mortgage should be considered as a more conservative investment than a good stock, for the only difference in practice is that the bond can never be worth more than its face value or return more than the interest, while a stock can be worth more than was paid for it and can return a limitless profit.

One may lose on either a bond or a stock. If a company fails it will usually be reorganized and in that case the bonds will have to give way to new money and possibly they will be scaled down. The common stockholders may lose all, or again they may get another kind of stock which may or may not eventually have a value. In a failure, neither the bondholders nor the stockholders will find any great cause for happiness—but there are very few failures among the larger corporations.

Beneficial Borrowing

A first mortgage on improved real estate is supposedly a very safe investment, but the value of realty shifts quickly and even the most experienced investors in real-estate mortgages have to foreclose an appreciable percentage of their mortgages and buy in the properties to protect themselves. It may be years before the property can be sold again.

I would rather buy real estate than buy mortgages on it, for then I have the chance of gaining more than I paid. On a mortgage I cannot get back more than I lend, but I may get back less.

The line between investment and speculation is a very hazy one, and a definition is not to be found in the legal form of a security or in limiting the possible return on the money. The difference is rather in the approach.

Placing a bet is very different from placing one's money with a corporation which has thoroughly demonstrated that it can normally earn profits and has a reasonable expectation of earning greater profits. That may be called speculation, but it would be more accurate to think of the operation as going into business with men who have demonstrated that they know how to do business.

The old view of debt was quite as illogical as the old view of investment. It was beyond the conception of anyone that debt could be constructive. Every old saw about debt—and there must be a thousand of them—is bound up with borrowing instead of earning. We now know that borrowing may be a method of earning and beneficial to everyone concerned. Suppose a man needs a certain amount of money in order to buy a set of tools or anything else which will increase his income. He can take one of two courses. He can save the money and in the course of time buy his tools, or he can, if the proper facilities are provided, borrow the money at a reasonable rate of interest, buy the tools and immediately so increase his income that he can pay off his debt and own the tools within half the time that it would have taken him to save the money and pay cash. That loan enables him at once to create more wealth than before and consequently makes him a more valuable citizen. By increasing his power to produce he also increases his power to consume and therefore he increases the power of others to produce in order to fill his new needs and naturally increases their power to consume, and so on and on. By borrowing the money instead of saving it he increases his ability to save and steps up prosperity at once.

The Way to Wealth

That is exactly what the automobile has done to the prosperity of the country through the plan of installment payments. The installment plan of paying for automobiles, when it was first launched, ran counter to the old notions of debt. It was opposed by bankers, who saw in it only an incentive for extravagance. It was opposed by manufacturers because they thought people would be led to buy automobiles instead of their products.

The results have been exactly opposite to the prediction. The ability to buy automobiles on credit gave an immediate step-up to their purchase. Manufacturing them, servicing them, building roads for them to run on, and caring for the people who used the roads have brought into existence about ten billion dollars of new wealth each year—which is roughly about the value of the farm crops. The creation of this new wealth gave a large increase to consumption and has brought on our present very solid prosperity.

But without the facility for going into debt or the facility for the consumer's getting credit—call it what you will—this great addition to wealth might never have taken place and certainly not for many years to come. Debt may be a burden, but it is more likely to be an incentive.

The great wealth of this country has been gained by the forces of production and consumption pushing each other for supremacy. The personal fortunes of this country have been made not by saving but by producing.

Mere saving is closely akin to the socialist policy of dividing and likewise runs up against the same objection that there is not enough around to save. The savings that count cannot be static. They must be going into the production of wealth. They may go in as debt and the managers of the wealth-making enterprises take all the profit over and above the interest paid. That has been the course recommended for saving and for the reasons that have been set out—the fallacy of conservative investment which is not conservative at all.

The way to wealth is to get into the profit end of wealth production in this country.

Questions

1. What essentially is Raskob's advice?
2. What problems does he believe face those who want to be rich?
3. Which problems does Raskob ignore?

25-3 Proposals for Recovery (1930–1931)

The depression hit with such force that the business community became confused and dispirited (see text pp. 772–773). Perhaps the real problem was a loss of nerve. Maybe a return to prosperity could be sparked by a National Sales Month—or by miniature golf. No one, including B. C. Forbes and Julius Klein, really knew.

Sources: "Snap Out of It!" in B. C. Forbes, "Fact and Comment," *Forbes*, September 15, 1930, p. 11; excerpts from Julius Klein, "New Business Will Arise!" *Forbes*, September 15, 1930, pp. 15–17; "National Sales Month Suggested," in B. C. Forbes, "Fact and Comment," *Forbes*, October 15, 1931, p. 10(?).

Snap Out Of It!

Snap out of it! Gloom has reigned long enough. It is time to drop cowardice and exercise courage. Deflation has run an ample course—to carry it much further would mean endless destruction, criminal destruction. The country is sound at the core, sound politically, sound financially, sound industrially, sound commercially. Agricultural prices, to, have been thoroughly deflated, even overde-pressed. The nation has its health. It has lost little or none of its real wealth. It is living saner than when everyone was unrestrainedly optimistic. The time has come to cast off our doubts and fears, our hesitancy and timidity, our spasm of "nerves". Summer, the season for holiday-making, is over. The season for fresh planning, new enterprise, hard work, driving force, initiative, concentration on business, is here. Let's go.

Snap out of it!

New Business Will Arise!

A Storehouse of Facts for Men Who Seek to Utilize Nation's Latent and Enormous Buying Power — The Example of Miniature Golf

By Julius Klein
Assistant Secretary of Commerce

Vigilance and vigor (as one need hardly say) are among the prime essentials of any business victory. Seldom, indeed, is the American business man deficient in the vigor with which he attacks a commercial problem. His energy, his briskness, his whirlwind tactics are proverbial. But such robust vitality is unfortunately not accompanied, in all cases, by a maximum of vigilance—if one includes in that term the painstaking, pertinacious scrutiny of every single fact, every collection of relevant data, that might bear upon his efforts. The value of such study is being realized increasingly—but do we not all know the business man who can be considered only as a mere slap-dash empiricist, with a breezy confidence in hunches and a deep, ingrained dislike of statistical tables and bar-charts?

Yet statistics are quite capable of proving his salvation. His business, in many instances, is dependent absolutely on his knowing commercial trends, economic movements, broad and sweeping social forces. In few decades in all history have such startling changes taken place as those that we have witnessed in the past ten years. A thorough knowledge of those changes may well provide the firmest conceivable basis for encouragement right now. Especially conducive to such optimism are the facts about the steady growth in American income and buying power.

The National Bureau of Economic Research tells us that the total realized income of the people of continental United States in 1928 was more than $89,000,000,000. And that did not include the income that might be imputed to housewives and householders for services rendered to their families, nor employees' expense accounts, nor the money earned through odd-job employment. That means a per capita income of $740. In the course of a year we are now earning nearly $25,000,000,000 more than we were ten years ago. And when we extend the comparison to 20 years ago, we find that the national income has more than trebled over that period. Even when we make all due allowance for price changes, the increase is very great.

Let us institute, for a moment, a comparison on the basis of "1913 dollars"—that is, dollars having a buying power equivalent to that which they had in 1913. We find that the purchasing power (in such 1913 dollars) of the total wages, salaries, pensions, etc., received by the employees of all American industries was $29,967,000,000 in 1928, as compared with $15,946,000,000 in 1909 and $18,822,000,000 in 1913. The purchasing power, in 1913 dollars, of the average annual earnings of the American wage-worker advanced from $556 in 1909, $594 in 1913, and $550 in 1921 to $705 in 1927 (the most recent year for which a dependable figure is available).

The National Bureau of Economic Research has well said that "the growth in per capita income since 1921 must be regarded as a remarkable phenomenon. The indications are that, in terms of immediate ability to buy goods for consumption purposes, the average American was approximately one-third better off in 1927 than he was in 1921." And the bureau goes on to draw the inevitable conclusions: "Under these circumstances it is not surprising that a tremendous market has developed for furs, automobiles, radios, and other luxuries which were previously beyond the reach of the masses of the population."

More recent, and undeniably significant, is the statement made just the other day by the United States Bureau of Labor Statistics, that the buying power of the dollar expanded more than a tenth in the year that ended June, 1930—and it is nearly a sixth greater than it was four years ago.

These are a few concrete facts (I shall speak later of

certain "intangibles") that indicate the rise of new markets for manufacturers and merchants who possess the vision to discern and develop them. . . .

[The] Census of Distribution will throw light on numerous domains of business which have been shrouded hitherto in an almost impenetrable obscurity. When integrated and coordinated with other Census data and relevant facts collected by governmental and able private agencies, these data should make it possible for every business man to evaluate his own position and methods in relation to his competitors, his customers and his sources of supply. From such information, any wide-awake industrialist or merchant can draw concretely useful conclusions as to the dominant commercial currents of a tangible sort.

To be sure, he needs also to be "*en rapport*" with the intangible currents—and this is a bit more difficult. Of one thing, however, he may be very certain: Some of the most potent of those currents spring from the general rise in human standards, attendant upon the growth in income that I mentioned a moment ago.

Customers are constantly displaying more discrimination. They are demanding not alone that an article shall work (that primary pragmatic test)—they are requiring also that it shall possess those intangible but unmistakable factors of distinction and of style.

Good taste among the buying public has been incalculably heightened during this past decade. It has advanced in a rapidly ascending spiral. Any given achievement in the creation of artistic merchandise has enhanced the public receptivity to many others—possibly in unrelated lines. There has been a tremendous stimulation, a restless, eager stirring of what I may call, perhaps, the "mass aesthetic sense."

It is perfectly obvious, of course, that the basic cause of this has been the rise in living standards—the widespread elevation of the scale of creature comforts that prove satisfying to the average man. And we must not be led for a single moment to believe that such standards have suffered any grave, enduring damage through the temporary business recession that had its beginning last October. No—that upward surge is too insistent—the typical desires and aptitudes arising from it have become too ineradicably implanted—to permit of any lasting impairment in this land!

The American people have been traveling, at home and in foreign countries, to a previously inconceivable extent, and their observation has been keen. Travel has been revealing once-unimagined vistas—poignant beauty, arresting design, novel treatment and applications of the articles of common use.

The almost miraculous advance in communication has contributed to this greater sensitiveness to style. Radio descriptions have awakened curiosity—have excited lively interest. A new and fascinating factor has appeared in the radio transmission, even across the broad Atlantic, of pictures of designs of goods that are peculiarly susceptible to style.

Entertainment plays a vital role—no less influential because it is subtle and, in many cases, not immediately perceived. Motion pictures especially (both the purely amusement subjects and the frankly industrial films) have intensified the public consciousness of style.

The Census has disclosed, once more, the seemingly almost irresistible impulse toward urbanization. Our titanic cities are expanding. And in those enormous masses of humanity—with their quick interchanges of ideas, their swirling complexity and immediacy of movement—the influence of style is singularly acute. In the ferment of this urban life, new conceptions are being incessantly produced. Many of these are significant—potentially very valuable—to manufacturers and merchants, if they will keep their eyes open and grasp the opportunities.

We now need, in the city, many things that we once associated only with the seashore or the countryside. This statement may seem strange at first (and I admit quite frankly that its application is restricted), but it is supported by ample facts.

Take, merely as an example, the case of sporting goods of certain types. Let us consider bathing-suits. Not so long ago, these were used almost solely in the open—at the beaches and along our streams. But to-day that condition has been absolutely changed by the building of many splendid urban pools (both indoor and outdoor), adorned with impressive names such as "Plage Biarritz," provided with bronzed lifeguards, and necessitating the wearing of good, attractive bathing-suits. At the old swimming-hole to which we resorted in the days of our youth, we were happy and hilarious in a cheap dingy garment (or maybe none at all)—but that, of course, would never do at the glittering, resplendent "Pompeian Pool" that now allures our patronage. Here we see the creation of a new market, a new demand—and one in which that factor of style-consciousness plays assuredly a potent part.

So, too, with the amazing rise of those miniature golf courses that are springing up by the thousands. The players are the cynosure of many eyes, in near-by structures and on the street. I think there can be no doubt that this new game has stimulated a demand for handsome sports attire on the part of countless persons who would not otherwise have cared so much to garb themselves in gaudy raiment.

Our researchers at the Department of Commerce have estimated that there are now (in the middle of August) no fewer than 25,000 of these bantam-size golf courses in the country, with a value of perhaps $125,000,000 (not including the real estate involved), and by the time this article appears in print there will undoubtedly be thousands more. Think of the market thus created for some rather unusual construction materials—for paints and oils—for electricity—for golf balls and, more especially, for putters! And the end is not in sight. Our Textile Division at Washington is putting forward right now the thoroughly sound idea that, as a protection in inclement weather, these miniature courses need a covering of tent or awning mater-

ial, which should prove a profitable investment at a cost of from $750 to $3,000 per course. This gives promise of developing a market for millions of dollars' worth of canvas, duck, and metal or wood supports. This entire situation illustrates forcefully the manner in which new businesses may arise unexpectedly and vigorously, in a way to hearten many trades. . . .

National Sales Month Suggested

H. E. Kranhold, vice-president of Brown & Bigelow, writes suggesting a National Sales Month. He says: "It is estimated that there are five million salesmen in the United States. Suppose it were possible to secure the interest and co-operation of every organization employing salesmen to put on a National Sales Month at the same time. Suppose that each one, through this extra effort, secured two additional orders during the month. Suppose these orders averaged $10. That would mean one hundred million dollars' worth of additional sales. It has been estimated that every dollar in a sale circulates approximately ten times in the course of producing what enters into the manufacture of the goods sold. That would represent, theoretically, a billion dollars. There isn't much questions but what, if every organization in the United States did put on a National Sales and a National Buying Month, business immediately

would turn for the better. Prosperity does not precede but follows sales."

He suggests December as the most appropriate month, as it is then that "thoughts are turning to Christmas, when retail stores are busy and the result of a big December business would make a happier Christmas for thousands and thousands of people. It would reflect itself in the new year by making business better in January."

Well, can it be organized?

Perhaps Mr. Gifford may see merit in this plan and, with his unique organizing ability, set in motion the machinery necessary for effective action, thus moving business off what Owen D. Young called its "dead center."

Doing nothing leads inevitably to everybody being undone.

Fear is failure—failure of faith.

Questions

1. Why would "snapping out of it" matter?
2. How would a National Sales Month work?
3. Explain how new businesses would have a ripple effect in generating prosperity.

Questions for Further Thought

1. How could Stuart Chase (Document 25-1) and John Raskob (Document 25-2) analyze the same economy yet reach such different conclusions?
2. Would Chase or Raskob have been more likely to endorse the proposals offered in Document 25-3?
3. What do these three documents suggest about the American people's level of understanding of economic matters?

Hard Times

The effects of the Great Depression could be measured in economic terms: so many workers unemployed, banks failed, mortgages foreclosed, and so on. The depression's effects also were felt in more personal and intimate ways. Marriages were postponed, the birth rate dropped, and suicides increased (see text pp. 776–777). Family life often changed dramatically as men were driven from the work force (Documents 25-4 and 25-5). Some men abandoned their families or took to the road to find work. Others stayed at home but struggled with a sense of personal failure when they could no longer fulfill the role of breadwinner (see text pp. 775–776). Millions of married women entered the work force, where their presence was sometimes resented (see text p. 777). Going "on the dole" could be a humiliating process for people who had once held good jobs and thought of themselves as secure and respectable. Young people found it hard to get started in life. Some stayed in school rather than enter the job market; others became homeless transients (see text pp. 777–778). Almost unnoticed amid the anxiety and the desire for release was a federal court hearing on the question of birth control (Document 25-6).

The often grim experience of day-to-day living could be forgotten for a while as Americans poured into movie houses to enjoy inexpensive entertainment. Gangster films, musicals, and "screwball comedies" were especially popular, suggesting that the last thing most moviegoers wanted to be reminded of was the depression (see text pp. 778–780). The popularity of *Grapes of Wrath* (Document 25-7) was an exception to this trend. The radio was another influential force in shaping an increasingly homogeneous national culture (Document 25-8).

25-4 "A Wise Economist Asks a Question" (1932)

John McCutcheon

In a career that spanned forty-three years at the Chicago *Tribune*, John T. McCutcheon (1870–1949) demonstrated a sense of compassion that was rare in political cartoonists. There is nothing obvious or partisan in this drawing, which may explain why it won a Pulitzer Prize.

Source: Copyright 1932, Reprinted by permission: Tribune Media Services.

Questions

1. How does McCutcheon make the man a sympathetic character?
2. Why does he have a squirrel ask the question?
3. What is McCutcheon saying about the American belief in personal responsibility?

25-5 "Mr. Patterson" (1940)

Mirra Komarovsky

The Barnard College sociologist Mirra Komarovsky measured the impact of hard times on men's self-esteem through case histories, such as that of "Mr. Patterson," in her 1940 book *The Unemployed Man and His Family* (see text pp. 775–776).

Source: Excerpted by permission of the author from Mirra Komarovsky, *The Unemployed Man and His Family* (New York: n.p., 1940; reprint, New York: Octagon, 1973), pp. 26–28.

Reaction to Unemployment and Relief. Prior to the depression Mr. Patterson was an inventory clerk earning from $35 to $40 a week. He lost his job in 1931. At the present time he does not earn anything, while his 18-year-old girl gets $12.50 a week working in Woolworth's, and his wife has part-time work cleaning a doctor's office. Unemployment and depression have hit Mr. Patterson much more than the rest of the family.

The hardest thing about unemployment, Mr. Patterson says, is the humiliation within the family. It makes him feel very useless to have his wife and daughter bring in money to the family while he does not contribute a nickel. It is awful to him, because now "the tables are turned," that is, he has to ask his daughter for a little money for tobacco, etc. He would rather walk miles than ask for carfare money. His daughter would want him to have it, but he cannot bring himself to ask for it. He had often thought that it would make it easier if he could have 25 cents a week that he could depend upon. He feels more irritable and morose than he ever did in his life. He doesn't enjoy eating. He hasn't slept well in months. He lies awake and tosses and tosses, wondering what he will do and what will happen to them if he doesn't ever get work any more. He feels that there is nothing to wake up for in the morning and nothing to live for. He often wonders what would happen if he put himself out of the picture, or just got out of the way of his wife. Perhaps she and the girl would get along better without him. He blames himself for being unemployed. While he tries all day long to find work and would take anything, he feels that he would be successful if he had taken advantage of his opportunities in youth and had secured an education.

Mr. Patterson believes that his wife and daughter have adjusted themselves to the depression better than he has. In fact, sometimes they seem so cheerful in the evening that he cannot stand it any more. He grabs his hat and says he is going out for a while, and walks hard for an hour before he comes home again. That is one thing he never did before unemployment, but he is so nervous and jumpy now he has to do something like that to prevent himself from exploding.

Mrs. Patterson says that they have not felt the depression so terribly themselves, or changed their way of living so very much.

Changes in Husband-Wife Relations Since Loss of Employment. The wife thinks it is her husband's fault that he is unemployed. Not that he doesn't run around and try

his very best to get a job, but he neglected his opportunities when he was young. If he had had a proper education and had a better personality, he would not be in his present state. Besides, he has changed for the worse. He has become irritable and very hard to get along with. He talks of nothing else, and isn't interested in anything else but his troubles. She and her daughter try to forget troubles and have a good time once in a while, but he just sits and broods. Of course that makes her impatient with him. She cannot sit at home and keep him company, so that during the past couple of years she and her daughter just go out together without him. It isn't that they leave him out—he just isn't interested and stays at home.

Mr. Patterson insists that his child is as sweet as ever and always tries to cheer him up, but the tenor of his conversation about his wife is different. She does go out more with the daughter, leaving him alone. He cannot stand it, worrying so and having them so lighthearted. "When you are not bringing in any money, you don't get as much attention. She doesn't nag all the time, the way some women do," but he knows she blames him for being unemployed. He intimates that they have fewer sex relations—"It's nothing that I do or don't do—no change in me—but when I tell her that I want more love, she just gets mad." It came about gradually, he said. He cannot point definitely to any time when he noticed the difference in her. But he knows that his advances are rebuffed now when they would not have been before the hard times.

The wife gives the impression that there might have been some decrease in sex relations, but declines to discuss them. She tells the following episode:

The day before the interview she was kissing and hugging the daughter. "I like to keep the girl sweet and young, and in the habit of kissing her mother good-night." The father walked in and said, "Don't you get enough of that?" Mrs. Patterson went on at great length as to how terribly that statement hurt her.

The interviewer also witnessed another episode. Towards the end of the interview with the wife, the husband walked into the living room and asked his wife if she thought the interviewer would be interested in talking to their neighbors. The woman said, "Don't bother us, we are talking about something else just now." He got up quietly and went into the kitchen. In a moment she called after him, "Oh, you can sit in here if you *want* to." Nevertheless, he stayed in the kitchen. . . .

Questions

1. Judging from Mr. Patterson's experience, what was the impact of prolonged unemployment on American families?
2. Compare the reaction to the depression of Mr. Patterson with that of his wife and daughter.

3. Some contemporary observers suggested that the solution to the depression would be for married women to say in the home and not "take jobs away from men." Judging from the Patterson family's experience, was this a realistic solution?

25-6 *United States v. One Package* (1936)

Hard times can change long-held beliefs, including those about birth control (see text pp. 776–777). This federal court decision made it easier for Americans to postpone bringing children into a very uncertain world.

Source: United States v. One Package, 86 F.2d 737 (1936).

AUGUSTUS N. HAND, Circuit Judge.

The United States filed this libel against a package containing 120 vaginal pessaries more or less, alleged to be imported contrary to section 305(a) of the Tariff Act of 1930 (*19 U.S.C.A. § 1305*(a). From the decree dismissing the libel the United States has appealed. In our opinion the decree should be affirmed.

The claimant Dr. Stone is a new York physician who has been licensed to practice for sixteen years and has specialized in gynecology. The package containing pessaries was sent to her by a physician in Japan for the purpose of trying them in her practice and giving her opinion as to their usefulness for contraceptive purposes. She testified that she prescribes the use of pessaries in cases where it would not be desirable for a patient to undertake a pregnancy. The accuracy and good faith of this testimony is not questioned. The New York Penal Law which makes it in general a misdemeanor to sell or give away or to advertise or offer for sale any articles for the prevention of conception excepts furnishing such articles to physicians who may in good faith prescribe their use for the cure or prevention of disease. *People v. Sanger, 222 N.Y. 192, 118 N.E. 637.* New York Penal Law (Consol. Laws, c. 40) § 1145. The witnesses for both the government and the claimant testified that the use of contraceptives was in many cases necessary for the health of women and that they employed articles of the general nature of the pessaries in their practice. There was no dispute as to the truth of these statements.

Section 305(a) of the Tariff Act of 1930 (*19 U.S.C.A. § 1305*(a) provides that: "All persons are prohibited from importing into the United States from any foreign country *** any article whatever for the prevention of conception or for causing unlawful abortion."

The question is whether physicians who import such articles as those involved in the present case in order to use them for the health of their patients are excepted by implication from the literal terms of the statute. Certainly they are excepted in the case of an abortive which is prescribed to save life, for section 305(a) of the Tariff Act only prohibits the importation of articles for causing "unlawful abortion." This was the very point decided in *Bours v. United States, 229 F. 960* (C.C.A. 7), where a similar statute (Cr. Code, § 211 [*18 U.S.C.A. § 334* and note]) declaring nonmailable "every article or thing designed, adapted, or intended for preventing conception or producing abortion, or for any indecent or immoral use," was held not to cover physicians using the mails in order to say that they will operate upon a patient if an examination shows the necessity of an operation to save life. And this result was reached even though the statute in forbidding the mailing of any article "intended for *** producing abortion" did not, as does section 305(a) of the Tariff Act, qualify the word "abortion" by the saving adjective "unlawful." In *Youngs Rubber Corporation v. C. I. Lee & Co., 45 F.(2d) 103* (C.C.A. 2), Judge Swan, writing for this court, construed the mailing statute in the same way. In referring to the mailing of contraceptive articles bearing the plaintiff's trade-mark, he adverted to the fact that the articles might be capable of legitimate use and said, at page 108 of 45 F.(2d), when discussing the incidence of the mailing statute:

"The intention to prevent a proper medical use of drugs or other articles merely because they are capable of illegal uses is not lightly to be ascribed to Congress. Section 334 forbids also the mailing of obscene books and writings; yet it has never been thought to bar from the mails medical writings sent to or by physicians for proper purposes, though of a character which would render them highly indecent if sent broadcast to all classes of persons.***It would seem reasonable to give the word 'adapted' a more limited meaning than that above suggested and to construe the whole phrase 'designed, adapted or intended' as requiring an intent on the part of the sender that the article mailed***be used for illegal contraception or abortion or for indecent or immoral purposes." . . .

Section 1 of the act of 1873 made it a crime to sell, lend, or give away, "any drug or medicine, or any article whatever, for the prevention of contraception, or for causing unlawful abortion." Section 2 prohibited sending through the mails "any article or thing designed or intended for the prevention of conception or procuring of abortion." Section 3 forbade the importation of "any of the hereinbefore-mentioned articles or things, except the drugs hereinbefore-mentioned when imported in bulk, and not put up for any of the purposes before mentioned." All the statutes we have referred to were part of a continuous scheme to suppress immoral articles and obscene literature and should so far as possible be construed together and consistently. If this be done, the articles here in question ought not to be forfeited when not intended for an immoral purpose. Such as the interpretation in the decisions of the Circuit Courts of Appeal of the Sixth and Seventh Circuits and of this court in Youngs Rubber Corporation v. C. I. Lee & Co., when construing the statute forbidding an improper use of the mails.

It is argued that section 305(a) of the Tariff Act of 1930 (*19 U.S.C.A. § 1305*(a) differs from the statutes prohibiting carriage by mail and in interstate commerce of articles "intended for preventing conception or producing abortion" because in section 305(a) the adjective "unlawful" is coupled with the word "abortion," but not with the words "prevention of conception." But in the Comstock Act, from which the others are derived, the word "unlawful" was sometimes inserted to qualify the word "abortion," and sometimes omitted. It seems hard to suppose that under the second and third sections articles intended for use in procuring abortions were prohibited in all cases while, under the first section, they were only prohibited when intended for use in an "unlawful abortion." Nor can we see why the statute should, at least in section 1, except articles for producing abortions if used to safeguard life, and bar articles for preventing conception though employed by a physician in the practice of his profession in order to protect the health of his patients or to save them from infection.

It is true that in 1873, when the Comstock Act was passed, information now available as to the evils resulting in many cases from conception was most limited, and accordingly it is argued that the language prohibiting the sale or mailing of contraceptives should be taken literally and that Congress intended to bar the use of such articles completely. While we may assume that section 305(a) of the Tariff Act of 1930 (*19 U.S.C.A. § 1305*(a) exempts only such articles as the act of 1873 excepted, yet we are satisfied that this statute, as well as all the acts we have referred to, embraced only such articles as Congress would have denounced as immoral if it had understood all the conditions under which they were to be used. Its design, in our opinion, was not to prevent the importation, sale, or carriage by mail of things which might intelligently be employed by conscientious and competent physicians for the purpose of saving life or promoting the well being of their patients. The word "unlawful" would make this clear as to articles for producing abortion, and the courts have read an exemption into the act covering such articles even where the word "unlawful" is not used. The same exception should apply to articles for preventing conception. While it is true that the policy of Congress has been to forbid the use of contraceptives altogether if the only purpose of using them be to prevent conception in cases where it would not be injurious to the welfare of the patient or her offspring, it is going far beyond such a policy to hold that abortions, which destroy incipient [*740] life, may be allowed in proper cases, and yet that no measures may be taken to prevent conception even though a likely result should be to require the termination of pregnancy by means of an operation. It seems unreasonable to suppose that the national scheme of legislation involves such inconsistencies and requires the complete suppression of articles, the use of which in many cases is advocated by such a weight of authority in the medical world.

The Comstock Bill, as originally introduced in the Senate, contained the words "except on a prescription of a physician in good standing, given in good faith," but those words were omitted from the bill as it was ultimately passed. The reason for amendment seems never to have been discussed on the floor of Congress, or in committee, and the remarks of Senator Conklin, when the bill was up for passage in final form, indicate that the scope of the measure was not well understood and that the language used was to be left largely for future interpretation. We see no ground for holding that the construction placed upon similar language in the decisions we have referred to is not applicable to the articles which the government seeks to forfeit, and common sense would seem to require a like interpretation in the case at bar.

The decree dismissing the libel is affirmed. . . .

Questions

1. What is the relevance of the Tariff Act of 1930 to this case?
2. What is the moral issue that faces the judges?
3. How do they settle it?

25-7 *The Grapes of Wrath* (1939)

John Steinbeck

John Steinbeck's novel *The Grapes of Wrath* portrayed the experiences of the Joad family, "Okies" who were displaced by the depression and tried to build a new life for themselves as agricultural workers in California. *The Grapes of Wrath* was a bestseller when it appeared in 1939 and was made into a successful Hollywood film the following year (see text pp. 779–780).

Source: Chapter 25 from *The Grapes of Wrath* (pp. 473–477) by John Steinbeck. Copyright 1939, renewed © 1967 by John Steinbeck. Used by permission of Viking Penguin, a division of Penguin Books USA Inc.

CHAPTER TWENTY-FIVE

The spring is beautiful in California. Valleys in which the fruit blossoms are fragrant pink and white waters in a shallow sea. Then the first tendrils of the grapes, swelling from the old gnarled vines, cascade down to cover the trunks. The full green hills are round and soft as breasts. And on the level vegetable lands are the mile-long rows of pale green lettuce and the spindly little cauliflowers, the gray-green unearthly artichoke plants.

And then the leaves break out on the trees, and the petals drop from the fruit trees and carpet the earth with pink and white. The centers of the blossoms swell and grow and color: cherries and apples, peaches and pears, figs which close the flower in the fruit. All California quickens with produce, and the fruit grows heavy, and the limbs bend gradually under the fruit so that little crutches must be placed under them to support the weight.

Behind the fruitfulness are men of understanding and knowledge and skill, men who experiment with seed, endlessly developing the techniques for greater crops of plants whose roots will resist the million enemies of the earth: the molds, the insects, the rusts, the blights. These men work carefully and endlessly to perfect the seed, the roots. And there are the men of chemistry who spray the trees against pests, who sulphur the grapes, who cut out disease and rots, mildews and sicknesses. Doctors of preventive medicine, men at the borders who look for fruit flies, for Japanese beetle, men who quarantine the sick trees and root them out and burn them, men of knowledge. The men who graft the young trees, the little vines, are the cleverest of all,

for theirs is a surgeon's job, as tender and delicate; and these men must have surgeons' hands and surgeons' hearts to slit the bark, to place the grafts, to bind the wounds and cover them from the air. These are great men.

Along the rows, the cultivators move, tearing the spring grass and turning it under to make a fertile earth, breaking the ground to hold the water up near the surface, ridging the ground in little pools for the irrigation, destroying the weed roots that may drink the water away from the trees.

And all the time the fruit swells and the flowers break out in long clusters on the vines. And in the growing year the warmth grows and the leaves turn dark green. The prunes lengthen like little green bird's eggs, and the limbs sag down against the crutches under the weight. And the hard little pears take shape, and the beginning of the fuzz comes out on the peaches. Grape blossoms shed their tiny petals and the hard little beads become green buttons, and the buttons grow heavy. The men who work in the fields, the owners of the little orchards, watch and calculate. The year is heavy with produce. And men are proud, for of their knowledge they can make the year heavy. They have transformed the world with their knowledge. The short, lean wheat has been made big and productive. Little sour apples have grown large and sweet, and that old grape that grew among the trees and fed the birds its tiny fruit has mothered a thousand varieties, red and black, green and pale pink, purple and yellow; and each variety with its own flavor. The men who work in the experimental farms have made new fruits: nectarines and forty kinds of plums, walnuts with paper shells. And always they work, selecting, grafting, changing, driving themselves, driving the earth to produce.

And first the cherries ripen. Cent and a half a pound. Hell, we can't pick 'em for that. Black cherries and red cherries, full and sweet, and the birds eat half of each cherry and the yellowjackets buzz into the holes the birds made. And on the ground the seeds drop and dry with black shreds hanging from them.

The purple prunes soften and sweeten. My God, we can't pick them and dry and sulphur them. We can't pay wages, no matter what wages. And the purple prunes carpet the ground. And first the skins wrinkle a little and swarms of flies come to feast, and the valley is filled with the odor of sweet decay. The meat turns dark and the crop shrivels on the ground.

And the pears grow yellow and soft. Five dollars a ton. Five dollars for forty fifty-pound boxes; trees pruned and sprayed, orchards cultivated—pick the fruit, put it in boxes, load the trucks, deliver the fruit to the cannery—forty boxes for five dollars. We can't do it. And the yellow fruit falls heavily to the ground and splashes on the ground. The yellowjackets dig in the soft meat, and there is a smell of ferment and rot.

Then the grapes—we can't make good wine. People can't buy good wine. Rip the grapes from the vines, good grapes, rotten grapes, wasp-stung grapes. Press stems, press dirt and rot.

But there's mildew and formic acid in the vats.

Add sulphur and tannic acid.

The smell from the ferment is not the rich odor of wine, but the smell of decay and chemicals.

Oh, well. It has alcohol in it, anyway, They can get drunk.

The little farmers watched debt creep up on them like the tide. They sprayed the trees and sold no crop, they pruned and grafted and could not pick the crop. And the men of knowledge have worked, have considered, and the fruit is rotting on the ground, and the decaying mash in the wine vats is poisoning the air. And taste the wine—no grape flavor at all, just sulphur and tannic acid and alcohol.

This little orchard will be a part of a great holding next year, for the debt will have choked the owner.

This vineyard will belong to the bank. Only the great owners can survive, for they own the canneries too. And four pears peeled and cut in half, cooked and canned, still cost fifteen cents. And the canned pears do not spoil. They will last for years.

The decay spreads over the State, and the sweet smell is a great sorrow on the land. Men who can graft the trees and make the seed fertile and big can find no way to let the hungry people eat their produce. Men who have created new fruits in the world cannot create a system whereby their fruits may be eaten. And the failure hangs over the State like a great sorrow.

The works of the roots of the vines, of the trees, must be destroyed to keep up the price, and this is the saddest, bitterest thing of all. Carloads of oranges dumped on the ground. The people came for miles to take the fruit, but this could not be. How would they buy oranges at twenty cents a dozen if they could drive out and pick them up? And men with hoses squirt kerosene on the oranges, and they are angry at the crime, angry at the people who have come to take the fruit. A million people hungry, needing the fruit— and kerosene sprayed over the golden mountains.

And the smell of rot fills the country.

Burn coffee for fuel in the ships. Burn corn to keep warm, it makes a hot fire. Dump potatoes in the rivers and place guards along the banks to keep the hungry people from fishing them out. Slaughter the pigs and bury them, and let the putrescence drip down into the earth.

There is a crime here that goes beyond denunciation. There is a sorrow here that weeping cannot symbolize. There is a failure here that topples all our success. The fertile earth, the straight tree rows, the sturdy trunks, and the ripe fruit. And children dying of pellagra must die because a profit cannot be taken from an orange. And coroners must fill in the certificates—died of malnutrition—because the food must rot, must be forced to rot.

The people come with nets to fish for potatoes in the river, and the guards hold them back; they come in rattling cars to get the dumped oranges, but the kerosene is sprayed. And they stand still and watch the potatoes float by, listen to the screaming pigs being killed in a ditch and covered with quicklime, watch the mountains of oranges slop down to a putrefying ooze; and in the eyes of the people there is the failure; and in the eyes of the hungry there is a growing wrath. In the souls of the people the grapes of wrath are filling and growing heavy, growing heavy for the vintage.

Questions

1. How does this chapter illustrate the paradox of hunger and want amid plenty?
2. Why did it seem more economical to the growers to destroy their crops than to bring them to market?
3. What does John Steinbeck mean when he ends the chapter with the warning that the "grapes of wrath are filling and growing heavy"?

25-8 Will Rogers on President Hoover (1930)

The depression did nothing to diminish the popularity of radio; if anything, it encouraged people to stay at home and get free entertainment (see text pp. 780–781). The humorist Will Rogers (1879–1935) provided the following view of Herbert Hoover on a broadcast that aired April 20, 1930.

Source: Reprinted by permission of the Will Rogers Museum of Oklahoma from Will Rogers, "President Hoover," E. R. Squibb & Sons Broadcast, April 20, 1930. In Steven K. Gragert, ed., *Radio Broadcasts of Will Rogers* (Stillwater: Oklahoma State University Press, 1983), pp. 10–14.

There is Orthodox Quakers and then the modern Quakers. The Orthodox stayed in Philadelphia and the modern ones got out. The further away from Philadelphia they got, the more modern they was. Mr. Hoover's is about the most modern of all of them. They got to Iowa. Of course, there was no California in those days. The motion picture camera hadn't been invented, and then climate was only a condition and not a sales commodity.

Mr. Hoover, he was left an orphan when he was a little boy, at a very early age, and he went to live for a while with an uncle. This uncle lived down in Pawhuska, Indian Territory, now Oklahoma, Pawhuska, Oklahoma. Pawhuska, to give you an idea—now of course maybe you never heard of it—Pawhuska is just fifty-five miles from Claremore, and it is near Tulsa, too, but it is fifty-five miles from Claremore, and he used to come to Claremore. People did from Tulsa, too. Pawhuska and Tulsa people used to come over to Claremore for their mail and to find out what time it was. We had a clock there.

Well, it has always been credited that this splendid association with these fine people that he met down in that country has really molded Mr. Hoover's future character. I mean, I think that is where he got his wonderful character, was in meeting those people. Just this touch of kind of artistic environment that he got in our country there, that has made him what he is, you know. He wouldn't have developed anything like that if he had stayed anywhere else. If he had stayed in Iowa or gone directly to California, he would have just turned out to be another real estate salesman, that is about all he would have been.

The next big step in Mr. Hoover's career, as I picture it and read about it, after having his character formed in Rogers County, Oklahoma, was to go to Leland Stanford School. It wasn't hardly known in those days because Pop Warner was still coaching the Carlisle Indians. They brought him away from Carlisle, and of course the Carlisle Indian School had to close, and Stanford became a university. There is no college now that has got a higher standing than Stanford has. Their stadium is just as big as anybody's stadium, and they can afford to pay as much for a good full-back or end as Harvard or Yale or Princeton or any of them.

In the days of course when Mr. Hoover went there,

there was no football, so if you wanted to work your way through school you had to work, you couldn't just play for it. You had to work, and that is what Mr. Hoover did. He worked his way through school and was really a self-made man that way. If there had been football in his day he would never have been president; he would have just turned out to be another coach.

Well, he not only picked up an education at Stanford but a wife, too, which is an education in itself. There was a mighty fine girl going to school there. Her name was Lou Henry. She was studying flowers and plants. She fell in love with Mr. Hoover. Now, if that strikes you as kind of strange, that is nothing. Look at Mrs. Coolidge, she was a teacher in a deaf and dumb school when she fell in love with Calvin.

He graduated, Mr. Hoover did, in 1895. The year he graduated there wasn't any filling stations for a college man to work in, so he took up engineering. He wasn't a stationary engineer; he was a locomotion engineer, I guess that is what you would call it, for he was always moving. He couldn't seem to make a go of it in any one place. He just prowled around all over the world.

The first job he got was in Australia. Well, he thought Australia was too wild a country to get married and take a wife to, that is, a new wife, so he decided to wait until he got to a more civilized place to go before he married. Then he figured, too, that after he got back from Australia, why he wouldn't have to go in debt for the license. So he waited until he finished this job in Australia, and he got a job in the interior of China. It was quiet and nice and fine there. He got married and went there. China gave him a wonderful reception. They put on the Boxer Rebellion for him when he arrived. They was barricaded in the town of Zin Zin or Tin Tin, or something like that, or Sen Sen, I don't know the name of it, one of those names, they all sound alike besides Hongkong. They was barricaded there for a long time, and the Chinamen shot at them for three months. That was for a honeymoon.

He went to South America and Siberia and Africa and Alaska and once in his early days he got as far away from civilization as to do some government surveying in Arkansas. That is my wife's state, I pulled that for her.

Through all these years of travel, Mrs. Hoover stuck

right with him and she helped him out in his work. He would think up new places to go, and she would look up the time table and see how to get there. If they stayed two weeks in any one place, why Mr. Hoover joined the Old Settlers Club.

Mrs. Hoover is not only a charming woman but a very brilliant woman. She helped him translate an old book on engineering that was written some four hundred years ago, and nobody knew what the book said, and they figured it out, and of course we don't know whether they figured it out right or not because nobody knows what the book said.

That brings him up to the war in 1914. He was chairman of the American Relief Association, and he helped feed Belgians, and a little later it was found we was worse off than the Belgians, so they brought him home to feed us. He is always feeding somebody. Now he is feeding the Republicans. No Armenian that every lived can eat more than one of them can.

I always did want to see him elected. I wanted to see how far a competent man could go in politics. It has never been tried before.

Women have always been very strong for Mr. Hoover, When his picture appeared on the screen, all the time the women have always applauded him. Even during the war, the women would drop their knitting to applaud for Mr. Hoover. Of course, they would be knitting on a sock that the soldier afterwards wore for a sweater, but, you know, their patriotism was better than their knitting, but they meant well.

He really won the war for us. Did you ever figure that out? He was our food dictator. He won the war for us, but he ruined our stomachs. He gave us liberty with indigestion.

You remember all the slogans we had during the war. Well, he is the inventor of all of them—"Butter it thin and you're bound to win;" and "Drink your coffee black and give the enemy a whack," and all of them. Mr. Hoover thought of all those things, you know.

One time I was down in the flooded area in the Mississippi Valley. I was shown around down there during the flood, and I saw some of the splendid work Mr. Hoover did. He really saved people's lives in that flood, he honestly did, he saved their lives. Out on a raft, he really pulled people out of the water with his own hands, you know, and then after he got them out and wrung them out, they was Democrats.

Well, that was wonderful, you know. Suppose you swam in and laid yourself liable to some personal injury and dragged something out and find it was only a Democrat, you would have a tendency to shove him back in again you know. But he didn't, you know, he didn't. He kept them out, you know, and that showed that he was really a humanitarian at heart, you know, because Congress ain't going to do nothing about the floods at all. Just be-

fore they closed the last session, they passed a resolution denouncing floods. They come out against them then. So if you have got any friends down in the Mississippi Valley, why, you had better advise them to get a row boat. I would put more dependence in a skiff during a flood than I would in the whole of the Senate or Government and all, you know.

Mr. Hoover, you know, he was originally a Democrat himself when he come back. When we was going to run him in 1920, we had him all framed up to run on our side. A lot of people tell you that Mr. Hoover ain't a politician. Well, he ain't a politician in a way, but he is a smart fellow all right, you know. You didn't see him running with the Democrats, did you? No, he liked us all right, but he didn't run with us. He waited until he got on the right side before he run, you know.

The politicians, you know, they have all been against him. That is really what elected him. The minute the people found out the politicians didn't want him, the whole nation said, He is the kind of fellow we want.

Of course, we kid about his commissions and all that, but I tell you in this late Wall Street crisis, I really believe that the way he got all those big men together, really saved a very delicate situation there, and you know there is quite a psychology in getting a lot of big men on commissions with you. You have just got that many more men working with you, you know. Any time you tell a fellow you will put him on some committee or something, he thinks, you know, it kind of makes him do a little better, you know, and I think that is one thing that Mr. Hoover did about that.

Of course, they talk about how everything is getting along and everything. He has only been in a year, and it all depends on what we do the last year. You know, the memory of a voter—you can give him three years of prosperity and then if you give him the last year and he ain't doing very well, a voter just goes to the polls and if he has got a dollar you stay in, and if he ain't got a dollar, you go out, you know. The memory of a voter is about as long as a billy goat. So it is all going to depend on how Mr. Hoover makes out the last year.

I guess I ought to say something about his recreation. Most men's recreation is golf, and their business is talking about it, talking about the golf, but he hasn't golfed in a long time, in years, in fact. He traded his niblick and putter for a can of worms, and now he goes to Virginia, you know. They used to raise presidents in Virginia, and now they just raise the fish that the presidents catch.

You know, when Mr. Coolidge was in and just let everything go along, that was wonderful. Nobody ever asked Coolidge to fix a thing. We just let everything go, and everybody grabbed off what he could and all, never fixed anything. We are great people to go to extremes. We just jump from one thing to another. Now Mr. Hoover is elected and we want him to fix everything. Farm relief—

we want him to fix the farmer. Now, the farmer never had relief. You know what I mean. He never had it even under Lincoln, he never had it. But he wants it under Hoover. He thinks Mr. Hoover ought to give him some relief.

Prohibition—they think Mr. Hoover ought to fix prohibition. Well, my goodness, Mr. Hoover can't—I don't know, but if I remember right, the boys had a couple of nips under Calvin's administration, I think they did.

Prosperity—millions of people never had it under nobody and never will have it under anybody, but they all want it under Mr. Hoover.

Women—women in this country, they think Mr. Hoover, my goodness, he ought to come in and wash the dishes, you know, and help take care of the baby or something. They are all wanting something from Mr. Hoover. If the weather is wrong, we blame it on Hoover. So all in all, I believe he is doing a pretty good job, and I only claim one distinction, and that is that I am the only person that I know of that is not on one of his commissions. And so good night.

Questions

1. What kind of humor does Rogers use in talking about President Hoover?
2. What is his opinion of Hoover?
3. Why does he seem to have a different opinion of the American public?

Questions for Further Thought

1. Judging by Documents 25-4 through 25-8, how did the American public hold up during the depression?
2. To what extent does John McCutcheon's cartoon (Document 25-4) describe the world of "Mr. Patterson" (Document 25-5)?
3. How might the depiction of conditions in Documents 25-5 and 25-7 have influenced popular attitudes about combating the depression?

The Social Fabric of Depression America and Herbert Hoover and the Great Depression

Hard times had come and gone in the history of the United States, but in the 1930s it seemed to many Americans that tough times were here to stay. African-Americans and Mexican-Americans were particularly hard hit by the depression, as were the residents of the "Dust Bowl" (see text pp. 781–787), but no group or region was exempt. Some Americans questioned whether capitalism and the nation's democratic political traditions could survive the crisis. When unemployed veterans of World War I camped in Washington, D.C., in the summer of 1932, demanding federal aid, it seemed to some observers that a revolution was at hand (see text pp. 790–792).

Some looked to the Soviet Union as a model for the future. Indeed, communism made inroads among displaced workers and intellectuals (Document 25-9), but its appeal was limited (see text p. 792). What most Americans wanted was their jobs, security, and sense of personal dignity, not a revolution. They were able to express their discontent by denouncing government leaders and policies. President Herbert Hoover (Document 25-10), not capitalism as a system, became the symbol of what was wrong with America. Hoover became identified in the public imagination with Secretary of the Treasury Andrew Mellon, who advised the president to "liquidate labor, liquidate stocks, liquidate the farmers, liquidate real estate." Milo Reno had something else in mind for American farmers (Document 25-11).

25-9   Richard Wright on Communism in the 1930s

With the publication of *Native Son* in 1940, Richard Wright became the best-known African-American novelist of his generation. In the mid-1930s Wright had been attracted to the Communist party (see text pp. 781–782). In this excerpt from his memoir *American Hunger*, published in 1977, he suggests why communism appealed to him for a time and why its appeal proved limited.

Source: Pages 60–65 from*American Hunger* by Richard Wright. Copyright © 1944 by Richard Wright. Copyright renewed 1977 by Ellen Wright. Reprinted by permission of HarperCollins, Publishers, Inc.

One Thursday night I received an invitation from a group of white boys I had known in the post office to meet in a South Side hotel and argue the state of the world. About ten of us gathered and ate salami sandwiches, drank beer, and talked. I was amazed to discover that many of them had joined the Communist party. I challenged them by reciting the antics of the Negro Communists I had seen in the parks, and I was told that those antics were "tactics" and were all right. I was dubious.

Then one Thursday night Sol, a Jewish chap, startled us by announcing that he had had a short story accepted by a little magazine called the *Anvil*, edited by Jack Conroy, and that he had joined a revolutionary artists' organization, the John Reed Club. Sol repeatedly begged me to attend the meetings of the club, but I always found an easy excuse for refusing.

"You'd like them," Sol said.

"I don't want to be organized," I said.

"They can help you to write," he said.

"Nobody can tell me how or what to write," I said.

"Come and see," he urged. "What have you to lose?"

I felt that Communists could not possibly have a sincere interest in Negroes. I was cynical and I would rather have heard a white man say that he hated Negroes, which I could have readily believed, then to have heard him say that he respected Negroes, which would have made me doubt him. I did not think that there existed many whites who, through intellectual effort, could lift themselves out of the traditions of their times and see the Negro objectively.

One Saturday night, sitting home idle, not caring to visit the girls I had met on my former insurance route, bored with reading, I decided to appear at the John Reed Club in the capacity of an amused spectator. I rode to the Loop and found the number. A dark stairway led upwards; it did not look welcoming. What on earth of importance could transpire in so dingy a place? Through the windows above me I saw vague murals along the walls. I mounted the stairs to a door that was lettered:

The Chicago John Reed Club

I opened it and stepped into the strangest room I had ever seen. Paper and cigarette butts lay on the floor. A few benches ran along the walls, above which were vivid colors depicting colossal figures of workers carrying streaming banners. The mouths of the workers gaped in wild cries; their legs were sprawled over cities.

"Hello."

I turned and saw a white man smiling at me.

"A friend of mine, who's a member of this club, asked me to visit here. His name is Sol———," I told him.

"You're welcome here," the white man said. "We're not having an affair tonight. We're holding an editorial meeting. Do you paint?" He was slightly gray and he had a mustache.

"No," I said. "I try to write."

"Then sit in on the editorial meeting of our magazine, *Left Front*," he suggested.

"I know nothing of editing," I said.

"You can learn," he said.

I stared at him, doubting.

"I don't want to be in the way here," I said.

"My name's Grimm," he said

I told him my name and we shook hands. He went to a closet and returned with an armful of magazines.

"Here are some back issues of the *Masses*," he said "Have you ever read it?"

"No," I said.

"Some of the best writers in America publish in it," he explained. He also gave me copies of a magazine called *International Literature*. "There's stuff here from Gide, Gorky . . ."

I assured him that I would read them. He took me to an office and introduced me to a Jewish boy who was to become one of the nation's leading painters, to a chap who was to become one of the eminent composers of his day, to a writer who was to create some of the best novels of his generation, to a young Jewish boy who was destined to film the Nazi invasion of Czechoslovakia. I was meeting men and women whom I would know for decades to come, who were to form the first sustained relationships in my life.

I sat in a corner and listened while they discussed their magazine, *Left Front*. Were they treating me courteously because I was a Negro? I must let cold reason guide me with these people, I told myself. I was asked to contribute something to the magazine, and I said vaguely that I would consider it. After the meeting I met an Irish girl who worked for an advertising agency, a girl who did social work, a schoolteacher, and the wife of a prominent university professor. I had once worked as a servant for people like these and I was skeptical. I tried to fathom their motives, but I could detect no condescension in them.

I went home full of reflection, probing the sincerity of the strange white people I had met, wondering how they *really* regarded Negroes. I lay on my bed and read the magazines and was amazed to find that there did exist in the world an organized search for the truth of the lives of the oppressed and the isolated. When I had begged bread from the officials, I had wondered dimly if the outcasts could become united in action, thought, and feeling. Now I knew. It was being done in one-sixth of the earth already. The revolutionary words leaped from the printed page and struck me with tremendous force.

It was not the economics of Communism, nor the great power of trade unions, nor the excitement of underground politics that claimed me; my attention was caught by the similarity of the experiences of workers in other lands, by the possibility of uniting scattered but kindred peoples into a whole. My cynicism—which had been my protection against an America that had cast me out—slid from me and, timidly, I began to wonder if a solution of unity was possible. My life as a Negro in America had led me to feel—though my helplessness had made me try to hide it from myself—that the problem of human unity was more important than bread, more important than physical living itself; for I felt that without a common bond uniting men, without a continuous current of shared thought and feeling circulating through the social system, like blood coursing through the body, there could be no living worthy of being called human.

I hungered to share the dominant assumptions of my time and act upon them. I did not want to feel, like an animal in a jungle, that the whole world was alien and hostile. I did not want to make individual war or individual peace. So far I had managed to keep humanly alive through transfusions from books. In my concrete relations with others I had encountered nothing to encourage me to believe in my feelings. It had been by denying what I saw with my eyes, disputing what I felt with my body, that I had managed to keep my identity intact. But it seemed to me that here at least in the realm of revolutionary expression was where Negro experience could find a home, a functioning value and role. Out of the magazines I read came a passionate call for the experiences of the disinherited, and there were none of the same lispings of the missionary in it. It did not say: "Be like us and we will like you, maybe." It said: "If you possess enough courage to speak out what you are,

you will find that you are not alone." It urged life to believe in life.

I read on into the night; then, toward dawn, I swung from bed and inserted paper into the typewriter. Feeling for the first time that I could speak to listening ears, I wrote a wild, crude poem in free verse, coining images of black hands playing, working, holding bayonets, stiffening finally in death . . . I read it and felt that in a clumsy way it linked white life with black, merged two streams of common experience.

I heard someone poking about the kitchen.

"Richard, are you ill?" my mother called.

"No. I'm reading."

My mother opened the door and stared curiously at the pile of magazines that lay upon my pillow.

"You're not throwing away money buying these magazines, are you?" she asked.

"No. They were given to me."

She hobbled to the bed on her crippled legs and picked up a copy of the *Masses* that carried a lurid May Day cartoon. She adjusted her glasses and peered at it for a long time.

"My God in heaven," she breathed in horror.

"What's the matter, mama?"

"What is this?" she asked, extending the magazine to me, pointing to the cover. "What's wrong with that man?"

With my mother standing at my side, lending me her eyes, I stared at a cartoon drawn by a Communist artist; it was the figure of a worker clad in ragged overalls and holding aloft a red banner. The man's eyes bulged; his mouth gaped as wide as his face; his teeth showed; the muscles of his neck were like ropes. Following the man was a horde of nondescript men, women, and children, waving clubs, stones, and pitchforks.

"What are those people going to do?" my mother asked.

"I don't know," I hedged.

"Are these Communist magazines?"

"Yes."

"And do they want people to act like this?"

"Well . . ." I hesitated.

My mother's face showed disgust and moral loathing. She was a gentle woman. Her ideal was Christ upon the cross. How could I tell her that the Communist party wanted her to march in the streets, chanting, singing?

"What do Communists think people are?" she asked.

"They don't quite mean what you see there," I said, fumbling with my words.

"Then what do they mean?"

"This is symbolic," I said.

"Then why don't they speak out what they mean?"

"Maybe they don't know how."

"Then why do they print this stuff?"

"They don't quite know how to appeal to people yet,"

I admitted, wondering whom I could convince of this if I could not convince my mother.

"That picture's enough to drive a body crazy," she said, dropping the magazine, turning to leave, then pausing at the door.

"You're not getting mixed up with those people?"

"I'm just reading, mama," I dodged.

Questions

1. Many Americans became dissatisfied with the status quo during the Great Depression. Which grievances shaped the response of African-Americans to the social and economic hardships of that era?
2. Why did communism appeal to Richard Wright as a possible solution to the problems he faced?
3. Judging from Wright's account, what factors prevented communism from becoming a more popular movement?

25-10 Herbert Hoover on Countering the Depression (1932)

In this statement at a press conference on May 13, 1932, President Herbert Hoover compared the actions his administration was taking to counter the effects of the depression with those the government would use in wartime. But in the same statement, Hoover identified balancing the budget (never a wartime priority) as the most important single step government could take to advance economic recovery (see text p. 790).

Source: State Papers of Herbert Hoover (Garden City, N.Y.: Doubleday, Doran, 1934), pp. 188–189.

Our job in the Government is unity of action to do our part in an unceasing campaign to reëstablish public confidence. That is fundamental to recovery. The imperative and immediate step is to balance the Budget and I am sure the Government will stay at this job until it is accomplished.

When our people recover from frozen confidence then our credit machinery will begin to function once more on a normal basis and there will be no need to exercise the emergency powers already vested in any of our governmental agencies or the further extensions we are proposing for the Reconstruction Corporation. If by unity of action these extensions of powers are kept within the limits I have proposed they do not affect the Budget. They do not constitute a drain on the taxpayer. They constitute temporary mobilization of timid capital for positive and definite purpose of speeding the recovery of business, agriculture and employment.

I have, however, no taste for any such emergency powers in the Government. But we are fighting the economic consequences of over liquidation and unjustified fear as to the future of the United States. The battle to set our economic machine in motion in this emergency takes new forms and requires new tactics from time to time. We used such emergency powers to win the war; we can use them to fight the depression, the misery and suffering from which are equally great.

Questions

1. Why does President Hoover believe that the restoration of public "confidence" is the solution to the country's economic problems?
2. Why does Hoover compare the country's economic crisis to the crisis of wartime?
3. Is there any contradiction between Hoover's call for balancing the budget and his request for "emergency" measures to combat the depression?

25-11 "Why the Farmers' Holiday?" (1932)

Milo Reno   Milo Reno (1866–1936) was the twelfth child of an Iowa farm couple (see text p. 791).
As a spokesman for farmers devastated by the depression, he became a controversial
figure. Once, after he had been hanged in effigy, Reno returned the following night to
inform his critics, "Here's the real man. Why don't you hang him?"

Source: Milo Reno, radio broadcast "Why the Farmers Holiday?" (July 20, 1932). In [R.
White], *Milo Reno, Farmers Union Pioneer: The Story of a Man and a Movement*, a memorial
volume (Iowa City, Iowa: Iowa Farmers Union, 1941), pp. 148–153.

In presenting to the listeners of KFNF the Farmers' National Holiday program, it is necessary to, as briefly as possible, review the causes which have led up to the most amazing and confounding situation in the history of the world—people starving in a land with an abundance of food; naked, because of a surplus of clothing; people bankrupt in the richest nation in the world.

This situation did not just happen. It is not because of an act of Providence! But is the result of a conspiracy as destructive and damnable as has ever occurred in this history of mankind.

Its correction can only be accomplished through heroic measures; a patriotic determination to faithfully carry out the objective for which this government was formed—a guarantee of life, liberty and the pursuit of happiness for the citizens of this Republic.

In 1920 as a result of the world's war, the debts of all nations engaged therein were multiplied many times, vast fortunes were made, with the power that attends the accumulation of great wealth. The conspirators against the peace and tranquility of this Republic, determined upon an unwarranted and drastic deflation that begun with agriculture and that in eighteen months had destroyed thirty billion dollars of farm values.

Farm organizations pled with congress for the correction of the situation that was strangling American agriculture, was destroying America's farm homes and which could only mean the final destruction of the foundation principles upon which this Government rests.

Many measures were proposed, alibis carefully prepared to excuse the pernicious program of the money lords of the nation, but the requests and prayers of the American farmer for economic equality were ignored.

In 1924, a pernicious program of propaganda, designed to excuse the do-nothing policy of those responsible for legislation was begun, leading the public to believe, that the farmer himself was to blame that he had not received the consideration that he was so evidently entitled to; that he was so contrary that he would not co-operate with his fellow farmer; that the farm leadership was selfish, envious, and jealous of each other to the extent that they could not agree upon a definite, positive legislative program and that, if the farm leaders would get together, lay aside their differences of opinion, their organization jealousies, and agree upon an agricultural program, how happy they would be to concede it.

The farm leadership of the United States met the challenge, and, in response to a call sent out by the national Farmers Union, a meeting was held in Des Moines, Iowa, on the 12th day of May 1925, in which 24 farm groups were represented. In this memorable conference, the Corn Belt committee was formed and a legislative program adopted, which embodied the McNary-Haugen bill. Splendid men were selected from all farm organizations, to present this legislative program to congress. So earnestly and valiantly the representatives of this group battled for the farmer's right to a square deal, that the bill twice passed the House and Senate and was twice vetoed by a unfriendly president. The second time the McNary-Haugen bill was vetoed, it had passed the house and senate by an overwhelming majority, in fact, it only lacked one vote of the necessary two-thirds to pass the measure over the president' veto.

The Corn Belt committee was called into session on July 6th, 1927, and after serious consideration of the situation and after fully realizing the money lords of the country, controlling the eastern vote, would never willingly grant the farmer an equal opportunity to exist with industry, the following resolution was passed:

"If we cannot obtain justice by legislation, the time will have arrived when no other course remains than organized refusal to deliver the products of the farm at less than production costs."

We had hoped in the nomination and election of a president in 1928 the country would concede the right of production costs, to those who produced the food and raw material for the rest of society, and the splendid representatives of 36 organized farm groups unanimously declared to the world in this resolution that unless we were conceded economic equality we would organize and refuse to deliver the products of our farms for less than production costs.

The absolute failure of the present congress, whether because of intellectual ability or a lack of patriotic courage, has miserably failed to correct a situation in this republic, unparalleled in history, consequently, we feel the time has arrived for the men and women, who live upon the farms, to resort to drastic measures to protect their homes from confiscation.

A meeting was called for May 3rd, 1932, in the city of Des Moines, Iowa, to which all groups were invited, both agriculture, business, professional and labor, to discuss the action necessary to save the farmers of this nation from complete destruction. It was a monster meeting of earnest men and women, and in this meeting the Farmers' Holiday association was born, and I wish to assure you that it is the last stand of American agriculture in defense of their rights and their homes. . . .

Congress has just ended a long and arduous session, but, seemingly, the objective aimed at by both the major political parties, was to prepare for the campaign of 1932, instead of relieving the situation of despair and desolation of the present time. Not a single measure of relief was passed that did not carry with it an increased burden of debt and usury. The one thing that would restore prosperity again to this nation was defeated each time it was proposed, that is, an inflation of the currency to that point that would reduce the value of the dollar as measured in other things practically to the same point that it was in 1920.

If we are ever able to obtain the legislation necessary to place agriculture on an economic equality with industry, it will be, when we use our economic power, which is the only power left the farmer today.

The Farmers' Holiday association proposes to fix a fair valuation on farm products, based on production costs, and to refuse to deliver until those prices are conceded. Some may call this a strike. Very well. If it is a strike for the farmers to refuse to deliver his products for less than production costs, it is also a strike when the merchant declines to deliver his goods for less than cost and carriage.

We propose that society, as a whole, shall recognize the farmer's right to be considered the same as other serving groups of society. Railroad corporations, because of the fact that they were performing a public service, were conceded by the federal government the cost of operation, plus a five and one-fourth per cent profit on their investment, and I wish to ask my listeners—Is it more of a public service to transport the food products of this nation than it is to produce them?

The utility corporations have, by the federal courts, been conceded the right to fix the price for their services, that, after all operating expenses are paid, they shall have from six to eight per cent return on their capital investment, and this is true of every other business.

Why should other groups of society expect the American farmer, to produce the food and raw material that makes existence possible for them, and deliver his product at a price below production costs, which inevitably means bankruptcy and destruction?

In calling a farmers' holiday, we are simply putting into operation a program that has been adopted by many cities in the middle west, to protect the assets of their banks.

No one should criticize either the banks or the officials of those cities, that adopted drastic methods to protect the property of those institutions from depreciation, in fact, destruction, neither should any group criticize the farmers for refusing to see the value of their holdings depreciated to the extent that the labor of a lifetime is destroyed and in their old age, they are left homeless and in poverty.

The governor of our state joined in with a group of Iowa farmers last September in an effort to stabilize the corn prices. This effort was commendable, but its failure was inevitable, because of its lack of militancy and universal support. For a movement of this kind to succeed, it should have the support and encouragement of the commercial and professional groups, as well as agriculture. It should be entirely divorced from any particular organization, because in order to succeed, it must have the same individual and organization support that prevailed in the old Corn Belt committee. This program means the restoration of the farmer's purchasing power, the power to pay his debts, the ability to purchase the things he so sadly needs, in the operation of his home and his farm. This will mean prosperity to the business institutions and to the professional world. For example, concede to the farmer production costs and he will pay his grocer, the grocer will pay the wholesaler, the wholesaler will pay the manufacturer and the manufacturer will be able to meet his obligations at the bank. Restore the farmer's purchasing power and you have re-established an endless chain of prosperity and happiness in this country. Continue the present policy and you will not only wreck the farmer's home, but in such wrecking, you will wreck every institution that is dependent upon the prosperity of the farmer.

We are at the parting of the ways. The time is too short to temporize longer. The people of the United States must be saved from the destructive desolation that is due us in the coming winter. Therefore, the national Farmers' Holiday association is appealing to the individual farmers, to the co-operative groups, and to all farm organizations to forget all their differences and join in a united effort to correct the situation before it is everlastingly too late to save the farm home, that has been builded by the sweat, the toil, the sacrifice, of those who occupy them.

To achieve these ends, some legislation will be necessary. There were a few bills introduced in the last session of congress that if enacted into law would have very materially corrected the present situation. It is not difficult to determine as to the effect of a bill that would provide an increase in the volume of money. . . .

The direct cause of the present distress was deflation of the currency or monopolization of the economic life blood of this nation. Any measure that would inflate the currency and assure us an honest dollar is the remedy. The legislators serving the money lords of the country very frequently use the term "honest dollar" in their opposition to the government exercising its sovereign perogative to provide the nations' currency.

In 1920, it required $3.00 to measure a bushel of wheat. Through the process of deflation or making money scarce, $1.00 would measure the same quantity of wheat. We did not hear this group of money servers, talking about a dishonest dollar, but, when we proposed to reverse the situation and bring the value of a dollar back to where it was when the great majority of our debts were created, immediately they sent up the cry for an "honest dollar".

Senator Borah, as reported in yesterday's paper (July 19th) says: "We can never pay out under the present program and under present conditions. There is nothing ahead but chaos and disaster, unless we boldly undertake to bring prices back to what they were when a substantial portion of our current debts were obligated, and that only an expansion of the currency would enable us to avoid chaos and disaster." In fact, every thinking man realizes that prices must be brought back by an expansion of the currency.

The farmer has a perfect right to insist that he be permitted to pay his obligation with a dollar of the same purchasing power as the one he borrowed.

How will we go about to accomplish this desired end?

Economists everywhere realize and frankly admit that the present economic system is entirely broken down—that not only the farmer is facing desolation and disaster, but our business and financial institutions are on the verge of universal collapse.

The farmer, by withholding his product, can not only restore a price that will cover production costs, but will have a powerful influence in shaping desired legislation.

In the perfecting of this Farmers' Holiday plan, we will have a marketing committee starting from the townships to the county, from the county to the state, and from the state to the national, without intervention, and it will be a farmer's marketing program built by himself, owned, controlled and operated by himself, without the obstruction of cumbersome federal machinery, that invariably degenerates into a political machine.

Farmers of the middle west, you are standing with your backs to the wall, you have pinned your faith in the past to parties and institutions provided for you by the men higher up. They have failed you in your hour of need—the time has arrived when, if your problems are solved and your right to prosperity and happiness restored, it will be through your own efforts.

Let's take the Farmers' Holiday program into every state, county and township that produces human food. I thank you.

Questions

1. What did the Farmers' Holiday Association hope to accomplish?
2. Why does Reno compare farmers to banks?
3. Which parts of this document make Reno appear radical?

Questions for Further Thought

1. How do the views of Richard Wright (Document 25-9) compare to those of Albert Parsons (Document 18-8)?
2. Compare Milo Reno (Document 25-11) with the Grangers and Populists (Documents 17-9, 17-10, and 19-5). What are the similarities and differences?
3. Could the ideas expressed in Documents 25-9 and 25-11 remain popular in the long run? Why or why not?
4. How would Herbert Hoover have responded to the ideas of Richard Wright and Milo Reno? In what ways, if any, were the beliefs of each typically American?

CHAPTER 26

The New Deal
1933–1939

★　　　★　　　★

The New Deal Takes Over, 1933–1935 and
The Second New Deal, 1935–1938

After Franklin Delano Roosevelt came to power in 1933 in the midst of the worst economic depression in American history, his policies and personality had a dramatic impact on the nation (see text pp. 798–799 and Document 26-1). Exuding confidence and energy, Roosevelt renewed the faith of millions of Americans in themselves and their nation; in his first inaugural address (Document 26-2), he told Americans that the only thing they had to fear "is fear itself."

In the first hundred days of his administration FDR bombarded Congress with proposals for new legislation, most of which passed in record time and with minimal debate (see text pp. 799–801). In the first months of his administration Roosevelt's popularity knew no bounds; businessmen, workers, farmers, homeowners, and others hailed him as an economic savior. Through his frequent press conferences and "fireside chats" Roosevelt fashioned a strong and direct rapport with both the press and the public. New Deal Washington was a beehive of activity as Roosevelt's advisers and administrators, many of them young and idealistic, grappled with the problems of the depression (Document 26-3).

Over the next two years, however, it became apparent that the early New Deal programs, designed to stimulate business recovery by restricting overproduction and stabilizing prices, were having only limited success. Faced with challenges from Populist demogogues such as Charles Coughlin and Huey Long (see text pp. 802–803 and Document 26-4) and aware that his support in the business community was eroding, Roosevelt pushed for farther-reaching reforms in the so-called Second New Deal of 1935–1938 (see text pp. 803–804).

In 1935 he proposed or endorsed the National Labor Relations Act, the Social Security Act, and the establishment of the Works Progress Administration. Those programs were meant to end the depression from the bottom up by protecting the right of workers to organize, providing pensions for the elderly, and creating jobs for the unemployed. By 1936 Roosevelt had constructed a coalition of the urban ethnic working class, southern and midwestern farmers, Catholics, Jews, African-Americans, and liberal intellectuals; that alliance that would wield tremendous power in American political life for decades afterward.

In his second inaugural address in 1937 Roosevelt reviewed the achievements of his first term and drew attention to the work that remained to be done. But owing to a downturn in the economy and a series of political miscalculations and setbacks, Roosevelt's second term was marked by a stalemate in domestic policy (see text pp. 805–807).

26-1 Candidate Attends World Series (1932)

Franklin Delano Roosevelt projected an image of such self-assurance and strength (see text pp. 798–799) that most Americans did not realize he was severely handicapped by polio or chose to ignore it. Roosevelt is pictured here throwing out the first pitch at Wrigley Field for the third game of the 1932 World Series between the Yankees and the Cubs (during which Babe Ruth might or might not have "called" his home run in the fifth inning). The presidential candidate is flanked by Mayor Anton Cermak of Chicago and son James Roosevelt.

Source: Franklin Delano Roosevelt at the 3rd Chicago Cubs baseball game of the 1932 World Series, October 15, 1932; the New York Yankees sweep the World Series 4–0. Reprinted by permission from the Joseph M. Jacobs Collection of Rooseveltiana, Special Collections, The University Library, The University of Illinois at Chicago.

Questions

1. What is FDR hoping to accomplish through his appearance?
2. How is he camouflaging his disability?
3. Why would he choose to appear at this particular event?

26-2   Franklin D. Roosevelt's First Inaugural Address (1933)

With so many Americans suffering in poverty through the winter of 1932–1933, President Roosevelt knew that he had to find a way to rekindle their spirits (see text pp. 798–799). Assisted by adviser Raymond Moley, Roosevelt crafted an inaugural address toward that end. The speech was a resounding success.

Source: In Samuel I. Rosenman, ed., *The Public Papers and Addresses of Franklin D. Roosevelt* (New York: Random House, 1938), vol. 2.

President Hoover, Mr. Chief Justice, my friends:

This is a day of national consecration, and I am certain that my fellow Americans expect that on my induction into the Presidency I will address them with a candor and a decision which the present situation of our nation impels.

This is pre-eminently the time to speak the truth, the whole truth, frankly and boldly. Nor need we shrink from honestly facing conditions in our country today. This great nation will endure as it has endured, will revive and will prosper.

So first of all let me assert my firm belief that the only thing we have to fear is fear itself—nameless, unreasoning, unjustified terror which paralyzes needed efforts to convert retreat into advance.

In every dark hour of our national life a leadership of frankness and vigor has met with that understanding and support of the people themselves which is essential to victory. I am convinced that you will again give that support to leadership in these critical days.

In such a spirit on my part and on yours we face our common difficulties. They concern, thank God, only material things. Values have shrunken to fantastic levels; taxes have risen; our ability to pay has fallen, government of all kinds is faced by serious curtailment of income; the means of exchange are frozen in the currents of trade; the withered leaves of industrial enterprise lie on every side; farmers find no markets for their produce; the savings of many years in thousands of families are gone.

More important, a host of unemployed citizens face the grim problem of existence, and an equally great number toil with little return. Only a foolish optimist can deny the dark realities of the moment.

Yet our distress comes from no failure of substance. We are stricken by no plague of locusts. Compared with the perils which our forefathers conquered because they believed and were not afraid, we have still much to be thankful for. Nature still offers her bounty and human efforts have multiplied it. Plenty is at our doorstop, but a generous use of it languishes in the very sight of the supply.

Primarily, this is because the rulers of the exchange of mankind's goods have failed through their own stubbornness and their own incompetence, have admitted their failure and abdicated. Practices of the unscrupulous money changers stand indicted in the court of public opinion, rejected by the hearts and minds of men.

True, they have tried, but their efforts have been cast in the pattern of an outworn tradition. Faced by failure of credit, they have proposed only the lending of more money.

Stripped of the lure of profit by which to induce our people to follow their false leadership, they have resorted to exhortations, pleading tearfully for restored confidence. They know only the rules of a generation of self-seekers.

They have no vision, and when there is no vision the people perish.

The money changers have fled from their high seats in the temple of our civilization. We may now restore that temple to the ancient truths.

The measure of the restoration lies in the extent to which we apply social values more noble than mere monetary profit.

Happiness lies not in the mere possession of money; it lies in the joy of achievement, in the thrill of creative effort.

The joy and moral stimulation of work no longer must be forgotten in the mad chase of evanescent profits. These dark days will be worth all they cost us if they teach us that our true destiny is not to be ministered unto but to minister to ourselves and to our fellow men.

Recognition of the falsity of material wealth as the standard of success goes hand in hand with the abandonment of the false belief that public office and high political position are to be valued only by the standards of pride of place and personal profit; and there must be an end to a conduct in banking and in business which too often has given to a sacred trust the likeness of callous and selfish wrongdoing.

Small wonder that confidence languishes, for it thrives only on honesty, on honor, on the sacredness of obligations, on faithful protection, on unselfish performance. Without them it cannot live.

Restoration calls, however, not for changes in ethics alone. This nation asks for action, and action now.

Our greatest primary task is to put people to work. This is no unsolvable problem if we face it wisely and courageously.

It can be accomplished in part by direct recruiting by

the government itself, treating the task as we would treat the emergency of a war, but at the same time, through this employment, accomplishing greatly needed projects to stimulate and reorganize the use of our natural resources.

Hand in hand with this, we must frankly recognize the overbalance of population in our industrial centers and, by engaging on a national scale in the redistribution, endeavor to provide a better use of the land for those best fitted for the land.

The task can be helped by definite efforts to raise the values of agricultural products and with this the power to purchase the output of our cities.

It can be helped by preventing realistically the tragedy of the growing loss, through foreclosure, of our small homes and our farms.

It can be helped by insistence that the Federal, State and local governments act forthwith on the demand that their cost be drastically reduced.

It can be helped by the unifying of relief activities which today are often scattered, uneconomical and unequal. It can be helped by national planning for and supervision of all forms of transportation and of communications and other utilities which have a definitely public character.

There are many ways in which it can be helped, but it can never be helped merely by talking about it. We must act, and act quickly.

Finally, in our progress toward a resumption of work we require two safeguards against a return of the evils of the old order; there must be a strict supervision of all banking and credits and investments; there must be an end to speculation with other people's money, and there must be provision for an adequate but sound currency.

There are the lines of attack. I shall presently urge upon a new Congress in special session detailed measures for their fulfillment, and I shall seek the immediate assistance of the several States.

Through this program of action we address ourselves to putting our own national house in order and making income balance outgo.

Our international trade relations, though vastly important, are, in point of time and necessity, secondary to the establishment of a sound national economy.

I favor as a practical policy the putting of first things first. I shall spare no effort to restore world trade by international economic readjustment, but the emergency at home cannot wait on that accomplishment.

The basic thought that guides these specific means of national recovery is not narrowly nationalistic.

It is the insistence, as a first consideration, upon the interdependence of the various elements in, and parts of, the United States—a recognition of the old and permanently important manifestation of the American spirit of the pioneer.

It is the way to recovery. It is the immediate way. It is the strongest assurance that the recovery will endure.

In the field of world policy I would dedicate this nation to the policy of the good neighbor—the neighbor who resolutely respects himself and, because he does so, respects the rights of others—the neighbor who respects his obligations and respects the sanctity of his agreements in and with a world of neighbors.

If I read the temper of our people correctly, we now realize as we have never before, our interdependence on each other; that we cannot merely take, but we must give as well; that if we are to go forward we must move as a trained and loyal army willing to sacrifice for the good of a common discipline, because, without such discipline, no progress is made, no leadership becomes effective.

We are, I know, ready and willing to submit our lives and property to such discipline because it makes possible a leadership which aims at a larger good.

This I propose to offer, pledging that the larger purposes will bind upon us all as a sacred obligation with a unity of duty hitherto evoked only in time of armed strife.

With this pledge taken, I assume unhesitatingly the leadership of this great army of our people, dedicated to a disciplined attack upon our common problems.

Action in this image and to this end is feasible under the form of government which we have inherited from our ancestors.

Our Constitution is so simple and practical that it is possible always to meet extraordinary needs by changes in emphasis and arrangement without loss of essential form.

That is why our constitutional system has proved itself the most superbly enduring political mechanism the modern world has produced. It has met every stress of vast expansion of territory, of foreign wars, of bitter internal strife, of world relations.

It is to be hoped that the normal balance of executive and legislative authority may be wholly adequate to meet the unprecedented task before us. But it may be that an unprecedented demand and need for undelayed action may call for temporary departure from that normal balance of public procedure.

I am prepared under my constitutional duty to recommend the measures that a stricken nation in the midst of a stricken world may require.

These measures, or such other measures as the Congress may build out of its experience and wisdom, I shall seek, within my constitutional authority, to bring to speedy adoption.

But in the event that the Congress shall fail to take one of these two courses, and in the event the national emergency is still critical, I shall not evade the clear course of duty that will then confront me.

I shall ask the Congress for the one remaining instrument to meet the crisis—broad executive power to wage a war against the emergency as great as the power that would be given me if we were in fact invaded by a foreign foe.

For the trust reposed in me I will return the courage and the devotion that befit the time, I can do no less.

We face the arduous days that lie before us in the warm courage of national unity; with the clear consciousness of seeking old and precious moral values; with the clean satisfaction that comes from the stern performance of duty by old and young alike.

We aim at the assurance of a rounded and permanent national life.

We do not distrust the future of essential democracy. The people of the United States have not failed. In their need they have registered a mandate that they want direct, vigorous action.

They have asked for discipline and direction under leadership. They have made me the present instrument of their wishes. In the spirit of the gift I take it.

In this dedication of a nation we humbly ask the blessing of God. May He protect each and every one of us! May He guide me in the days to come!

Questions

1. How does Roosevelt achieve a sense of community in this speech?
2. Who receives his strongest criticism? Why?
3. Are the religious elements in the speech appropriate? Why or why not?

26-3 Inside the New Deal (1936)

Joe Marcus

In the mid-1930s, Washington, D.C., was filled with new faces and new ideas. Young people flocked to public service in the Roosevelt administration, believing that they could make a better world. Joe Marcus was an economist who went to Washington to work for Harry Hopkins (see text pp. 800, 804) on a study of the effect of technology on reemployment opportunities. Marcus reflected on his experience in the New Deal in an interview with Studs Terkel that was included in Terkel's oral history of the depression, *Hard Times*.

Source: From *Hard Times: An Oral History of the Great Depression in America*, pp. 255–259, by Studs Terkel. Copyright © 1970 by Studs Terkel. Reprinted by permission of Pantheon Books, a division of Random House, Inc.

I think it was '31 or '32. I was attending the City College of New York. Most were students whose parents were workers or small businessmen hit by the Depression. In the public speaking class, I was called upon to talk about unemployment insurance. I was attacked by most of the students . . . this was Socialism. I was shocked by their vehemence. If I remember, the American Federation of Labor at its national convention voted it down. The idea of social security was very advanced. Those who were really hungry wanted something. But the intellectuals, the students, the bureaucratic elements—to them it was a horrible thought. It was something subversive. At first.

But they learned quickly. It was a shock to them. When Roosevelt came out with the ideas, it was not a clearly thought-out program. There was much improvisa-

tion. What you had was a deep-seated emotional feeling as far as the people were concerned. A willingness to change society, just out of outrage, out of need. I think they would have accepted even more radical ideas.

Roosevelt was reflecting the temper of the time—the emotional more than the intellectual. It wasn't merely a question of the king bestowing favors. The pressure from below was a reality. It was not a concentrated campaign effort. There was no organization with a program that commanded the majority of the people. This was part of the political strangeness of our society. The actions below were very revolutionary. Yet some of the ideas of the people, generally, were very backward.

I graduated college in '35. I went down to Washington and started to work in the spring of '36. The New Deal was a young man's world. Young people, if they showed any ability, got an opportunity. I was a kid, twenty-two or twenty-three. In a few months I was made head of the department. We had a meeting with hot shots: What's to be done? I pointed out some problems: let's define what we're looking for. They immediately had me take over. I had to set up the organization and hire seventy-five people. Given a chance as a youngster to try out ideas, I learned a fantastic amount. The challenge itself was great.

It was the idea of being asked big questions. The technical problems were small. These you had to solve by yourself. But the context was broad: Where was society going? Your statistical questions became questions of full employment. You were not prepared for it in school. If you wanted new answers, you needed a new kind of people. This is what was exciting.

Ordinarily, I might have had a job at the university, marking papers or helping a professor. All of a sudden, I'm doing original research and asking basic questions about how our society works. What makes a Depression? What makes for pulling out of it? Once you start thinking in these terms, you're in a different ball game.

The climate was exciting. You were part of a society that was on the move. You were involved in something that could make a difference. Laws could be changed. So could the conditions of people.

The idea of being involved close to the center of political life was unthinkable, just two or three years before all this happened. Unthinkable for someone like me, of lower middle-class, close to ghetto, Jewish life. Suddenly you were a significant member of society. It was not the kind of closed society you had lived in before. . . .

You were really part of something, changes could be made. Bringing *immediate* results to people who were starving. You could do something about it: that was the most important thing. This you felt.

A feeling that if you had something to say, it would get to the top. As I look back now, memoranda I had written reached the White House, one way or another. The biggest thrill of my life was hearing a speech of Roosevelt's using a selection from a memorandum I had written.

Everybody was searching for ideas. A lot of guys were opportunists, some were crackpots. But there was a search, a sense of values . . . that would make a difference in the lives of people.

We weren't thinking of remaking society. That wasn't it. I didn't buy this dream stuff. What was happening was a complete change in social attitudes at the central government level. The question was: How can you do it within this system? People working in all the New Deal agencies were dominated by this spirit. . . .

It was an exciting community, where we lived in Washington. The basic feeling—and I don't think this is just nostalgia—was one of excitement, of achievement, of happiness. Life was important, life was significant.

Were there questions in Washington about the nature of our society?

I don't think revolution as a topic of the day existed. The fact that people acted as they did, in violation of law and order, was itself a revolutionary act. People suddenly heard there was a Communist Party. It was insignificant before then. Suddenly, the more active people, the more concerned people, were in one way or another exposed to it. It never did command any real popular support, though it had influence in key places. This was a new set of ideas, but revolution was never really on the agenda.

F.D.R. was very significant in understanding how best to lead this sort of situation. Not by himself, but he mobilized those elements ready to develop these programs.

Questions

1. According to Joe Marcus, what was distinctive about the spirit and approach to governing of New Deal bureaucrats?
2. Marcus argues that Roosevelt was not a "king bestowing favors" on the populace. How does he account for the cornucopia of reforms that characterized the New Deal era?
3. Did the New Deal represent a "revolutionary" change in American society?

26-4 "The Long Plan" (1933)

To his supporters, Senator Huey P. Long of Louisiana (see text pp. 802–803) was a saint; to his enemies, he was Satan. Long simply referred to himself as "the Kingfish." Until an assassin murdered him in 1935, Long and his brand of Populism seemed strong enough to pose a threat to FDR's winning a second term.

Long titled his autobiography *Every Man a King*. Following is the plan to make that vision a reality.

Source: Reprinted by permission of Palmer R. Long, Sr., from [Huey P. Long], *Every Man a King: The Autobiography of Huey P. Long* (New Orleans: National Book Company, 1933; reprint: Chicago: Quadrangle Books, 1964), pp. 338–340.

THE MADDENED FORTUNE HOLDERS AND THEIR INFURIATED PUBLIC PRESS!

The increasing fury with which I have been, and am to be, assailed by reason of the fight and growth of support for limiting the size of fortunes can only be explained by the madness which human nature attaches to the holders of accumulated wealth.

What I have proposed is:—

THE LONG PLAN

1. A capital levy tax on the property owned by any one person of 1% of all over $1,000,000; 2% of all over $2,000,000 etc., until, when it reaches fortunes of over $100,000,000, the government takes all above that figure; which means a limit on the size of any one man's fortune to something like $50,000,000—the balance to go to the government to spread out in its work among all the people.

2. An inheritance tax which does not allow any one person to receive more than $5,000,000 in a lifetime without working for it, all over that amount to go to the government to be spread among the people for its work.

3. An income tax which does not allow any one man to make more than $1,000,000 in one year, exclusive of taxes, the balance to go to the United States for general work among the people.

The foregoing program means all taxes paid by the fortune holders at the top and none by the people at the bottom; the spreading of wealth among all the people and the breaking up of a system of Lords and Slaves in our eco-

nomic life. It allows the millionaires to have, however, more than they can use for any luxury they can enjoy on earth. But, with such limits, all else can survive.

That the public press should regard my plan and effort as a calamity and me as a menace is no more than should be expected, gauged in the light of past events. . . .

In 1932, the vote for my resolution showed possibly a half dozen other Senators back of it. It grew in the last Congress to nearly twenty Senators. Such growth through one other year will mean the success of a venture, the completion of everything I have undertaken,—the time when I can and will retire from the stress and fury of my public life, maybe as my forties begin,—a contemplation so serene as to appear impossible.

That day will reflect credit on the States whose Senators took the early lead to spread the wealth of the land among all the people.

Then no tear dimmed eyes of a small child will be lifted into the saddened face of a father or mother unable to give it the necessities required by its soul and body for life; then the powerful will be rebuked in the sight of man for holding that which they cannot consume, but which is craved to sustain humanity; the food of the land will feed, the raiment clothe, and the houses shelter all the people; the powerful will be elated by the well being of all, rather than through their greed.

Then, those of us who have pursued that phantom of Jefferson, Jackson, Webster, Theodore Roosevelt and Bryan may hear wafted from their lips in Valhalla:

EVERY MAN A KING

Questions

1. What is Long proposing?
2. Who was most likely to support him? Why?
3. Is Long arguing for reform or revolution? In your answer consider the status of the rich under the Long Plan.

Questions for Further Thought

1. Compare FDR's inaugural address (Document 26-2) with Document 25-3, the *Forbes* magazine editorial "Snap Out Of It!" To what extent do they make the same argument? Why did one succeed where the other failed?

2. Using Documents 26-1 and 26-2, consider the importance of image and rhetoric for a political leader. Is popular success possible without them?

3. How does the Long Plan compare with the ideas of William Jennings Bryan (Document 19-7) and the Progressive party platform of 1912 (Document 21-9)? What makes an idea "radical"?

The New Deal's Impact on Society

The New Deal has had an enduring impact on American government and society by instituting a vast expansion of the federal bureaucracy and laying the groundwork for the modern welfare state. For the first time ordinary Americans felt the impact of federal decisions in their everyday lives. In addition, new groups were brought into the political community. Women played an important and unprecedented role in shaping the policies of the New Deal, and African-Americans found themselves the beneficiaries of government social welfare programs (see text pp. 807–811).

Some of Roosevelt's critics accused him of seeking to replace capitalism with socialism. Roosevelt always insisted that his goal was to preserve capitalism by saving it from its own excesses. He had no master plan to remake American society. Instead, he prided himself on his pragmatic willingness to experiment with a variety of policies, continuing those which worked and discarding those which failed. Many New Deal programs, such as the Civilian Conservation Corps and the Works Progress Administration, were abandoned as soon as the economic crisis eased. Others, such as the Social Security Act, the National Labor Relations Act, and federal regulation of the stock market, banking, and mortgage lending, have had a continuing impact on the American economy and society.

The labor movement, which had revived during Roosevelt's first term in office, threw its enthusiastic support to the president in his bid for reelection. (see text pp. 811–813); it appeared that labor had an ally in the White House in the person of Eleanor Roosevelt (Document 26-5). Within weeks of Roosevelt's landslide victory a wave of sit-down strikes broke out which resulted in the organization of unions in the nation's mass-production industries (Document 26-6). However, success did not come easily or without bloodshed (Document 26-7).

26-5   "The State's Responsibility for Fair Working Conditions" (1933)

Eleanor Roosevelt

Although the newspaper columnist Westbook Pegler dismissed Eleanor Roosevelt as "Empress Eleanor," the first lady did not mind criticism. She was a longtime social reformer (see text pp. 807, 810) who spoke her mind and argued for change, as she did in *Scribner's Magazine* in 1933.

Source: "The State's Responsibility for Fair Working Conditions" by Eleanor Roosevelt is reprinted with the permission of Scribner, a Division of Simon & Schuster, from *Scribner's Magazine*, March 1933, p. 140. Copyright 1933 by Charles Scribner's Sons; copyright renewed © 1961 by Charles Scribner's Sons. In Allida M. Black, ed., *What I Hope to Leave Behind: The Essential Essays of Eleanor Roosevelt* (Brooklyn, N.Y.: Carlson Publishing, 1995), pp. 57–58.

No matter how fair employers wish to be, there are always some who will take advantage of times such as these to lower unnecessarily the standards of labor, thereby subjecting him to unfair competition. It is necessary to stress the regulation by law of these unhealthy conditions in industry. It is quite obvious that one cannot depend upon the worker in such times as these to take care of things in the usual way. Many women, particularly, are not unionized and even unions have temporarily lowered their standards in order to keep their people at work. If you face starvation, it is better to accept almost anything than to feel that you and your children are going to be evicted from the last and the cheapest rooms which you have been able to find and that there will be no food.

Cut after cut has been accepted by workers in their wages, they have shared their work by accepting fewer days a week in order that others might be kept on a few days also, until many of them have fallen far below what I would consider the normal and proper standard for healthful living. If the future of our country is to be safe and the next generation is to grow up to healthy and good citizens, it is absolutely necessary to protect the health of our workers now and at all times.

It has been found, for instance, in Germany, in spite of the depression and the difficulty in making wages cover good food, that sickness and mortality rates have been surprisingly low amongst the workers, probably because of the fact that they have not been obliged to work an unhealthy number of hours.

Limiting the number of working hours by law has a twofold result. It spreads the employment, thereby giving more people work, and it protects the health of the workers. Instead of keeping a few people working a great many hours and even asking them to share their work with others by working fewer days, it limits all work to a reasonable number of hours and makes it necessary to employ the number of people required to cover the work.

Refusing to allow people to be paid less than a living wage preserves to us our own market. There is absolutely no use in producing anything if you gradually reduce the number of people able to buy even the cheapest products. The only way to preserve our markets is to pay an adequate wage.

It seems to me that all fair-minded people will realize that it is self-preservation to treat the industrial worker with consideration and fairness at the present time and to uphold the fair employer in his efforts to treat his employees well by preventing unfair competition.

Questions

1. What group is Eleanor Roosevelt attacking?
2. Who is she aligning herself with?
3. What kind of political fallout could such views have for her husband? Should that have been a consideration for her? Why or why not?

26-6 The Sit-Down Strike at General Motors (1937)

Mary Heaton Vorse

The Flint sit-down strike, which began on December 31, 1936, was one of the most dramatic and significant incidents in American labor history (see text pp. 811–813). Workers in Flint, Michigan, occupied the General Motors plant to support their demand for union recognition, defying court injunctions and police attacks. In the end their victory paved the way for the unionization of the entire automobile industry. The journalist Mary Heaton Vorse captured the mood in Flint the day the workers left the factories in victory on February 11, 1937, in her 1938 book *Labor's New Millions*.

Source: From Mary Heaton Vorse, *Labor's New Millions* (New York: Modern Age Books, 1938; reprint, New York: Ayer Company Publications, 1969), pp. 76–77, 88–90.

I went down to the Chevrolet plant with two members of the Emergency Brigade. The workers had now captured plant No. 4. The street was full of people—there were about twenty policemen between the bridge and the high gate of the plant. They were quiet and unprovocative, so the crowd of pickets was good-natured. The sound car was directing operations.

The use of the sound truck is new in strike procedure and it is hard to know how a strike was ever conducted without it. As we came down past the policemen a great voice, calm and benign, proclaimed that everything was in hand—the plant was under control.

Next the great disembodied voice, really the voice of auburn-haired young Roy Reuther, urged the men in the plant to barricade themselves from tear gas. Every now and then the voice boomed:

"Protection squad. Attention! Guard your sound car. Protection squad. Attention!"

Then the voice addressed the workers who crowded the windows of the lower levels. At the top of the steep flight of steps were the workers of the plant, lunch buckets under their arms, waving at the pickets in the street. A crowd of workers fringed the roof. The sound car inquired if they were union men. They shouted, "Yes." The crowd cheered.

The measured soothing voice of the sound car boomed:

"Word has come to us that there are men in the crowd anxious to join the union. Go to the last car, you will find the cards ready to sign. If you have no money for dues with you you can come to Pengally Hall later." The sound car struck up *Solidarity* and the men at the top of the steps, on top of the plant, in the street, all sang.

A woman's voice next—Genora Johnson. She told the crowd that the women had gone to the Hall to wipe their eyes clear of tear gas and would soon be back. "We don't want any violence; we don't want any trouble. We are going to do everything we can to keep from trouble, but we are going to protect our husbands."

Down the hill presently came a procession, preceded by an American flag. The women's bright red caps showed dramatically in the dark crowd. They were singing, *Hold the Fort.*

To all the crowd there was something moving about seeing the women return to the picket line after having been gassed in front of plant No. 9. A cheer went up; the crowd took up the song. The line of bright-capped women spread itself out in front of the high gate. Clasping hands, they struck up the song, *We Shall Not Be Moved.* Some of the men who had jumped over the gate went back, amid the cheers of the crowd.

I went to the top of the little hill and a file of men were coming out of the back of the building.

"Are you going home?"

"Home—Hell no! We're going back to picket the plant. Half of us are sitting down inside, and half of us are coming out to picket from the street."

"How many of you are for the sit-down?"

"Ninety per cent," a group of them chorused. . . .

What happened that day in Flint was something that no one who ever saw it could possibly forget. Never since Armistice Day has anything been seen comparable to its intensity. A mighty emotion shook the working people of that town. Joy and freedom dominated Flint's commonplace streets.

It was as if Flint had been under a spell for a long time, perhaps always. Fear and suspicion had walked through Flint's streets. People didn't dare to join unions. They'd get fired, they'd lose their jobs. Your next door neighbor might be a spy. No one knew who the stool pigeons were. The people who had got used to living that way didn't know how maimed they were.

General Motors had come into Flint and made a city out of a crossroads. General Motors had dominated the town. It had ruled its political life and it had set its face against unions. Men had organized on their peril. Unions were kept out by fear. And now that fear was over. No wonder that the people marching in the line stretched out their hands to their friends on the sidewalk and said:

"You can join now, you can join now, we are free!"

Freedom to join your own union seems a little thing. But one has to live in a town dominated by a great industry to see how far off a union can seem and how powerful the industry.

Now General Motors had bargained with the union officials. The long days of suspended violence were over. Here was the antithesis of a mob: the gathering together of people to express a great emotion. Such gathering together is at the very basis of civilization. It is the intensification of the individual, the raising of his power for good to a thousandth degree.

No one in that crowd remained isolated. People's small personalities were lost in this great Halleluiah.

When the men from Fisher No. 1 had accepted the agreement they marched in a parade to the plants at the other end of the town which were still guarded by the militia. The barrier of soldiers drew aside.

The crowd with flags marched cheering into the guarded zone.

The strikers were coming out of Chevrolet No. 4, flags preceding them. There were flags on the steps and flags on the street. Flares lighted up the scene. Cheers for Governor Murphy filled the air. Strikers' wives were waving to husbands they had not seen for days. A woman held up a baby. The procession marched down the street. Another roar filled all space.

The Fisher No. 2 boys marched out. They marched out in military formation from the quiet of the empty, waiting plant, carrying neat bundles of their things. They became part of the crowd that was now bright with confetti. People carried toy balloons. The whole scene was lit up by the burst of glory of the photographers' flares. The big flags punctuated the crowd with color.

They shouted to the rhythm of "Freedom, Freedom, Freedom!"

Chevrolet Avenue was packed from bridge to bridge. People swarmed over the murky little Flint River with its new barbed wire fences. They came past Chevrolet No. 4 and they came up the street past Fisher No. 2. They came, flags at their head, singing. They marched from the plants back to union headquarters. The streets were lined all the way with cheering people. Men and women from the cars and marchers shouted to the groups of other working people who lined the streets, "Join the union! We are free!"

The marchers arrived in front of Pengally Hall. They gathered in increasing thousands. The hall itself was jammed. They no longer let people into the building. Inside and outside, the loud speakers were going. Homer Martin, Wyndham Mortimer, Bob Travis and the other strike leaders addressed the roaring crowds.

The joy of victory tore through Flint. It was more than the joy of war ceasing, it was the joy of creation. The workers were creating a new life. The wind of Freedom had roared down Flint's streets. The strike had ended! The working people of Flint had begun to forge a new life out of their historic victory.

Questions

1. According to Vorse, why had Flint's workers remained nonunionized for so many years?
2. Which tactics brought victory to the union?
3. Why does Vorse compare the emotions of the workers after winning the strike to those on Armistice Day (the day which ended World War I)?

26-7 Memorial Day Massacre (1937)

Despite support from Washington, organized labor in the 1930s faced a good deal of hostility, some of it violent (see text pp. 811–813). One incident of armed conflict occurred in Chicago on Memorial Day in 1937. The police fired on a strike rally outside a Republic Steel plant, and ten people were left dead (see text p. 812). This newspaper account affords little sympathy to the victims.

Source: "Riots Blamed on Red Chiefs: Coroner Moves Today to Seize Mob's Leaders," and "Chicagoans Led in Steel Strike by Outsiders: Union Organizers Come from Far Points," *Chicago Daily Tribune*, June 1, 1937. © copyrighted Chicago Tribune Company. All rights reserved. Used with permission.

RIOTS BLAMED ON RED CHIEFS

CORONER MOVES TODAY TO SEIZE MOB'S LEADERS

Impasse Reached in Horner Parley.

Blaming communist agitators in the Committee for Industrial Organization ranks for the Memorial day bloodshed at the Republic Steel corporation plant in South Chicago, Coroner Frank J. Walsh took personal charge of the investigation last night.

The coroner said he is determined to fix the blame for the mob attack on the police who were guarding the company's property rights—an attack which precipitated a riot whose death toll rose yesterday to five.

First Step Toward Punishment.

He will begin that task when the inquest into the deaths opens at 1 p.m. today in the county morgue. The coroner's action is regarded as the first step toward punishment of those who incited the strikers to assail the police with firearms, clubs, and brick-bats in an attempted invasion of the plant.

Coroner Walsh said he had been given definite information that communists inspired the mob.

At the same time communists in John L. Lewis' C. I. O. were flatly charged with responsibility by James L. Mooney, supervising captain, who was in command of the police when the mob attacked.

Capt. Mooney Accuses Reds.

Capt. Mooney said he has been given information that known communists fomented the attack, in which ninety persons other than those killed suffered gunshot wounds and other injuries that sent them to hospitals. Twenty-six of the injured were policemen.

Capt. Mooney said he would present his information to State's Attorney Courtney. This was believed to assure grand jury action leading to punishment of the mob leaders—the same objective as that of Coroner Walsh.

Cites Handbills as Evidence.

The police captain cited inflammatory handbills issued by the Illinois state committee of the communist party as evidence of the communist activities in the riot. These circulars, upholding the rioters, were issued early yesterday, a few hours after the riot.

"The speed with which the handbills were issued, and the accusations they contained," Capt. Mooney said, "show definitely that the communists knew in advance that the workers were going to be led into attacking the police, and that they encouraged the attack."

No Progress at Parley.

A peace conference called by Gov. Horner reached an impasse in the Congress hotel last night when the conferees decided no further progress could be made until an interpretation of certain puzzling provisions of the Wagner labor relations act could be obtained by Robert Pilkington, federal labor conciliator.

When the five hour conference closed just before midnight the governor said another would be held as soon as Pilkington received the required information.

Among those at the meeting were James L. Hyland, western manager of the Republic corporation; Van A. Bittner, regional director of the S. W. O. C; Martin Durkin, director of the state department of labor; Warren Canaday, assistant United States attorney, and Pilkington.

Bittner to Continue Fight.

After taking leave of the governor Bittner spoke emphatically of the conference.

"Progress made here tonight is not worth a thin dime to anybody," he said. "The company has said that even though a majority vote is taken under the labor relations act it will not sign contracts with the men. The strike will go on until the vote is taken and until the company signs. We will increase picketing at once."

The strike was called by the Steel Workers' Organizing committee of Lewis' C. I. O. against the Republic, Inland, and Youngstown Sheet and Tube companies to win collective bargaining contracts.

Official action did not end with that of Gov. Horner, Coroner Walsh, and Capt. Mooney.

Capt. Thomas Kilroy of the East Chicago police, another commanding officer at the time the mob attacked the bluecoats, announced that sixty seven persons now in custody will be formally charged this morning with conspiracy to commit an illegal act.

This constitutes a felony, Capt. Kilroy said, and is punishable by a maximum penalty of five years in prison and a $2,000 fine.

Thirty four of those against whom the charge is to be leveled are under guard in hospitals, where they are being treated for wounds and injuries suffered in the riot. The others have been removed from hospitals to lockups.

Eight young men and eight girls, who said they are students at the University of Chicago, eluded police guards and joined the ranks of the picketers at the South Chicago plant last night. They carried banners condemning the police for protecting themselves against gunfire, brickbats, and clubs of the mob. One banner said University of Chicago students are protesting the police action. The spokesman for the professed students said he was Paul Bradley, 20 years old, of New York City.

The Fifth Victim.

At the time the strike began last Wednesday, police agreed to permit the strikers to maintain eight pickets. The arrival of the professed students tripled the number authorized, but no action was taken to halt the picketers.

The fifth victim of the riot was Joseph Rothmund, 47 years old, of 2857 Belmont avenue, a Works Progress administration employee, who had been shot. Rothmund died in the Bridewell hospital.

Two of the previously unidentified dead were identified yesterday.

One was Alfred Causey, 43 years old, 7050 Arizona avenue, a Republic carpenter. He was the father of three children. His widow, Gladys, identified him. She said he recently came here after losing a job with another steel company because of labor activities.

The other was Kenneth Reed, 23 years old, 3921 Deal street, Indiana Harbor, the father of two children. He was an Inland Steel company electrician.

A relative tentatively identified another victim as Sam Popovich, address unknown.

Two men were reported in a critical condition in the South Chicago hospital. They were Hilding Anderson, 38 years old, 9804 Avenue D; and Anthony Tagliere, 26, of 615 East 74th street.

Plant Still Working.

The Republic plant, at 115th street and Burley avenue, is still turning out steel despite the strike, which has closed other mills in the Calumet-South Chicago area. It is estimated 22,000 of the 70,000 steel strikers in five states are in this area. Some 1,400 loyal employe[e]s are still working in the Republic's plant.

Some 5,000 strikers and sympathizers met yesterday in Washington park, Indiana Harbor, East Chicago. Speakers were Bittner and Nicholas Fontecchio, who was one of the speakers at the meeting which preceded the riot.

CHICAGOANS LED IN STEEL STRIKE BY OUTSIDERS

Union Organizers Come from Far Points.

Leaders of the steel strike in the Chicago district, whose rabid oratory inflamed the strike mob to fighting pitch before the battle with police at the Republic Steel company plant Sunday, neither live in this area nor are they steel workers.

All are veterans in union organization work. Most of them come from the United Mine Workers of America, which produced John L. Lewis, whose Committee for Industrial Organization is sponsoring the steel strike. All local strike executives are close associates of the beetle-browed Lewis, the labor dictator, who once fought communists in the U. M. W. of A., but now welcomes them with open arms to the C. I. O.

Van A. Bittner is the high mogul of the Steel Workers' Organizing committee in the Great Lakes region. He takes his orders from Philip Murray, the national S. W. O. C. head, and from Lewis. When Lewis speaks, Bittner acts in the territory from Buffalo to the Pacific coast.

Bittner is president of one of the two West Virginia districts of the U. M. W. of A., is a member of the U. M. W. of A. policy committee and sits in on the Appalachian district wage conferences.

Krzycki Is Socialist.

It was after Leo Krzycki's rabble rousing speech that the strike mob marched on the Republic plant Sunday.

He is an old time Socialist from Milwaukee, where he was an under-sherif, former alderman, and unsuccessful candidate for senator.

Born in Poland, Krzycki now is a member of the C. I. O. advisory board, a member of the national executive committee of the Socialist party, and is second in command to Bittner in the western territory of the S. W. O. C.

He called for a world uprising of workers after the bloody civil war in Austria a few years ago. In 1919 he first used his rabble rousing technique to inflame workers in the American Steel and Wire company strike at Waukegan.

Nicholas Fontecchio is the chief commissar for the S. W. O. C. in the Calumet industrial district. He has been an international representative of the U. M. W. of A. for thirty-five years and in 1924 and 1925 led the West Virginia miners in their strike.

Fontecchio and Krzycki were active in the abortive attempt to organize the Fansteel Metallurgical corporation in North Chicago last March.

Two Others from East.

Leo Wisniewski and John Riffe are Fontecchio's assistants. The former, a district representative of the U. M. W. of A. for fourteen years, lives in Fairmont, W. Va., but runs the Gary district for the S. W. O. C. Riffe, a West Virginia officer of the U. M. W. of A., with which he has been connected for ten years, rules the South Chicago district of the S. W. O. C. and lives now at 9233 Huston avenue.

Although not active in the Republic district steel strike, Meyer Adelman became a prominent figure [he weighs 300 pounds] in the Fansteel strike. For his flagrant law flouting activities there he was arrested by Lake county officials. The charges are still pending.

Questions

1. What biases do the stories contain?
2. What does the article imply about the strikers' political affiliation?

3. Under the First Amendment, does the press have the right to print such a distorted account? Why or why not?

Questions for Further Thought

1. Why were employers so strongly opposed to organized labor while so many Americans were sympathetic?
2. Did Eleanor Roosevelt (Document 26-5) help or hurt labor's cause? How?
3. Why did workers risk so much when jobs were scarce whereas they had been passive in the more prosperous 1920s?

Culture and Commitment

In the 1930s American artists and writers abandoned the stance of personal alienation that had characterized intellectual life in the 1920s. The New Deal encouraged Americans to embrace the ideal of "commitment" to solve the nation's problems. Government agencies, most notably the Works Progress Administration, hired writers and artists to research and celebrate America's democratic past (see text pp. 819–823).

Some intellectuals, believing that capitalism was doomed, looked for alternatives on the left. In the early 1930s, some became socialists and others became communists. Many did not join any of the radical parties, but increasingly allied themselves with the communists as "fellow travelers." The 1930s would be the period of communism's greatest appeal in American history (see text pp. 822–823). The Communist party won credibility among intellectuals as a militant advocate for trade unionism and equal rights for blacks and, particularly after 1935, an outspoken opponent of fascism.

The communists were by no means alone in chronicling the struggles of everyday America; the government did an exceptional job of this through agencies such as the Federal Writers' Project and the Farm Security Administration (Documents 26-8 and 26-9). At the same time intellectuals such as Alfred Kazin (Document 26-10) believed that the same struggle—though more starkly drawn—was occurring throughout the world.

26-8   The Federal Writers' Project: Barre, Vermont

New Deal agencies attempted to generate employment in virtually every field from masonry to acting. Some of the most interesting activity involved the Federal Writers' Project (see text p. 820), which collected folklore and oral histories, among its other assignments.

A team of FWP writers spent over a year in Barre, Vermont, interviewing people who made a living from granite.

Source: "Alfred Tornazzi" (interview conducted by Mari Tomasi) and "Anthony Tonelli" (interview conducted by John Lynch), in Ann Banks, ed., *First-Person America* (New York: Knopf, 1980), pp. 101–102, 104–105.

Alfred Tornazzi

Shed-owner Alfred Tornazzi studied sculpture for eight years at the Reale Accademia di Belle Arti di Brera *before coming to the United States. Tornazzi carved the monument he described as his masterpiece around the turn of the century. A statue of a little girl wearing a dress trimmed with delicate eyelet lace, it still stands in a Montpelier cemetery.*

I didn't start operating a shed of my own right away, although I could have. I wanted to learn more of this country, the way the sheds did business. I did carving for a shed in Barre the first year. The second year I went out to our western granite states. I found you could do better, more delicate work with the hard Barre stone, and I learned that it rated high in eastern markets and was quickly becoming known further west, so I decided to settle in or near Barre.

My brother, who had come to this country two years before I did, suggested that we start a shed of our own. It went under the name of Tornazzi Brothers. We've had our ups and downs, but we've made money and we've put out plenty of memorials that we're proud of.

My favorite memorial and what I believe is my masterpiece is one of my very early statues. It's called *The Little Margaret*. It stands in the Green Mount Cemetery in Montpelier. There's a story to that, too. I won't tell the cus-tomer's name, although you can easily find out by going to the cemetery and looking at the memorial. This customer wanted me to carve a statue of his little daughter who was dead. I'd never seen the girl. Her family produced a full-length picture of her and asked me to make the statue identical in clothing, posture, et cetera. I said it would be difficult since the picture was a poor one, and faint, but I'd do my best. I completed it, and was justly proud of it. The parents liked it, too. I remember the mother cried and said it looked real. But in spite of their satisfaction, they hated to pay the price agreed upon. I admit it was a steep price, but it was good work, and hard, and they could afford it. Well, the father came to me one day. He pointed to the picture and said, "Look, you promised to make the statue exactly like this picture. You didn't. On the memorial there's a button missing on one shoe. Since they aren't identical you should lower the price." It made me mad. I'd been very careful in carving those shoes; they were those old-fashioned, high-buttoned shoes the girls wore at that time, and since the picture was so dim I'd been careful to make sure of each detail. "They *are* identical," I assured him, and proceeded to prove it. A magnifying glass held over the picture showed that sure enough one button was missing on the shoe. Well, the short of it is the man stopped quibbling and paid the price I'd asked.

Mari Tomasi [conducted interview]

Anthony Tonelli

Anthony Tonelli learned the trade of stonecutting in Viggiu, Italy. Silicosis was not an occupational hazard there because the stonecutters worked on marble—softer than granite—in open-air sheds. Tonelli expected to send all his children to college. "At least that will take them away from the sheds," he said, "and after they get out of college they won't want to work with granite. I have planned that."

The life of a stonecutter is fifty years. No more. Every one of them, they all die in their fifties, they are through before that. I am near fifty. I die soon. I expect it. You got to expect it when you work with granite. You can get up any morning and go to work and say to yourself, "I am going to die very soon"; when you see your kids, you can say, "Yes, I am going to leave them soon." And other people are saying, "I am going to retire because I am in my fifties and I want to enjoy life a little," but you say, "I can not retire. I am in the granite business and it will retire me." But I hate like hell to leave my family when I am fifty. Just beginning to live. No children of mine will ever go into the granite sheds. Too much dust. I want them to have fresh air, and good jobs. I don't care what they do, so long as they keep away from the dust of granite.

I have seen big, strong, healthy men come to work. They have laughing eyes, they show they love life, they enjoy themselves. They are good workers. They have strength and knowledge of the job. Skill. And they don't last long. And this keeps up for many years. People grumble. The grumble increases. People lose their heads. I see children with tears in their eyes as they follow the casket to the grave. The big strong men do not last long against stone dust. They die and people cry and the family starves for a while, but all the time I keep saying, "The problem will be solved, this dust will end in the sheds," and they say, "You are a fool, dust will stay here forever, you can't end dust." I laugh now. It is coming to an end but nobody says to me, "You are smart, you tell us years ago that dust problem, this silicosis will be over with." No, I am not smart. I think a lot. I see improvements in every line.

I say the scientists are brilliant. They study when we are not thinking of them. They solve disease when it has killed millions, and they make autos and they get better every year. Look at the children. They get better care. Doctors know more. Why wouldn't they end this big problem of ours? It has caused a lot of suffering. Everybody in the granite business has been sad because of dust, deaths in all families, but now it is near the end. You will see men work longer in the sheds. They will not grow old so fast.

I have gone to work in the morning and after a little while in the shed I couldn't recognize my own body. It was covered from head to foot with dust. Of course we have to breathe that dust in. That is what does it. We give our whole strength, our hearing, our hands, our sight, the eyes, everything we possess to the business. We give our lives, our family, we give everything we have and love, and then what do we get out of it? Just a little money. Granite cutters have always been underpaid. You can't get around it. You go in there and die young. Do you see any of them rich?

You want to know what I do? I am a letterer. I have responsibility. If I cut one little piece from a stone, just when it is nearing completion, that spoils the whole works. It is all destroyed. And I get the gate. I can't take any chances getting drunk with all that at stake. It takes everything I got, everything. After a day in the sheds I am no good for anything, or for anybody. I guess most men wouldn't like it. You got to be strong. How many men can stand it? By the time you become good at your trade, you are ready to die.

John Lynch [conducted interview]

Questions

1. What is the work of stonecutters like?
2. What is the greatest danger?
3. Why do people do this kind of work?

26-9 "A Miner's Home: Vicinity Morgantown, West Virginia, July 1935"

Walker Evans

The photographer Walker Evans had the ability to take a simple subject and make it profound. Evans (1903–1975) worked periodically for the Farm Security Administration from 1935 to 1938 (see text p. 822). His assignment was to record poverty in America.

Source: Farm Security Administration Collection, Library of Congress. In *Walker Evans: Photographs for the Farm Security Administration, 1935–1938* (New York: Da Capo Press, 1973), p. 127.

Questions

1. Describe the scene. Does the boy appear happy?
2. What might be the purpose of the cardboard advertising on the wall?
3. What is the overall effect of the photograph?

26-10 "Starting Out in the Thirties"

Alfred Kazin

Alfred Kazin grew up in New York City during the depression. He supported himself through a variety of literary odd jobs, including working for *The New Republic*. The excerpt that follows, from Kazin's memoir *Starting Out in the Thirties* (1965), suggests how radical political idealism gave way to disillusionment among many intellectuals at the end of the decade (see text pp. 822–823).

Source: Excerpted by permission of the author from Alfred Kazin, *Starting Out in the Thirties* (Boston: Little, Brown, 1965), pp. 82–87, 138–139.

[1936]

History was going our way, and in our need was the very lifeblood of history. Everything in the outside world seemed to be moving toward some final decision, for by now the Spanish Civil War had begun, and every day felt choked with struggle. It was as if the planet had locked in combat. In the same way the unrest and unemployment, the political struggles inside the New Deal, suddenly became part of the single pattern of struggle in Europe against Franco and his allies Hitler and Mussolini, so I sensed that I could become a writer without giving up my people. The unmistakable and surging march of history might yet pass through me. There seemed to be no division between my effort at personal liberation and the apparent effort of humanity to deliver itself. Reading [Italian Communist novelist Ignazio] Silone and [French novelist André] Malraux, discovering the Beethoven string quartets and having love affairs were part of the great pattern in Spain, in Nazi concentration camps, in Fontamars and in the Valley of the Ebro, in the Salinas Valley of California that Steinbeck was describing with love for the oppressed, in the boilers of Chinese locomotives where Chiang Kai-shek was burning the brave and sacrificial militants of the Chinese Communists. Wherever I went now, I felt the moral contagion of a single idea. . . .

More than twenty years later, I was to hear young intellectuals in Moscow laugh at the show trials of the Thirties, and in their proud American English dismiss them as "phonies." The Moscow airfield was lined with gleaming white jets, and the young intellectuals born in 1936 now know all about Stalin. But in 1936 the issue was not quite so simple even for those who knew that the trials were *wrong*. The danger was Hitler, Mussolini, Franco. And because the Fascist assault on Spain and the ever-growing strength of Hitler had made the United Front necessary, I found myself more sympathetic to the Communists. They had, they had just had, they still seemed to have, Silone, Malraux, Hemingway, Gide, [Romain] Rolland, Gorky, [Louis] Aragon, Picasso, [Paul] Eluard, Auden, Spender, Barbusse, Dreiser, [James T.] Farrell, while the Socialists seemed to have only their own virtue. I was tired of virtue, and now wanted to see some action. In the midst of the vi-

olent labor unrest in France, the great sitdown strikes in American factories, the beginnings of the CIO, everything at home and abroad seemed to call for the same revolutionary energy. On Inaugural Day 1937, I went down to Washington to do an article on the great day, and though that morning of rain the flags flapped wetly against the posts and the streets seemed strangely empty, there, in the back of the car as it came out of the White House drive, was the fixedly smiling face that presided over our generation, and standing in the rain we cheered our President and all our own hopes. Like all my friends, I distrusted Roosevelt as a wily politician and a professional charmer. Who was he behind that ever-smiling public face, and what reason did *he* have to care? But I could almost believe in him now, there was so much need of him to do the right thing. FDR's historical function was destined; everybody's was. Not even the hack jobs I did for a living now seemed unworthy, for the issue raised in a book review, a street scene studied for an article, always fitted into my sense of the destiny and inclusiveness of history. So my parents' poverty had a mystique for me, and our loneliness a definite heroism—we were usually unhappy and always on each other's necks, but I saw us all moving forward on the sweep of great events. I believed that everyone was engulfed in politics, absorbed in issues that were the noble part of themselves. Despite the daily anxiety of trying to get a push up the inhumanly smooth wall of other people's jobs, I felt, with the outbreak of the Spanish Civil War, that the outrage of Franco, Mussolini and Hitler working together was a challenge, not a defeat; I trusted to the righteousness of history. Just as I was trying to break through, so history was seeking its appointed consummation. My interest and the genius of history simply had to coincide. It did not matter how deceitful and murderous Stalin was showing himself to be in the purges; the Soviet Union, a "workers' state" stained only with the unaccountable sins of its leadership, still represented the irreversible movement of human progress. Even Hitler, by his total infamy, obviously represented a *deliberate* attempt to put the clock back; believing that the Jews, and especially Jewish intellectuals, had a mission to humanity, I never wondered why Jewish intellectuals particularly were hated by the Nazis.

We were a moral ferment; easy to kill off, but an unsettling influence. Hitler destroyed German democracy, Dollfuss the Austrian Socialists, Franco was destroying the Spanish Republic and Mussolini thousands of Ethiopians: the daily onrush of events fitted so easily into a general pattern of meaning, seemingly supplied by the age itself, that every day was like a smoothly rushing movie of the time—and I loved newsreels, the documentary novels of Dos Passos with their own newsreels, documentary movies, especially now that in tribute to the emergency of the times there were movie houses in Times Square that showed nothing but newsreels. I was as excited by history as if it were a newsreel, and I saw history in every newsreel, my love and hated of the historical actors rising to the music on the sound track like a swimmer to the surf. . . .

[1938, 1939]

I could not believe that Fascism was anything but a temporary aberration; given a fair chance, the people under Nazi rule and Fascist rule would get rid of their oppressors and give themselves to the historical destiny so clearly forseen by liberals and socialists in the nineteenth century. When a classmate of mine just back from the front told me of the massacre by the GPU in Barcelona of Anarchists and anti-Stalinist Communists, I was reluctant to believe him. Although, after years of writing for Cowley at the *New Republic*, I liked him as little as ever and resented his protective benevolence toward "proletarian" literature, which I despised, I shared his feeling that Fascism was the main enemy and I feared any division on the left that might limit maximum resistance to Franco and Hitler. As an influence in literature, the Communists seemed to me idiotic; even Party members now made a point of laughing at the obtuseness of the professional Communist critics. My teaching in the evening session at City College became wearisome as the faithful in my classes resisted every example of free thought, of literary originality. In giving a course on modern fiction, I found to my disgust that half the class refused to read anything by H. G. Wells—he was a "bourgeois liberal." The arrogant stupidity of Communist instructors at this time passed beyond anything I had ever known before. The college *Führer* of the Party was an English instructor with a bad stammer, large spectacles, and a little beard; his middle name was Ulysses, and as he horribly choked out each word in a pronunciamento on the relation of *The Canterbury Tales* to the wool trade in fourteenth-century England, his bearded chin would quiver with agony and his weak frightened eyes would stare up at you while obstinately he ground out the literary law. And one day, when I was offered an editor's job in Washington with the WPA Writers' Project, I went down for my interview in the New York office, somewhere along the waterfront, to enter a room crowded with men and women lying face down on the floor, screaming that they were on strike. In order to get to the supervisor's office at the other end of the hall, I had to make my way over bodies stacked as if after a battle; and as I sat in the supervisor's office, he calmly discussed the job while shouts and screams came from the long hall outside. I made my way out again between and over the bodies.

It was the summer of 1939 now. After Hitler's seizure of Czechoslovakia in March, it still seemed to me inconceivable that Russia would not come out against Hitler, and in August, when English and French military missions arrived in Moscow, I took it for granted that some agreement would be made, since of course the Soviet Union wanted peace. On the morning of August 22, I was working happily away at my book and had interrupted myself at noon for a cup of coffee and the news broadcast when it was announced that Ribbentrop was flying to Moscow to sign a non-aggression pact with Stalin the next day, and that the Swastika was already flying over Moscow airport. "No!" I shouted at the radio. "It's not true!" The announcer calmly went on giving the details. . . .

Questions

1. What does Kazin mean when he writes about the "moral contagion of a single idea"?
2. Why does Kazin "love" the newsreels of the 1930s?
3. Why was the Nazi-Soviet pact of August 1939 so shocking to Kazin?

Questions for Further Thought

1. Why would artists be interested in people such as those in Barre (Document 26-8) and Morgantown (Document 26-9)? Could ordinary people be expected to reciprocate that interest? Why or why not?

2. The New Deal was a political coalition. How could it appeal to a diverse group that included artists, intellectuals, and coal miners? What problems were inevitable?
3. What kind of gulf existed between working people and sympathetic intellectuals such as Alfred Kazin (Document 26-10)? Could anything have bridged it?

CHAPTER 27

The World at War 1939–1945

★　　　　★　　　　★

The Road to War

The origins of World War II lay in the aftermath of the Great War of 1914–1918. As Adolf Hitler and the Nazis rose to power in the 1920s, they played on German resentment of the Treaty of Versailles and the harsh terms of a "conquerors' peace." In his speeches and writings, especially in *Mein Kampf* (1923), Hitler served up heavy doses of fanatical nationalism and anti-Semitism (see text p. 829). He reminded Germans of their loss of territory, their forced disarmament, the heavy reparations assessed by the victors, and the war guilt clause that placed full blame for the war on Germany. When he finally attained power as chancellor, Hitler was ready to move quickly to rebuild Germany in accordance with his own plan.

Between January 1933 and August 1939 Hitler took carefully measured steps to revive German power, setting the stage for another world war. In violation of the Treaty of Versailles and in a direct challenge to the League of Nations, Hitler rearmed Germany and remilitarized the Rhineland. He designed the Axis to link Germany, Italy, and Japan in a tripartite alliance. He engineered the forced union of Austria with Germany in March 1938, took the Sudetenland from Czechoslovakia in the fall of 1938, and seized the rest of the Czech state early in 1939. On September 1, 1939, Hitler launched a *Blitzkrieg* against Poland and began World War II in Europe. With Japan and China already at war in Asia since a Japanese attack on China in 1937 (see text p. 829), the new war had truly global proportions.

Despite the internationalist preferences of President Franklin D. Roosevelt, the United States stayed away from the troubles in Europe and Asia and concentrated on the economic crisis at home (see text p. 830). The American people did not want to repeat what they regarded as the mistakes of 1914–1917 that had drawn their country into the Great War. They wanted to stay isolated—*neutral* was the popular word of the time—and set those sentiments into legislation in the Neutrality Acts of 1935, 1936, and 1937. Among several provisions, those laws prohibited arms shipments and loans to belligerents. The third Neutrality Act (Document 27-1) extended the restrictions to nations experiencing civil wars. Despite an occasional attempt to challenge the isolationist bent of the people, notably in the quarantine speech of October 1937 (Document 27-2), the president fell into line with the isolationists.

After the onset of war in Europe, Congress modified the Neutrality Act of 1937 to allow for the purchase of arms on a "cash and carry" basis; war supplies could not be bought on credit or be transported on American ships. Through 1940 President Roosevelt stepped up aid to Great Britain (see text p. 831), but the British needed more if they were to keep Hitler away from their home islands. In late December 1940, after his election to a third term as president, Roosevelt told the American people in one of his "fireside chats" that the United States had to become "the great arsenal of democracy" (Document 27-3). This led to a Lend-Lease program that would pour billions of dollars in military aid into countries at war with the Axis (see text pp. 831–832). Isolationists opposed these aid programs, and the president just as avidly defended them, for example, in his "Four Freedoms" speech (Document 27-4). In August 1941 President Roosevelt and the British prime minister, Winston Churchill, announced the signing of the Atlantic Charter (Document 27-5), which outlined common Anglo-American interests and potential war aims (see text p. 832). As the United States expanded its efforts to aid Great Britain through 1941, neutrality evolved into nonbelligerency. Critics continued to rail against the president until December 7, 1941, when a Japanese sneak attack on Pearl Harbor (see text pp. 832–833) silenced the isolationists and plunged the United States into war (Document 27-6).

27-1   The Neutrality Act of 1937

Many Americans were deeply disappointed by the outcome of U.S. participation in World War I, the persistence of traditional power politics in Europe, and the intensification of military and diplomatic conflict in Asia. Many were outraged at the evidence, publicized by the hearings of the Nye Committee on Munitions Manufactures, that weapons makers had earned large profits from that war. In the face of the rise of fascism in Europe, Congress moved quickly to keep the United States out of any new international conflict by passing a Neutrality Act. It responded to the increasing conflicts of the next two years by passing increasingly stringent Neutrality Acts in 1935, 1936, and 1937 (see text p. 838).

Source: United States, *Statutes at Large*, vol. 50, p. 121.

EXPORT OF ARMS, AMMUNITION, AND
IMPLEMENTS OF WAR

SECTION 1. (a) Whenever the President shall find that there exists a state of war between, or among, two or more foreign states, the President shall proclaim such fact, and it shall thereafter be unlawful to export, or attempt to export, or cause to be exported, arms, ammunition, or implements of war from any place in the United States to any belligerent state named in such proclamation, or to any neutral state for transshipment to, or for the use of, any such belligerent state.

(b) The President shall, from time to time, by proclamation, extend such embargo upon the export of arms, ammunition, or implements of war to other states as and when they may become involved in such war.

(c) Whenever the President shall find that a state of civil strife exists in a foreign state and that such civil strife is of a magnitude or is being conducted under such conditions that the export of arms, ammunition, or implements of war from the United States to such foreign state would threaten or endanger the peace of the United States, the President shall proclaim such fact, and it shall thereafter be unlawful to export, or attempt to export, or cause to be exported, arms, ammunition, or implements of war from any place in the United States to such foreign state, or to any neutral state for transshipment to, or for the use of, such foreign state.

(d) The President shall, from time to time by proclamation definitely enumerate the arms, ammunition, and implements of war, the export of which is prohibited by this section.

EXPORT OF OTHER ARTICLES AND MATERIALS

SEC. 2. (a) Whenever the President shall have issued a proclamation under the authority of section 1 of this Act and he shall thereafter find that the placing of restrictions on the shipment of certain articles or materials in addition to arms, ammunition, and implements of war from the United States to belligerent states, or to a state wherein civil strife exists, is necessary to promote the security or preserve the peace of the United States or to protect the lives of citizens of the United States, he shall so proclaim, and it shall thereafter be unlawful, for any American vessel to carry such articles or materials to any belligerent state, or to any state wherein civil strife exists, named in such proclamation issued under the authority of section 1 of this Act, or to any neutral state for transshipment to, or for the use of, any such belligerent state or any such state wherein civil strife exists, named in such proclamation issued under the authority of section 1 of this Act, or to any neutral state for transshipment to, or for the use of, any such belligerent state or any such state wherein civil strife exists. The President shall ... definitely enumerate the articles and materials which it shall be unlawful for American vessels to so transport. . . .

FINANCIAL TRANSACTIONS

SEC. 3. (a) Whenever the President shall have issued a proclamation under the authority of section 1 of this Act, it shall thereafter be unlawful for any person within the United States to purchase, sell, or exchange bonds, securities, or other obligations of the government of any belligerent state or of any state wherein civil strife exists, named in such proclamation, or of any political subdivision of any such state, or of any person acting for or on behalf of the government of any such state, or of any faction or asserted government within any such state wherein civil strife exists, or of any person acting for or on behalf of any faction or asserted government within any such state wherein civil strife exists, issued after the date of such proclamation, or to make any loan or extend any credit to any such government, political subdivision, faction, asserted government, or person: *Provided*, That if the President shall find that such action will serve to protect the commercial or other interests of the United States or its citizens, he may, in his discretion, and to such extent and under such regulations

as he may prescribe, except from the operation of his section ordinary commercial credits and short-time obligations in aid of legal transactions and of a character customarily used in normal peacetime commercial transactions. Nothing in this subsection shall be construed to prohibit the solicitation or collection of funds to be used for medical aid and assistance, or for food and clothing to relieve human suffering, when such solicitation or collection of funds is made on behalf of any such government, political subdivision, faction, or asserted government, but all such solicitations and collections of funds shall be subject to the approval of the President and shall be made under such rules and regulations as he shall prescribe. . . .

(c). Whoever shall violate the provisions of this section or of any regulations issued hereunder shall, upon conviction thereof, be fined not more than $50,000 or imprisoned for not more than five years, or both. . . .

EXCEPTIONS—AMERICAN REPUBLICS

SEC. 4. This Act shall not apply to an American republic or republics engaged in war against a non-American state or states, provided the American republic is not cooperating with a non-American state or states in such war.

USE OF AMERICAN PORTS AS BASE OF SUPPLY

SEC. 7. (a) Whenever, during any war in which the United States is neutral, the President, or any person thereunto authorized by him, shall have cause to believe that any vessel, domestic or foreign, whether requiring clearance or not, is about to carry out of a port of the United States, fuel, men, arms, ammunition, implements of war, or other supplies to any warship, tender, or supply ship of a belligerent state, but the evidence is not deemed sufficient to justify forbidding the departure of the vessel as provided for by section 1, title V, chapter 30, of the Act approved June 15, 1917, and if in the President's judgment, such action will serve to maintain peace between the United States and foreign states, or to protect the commercial interests of the United States and its citizens, or to promote the security or neutrality of the United States, he shall have the power and it shall be his duty to require the owner, master, or person in command thereof, before departing from a port of the United States, to give a bond to the United States, with sufficient sureties, in such amount as he shall deem proper, conditioned that the vessel will not deliver the men, or any part of the cargo, to any warship, tender, or supply ship of a belligerent state.

(b) If the President, or any person thereunto authorized by him, shall find that a vessel, domestic or foreign, in a port of the United States, has previously cleared from a port of the United States during such war and delivered its cargo or any part thereof to a warship, tender, or supply ship of a belligerent state, he may prohibit the departure of such vessel during the duration of the war.

TRAVEL ON VESSELS OF BELLIGERENT STATES

SEC. 9. Whenever the President shall have issued a proclamation under the authority of section 1 of this Act it shall thereafter be unlawful for any citizen of the United States to travel on any vessel of the state or states named in such proclamation, except in accordance with such rules and regulations as the President shall prescribe: . . .

ARMING OF AMERICAN MERCHANT VESSELS PROHIBITED

SEC. 10. Whenever the President shall have issued a proclamation under the authority of section 1, it shall

thereafter be unlawful, until such proclamation is revoked, for any American vessel engaged in commerce with any belligerent state, or any state wherein civil strife exists, named in such proclamation, to be armed or to carry any armament, arms, ammunition, or implements of war, except small arms and ammunition therefor [for the vessel] which the President may deem necessary.

Questions

1. How was this act designed to keep the United States out of international conflicts?
2. Does this act distinguish in any way between aggressors and victims? Why or why not?
3. Does this act identify any U.S. interests in international affairs? If any, what are they?

27-2   The Quarantine Speech (1937)

Franklin D. Roosevelt

In the summer of 1937 Japan launched an attack against China (see text p. 829) that marked the onset of a second world war in Asia. President Roosevelt feared the long-range consequences of international aggression but knew that the American people and Congress preferred isolationism to involvement. On October 7, 1937, in a speech dedicating a bridge across the Chicago River, Roosevelt decided to test public opinion and determine whether the mood of the nation was changing. The public outcry that followed caused Roosevelt to back away and wait for another time to get the United States involved in international affairs.

Source: In Samuel I. Rosenman, ed., *The Public Papers and Addresses of Franklin D. Roosevelt, 1937* (New York: Macmillan, 1941), pp. 406–411.

Speech at Chicago
October 5 1937

. . . On my trip across the continent and back. . . . I have seen with my own eyes the prosperous farms, the thriving factories, and the busy railroads, as I have seen the happiness and security and peace which covers our wide land, [and] almost inevitably I have been compelled to contrast our peace with very different scenes being enacted in other parts of the world.

It is because the people of the United States under modern conditions must, for the sake of their own future, give thought to the rest of the world, that I, as the responsible executive head of the nation, have chosen this great

inland city . . . to speak to you on a subject of definite national importance.

The political situation in the world, which of late has been growing progressively worse, is such as to cause grave concern and anxiety to all the peoples and nations who wish to live in peace and amity with their neighbors.

Some fifteen years ago the hopes of mankind for a continuing era of international peace were raised to great heights when more than sixty nations solemnly pledged themselves not to resort to arms in furtherance of their national aims and policies. The high aspirations expressed in the Briand-Kellogg Peace Pact, and the hopes for peace thus raised, have of late given way to a haunting fear of calamity. The present reign of terror and international lawlessness began a few years ago.

It began through unjustified interference in the internal affairs of other nations or the invasion of alien territory in violation of treaties; and has now reached a stage where the very foundations of civilization are seriously threatened. The landmarks and traditions which have marked the progress of civilization toward a condition of law, order, and justice are being wiped away.

Without a declaration of war, and without warning or justification of any kind, civilians, including vast numbers of women and children, are being ruthlessly murdered with bombs from the air. In times of so-called peace, ships are being attacked and sunk by submarines without cause or notice. Nations are fomenting and taking sides in civil warfare in nations that have never done them any harm. Nations claiming freedom for themselves deny it to others.

Innocent peoples, innocent nations, are being cruelly sacrificed to a greed for power and supremacy which is devoid of all sense of justice and humane considerations. . . .

If those things come to pass in other parts of the world, let no one imagine that America will escape, that America may expect mercy, that this Western Hemisphere will not be attacked, and that it will continue tranquilly and peacefully to carry on the ethics and the arts of civilization. . . . if we are to have a world in which we can breathe freely and live in amity without fear—the peace-loving nations must make a concerted effort to uphold laws and principles on which alone peace can rest secure.

The peace-loving nations must make a concerted effort in opposition to those violations of treaties and those ignorings of humane instincts which today are creating a state of international anarchy and instability from which there is no escape through mere isolation or neutrality.

Those who cherish their freedom and recognize and respect the equal right of their neighbors to be free and live in peace must work together for the triumph of law and moral principles in order that peace, justice, and confidence may prevail in the world. There must be a return to a belief in the pledged word, in the value of a signed treaty. There must be recognition of the fact that national morality is as vital as private morality. . . .

There is a solidarity and interdependence about the modern world, both technically and morally, which makes it impossible for any nation completely to isolate itself from economic and political upheavals in the rest of the world, especially when such upheavals appear to be spreading and not declining. There can be no stability or peace either within nations or between nations except under laws and moral standards adhered to by all. International anarchy destroys every foundation for peace. It jeopardizes either the immediate or the future security of every nation, large or small. It is, therefore, a matter of vital interest and concern to the people of the United States that the sanctity of international treaties and the maintenance of international morality be restored.

The overwhelming majority of the peoples and nations of the world today want to live in peace. They seek the removal of barriers against trade. They want to exert themselves in industry, in agriculture, and in business that they may increase their wealth through the production of wealth-producing goods rather than striving to produce military planes and bombs and machine guns and cannon for the destruction of human lives and useful property.

In those nations of the world which seem to be piling armament on armament for purposes of aggression, and those other nations which fear acts of aggression against them and their security, a very high proportion of their national income is being spent directly for armaments. It runs from thirty to as high as fifty per cent. We are fortunate. The proportion that we in the United States spend is far less—eleven or twelve per cent. . . .

I am compelled and you are compelled . . . to look ahead. The peace, the freedom, and the security of ninety per cent of the population of the world is being jeopardized by the remaining ten per cent who are threatening a breakdown of all international order and law. Surely the ninety per cent who want to live in peace under law and in accordance with moral standards that have received almost universal acceptance through the centuries can and must find some way to make their will prevail.

The situation is definitely of universal concern. The questions involved relate not merely to violations of specific provisions of particular treaties; they are questions of war and of peace, of international law and especially of principles of humanity. It is true that they involve definite violations of agreements, and especially of the Covenant of the League of Nations, the Briand-Kellogg Pact, and the Nine Power Treaty. But they also involve problems of world economy, world security, and world humanity.

It is true that the moral consciousness of the world must recognize the importance of removing injustices and well-founded grievances; but at the same time it must be aroused to the cardinal necessity of honoring sanctity of treaties, of respecting the rights and liberties of others, and of putting an end to acts of international aggression.

It seems to be unfortunately true that the epidemic of world lawlessness is spreading.

When an epidemic of physical disease starts to spread, the community approves and joins in a quarantine of the patients in order to protect the health of the community against the spread of the disease.

It is my determination to pursue a policy of peace. It is my determination to adopt every practicable measure to avoid involvement in war. It ought to be inconceivable that in this modern era, and in the face of experience, any nation could be so foolish and ruthless as to run the risk of plunging the whole world into war by invading and violating, in contravention of solemn treaties, the territory of other nations that have done them no real harm and are too weak to protect themselves adequately. Yet the peace of the world and the welfare and security of every nation, including our own, is today being threatened by that very thing.

No nation which refuses to exercise forbearance and to respect the freedom and rights of others can long remain strong and retain the confidence and respect of other nations. No nation ever loses its dignity or its good standing by conciliating its differences, and by exercising great patience with, and consideration for, the rights of other nations.

War is a contagion, whether it be declared or undeclared. It can engulf states and peoples remote from the original scene of hostilities. We are determined to keep out of war, yet we cannot insure ourselves against the disastrous effects of war and the dangers of involvement. We are adopting such measures as will minimize our risk of involvement, but we cannot have complete protection in a world of disorder in which confidence and security have broken down.

If civilization is to survive, the principles of the Prince of Peace must be restored. Trust between nations must be revived.

Most important of all, the will for peace on the part of peace-loving nations must express itself to the end that nations that may be tempted to violate their agreements and the rights of others will desist from such a course. There must be positive endeavors to preserve peace.

America hates war. America hopes for peace. Therefore, America actively engages in the search for peace.

Questions

1. Which world events convinced President Roosevelt that peace was in jeopardy and that the United States should feel threatened?
2. What specific benefits could the United States and other nations expect to enjoy in a world where peace reigned?
3. What specific steps does Roosevelt propose to take to preserve peace?

27-3 "Fireside Chat" on "The Great Arsenal of Democracy" (1940)

Franklin D. Roosevelt

The United States reaffirmed its neutrality when World War II began in Europe with the German invasion of Poland in September 1939. But President Roosevelt did persuade Congress to repeal the arms embargo of the Neutrality Acts, replacing it with a plan, called "cash and carry," that worked to the advantage of Great Britain. One year later, in September 1940, the United States and Great Britain engineered a destroyers-bases exchange: Roosevelt transferred to Great Britain fifty World War I–vintage destroyers that had been declared surplus by the Navy Department in return for ninety-nine-year leases on eight British territories in the Atlantic that could be used for air and naval bases. By the end of 1940 Great Britain needed even more help. In a fireside chat (see text p. 831) that the president called "a talk on national security" delivered "in the presence of a world crisis," Roosevelt described the role he envisioned for the United States over the next several months.

Source: In Samuel I. Rosenman, ed., *The Public Papers and Addresses of Franklin D. Roosevelt, 1940* (New York: Macmillan, 1941), pp. 633–644.

Never before since Jamestown and Plymouth Rock has our American civilization been in such danger as now.

For, on September 27, 1940, by an agreement signed in Berlin, three powerful nations, two in Europe and one in Asia, joined themselves together in the threat that if the United States of America interfered with or blocked the expansion program of these three nations—a program aimed at world control—they would unite in ultimate action against the United States.

The Nazi masters of Germany have made it clear that

they intend not only to dominate all life and thought in their own country, but also to enslave the whole of Europe, and then to use the resources of Europe to dominate the rest of the world. . . .

Some of our people like to believe that wars in Asia and in Europe are of no concern to us. But it is a matter of most vital concern to us that European and Asiatic war-makers should not gain control of the oceans which lead to this hemisphere. . . .

Does anyone seriously believe that we need to fear attack anywhere in the Americas while a free Britain remains our most powerful naval neighbor in the Atlantic? Does anyone seriously believe, on the other hand, that we could rest easy if the Axis powers were our neighbors there?

If Great Britain goes down, the Axis powers will control the continents of Europe, Asia, Africa, Australia, and the high seas—and they will be in a position to bring enormous military and naval resources against this hemisphere. It is no exaggeration to say that all of us, in all the Americas, would be living at the point of a gun—a gun loaded with explosive bullets, economic as well as military.

We should enter upon a new and terrible era in which the whole world, our hemisphere included, would be run by threats of brute force. To survive in such a world, we would have to convert ourselves permanently into a militaristic power on the basis of war economy.

Some of us like to believe that even if Great Britain falls, we are still safe, because of the broad expanse of the Atlantic and of the Pacific.

But the width of those oceans is not what it was in the days of clipper ships. At one point between Africa and Brazil the distance is less than from Washington to Denver, Colorado—five hours for the latest type of bomber. And at the North end of the Pacific Ocean America and Asia almost touch each other. . . .

There are those who say that the Axis powers would never have any desire to attack the Western Hemisphere. That is the same dangerous form of wishful thinking which has destroyed the powers of resistance of so many conquered peoples. The plain facts are that the Nazis have proclaimed, time and again, that all other races are their inferiors and therefore subject to their orders. And most important of all, the vast resources and wealth of this American Hemisphere constitute the most tempting loot in all the round world. . . .

The experience of the past two years has proven beyond doubt that no nation can appease the Nazis. . . . There can be no appeasement with ruthlessness. There can be no reasoning with an incendiary bomb. We know now that a nation can have peace with the Nazis only at the price of total surrender. . . .

The history of recent years proves that shootings and chains and concentration camps are not simply the tran-sient tools but the very altars of modern dictatorships. They may talk of a "new order" in the world, but what they have in mind is only a revival of the oldest and the worst tyranny. In that there is no liberty, no religion, no hope.

The proposed "new order" is the very opposite of a United States of Europe or a United States of Asia. It is not a Government based upon the consent of the governed. It is not a union of ordinary, self-respecting men and women to protect themselves and their freedom and their dignity from oppression. It is an unholy alliance of power and pelf to dominate and enslave the human race.

The British people and their allies today are conducting an active war against this unholy alliance. Our own future security is greatly dependent on the outcome of that fight. Our ability to "keep out of war" is going to be affected by that outcome.

Thinking in terms of today and tomorrow, I make the direct statement to the American people that there is far less chance of the United States getting into war, if we do all we can now to support the nations defending themselves against attack by the Axis than if we acquiesce in their defeat, submit tamely to an Axis victory, and wait our turn to be the object of attack in another war later on.

If we are to be completely honest with ourselves, we must admit that there is risk in any course we may take. But I deeply believe that the great majority of our people agree that the course that I advocate involves the least risk now and the greatest hope for world peace in the future.

The people of Europe who are defending themselves do not ask us to do their fighting. They ask us for the implements of war . . . which will enable them to fight for their liberty and for our security. Emphatically we must get these weapons to them in sufficient volume and quickly enough, so that we and our children will be saved the agony and suffering of war which others have had to endure. . . .

We must be the great arsenal of democracy. For us this is an emergency as serious as war itself. We must apply ourselves to our task with the same resolution, the same sense of urgency, the same spirit of patriotism and sacrifice as we would show were we at war.

We have furnished the British great material support and we will furnish far more in the future.

There will be no "bottlenecks" in our determination to aid Great Britain. No dictator, no combination of dictators, will weaken that determination by threats of how they will construe that determination.

The British have received invaluable military support from the heroic Greek army, and from the forces of all the governments in exile. Their strength is growing. It is the strength of men and women who value their freedom more highly than they value their lives.

Questions

1. According to Roosevelt, how have events in Europe and Asia threatened American interests?
2. How does Roosevelt describe Great Britain's role in the international conflict?
3. What actions does Roosevelt propose?

27-4   Franklin D. Roosevelt's "Four Freedoms" Speech (1941)

President Roosevelt stated his opposition to isolationism (see text pp. 830–832) more strongly than ever in his State of the Union message to Congress at the beginning of 1941. In this speech he tied Lend-Lease and other international initiatives to his agenda for domestic politics. His concluding paragraphs on the "Four Freedoms" soon became the most famous rationale for American participation in the war. These paragraphs also put forth a striking agenda for a postwar debate both at home and abroad.

Source: In Samuel I. Rosenman, ed., *The Public Papers and Addresses of Franklin D. Roosevelt, 1940* (New York: Macmillan, 1941), pp. 663–672.

I address you, the Members of the Seventy-Seventh Congress, at a moment unprecedented in the history of the Union. I use the word "unprecedented," because at no previous time has American security been as seriously threatened from without as it is today. . . .

It is true that prior to 1914 the United States often had been disturbed by events in other Continents. We had even engaged in two wars with European nations and in a number of undeclared wars in the West Indies, in the Mediterranean and in the Pacific for the maintenance of American rights and for the principles of peaceful commerce. In no case, however, had a serious threat been raised against our national safety or our independence.

What I seek to convey is the historic truth that the United States as a nation has at all times maintained opposition to any attempt to lock us in behind an ancient Chinese wall while the procession of civilization went past. Today, thinking of our children and their children, we oppose enforced isolation for ourselves or for any part of the Americas.

Even when the World War broke out in 1914, it seemed to contain only small threat of danger to our own American future. But, as time went on, the American people began to visualize what the downfall of democratic nations might mean to our own democracy.

We need not over-emphasize imperfections in the Peace of Versailles. We need not harp on failure of the democracies to deal with problems of world deconstruction. We should remember that the Peace of 1919 was far less unjust than the kind of "pacification" which began even before Munich, and which is being carried on under the new order of tyranny that seeks to spread over every continent today. The American people have unalterably set their faces against that tyranny.

Every realist knows that the democratic way of life is at this moment being directly assailed in every part of the world—assailed either by arms, or by secret spreading of poisonous propaganda by those who seek to destroy unity and promote discord in nations still at peace. During sixteen months this assault has blotted out the whole pattern of democratic life in an appalling number of independent nations, great and small. The assailants are still on the march, threatening other nations, great and small.

Therefore, as your President, performing my constitutional duty to "give to the Congress information of the state of the Union," I find it necessary to report that the future and the safety of our country and of our democracy are overwhelmingly involved in events far beyond our borders.

Armed defense of democratic existence is now being gallantly waged in four continents. If that defense fails, all the population and all the resources of Europe, Asia, Africa and Australasia will be dominated by the conquerors. The total of those populations and their resources greatly exceeds the sum total of the population and resources of the whole of the Western Hemisphere—many times over.

In times like these it is immature—and incidentally untrue—for anybody to brag that an unprepared America, single-handed, and with one hand tied behind its back, can hold off the whole world. . . .

A free nation has the right to expect full cooperation from all groups. A free nation has the right to look to the leaders of business, of labor, and of agriculture to take the lead in stimulating effort, not among other groups but within their own groups. The best way of dealing with the few slackers or trouble makers in our midst is, first, to shame them by patriotic example, and, if that fails, to use the sovereignty of government to save government.

As men do not live by bread alone, they do not fight by armaments alone. Those who man our defenses, and those behind them who build our defenses, must have the stamina and courage which come from an unshakable belief in the manner of life which they are defending. The mighty action which we are calling for cannot be based on a disregard of all things worth fighting for.

The Nation takes great satisfaction and much strength from the things which have been done to make its people conscious of their individual stake in the preservation of democratic life in America. Those things have toughened the fibre of our people, have renewed their faith and strengthened their devotion to the institutions we make ready to protect. Certainly this is no time to stop thinking about the social and economic problems which are the root cause of the social revolution which is today a supreme factor in the world.

There is nothing mysterious about the foundations of a healthy and strong democracy. The basic things expected by our people of their political and economic systems are simple. They are: equality of opportunity for youth and for others; jobs for those who can work; security for those who need it; the ending of special privilege for the few; the preservation of civil liberties for all; the enjoyment of the fruits of scientific progress in a wider and constantly rising standard of living.

These are the simple and basic things that must never be lost sight of in the turmoil and unbelievable complexity of our modern world. The inner and abiding strength of our economic and political systems is dependent upon the degree to which they fulfill these expectations.

Many subjects connected with our social economy call for immediate improvement. As examples: We should bring more citizens under the coverage of old age pensions and unemployment insurance. We should widen the opportunities for adequate medical care. We should plan a better system by which persons deserving or needing gainful employment may obtain it.

I have called for personal sacrifice. I am assured of the willingness of almost all Americans to respond to that call. . . .

In the future days, which we seek to make secure, we look forward to a world founded upon four essential human freedoms.

The first is freedom of speech and expression—everywhere in the world.

The second is freedom of every person to worship God in his own way—everywhere in the world.

The third is freedom from want—which, translated into world terms, means economic understandings which will secure to every nation a healthy peace time life for its inhabitants—everywhere in the world.

The fourth is freedom from fear—which, translated into world terms, means a world-wide reduction of armaments to such a point and in such a thorough fashion that no nation will be in a position to commit an act of physical aggression against any neighbor—anywhere in the world.

That is no vision of a distant millenium. It is a definite basis for a kind of world attainable in our own time and generation. That kind of world is the very antithesis of the so-called new order of tyranny which the dictators seek to create with the crash of a bomb.

To that new order we oppose the greater conception—the moral order. A good society is able to face schemes of world domination and foreign revolutions alike without fear.

Since the beginning of our American history we have been engaged in change—in a perpetual peaceful revolution—a revolution which goes on steadily, quietly adjusting itself to changing conditions—without the concentration camp or the quick-lime in the ditch. The world order which we seek is the cooperation of free countries, working together in a friendly, civilized society.

This nation has placed its destiny in the hands and heads and hearts of its millions of free men and women; and its faith in freedom under the guidance of God. Freedom means the supremacy of human rights everywhere. Our support goes to those who struggle to gain those rights or keep them. Our strength is in our unity of purpose.

To that high concept there can be no end save victory.

Questions

1. What "four freedoms" does Roosevelt identify?
2. How does Roosevelt link domestic and foreign concerns in this speech?
3. How does Roosevelt extend his argument against the principles of the Neutrality Acts and in favor of an internationalist foreign policy?

27-5 The Atlantic Charter (1941)

President Roosevelt met with British Prime Minister Winston Churchill in August 1941 at sea off the coast of Newfoundland (see text p. 832). The United States and Britain were already allies against Germany, Italy, and Japan, although the United States had not yet declared war. Their Atlantic Charter statement combined some of the points Roosevelt had made in his "Four Freedoms" speech with the long-standing British and American commitment to freedom of the seas.

Source: In Samuel I. Rosenman, ed., *The Public Papers and Addresses of Franklin D. Roosevelt, 1941* (New York: Harper & Bros., 1950), p. 314.

The President of the United States of America and the Prime Minister, Mr. Churchill, representing His Majesty's Government in the United Kingdom, being met together, deem it right to make known certain common principles in the national policies of their respective countries on which they base their hopes for a better future for the world.

First, their countries seek no aggrandizement, territorial or other;

Second, they desire to see no territorial changes that do not accord with the freely expressed wishes of the peoples concerned;

Third, they respect the right of all peoples to choose the form of government under which they will live; and they wish to see sovereign rights and self government restored to those who have been forcibly deprived of them;

Fourth, they will endeavor, with due respect for their existing obligations to further the enjoyment by all States, great or small, victor or vanquished, of access, on equal terms, to the trade and to the raw materials of the world which are needed for their economic prosperity;

Fifth, they desire to bring about the fullest collaboration between all nations in the economic field with the object of securing, for all, improved labor standards, economic advancement and social security;

Sixth, after the final destruction of the Nazi tyranny, they hope to see established a peace which will afford to all nations the means of dwelling in safety within their own boundaries, and which will afford assurance that all the men in all the lands may live out their lives in freedom from fear and want;

Seventh, such a peace should enable all men to traverse the high seas and oceans without hindrance;

Eighth, they believe that all of the nations of the world, for realistic as well as spiritual reasons must come to the abandonment of the use of force. Since no future peace can be maintained if land, sea or air armaments continue to be employed by nations which threaten, or may threaten, aggression outside of their frontiers, they believe, pending the establishment of a wider and permanent system of general security, that the disarmament of such nations is essential. They will likewise aid and encourage all other practicable measures which will lighten for peace-loving peoples the crushing burden of armaments.

FRANKLIN D. ROOSEVELT
WINSTON S. CHURCHILL

Questions

1. How does the Atlantic Charter balance economic and political concerns?
2. How do Roosevelt and Churchill envision the world order that will follow the war?
3. Does the Atlantic Charter include principles that were likely to pose significant problems after the war for the British empire or for American possessions such as Puerto Rico, Hawaii, Guam, and the Philippines?

27-6 Franklin D. Roosevelt's War Message against Japan (1941)

Persuaded that war with the United States was inevitable, the Japanese attacked Pearl Harbor on December 7, 1941. The next morning, President Roosevelt addressed the following request for a declaration of war to a joint session of Congress (see text p. 833).

Source: In Samuel I. Rosenman, ed., *The Public Papers and Addresses of Franklin D. Roosevelt, 1941* (New York: Harper & Bros., 1950), pp. 514–515.

Yesterday, December 7, 1941—a date which will live in infamy—the United States of America was suddenly and deliberately attacked by naval and air forces of the empire of Japan.

The United States was at peace with that nation and, at the solicitation of Japan, was still in conversation with its government and its emperor looking toward the maintenance of peace in the Pacific.

Indeed, one hour after Japanese air squadrons had commenced bombing in the American Island of Oahu the Japanese Ambassador to the United States and his colleague delivered to our Secretary of State a formal reply to a recent American message. And, while this reply stated that it seemed useless to continue the existing diplomatic negotiations, it contained no threat or hint of war or of armed attack.

It will be recorded that the distance of Hawaii from Japan makes it obvious that the attack was deliberately planned many days or even weeks ago. During the intervening time the Japanese Government has deliberately sought to deceive the United States by false statements and expressions of hope for continued peace.

The attack yesterday on the Hawaiian Islands has caused severe damage to American naval and military forces. I regret to tell you that very many American lives have been lost. In addition American ships have been reported torpedoed on the high seas between San Francisco and Honolulu.

Yesterday the Japanese Government also launched an attack against Malaya.

Last night Japanese forces attacked Hong Kong.

Last night Japanese forces attacked Guam.

Last night Japanese forces attacked the Philippine Islands.

Last night the Japanese attacked Wake Island.

And this morning the Japanese attacked Midway Island.

Japan has therefore undertaken a surprise offensive extending throughout the Pacific area. The facts of yesterday and today speak for themselves. The people of the United States have already formed their opinions and well understand the implications to the very life and safety of our nation.

As Commander in Chief of the Army and Navy I have directed that all measures be taken for our defense.

Always will our whole nation remember the character of the onslaught against us.

No matter how long it may take us to overcome this premeditated invasion, the American people, in their righteous might, will win through to absolute victory.

I believe that I interpret the will of the Congress and of the people when I assert that we will not only defend ourselves to the uttermost but will make it very certain that this form of treachery shall never again endanger us.

Hostilities exist. There is no blinking at the fact that our people, our territory and our interests are in grave danger.

With confidence in our armed forces, with the unbounding determination of our people, we will gain the inevitable triumph. So help us God.

I ask that the Congress declare that since the unprovoked and dastardly attack by Japan on Sunday, December 7, 1941, a state of war has existed between the United States and the Japanese Empire.

Questions

1. What arguments does Roosevelt use in this speech to rally the American people for war against Japan?
2. What pattern of Japanese actions does Roosevelt describe?
3. How does this speech relate to Roosevelt's earlier statements of support for an active American response to the rise of Japan and Germany (see Documents 27-2 through 27-4)?

Questions for Further Thought

1. The Neutrality Act (Document 27-1) and the policies advocated by isolationists in the United States placed certain limits on the activities of Americans. How did those limits affect the economic interests of Americans? How did they define the limits of American diplomatic interests?

2. Even at a time when isolationism was dominant, President Franklin D. Roosevelt believed that the United States should be involved in world affairs. How did the president define the interests of the United States in the world (see Documents 27-2 through 27-6)?

3. How did the Neutrality Acts and the views of isolationists temper the war aims announced by Roosevelt and Churchill in the Atlantic Charter (Document 27-5) and defined by Roosevelt in his war message?

Mobilizing for Victory and *Life on the Home Front*

The preparedness campaign of 1940 paid quick dividends after the Japanese attack on Pearl Harbor. Defense mobilization enabled the United States to mount a relentless campaign against Japan in the Pacific and to provide supplies that allowed Great Britain to hold on and the Soviet Union to launch a powerful counteroffensive against the German invaders. Mobilization accelerated the development of the alliance between government and business that had started in the 1920s and permanently increased the size and powers of the federal government (see text p. 833). Congress and the general public accepted the expansion of federal power and activity because they viewed it as a military and patriotic necessity and because wartime conditions restored the full employment and prosperity of the 1920s.

For large numbers of American men and women the world war meant military service. For many others it opened opportunities in the work force, especially in defense industries; by late 1943 two-thirds of the economy revolved around the war effort. Many of those who found jobs were women who left their homes to work in munitions plants, shipyards, and aircraft factories. One striking effect of the war was a permanent increase in women's participation in the out-of-household labor market (see text p. 838). As a letter from one woman worker suggests, federal officials had not anticipated this (Document 27-8).

Wartime reaffirmation of America's fundamental political values undermined racial segregation and disfranchisement in the South (Document 27-9). But if World War II proved to be a "good war" for African-Americans (see text pp. 840–841)—with increased job opportunities and support for civil rights—not all minority groups benefited. For Japanese-Americans on the West Coast (see text pp. 845–847) war mobilization meant a stark confrontation with popular fear and federal power, a loss of individual rights, and forced relocation (Document 27-7). Although Japanese internment flew in the face of the country's professed commitment to liberty and freedom, the U.S. Supreme Court upheld the policy in rulings delivered in 1943 and 1944.

27-7   Executive Order 9066 "to Prescribe Military Areas" (1942)

After the surprise attack on Pearl Harbor, amid rumors of espionage and subversion in Hawaii, the American people grew fearful of enemy aliens. On February 19, 1942, President Roosevelt issued an executive order authorizing the secretary of war to identify areas of the country where movements of people could be controlled or restricted. This presidential directive evolved into legislation passed on March 21 that was used to limit the freedom of and eventually intern Japanese and Japanese-Americans along the West Coast (see text pp. 845–846).

Source: Executive Order No. 9066, "Authorizing the Secretary of War to Prescribe Military Areas," 7 *Federal Register*, no. 38, p. 1407 (February 25, 1942).

AUTHORIZING THE SECRETARY OF WAR TO PRESCRIBE MILITARY AREAS

WHEREAS the successful prosecution of the war requires every possible protection against espionage and against sabotage to national-defense material, national-defense premises, and national-defense utilities. . . .

NOW, THEREFORE, by virtue of the authority vested in me as President of the United States, and Commander in Chief of the Army and Navy, I hereby authorize and direct the Secretary of War, and the Military Commanders whom he may from time to time designate, whenever he or any designated Commander deems such actions necessary or desirable, to prescribe military areas in such places and of such extent as he or the appropriate Military Commanders may determine, from which any or all persons may be excluded, and with such respect to which, the right of any person to enter, remain in, or leave shall be subject to whatever restrictions the Secretary of War or the appropriate Military Commander may impose in his discretion. The Secretary of War is hereby authorized to provide for residents of any such area who are excluded therefrom, such transportation, food, shelter, and other accommodations as may be necessary, in the judgement of the Secretary of War or the said Military Commander, and until other arrangements are made, to accomplish the purpose of this order. The designation of military areas in any region or locality shall supersede designations of prohibited and restricted areas by the Attorney General under the Proclamations of December 7 and 8, 1941, and shall supersede the responsibility and authority of the Attorney General under the said Proclamations in respect of such prohibited and restricted areas.

I hereby further authorize and direct the Secretary of War and the said Military Commanders to take such other steps as he or the appropriate Military Commander may deem advisable to enforce compliance with the restrictions applicable to each Military area hereinabove authorized to be designated, including the use of Federal troops and other Federal Agencies, with authority to accept assistance of state and local agencies.

I hereby further authorize and direct all Executive Departments, independent establishments and other Federal Agencies, to assist the Secretary of War or the said Military Commanders in carrying out this Executive Order, including the furnishing of medical aid, hospitalization, food, clothing, transportation, use of land, shelter, and other supplies, equipment, utilities, facilities and services.

This order shall not be construed as modifying or limiting in any way the authority heretofore granted under Executive Order No. 8972, dated December 12, 1941, nor shall it be construed as limiting or modifying the duty and responsibility of the Federal Bureau of Investigation, with respect to the investigation of alleged acts of sabotage or the duty and responsibility of the Attorney General and the Department of Justice under the Proclamations of December 7 and 8, 1941, prescribing regulations for the conduct and control of alien enemies, except as such duty and responsibility is superseded by the designation of military areas hereunder.

FRANKLIN D. ROOSEVELT
The White House
February 19, 1942.

Questions

1. What specific concerns about national security led to the issuance of Executive Order 9066?

2. Is the order restricting the actions of residents of prescribed military areas specific in identifying individuals or groups? In your opinion, why was it written this way?
3. What limitations does the order place on the secretary of war and others authorized to enforce its provisions?

27-8 Women on the Home Front (1944)

Norma Yerger Queen

During World War II the U.S. Office of War Information gathered information to help shape government policy and to use in wartime propaganda. Norma Yerger Queen of Utah wrote a long letter in response to a request from the office. The letter makes it clear that she knew many women in farm and city families in Utah as well as at the military hospital where she worked. She describes both the wartime work experiences of many women and the way they and their families viewed women's roles at work and at home (see text p. 838).

Source: Norma Yerger Queen to the Office of War Information, 1944.

The people of this community all respect women who work regardless of the type of work. Women from the best families & many officers' wives work at our hospital. It is not at all uncommon to meet at evening parties in town women who work in the kitchens or offices of our hospital (Army-Bushnell-large general). The city mayor's wife too works there.

The church disapproves of women working who have small children. The church has a strong influence in our county.

For the canning season in our county men's & women's clubs & the church all recruited vigorously for women for the canneries. . . .

I personally have encouraged officers' wives who have no children to get out and work. Those of us who have done so have been highly respected by the others and we have not lost social standing. In fact many of the social affairs are arranged at our convenience.

Some husbands do not approve of wives working & this has kept home some who do not have small children. Some of the women just do not wish to put forth the effort.

The financial incentive has been the strongest influence among most economic groups but especially among those families who were on relief for many years. Patriotic motivation is sometimes present but sometimes it really is a front for the financial one. A few women work to keep their minds from worrying about sons or husbands in the service.

In this county, the hospital is the chief employer of women. A few go to Ogden (20 miles away) to work in an arsenal, the depot, or the air field. When these Ogden plants first opened quite a few women started to work there, but the long commuting plus the labor at the plants plus their housework proved too much.

Many women thoroughly enjoy working & getting away from the home. They seem to get much more satisfaction out of it than out of housework or bringing up children. Those who quit have done so because of lack of good care for their children, or of inability to do the housework & the job. . . .

I am convinced that if women could work 4 days a week instead of $5\frac{1}{2}$ or 6 that more could take jobs. I found it impossible to work $5\frac{1}{2}$ days & do my housework but when I arranged for 4 days I could manage both. These days one has to do everything—one cannot buy services as formerly. For instance—laundry. I'm lucky. I can send out much of our laundry to the hospital but even so there is a goodly amount that must be done at home—all the ironing of summer dresses is very tiring. I even have to press my husband's trousers—a thing I never did in all my married life. The weekly housecleaning—shoe shining—all things we formerly had done by others. Now we also do home canning. I never in the 14 yrs. of my married life canned 1 jar. Last summer I put up dozens of quarts per instructions of Uncle Sam. I'm only one among many who is now doing a lot of manual labor foreign to our usual custom. I just could not take on all that & an outside job too. It is no fun to eat out—you wait so long for service & the restaurants cannot be immaculately kept—therefore it is more pleasant & quicker to cook & eat at home even after a long day's work. I've talked with the personnel manager at the hospital & he agrees that fewer days a week would be better. The canneries finally took women for as little as 3 hrs. a day.

This is a farming area & many farm wives could not under any arrangements take a war job. They have too much to do at their farm jobs & many now have to go into the fields, run tractors & do other jobs formerly done by men. I marvel at all these women are able to do & feel very inadequate next to them. . . .

Here is the difference between a man working & a woman as seen in our home—while I prepare the evening meal, my husband reads the evening paper. We then do the dishes together after which he reads his medical journal or cogitates over some lecture he is to give or some problem at his lab. I have to make up grocery lists, mend, straighten up a drawer, clean out the ice box, press clothes, put away anything strewn about the house, wash bric a brac, or do several of hundreds of small "woman's work is never done stuff." This consumes from 1 to 2 hrs. each evening after which I'm too weary to read any professional social work literature & think I'm lucky if I can keep up with the daily paper, Time Life or Reader's Digest. All this while my husband is relaxing & resting. When I worked full time, we tried doing the housecleaning together but it just didn't click. He is responsible for introducing penicillin into Bushnell & thus into the army & there were so many visiting brass hats & night conferences he couldn't give even one night a week to the house. Then came a mess of lectures of all kinds of medical meetings—he had to prepare those at home. I got so worn out it was either quit work or do it part time.

This has been a lot of personal experience but I'm sure we are no exception. I thought I was thro[ugh] working in 1938. My husband urged me to help out for the war effort—he's all out for getting the war work done & he agreed to do his share of the housework. He is not lazy but he found we could not do it. I hope this personal experience will help to give you an idea of some of the problems.

Questions

1. According to Queen, why did women take jobs during the war? Which reasons were especially important?
2. What practical factors limited women's participation in the labor force? How did practical factors affect women who came from different circumstances—farms, towns, the military base?
3. How did their outside jobs affect women's work at home? What problems and options does Queen mention?

27-9 The Supreme Court on Black Disfranchisement in the South (1944)

In 1944 Lonnie E. Smith, an African-American citizen, sued S. E. Allwright, an election judge in Harris County (Houston), Texas. Smith asserted that he had been denied the right to vote in the Democratic primary because he was not a "white citizen" (see text pp. 840–841). The Supreme Court agreed to hear this case and overruled lower courts that had relied on an early Court decision (*Grovey v. Townsend*) allowing the all-white primary.

Source: Smith v. Allwright, 321 U.S. 649 (1944).

The State of Texas by its Constitution and statutes provides that every person, if certain other requirements are met which are not here in issue, qualified by residence in the district or county "shall be deemed a qualified elector." Primary elections for United States Senators, Congressmen and state officers are provided for by Chapters Twelve and Thirteen of the statutes. Under these chapters, the Democratic Party was required to hold the primary which was the occasion of the alleged wrong to petitioned. . . . These nominations are to be made by the qualified voters of the party.

The Democratic Party of Texas is held by the Supreme Court of that state to be a "voluntary association," protected by Section 27 of the Bill of Rights, Art. 1, Constitution of Texas, from interference by the state except that:

"In the interest of fair methods and a fair expression by their members of their preferences in the selection of their nominees, the State may regulate such elections by proper laws."

The Democratic party on May 24, 1932 in a State Convention adopted the following resolution, which has not since been "amended, abrogated, annulled or avoided":

"Be it resolved that all white citizens of the State of Texas who are qualified to vote under the Constitution and laws of the State shall be eligible to membership in the Democratic party and, as such, entitled to participate in its deliberations."

It was by virtue of this resolution that the respondents refused to permit the petitioner to vote.

Texas is free to conduct her elections and limit her electorate as she may deem wise, save only as her action may be affected by the prohibitions of the United States Constitution or in conflict with powers delegated to and exercised by the National Government. The Fourteenth Amendment forbids a state from making or enforcing any law which abridges the privileges or immunities of citizens of the United States and the Fifteenth Amendment specifically interdicts any denial or abridgement by a state of the right of citizens to vote on account of color. . . .

When *Grovey v. Townsend* was written, the Court looked upon the denial of a vote in a primary as a mere refusal by a party of party membership. As the Louisiana statutes for holding primaries are similar to those of Texas, our ruling in *Classic* [another similar case] as to the unitary character of the electoral process calls for a reëxamination as to whether or not the exclusion of Negroes from a Texas party primary was state action.

It may now be taken as a postulate that the right to vote in such a primary for the nomination of candidates without discrimination by the State, like the right to vote in a general election, is a right secured by the Constitution.

We are thus brought to an examination of the qualifications for Democratic primary electors in Texas, to determine whether state action or private action has excluded Negroes from participation.

We think that this statutory system for the selection of party nominees for inclusion on the general election ballot makes the party which is required to follow these legislative directions an agency of the state in so far as it determines the participants in a primary election. The party takes its character as a state agency from the duties imposed upon it by state statutes; the duties do not become matters of private law because they are performed by a political party. . . .

The United States is a constitutional democracy. Its organic law grants to all citizens a right to participate in the choice of elected officials without restriction by any state because of race. This grant to the people of the opportunity for choice is not to be nullified by a state through casting its electoral process in a form which permits a private organization to practice racial discrimination in the election. Constitutional rights would be of little value if they could be thus indirectly denied. . . .

Questions

1. According to this Supreme Court decision, what limits was Texas bound to observe in arranging its primary elections?

2. Texas had argued that the all-white Democratic primary was a *private*, not a public, activity. How did it make this argument? Why did the Court rule against it?

3. What influence, if any, might U.S. war aims as stated by President Roosevelt have had on the Supreme Court's decision to hear this case or on the language used in the decision?

Questions for Further Thought

1. War mobilization brought nearly every American citizen into closer contact with the federal government. To judge from these documents, what impact did the federal government have on women (Document 27-8) and members of racial minority groups during mobilization for World War II?

2. President Roosevelt offered a broad rationale for U.S. participation in World War II. To what extent did the federal government rely on this rationale in its treatment of racial minorities during the war, as suggested in Documents 27-7 and 27-9?

3. President Roosevelt's war rationale and federal actions during World War II may well have shaped the expectations that women and members of racial minorities had in regard to government policy after the war. What new expectations do you think women and members of racial minority groups might have developed during the war?

Fighting and Winning the War

The broad war aims stated by Roosevelt and Churchill in the Atlantic Charter (Document 27-5) were not fully acceptable to Soviet Premier Josef Stalin, whose views had to be considered because the Soviet Union was bearing the brunt of battle against Germany, certainly on the Eastern Front. The president and prime minister held their first meeting with Stalin at Teheran, Iran, in November 1943 (see text p. 848). By that time, Soviet forces were driving German armies out of western Russia, but the fighting was still intense and costly, especially in casualties, for the Soviet Union. Stalin insisted that the Allies open a second front in Europe to take the pressure off Russian armies. Roosevelt and Churchill agreed in return for Stalin's promise to enter the war against Japan after the European war ended. The western leaders found it impossible, however, to agree with Stalin about postwar control of Poland and other areas of Eastern Europe (see text pp. 848, 854).

The "Big Three" leaders met again in February 1945 at Yalta, a Black Sea resort in Russian territory on the Crimean peninsula, where they tried to establish postwar arrangements (see text p. 854). Stalin reaffirmed his commitment to go to war against Japan, and the three leaders agreed to divide Germany and the German capital of Berlin after the war. They also agreed on plans for a United Nations. But intransigent demands by the Soviets for security on their own terms—backed up by the fact that the Soviet army already controlled most of Poland, Hungary, and the Balkans—forced Roosevelt and Churchill to accept vague language on the future of Eastern Europe. On his return to Washington, Roosevelt told Congress that the Yalta Conference had produced "a compromise" that held great hope for "a world of peace" (Document 27-10).

But even at the war's end Eastern Europe remained a land of misery and death. As American and Russian troops advanced into eastern Germany and Poland, they witnessed the horrors of the Holocaust (see text pp. 850–851) that had killed 6 million Jews and at least as many other "undesirables." They told their stories, sometimes long after the fact (Document 27-11), and made people understand that the war against Hitler truly had been a war to save civilization.

27-10   Franklin D. Roosevelt on the Yalta Conference (1945)

After the Yalta Conference Roosevelt sailed back through the Mediterranean, meeting briefly with Egypt's King Farouk, Ethiopia's Emperor Haile Selassie, Saudi Arabia's King Ibn Saud, and (at Alexandria) once again with Churchill. He stopped at Algiers for a discussion with French General Charles De Gaulle, but De Gaulle chose to protest his exclusion from the Yalta Conference by refusing to meet the president. Exhausted and increasingly ill, Roosevelt mostly remained in his cabin during the journey across the Atlantic. He met only briefly with Samuel Rosenman, his speechwriter, to review a draft of his address, which he delivered to Congress and the American people while sitting down, contrary to his usual practice of standing. This was Roosevelt's last major speech; he died six weeks later, just before the final victory of allied forces in Europe (see text p. 854).

Source: In Samuel I. Rosenman, ed., *The Public Papers and Addresses of Franklin D. Roosevelt, 1944–1945* (New York: Harper & Bros., 1950), pp. 571–586.

I come from the Crimea Conference with a firm belief that we have made a good start on the road to a world of peace.

There were two main purposes in this Crimea Conference. The first was to bring defeat to Germany with the greatest possible speed, and the smallest possible lost of Allied men. That purpose is now being carried out in great force. The German Army, and the German people, are feeling the ever-increasing might of our fighting men and of the Allied armies. Every hour gives us added pride in the heroic advance of our troops in Germany—on German soil—toward a meeting with the gallant Red Army.

The second purpose was to continue to build the foundation for an international accord that would being order and security after the chaos of the war, that would give some assurance of lasting peace among the Nations of the world.

Toward that goal also, a tremendous stride was made.

. . .

When we met at Yalta, in addition to laying our strategic and tactical plans for the complete and final military victory over Germany, there were other problems of vital political consequence.

For instance, first, there were the problems of the occupation and control of Germany—after victory—the complete destruction of her military power, and the assurance that neither the Nazis nor Prussian militarism could again be revived to threaten the peace and the civilization of the world.

Second—again for example—there was the settlement of the few differences that remained among us with respect to the International Security Organization after the Dumbarton Oaks Conference [see text p. 854]. As you remember, at that time, I said that we had agreed ninety percent.

Well, that's a pretty good percentage. I think the other ten percent was ironed out at Yalta.

Third, there were the general political and economic problems common to all of the areas which had been or would be liberated from the Nazi yoke. This is a very special problem. We over here find it difficult to understand the ramifications of many of these problems in foreign lands, but we are trying to.

Fourth, there were the special problems created by a few instances such as Poland and Yugoslavia.

Days were spent in discussing these momentous matters and we argued freely and frankly across the table. But at the end, on every point, unanimous agreement was reached. And more important even than the agreement of words, I may say we achieved a unity of thought and a way of getting along together.

Of course, we know that it was Hitler's hope—and the German war lords'—that we would not agree—that some slight crack might appear in the solid wall of Allied unity, a crack that would give him and his fellow gangsters one last hope of escaping their just doom. That is the objective for which his propaganda machine has been working for many months.

But Hitler has failed.

Never before have the major allies been more closely united—not only in their war aims but also in their peace aims. And they are determined to continue to be united with each other—and with all peace-loving Nations—so that the ideal of lasting peace will become a reality.

The Soviet, British, and United States Chiefs of Staff held daily meetings with each other. They conferred frequently with Marshal Stalin, and with Prime Minister Churchill and with me, on the problem of coordinating the strategic and tactical efforts of the Allied powers. They completed their plans for the final knock-out blows to Germany. . . .

Of equal importance with the military arrangements at the Crimea Conference were the agreements reached with respect to a general international organization for lasting world peace. The foundations were laid at Dumbarton Oaks. There was one point, however, on which agreement was not reached at Dumbarton Oaks. It involved the procedure of voting in the Security Council. . . .

At the Crimea Conference, the Americans made a proposal on this subject which, after full discussion was, I am glad to say, unanimously adopted by the other two Nations.

It is not yet possible to announce the terms of that agreement publicly, but it will be in a very short time.

When the conclusions reached with respect to voting in the Security Council are made known, I think and I hope you will find them a fair solution of this complicated and difficult problem. They are founded in justice, and will go far to assure international cooperation in the maintenance of peace.

A conference of all the United Nations of the world will meet in San Francisco on April 25, 1945. There, we all hope, and confidently expect, to execute a definite charter of organization under which the peace of the world will be preserved and the forces of aggression permanently outlawed.

This time we are not making the mistake of waiting until the end of the war to set up the machinery of peace. This time, as we fight together to win the war finally, we work together to keep it from happening again. . . .

One outstanding example of joint action by the three major Allied powers in the liberated areas was the solution reached on Poland. The whole Polish question was a potential source of trouble in postwar Europe—as it has been sometimes before—and we came to the Conference determined to find a common ground for its solution. And we did—even though everybody does not agree with us, obviously.

Our objective was to help create a strong, independent, and prosperous Nation. That is the thing we must always remember, those words, agreed to by Russia, by Britain, and by the United States: the objective of making Poland a strong, independent, and prosperous Nation, with a government ultimately to be selected by the Polish people themselves.

To achieve that objective, it was necessary to provide for the formation of a new government much more representative than had been possible while Poland was enslaved. There were, as you know, two governments—one in London, one in Lublin—practically in Russia. Accordingly, steps were taken at Yalta to reorganize the existing Provisional Government in Poland on a broader democra-

tic basis, so as to include democratic leaders now in Poland and those abroad. This new, reorganized government will be recognized by all of us as the temporary government of Poland. Poland needs a temporary government in the worst way—an ad interim government, I think is another way of putting it.

However, the new Polish Provisional Government of National Unity will be pledged to holding a free election as soon as possible on the basis of universal suffrage and a secret ballot.

Throughout history, Poland has been the corridor through which attacks on Russia have been made. Twice in this generation, Germany has struck at Russia through this corridor. To insure European security and world peace, a strong and independent Poland is necessary to prevent that from happening again.

The decision with respect to the boundaries of Poland was, frankly, a compromise. I did not agree with all of it, by any means, but we did not go as far as Britain wanted, in certain areas; we did not go as far as Russia wanted, in certain areas; and we did not go as far as I wanted, in certain areas. It *was* a compromise. The decision is one, however, under which the Poles will receive compensation in territory in the North and West in exchange for what they lose by the Curzon Line in the East. The limits of the western border will be permanently fixed in the final Peace Conference. We know, roughly, that it will include—in the new, strong Poland—quite a large slice of what now is called Germany. And it was agreed, also, that the new Poland will have a large and long coast line, and many new harbors. Also, that most of East Prussia will go to Poland. A corner of it will go to Russia. Also, that the anomaly of the Free State of Danzig (now Gdansk] will come to an end; I think Danzig would be a lot better if it were Polish.

It is well known that the people east of the Curzon Line—just for example, here is why I compromised—are predominantly white Russian and Ukranian—they are not Polish; and a very great majority of the people west of the line are predominantly Polish, except in that part of East Prussia and eastern Germany, which will go to the new Poland. As far back as 1919, representatives of the Allies agreed that the Curzon Line represented a fair boundary between the two peoples. And you must remember, also, that there had not been any Polish government before 1919 for a great many generations.

I am convinced that the agreement on Poland, under the circumstances, is the most hopeful agreement possible for a free, independent, and prosperous Polish state. . . .

The Conference in the Crimea was a turning point—I hope in our history and therefore in the history of the world. There will soon be presented to the Senate of the United States and to the American people a great decision that will determine the fate of the United States—and of the world—for generations to come.

Questions

1. What did Roosevelt believe he accomplished at Yalta?
2. What problems does Roosevelt acknowledge are still unresolved?
3. What problems, if any, did Roosevelt omit in this report to Congress on the Yalta Conference?

27-11 Remembering the Holocaust (1945)

In the spring of 1945, as Allied forces closed the circle around the Third Reich, the horrors of the Holocaust finally came to light (see text pp. 850–851). When American armies entered the death camps of Eastern Europe, they pierced the dark heart of Hitler's world and saw sights that would change their lives forever. The following recollections from a doctor and nurse were recorded in the early 1980s as part of an oral history project in Minnesota to tap the memories of the survivors and liberators of the death camps.

Source: Recollections of Dr. William McConahey and Dorothy Wahlstrom, excerpted with permission of Twayne Publishers, an imprint of Simon & Schuster Macmillan, from *Witnesses to the Holocaust: An Oral History*, edited by Rhoda G. Lewin, pp. 202–203, 214–215. Copyright © 1990 by Jewish Community Relations Council/Anti-Defamation League of Minnesota and the Dakotas.

Dr. William McConahey, medical officer at Flossenburg with the 337th Infantry:

. . . As we moved into Germany we started hearing about the concentration camps at army briefings. April 23 our division liberated Flossenburg, and I went in there next day.

Flossenburg held 15,000 prisoners but there were only about 1,500 left. The German guards had marched out about 13,000 toward Dachau, to get away from our advancing army. It was a very poignant, sad-looking road because they were marched out carrying blankets or maybe a jacket, but they were too weak to carry things, and they'd dropped them along the way.

A few very emaciated prisoners were wandering around in blue and white striped prison garb. My jeep driver spoke German, so he had conversations with many of the prisoners. They were from all over Europe—Poles, Russians, Czechs, French, Belgian, Spanish. They had a lot of Jewish people there, of course, but many were political prisoners, from the underground, or just people picked up by the Gestapo because they thought they were anti-Hitler. They all bore the scars of beatings and being knocked around.

The camp was laid out in very neat barracks style, with two big barbed wire fences around it. Running through it was a little railroad with a little pushcart like you see in coal mines, pushed by hand, to haul bodies to the crematory.

Three inmates, pretty much zombies, were still burning bodies in the crematory because prisoners were still dying left and right, and for sanitation you had to do something! About sixteen corpses were lined up to be burned. They were just skin and bone, each one weighing about forty pounds, I'd guess, because you could pick them up with one hand. One fellow opened the furnace door, and there were a couple of bodies in there, sizzling away.

We saw the beautiful houses where the S.S. guards lived with their women. Then I walked into the barracks, very drab and cold, with three tiers of bunks on each side. It was nothing but boards—no mattresses, no straw, nothing. Each bunk was big enough for one, but they said three slept there every night.

I visited the "hospital" where they brought prisoners to die. They'd put them on the bare wooden floor with straw on it, and they'd lie there in their own excrement and vomitus, until they died.

Some prisoners, their spirits were broken, they were just shells and they'd lost the will to live. Some were so close to death you couldn't feed them because they hadn't eaten for so long their stomachs were atrophied, and if they got food in, they vomited and bloated and obstructed.

We tried to get them back on small feedings very slowly, over a period of weeks, but we couldn't save them. We felt terrible. They were dying under our eyes, and there was nothing we could do.

After the war ended, we drove to Dachau one day. Dachau was much bigger than Flossenburg. Again, we toured the barracks and saw the crematories, six big ovens. Outside were thousands of jars stacked up, the charred bones and ashes of people who had been burned there. I was told they used these for fertilizing the gardens, and that sometimes they would send a political prisoner's family a box of bones, anybody's bones. We saw the whipping posts, the torture chambers. It was obviously degradation and terror and horror and suffering, just like Flossenburg, only on a bigger scale.

It was those concentration camps that made us realize what we were fighting for. We really felt this was a holy crusade to wipe out this diabolical regime. We have sadistic bums and misfits and psychopaths in this country who could do what the S.S. did in Germany, but Hitler gave them a rank, a uniform, a purpose and a mission, and encouraged them.

The infantry medical corps was not like "M.A.S.H." or the movies. Unless you're there, unless you're in combat, and fight the battle, and crawl on your belly under machine gun bullets, and dig a foxhole in the rain, and get shelled, you can't understand what it's like. We were with the infantry, having the same life as they were having, and the same death they were having, too.

The war marked me for life. I realized that making a lot of money or being a big shot, that wasn't as important as doing something worthwhile. To really be a person was what counted.

Dorothy Wahlstrom, a captain with the 127th Evac Hospital, whose unit entered Dachau on May 3, 1945:

The dead and dying were all around us. Piles of naked dead were stacked beside the crematorium and inside. Dachau was certainly a calculated attempt by the Nazis to desecrate not only the body, but also the mind and spirit.

We set up ward units in the S.S. barracks. Dead dogs lay in the kennels nearby, killed by our military after survivors told us they were used to tear away parts of prisoners' bodies on command. Survivors told us infants were torn limb from limb as their mothers watched. They told us that prisoners who could no longer work were used as live targets for machine gun practice. They mentioned other unspeakable atrocities—medical experiments, torture chambers—horrors too terrible to think up without having experienced them.

Each of the two hospital units at Dachau, the 127th and the 116th, was equipped to care for 450 patients at one time, but each unit cared for 1,500 or more at peak times.

We felt we were dancing with death. We couldn't get away from it, and wondered if it would ever stop. We couldn't care for everyone, and often we could not admit a patient until another one died or was discharged from the hospital. It was truly heartbreaking for our medical officers to have to choose the people they thought might live and leave the sickest ones to die. Of those we thought would live, seven or eight stretchers were lined up in front of each ward in the morning—people who had died during the night.

The severely malnourished did not tolerate increased rations too well, and dysentery was out of control. We had double bunk beds for our patients, and the diarrhea was so severe it leaked from bed to bed. Many were so emaciated that even with the care we gave them, it was too late.

The diseases were those that go with filth and lack of sanitation. One and one-half tons of DDT powder were used in dusting the camp to get control of the infected lice that spread typhus. Perhaps 20 percent of the camp population had active tuberculosis.

I wish I could describe the smells and the silence of death. Even now, certain sights and sound can remind me of that pain, that suffering, that sorrow and loss and anguish and degradation.

I find comfort in the sacred Scriptures that record that the Lord will vindicate His Israel, and that there will always be a House of David. I am truly grateful to the Lord for having allowed me to serve His people.

Questions

1. For both McConahey and Wahlstrom, which sights and smells affected them the most as they toured the death camps?
2. Why did medical personnel feel so frustrated in their efforts to save the victims they found in the camps?
3. How did their experiences with the victims of the Holocaust change the lives of McConahey and Wahlstrom?

Questions for Further Thought

1. Why was there such concern about the future of Eastern Europe after World War II? Did anyone—notably the president—provide any hint of the horrors that might be uncovered in that area after the war (Document 27-11)?

2. Do you think the realities of wartime, including the necessity of forming an alliance with the Soviet Union, forced Roosevelt and Churchill to compromise the principles in the Atlantic Charter (Document 27-5)? If so, what changes did they have to make?

3. Did President Roosevelt achieve the aims stated in his "Four Freedoms" speech and in the Atlantic Charter (Documents 27-4 and 27-5)? Why or why not? Might he have spoken differently if he had known about Hitler's plans to exterminate the Jewish population of Europe?

CHAPTER *28*

Cold War America 1945–1960

★   ★   ★

The Early Cold War

The American people regarded the end of World War II as the successful resolution of what General Dwight Eisenhower had called a "crusade." This was thought to be different from the lost crusade of Woodrow Wilson and the United States in World War I. Yet even in the afterglow of victory over the Axis the American people shuddered at the thought of rising tensions with one wartime ally, the Soviet Union (see text pp. 862–864). In the climate of what came to be known as the Cold War, the United States experienced a revolution that changed the style and content of American foreign policy. Throwing over a traditional aversion to entanglement that can be traced to George Washington's Farewell Address in 1796, the United States made long-term commitments to its allies to keep the Soviet Union in check. This new foreign policy approach, called containment (Document 28-1), became the primary way to deal with the Soviets in the early stages of the Cold War.

In 1947 Great Britain announced that an economic crisis at home would force a cutoff of aid to Greece and Turkey in their fight against communism (see text pp. 864–865). President Harry Truman, who saw this as a "turning point" for American foreign policy, asked Congress to appropriate millions of dollars to protect "free peoples" from this new danger (Document 28-2). The Truman Doctrine later was extended to Western Europe through the Marshall Plan (see text pp. 865, 868), a multi-billion-dollar aid program that was intended to arrest communism in countries such as France and Italy. There was no doubt in Truman's mind that Soviet communism was a threat to the stability of world order, and subsequent actions by the Soviets appeared to prove him right. The Berlin blockade that began in June 1948 was broken within a year by an ambitious airlift that brought 2.3 million tons of food and other supplies into the divided city (see text pp. 868–869).

The Western European states knew that they could count on strong support through the Truman years, but they could not be certain that later presidents would not retreat to the old foreign policy of nonentanglement. To provide some protection for themselves, Great Britain, France, and the Benelux states signed the Brussels Pact in 1948. By 1949 that agreement had been expanded into the North Atlantic Treaty Organization, which included the United States in a long-term defensive alliance to protect Western Europe (see text p. 869 and Document 28-3).

Foreign policy crises also developed in Asia. In December 1949 the flight of the forces of Jiang Jieshi (Chaing Kai-shek) from mainland China to Taiwan signaled the victory of the Communist Chinese and the virtual expulsion of the Nationalists (see text pp. 869–870). In June 1950 the stakes in Asia escalated when North Korean armies crossed the 38th parallel in an attempt to take military control of South Korea. The United States, with a recent record of economic aid (the Truman Doctrine and the Marshall Plan) and military assistance (the Berlin airlift) in Europe, found itself committing military forces to a land war in Asia (see text pp. 871–874).

By 1950 the lines had been drawn for American policy makers. National Security Paper 68 (see text pp. 870–871) clearly marked communism as the enemy (Document 28-4). The Soviets were no longer former allies with whom an amicable agreement might be arranged (as some of George Kennan's writings suggested) but implacable opponents who might draw the United States into a war. NSC-68 suggested possible attack strategies that went beyond anything previous planners had been willing to consider.

28-1   George Kennan Formulates "Containment" Policy (1947)

George Kennan, a career diplomat attached to the American embassy in Moscow (see *American Lives*, text pp. 866–867) sent a lengthy telegram to the State Department early in 1946 in which he warned American policy makers about Soviet aggression in the future. Those ideas evolved into a position paper that helped shape the cold war policy of containment of the Soviet Union (see text p. 864). In July 1947 Kennan made his views public when he published an essay titled "The Sources of Soviet Conduct" in the influential journal *Foreign Affairs* under the pseudonym "X."

Source: X [George Kennan], "The Sources of Soviet Conduct." Reprinted by permission of *Foreign Affairs*, July 1947, pp. 566–582. Copyright © 1947 by the Council on Foreign Relations, Inc.

The political personality of Soviet power as we know it today is the product of ideology and circumstances: ideology inherited by the present Soviet leaders from the movement in which they had their political origin, and circumstances of the power which they now have exercised for nearly three decades in Russia. . . .

It is difficult to summarize the set of ideological concepts with which the Soviet leaders came into power. Marxian ideology, in its Russian-Communist projection, has always been in process of subtle evolution. The materials on which it bases itself are extensive and complex. But the outstanding features of Communist thought as it existed in 1916 may perhaps be summarized as follows:

(a) that the central factor in the life of man, the factor which determines the character of public life and the "physiognomy of society," is the system by which material goods are produced and exchanged; (b) that the capitalist system of production is a nefarious one which inevitably leads to the exploitation of working class by the capital-owning class and is incapable of developing adequately the economic resources of society or of distributing fairly the material goods produced by human labor; (c) that capitalism contains the seeds of its own destruction and must, in view of the inability of the capital-owning class to adjust itself to economic change, result eventually and inescapably in a revolutionary transfer of power to the working class; and (d) that imperialism, the final phase of capitalism, leads directly to war and revolution.

The rest may be outlined in Lenin's own words: "Unevenness of economic and political development is the inflexible law of capitalism. It follows from this that the victory of Socialism may come originally in a few capitalist countries or even in a single capitalist country. The victorious proletariat of that country, having expropriated the capitalists and having organized Socialist production at home, would rise against the remaining capitalist world, drawing to itself in the process the oppressed classes of other countries." It must be noted that there was no assumption that capitalism would perish without proletarian revolution. A final push was needed from a revolutionary proletariat movement in order to tip over the tottering structure. But it was regarded as inevitable that sooner or later that push be given....

The circumstances of the immediate post-revolution period—the existence in Russia of civil war and foreign intervention, together with the obvious fact that the Communists represented only a tiny minority of the Russian people—made the establishment of dictatorial power a necessity. The experiment with "war Communism" and the abrupt attempt to eliminate private production and trade had unfortunate economic consequences and caused further bitterness against the new revolutionary régime. While the temporary relaxation of the effort to communize Russia, represented by the New Economic Policy, alleviated some of this economic distress and thereby served its purpose, it also made evident that the "capitalist sector of society" was still prepared to profit at once from any relaxation of governmental pressure, and would, if permitted to continue to exist, always constitute a powerful opposing element to the Soviet régime and a serious rival for influence in the country. Somewhat the same situation prevailed with respect to the individual peasant who, in his own small way, was also a private producer....

Now the outstanding circumstance concerning the Soviet régime is that down to the present day this process of political consolidation has never been completed and the men in the Kremlin have continued to be predominantly absorbed with the struggle to secure and make absolute the power which they seized in November 1917. They have endeavored to secure it primarily against forces at home, within Soviet society itself. But they have also endeavored to secure it against the outside world. For ideology, as we have seen, taught them that the outside world was hostile and that it was their duty eventually to overthrow the political forces beyond their borders. The powerful hands of Russian history and tradition reached up to sustain them in this feeling. Finally, their own aggressive intransigence with respect to the outside world began to find its own reaction; and they were soon forced, to use another Gibbonesque phrase, "to chastise the contumacy" which they themselves had provoked. It is an undeniable privilege of every man to prove himself right in the thesis that the world is his enemy; for if he reiterates it frequently enough and makes it the background of his conduct he is bound eventually to be right....

Now the maintenance of this pattern of Soviet power, namely, the pursuit of unlimited authority domestically, accompanied by the cultivation of the semi-myth of implacable foreign hostility, has gone far to shape the actual machinery of Soviet power as we know it today. Internal organs of administration which did not serve this purpose withered on the vine. Organs which did serve this purpose became vastly swollen. The security of Soviet power came to rest on the iron discipline of the Party, on the severity and ubiquity of the secret police, and on the uncompromising economic monopolism of the state. The "organs of suppression," in which the Soviet leaders had sought security from rival forces, became in large measure the masters of those whom they were designed to serve. Today the major part of the structure of Soviet power is committed to the perfection of the dictatorship and to the maintenance of the concept of Russia as in a state of siege, with the enemy lowering beyond the walls. And the millions of human beings who form that part of the structure of power must defend at all costs this concept of Russia's position, for without it they are themselves superfluous.

As things stand today, the rulers can no longer dream of parting with these organs of suppression. The quest for absolute power, pursued now for nearly three decades with a ruthlessness unparalleled (in scope at least) in modern times, has again produced internally, as it did externally, its own reaction. The excesses of the police apparatus have fanned the potential opposition to the régime into something far greater and more dangerous than it could have been before those excesses began.

But least of all can the rulers dispense with the fiction by which the maintenance of dictatorial power has been defended. For this fiction has been canonized in Soviet philosophy by the excesses already committed in its name; and it is now anchored in the Soviet structure of thought by bonds far greater than those of mere ideology.

II

... Once a given party line has been laid down on a given issue of current policy, the whole Soviet governmental machine, including the mechanism of diplomacy, moves inexorably along the prescribed path, like a persistent toy automobile wound up and headed in a given direction, stopping only when it meets with some unanswerable force. The individuals who are the components of this machine are unamenable to argument or reason which comes to them from outside sources. Their whole training has taught them to mistrust and discount the glib persuasiveness of the outside world. Like the white dog before the phonograph, they hear only the "master's voice." And if they are to be called off from the purposes last dictated to them, it is the master who must call them off. Thus the foreign representative cannot hope that his words will make any impression on them. The most that he can hope is that they will be transmitted to those at the top, who are capable of changing the party line. But even those are not likely to be swayed by any normal logic in the words of the bourgeois representative. Since there can be no appeal to common purposes, there can be no appeal to common mental approaches. For this reason, facts speak louder than words to the ears of the Kremlin; and words carry the greatest weight when they have the ring of reflecting, or being backed up by, facts of unchallengeable validity.

But we have seen that the Kremlin is under no ideological compulsion to accomplish its purposes in a hurry. Like the Church, it is dealing in ideological concepts which are of long-term validity, and it can afford to be patient. It has no right to risk the existing achievements of the revolution for the sake of vain baubles of the future. The very teachings of Lenin himself require great caution and flexibility in the pursuit of Communist purposes. Again, these precepts are fortified by the lessons of Russian history: of centuries of obscure battles between nomadic forces over the stretches of a vast unfortified plain. Here caution, circumspection, flexibility and deception are the valuable qualities; and their value finds natural appreciation in the Russian or the oriental mind. Thus the Kremlin has no compunction about retreating in the face of superior force. And being under the compulsion of no timetable, it does not get panicky under the necessity for such retreat. Its political action is a fluid stream which moves constantly, wherever it is permitted to move, toward a given goal. Its main concern is to make sure that it has filled every nook and cranny available to it in the basin of world power. But if it finds unassailable barriers in its path, it accepts these philosophically and accommodates itself to them. The main thing is that there should always be pressure, unceasing constant pressure, toward the desired goal. . . .

In these circumstances it is clear that the main element of any United States policy toward the Soviet Union must be that of a long-term, patient but firm and vigilant containment of Russian expansive tendencies. It is important to note, however, that such a policy has nothing to do with outward histrionics: with threats or blustering or superfluous gestures of outward "toughness." . . .

III

In the light of the above, it will be clearly seen that the Soviet pressure against the free institutions of the western world is something that can be contained by the adroit and vigilant application of counter-force at a series of constantly shifting geographical and political points, corresponding to the shifts and manœuvres of Soviet policy, but which cannot be charmed or talked out of existence. . . .

Thus the future of Soviet power may not be by any means as secure as Russian capacity for self-delusion would make it appear to the men in the Kremlin. That they can keep power themselves, they have demonstrated. That they can quietly and easily turn it over to others remains to be proved. Meanwhile, the hardships of their rule and the vicissitudes of international life have taken a heavy toll of the strength and hopes of the great people on whom their power rests. . . . This cannot be proved. And it cannot be disproved: But the possibility remains (and in the opinion of this writer it is a strong one) that Soviet power, like the capitalist world of its conception, bears within it the seeds of its own decay, and that the sprouting of these seeds is well advanced.

IV

It is clear that the United States cannot expect in the foreseeable future to enjoy political intimacy with the Soviet régime. It must continue to regard the Soviet Union as a rival, not a partner, in the political arena. It must continue to expect that Soviet policies will reflect no abstract love of peace and stability, no real faith in the possibility of a permanent happy coexistence of the Socialist and capitalist worlds, but rather a cautious, persistent pressure toward the disruption and weakening of all rival influence and rival power.

Balanced against this are the facts that Russia, as opposed to the western world in general, is still by far the weaker party, that Soviet policy is highly flexible, and that Soviet society may well contain deficiencies which will eventually weaken its own total potential. This would of itself warrant the United States entering with reasonable confidence upon a policy of firm containment, designed to confront the Russians with unalterable counter-force at every point where they show signs of encroaching upon the interests of a peaceful and stable world.

But in actuality the possibilities for American policy are by no means limited to holding the line and hoping for the best. It is entirely possible for the United States to influence by its actions the internal developments, both within Russia and throughout the international Communist movement, by which Russian policy is largely determined. This is not only a question of the modest measure of informational activity which this government can conduct in the Soviet Union and elsewhere, although that, too, is important. It is rather a question of the degree to which the United States can create among the peoples of the world generally the impression of a country which knows what it wants, which is coping successfully with the problems of its internal life and with the responsibilities of a World Power, and which has a spiritual vitality capable of holding its own among the major ideological currents of the time. To the extent that such an impression can be created and maintained, the aims of Russian Communism must appear sterile and quixotic, the hopes and enthusiasm of

Moscow's supporters must wane, and added strain must be imposed on the Kremlin's foreign policies. For the palsied decrepitude of the capitalist world is the keystone of Communist philosophy. Even the failure of the United States to experience the early economic depression which the ravens of the Red Square have been predicting with such complacent confidence since hostilities ceased would have deep and important repercussions throughout the Communist world. . . .

It would be an exaggeration to say that American behavior unassisted and alone could exercise a power of life and death over the Communist movement and bring about the early fall of Soviet power in Russia. But the United States has it in its power to increase enormously the strains under which Soviet policy must operate, to force upon the Kremlin a far greater degree of moderation and circumspection than it has had to observe in recent years, and in this way to promote tendencies which must eventually find their outlet in either the break-up or the gradual mellowing of Soviet power. For no mystical, Messianic movement—

and particularly not that of the Kremlin—can face frustration indefinitely without eventually adjusting itself in one way or another to the logic of that state of affairs.

Thus the decision will really fall in large measure in this country itself. The issue of Soviet-American relations is in essence a test of the over-all worth of the United States as a nation among nations. To avoid destruction the United States need only measure up to its own best traditions and prove itself worthy of preservation as a great nation.

Surely, there was never a fairer test of national quality than this. In the light of these circumstances, the thoughtful observer of Russian-American relations will find no cause for complaint in the Kremlin's challenge to American society. He will rather experience a certain gratitude to a Providence which, by providing the American people with this implacable challenge, has made their entire security as a nation dependent on their pulling themselves together and accepting the responsibilities of moral and political leadership that history plainly intended them to bear.

Questions

1. Kennan's title is a curious one. Could or should one speak of sources of *American* conduct?
2. How much does Soviet communism really have to do with the history Kennan is describing? What role does history play in Kennan's analysis?
3. What specific strategies does Kennan propose for carrying out a policy of containment?

28-2 Harry Truman Remembers the Truman Doctrine (1947)

The new American foreign policy of containment got its first real test in Greece and Turkey (see text pp. 864–865), where the Soviet Union had taken aggressive actions in 1946. President Harry Truman, a long-time hard-liner toward the Soviet Union, determined that the United States could not allow Greece and Turkey to fall into the Soviet sphere. In March 1947 he asked Congress to appropriate $400 million in aid to those two states. Some years later, writing in his memoirs, Truman explained his thinking in 1947 and laid out a good explanation of American foreign policy for the future.

Source: Excerpted by permission of Margaret Truman Daniel from Harry S. Truman, *Memoirs by Harry S. Truman*, vol. 2: *Years of Trial and Hope* (Garden City, N.Y.: Doubleday, 1956), pp. 93, 95–106.

In early 1946 Russian activities in Iran threatened the peace of the world. . . .

As I saw it, three things were involved. One was the security of Turkey. Russia had been pressing Turkey for special privileges and for territorial concessions for several months. The Turks had resisted all these demands, but their position would be infinitely more difficult if Russia,

or a Russian puppet state, were able to outflank her in the east.

The second problem was the control of Iran's oil reserves. That Russia had an eye on these vast deposits seemed beyond question. If the Russians were to control Iran's oil, either directly or indirectly, the raw-material balance of the world would undergo a serious change, and it would be a serious loss for the economy of the Western world.

What perturbed me most, however, was Russia's callous disregard of the rights of a small nation and of her own solemn promises. International co-operation was impossible if national obligations could be ignored and the U.N. bypassed as if it did not exist.

I talked over all these points with Secretary Byrnes and Admiral Leahy. Then I told Byrnes to send a blunt message to Premier Stalin. On March 24 Moscow announced that all Russian troops would be withdrawn from Iran at once. The threat to Turkey had been removed, although it had not vanished and continued to demand our attention. Iran could negotiate with Russia without feeling threatened; indeed, its parliament rejected later the accord entered into by its government, a clear sign that fear had been removed from the land.

The world was now able to look more hopefully toward the United Nations. But Russia's ambitions would not be halted by friendly reminders of promises made. The Russians would press wherever weakness showed—and we would have to meet that pressure wherever it occurred, in a manner that Russia and the world would understand. When Communist pressure began to endanger Greece and Turkey, I moved to make this policy clear and firm.

It was not long before the same issue was presented to us again in the same part of the world. Turkey and Greece had become subjected to heavy pressures from the Russian bloc. Each of them had valiantly sought to repel these pressures, but now their strength was waning and they were in need of aid.

Turkey was, of course, an age-old objective of Russian ambitions. The Communists were only continuing what the Czars had practiced when they tried to gain control of the area that blocked Russian exit into the Mediterranean Sea. . . .

[T]he Russians, in addition to their efforts to outflank Turkey through Iran, were beginning to exert pressure on Turkey for territorial concessions. In July 1946, Moscow sent a note to Ankara proposing a new regime for the Dardanelles that would have excluded all nations except the Black Sea powers. In other words, both we and the British would have been eliminated from any future agreement, and Turkey would have been faced by a combination of three Communist states: Russia, Rumania, and Bulgaria. The second and far more ominous part of the Soviet proposal was that the straits should be put under joint Turkish-Russian defense.

This was indeed an open bid to obtain control of Turkey. If Russian troops entered Turkey with the ostensible purpose of enforcing joint control of the straits, it would only be a short time before these troops would be used for the control of all of Turkey. We had learned from the experience of the past two years that Soviet intervention inevitably meant Soviet occupation and control. To allow Russia to set up bases in the Dardanelles or to bring troops into Turkey, ostensibly for the defense of the straits, would, in the natural course of events, result in Greece and the whole Near and Middle East falling under Soviet control.

The Turkish government sought our advice, and Acting Secretary of State Acheson placed the matter before me. I directed the State, War, and Navy Departments to make a careful study of the situation. The Secretaries of the three departments, with the Chiefs of Staff, moved with speed and brought me a unanimous recommendation that we take a strong position. I met with the Secretaries and the Chiefs of Staff and discussed the development thoroughly around a map on my desk to evaluate the situation in the Middle East. I approved the recommendations submitted. We co-ordinated our views with those of our allies, taking a strong position, which was at once communicated to the Turkish government. At the same time, the Turkish government received similar views and support from the British and French. . . .

While Turkey's plight was entirely due to Russia's postwar intransigence, the condition of Greece had its beginning in the World War II occupation of that nation.

Greece had suffered tragically in World War II. Her people had offered heroic resistance to Mussolini's army, but at last the combined might of Germany and Italy had broken the Greek armies.

Resistance continued, however, throughout the country, and soon it had come to crystallize around two principal groups. One of these, the so-called EAM, was under Communist domination; the other remained loyal to the King and his government in exile. Between the vicious practices of the German forces of occupation and the constant fighting between the resistance groups, normal life in Greece virtually ceased. Fields and factories were idle. People starved, and disease took untold numbers. . . .

The Communists, of course, thrived on the continuing conditions of misery, starvation, and economic ruin. Moscow and the Balkan satellite countries were now rendering open support to the EAM. Intelligence reports which I received stated that many of the insurgents had been trained, indoctrinated, armed, and equipped at various camps beyond the Greek borders. Under Soviet direction, the reports said, Greece's northern neighbors—Yugoslavia, Bulgaria, and Albania—were conducting a drive to establish a Communist Greece.

What little stability and order could be found in Greece was due primarily to the presence there of forty thousand British troops and to the counsel and support given to the Greek government by the British. But as early as the fall of 1945 the British had suggested to us that they would like our assistance in Greece, especially financial help to the Greek government.

I had authorized the State Department to enter into discussions with the British on terms of economic aid to Greece. . . .

Greece needed aid, and needed it quickly and in substantial amounts. The alternative was the loss of Greece and the extension of the iron curtain across the eastern Mediterranean. If Greece was lost, Turkey would become an untenable outpost in a sea of Communism. Similarly, if Turkey yielded to Soviet demands, the position of Greece would be extremely endangered.

But the situation had even wider implications. Poland, Rumania, and the other satellite nations of eastern Europe had been turned into Communist camps because, in the course of the war, they had been occupied by the Russian Army. We had tried, vainly, to persuade the Soviets to permit political freedom in these countries, but we had no means to compel them to relinquish their control, unless we were prepared to wage war.

Greece and Turkey were still free countries being challenged by Communist threats both from within and without. These free peoples were now engaged in a valiant struggle to preserve their liberties and their independence.

America could not, and should not, let these free countries stand unaided. To do so would carry the clearest implications in the Middle East and in Italy, Germany, and France. The ideals and the traditions of our nation demanded that we come to the aid of Greece and Turkey and that we put the world on notice that it would be our policy to support the cause of freedom wherever it was threatened.

The risks which such a course might entail were risks which a great nation had to take if it cherished freedom at all. The studies which Marshall and Acheson brought to me and which we examined together made it plain that serious risks would be involved. But the alternative would be disastrous to our security and to the security of free nations everywhere.

What course the free world should take in the face of the threat of Russian totalitarianism was a subject I had discussed with my foreign policy advisers on many occasions in the year just passed. To foster our thinking in long-range terms I had approved the establishment in the State Department of a Policy Planning Staff. George F. Kennan, one of our foremost experts on Russia, was to head this group.

A President has little enough time to meditate, but whenever such moments occurred I was more than likely to turn my thoughts toward this key problem that confronted our nation.

We had fought a long and costly war to crush the totalitarianism of Hitler, the insolence of Mussolini, and the arrogance of the warlords of Japan. Yet the new menace facing us seemed every bit as grave as Nazi Germany and her allies had been.

I could never quite forget the strong hold which isolationism had gained over our country after World War I. Throughout my years in the Senate I listened each year as one of the senators would read Washington's Farewell Address. It served little purpose to point out to the isolationists that Washington had advised a method suitable under the conditions of *his* day to achieve the great end of preserving the nation, and that although conditions and our international position had changed, the objectives of our policy—peace and security—were still the same. For the isolationists this address was like a biblical text. The America First organization of 1940–41, the Ku Klux Klan, Pelley and his Silver Shirts—they all quoted the first President in support of their assorted aims.

I had a very good picture of what a revival of American isolationism would mean for the world. After World War II it was clear that without American participation there was no power capable of meeting Russia as an equal. If we were to turn our back on the world, areas such as Greece, weakened and divided as a result of the war, would fall into the Soviet orbit without much effort on the part of the Russians. The success of Russia in such areas and our avowed lack of interest would lead to the growth of domestic Communist parties in such European countries as France and Italy, where they were already significant threats. Inaction, withdrawal, "Fortress America" notions could only result in handing to the Russians vast areas of the globe now denied to them.

This was the time to align the United States of America clearly on the side, and the head, of the free world. I knew that George Washington's spirit would be invoked against me, and Henry Clay's, and all the other patron saints of the isolationists. But I was convinced that the policy I was about to proclaim was indeed as much required by the conditions of my day as was Washington's by the situation in his era and Monroe's doctrine by the circumstances which he then faced. . . .

The drafting of the actual message which I would deliver to the Congress had meanwhile been started by the State Department. . . . I wanted no hedging in this speech. This was America's answer to the surge of expansion of Communist tyranny. It had to be clear and free of hesitation or double talk.

On Wednesday, March 12, 1947, at one o'clock in the afternoon, I stepped to the rostrum in the hall of the House of Representatives and addressed a joint session of the Congress. I had asked the senators and representatives to meet together so that I might place before them what I believed was an extremely critical situation.

To cope with this situation, I recommended immediate action by the Congress. But I also wished to state, for all the world to know, what the position of the United States was in the face of the new totalitarian challenge. This declaration of policy soon began to be referred to as the "Truman Doctrine." This was, I believe, the turning point in America's foreign policy, which now declared that wherever aggression, direct or indirect, threatened the peace, the security of the United States was involved.

Questions

1. What specific concerns did President Truman have in mind when he began to consider the need to provide financial aid to Greece and Turkey? Were these new problems, or did they reflect long-term issues?
2. Was the United States worried specifically about a Soviet presence in Greece and Turkey or the opportunities that presence might give the Soviet Union to threaten other parts of Europe?
3. In Truman's mind, why was traditional isolationism no longer a viable policy for the United States?
4. Why did Truman view this moment as a "turning point" for the United States?

28-3 Senator Arthur Vandenberg on NATO

By 1948 several European states had begun to plan for their own defense through the the Brussels Pact. Great Britain, France, Belgium, the Netherlands, and Luxembourg agreed to come to one another's defense in case of aggression by an outsider. Senator Arthur Vandenberg (R-Michigan), at one time an ardent isolationist, used his position as chairman of the Senate Foreign Relations Committee to bring the United States into the orbit of this new European defense system. The Vandenberg Resolution called for the United States to enter into negotiations with the Brussels Pact signatories to develop a wider defensive arrangement for Western Europe. The outgrowth was the North Atlantic Treaty Organization (see text p. 869). Vandenberg took great pleasure in helping to create NATO: "Rarely in our nation's history has such a small egg hatched so quickly into such a large chicken," he wrote in his memoirs. In letters to constituents he expressed his hopes for NATO.

Source: Excerpts from *The Private Papers of Senator Vandenberg,* edited by Arthur H. Vandenberg, Jr., with the collaboration of Joe Alex Morris, pp. 475, 477–480, 499–500. Copyright 1952 by Arthur Vandenberg, Jr., © renewed 1980. Reprinted by permission of Houghton Mifflin Company. All rights reserved.

January 27, 1949

There is no doubt about the fact that it is a "calculated risk" for us to even partially arm the countries of Western Europe. It is also very much of a "calculated risk" if we do *not.* One risk will have to be weighed against the other. You suggest that it will be a safe thing to do "when the economic stability of these countries shall have improved." The basic question we have to settle is whether "economic stability" can precede the creation of a greater sense of physical security. I am inclined to think that "physical security" is a prerequisite to the kind of long-range economic planning which Western Europe requires. The fact remains that the problem is fraught with many hazardous imponderables. I am withholding my own final judgment until I see the precise terms of the treaty under which this new co-operation will be proposed. I think we ought to have wit enough to write it on a basis which is relatively safe. . . .

February 21, 1949

. . . in my opinion, when Mr. Hitler was contemplating World War Two, I believe he would have never launched it if he had had any serious reasons to believe that it might bring him into armed collision with the United States. I think he was sure it would not do so because of our then existing neutrality laws. If an appropriate North Atlantic Pact is written, I think it will exactly reverse this psychology so far as Mr. Stalin is concerned if, as and when he contemplates World War Three. Under such circumstances, I very much doubt whether World War Three happens. . . .

February 22, 1949

I am one of its [the Pact's] authors. I heartily believe in it. I want to give it a maximum chance to help prevent World War Three before it starts. But this requires absolute candor as to what it does and does not promise. I can think of no greater tragedy than to permit our friends in Western Europe to interpret the Pact beyond its actual realities. One reality is that we cannot commit ourselves to automatic war in the future. . . . We are recognizing facts of life as established in the Constitution of the United States. I will go as far as I can within the Constitution. I will not go farther because it would be an imposition upon our own good faith and a false reliance for our friends abroad. I hasten to add that I think we can achieve every essential result for the North Atlantic Pact by staying strictly within the Constitution of the United States and within the Charter of the United Nations. . . .

March 18, 1949

. . . I am glad to know your preliminary reaction to the North Atlantic pact. I agree with you one thousand percent that "this world cannot stand another war." Every effort of my remaining days will be dedicated to this truth. My greatest fear in this connection is that we will somehow drift into another war. . . . If Soviet Russia does start to march it would seem to be completely inevitable that the United States will be the ultimate target and that we shall inevitably be in that war—Pact or no Pact. So it seems to me that our best insurance is to make our position plan in advance. This includes above all else a clear demonstration that our objectives are totally defensive; that we have no goal except peace with honor and justice in a live-and-let-live world.

If you are right and this proposed North Atlantic Pact is "another provocation to another World War" then the Pact ought to be rejected. If I am right in believing that the Pact is our best protection against another World War then the Pact ought to be ratified. Therefore, our current problem is to fully and publicly explore every phase and every angle of the Pact. You may be very sure that I shall insist upon extensive public hearings which will clarify the issue. I wan everything ventilated in this connection so that we may reach the wisest possible decision in a situation where we must take a "calculated risk" whichever way the decision goes. . . .

[July 21, 1949]

Well—as you know we won the big battle [over the North Atlantic Treaty] today by a vote of 82 to 13 . . . It's a great relief to have the battle over—yet I seem to feel a greater responsibility than ever tonight—how will it all work out? At best, it's a calculated risk. But I have a feeling that this day will go down in history as one of the big dates. . . .

Questions

1. According to Senator Vandenberg, what kinds of dangers did the United States face in the Cold War?
2. What risks did the United States run by aligning itself so closely with the states of Western Europe? What kinds of gains did NATO make possible?
3. What lessons did Vandenberg learn from the events preceding World War II? How does he put them to use in his support for NATO?

28-4 NSC-68 (1950)

The National Security Council (NSC) was established as part of the 1947 legislation that created the Department of Defense and the Central Intelligence Agency. The purpose of the NSC was to provide the president with top-secret advice on matters related to foreign affairs. The NSC's report to President Truman known as NSC-68 (written in 1950 but not made public until 1973) left no doubt that from the American perspective, cooperation between the United States and the Soviet Union was no longer possible (see text pp. 870–871).

NSC-68 is an extensive, carefully thought-out document. To show its scope, an outline of the document is given below, followed by selected excerpts.

Source: Foreign Relations of the United States (1950), no. 1, pp. 237–292.

Analysis

ANALYSIS

I. Background of the Present Crisis

. . . During the span of one generation, the international distribution of power has been fundamentally altered. . . .

Two complex sets of factors have now basically altered this historical distribution of power. First, the defeat of Germany and Japan and the decline of the British and French Empires have interacted with the development of the United States and the Soviet Union in such a way that power has increasingly gravitated to these two centers. Second, the Soviet Union, unlike previous aspirants to hege-

mony, is animated by a new fanatic faith, antithetical to our own, and seeks to impose its absolute authority over the rest of the world. Conflict has, therefore, become endemic and is waged, on the part of the Soviet Union, by violent or non-violent methods in accordance with the dictates of expediency. With the development of increasingly terrifying weapons of mass destruction, every individual faces the ever-present possibility of annihilation should the conflict enter the phase of total war.

On the one hand, the people of the world yearn for relief from the anxiety arising from the risk of atomic war. On the other hand, any substantial further extension of the area under the domination of the Kremlin would raise the possibility that no coalition adequate to confront the Kremlin with greater strength could be assembled. It is in this context that this Republic and its citizens in the ascendancy of their strength stand in their deepest peril. . . .

II. Fundamental Purpose of the United States

The fundamental purpose of the United States is laid down in the Preamble to the Constitution. . . . In essence, the fundamental purpose is to assure the integrity and vitality of our free society, which is founded upon the dignity and worth of the individual.

Three realities emerge as a consequence of this purpose: Our determination to maintain the essential elements of individual freedom, as set forth in the Constitution and Bill of Rights; our determination to create conditions under which our free and democratic system can live and prosper; and our determination to fight if necessary to defend our way of life. . . .

III. Fundamental Design of the Kremlin

The fundamental design of those who control the Soviet Union and the international communist movement is to retain and solidify their absolute power, first in the Soviet Union and second in the areas now under their control. In the minds of the Soviet leaders, however, achievement of this design requires the dynamic extension of their authority and the ultimate elimination of any effective opposition to their authority.

The design, therefore, calls for the complete subversion or forcible destruction of the machinery of government and structure of society in the countries of the non-Soviet world and their replacement by an apparatus and structure subservient to and controlled from the Kremlin. To that end Soviet efforts are now directed toward the domination of the Eurasian land mass. The United States, as the principal center of power in the non-Soviet world and the bulwark of opposition to Soviet expansion, is the principal enemy whose integrity and vitality must be subverted or destroyed by one means or another if the Kremlin is to achieve its fundamental design.

IV. The Underlying Conflict in the Realm of Ideas and Values between the U.S. Purpose and the Kremlin Design

A. NATURE OF CONFLICT

The Kremlin regards the United States as the only major threat to the achievement of its fundamental design. There is a basic conflict between the idea of freedom under a government of laws, and the idea of slavery under the grim oligarchy of the Kremlin, which has come to a crisis with the polarization of power described in Section I, and the exclusive possession of atomic weapons by the two protagonists. The idea of freedom, moreover, is peculiarly and intolerably subversive of the idea of slavery. But the converse is not true. The implacable purpose of the slave state to eliminate the challenge of freedom has placed the two great powers at opposite poles. It is this fact which gives the present polarization of power the quality of crisis. . . .

B. OBJECTIVES

In a shrinking world, which now faces the threat of atomic warfare, it is not an adequate objective merely to seek to check the Kremlin design, for the absence of order among nations is becoming less and less tolerable. This fact imposes on us, in our own interests, the responsibility of world leadership. It demands that we make the attempt, and accept the risks inherent in it, to bring about order and justice by means consistent with the principles of freedom and democracy. We should limit our requirement of the Soviet Union to its participation with other nations on the basis of equality and respect for the rights of others. Subject to this requirement, we must with our allies and the former subject peoples seek to create a world society based on the principle of consent. Its framework cannot be inflexible. It will consist of many national communities of great and varying abilities and resources, and hence of war potential. The seeds of conflicts will inevitably exist or will come into being. To acknowledge this is only to acknowledge the impossibility of a final solution. Not to acknowledge it can be fatally dangerous in a world in which there are no final solutions. . . .

V. Soviet Intentions and Capabilities— Actual and Potential

A. POLITICAL AND PSYCHOLOGICAL

. . . Soviet ideas and practices run counter to the best and potentially the strongest instincts of men, and deny their most fundamental aspirations. Against an adversary which effectively affirmed the constructive and hopeful instincts of men and was capable of fulfilling their fundamental aspirations, the Soviet system might prove to be fatally weak. . . .

C. MILITARY

The Soviet Union is developing the military capacity to support its design for world domination. The Soviet Union actually possesses armed forces far in excess of those necessary to defend its national territory. These armed forces are probably not yet considered by the Soviet Union to be sufficient to initiate a war which would involve the United States. This excessive strength, coupled now with an atomic capability, provides the Soviet Union with great coercive power for use in time of peace in furtherance of its objectives and serves as a deterrent to the victims of its aggression from taking any action in opposition to its tactics which would risk war.

Should a major war occur in 1950 the Soviet Union and its satellites are considered by the Joint Chiefs of Staff to be in a sufficiently advanced state of preparation immediately to undertake and carry out the following campaigns.

a. To overrun Western Europe, with the possible exception of the Iberian and Scandinavian Peninsulas; to drive toward the oil-bearing areas of the Near and Middle East; and to consolidate Communist gains in the Far East;

b. To launch air attacks against the British Isles and air and sea attacks against the lines of communications of the Western Powers in the Atlantic and the Pacific;

c. To attack selected targets with atomic weapons, now including the likelihood of such attacks against targets in Alaska, Canada, and the United States. Alternatively, this capability, coupled with other actions open to the Soviet Union, might deny the United Kingdom as an effective base of operations for allied forces. It also should be possible for the Soviet Union to prevent any allied "Normandy" type amphibious operations intended to force a reentry into the continent of Europe.

After the Soviet Union completed its initial campaigns and consolidated its positions in the Western European area, it could simultaneously conduct:

a. Full-scale air and limited sea operations against the British Isles;

b. Invasions of the Iberian and Scandinavian Peninsulas;

c. Further operations in the Near and Middle East, continued air operations against the North American continent, and air and sea operations against Atlantic and Pacific lines of communication; and

d. Diversionary attacks in other areas. . . .

For planning purposes, therefore, the date the Soviets possess an atomic stockpile of 200 bombs would be a critical date for the United States, for the delivery of 100 atomic bombs on targets in the United States would seriously damage this country.

At the time the Soviet Union has a substantial atomic stockpile and if it is assumed that it will strike a strong surprise blow and if it is assumed further that its atomic attacks will be met with no more effective defense opposition than the United States and its allies have programmed, results of those attacks could include:

a. Laying waste to the British Isles and thus depriving the Western Powers of their use as a base;

b. Destruction of the vital centers and of the communications of Western Europe, thus precluding effective defense by the Western Powers; and

c. Delivering devastating attacks on certain vital centers of the United States and Canada.

The possession by the Soviet Union of a thermonuclear capability in addition to this substantial atomic stockpile would result in tremendously increased damage.

During this decade, the defensive capabilities of the Soviet Union will probably be strengthened, particularly by the development and use of modern aircraft, aircraft warning and communications devices, and defensive guided missiles. . . .

VI. U.S. Intentions and Capabilities—Actual and Potential

A. POLITICAL AND PSYCHOLOGICAL

In a world of polarized power, policies designed to develop a healthy international community are more than ever necessary to our own strength.

As for the policy of "containment," it is one which seeks by all means short of war to (1) block further expansion of Soviet power, (2) expose the falsities of Soviet pretensions, (3) induce a retraction of the Kremlin's control and influence, and (4) in general, so foster the seeds of destruction within the Soviet system that the Kremlin is brought at least to the point of modifying its behavior to conform to generally accepted international standards.

It was and continues to be cardinal in this policy that we possess superior overall power in ourselves or in dependable combination with other like-minded nations. One of the most important ingredients of power is military strength. In the concept of "containment," the maintenance of a strong military posture is deemed to be essential for two reasons: (1) as an ultimate guarantee of our national security and (2) as an indispensable backdrop to the conduct of the policy of "containment." Without superior aggregate military strength, in being and readily mobilizable, a policy of "containment"—which is in effect a policy of calculated and gradual coercion—is no more than a policy of bluff. . . .

VII. Present Risks

B. SPECIFIC

It is quite clear from Soviet theory and practice that the Kremlin seeks to bring the free world under its dominion by the methods of the cold war. The preferred technique is to subvert by infiltration and intimidation. Every institution of our society is an instrument which it is sought to stultify and turn against our purposes. Those that touch most closely our material and moral strength are obviously the prime targets, labor unions, civic enterprises, schools, churches, and all media for influencing opinion. The effort is not so much to make them serve obvious Soviet ends as to prevent them from serving our ends, and thus to make them sources of confusion in our economy, our culture, and our body politic. The doubts and diversities that in terms of our values are part of the merit of a free system, the weaknesses and the problems that are peculiar to it, the rights and privileges that free men enjoy, and the disorganization and destruction left in the wake of the last attack on our freedoms, all are but opportunities for the Kremlin to do its evil work. Every advantage is taken of the fact that our means of prevention and retaliation are limited by those principles and scruples which are precisely the ones that give our freedom and democracy its meaning for us. None of our scruples deter those whose only code is "morality is that which serves the revolution."

Since everything that gives us or others respect for our institutions is a suitable object for attack, it also fits the Kremlin's design that where, with impunity, we can be insulted and made to suffer indignity the opportunity shall not be missed, particularly in any context which can be used to cast dishonor on our country, our system, our motives, or our methods. Thus the means by which we sought to restore our own economic health in the '30's, and now seek to restore that of the free world, come equally under attack. The military aid by which we sought to help the free world was frantically denounced by the Communists in the early days of the last war, and of course our present efforts to develop adequate military strength for ourselves and our allies are equally denounced.

At the same time the Soviet Union is seeking to create overwhelming military force, in order to back up infiltration with intimidation. In the only terms in which it understands strength, it is seeking to demonstrate to the free world that force and the will to use it are on the side of the Kremlin, that those who lack it are decadent and doomed. In local incidents it threatens and encroaches both for the sake of local gains and to increase anxiety and defeatism in all the free world. . . .

VIII. Atomic Armaments

A. MILITARY EVALUATION OF U.S.
AND USSR ATOMIC CAPABILITIES

. . . As the atomic capability of the USSR increases, it will have an increased ability to hit at our atomic bases and installations and thus seriously hamper the ability of the United States to carry out an attack such as that outlined above. It is quite possible that in the near future the USSR will have a sufficient number of atomic bombs and a sufficient deliverability to raise a question whether Britain with its present inadequate air defense could be relied upon as an advance base from which a major portion of the U.S. attack could be launched.

It is estimated that, within the next four years, the USSR will attain the capability of seriously damaging vital centers of the United States, provided it strikes a surprise blow and provided further that the blow is opposed by no more effective opposition than we now have programmed. Such a blow could so seriously damage the United States as to greatly reduce its superiority in economic potential.

Effective opposition to this Soviet capability will require among other measures greatly increased air warning systems, air defenses, and vigorous development and implementation of a civilian defense program which has been thoroughly integrated with the military defense systems.

In time the atomic capability of the USSR can be expected to grow to a point where, given surprise and no more effective opposition than we now have programmed, the possibility of a decisive initial attack [by the USSR] cannot be excluded. . . .

B. STOCKPILING AND USE OF ATOMIC WEAPONS

In the event the USSR develops by 1954 the atomic capability which we now anticipate, it is hardly conceivable that, if war comes, the Soviet leaders would refrain from the use of atomic weapons unless they felt fully confident of attaining their objectives by other means.

In the event we use atomic weapons either in retaliation for their prior use by the USSR or because there is no alternative method by which we can attain our objectives, it is imperative that the strategic and tactical targets against which they are used be appropriate and the manner in which they are used be consistent with those objectives.

It appears to follow from the above that we should produce and stockpile thermonuclear weapons in the event they prove feasible and would add significantly to our net capability. Not enough is yet known of their potentialities to warrant a judgment at this time regarding their use in war to attain our objectives. . . .

C. INTERNATIONAL CONTROL OF ATOMIC ENERGY

The principal immediate benefit of international control would be to make a surprise atomic attack impossible, as-

suming the elimination of large reactors and the effective disposal of stockpiles of fissionable materials. But it is almost certain that the Soviet Union would not agree to the elimination of large reactors, unless the impracticability of producing atomic power for peaceful purposes had been demonstrated beyond a doubt. By the same token, it would not now agree to elimination of its stockpile of fissionable materials. . . .

[T]he absence of good faith on the part of the USSR must be assumed until there is concrete evidence that there has been a decisive change in Soviet policies. It is to be doubted whether such a change can take place without a change in the nature of the Soviet system itself. . . .

IX. Possible Courses of Action

Introduction. Four possible courses of action by the United States in the present situation can be distinguished. They are:

a. Continuation of current policies, with current and currently projected programs for carrying out these policies;
b. Isolation;
c. War; and
d. A more rapid building up of the political, economic, and military strength of the free world than provided under a, with the purpose of reaching, if possible, a tolerable state of order among nations without war and of preparing to defend ourselves in the event that the free world is attacked. . . .

The Kremlin will have three major objectives in negotiations with the United States. The first is to eliminate the atomic capabilities of the United States; the second is to prevent the effective mobilization of the superior potential of the free world in human and material resources; and the third is to secure a withdrawal of United States forces from, and commitments to, Europe and Japan. Depending on its evaluation of its own strengths and weaknesses as against the West's (particularly the ability and will of the West to sustain its efforts), it will or will not be prepared to make important concessions to achieve these major objectives. It is unlikely that the Kremlin's evaluation is such that it would now be prepared to make significant concessions.

It must be presumed that for some time the Kremlin will accept agreements only if it is convinced that by acting in bad faith whenever and wherever there is an opportunity to do so with impunity, it can derive greater advantage from the agreements than the free world. For this reason, we must take care that any agreements are enforceable or that they are not susceptible of violation without detection and the possibility of effective counter-measures. . . .

A. THE FIRST COURSE—CONTINUATION OF CURRENT POLICIES, WITH CURRENT AND CURRENTLY PROJECTED PROGRAMS FOR CARRYING OUT THESE POLICIES

1. Military aspects. . . . A review of Soviet policy shows that the military capabilities, actual and potential, of the United States and the rest of the free world, together with the apparent determination of the free world to resist further Soviet expansion, have not induced the Kremlin to relax its pressures generally or to give up the initiative in the cold war. On the contrary, the Soviet Union has consistently pursued a bold foreign policy, modified only when its probing revealed a determination and an ability of the free world to resist encroachment upon it. The relative military capabilities of the free world are declining, with the result that its determination to resist may also decline and that the security of the United States and the free world as a whole will be jeopardized.

From the military point of view, the actual and potential capabilities of the United States, given a continuation of current and projected programs, will become less and less effective as a war deterrent. Improvement of the state of readiness will become more and more important not only to inhibit the launching of war by the Soviet Union but also to support a national policy designed to reverse the present ominous trends in international relations. A building up of the military capabilities of the United States and the free world is a pre-condition to the achievement of the objectives outlined in this report and to the protection of the United States against disaster.

Fortunately, the United States military establishment has been developed into a unified and effective force as a result of the policies laid down by the Congress and the vigorous carrying out of these policies by the Administration in the fields of both organization and economy. It is, therefore, a base upon which increased strength can be rapidly built with maximum efficiency and economy.

2. Political aspects. . . . Politically, recognition of the military implications of a continuation of present trends will mean that the United States and especially other free countries will tend to shift to the defensive, or to follow a dangerous policy of bluff, because the maintenance of a firm initiative in the cold war is closely related to aggregate strength in being and readily available. . . .

3. Economic and social aspects. As was pointed out in Chapter VI, the present foreign economic policies and programs of the United States will not produce a solution to the problem of international economic equilibrium, notably the problem of the dollar gap, and will not create an economic base conducive to political stability in many important free countries. . . .

The Executive Branch is now undertaking a study of the problem of the United States balance of payments and of the measures which might be taken by the United States to assist in establishing international economic equilibrium. This is a very important project and work on it should have a high priority. However, unless such an economic program is matched and supplemented by an equally far-sighted and vigorous political and military program, we will not be successful in checking and rolling back the Kremlin's drive.

4. Negotiation. In short, by continuing along its present course the free world will not succeed in making effective use of its vastly superior political, economic, and military potential to build a tolerable state of order among nations. On the contrary, the political, economic, and military situation of the free world is already unsatisfactory and will become less favorable unless we act to reverse present trends. . . .

The idea that Germany or Japan or other important areas can exist as islands of neutrality in a divided world is unreal, given the Kremlin design for world domination.

B. THE SECOND COURSE—ISOLATION

[A policy of isolation] overlooks the relativity of capabilities. With the United States in an isolated position, we would have to face the probability that the Soviet Union would quickly dominate most of Eurasia, probably without meeting armed resistance. It would thus acquire a potential far superior to our own, and would promptly proceed to develop this potential with the purpose of eliminating our power, which would, even in isolation, remain as a challenge to it and as an obstacle to the imposition of its kind of order in the world. There is no way to make ourselves inoffensive to the Kremlin except by complete submission to its will. Therefore isolation would in the end condemn us to capitulate or to fight alone and on the defensive, with drastically limited offensive and retaliatory capabilities in comparison with the Soviet Union. (These are the only possibilities, unless we are prepared to risk the future on the hazard that the Soviet Empire, because of overextension or other reasons, will spontaneously destroy itself from within. . . .

C. THE THIRD COURSE—WAR

. . . [A] surprise attack upon the Soviet Union, despite the provocativeness of recent Soviet behavior, would be repugnant to many Americans. Although the American people would probably rally in support of the war effort, the shock of responsibility for a surprise attack would be morally corrosive. . . .

. . . If the argument of Chapter IV is accepted, it follows that there is no "easy" solution and that the only sure victory lies in the frustration of the Kremlin design by the steady development of the moral and material strength of the free world and its projection into the Soviet world in such a way as to bring about an internal change in the Soviet system.

D. THE REMAINING COURSE OF ACTION—A RAPID BUILD-UP OF POLITICAL, ECONOMIC, AND MILITARY STRENGTH IN THE FREE WORLD

A more rapid build-up of political, economic, and military strength and thereby of confidence in the free world than is now contemplated is the only course which is consistent with progress toward achieving our fundamental purpose. . . .

The threat to the free world involved in the development of the Soviet Union's atomic and other capabilities will rise steadily and rather rapidly. For the time being, the United States possesses a marked atomic superiority over the Soviet Union which, together with the potential capabilities of the United States and other free countries in other forces and weapons, inhibits aggressive Soviet action. This provides an opportunity for the United States, in cooperation with other free countries, to launch a build-up of strength which will support a firm policy directed to the frustration of the Kremlin design. The immediate goal of our efforts to build a successfully functioning political and economic system in the free world backed by adequate military strength is to postpone and avert the disastrous situation which, in light of the Soviet Union's probable fission bomb capability and possible thermonuclear bomb capability, might arise in 1954 on a continuation of our present programs. By acting promptly and vigorously in such a way that this date is, so to speak, pushed into the future, we would permit time for the process of accommodation, withdrawal and frustration to produce the necessary changes in the Soviet system. Time is short, however, and the risks of war attendant upon a decision to build up strength will steadily increase the longer we defer it.

CONCLUSIONS

The foregoing analysis indicates that the probable fission bomb capability and possible thermonuclear bomb capability of the Soviet Union have greatly intensified the Soviet threat to the security of the United States. This threat is of the same character as that described in NSC 20/4 (approved by the President on November 24, 1948) but is more immediate than had previously been estimated. In particular, the United States now faces the contingency that within the next four or five years the Soviet Union will possess the military capability of delivering a surprise atomic attack of such weight that the United States must have substantially increased general air, ground, and sea strength, atomic capabilities, and air and civilian defenses to deter war and to provide reasonable assurance, in the event of war, that it could survive the initial blow and go on to the eventual attainment of its objectives. In return,

this contingency requires the intensification of our efforts in the fields of intelligence and research and development. . . .

Allowing for the immediacy of the danger, the following statement of Soviet threats contained in NSC 20/4, remains valid:

14. The gravest threat to the security of the United States within the foreseeable future stems from the hostile designs and formidable power of the USSR, and from the nature of the Soviet system.

15. The political, economic, and psychological warfare which the USSR is now waging has dangerous potentialities for weakening the relative world position of the United States and disrupting its traditional institutions by means short of war, unless sufficient resistance is encountered in the policies of this and other non-communist countries.

16. The risk of war with the USSR is sufficient to warrant, in common prudence, timely and adequate preparation by the United States.

a. Even though present estimates indicate that the Soviet leaders do not intend deliberate armed action involving the United States at this time, the possibility of such deliberate resort to war cannot be ruled out.

b. Now and for the foreseeable future there is a continuing danger that war will arise either through Soviet miscalculation of the determination of the United States to use all the means at its command to safeguard its security, through Soviet misinterpretation of our intentions, or through U.S. miscalculation of Soviet reactions to measures which we might take.

17. Soviet domination of the potential power of Eurasia, whether achieved by armed aggression or by political and subversive means, would be strategically and politically unacceptable to the United States.

18. The capability of the United States either in peace or in the event of war to cope with threats to its security or to gain its objectives would be severely weakened by internal development, important among which are:

a. Serious espionage, subversion and sabotage, particularly by concerted and well-directed communist activity.

b. Prolonged or exaggerated economic instability.

c. Internal political and social disunity.

d. Inadequate or excessive armament or foreign aid expenditures.

e. An excessive or wasteful usage of our resources in time of peace.

f. Lessening of U.S. prestige and influence through vacillation or appeasement or lack of skill and imagination in the conduct of its foreign policy or by shirking world responsibilities.

g. Development of a false sense of security through a deceptive change in Soviet tactics. . . .

19.

a. To reduce the power and influence of the USSR to limits which no longer constitute a threat to the peace, national independence, and stability of the world family of nations.

b. To bring about a basic change in the conduct of international relations by the government in power in Russia, to conform with the purposes and principles set forth in the UN Charter.

In pursuing these objectives, due care must be taken to avoid permanently impairing our economy and the fundamental values and institutions inherent in our way of life.

20. We should endeavor to achieve our general objectives by methods short of war through the pursuit of the following aims:

a. To encourage and promote the gradual retraction of undue Russian power and influence from the present perimeter areas around traditional Russian boundaries and the emergence of the satellite countries as entities independent of the USSR.

b. To encourage the development among the Russian peoples of attitudes which may help to modify current Soviet behavior and permit a revival of the national life of groups evidencing the ability and determination to achieve and maintain national independence.

c. To eradicate the myth by which people remote from Soviet military influence are held in a position of subservience to Moscow and to cause the world at large to see and understand the true nature of the USSR and the Soviet-directed world communist party, and to adopt a logical and realistic attitude toward them.

d. To create situations which will compel the Soviet Government to recognize the practical undesirability of acting on the basis of its present concepts and the necessity of behaving in accordance with precepts of international conduct, as set forth in the purposes and principles of the UN Charter.

21. Attainment of these aims requires that the United States:

a. Develop a level of military readiness which can be maintained as long as necessary as a deterrent to Soviet aggression, as indispensable support to our political attitude toward the USSR, as a source of encouragement to nations resisting Soviet political aggression, and as an adequate basis for immediate military commitments and for rapid mobilization should war prove unavoidable.

b. Assure the internal security of the United States against dangers of sabotage, subversion, and espionage.

c. Maximize our economic potential, including the strengthening of our peacetime economy and the establishment of essential reserves readily available in the event of war.

d. Strengthen the orientation toward the United States of the non-Soviet nations; and help such of those nations as are able and willing to make an important contribution to U.S. security, to increase their economic and political stability and their military capability.

e. Place the maximum strain on the Soviet structure of power and particularly on the relationship between Moscow and the satellite countries.

f. Keep the U.S. public fully informed and cognizant of the threats to our national security so that it will be prepared to support the measures which we must accordingly adopt.

In the light of present and prospective Soviet atomic capabilities, the action which can be taken under present programs and plans, however, becomes dangerously inadequate, in both timing and scope, to accomplish the rapid progress toward the attainment of the United States political, economic, and military objectives which is now imperative.

A continuation of present trends would result in a serious decline in the strength of the free world relative to the Soviet Union and its satellites. This unfavorable trend arises from the inadequacy of current programs and plans rather than from any error in our objectives and aims. These trends lead in the direction of isolation, not by deliberate decision but by lack of the necessary basis for a vigorous initiative in the conflict with the Soviet Union.

Our position as the center of power in the free world places a heavy responsibility upon the United States for leadership. We must organize and enlist the energies and resources of the free world in a positive program for peace which will frustrate the Kremlin design for world domination by creating a situation in the free world to which the Kremlin will be compelled to adjust. Without such a cooperative effort, led by the United States, we will have to make gradual withdrawals under pressure until we discover one day that we have sacrificed positions of vital interest.

It is imperative that this trend be reversed by a much more rapid and concerted build-up of the actual strength of both the United States and the other nations of the free world. The analysis shows that this will be costly and will involve significant domestic financial and economic adjustments.

The execution of such a build-up, however, requires that the United States have an affirmative program beyond the solely defensive one of countering the threat posed by the Soviet Union. This program must light the path of peace and order among nations in a system based on freedom and justice, as contemplated in the Charter of the United Nations. Further, it must envisage the political and economic measures with which and the military shield behind which the free world can work to frustrate the Kremlin design by the strategy of the cold war; for every consideration of devotion to our fundamental values and to our national security demands that we achieve our objectives by the strategy of the cold war, building up our military strength in order that it may not have to be used. The only sure victory lies in the frustration of the Kremlin design by the steady development of the moral and material strength of the free world and its projection into the Soviet world in such a way as to bring about an internal change in the Soviet system. Such a positive program—harmonious with our fundamental national purpose and our objectives—is necessary if we are to regain and retain the initiative and to win and hold the necessary popular support and cooperation in the United States and the rest of the free world.

This program should include a plan for negotiation with the Soviet Union, developed and agreed with our allies and which is consonant with our objectives. The United States and its allies, particularly the United Kingdom and France, should always be ready to negotiate with the Soviet Union on terms consistent with our objectives. The present world situation, however, is one which militates against successful negotiations with the Kremlin—for the terms of agreements on important pending issues would reflect present realities and would therefore be unacceptable, if not disastrous, to the United States and the rest of the free world. After a decision and a start on building up the strength of the free world has been made, it might then be desirable for the United States to take an initiative in seeking negotiations in the hope that it might facilitate the process of accommodation by the Kremlin to the new situation. Failing that, the unwillingness of the Kremlin to accept equitable terms or its bad faith in observing them would assist in consolidating popular opinion in the free world in support of the measures necessary to sustain the build-up.

In summary, we must, by means of a rapid and sustained build-up of the political, economic, and military strength of the free world, and by means of an affirmative program intended to wrest the initiative from the Soviet Union, confront it with convincing evidence of the determination and ability of the free world to frustrate the Kremlin design of a world dominated by its will. Such evidence is the only means short of war which eventually may force the Kremlin to abandon its present course of action and to negotiate acceptable agreements on issues of major importance.

The whole success of the proposed program hangs ultimately on recognition by this Government, the American people, and all free peoples, that the cold war is in fact a real war in which the survival of the free world is at stake. Essential prerequisites to success are consultations with Congressional leaders designed to make the program the object of non-partisan legislative support, and a presentation to the public of a full explanation of the facts and implications of the present international situation. The prosecution of the program will require of us all the ingenuity, sacrifice, and unity demanded by the vital importance of the issue and the tenacity to persevere until our national objectives have been attained. . . .

Questions

1. NSC-68 established a real opposition between the United States and the Soviet Union. What fundamental sources of that conflict are mentioned in this document?
2. What basic assumptions does this document make about the relationship between the United States and the Soviet Union?
3. How does the new stance outlined in NSC-68 differ from containment? Could containment and the stance of NSC-68 have been reconciled? If so, how?

Questions for Further Thought

1. How is the threat posed by the Soviet Union portrayed in Documents 28-1 through 28-4?
2. How did containment policy evolve from Kennan's early formulation (Document 28-1) to the more formal NSC-68 (Document 28-4)?
3. Did the Truman Doctrine (Document 28-2), NATO (Document 28-3), and NSC-68 (Document 28-4) serve the aims of containment?

Harry Truman and the Fair Deal

Years of seemingly intractable economic depression left few American policy makers confident that the postwar economic future had been secured by the New Deal or by artificial wartime prosperity. Congressional leaders, including many who had opposed the New Deal all along, were reluctant to rethink economic and social programs for the postwar years, particularly if they echoed New Deal programs.

Truman's handling of post–World War II reconversion was in part an inheritance from Franklin Delano Roosevelt. After twelve years of depression the United States had not been in a position to mount a major wartime industrial expansion, although it was in much better shape than Britain and France. However, the legacy of unfinished social programs was important: whether Social Security would be expanded and medical care added to it, for example, and the question of how to deal with organized labor, given its mandate by the New Deal and its expansion during the war (see text pp. 874–876).

Even for a Democratic president labor relations could be difficult as the uneasy wartime truce kept coming unstuck. The suspicions Truman harbored about labor giants such as John L. Lewis (see text pp. 875–876) were similar to those of Roosevelt (Document 28-6). There were major strikes in the coal industry, steel, and the railroads. Truman was prepared to use military intervention when he felt national interests were at stake (see text p. 875). One of the most important legacies of the New Deal and the production boom during World War II concerned the promise of full employment, which for generations had been a progressive-liberal pledge to the nation's workers. The Employment Act of 1946 was an attempt to keep this promise (Document 28-5; see text p. 875).

The war had promised improved conditions for American blacks. African-American workers who had worked in factories during the war were barred from unions, laid off, and replaced by whites afterward. Black soldiers returning from the war faced discrimination that often involved violence. Truman pledged himself to protect the rights of all Americans (Document 28-7), but his proposals floundered in a Congress controlled by a conservative coalition of northern Republicans and southern Democrats. His one action of substance came when he ordered the desegregation of American military services.

The perceived threat of Soviet expansion abroad was reflected in anxiety over domestic communist activities, real or imagined. Senator Joseph R. McCarthy of Wisconsin became both the symbol and the practitioner of a form of Red-baiting Americans had not seen since the 1930s. Accommodation with the Soviet Union had been a necessary element in the wartime alliance, and the emergence of the Cold War created a fear of Soviet influence that could be used to attack anyone perceived as favoring liberal social programs, let alone sympathizing with the Soviet Union. McCarthy committed himself to evicting from the government anyone he could accuse of Soviet sympathies, turning what might have been a legitimate interest in the Soviet Union into implications of active espionage (Document 28-8; see text pp. 878–881).

28-5 The Employment Act of 1946

The Employment Act of 1946 signaled the beginning of permanent government involvement in the American economy. It integrated Keynesian ideas into economic policy (see text pp. 874–875), supporting government spending to spur economic growth and envisioning the use of taxes as a tool to manage the economy. It also called for the president to appoint a Council of Economic Advisers who would be directly accountable to the White House.

Source: United States, *Statutes at Large*, vol. 60, pp. 23–26.

DECLARATION OF POLICY

SEC. 2. The Congress hereby declares that it is the continuing policy and responsibility of the Federal Government to use all practicable means consistent with its needs and obligations and other essential considerations of national policy, with the assistance and cooperation of industry, agriculture, labor, and State and local governments, to coordinate and utilize all its plans, functions, and resources for the purpose of creating and maintaining, in a manner calculated to foster and promote free competitive enterprise and the general welfare, conditions under which there will be afforded useful employment opportunities, including self-employment, for those able, willing, and seeking to work, and to promote maximum employment, production, and purchasing power.

ECONOMIC REPORT OF THE PRESIDENT

SEC. 3. (a) The President shall transmit to the Congress within sixty days after the beginning of each regular session (commencing with the year 1947) an economic report (hereinafter called the "Economic Report") setting forth (1) the levels of employment, production, and purchasing power obtaining in the United States and such levels needed to carry out the policy declared in section 2; (2) current and foreseeable trends in the levels of employment, production, and purchasing power; (3) a review of the economic program of the Federal Government and a review of economic conditions affecting employment in the United States or any considerable portion thereof during the preceding year and of their effect upon employment, production, and purchasing power; and (4) a program for carrying out the policy declared in section 2, together with such recommendations for legislation as he may deem necessary or desirable.

(b) The President may transmit from time to time to the Congress reports supplementary to the Economic Report, each of which shall include such supplementary or revised recommendations as he may deem necessary or desirable to achieve the policy declared in section 2.

(c) The Economic Report, and all supplementary reports transmitted under subsection (b), shall, when transmitted to Congress, be referred to the joint committee created by section 5.

COUNCIL OF ECONOMIC ADVISERS TO THE PRESIDENT

SEC. 4. (a) There is hereby created in the Executive Office of the President, a Council of Economic Advisers (hereinafter called the "Council"). The Council shall be composed of three members who shall be appointed by the President, by and with the advice and consent of the Senate, and each of whom shall be a person who, as a result of his training, experience, and attainments, is exceptionally qualified to analyze and interpret economic developments, to appraise programs and activities of the Government in the light of the policy declared in section 2, and to formulate and recommend national economy policy to promote employment, production, and purchasing power under free competitive enterprise. Each member of the Council shall receive compensation at the rate of $15,000 per annum. The President shall designate one of the members of the Council as chairman and one as vice chairman, who shall act as chairman in the absence of the chairman.

(b) The Council is authorized to employ, and fix the compensation of, such specialists and other experts as may be necessary for the carrying out of its functions under this Act, without regard to the civil-service laws and the Classification Act of 1923, as amended, and is authorized, subject to the civil-service laws, to employ such other officers and employees as may be necessary for carrying out its functions under this Act, and fix their compensation in accordance with the Classification Act of 1923, as amended.

(c) It shall be the duty and function of the Council–

(1) to assist and advise the President in the preparation of the Economic Report;

(2) to gather timely and authoritative information concerning economic developments and economic trends, both current and prospective, to analyze and interpret such information in the light of the policy declared in section 2 for the purpose of determining whether such developments and trends are interfering, or are likely to interfere, with the achievement of such policy, and to compile and submit to the President studies relating to such developments and trends;

(3) to appraise the various programs and activities of the Federal Government in the light of the policy declared in section 2 for the purpose of determining the extent to which such programs and activities are

contributing, and the extent to which they are not contributing, to the achievement of such policy, and to make recommendations to the President with respect thereto;

(4) to develop and recommend to the President national economic policies to foster and promote free competitive enterprise, to avoid economic fluctuations or to diminish the effects thereof, and to maintain employment, production, and purchasing power;

(5) to make and furnish such studies, report thereon, and recommendations with respect to matters of Federal economic policy and legislation as the President may request.

(d) The Council shall make an annual report to the President in December of each year.

(e) In exercising its powers, functions and duties under this Act—

(1) the Council may constitute such advisory committees and may consult with such representatives of industry, agriculture, labor, consumers, State and local governments, and other groups, as it deems advisable;

(2) the Council shall, to the fullest extent possible, utilize the services, facilities, and information (including statistical information) of other Government agencies as well as of private research agencies, in order that duplication of effort and expense may be avoided.

(f) To enable the Council to exercise its powers, functions, and duties under this Act, there are authorized to be appropriate (except for the salaries of the members and the salaries of officers and employees of the Council) such sums as may be necessary. For the salaries of the members and the salaries of officers and employees of the Council, there is authorized to be appropriated not exceeding $345,000 in the aggregate for each fiscal year.

JOINT COMMITTEE ON THE ECONOMIC REPORT

Sec. 5. (a) There is hereby established a Joint Committee on the Economic Report, to be composed of seven Members of the Senate, to be appointed by the President of the Senate, and seven Members of the House of Representatives, to be appointed by the Speaker of the House of Representatives. The party representation on the joint committee shall as nearly as may be feasible reflect the relative membership of the majority and minority parties in the Senate and House of Representatives.

(b) It shall be the function of the joint committee—

(1) to make a continuing study of matters relating to the Economic Report;

(2) to study means of coordinating programs in order to further the policy of this Act; and

(3) as a guide to the several committees of the Congress dealing with legislation relating to the Economic Report, not later than May 1 of each year (beginning with the year 1947) to file a report with the Senate and the House of Representatives containing its findings and recommendations with respect to each of the main recommendations made by the President in the Economic Report, and from time to time to make such other reports and recommendations to the Senate and House of Representatives as it deems advisable.

(c) Vacancies in the membership of the joint committee shall not affect the power of the remaining members to execute the functions of the joint committee, and shall be filled in the same manner as in the case of the original selection. The joint committee shall select a chairman and a vice chairman from among its members.

(d) The joint committee, or any duly authorized subcommittee thereof, is authorized to hold such hearings as it deems advisable, and, within the limitations of its appropriations, the joint committee is empowered to appoint and fix the compensation of such experts, consultants, technicians, and clerical and stenographic assistants, to procure such printing and binding, and to make such expenditures, as it deems necessary and advisable. The cost of stenographic services to report hearings of the joint committee, or any subcommittee thereof, shall not exceed 25 cents per hundred words. The joint committee is authorized to utilize the services, information, and facilities of the departments and establishments of the Government, and also of private research agencies.

(e) There is hereby authorized to be appropriated for each fiscal year, the sum of $50,000, or so much thereof as may be necessary, to carry out the provisions of this section, to be disbursed by the Secretary of the Senate on vouchers signed by the chairman or vice chairman.

Approved February 20, 1946.

Questions

1. At several points the textbook refers to the influence of the English economist John Maynard Keynes on American economic policy. What were Keynes's economic beliefs?

2. What evidence is there in the act to indicate that it integrated Keynesian ideas into American economic policy?

3. What are the president's responsibilities for dealing with unemployment under this legislation? How does Congress control economic policy making under this law?

28-6   Harry S Truman on John L. Lewis and the Coal Strike of 1946

President Harry Truman and the United Mine Workers leader John L. Lewis had crossed swords during World War II. Truman, then the chairman of a Senate committee investigating the carrying out of war contracts, had called Lewis "sassy" for what Truman considered his defiance of the committee's authority. Lewis, remembering the treatment accorded to labor in the aftermath of World War I (see text pp. 732–733, 745), was not inclined to bend to Truman's will (see text p. 875).

Source: Harry S. Truman, diary entry for December 11, 1946, in *Off the Record: The Private Papers of Harry S. Truman*, ed. Robert H. Ferrell (New York: Harper & Row, 1980), pp. 103–104.

DIARY

December 11, 1946

Lewis called a coal strike in the spring of 1946. For no good reason. He called it after agreeing to carry on negotiations without calling it. At least he told John Steelman [special assistant to the president] to tell me there would be no strike. He called one on the old gag that the miners do not work when they have no contract.

After prolonged negotiation I decided to exercise the powers under the second war power act and take over the mines. After they were taken over a contract was negotiated between the Secretary of the Interior, Mr. Krug, and John L. Lewis.

The contract was signed in my office on the 5th of May and Mr. Lewis stated for the movies that it was his best contract and would not be broken during the time of Government control of the mines.

Along in September and October 1946 there arose some minor disputes between the Solid Fuels Administrator and Mr. Lewis. Nothing of vital importance—purely details of interpretation of the contract with regard to coal weights on which the new welfare fund is based and some other small details that could have been settled easily by a half hour discussion.

But Mr. Lewis wanted to be sure that the President would be in the most embarrassing position possible for the Congressional elections on Nov. 6. So he served a notice on the first day of November that he would consider his contract at an end on a certain date. Which was, in effect, calling a strike on that date. He called his strike by a subterfuge in order to avoid prosecution under the Smith-Connally Act. But he'll be prosecuted never the less. [This last sentence was written in later.]

The strike took place as planned by Mr. Lewis. It lasted seventeen days and then Mr. Lewis decided for the first time in his life that he had "over-reached himself." He is a Hitler at heart, a demagogue in action and a traitor in fact. In 1942 he should have been hanged for treason. In Germany under Hitler, his ideal, in Italy under the great castor oil giver, or in Russia now he would have been "eliminated." Only in the greatest country on earth could he operate and have the support of such harmless wonders as [Philip] Murray [president of the Congress of Industrial Organizations] and [William] Green [president of the American Federation of Labor], [Alexander F.] Whitney [head of the Brotherhood of Railway Trainmen] and [Alvanley] Johnson [head of the Brotherhood of Locomotive Engineers].

There was only one thing for me to do when he called his strike by indirection and that was to take him to a cleaning.

I discussed the situation with the secretaries in the White House at the morning meeting after the fake strike call and warned them that it was a fight to the finish. At the Cabinet meeting on Friday before the election the Attorney General was instructed to take such legal steps as would protect the Government. Discussions were held with all the Cabinet and special meetings were called at which the Solid Fuels Administrator, Mr. Krug, the Secretary of Labor, Mr. Schwellenbach, the Attorney General, Mr. Clark, the Special Counselor to the President, Mr. Clifford, and the Special Assistant to the President, Dr. John Steelman, were present.

The instructions were a fight to the finish, by every legal means available, and in the end to open the mines by force if that became necessary.

Mr. Lewis was hauled in to Federal Court, fined no mean sum for contempt. Action was started to enforce the contract and I had prepared an address to the country to be delivered on Sunday evening Dec. 8, [to commemorate the] anniversary of Pearl Harbor.

Mr. Lewis folded up on Saturday afternoon Dec. 7 at 3 P.M. He is, as all bullies are, as yellow as a dog pound pup. He cannot face the music when the tune is not to his liking. On the front under shell fire he'd crack up. But he can direct the murder, assault and battery goon squads as long as he doesn't have to face them.

He tried to get into communication with me while I was taking a sun treatment at Key West for a cold. He tried to talk to Dr. Steelman; he tried to approach the Secretary of the Navy, Mr. Forrestal; he tried to get in touch with the

Secretary of Labor on the night before the fold up. For [the] first time he found no pipe line to the White House. I had a fully loyal team and that team whipped a damned traitor.

Questions

1. What is the significance of Truman's use of the concepts of patriotism and loyalty in response to Lewis's behavior?
2. The New Deal is generally interpreted as having achieved the liberation of organized labor. Was Truman stepping back from that?
3. How should a diary be read as a historical document? What are a diary's advantages over a public document? Its disadvantages?

28-7   Harry S Truman on Civil Rights (1947)

President Truman's attitude toward civil rights is remarkable for its combination of political pragmatism and honest morality. As he wrote to an old friend and opponent of racial integration: "I am not asking for social equality, because no such thing exists, but I am asking for equality of opportunity for all human beings and, as long as I stay here [remain president], I am going to continue that fight." This attitude rings clearly through Truman's speech before the National Association for the Advancement of Colored People on June 29, 1947. Speaking at the Lincoln Memorial—the same site as Martin Luther King, Jr.'s "I Have a Dream" speech in 1963—Truman expressed his hope that all Americans could be granted an opportunity to enjoy civil rights under the law (see text p. 878).

Source: Public Papers of the Presidents of the United States: Harry S. Truman, 1947 (Washington, D.C.: U.S. Government Printing Office, 1963), pp. 311–313.

I am happy to be present at the closing session of the 38th Annual Conference of the National Association for the Advancement of Colored People. The occasion of meeting with you here at the Lincoln Memorial affords me the opportunity to congratulate the association upon its effective work for the improvement of our democratic processes.

I should like to talk to you briefly about civil rights and human freedom. It is my deep conviction that we have reached a turning point in the long history of our country's efforts to guarantee freedom and equality to all our citizens. Recent events in the United States and abroad have made us realize that it is more important today than ever before to insure that all Americans enjoy these rights.

When I say all Americans I mean all Americans.

The civil rights laws written in the early years of our Republic, and the traditions which have been built upon them, are precious to us. Those laws were drawn up with

the memory still fresh in men's minds of the tyranny of an absentee government. They were written to protect the citizen against any possible tyrannical act by the new government in this country.

But we cannot be content with a civil liberties program which emphasizes only the need of protection against the possibility of tyranny by the Government.

We cannot stop there.

We must keep moving forward, with new concepts of civil rights to safeguard our heritage. The extension of civil rights today means, not protection of the people *against* the Government, but protection of the people *by* the Government.

We must make the Federal Government a friendly, vigilant defender of the rights and equalities of all Americans. And again I mean all Americans.

As Americans, we believe that every man should be

free to live his life as he wishes. He should be limited only by his responsibility to his fellow countrymen. If this freedom is to be more than a dream, each man must be guaranteed equality of opportunity. The only limit to an American's achievement should be his ability, his industry, and his character. These rewards for his effort should be determined only by those truly relevant qualities.

Our immediate task is to remove the last remnants of the barriers which stand between millions of our citizens and their birthright. There is no justifiable reason for discrimination because of ancestry, or religion, or race, or color.

We must not tolerate such limitations on the freedom of any of our people and on their enjoyment of basic rights which every citizen in a truly democratic society must possess.

Every man should have the right to a decent home, the right to an education, the right to adequate medical care, the right to a worthwhile job, the right to an equal share in making the public decisions through the ballot, and the right to a fair trial in a fair court.

We must insure that these rights—on equal terms—are enjoyed by every citizen.

To these principles I pledge my full and continued support.

Many of our people still suffer the indignity of insult, the narrowing fear of intimidation, and, I regret to say, the threat of physical injury and mob violence. Prejudice and intolerance in which these evils are rooted still exist. The conscience of our Nation, and the legal machinery which enforces it, have not yet secured to each citizen full freedom from fear.

We cannot wait another decade or another generation to remedy these evils. We must work, as never before, to cure them now. The aftermath of war and the desire to keep faith with our Nation's historic principles make the need a pressing one.

The support of desperate populations of battle-ravaged countries must be won for the free way of life. We must have them as allies in our continuing struggle for the peaceful solution of the world's problems. Freedom is not an easy lesson to teach, nor an easy cause to sell, to peoples beset by every kind of privation. They may surrender to the false security offered so temptingly by totalitarian regimes unless we can prove the superiority of democracy.

Our case for democracy should be as strong as we can make it. It should rest on practical evidence that we have been able to put our own house in order.

For these compelling reasons, we can no longer afford the luxury of a leisurely attack upon prejudice and discrimination. There is much that State and local governments can do in providing positive safeguards for civil rights. But we cannot, any longer, await the growth of a will to action in the slowest State or the most backward community.

Our National Government must show the way.

This is a difficult and complex undertaking. Federal laws and administrative machineries must be improved and expanded. We must provide the Government with better tools to do the job. As a first step, I appointed an Advisory Committee on Civil Rights last December. Its members, fifteen distinguished private citizens, have been surveying our civil rights difficulties and needs for several months. I am confident that the product of their work will be a sensible and vigorous program for action by all of us.

We must strive to advance civil rights wherever it lies within our power. For example, I have asked the Congress to pass legislation extending basic civil rights to the people of Guam and American Samoa so that these people can share our ideals of freedom and self-government. This step, with others which will follow, is evidence to the rest of the world of our confidence in the ability of all men to build free institutions.

The way ahead is not easy. We shall need all the wisdom, imagination and courage we can muster. We must and shall guarantee the civil rights of all our citizens. Never before has the need been so urgent for skillful and vigorous action to bring us closer to our ideal.

We can reach the goal. When past difficulties faced our Nation we met the challenge with inspiring charters of human rights—the Declaration of Independence, the Constitution, the Bill of Rights, and the Emancipation Proclamation. Today our representatives, and those of other liberty-loving countries on the United Nations Commission on Civil Rights, are preparing an International Bill of Rights. We can be confident that it will be a great landmark in man's long search for freedom since its members consist of such distinguished citizens of the world as Mrs. Franklin D. Roosevelt.

With these noble characters to guide us, and with faith in our hearts, we shall make our land a happier home for our people, a symbol of hope for all men, and a rock of security in a troubled world.

Abraham Lincoln understood as well the ideal which you and I seek today. As this conference closes we would do well to keep in mind his words, when he said,

". . . . if it shall please the Divine Being who determines the destinies of nations, we shall remain a united people, and we will, humbly seeking the Divine Guidance, make their prolonged national existence a source of new benefits to themselves and their successors, and to all classes and conditions of mankind."

Questions

1. What role does President Truman believe the federal government should play in the field of civil rights? Does this reflect a changed role for the government?
2. What basic rights does Truman make a commitment to protect for all Americans?
3. What steps has the president taken or does he propose to take to advance civil rights in the United States?

28-8   Joseph R. McCarthy on Communists in the U.S. Government (1950)

Senator Joseph R. McCarthy (R–Wisconsin), who preferred the all-American name Joe, kept a low profile in the Senate through the early years of a term that began in 1947. Figuring that to win reelection in 1952 he would need an issue to bring him national attention, in 1950 he hit on the idea of "communists in government." What began as a campaign issue quickly took on a new life at a time when Americans had grown fearful of communist subversion at home and aggression abroad (see text p. 878). On February 9, 1950, in a speech before Republican women in Wheeling, West Virginia, McCarthy tried out his idea, claiming to have a list of 205 known Communists in the State Department (see text p. 881). In the version of the speech he read into the *Congressional Record* on February 20, 1950 (the version given here), he revised the number to 57, and an investigating committee of the Senate later rejected all his accusations. For four years McCarthy remained in the spotlight with an anticommunist crusade that generated such notoriety that it gave rise to a new noun in the political lexicon, *McCarthyism*.

Source: Congressional Record, 81st Cong., 2d sess., 1950, vol. 96, pt. 2, pp. 1954–1957.

Five years after a world war has been won, men's hearts should anticipate a long peace, and men's minds should be free from the heavy weight that comes with war. But this is not such a period—for this is not a period of peace. This is a time of the "cold war." This is a time when all the world is split into two vast, increasingly hostile armed camps—a time of a great armaments race.

Today we can almost physically hear the mutterings and rumblings of an invigorated god of war. You can see it, feel it, and hear it all the way from the hills of Indochina, from the shores of Formosa, right over into the very heart of Europe itself. . . .

[W]e are now engaged in a show-down fight—not the usual war between nations for land areas or other material gains, but a war between two diametrically opposed ideologies.

The great difference between our western Christian world and the atheistic Communist world is not political, ladies and gentlemen, it is moral. . . .

The real, basic difference, however, lies in the religion of immoralism—invented by Marx, preached feverishly by Lenin, and carried to unimaginable extremes by Stalin. This religion of immoralism, if the Red half of the world wins—and well it may—this religion of immoralism will more deeply wound and damage mankind than any conceivable economic or political system.

Karl Marx dismissed God as a hoax, and Lenin and Stalin have added in clear-cut, unmistakable language their resolve that no nation, no people who believe in a God, can exist side by side with their communistic state.

Karl Marx, for example, expelled people from his Communist Party for mentioning such things as justice, humanity, or morality. He called this soulful ravings and sloppy sentimentality.

While Lincoln was a relatively young man in his late thirties, Karl Marx boasted that the Communist specter was haunting Europe. Since that time, hundreds of millions of people and vast areas of the world have fallen under Communist domination. Today, less than 100 years after Lincoln's death, Stalin brags that this Communist specter is not only haunting the world, but is about to completely subjugate it.

Today we are engaged in a final, all-out battle between communistic atheism and Christianity. The modern champions of communism have selected this as the time. And, ladies and gentlemen, the chips are down—they are truly down. . . .

Ladies and gentlemen, can there be anyone here tonight who is so blind as to say that the war is not on? Can there be anyone who fails to realize that the Communist world has said, "The time is now"—and that this is the time for the show-down between the democratic Christian world and the Communist atheistic world?

Unless we face this fact, we shall pay the price that must be paid by those who wait too long.

Six years ago, at the time of the first conference to map out the peace—Dumbarton Oaks—there was within the Soviet orbit 180,000,000 people. Lined up on the anti-totalitarian side there were in the world at that time roughly 1,625,000,000 people. Today only 6 years later, there are 800,000,000 people under the absolute domination of Soviet Russia—an increase of over 400 percent. On our side, the figure has shrunk to around 500,000,000. In other words, in less than 6 years the odds have changed from 9 to 1 in our favor to 8 to 5 against us. This indicates the swiftness of the tempo of Communist victories and American defeats in the cold war. As one of our outstanding historical figures once said, "When a great democracy is destroyed, it will not be because of enemies from without, but rather because of enemies from within."

The truth of this statement is becoming terrifyingly clear as we see this country each day losing on every front.

At war's end we were physically the strongest nation on earth and, at least potentially, the most powerful intellectually and morally. Ours could have been the honor of being a beacon in the desert of destruction, a shining living proof that civilization was not yet ready to destroy itself. Unfortunately, we have failed miserably and tragically to arise to the opportunity.

The reason why we find ourselves in a position of impotency is not because our only powerful potential enemy has sent men to invade our shores, but rather because of the traitorous actions of those who have been treated so well by this Nation. It has not been the less fortunate or members of minority groups who have been selling this Nation out, but rather those who have had all the benefits that the wealthiest nation on earth has had to offer—the finest homes, the finest college education, and the finest jobs in Government we can give.

This is glaringly true in the State Department. There the bright young men who are born with silver spoons in their mouths are the ones who have been worst. . . .

When Chiang Kai-shek [Jiang Jieshi] was fighting our war, the State Department had in China a young man named John S. Service. His task, obviously, was not to work for the communization of China. Strangely, however, he sent official reports back to the State Department urging that we torpedo our ally Chiang Kai-shek and stating, in effect, that communism was the best hope of China.

Later, this man—John Service—was picked up by the Federal Bureau of Investigation for turning over to the Communists secret State Department information. Strangely, however, he was never prosecuted. However, Joseph Grew, the Under Secretary of State, who insisted on his prosecution, was forced to resign. Two days after Grew's successor, Dean Acheson, took over as Under Secretary of State, this man—John Service—who had been picked up by the FBI and who had previously urged that communism was the best hope of China, was not only reinstated in the State Department but promoted. And finally, under Acheson, placed in charge of all placements and promotions.

Today, ladies and gentlemen, this man Service is on his way to represent the State Department and Acheson in Calcutta—by far and away the most important listening post in the Far East. . . .

This, ladies and gentlemen, gives you somewhat of a picture of the type of individuals who have been helping to shape our foreign policy. In my opinion the State Department, which is one of the most important government departments, is thoroughly infested with Communists.

I have in my hand 57 cases of individuals who would appear to be either card carrying members or certainly loyal to the Communist Party, but who nevertheless are still helping to shape our foreign policy.

One thing to remember in discussing the Communists in our Government is that we are not dealing with spies who get 30 pieces of silver to steal the blueprints of a new weapon. We are dealing with a far more sinister type of activity because it permits the enemy to guide and shape our policy. . . .

It is the result of an emotional hang-over and a temporary moral lapse which follows every war. It is the apathy to evil which people who have been subjected to the tremendous evils of war feel. As the people of the world see mass murder, the destruction of defenseless and innocent people, and all of the crime and lack of morals which go with war, they become numb and apathetic. It has always been thus after war.

However, the morals of our people have not been destroyed. They still exist. This cloak of numbness and apathy has only needed a spark to rekindle them. Happily, this spark has finally been supplied.

As you know, very recently the Secretary of State proclaimed his loyalty to a man guilty of what has always been considered as the most abominable of all crimes—of being a traitor to the people who gave him a position of great trust. The Secretary of State in attempting to justify his continued devotion to the man who sold out the Christian world to the atheistic world, referred to Christ's Sermon on the Mount as a justification and reason therefor, and the reaction of the American people to this would have made the heart of Abraham Lincoln happy.

When this pompous diplomat in striped pants, with a phony British accent, proclaimed to the American people that Christ on the Mount endorsed communism, high treason, and betrayal of a sacred trust, the blasphemy was so great that it awakened the dormant indignation of the American people.

He has lighted the spark which is resulting in a moral uprising and will end only when the whole sorry mess of twisted, warped thinkers are swept from the national scene so that we may have a new birth of national honesty and decency in Government.

Questions

1. What do the changes in Senator McCarthy's numbers seem to signify?
2. What do you take the biblical references to mean? Do they seem appropriate? Who might have been the intended audience?
3. The fact that the enemies mentioned in this speech are not poor but are members of a privileged class seems significant to McCarthy. What do you take that to mean?

Questions for Further Thought

1. What do Documents 28-6 through 28-8 say about challenges to civil liberties and the expansion of civil rights during the Truman era?
2. Personal relationships and personalities seem at least as important as issues in these documents. Explain.
3. What constituencies did Truman and McCarthy represent? What groups are they addressing in these documents? What constituencies are they willing to take as their opposition?

"Modern Republicanism"

In the presidential election of 1952 Dwight Eisenhower's personal popularity and the political troubles that plagued the Democrats assured "Ike" a great victory (see text p. 882). Some Republican leaders hoped that the GOP's return to the White House would signal the end of social and economic reforms and the dismantling of the New Deal. Eisenhower refused to turn back the political clock but did promise a modern Republicanism that would bring prosperity at home and maintain strength abroad. The continuing Cold War demanded that much of the new president's attention be paid to foreign policy.

Searching for a method to deal with international issues without involving U.S. ground troops, Eisenhower and his secretary of state, John Foster Dulles, formulated a conception of foreign policy that proposed "massive retaliation" and limited nuclear warfare to provide "more bang for the buck." The resulting "New Look" could establish superior military power without threatening the nation with bankruptcy (Document 28-9; see text pp. 885–886).

Many of Eisenhower's challenges in foreign policy involved postcolonial problems in Egypt, India, and Pakistan. Later crises in Iran, Iraq, and Vietnam had their beginnings in the Eisenhower administration's efforts to maintain a strong defense against Soviet expansion, including the creation of regional military alliances (see text p. 886).

The decision to maintain a permanent and expanding military machine in the climate of the Cold War required financial support from Congress and a commitment by private industry, corporate laboratories, and research universities to supply new ideas and military equipment. This alliance among government, industry, and education gave rise to what became known as "the military-industrial complex," a new entity that received a good deal of attention in President Eisenhower's farewell address (Document 28-10) in 1961 (see text p. 889).

28-9 John Foster Dulles on American Foreign Policy (1958)

The idea of the threat of global communism was fed by interpretations of the Korean War as a conspiracy of the Soviet Union and China. Knowledge that the relationship between the two communist superpowers was not that strong and that cracks were developing in it did little to influence American foreign policy. Secretary of State John Foster Dulles sought a balance that would continue to support calls for freedom without promising more American military aid than the American public in the post-Korea era would be willing to sustain (see text pp. 885–886). However, a land war on the European continent against Soviet troops would be a different matter. The excerpts that follow indicate the ambivalence inherent in promoting a containment policy while trying to avoid military conflict.

Source: Department of State Bulletin, February 17, 1958, pp. 250–254.

Gentlemen, the close of World War II raised mankind's hopes that a new era of peace and security for all might now prevail. Unfortunately, these hopes were soon dashed. Instead, free men and free nations found themselves faced with a struggle to preserve their independence from the predatory ambitions of Communist imperialism. Moscow and Peiping [Beijing] directly or through local Communist parties, have relentlessly sought to extend their control in every direction. Where they have succeeded, freedom of choice has become a sham, the dignity of the individual a hollow mockery. The list of once free and proud nations that must today wear the Communist yoke is painful to recall. They are nearly a score in number. Coercion alone keeps them in this state of bondage, as was demonstrated by the recent revolt of the Hungarian people against their alien masters. Yet the parties of international communism continue openly to proclaim their goal of world domination. They did so again, only last November, at Moscow.

Currently the use and threat of military power are supplemented by intensified and enlarged efforts at subversion and seduction. These efforts are insidious and decep-

tive. They seize upon mankind's yearning for economic and social betterment to undermine his vigilance to resist enslavement. . . .

Fortunately, there is, in general, a clear perception of the threat to independence posed by Communist imperialism. Around the world, the free nations have drawn together in collective regional associations as authorized and encouraged by the charter of the United Nations. These associations would, I believe, profit from exchange of information and of experience as between themselves. . . .

We are well aware of the fact that in this general area political independence, always an aspiration, has sometimes been lost and oftentimes been threatened, as indeed it is threatened today.

Also we recognize that it is not enough merely to want, or now have, independence. Reliable independence rests on two pillars: the pillar of defensive security and the pillar of economic health. The United States is prepared to cooperate, where desired, in assisting in these two ways any nation or group of nations in the general area of the Middle East to maintain national independence.

DEFENSIVE SECURITY

Let me speak first of security.

Security cannot be taken for granted. It must be won by positive efforts. It is not won by pacifism, by weakness, or by appeasement. That has been demonstrated time after time. Security is won by conditions which make it apparent that aggression does not pay. If a potential aggressor realizes that he will, by aggression, lose more than he could gain, it can be reliably assumed that he will not attempt aggression. That is where collective security plays its indispensable role. Few nations, by themselves, possess the resources needed to deter aggression. Collectively they can do so. Therefore, sometimes by treaty, sometimes by congressional resolution, the United States has associated itself with over 40 nations in defense of national independence and of peace. . . .

The Baghdad Pact group of countries can be confident that mobile power of great force would, as needed, be brought to bear against any Communist aggressor. And by the same token any such potential aggressor knows in advance that his losses from aggression would far exceed any possible gains. That is an effective deterrent to aggression and a guaranty of peace.

Also, it is vital that there be forces of national defense. These constitute indispensable, visible evidence of the will of people to fight and die, if need be, for their homes, their nation, and their faith. There is no "pushbutton" substitute for this. Furthermore, such forces, with the reinforcement where needed of mobile power, can save the people from the scourge of invasion if, perchance, deterrence fails. The United States has contributed, and will contribute, to this aspect of defense. . . .

I assure you that the United States strives earnestly both to end the nuclear menace and to limit conventional armaments. I recall that a decade ago the United States, possessing a monopoly of atomic weapons, offered to forgo that monopoly and to join in establishing a system to assure that atomic power would be used only for peaceful purposes. The Soviet Union alone blocked that peaceful and humanitarian measure.

And we act in the same spirit today. Outer space is becoming, for the first time, usable, and both the United States and the Soviet Union are experimentally using outer space for weapons purposes. So the United States has proposed to the Soviet Union that the nations forgo the use of outer space for war and dedicate it for all time to the peaceful purposes of mankind, to man's fuller life, not to his greater peril. So far that proposal remains without positive response.

The Soviet Union has, however, by a statement made last week, advanced the grotesque theory that only atheistic governments, as are the Communists, can properly possess modern weapons. The argument is that it would be a sacrilege for religious peoples, for defenders of the faith, to have such weapons; thus only the atheists, the Communists, can have them.

The United States ardently seeks limitation of armament on the basis of equality. But never will the United States accept the Soviet Communist thesis that men, because they are religious, must deny themselves the means to defend their religious freedom.

ECONOMIC HEALTH

Let me speak now of economic health. This is an equally indispensable pillar of independence. Without it no nation can maintain adequate and dependable security forces or be able surely to resist subversion.

Large military establishments are not easily reconciled with economic welfare. One of the merits of collective self-defense is that it reduces the requirements for individual self-defense. For under a collective system the mobile power that protects one can equally protect many. In this way, and only in this way, is it made possible for nations confronted by superior hostile power to avoid making the people fear an excessive nonproductive military burden and enable them to combine military security with economic health.

Military authorities can advise us about military security. But there is need also for a broad political judgment that comprehends both military and economic factors. Some economic sacrifices are needed for military security. We dare not give so absolute a priority to military requirements that economic health collapses. Indeed a sound and developing economy is the indispensable foundation for sustained military effort. Furthermore, given the deterrent military power that exists in the world today, there may be greater risk to independence in economic weakness than in local military weakness. It is not easy to strike the proper balance between military and economic effort. To achieve that is, however, the paramount duty of statesmanship. . . .

Social and economic progress is a universal desire. It is understandably most acute among those peoples who, for various historical reasons, do not yet fully share in the benefits of modern technology and science. These improve man's health, ease his labor, and afford him greater opportunities to develop his own talents and spiritual resources. . . .

MEETING THE COMMUNIST THREAT

Gentlemen, we live in difficult days. By great efforts over the centuries—efforts marked by successes and failures—men have reached a great appreciation of the dignity of the human individual and the need for an organization of the society of nations in accordance with the tested principles of collective security and friendly cooperation. Yet at the moment, when so much seems possible, all is endangered. A small group believes fanatically in a materialistic, atheistic society. It believes in mechanistic conformity, both in terms of human beings and of national groups. It would turn men into cogs in a materialistic machine, thinking and acting under central dictatorship. It boasts that it is "internationalist" in the sense of bringing all governments everywhere under the domination of a single power, that of international communism, acting under the guiding direction of the Communist Party of the Soviet Union.

This fanatical group, using every device without moral restraint—for they deny the existence of a moral law—by use of revolution, military conquest, and subversion have come to rule a great part of the world, and they exploit the human and material resources they now control to extend their domination over the rest of us.

That is a threat of immense proportions. We need not,

however, be dismayed. The greatest danger is always the danger which comes from blindness to danger. Today we see the danger, and we are allied with forces that have repeatedly demonstrated their ability to prevail as against materialistic despotisms. There are, we know, God-given aspirations for freedom of mind and spirit and for opportunity. These are beyond the power of man to destroy. So long as we ally ourselves loyally and sacrificially with what is good, what is true, our cause surely will prevail.

Gentlemen, the United States observer delegation, animated by these sentiments, will endeavor to make a constructive contribution to your deliberations.

Thank you.

Questions

1. Dulles sees a significant difference between what had been anticipated at the end of World War II and what actually occurred. How does he account for that difference?

2. How does Dulles explain the fact that military strength and economic well-being are in opposition to each other? What economic benefits of collective security does he mention?

3. How does this document relate to the "New Look"?

28-10   Dwight D. Eisenhower, Farewell Address (1961)

In the second Eisenhower administration it became increasingly clear that science and technology were going to play an essential role in maintaining America's position in the world order. But what would the elements in that order be, and how would Americans cope with them? The difference between "pure" science and technology and engineering was not clear to the public. Science came under political pressure and ideological scrutiny, whereas technology and engineering seemed to be confined to providing solutions to practical problems. Eisenhower's farewell address tried to make clear at least some of the misunderstandings that were bound to arise. The involvement of private industry in militarily useful technological developments and the interest of military managers in the same issues raised "science" and scientists to new levels of political responsibility (see text pp. 888–889).

Source: Public Papers of the Presidents of the United States: Dwight D. Eisenhower, 1960–1961 (Washington, D.C.: U.S. Government Printing Office, 1961), pp. 1035–1040.

We now stand ten years past the midpoint of a century that has witnessed four major wars among great nations. Three of these involved our own country. Despite these holocausts America is today the strongest, the most influential and most productive nation in the world. Understandably proud of this pre-eminence, we yet realize that America's

leadership and prestige depend, not merely upon our unmatched material progress, riches and military strength, but on how we use our power in the interests of world peace and human betterment.

Throughout America's adventure in free government, our basic purposes have been to keep the peace; to foster progress in human achievement, and to enhance liberty, dignity and integrity among people and among nations. To strive for less would be unworthy of a free and religious people. Any failure traceable to arrogance, or our lack of comprehension or readiness to sacrifice would inflict upon us grievous hurt both at home and abroad.

Progress toward these noble goals is persistently threatened by the conflict now engulfing the world. It commands our whole attention, absorbs our very beings. We face a hostile ideology—global in scope, atheistic in character, ruthless in purpose, and insidious in method. Unhappily the danger it poses promises to be of indefinite duration. To meet it successfully, there is called for, not so much the emotional and transitory sacrifices of crisis, but rather those which enable us to carry forward steadily, surely, and without complaint the burdens of a prolonged and complex struggle—with liberty the stake. Only thus shall we remain, despite every provocation, on our charted course toward permanent peace and human betterment. . . .

A vital element in keeping the peace is our military establishment. Our arms must be mighty, ready for instant action, so that no potential aggressor may be tempted to risk his own destruction.

Our military organization today bears little relation to that known by any of my predecessors in peacetime, or indeed by the fighting men of World War II or Korea.

Until the latest of our world conflicts, the United States had no armaments industry. American makers of plowshares could, with time and as required, make swords as well. But now we can no longer risk emergency improvisation of national defense; we have been compelled to create a permanent armaments industry of vast proportions. Added to this, three and a half million men and women are directly engaged in the defense establishment. We annually spend on military security more than the net income of all United States corporations.

This conjunction of an immense military establishment and a large arms industry is new in the American experience. The total influence—economic, political, even spiritual—is felt in every city, every State house, every office of the Federal government. We recognize the imperative need for this development. Yet we must not fail to comprehend its grave implications. Our toil, resources and livelihood are all involved; so is the very structure of our society.

In the councils of government, we must guard against the acquisition of unwarranted influence, whether sought or unsought, by the military-industrial complex. The potential for the disastrous rise of misplaced power exists and will persist.

We must never let the weight of this combination endanger our liberties or democratic processes. We should take nothing for granted. Only an alert and knowledgeable citizenry can compel the proper meshing of the huge industrial and military machinery of defense with our peaceful methods and goals, so that security and liberty may prosper together.

Akin to, and largely responsible for the sweeping changes in our industrial-military posture, has been the technological revolution during recent decades.

In this revolution, research has become central; it also becomes more formalized, complex, and costly. A steadily increasing share is conducted for, by, or at the direction of, the Federal government.

Today, the solitary inventor, tinkering in his shop, has been overshadowed by task forces of scientists in laboratories and testing fields. In the same fashion, the free university, historically the fountainhead of free ideas and scientific discovery, has experienced a revolution in the conduct of research. Partly because of the huge costs involved, a government contract becomes virtually a substitute for intellectual curiosity. For every old blackboard there are now hundreds of new electronic computers.

The prospect of domination of the nation's scholars by Federal employment, project allocations, and the power of money is ever present—and is gravely to be regarded.

Yet, in holding scientific research and discovery in respect, as we should, we must also be alert to the equal and opposite danger that public policy could itself become the captive of a scientific-technological elite.

It is the task of statesmanship to mold, to balance, and to integrate these and other forces, new and old, within the principles of our democratic system—ever aiming toward the supreme goals of our free society.

Another factor in maintaining balance involves the element of time. As we peer into society's future, we—you and I, and our government—must avoid the impulse to live only for today, plundering, for our own ease and convenience, the precious resources of tomorrow. We cannot mortgage the material assets of our grandchildren without risking the loss also of their political and spiritual heritage. We want democracy to survive for all generations to come, not to become the insolvent phantom of tomorrow.

Down the long lane of the history yet to be written America knows that this world of ours, ever growing smaller, must avoid becoming a community of dreadful fear and hate, and be, instead, a proud confederation of mutual trust and respect.

Such a confederation must be one of equals. The weakest must come to the conference table with the same confidence as do we, protected as we are by our moral, economic, and military strength. That table, though scarred by many past frustrations, cannot be abandoned for the certain agony of the battlefield.

Disarmament, with mutual honor and confidence, is a continuing imperative. Together we must learn how to compose differences, not with arms, but with intellect and decent purpose. Because this need is so sharp and apparent I confess that I lay down my official responsibilities in this field with a definite sense of disappointment. As one who has witnessed the horror and the lingering sadness of war—as one who knows that another war could utterly destroy this civilization which as been so slowly and painfully built over thousands of years—I wish I could say tonight that a lasting peace is in sight.

Happily, I can say that war has been avoided. Steady progress toward our ultimate goal has been made. But, so much remains to be done. As a private citizen, I shall never cease to do what little I can to help the world advance along that road. . . .

You and I—my fellow citizens—need to be strong in our faith that all nations, under God, will reach the goal of peace with justice. May we be ever unswerving in devotion to principle, confident but humble with power, diligent in pursuit of the Nation's great goals.

To all the peoples of the world, I once more give expression to America's prayerful and continuing aspiration:

We pray that peoples of all faiths, all races, all nations, may have their great human needs satisfied; that those now denied opportunity shall come to enjoy it to the full; that all who yearn for freedom may experience its spiritual blessings; that those who have freedom will understand, also, its heavy responsibilities; that all who are insensitive to the needs of others will learn charity; that the scourges of poverty, disease and ignorance will be made to disappear from the earth, and that, in the goodness of time, all peoples will come to live together in a peace guaranteed by the binding force of mutual respect and love.

Questions

1. Eisenhower seems to see a threat to the independence of universities and the sciences as a result of governmental invasion of university laboratories. How does he describe changes in laboratories that would make them subject to such an invasion?

2. Eisenhower's use of the term *military-industrial complex* suggests the potential for a conspiracy against the public interest. How does he relate the military to public and governmental concerns? What role does government play in the development of industrial power?

3. Liberty, Eisenhower states, is at stake. From his speech, which institutions seem to be involved? Who is threatening liberty, and what can be done to protect it?

Questions for Further Thought

1. Dulles (Document 28-9) and Eisenhower (Document 28-10) discern both foreign and domestic threats to which they want to call attention. What are those threats, and what responses do they want their audiences to have?

2. Both Dulles and Eisenhower are concerned with the expansion of American military power and its effect on the national and the international roles of the United States. This is a new, post–World War II issue for Americans. How is it defined for them by both men? Are they saying essentially the same things?

3. Eisenhower's farewell address represents one of the earliest uses of political television. How well did he do? What rhetorical techniques did he seem to apply or avoid that are characteristic of the medium of television?

CHAPTER *29*

Affluence and Its Contradictions 1945–1965

★   ★   ★

Technology and Economic Change and *A Suburban Society*

The unprecedented prosperity Americans enjoyed after World War II resulted primarily from three factors: pent-up consumer demand, the wartime avoidance of massive destruction, and the absence of international competition for consumer markets (see text pp. 894–895 and Document 29-1). Several other developments rooted in wartime mobilization and central to the budding military-industrial complex (see text pp. 895–896) also shaped postwar American society. The fusion of science and production encouraged technological change, and the close relationship between government and business assured a public commitment to economic growth and security.

Although the first twenty years of the postwar era were prosperous, they were accompanied by economic anxieties. Many people feared the loss of their jobs to automation. There was also a vague sense that computers would transform society—but to what extent? If one watched television and believed the stories on "The Twilight Zone," the future was indeed frightening.

Postwar America underwent significant and often wrenching change. Women were expected to stay at home and raise families (see text p. 900) at the same time that they were encouraged to seek employment outside the home (Document 29-2). The exact location of home was another important issue. After the war Americans began leaving the cities in massive numbers. They received a good deal of help from the federal government, especially through programs such as the GI Bill, Housing Administration home mortgage guarantees, and the interstate highway system.

At least part of the American dream became connected to places such as Green Acres (Document 29-3), courtesy of the interstate highway system (Document 29-4), which allowed for the movement of commuters as well as troops (see text p. 905).

29-1 "When You Meet Again . . ." (1945)

War was all-consuming in Europe and Asia but not in the United States, where there had been no combat and relatively light casualties (see text p. 894). As World War II neared an end in 1945, many Americans were impatient to see what the future had in store—and what stores would have in the future. Nash Motors offered a hint that May.

Source: Ad for Nash Motors, Division of Nash-Kelvinator Corporation, in *Time*, April 30, 1945.

Questions

1. How does this advertisement balance consumer appeal and patriotism?
2. According to Nash, what appears to be the essence of peace?
3. Given that there were three months of fighting left, was the ad appropriate? Why or why not?

WHEN YOU MEET AGAIN . . .

It will be you again,
just you, together again . . .

The road's a ribbon of white in the pale moonlight, and the trees whisper "Everything's going to be all right" and the sound of the wind rushing past is a voice crooning "home, home again, home at last . . ."

Home, at last with the wind and the stars and the girl and the car you've been longing for.

The panel's glow and the wheel in your hands and the feel of her shoulder warm against yours . . . and the lift and power of singing speed and the long, bright beams exploring the night . . . and the deep, sleepy hush of the motor's murmur . . .

All tell you again what you've needed, wanted, waited for . . . you have.

And your heart beats fast for now you know there's *nothing* ahead but the open road and the far-off places where a blue sky rolls to the horizon's edges.

•   •   •

Though here at Nash our entire effort has been devoted to production for war . . . we believe we can look ahead now, think ahead now, to the time when we'll be building cars again, to the time when we'll be making two great new Nash cars designed to be the finest, biggest, most dependable and economical automobiles in their respective fields . . . the new medium-priced Nash Ambassador and the new low-priced Nash "600". And Nash will build these new, advanced cars in numbers three times greater than our 1941 peak. In this way Nash will contribute the jobs, the opportunities, the futures that will help insure the strong, the growing, the prosperous America we owe to those who now work and fight to preserve it.

*A New Radio Hit Show! Tune in
"The Andrews Sisters" and Guest Stars
Sundays 4:30 P.M. E.W.T. Blue Network*

29-2 "Help Wanted—Women" (1957)

The 1950s was a transitional decade for American women. Employers were eager to hire (see text p. 900), but the want ads did not promise the same kind of jobs men sought.

Source: Classified ads from the *Chicago Sunday Tribune*, May 12, 1957, part 5, pp. 36, 40.

Executive Secretary
$100 Week

$100 paid weekly to the PRESIDENT'S private secretary. Your own carpeted private office. Average skills nec. as you'll be handling most of your own correspondence. Ability to deal with people important, heavy public contact work involved. FREE at CHICAGO Personnel. 6 E. Randolph [Above Walgreens.] RAndolph 6-2355.

Arrange
Social Functions

Famous college fraternity needs you to take over in their beautiful new national headquarters office. Make arrangements for social functions, send invitations to members, handle enrollments and all convention plans. $70 to start with raise in 30 days for this unusually different position. FREE at LAKE Personnel. 29 E. Madison.
RAndolph 6-4650   11th Fl.

RECEPTION
LITE TYPING

No exp. nec. for this front office reception position. Answer pushbutton phones, greet visitors in beautiful modern office from 9-5. Lt. typing. Sal. high. FREE at LAKE Personnel. 29 E. Madison.
RAndolph 6-4650   11th Fl.

Reservation
Secretary

Lite steno desired for unique position as secretary in charge of reservations for beautiful hotel. Handle accommodations for important people in the public eye. Poise and ability to deal with people important. Extremely high starting salary. FREE at LAKE Personnel. 29 E. Madison.
RAndolph 6-4650   11th Fl.

AIRLINE TICKET
SALES GIRL

$305 mo. even during 10 day training period as ticket sales girl with high paying airline. All public contact—no office skills. Single girls receive travel passes for themselves and their families. Absolutely no exp. nec. For details see
BOULEVARD   22 W. Madison st.
5th Floor   FInancial 6-3780

RECEPTION
WILL TEACH SWBD.

No experience or typing needed to be front office girl in well known commercial art studio. Your nice appearance, friendly manner, interest in public contact qualify. Salary open and high! Vacation this summer! Beginner qualifies. No fee at
BOULEVARD   22 W. Madison st.
5th Floor   FInancial 6-3780

SECRETARY

Permanent position available for girl to perform secretarial work of a varied nature. Requires person with pleasing personality, experience and ability. Modern air conditioned office located for convenient transportation.

GOSS
PRINTING PRESS CO.
5601 W. 31ST-ST.
BIshop 2-3300   Ext. 311

SECRETARY
PUBLIC RELATIONS DIR.

Must have good stenographic skills and like to do a variety of work. Age 22-30. Paid vacations, holidays, company cafeteria, and other employee benefits.
ILLINOIS TOOL WORKS
2501 N. Keeler [4200 W.]

SECRETARY
VACATION WITH PAY THIS SUMMER!

If you're not happy where you are, but don't want to lose your vacation this summer, here's your chance. We need a secretary for a vice president of this advertising agency, one who's neat, accurate taking and transcribing heavy copy dictation on electric typewriter, who can handle details herself, keep her boss on the beam, help out elsewhere in this six-girl office. We're in a spanking new office just a few steps from Van Buren I. C. station. A happy place to work in an expanding organization. Salary starts at $70 per week, but you must work 1 month before vacation starts. We'll test you before hiring—to start at once.

CALL MR. DEAN
WAbash 2-8056

SALES POSITIONS

HOUSEWIVES

NO EXPERIENCE NECESSARY

EARN EXTRA MONEY FOR VACATION

WORK FULL TIME

PART TIME

SALARY + COMMISSION

GOOD EARNINGS

IMMEDIATE MERCHANDISE DISCOUNT

APPLY NOW!

GOLDBLATTS

LOOP

STATE AND VAN BUREN

NORTH
4722 N. BROADWAY
3149 N. LINCOLN-AV.

SOUTH
250 PLAZA—PARK FOREST
7975 S. CICERO

Brides! Housewives!

Have You 2 or 3 days to Spare, Each Week?

This part-time job—in a pleasant, air conditioned Michigan avenue office—will take you away from home just enough each week, to sharpen up your interest in your household tasks.

Type of duties in this job? You will alternate chiefly between telephone work and general office work. You'll be working with nice people, and you'll find the days go quickly.

You have your choice of working either 2 or 3 full days [8 hours] each week, but one of the days must be Friday. Also, we have one opening for Sunday work, combined with 2-3 other weekdays.

No previous experience is necessary, but an alert, intelligent attitude and liking for people are important.

If you find this offer appealing—and you're between the ages of 22 and 45 with a high school education—apply Monday through Friday, 9 to 11 a.m. or 1 to 4 p.m.

ROOM 635

CHICAGO TRIBUNE

435 N. Michigan

APPAREL STORE MANAGER or DEPT. MGR.
EXPERIENCED for store at GRAND AND HARLEM

REAL FUTURE FOR AGGRESSIVE LADIES. RTW. MGR. GOOD SALARY, COMMISSIONS. COMPANY BENEFITS AND FUTURE. WILL TRAIN. WRITE FULLY.

Write MDV 397, Tribune

GIRLS!

Now That Spring's Here
Why Not Put Your
EXTRA ENERGY
into a Job at

Motorola

where
YOU ARE NEEDED IN
Work You'll Enjoy

WE HAVE OPENINGS FOR

Wirers and Solderers

TO WORK DAY SHIFT ON
TV.

HIGH WAGES
FREE INSURANCE
PROFIT SHARING

FOR THOSE WHO CAN QUALIFY

EMPLOYMENT OFFICE OPEN DAILY
8:30 A.M.-4 P.M.
APPLY AT

Motorola

4545 W. AUGUSTA-BLVD.
OR 1450 N. CICERO

Questions

1. What do these ads stress as benefits?
2. To what extent are these jobs professional?
3. Why were there separate want-ad sections for men and women?

29-3 "Green Acres" (1950)

Green Acres was the place for New Yorkers to be in June 1950, or so the developers of this Long Island subdivision hoped. The ad reprinted here was one of countless appeals to city people to become suburbanites (see text pp. 902–906).

Source: Green Acres ad from *New York Times*, June 25, 1950, sec. 8, p. 6.

Questions

1. What was the appeal of Green Acres?
2. How does this advertisement both separate and link the subdivision and the city?
3. Why would New Yorkers be interested in living in Green Acres?

A New Home by CHANIN

Six rooms, all on one floor, attached garage, full basement, 34x25, exclusive of laundry space, make this a *complete* home for all the family—comfortable to live in, easy to keep, interesting and inviting to your friends.

Chanin skill of design has given it graciousness and luxury. Rooms are well-proportioned. Friendly entrance vestibule with guest closet, picture windows, front and rear, venetian blinds, china closet with service bar between dining room and kitchen, combination linen closet and laundry hamper, color-harmonized bath with vanitory, medicine cabinet with 14 feet of shelf-room, ceramic tile wainscoting and floor add finish and charm.

The basement easily becomes a recreation or hobby room, a play place for the children.

Chanin precision construction—poured concrete foundation and basement walls, full insulation, weather stripping, copper piping—mean low-cost maintenance. Oil-fired hot water circulating heat provides winter comfort; keeps down fuel bills.

The Hotpoint all-electric kitchen lightens housework. Steel cabinets have 23 square feet of textolite work surfaces. Refrigerator, range, dishwasher, ventilating fan and washing machine (in the basement) all are included in the purchase price.

But more important than details are the experience and integrity of the designer and builder. The Chanin Organization has created more than 6,000 dwelling units. Chanin "know-how" means lasting charm, sturdy lifetime quality.

The purchase price is less than you may think— $14,790 for everything mentioned, plus your choice of several exteriors, 6,000-square foot landscaped plot, sewers, curb, paved street, sidewalk. Veterans pay nothing down. Their 30-year mortgages bear 4 percent interest. Terms to nonveterans are equally attractive.

Compare this house with anything you have seen anywhere near its price range. Compare its location, in a planned, established community, 5 minutes walk from the Valley Stream station, 29 minutes from Penn Station, 17 miles from midtown New York or Brooklyn, near main highways, parkways, schools, churches, stores.

Then walk around Green Acres a bit. Hundreds of other homes, now 8 to 14 years old themselves will tell you that "Chanin-built is well-built" and much more than a phrase. It is a hallmark, a guarantee of building perfection.

Hotpoint appliances used exclusively

BY TRAIN: *Long Island train from Penn Station or Brooklyn to Valley Stream; walk back through park to property.* BY CAR: *Sunrise Highway to Central Avenue; from Merrick Road or Southern State Parkway, turn on Central Avenue to Sunrise Highway.* BY SUBWAY AND BUS: *6th Avenue or 8th Avenue IND train to Parsons Boulevard, Queens. Change to Bee Line's Grant Park bus which passes entrance gates.*

•GREEN ACRES•

"The Planned Residential Community"

SUNRISE HIGHWAY AT CENTRAL AVE., VALLEY STREAM, L. I.

29-4 The Interstate Highway System (1955)

George M. Humphrey   Few better examples of the Eisenhower administration's close relationship with big business can be found than defense secretary Charles Wilson's connections with General Motors. Wilson's nomination was held up in Congress because he refused to part with $2.5 million in G.M. stock even though the company was a major defense contractor. In his Senate testimony Wilson reasoned that he could not conceive of ever having to make a decision that ran counter to his financial interests in the company. "For years I thought," he remarked, "what was good for our country was good for General Motors, and *vice versa.*" Wilson was forced to sell his stock before the Senate consented to his appointment, but his remark about the similarity of corporate and national welfare testified to the administration's view of economic policy.

The construction of the interstate highway system symbolized the relationship between corporate interests, public welfare, and governmental policy. The highway system was both a response and a spur to the growth of automobile ownership. Highways made it easier to commute from the suburbs into the city, severed people's reliance on mass transit, and made suburban shopping areas more convenient and appealing than downtown stores. Not even the military-industrial complex was quite so integral to the politics and economics of postwar America (see text p. 905). Indeed, the administration defended the highway program as necessary both to economic growth and to national defense, as Treasury Secretary George M. Humphrey argued before a House subcommittee.

Source: Treasury Secretary George M. Humphrey, testimony before a House Subcommittee, 1955. In Nathaniel Howard, ed., *The Basic Papers of George M. Humphrey* (Cleveland: Western Reserve Historical Society, 1965), pp. 513–515.

In my view, the new highways will be earning assets, making possible a continuation of expansion in the case of motor transportation which would otherwise be seriously handicapped by the growing inadequacy of our highway network. You already know of the savings possible from improved safety, reduced time delays, greater vehicle efficiency, and lower repair and maintenance costs. . . .

There is probably. . . no thinking person in America who does not know that the nation needs better highways. We need them for the daily business and safety of everyone. And we need them to help our defense should this nation ever be attacked by a foreign power. This being the

case, I believe that men of good will and good intentions must be able to get together on a plan for starting these better highways—not on a small scale, and not just a little amount a year—but on a major scale, and right now. Every year, every month lost in having these extra miles of better highways means loss to our economy and so less better living for our citizens. It means loss of lives through loss of the safety these better highways would bring. It means loss of the best possible transportation of our defense equipment and evacuation of our people in the event of an enemy attack.

Questions

1. According to Humphrey, why would highways be "earning assets"?
2. In Humphrey's view, why were highways necessary for national defense?
3. Humphrey claims that "no thinking person in America" would oppose the highway program. Are there any sound arguments against it?

Questions for Further Thought

1. Use Documents 29-1 and 29-2 to consider how advertising influences people's attitudes about the future.
2. How did the federal government encourage suburbanization?
3. What do Documents 29-3 and 29-4 suggest about the views Americans held about cities?

The Other America

Many critics of postwar American society attacked the suburbs for their cultural and psychological sterility. Suburban life, those critics charged, mired people in neurotic relationships and amounted to a futile attempt to re-create an individualistic past; in a bureaucratic society such attempts were laughable. By focusing on the supposedly humdrum aspects of suburban life, the critics often ignored the darker side of suburbanization: realtors, builders, and bankers all followed business practices that ensured racial segregation in American housing patterns. Suburbanization drained the cities of tax revenue and strained city services for all urban dwellers, thus encouraging more flight to the suburbs while creating multiple layers of local, county, and state administration that made it difficult to address mutual problems efficiently (see text pp. 909–910).

By the mid-1960s every American city was struggling with the multitude of social problems associated with flight and decay (see text pp. 906–908). Not the least of such problems was the emergence of grim slum areas that conformed to Kenneth Clark's description of Harlem as a "dark ghetto." Herbert Gans reminds us that there were also large pockets of poor whites who struggled against the same pressures (Document 29-5). As a means of dealing with poor urban neighborhoods, municipal and federal officials turned to urban renewal projects (Document 29-6), which in theory were intended to replace slums with new and decent housing. Because urban renewal relied on real-estate developers for both the planning and the execution of renewal projects, the program more often resulted in luxury apartments, office space, and government buildings than in low-income housing (see text pp. 909–910). Urban renewal not only displaced poor residents but increased the cost of low-income housing by decreasing the supply.

It was not easy to exist outside the cultural mainstream in the 1950s. African-Americans, for example, came north in search of opportunity, only to be labeled an urban problem. For policy makers blacks were yet another drain on the resources of city governments. In the South African-Americans emerged as both a puzzle and a threat. They had endured segregation for so long that whites could not comprehend how anyone, least of all a black seamstress, could challenge Jim Crow. But that is exactly what Rosa Parks did (Document 29-7).

29-5   The West Enders of Boston (1962)

Herbert Gans

Just as American metropolitan life as a whole became more segregated in the 1950s and 1960s, urban and suburban residential patterns differed according to class. In addition to the growing "dark ghettos," most cities had lower-class white areas that suffered through the urban crisis.

In contrast to the sense of stifling oppression the "dark ghetto" engendered, working-class white neighborhoods such as Philadelphia's Kensington and Chicago's suburb of Cicero gave rise to a tenacious loyalty in their residents. Herbert Gans (b. 1927) found the "urban villagers" of Boston's mostly Italian West End (see text pp. 909–910) indifferent to the seductions of middle-class suburban culture. So long as they had steady work and were left alone, so long as outsiders—blacks included—did not try to settle in their neighborhood, they were content to remain in the city, living pretty much as their immigrant parents had. As it happened, Gans's subjects were forced out of their beloved neighborhood when the West End was declared an irredeemable slum and replaced with luxury apartments.

Source: Abridged with the permission of The Free Press, a division of Simon & Schuster, from *The Urban Villagers*, Expanded Edition, by Herbert J. Gans, pp. 20–24. Copyright © 1962 by The Free Press. Copyright © 1982 by Herbert J. Gans.

West Enders did not think of their area as a slum and resented the city's description of the area because it cast aspersions on them as slum dwellers. They were not pleased that the apartment buildings were not well kept up outside, but, as long as the landlord kept the building clean, maintained the mechanical system, and did not bother his tenants, they were not seriously disturbed about it. People kept their apartments up-to-date as they could afford to, and most of the ones I saw differed little from lower-middle-class ones in urban and suburban neighborhoods.

Housing is not the same kind of status symbol for the West Enders that it is for middle-class people. They are as concerned about making a good impression on others as anyone else, but the people to be impressed and the ways of impressing them do differ. The people who are entertained in the apartment are intimates. Moreover, they all live in similar circumstances. As a result they evaluate the host not on the basis of his housing, but on his friendliness, his moral qualities, and his ability as a host. Not only are acquaintances and strangers invited less freely to the home than in the middle class, but they are also less important to the West Enders' way of life, and therefore less significant judges of their status. Thus, West Enders, unlike the middle class, do not have to put on as impressive a front for such people. . . .

Whereas most West Enders have no objection to the older suburban towns that surround the Boston city limits, they have little use for the newer suburbs. They described these as too quiet for their tastes, lonely—that is, without street life—and occupied by people concerned only with trying to appear better than they are. West Enders avoid "the country." . . . They do not like its isolation. . . . I was told by one social worker of an experiment some years back to expose West End children to nature by taking them on a trip to Cape Cod. The experiment failed, for the young West Enders found no pleasure in the loneliness of natural surroundings and wanted to get back to the West End as quickly as possible. They were incredulous that anyone could live without people around them. . . .

Many West Enders impressed me as being true urbanites, with empathy for the pace, crowding, and excitement of city life. . . . They are not [cosmopolitan], however; the parts of the city that they use and enjoy are socially, culturally, and physically far different from those frequented by the upper-middle class. . . .

Questions

1. According to Gans, how was home life connected to status for West Enders?
2. Why did West Enders criticize the suburbs?
3. What does Gans mean when he calls West Enders "true urbanites"?

29-6   "What Does Chicago's Renewal Program Mean . . ."

By the early 1960s American cities were using urban renewal as a weapon of desperation in an attempt to hold on to their middle-class population (see text pp. 909–910). The city of Chicago printed this pamphlet in the hope that the upbeat tone would allay fears of urban decline.

Source: Pamphlet *What Does Chicago's Renewal Program Mean . . . to You . . . to Your Family . . . Your Neighbors . . . and Your Chicago?* (Chicago: City of Chicago, 1963). Courtesy of the Municipal Reference Collection, Chicago Public Library.

What Does Chicago's Renewal Program Mean . . .

To You . . . To Your Family . . . Your Neighbors . . . And Your Chicago?

IT MEANS MANY THINGS

Chicago is a great city. It is a city of fine neighborhoods, providing its citizens with homes and apartments of all sizes and at all prices. It is a city of magnificent parks. It offers unequalled cultural activities. Your children are provided with good schools. Good public transportation, super highways and well-lighted, clean streets provide easy access to and from your job.

But as great as Chicago is, it needs constant improvement and renewal to serve its people well.

Chicago—like all cities—must keep pace in the modern world BY SOLVING PROBLEMS of congestion and blight, BY PROTECTING THE GOOD THINGS we

have, and by TAKING ADVANTAGE OF THE BIG OPPORTUNITIES that Chicago enjoys. This can mean better homes, more and better jobs, a better life for everyone. And the job of making Chicago a better place in which to live is a team effort requiring the help of all its citizens. It is the responsibility of each neighborhood and community.

In this great effort there is a role for all citizens.

They can do their part through their local neighborhood organization, civic groups, perhaps as a member of the conservation community councils, and various other citizen boards and commissions. Through these groups people work with those agencies directly concerned with the overall planning and execution of renewal and conservation.

Only when people—tenants, homeowners, businessmen, industrialists—all of them taxpayers—participate, is renewal and community improvement truly representative of their desires and needs for a better life.

Every taxpayer should be aware of the fact that slums and blight cost Chicago money.

More than 75 per cent of Chicago's corporate budget goes for police, fire, health, sanitation and Building Department operations.

To render these services in slums costs much more than it does in good neighborhoods.

RENEWAL CLEARS AND PREVENTS SLUMS.

DO YOU KNOW—the Chicago Renewal Program has already added $18,700,000 in new assessed valuation and current projects are expected to add $13,000,000 in the next two years.

Renewal ENCOURAGES PRIVATE INVESTMENT IN EXISTING NEIGHBORHOODS AND PROVIDES LAND FOR NEW INDUSTRIAL, COMMERCIAL, AND RESIDENTIAL DEVELOPMENT.

The Chicago Renewal Program costs money. BUT—MONEY SPENT FOR RENEWAL IS QUICKLY RECAPTURED THROUGH TAX RETURNS FROM THE ADDED VALUE OF THE NEW BUILDINGS WHICH ARE BUILT.

AFTER REDEVELOPMENT

$4,794,368

BEFORE REDEVELOPMENT

$2,321,442

Tax yields in clearance projects before and after redevelopment.

IF YOU ARE A HOMEOWNER . . .

Chances are your home represents the biggest single purchase you will ever make. Renewal protects not only your home but that of your neighbor as well. Enforcement of the building, housing and zoning codes prevents blight. Conservation projects and slum clearance in any neighborhood improves all of Chicago by providing space for schools, parks, streets, street lighting, and churches.

IF YOU ARE A TENANT . . .

Renewal, whether slum clearance or conservation, helps YOU by eliminating dilapidated buildings and replacing them with apartments and homes thus giving everyone a bigger choice of housing accommodations, or by rehabilitation of existing buildings. Renewal brings about street improvements, helps with parking problems, and provides you with all types of public improvements you need for good city living.

IF YOU ARE A BUSINESSMAN . . .

Either as an industrialist or a merchant, Chicago's Renewal Program benefits you directly. To-date, Chicago's Renewal Program means that $150,000,000 worth of investment has gone into industrial plants, commercial properties and homes.

Renewal can provide major new industrial sites.

Renewal can aid in the conservation of industrial districts.

Renewal provides the new homes and conserves existing neighborhoods from which business and factories draw for their labor force.

To the merchant, renewal adds in modernizing you business district.

Renewal improves traffic and parking conditions.

Renewal helps you and your customers.

Renewal helps provide jobs and assists Chicago's economy so that people in your community can continue to patronize your store, your bank and your place of entertainment.

IF YOU ARE A WAGE EARNER . . .

Renewal means more jobs and better jobs.

Renewal not only adds jobs, but saves jobs through industrial redevelopment that otherwise might be lost.

IF YOU ARE A CONSTRUCTION WORKER . . .

The renewal program is a major factor in rebuilding—homes and other construction projects requiring large amounts of land—which has already generated over $150,000,000 worth of building activity.

IF YOU ARE A PARENT . . .

Physical—Renewal eliminates conditions that breed juvenile delinquency and disease.

Social—Renewal provides land for improved parks, schools, churches and provides safer streets. It plays a vital role in reducing juvenile delinquency and contributes directly in making a better, cleaner, healthier neighborhood environment.

Your youngsters will benefit from renewal by attending the University of Illinois, the University of Chicago, Illinois Institute of Technology, DePaul University, Chicago Teachers College, and other fine colleges which are directly benefiting from Chicago's Renewal program.

Questions

1. How is urban renewal defined here?
2. What does it promise?
3. Which consequences of urban renewal are ignored?

29-7   Rosa Parks Describes Her Arrest (1955)

While women such as Ella Baker and Fanny Lou Hamer played prominent, if often underestimated, roles in the civil rights movement, Rosa Parks was truly the mother of the movement. Her decision to refuse to give her seat on a segregated bus to a white rider set the stage for the nonviolent protest that became so central to the civil rights movement (see text pp. 911–912). Rosa Parks recounted that historic event in an interview with Howell Raines.

Source: Rosa L. Parks interview by Howell Raines. Reprinted by permission of The Putnam Publishing Group from *My Soul Is Rested: The Story of the Civil Rights Movement in the Deep South* by Howell Raines, pp. 40–41. Copyright © 1977 by Howell Raines.

I had left my work at the men's alteration shop . . . in the Montgomery Fair department store . . . . I came across the street and looked for a Cleveland Avenue bus that apparently had some seats on it. At that time it was a little hard to get a seat on the bus. . . .

As I got up on the bus and walked to the seat I saw there was only one vacancy that was just back of where it was considered the white section. So this was the seat that I took, next to the aisle, and a man was sitting next to me. Across the aisle there were two women, and there were a few seats at this point in the very front of the bus that was called the white section. . . . And on the third stop there were some people getting on, and at this point all of the front seats were taken. Now in the beginning, at the very first stop I had got on the bus, the back of the bus was filled up with people standing in the aisle and I don't know why this one vacancy that I took was left, because there were quite a few people already standing toward the back of the bus. The third stop is when all the front seats were taken, and this one man was standing and when the driver looked around and saw he was standing, he asked the four of us, the man in the seat with me and the two women across the aisle, to let him have those front seats.

At his first request, didn't any of us move. Then he spoke again and said, "You'd better make it light on your-

selves and let me have those seats." At this point, of course, the passenger who would have taken the seat hadn't said anything. In fact, he never did speak to my knowledge. When the three people, the man who was in the seat with me and the two women, stood up and moved into the aisle, I remained where I was. When the driver saw that I was still sitting there, he asked if I was going to stand up. I told him, no, I wasn't. He said, "Well, if you don't stand up, I'm going to have you arrested." I told him to go on and have me arrested.

He got off the bus and came back shortly. A few minutes later, two policemen got on the bus, and they approached me and asked if the driver had asked me to stand up, and I said yes, and they wanted to know why I didn't. I told them I didn't think I should have to stand up. . . . They placed me under arrest then and had me get in the police car, and I was taken to jail and booked on suspicion. . . . They had to determine whether or not the driver wanted to press charges or swear out a warrant, which he did. Then they took me to jail and I was placed in a cell. In a little while I was taken from the cell, and my picture was made and fingerprints taken. I went back to the cell then, and a few minutes later I was called back again, and when this happened I found out that Mr. E. D. Nixon and Attorney and Mrs. Clifford Durr had come to make bond for me.

Questions

1. What elements of nonviolent protest are evident in Rosa Parks's recollection?
2. Do you think that the fact that Parks was a woman was an important element in this event? Why or why not?
3. What does Parks's story indicate about whites in Montgomery and their attitudes—the bus driver and the passenger who was supposed to take Parks's seat, for example?

Questions for Further Thought

1. Do the people of Boston's West End (Document 29-5) have anything in common with Rosa Parks and the African-Americans of Montgomery (Document 29-7)? What?
2. Was the clearing of slums (Document 29-6) necessary for cities to stem the exodus to the suburbs? Why or why not? In your answer, be sure to define what constitutes a slum.
3. Imagine that you are a big-city mayor in the 1950s. How should you respond to the simultaneous challenges of urban decline and civil rights?

American Society during the Baby Boom

Writing at the tail end of the baby–boom years, the sociologist Daniel Bell argued that modern capitalism had been built on a basic contradiction. On the one hand, capitalist society continued to exhort its citizens to uphold traditional values such as the work ethic. On the other hand, the economy thrived on the new value of consumerism, which called on people to discard traditional injunctions against self-gratification and seek personal fulfillment through buying rather than through working, through consuming rather than through producing (see text pp. 912–913). Television, the dominant medium of consumerism, presented these contradictory values: viewers could watch "Father Knows Best," with its self-sacrificing mother, hard-working father, and obedient children, only to have the program broken up by commercials instructing them in self-indulgence (see text pp. 913–914).

What held for television appeared throughout American culture. The 1950s was the heyday of the traditional nuclear family: the historic decline in American birth rates was reversed temporarily, and women were expected to find fulfillment in maternal duties. At the same time, however, the constant increase in white-collar and office work, along with the mounting need for income to satisfy the desire for consumer goods, drew more and more women out of the home and into the workplace (see text pp. 916–918). Similarly, the discovery of the youth market encouraged advertisers to shape messages for young people, thus encouraging a rebellious identity among youth that ran against the stereotype of traditional family life (see text p. 918). Advertisers were clever enough to note important social changes and to channel their appeals accordingly (Document 29-8).

Despite their power, television and advertising images did not entirely dominate American society in the 1950s. This was a vibrant decade for art and literature. The so-called beat generation seemed to experience the same alienation that American artists had felt in the 1920s (see text pp. 918–919), but no one went to Paris. Instead, artists mostly stayed in the United States to work and, like Jackson Pollock (Document 29-9), comment on their efforts.

Popular culture flourished. A look at the 1950s would be incomplete without recognizing that mad iconoclast who refused to worry (Document 29-10).

29-8 *The Hidden Persuaders* (1957)

Vance Packard   Were products that good in the 1950s, or was advertising exceptionally effective (see text pp. 912–913)? Vance Packard (b. 1914) thought it was the latter, which he saw as cause for concern. Packard warned that the manipulation of consumer tastes could lead to "the chilling world of George Orwell" in *1984*.

    This excerpt notes how advertisers appeal to the consumer's subconscious.

Source: Excerpted from Vance Packard, *The Hidden Persuaders* (New York: Van Rees Press, 1957), pp. 72–82.

Marketing Eight Hidden Needs

. . . *Selling emotional security.* The Weiss and Geller advertising agency became suspicious of the conventional reasons people gave for buying home freezers. In many cases it found that economically, the freezers didn't make sense when you added up the initial cost, the monthly cost added on the electric bill, and the amount of frozen leftovers in the box that eventually would be thrown out. When all factors were added, the food that was consumed from the freezer often became very costly indeed.

Its curiosity aroused, the agency made a psychiatric pilot study. The probers found significance in the fact that the home freezer first came into widespread popularity after World War II when many families were filled with inner anxieties because of uncertainties involving not only food but just about everything else in their lives. These people began thinking fondly of former periods of safety and security, which subconsciously took them back to childhood where there was the mother who never disappointed and love was closely related with the giving of food. The probers concluded: "The freezer represents to many the assurance that there is always food in the house, and food in the home represents security, warmth, and safety." People who feel insecure, they found, need more food around than they can eat. The agency decided that the merchandising of freezers should take this squirrel factor into account in shaping campaigns. . . .

Selling reassurance of worth. In the mid-fifties *The Chicago Tribune* made a depth study of the detergent and soap market to try to find out why these products had failed to build brand loyalty, as many other products have done. Housewives tend to switch from one brand to another. This, the *Tribune* felt, was lamentable and concluded that the soap and detergent makers were themselves clearly to blame. They had been old-fashioned in their approach. "Most advertising," it found, "now shows practically no awareness that women have any other motive for using their products than to be clean, to protect the hands, and to keep objects clean." The depth-wise soap maker, the report advised, will realize that many housewives feel they are engaged in unrewarded and unappreciated drudgery when they clean. The advertiser should thus foster the wife's feeling of "worth and esteem." His "advertising should exalt the role of housekeeping—not in self-conscious, stodgy ways or with embarrassingly direct praise—but by various implications making it known what an important and proud thing it is or should be to be a housewife performing a role often regarded . . . as drudger." . . .

Selling ego-gratification. This in a sense is akin to selling reassurance or worth. A maker of steam shovels found that sales were lagging. It had been showing in its ads magnificent photos of its mammoth machines lifting great loads of rock and dirt. A motivation study of prospective customers was made to find what was wrong. The first fact uncovered was that purchasing agents, in buying such machines, were strongly influenced by the comments and recommendations of their steam-shovel operators, and the operators showed considerable hostility to this company's brand. Probing the operators, the investigators quickly found the reason. The operators resented pictures in the ad that put all the glory on the huge machine and showed the operator as a barely visible figure inside the distant cab. The shovel maker, armed with this insight, changed its ad approach and began taking its photographs from over the operator's shoulder. He was shown as the complete master of the mammoth machine. This new approach, *Tide* magazine reported, is "easing the operators' hostility." . . .

Selling creative outlets. The director of psychological research at a Chicago ad agency mentioned casually in a conversation that gardening is a "pregnancy activity." When questioned about this she responded, as if explaining the most obvious thing in the world, that gardening gives older women a chance to keep on growing things after they have passed the child-bearing stage. This explains, she said, why gardening has particular appeal to older women and to men, who of course can't have babies. She cited the case of a woman with eleven children who, when she passed through menopause, nearly had a nervous collapse until she discovered gardening, which she took to for the first time in her life and with obvious and intense delight.

Housewives consistently report that one of the most pleasurable tasks of the home is making a cake. Psychologists were put to work exploring this phenomenon for merchandising clues. James Vicary made a study of cake symbolism and came up with the conclusion that "baking a cake traditionally is acting out the birth of a child" so that when a woman bakes a cake for her family she is symbolically presenting the family with a new baby, an idea she likes very much. Mr. Vicary cited the many jokes and old wives tales about cake making as evidence: the quip that brides whose cakes fall obviously can't produce a baby yet; the married jest about "leaving a cake in the oven"; the myth that a cake is likely to fall if the woman baking it is menstruating. A psychological consulting firm in Chicago also made a study of cake symbolism and found that "women experience making a cake as making a gift of themselves to their family," which suggests much the same thing.

The food mixes—particularly the cake mixes—soon found themselves deeply involved in this problem of feminine creativity and encountered much more resistance than the makers, being logical people, ever dreamed possible. The makers found themselves trying to cope with negative and guilt feelings on the part of women who felt that use of ready mixes was a sign of poor housekeeping and threatened to deprive them of a traditional source of praise.

In the early days the cake-mix packages instructed, "Do not add milk, just add water." Still many wives insisted on adding milk as their creative touch, overloaded the cakes or muffins with calcium, and often the cakes or muffins fell, and the wives would blame the cake mix. Or the package would say, "Do not add eggs." Typically the milk and eggs had already been added by the manufacturer in dried form. But wives who were interviewed in depth studies would exclaim: "What kind of cake is it if you just need to add tap water!" Several different psychological firms wrestled with this problem and came up with essentially the same answer. The mix makers should always leave the housewife something to do. Thus Dr. Dichter counseled General Mills that it should start telling the housewife that she and Bisquick *together* could do the job and not Bisquick alone. Swansdown White Cake Mix began telling wives in large type: "You Add Fresh Eggs . . ." Some mixes have the wife add both fresh eggs and fresh milk. . . .

Selling love objects. This might seem a weird kind of merchandising but the promoters of Liberace, the TV pianist, have manipulated—with apparent premeditation—the trappings of Oedipus symbolism in selling him to women past the child-bearing age (where much of his following is concentrated). The TV columnist John Crosby alluded to this when he described the reception Liberace was receiving in England, where, according to Mr. Crosby, he was "visible in all his redundant dimples" on British commercial TV. Mr. Crosby quoted the *New Statesman*

and Nation as follows: "Every American mom is longing to stroke the greasy, roguish curls. The wide, trustful child-like smile persists, even when the voice is in full song." TV viewers who have had an opportunity to sit in Mr. Liberace's TV presence may recall that in his TV presentations a picture of his real-life mom is frequently flashed on the screen, beaming in her rocking chair or divan while her son performs.

Selling sense of power. The fascination Americans show for any product that seems to offer them a personal extension of power has offered a rich field for exploitation by merchandisers. Automobile makers have strained to produce cars with ever-higher horsepower. After psychiatric probing a Midwestern ad agency concluded that a major appeal of buying a shiny new and more powerful car every couple of years is that "it gives him [the buyer] a renewed sense of power and reassures him of his own masculinity, an emotional need which his old car fails to deliver."

One complication of the power appeal of a powerful new car, the Institute for Motivational Research found, was that the man buying it often feels guilty about indulging himself with power that might be regarded as needless. The buyer needs some rational reassurance for indulging his deep-seated desires. A good solution, the institute decided, was to give the power appeals but stress that all that wonderful surging power would provide "the extra margin of safety in an emergency." This, an institute official explains, provides "the illusion of rationality" that the buyer needs.

The McCann-Erickson advertising agency made a study for Esso gasoline to discover what motivates consumers, in order more effectively to win new friends for Esso. The agency found there is considerable magic in the word power. After many depth interviews with gasoline buyers the agency perfected an ad strategy that hammered at two words, with all letters capitalized: TOTAL POWER. . . .

Selling a sense of roots. When the Mogen David wine people were seeking some way to add magic to their wine's sales appeal (while it was still an obscure brand), they turned to motivation research via its ad agency. Psychiatrists and other probers listening to people talk at random about wine found that many related it to old family-centered or festive occasions. Some talked in an almost homesick way about wine and the good old days that went with it. A hard-hitting copy platform was erected based on these homey associations. The campaign tied home and mother into the selling themes. One line was: "The good old days—the home sweet home wine—the wine that grandma used to make." As a result of these carefully "motivated" slogans, the sales of Mogen David doubled within a year and soon the company was budgeting $2,000,000 just for advertising—the biggest ad campaign in the history of the wine industry.

Selling immortality. Perhaps the most astounding of all the efforts to merchandise hidden needs was that proposed to a conference of Midwestern life-insurance men. The conference invited Edward Weiss, head of Weiss and Geller, to tell members of the assembled North Central Life Advertisers Association (meeting in Omaha in April, 1955) how to put more impact into their messages advertising insurance. In his speech, called "Hidden Attitudes Toward Life Insurance" he reported on a study in depth made by several psychologists. . . .

The heart of his presentation was the findings on selling life insurance to the male, who is the breadwinner in most families and the one whose life is to be insured. Weiss criticized many of the current selling messages as being blind to the realities of this man who usually makes the buying decision. Typically, he demonstrated, current ads either glorified the persistence and helpfulness of the insurance agent or else portrayed the comfortable patter of life the family had managed to achieve after the breadwinner's death, thanks to the insurance. Both approaches, said Mr. Weiss, are dead wrong. In a few cases, he conceded, the breadwinner may be praised for his foresight, but still he is always depicted as someone now dead and gone.

One of the real appeals of life insurance to a man, his probers found, is that it assures the buyer of "the prospect of immortality through the perpetuation of his influence for it is not the fact of his own *physical* death that is inconceivable; it is the prospect of his *obliteration*." The man can't stand the thought of obliteration. Weiss reported that when men talked at the conscious and more formal level about insurance they talked of their great desire to protect their loved ones in case of any "eventuality." In this their desire for immortality was plain enough. But Weiss said there was strong evidence that this socially commendable acceptance of responsibility was not always the real and main desire of the prospective customer. Weiss said it appeared to be true for many men but not all. "In many instances," he went on, "our projective tests revealed the respondent's fierce desire to achieve immortality in order to *control* his family after death. These men obtain insurance against obliteration through the knowledge that they will continue to *dominate* their families; to *control* the family standard of living, and to guide the education of their children long after they are gone."

Questions

1. What difference does it make if advertisers work on a subliminal level?
2. What is the most troubling of the eight appeals outlined here?
3. How could the same strategies be applied to politics?

29-9   Barnett Newman and Jackson Pollock on Painting

The abstract expressionists Barnett Newman (1905–1970) and Jackson Pollock (1912–1956) were part of an artistic movement little concerned with reassuring a public that had problems with modern art in the 1950s. Newman's and Pollock's views show the changes that occurred in American art after the Gilded Age (see text pp. 918–919).

Source: Excerpts (1) from an interview with Barnett Newman by Dorothy Seckler, "Frontiers in Space," *Art in America*, vol. 50, no. 2 (Summer 1962), pp. 86–87; (2) from Jackson Pollock in the *New Yorker*, August 5, 1950, p. 16; and (3) from an unpublished letter from Jackson Pollock to Alfonso Ossorio and Edward Dragon, June 7, 1951. All three in Los Angeles County Museum of Art, *New York School: The First Generation—Paintings of the 1940s and 1950s* (a catalogue of the exhibition with statements by the artists and critics), ed. Maurice Tuchman (July 16 to August 1, 1965, Lytton Gallery), pp. 23–25.

The central issue of painting is the subject-matter. Most people think of subject-matter as what Meyer Schapiro has called "object-matter." It is the "object-matter" that most people want to see in a painting. That is what, for them, makes the painting seem full. For me both the use of objects and the manipulation of areas for the sake of the

areas themselves must end up being anecdotal. My subject is anti-anecdotal. An anecdote can be subjective and internal as well as of the external world so that the expression of the biography of self or the intoxicated moment of glowing ecstasy must in the end also become anecdotal. All such painting is essentially episodic which means it calls for a sequel. This must happen if a painting does not give a sensation of wholeness or fulfillment. That is why I have no interest in the episodic or ecstatic, however abstract. . . .

I am always referred to in relation to my color. Yet I know that if I have made a contribution, it is primarily in my drawing. The impressionists changed the way of seeing the world through their kind of drawing; the cubists saw the world anew in their drawing, and I hope that I have contributed a new way of seeing through drawing. Instead of using outlines, instead of making shapes or setting off spaces, my drawings declare the space. Instead of working with the remnants of space, I work with the whole space. . . .

It is full of meaning, but the meaning must come from the seeing, not from the talking. I feel, however, that one of its implications is its assertion of freedom, its denial of dogmatic principles, its repudiation of all dogmatic life. Almost 15 years ago, Harold Rosenberg challenged me to explain what one of my paintings could possibly mean to the world. My answer was that if he and others could read it properly it would mean the end of all state capitalism and totalitarianism. That answer still goes.

Abstract painting is abstract. It confronts you. There was a reviewer a while back who wrote that my pictures didn't have any beginning or any end. He didn't mean it as a compliment, but it was. It was a fine compliment.

I've had a period of drawing on canvas in black—with some of my early images coming thru—think the non-objectionists will find them disturbing—and the kids who think it simple to splash a Pollock out.

Questions

1. Why does Newman avoid "object-matter" in his work?
2. What kind of meaning do these artists say their art has?
3. Are Pollock and Newman obliged to make their work understandable to a mass audience? Why or why not?

29-10 "Handy Phrases for Traveling in Russia" (1959)

Mad debuted as a comic in 1952 and switched to a magazine format three years later. The humor was as irreverant as the rest of the 1950s was serious, a contrast that often irritated authority figures—not least of all parents—as it amused others. The following is *Mad*'s take on the Soviet Union in 1959 (see text p. 918).

HANDY PHRASES FOR TRAVELING IN
RUSSIA

When will I get my camera back?	Спальни—комнаты, принимаютъ гостеи въ которыхъ	Hchoo-vastat *lay-dee* hchye *tsaw* yoo veet lest-ni-yit?
Has the chamber-maid finished searching my luggage?	Полъ ея устланъ коврами, и на спятъ люди.	Dyit-yoo hav yoor tsoop too-dyay?
Which corner of the room is mine?	Въ гостинной вис кухнѣ приготовля ютъ кушанье.	Izz dere hay dock-tur hin tzee howze?
What time is the ex-Commissar's funeral?	Столовая—комната, которой кушаютъ.	*Vhat* har lit-teel gowrls may-de huv?
What time is the new Commissar's funeral?	Около стола	Vhat ist diss *tzing* corld luff?
Our guide is very friendly.	Въ столовой стоя стоятъ нѣсколько	Tzee cho *muz* gho hon.

Why was our guide liquidated?	Въ выхъ или въ круглый столъ и высокіи буфетъ.	Iz *hev-ree* budd-hee hap-hee?
Waiter, there's a dictaphone in my borscht!	Въ гостинной при съѣстные припасы хранятся въ	Tsam, hyu med tsee pahntz *tu* lungl
The handcuffs are chafing my wrists.	Полъ ея устланъ стѣнахъ висятъ пр коврами, и на	Cluz cuh-vor bee-fohr strah-kink.
Do you have a cell with a view?	Спальни ятъ люди; спальняхъ стоятъ кухнѣ приготово	Vye du fahr-menz vhere *rähd* suz-pehn-derz?
Will I need my galoshes in Siberia?	Въ столовоі стоя которой кушаютъ: и ужинаютъ.	Hchow har tzings een Glock-hcha-mohr-hcha?
Is this how you treated Adlai Stevenson?	Около стола	Veel tsöck-tsess *spowrl* Hchrock Hchun-tahr?
I demand to see the American Consul!	Столовая—комната, высокіи буфетъ.	Hchew kent *du* dzits tu mhee!

Questions

1. What stereotypes are used here?
2. To what extent is the piece political?
3. How well does the humor hold up today?

Questions for Further Thought

1. How do Documents 29-8 through 29-10 belie the notion of the 1950s as a simple time, free of conflict and controversy?
2. Apply the ideas of Vance Packard (Document 29-8) to the 1920s ads in Documents 24-4 and 24-5. Was hidden persuasion new to the 1950s, or is it the essence of advertising? If flag burning is afforded First Amendment protection, should all forms of advertising also be protected? Why or why not?
3. What is the relationship between an era's politics, popular culture, and art? Is one more important than the others for understanding a particular period? Why or why not?

CHAPTER 30

The Ascent of Liberalism
1960–1970

★   ★   ★

John Kennedy and the Politics of Expectation

After Adlai Stevenson's two unsuccessful presidential campaigns in the 1950s, the Democratic party turned to John F. Kennedy for the 1960 election. Kennedy had Stevenson's penchant for high-minded idealism and even took on many of Stevenson's liberal advisers, but he had several qualities that Stevenson lacked. An Irish Catholic from an urban constituency, he was more appealing to ethnic and blue-collar Democrats, even though his Catholicism was a problem for many other Americans. A war hero with a conservative Congressional record, he could pose as a tough cold warrior. His relative youth and handsome features made him ideal as a candidate of the new politics of televised imagery and style (see text pp. 926–928).

He bound these strengths together with promises to "get America moving again" by shaking up the country and unleashing the national spirit. Underneath his calls to idealism Kennedy was an extremely cautious politician, particularly because his margin of victory in 1960 was so slim (see text p. 928). During his brief presidency, JFK's domestic agenda was limited, and he failed to provide decisive leadership. He also moved very cautiously on the civil rights front (see text pp. 935, 938).

Television seemed made to order for John Kennedy. It captured his good looks and Richard Nixon's haggard features (Document 30-1) just as it elevated his inaugural address (Document 30-2). Television also conveyed just how critical the Cuban missile crisis was (Document 30-3).

30-1 "The Television Debates" (1960)

Theodore H. White

The journalist Theodore H. White believed that "the central fact of politics has always been the quality of leadership under the pressure of great forces." White (1915–1986) tested his hypothesis during the presidential campaign of 1960, when the television cameras created their own great pressure during a series of debates between John F. Kennedy and Richard M. Nixon (see text p. 927).

Source: Abridged and reprinted with the permission of Scribner, a Division of Simon & Schuster, from *The Making of the President, 1960* by Theodore H. White, pp. 279–287. Copyright 1961 Atheneum House, Inc.

At 8:30 P.M., Chicago time, on the evening of September 26th, 1960, the voice and shadow of the previous show faded from the screen; in a few seconds it was followed by another voice and by a visual clip extolling the virtues of Liggett and Myers cigarettes; fifteen seconds were then devoted to Maybelline, the mascara "devoted exclusively to eye beauty, velvety soft and smooth." Then a deep voice regretfully announced that the viewers who turned to this channel would tonight be denied the privilege of viewing the Andy Griffith Show—and the screen dissolved to three men who were about to confirm a revolution in American Presidential politics.

This revolution had been made by no one of the three men on screen—John F. Kennedy, Richard M. Nixon or Howard K. Smith, the moderator. It was a revolution born of the ceaseless American genius in technology; its sole agent and organizer had been the common American television set. Tonight it was to permit the simultaneous gathering of all the tribes of America to ponder their choice between two chieftains in the largest political convocation in the history of man.

Again, it is the census that best describes this revolution. Ten years earlier (in 1950) of America's then 40,000,000 families only 11 percent (or 4,400,000) enjoyed the pleasures of a television set. By 1960 the number of American families had grown to 44,000,000, and of these *no less than 88 per cent, or 40,000,000, possessed a television set*. The installation of this equipment had in some years of the previous decade partaken of the quality of stampede—and in the peak stampede years of 1954–1955–1956 no fewer than 10,000 American homes had each been installing a new television set for the first time *every single day of the year*. The change that came about with this stampede is almost immeasurable. By the summer of 1960 the average use of the television set in the American home was four or five hours out of the twenty-four in each day. The best judgment on what television had done to America comes from the research departments of the large television networks. According to them, it is now possible for the first time to answer an inquiring foreign visitor as to what Americans do in the evening. The answer is clear: *they watch television*. Within a single decade the medium has exploded to a dimension in shaping the American mind that rivals that of America's schools and churches. . . .

In 1960 this yearning of the television networks to show their best was particularly acute. For the men who direct television are sensitive to public criticism; they wince and weep in public like adolescents at the slightest touch of hostility in print—and in 1959 they had suffered the worst round of public criticism and contempt since their industry was founded. The shock of the "payola" scandals of 1959; the Congressional hearings on these scandals; the editorial indignation in the "Gutenberg" media not only at these scandals but at the drenching of the air by violence, vulgarity and horse opera—all these had not only given the masters of television an inferiority complex but also frightened them with the prospect that the franchise on the air given to them so freely in return for their legal obligation of "public service" might be withdrawn, curtailed or abolished. It was a time for the "upgrading" of television; and the Presidential campaign of 1960 seemed to offer a fine opportunity for public service—if only Congress would relax those regulations and laws that had manacled and *prevented* television from doing its best. . . .

It is important to understand why the debates of 1960 were to be different from previous political use of the medium.

Television had already demonstrated its primitive power in politics from, at least, the fall of 1952, when, in one broadcast, it had transformed Richard M. Nixon from a negative Vice-Presidential candidate, under attack, into a martyr and an asset to Dwight D. Eisenhower's Presidential campaign. But from 1952 until 1960 television could be used only as an expensive partisan instrument; its time had to be bought and paid for by political parties for their own candidates. The audiences such partisan broadcasts assembled, like the audiences at political rallies, were audiences of the convinced—of convinced Republicans for Republican candidates, of convinced Democrats for Democratic candidates. Generally, the most effective political broadcast could assemble hardly more than half the audience of the commercial show that it replaced. This was why so many candidates and their television advisers sought two-minute or five-minute spots tacked on to the major programs that engaged the nation's fancy; the general audience would not tune out a hostile candidate if he appeared for only two or three minutes, and thus a candidate, using TV "spots" had a much better chance of reaching the members of the opposition party and the "independents," whom he must lure to listen to and then vote for him. The 1960 idea of a "debate," in which both major candidates would appear simultaneously, thus promised to bring both Democrats and Republicans together in the same viewing audience for the first time. Some optimists thought the debates would at least double the exposure of both candidates. How much more they would do than "double" the exposure no one, in the summer of 1960, dreamed.

The future was thus still obscure when the representatives of the two candidates and the spokesmen for the broadcasting networks first met at the Waldorf-Astoria Hotel in New York in September to discuss the conditions and circumstances of the meetings. By this time each of the two major networks had offered eight hours of free time to the campaign, and the third had offered three hours, for a total of nineteen hours of nationwide broadcasting, worth about $2,000,000; they had also made it clear to the candidates that this was not "gift" time but time over which they, the networks, meant to exercise an editorial control to insure maximum viewing interest. Slowly, in discussion, the shape and form of the debates emerged—a controlled panel of four press interlocutors; no notes; dignity to be safeguarded; opening statements of eight minutes by each candidate in the first and last debates; two-and-one-half minute responses to questions. The Nixon negotiators fought to restrict the number of debates—their man, they felt, was the master of the form and one "sudden-death" debate could eliminate Kennedy with a roundhouse swing. They viewed the insistence of the Kennedy negotiators on the maximum possible number of debates as weakness. ("If they weren't scared," said one Nixon staffman, "why shouldn't they be willing to pin everything on one show?") The Kennedy negotiators insisted on at least five debates, then let themselves be whittled to four. ("Every time we get those two fellows on the screen side by side," said J. Leonard Reinsch, Kennedy's TV maestro, "we're going to gain and he's going to lose.")

By mid-September all had been arranged. There would be four debates—on September 26th, October 7th, October 13th and October 21st. The first would be produced by CBS out of Chicago, the second by NBC out of Washington, the third by ABC out of New York and Los Angeles and the fourth, again by ABC, out of New York.

In the event, when all was over, the audience exceeded the wildest fancies and claims of the television networks. Each individual broadcast averaged an audience set at a low of 65,000,000 and a high of 70,000,000. The greatest previous audience in television history had been for the climactic game of the 1959 World Series, when an estimated 90,000,000 Americans had tuned in to watch the White Sox play the Dodgers. When, finally, figures were assembled for all four debates, the total audience for the television debates on the Presidency exceeded even this figure.

All this, of course, was far in the future when, on Sunday, September 25th, 1960, John F. Kennedy arrived in Chicago from Cleveland, Ohio, to stay at the Ambassador East Hotel, and Richard M. Nixon came from Washington, D.C., to stop at the Pick-Congress Hotel, to prepare, each in his own way, for the confrontation.

Kennedy's preparation was marked by his typical attention to organization and his air of casual self-possession; the man behaves, in any crisis, as if it consisted only of a sequence of necessary things to be done that will become complicated if emotions intrude. His personal Brain Trust of three had arrived and assembled at the Knickerbocker Hotel in Chicago on Sunday, the day before. The chief of these three was, of course, Ted Sorensen; with Sorensen was Richard Goodwin, a twenty-eight-year-old lawyer, an elongated elfin man with a capacity for fact and reasoning that had made him Number One man only two years before at the Harvard Law School; and Mike Feldman, a burly and impressive man, a one-time instructor of law at the University of Pennsylvania, later a highly successful businessman, who had abandoned business to follow Kennedy's star as Chief of the Senator's Legislative Research. With them, they had brought the portable Kennedy campaign research library—a Sears Roebuck foot locker of documents—and now, for a twenty-four-hour session at the Knickerbocker Hotel, stretching around the clock, they operated like young men at college cramming for an exam. When they had finished, they had prepared fifteen pages of copy boiling down into twelve or thirteen subject areas the relevant facts and probable questions they thought the correspondents on the panel, or Mr. Nixon, might raise. All three had worked with Kennedy closely for years. They knew that as a member of the House and the Senate Committees on Labor he was fully familiar with all the issues that might arise on domestic policy (the subject of the first debate) and that it was necessary to fix in his mind, not the issues or understanding, but only the latest data.

Early on Monday they met the candidate in his suite for a morning session of questions and answers. The candidate read their suggestions for his opening eight-minute statement, disagreed, tossed their suggestions out, called his secretary, dictated another of his own; and then for four hours Kennedy and the Brain Trust considered together the Nixon position and the Kennedy position, with the accent constantly on fact: What was the latest rate of unemployment? What was steel production rate? What was the Nixon stand on this or that particular? The conversation, according to those present, was not only easy but rather comic and rambling, covering a vast number of issues entirely irrelevant to the debate. Shortly before one o'clock Goodwin and Feldman disappeared to a basement office in the Ambassador East to answer new questions the candidate had raised, and the candidate then had a gay lunch with Ted Sorensen, his brother Robert and public-opinion analyst Louis Harris. The candidate left shortly thereafter for a quick address to the United Brotherhood of Carpenters and Joiners of America (which Nixon had addressed in the morning) and came back to his hotel room for a nap. About five o'clock he rose from his nap, quite refreshed, and assembled brother Robert, Sorensen, Harris, Goodwin and Feldman for another Harvard tutorial skull session.

Several who were present remember the performance as vividly as those who were present at the Hyannisport meeting in October, 1959. The candidate lay on his bed in a white, open-necked T shirt and army suntan pants, and fired questions at his intimates. He held in his hand the fact cards that Goodwin and Feldman had prepared for him during the afternoon, and as he finished each, he sent it spinning off the bed to the floor. Finally, at about 6:30, he rose from his bed and decided to have dinner. He ate what is called "a splendid dinner" all by himself in his room, then emerged in a white shirt and dark-gray suit, called for a stop watch and proceeded to the old converted sports arena that is now CBS Station WBBM at McClurg Court in Chicago, to face his rival for the Presidency of the United States.

Richard M. Nixon had preceded him to the studio. Nixon had spent the day in solitude without companions in the loneliness of his room at the Pick-Congress. The Vice-President was tired; the drive of campaigning in the previous two weeks had caused him to lose another five pounds since he had left the hospital; his TV advisers had urged that he arrive in Chicago on Saturday and have a full day of rest before he went on the air on Monday, but they had been unable to get through to him, and had not even been able to reach his press secretary, Herbert Klein. Mr. Nixon thus arrived in Chicago late on Sunday evening, unbriefed on the magnitude of the trial he was approaching; on Monday he spoke during the morning to the United Brotherhood of Carpenters and Joiners, an appearance his TV advisers considered a misfortune—the Brotherhood was a hostile union audience, whose negative reaction, they knew, would psychologically disturb their contender.

When Nixon returned to his hotel from the Brotherhood appearance at 12:30, he became incommunicado while his frantic TV technicians tried to reach him or brief him on the setting of the debate, the staging, the problems he might encounter. The Vice-President received one visitor for five minutes that afternoon in his suite, and he received one long telephone call—from Henry Cabot Lodge, who, reportedly, urged him to be careful to erase the "assassin

image" when he went on the air. For the rest, the Vice-President was alone, in consultation with no one. Finally, as he emerged from the hotel to drive through Chicago traffic to the studio, one TV adviser was permitted to ride with him and hastily brief him in the ten-minute drive. The adviser urged that the Vice-President come out swinging—that this was a contest, a fight, and that Kennedy must be jolted at the first exchange. The Vice-President was of another mind, however—and wondered whether the suggestion had originated with his adviser or with someone else, like Frank Stanton, President of CBS, who, said the Vice-President, only wanted a good show. Thus they arrived at the studio; as Nixon got out, he struck his knee again—a nasty crack—on the edge of the automobile door, just as he had on his first accident to the knee at Greensboro, North Carolina. An observer reports that his face went all "white and pasty" but that he quickly recovered and entered the studio. . . .

Mr. Nixon's advisers and representatives, understandably nervous since they could not communicate with their principal, had made the best preparation they could. They had earlier requested that both candidates talk from a lectern, standing—and Kennedy had agreed. They had asked several days earlier that the two candidates be seated farther apart from each other than originally planned—and that had been agreed on too. Now, on the day of the debate, they paid meticulous attention to each detail. They were worried about the deep eye shadows in Nixon's face and they requested and adjusted two tiny spotlights ("inkies" in television parlance) to shine directly into his eye wells and illuminate the darkness there; they asked that a table be placed in front of the moderator, and this was agreed to also; they requested that no shots be taken of Nixon's left profile during the debate; and this was also agreed to.

The Kennedy advisers had no requests; they seemed as cocky and confident as their chief.

Nixon entered the studio about an hour before air time and inspected the setting, let himself be televised on an interior camera briefly for the inspection of his advisers, then paced moodily about in the back of the studio. He beckoned the producer to him at one point as he paced and asked as a personal favor that he not be on camera if he happened to be mopping sweat from his face. (That night, contrary to most reports, Nixon was wearing no theatrical make-up. In order to tone down his dark beard stubble on the screen, an adviser had applied only a light coating of "Lazy Shave," a pancake make-up with which a man who has heavy afternoon beard growth may powder his face to conceal the growth.)

Senator Kennedy arrived about fifteen minutes after the Vice-President; he inspected the set; sat for the camera; and his advisers inspected him, then declared they were satisfied. The producer made a remark about the glare of the Senator's white shirt, and Kennedy sent an aide back to his hotel to bring back a blue one, into which he changed just before air time. The men took their seats, the tally lights on the cameras blinked red to show they were live now.

"Good evening," said Howard K. Smith, the gray and handsome moderator. "The television and radio stations of the United States . . . are proud to provide for a discussion of issues in the current political campaign by the two major candidates for the Presidency. The candidates need no introduction. . . ."

And they were on air, before seventy million Americans.

Questions

1. By 1960, how important had television become in national politics?
2. What problems did candidate Nixon experience going into the debate which might have affected viewers' perception of his performance?
3. Are televised debates a fair and accurate measure of a candidate's abilities? Why or why not?

30-2 Inaugural Address (1961)

John F. Kennedy

President Kennedy's inaugural address is best known for his call to national self-sacrifice: "Ask not what your country can do for you—ask what you can do for your country." It was the sort of broad appeal for which he was famous. The call to national sacrifice thus included efforts, as he put it, to "explore the stars, conquer the deserts, eradicate disease, tap the ocean depths, and encourage the arts and commerce." In more concrete terms sacrifice meant everything from prevailing in the space race to joining the new President's Council on Physical Fitness; it could inspire people to devote themselves to humanitarian work in the Peace Corps or to train for counterinsurgency (see text pp. 928–929).

The inaugural address showed clearly Kennedy's devotion to foreign policy (see text pp. 928–931). Kennedy affirmed the western alliance, warned off the Soviets, and appealed to the Third World, which, only then emerging from its colonial past, was the prime object of superpower competition.

Source: Public Papers of the Presidents of the United States: John F. Kennedy, 1961 (Washington, D.C.: U.S. Government Printing Office, 1962), pp. 1–3.

We observe today not a victory of party but a celebration of freedom—symbolizing an end as well as a beginning—signifying renewal as well as change. For I have sworn before you and Almighty God the same solemn oath our forebears prescribed nearly a century and three quarters ago.

The world is very different now. For man holds in his mortal hands the power to abolish all forms of human poverty and all forms of human life. And yet the same revolutionary beliefs for which our forebears fought are still at issue around the globe—the belief that the rights of man come not from the generosity of the state but from the hand of God.

We dare not forget today that we are the heirs of that first revolution. Let the word go forth from this time and place, to friend and foe alike, that the torch has been passed to a new generation of Americans—born in this century, tempered by war, disciplined by a hard and bitter peace, proud of our ancient heritage—and unwilling to witness or permit the slow undoing of those human rights to which this nation has always been committed, and to which we are committed today at home and around the world.

Let every nation know, whether it wishes us well or ill, that we shall bear any burden, meet any hardship, support any friend, oppose any foe, to assure the survival and the success of liberty.

This we pledge and more.

To those allies whose cultural and spiritual origins we share, we pledge the loyalty of faithful friends. United, there is little we cannot do in a host of cooperative ventures. Divided, there is little we can do—for we do not meet a powerful challenge at odds and split asunder.

To those new states whom we welcome to the ranks of the free, we pledge our word that one form of colonial control shall not have passed away merely to be replaced by a far more iron tyranny. We shall not always expect to find them supporting our view. But we shall always hope to find them strongly supporting their own freedom—and to remember that in the past, those who foolishly sought power by riding the back of the tiger ended up inside.

To those peoples in the huts and villages of half the globe struggling to break the bonds of mass misery, we pledge our best efforts to help them help themselves . . .

not because the Communists may be doing it, not because we seek their votes, but because it is right. If a free society cannot help the many who are poor, it cannot save the few who are rich. . . .

Finally, to those nations who would make themselves our adversary, we offer not a pledge but a request: that both sides begin anew the quest for peace, before the dark powers of destruction unleashed by science engulf all humanity in planned or accidental self-destruction.

We dare not tempt them with weakness. For only when our arms are sufficient beyond doubt can we be certain beyond doubt that they will never be employed. . . .

In the long history of the world, only a few generations have been granted the role of defending freedom in its hour of maximum danger. I do not shrink from this responsibility—I welcome it.

Questions

1. Kennedy begins his speech with appeals to the "revolutionary beliefs for which our forebears fought." How could those beliefs be used to fight the Cold War in the Third World?
2. What parts of the address are aimed at the communist superpowers, and what is Kennedy's posture toward them?
3. Kennedy is asking Americans to sacrifice for American ideals. How does he promise to live up to those ideals himself?

30-3　The Cuban Missile Crisis (1962)

In October 1962 the Cuban missile crisis brought to a head more than a year of difficult confrontations between the Kennedy administration and the Soviets over Cuba, Berlin, the Congo, and Southeast Asia (see text pp. 929–930). Up to that point Kennedy had been on the losing end of most of the confrontations, and he was enormously frustrated. When U.S. reconnaissance flights discovered the Soviets' construction of missile sites in Cuba, Kennedy not only took it as a serious threat but was determined to prevail in his struggle for diplomatic momentum.

Hence, rather than keeping the information secret and negotiating with the Russians behind closed doors, he turned the matter into a public confrontation. He went on national television and announced his policy: until the Soviet missiles were removed there would be a naval quarantine of Cuba, reinforcement of the American base at Guantánamo, and an intention to regard any attack from Cuba as an attack from the Soviet Union. In effect, Kennedy dared the Russians to maintain missiles on the island, and in this case they backed down (see text pp. 930–931).

Source: Public Papers of the Presidents of the United States: John F. Kennedy, 1962 (Washington, D.C.: U.S. Government Printing Office, 1963), pp. 806–809.

This government, as promised, has maintained the closest surveillance of the Soviet military build-up on the island of Cuba. Within the past week, unmistakable evidence has established the fact that a series of offensive missile sites is now in preparation on that imprisoned island. The purpose of these bases can be none other than to provide a nuclear strike capability against the Western Hemisphere. . . .

For many years, both the Soviet Union and the United

States . . . have deployed strategic nuclear weapons with great care, never upsetting the precarious status quo which insured that these weapons would not be used in the absence of some vital challenge. Our own strategic missiles have never been transferred to the territory of any other nation under a cloak of secrecy and deception; and our history—unlike that of the Soviets since the end of World War II—demonstrates that we have no desire to dominate or conquer any other nation or impose our system upon its people. Nevertheless, American citizens have become adjusted to living daily on the bull's-eye of Soviet missiles located inside the U.S.S.R. or in submarines.

In that sense, missiles in Cuba add to an already clear and present danger. . . .

But this secret, swift, and extraordinary buildup of Communist missiles—in an area well known to have a special and historical relationship to the United States and the nations of the Western Hemisphere, in violation of Soviet assurances, and in defiance of American and hemispheric policy—this sudden, clandestine decision to station strategic weapons for the first time outside of Soviet soil—is a deliberately provocative and unjustified change in the status quo which cannot be accepted by this country, if our courage and our commitments are ever to be trusted again by either friend or foe. . . .

Our policy has been one of patience and restraint, as befits a peaceful and powerful nation, which leads a worldwide alliance. . . . We will not prematurely or unnecessarily risk the costs of worldwide nuclear war in which even the fruits of victory would be ashes in our mouth—but neither will we shrink from that risk at any time it must be faced. . . .

The path we have chosen for the present is full of hazards, as all paths are—but it is the one most consistent with our character and our courage as a nation and our commitments around the world. The cost of freedom is always high—but Americans have always paid it. And one path we shall never choose, and that is the path of surrender or submission.

Questions

1. What purpose can Soviet missiles serve in Cuba, according to Kennedy?
2. Why, according to the President, was the installation of missiles in Cuba a greater provocation than the continued existence of Soviet missiles on submarines?
3. In what ways does Kennedy relate the installation of missiles in Cuba to the political and ideological confrontation of the Cold War?

Questions for Further Thought

1. Using Documents 30-1 and 30-3, consider how television has changed the course of politics and government. Is there cause for concern? Why or why not?
2. How does JFK's inaugural address (Document 30-2) compare to FDR's (Document 26-2)? Note especially the way each speaker appeals to his audience.
3. To what extent should a president be judged by the promises made in an inaugural address?

The Civil Rights Movement and Lyndon Johnson and the Great Society

In the period 1954–1975, groups of Americans who traditionally had been outside the mainstream of society and culture tried to make inroads into it. African-Americans were at the vanguard of this social movement. At first blacks patiently lobbied for their rightful place in society as a matter of justice. However, when confronted with the entrenched opposition of some whites, African-Americans became more assertive and their demands grew more militant. These trends were manifested first in the South, where segregation by law presented a particular affront to African-American sensibilities (see text p. 934).

A year after the *Brown* decision (see text p. 934) events in Montgomery, Alabama, gave impetus to the modern civil rights movement. Rosa Parks's refusal to give up her bus seat on December 1, 1955, was both a heroic and a historic act. In response to

Parks's arrest and to protest segregation in transportation, Montgomery's black community boycotted the city's bus system. The boycott launched the career of the Reverend Martin Luther King, Jr., whose name became synonymous with the civil rights movement. King's nonviolent approach was closely associated with the movement. He discussed his philosophy and tactics in his "Letter from Birmingham City Jail" (Document 30-4). Dr. King and his organization, the Southern Christian Leadership Conference, continued to practice nonviolent protest for the next decade.

A confluence of events, some of them tragic, moved the struggle for civil rights forward. Although John Kennedy had approached the issue cautiously, his death allowed Lyndon Johnson to argue that his legislative initiatives were actually those of Kennedy, the martyred president. Congress responded by embracing Johnson's call for a Great Society, including the Voting Rights Act of 1965 (Document 30-5). The murders of several civil rights workers (see text p. 940) also contributed to a climate favorable to its passage.

If for only an instant, it appeared that Americans had reached a consensus that poverty must be abolished. Again, Kennedy's death made Americans sympathetic to the War on Poverty, as did Michael Harrington's examination of poverty amid plenty (Document 30-6). But for all Johnson's political talents (no president had greater legislative ability than this former Senate leader) the moment passed, and Americans got interested in other issues. The acceptance speech of Senator Barry Goldwater (Document 30-7) outlined where those interests would lie in the decades ahead.

30-4   Letter from Birmingham City Jail (1963)

Martin Luther King, Jr.   In April and May of 1963 the Reverend Martin Luther King, Jr., and the Southern Christian Leadership Conference led a series of mass protests in Birmingham, Alabama (see text pp. 935, 938). On Good Friday, April 12, King allowed himself to be arrested and jailed for leading a demonstration. He explained his actions and ideas about nonviolence in the now famous "Letter from Birmingham City Jail" addressed to other members of the clergy.

Source: Excerpted from Martin Luther King, Jr., "Letter from Birmingham City Jail," April 16, 1963. In *A Testament of Hope: The Essential Writings of Martin Luther King, Jr.*, ed. James Melvin Washington (New York: HarperCollins, 1991), pp. 289–302. Reprinted by arrangement with The Heirs to the Estate of Martin Luther King, Jr., c/o Writers House, Inc., as agent for the proprietor. Copyright 1963 by Martin Luther King, Jr.; copyright renewed 1991 by Coretta Scott King.

My dear Fellow Clergymen,

While confined here in the Birmingham city jail, I came across your recent statement calling our present activities "unwise and untimely." Seldom, if ever, do I pause to answer criticism of my work and ideas. If I sought to answer all of the criticisms that cross my desk, my secretaries would be engaged in little else in the course of the day, and I would have no time for constructive work. But since I feel that you are men of genuine good will and your criticisms are sincerely set forth, I would like to answer your statement in what I hope will be patient and reasonable terms.

I think I should give the reason for my being in Birmingham, since you have been influenced by the argument of "outsiders coming in." I have the honor of serving as president of the Southern Christian Leadership Conference, an organization operating in every southern state, with headquarters in Atlanta, Georgia. We have some eighty-five affiliate organizations all across the South—one being the Alabama Christian Movement for Human Rights. Whenever necessary and possible we share staff, educational and financial resources with our affiliates. Several months ago our local affiliate here in Birmingham invited us to be on call to engage in a nonviolent direct-action program if such were deemed necessary. We readily consented and when the hour came we lived up to our promises. So I am here, along with several members of my staff, because we were invited here. I am here because I have basic organizational ties here. . . .

In any nonviolent campaign there are four basic steps: (1) collection of the facts to determine whether injustices are alive, (2) negotiation, (3) self-purification, and (4) direct action. We have gone through all of these steps in Birmingham. There can be no gainsaying of the fact that racial injustice engulfs this community.

Birmingham is probably the most thoroughly segregated city in the United States. Its ugly record of police brutality is known in every section of this country. Its injust treatment of Negroes in the courts is a notorious reality. There have been more unsolved bombings of Negro homes and churches in Birmingham than any city in this nation. These are the hard, brutal and unbelievable facts. On the basis of these conditions Negro leaders sought to negotiate with the city fathers. But the political leaders consistently refused to engage in good faith negotiation.

Then came the opportunity last September to talk with some of the leaders of the economic community. In these negotiating sessions certain promises were made by the merchants—such as the promise to remove the humiliating racial signs from the stores. On the basis of these promises Rev. Shuttlesworth and the leaders of the Alabama Christian Movement for Human Rights agreed to call a moratorium on any type of demonstrations. As the weeks and months unfolded we realized that we were the victims of a broken promise. The signs remained. Like so many experiences of the past we were confronted with blasted hopes, and the dark shadow of a deep disappointment settled upon us. So we had no alternative except that of preparing for direct action, whereby we would present our very bodies as a means of laying our case before the conscience of the local and national community. We were not unmindful of the difficulties involved. So we decided to go through a process of self-purification. We started having workshops on nonviolence and repeatedly asked ourselves the questions, "Are you able to accept blows without retaliating?" "Are you able to endure the ordeals of jail?" We decided to set our direct-action program around the Easter season, realizing that with the exception of Christmas, this was the largest shopping period of the year. . . .

You may well ask, "Why direct action? Why sit-ins, marches, etc.? Isn't negotiation a better path?" You are exactly right in your call for negotiation. Indeed, this is the purpose of direct action. Nonviolent direct action seeks to create such a crisis and establish such creative tension that a community that has constantly refused to negotiate is forced to confront the issue. It seeks so to dramatize the issue that it can no longer be ignored. . . . So the purpose of the direct action is to create a situation so crisis-packed that it will inevitably open the door to negotiation. We, therefore, concur with you in your call for negotiation. Too long has our beloved Southland been bogged down in the tragic attempt to live in monologue rather than dialogue.

My friends, I must say to you that we have not made a single gain in civil rights without determined legal and nonviolent pressure. History is the long and tragic story of the fact that privileged groups seldom give up their privileges voluntarily. Individuals may see the moral light and voluntarily give up their unjust posture; but as Reinhold Niebuhr has reminded us, groups are more immoral than individuals.

We know through painful experience that freedom is never voluntarily given by the oppressor; it must be demanded by the oppressed. Frankly, I have never yet engaged in a direct action movement that was "well-timed," according to the timetable of those who have not suffered unduly from the disease of segregation. For years now I have heard the words "Wait!" It rings in the ear of every Negro with a piercing familiarity. This "Wait" has almost always meant "Never." . . . We must come to see with the distinguished jurist of yesterday that "justice too long delayed is justice denied." We have waited for more than 340 years for our constitutional and God-given rights. The nations of Asia and Africa are moving with jetlike speed toward the goal of political independence, and we still creep at horse and buggy pace toward the gaining of a cup of coffee at a lunch counter. I guess it is easy for those who have never felt the stinging darts of segregation to say, "Wait." But when you have seen vicious mobs lynch your mothers and fathers at will and drown your sisters and brothers at whim; when you have seen hate-filled policemen curse, kick, brutalize and even kill your black brothers and sisters with impunity; when you see the vast majority of your twenty million Negro brothers smothering in an airtight cage of poverty in the midst of an affluent society; when you suddenly find your tongue twisted and your speech stammering as you seek to explain to your six-year-old daughter why she can't go to the public amusement park that has just been advertised on television, and see tears welling up in her little eyes when she is told that Funtown is closed to colored children, and see the depressing clouds of inferiority begin to form in her little mental sky, and see her begin to distort her little personality by unconsciously developing a bitterness toward white people; when you have to concoct an answer for a five-year-old son asking in agonizing pathos: "Daddy, why do white people treat colored people so mean?"; when you take a cross-country drive and find it necessary to sleep night after night in the uncomfortable corners of your automobile because no motel will accept you; when you are humiliated day in and day out by nagging signs reading "white" and "colored"; when your first name becomes "nigger" and your middle name becomes "boy" (however old you are) and your last name becomes "John," and when your wife and mother are never given the respected title "Mrs."; when you are harried by day and haunted by night by the fact that you are a Negro, living constantly at tiptoe stance never quite knowing what to expect next, and plagued with inner fears and outer resentments; when you are forever fighting a degenerating sense of "nobodiness"; then you will understand why we find it difficult to wait. There comes a time when the cup of endurance runs over, and men are no longer willing to be plunged into an abyss of injustice where they experience the blackness of corroding despair. I hope, sirs, you can understand our legitimate and unavoidable impatience. . . .

We must come to see that human progress never rolls in on wheels of inevitability. It comes through the tireless efforts and persistent work of men willing to be co-workers with God, and without this hard word time itself becomes an ally of the forces of social stagnation. We must use time creatively, and forever realize that the time is always ripe to do right. Now is the time to make real the promise of democracy, and transform our pending national elegy into a creative psalm of brotherhood. Now is the time to lift our national policy from the quicksand of racial injustice to the solid rock of human dignity.

You spoke of our activity in Birmingham as extreme. At first I was rather disappointed that fellow clergymen would see my nonviolent efforts as those of the extremist. I started thinking about the fact that I stand in the middle of two opposing forces in the Negro community. One is a force of complacency made up of Negroes who, as a result of long years of oppression, have been so completely drained of self-respect and a sense of "somebodiness" that they have adjusted to segregation, and, of a few Negroes in the middle class who, because of a degree of academic and economic security, and because at points they profit by segregation, have unconsciously become insensitive to the problems of the masses. The other force is one of bitterness and hatred, and comes perilously close to advocating violence. It is expressed in the various black nationalist groups that are springing up over the nation, the largest and best known being Elijah Muhammad's Muslim movement. This movement is nourished by the contemporary frustration over the continued existence of racial discrimination. It is made up of people who have lost faith in America, who have absolutely repudiated Christianity, and

who have concluded that the white man is an incurable "devil." I have tried to stand between these two forces, saying that we need not follow the "do-nothingism" of the complacent or the hatred and despair of the black nationalist. There is the more excellent way of love and nonviolent protest. I'm grateful to God that, through the Negro church, the dimension of nonviolence entered our struggle. If this philosophy had not emerged, I am convinced that by now many streets of the South would be flowing with floods of blood. And I am further convinced that if our white brothers dismiss us as "rabble-rousers" and "outside agitators" those of us who are working through the channels of nonviolent direct action and refuse to support our nonviolent efforts, millions of Negroes, out of frustration and despair, will seek solace and security in black nationalist ideologies, a development that will lead inevitably to a frightening racial nightmare.

Oppressed people cannot remain oppressed forever. The urge for freedom will eventually come. This is what happened to the American Negro. Something within has reminded him of his birthright of freedom; something without has reminded him that he can gain it. . . .

In spite of my shattered dreams of the past, I came to Birmingham with the hope that the white religious leadership of this community would see the justice of our cause, and with deep moral concern, serve as the channel through which our just grievances would get to the power structure. I had hoped that each of you would understand. But again I have been disappointed. I have heard numerous religious leaders of the South call upon their worshippers to comply with a desegregation decision because it is the *law*, but I have longed to hear white ministers say, "Follow this decree because integration is morally *right* and the Negro is your brother." In the midst of blatant injustice inflicted upon the Negro, I have watched white churches stand on the sideline and merely mouth pious irrelevancies and sanctimonious trivialities. In the midst of a mighty struggle to rid our nation of racial and economic injustice, I have heard so many ministers say, "Those are social issues with which the gospel has no real concern," and I have watched so many churches commit themselves to a completely otherworldly religion which made a strange distinction between body and soul, the sacred and the secular. . . .

I'm sorry that I can't join you in your praise for the police department.

It is true that they have been rather disciplined in their public handling of the demonstrators. In this sense they have been rather publicly "nonviolent." But for what purpose? To preserve the evil system of segregation. Over the last few years I have consistently preached that nonviolence demands that the means we use must be as pure as the ends we seek. So I have tried to make it clear that it is wrong to use immoral means to attain moral ends. But now I must affirm that it is just as wrong, or even more so, to use moral means to preserve immoral ends. Maybe Mr.

Connor and his policemen have been rather publicly non-violent, as Chief Pritchett was in Albany, Georgia, but they have used the moral means of nonviolence to maintain the immoral end of flagrant racial injustice. T.S. Eliot has said that there is no greater treason than to do the right deed for the wrong reason.

I wish you had commended the Negro sit-inners and demonstrators of Birmingham for their sublime courage, their willingness to suffer and their amazing discipline in the midst of the most inhuman provocation. . . .

One day the South will know that when these disinherited children of God sat down at lunch counters they were in reality standing up for the best in the American dream and the most sacred values in our Judeo-Christian heritage, and thusly, carrying our whole nation back to those great wells of democracy which were dug deep by the Founding Fathers in the formulation of the Constitution and the Declaration of Independence. . . .

I hope this letter finds you strong in the faith. I also hope that circumstances will soon make it possible for me to meet each of you, not as an integrationist or a civil rights leader, but as a fellow clergyman and a Christian brother. Let us all hope that the dark clouds of racial prejudice will soon pass away and the deep fog of misunderstanding will be lifted from our fear-drenched communities and in some not too distant tomorrow the radiant stars of love and brotherhood will shine over our great nation with all of their scintillating beauty.

Yours for the cause of Peace and Brotherhood,
Martin Luther King, Jr.

Questions

1. What does this letter indicate about the major tenets of King's philosophy of non-violence?
2. What was King's attitude toward moderate members of the white clergy? How did he hope to alter the position of his white colleagues?
3. Do you find the overall tone of the letter to be optimistic or pessimistic? What evidence can you cite to support your conclusion? What does this tell you about the civil rights movement in 1963?

30-5 Voting Rights Act of 1965

The Voting Rights Act of 1965 (see text p. 940) was passed 100 years after the start of Reconstruction; the legislation outlawed tactics southern states had used to deny civil rights to African-Americans since the late nineteenth century. The act also had at least one unintended result—it furthered white backlash against the Democratic party in the South.

Source: Excerpted from United States, *Statutes at Large*, vol. 79, pp. 437–446 (Public Law 89–110).

Public Law 89-110

AN ACT

To enforce the fifteenth amendment to the Constitution of the United States, and for other purposes.

Be it enacted by the Senate and House of Representatives of the United States of America in Congress assembled, That this Act shall be known as the "Voting Rights Act of 1965".

SEC. 2. No voting qualification or prerequisite to voting, or standard, practice, or procedure shall be imposed or applied by any State or political subdivision to deny or abridge the right of any citizen of the United States to vote on account of race or color.

SEC. 3. (a) Whenever the Attorney General institutes a proceeding under any statute to enforce the guarantees of the fifteenth amendment in any State or political subdivision the court shall authorize the appointment of Federal examiners by the United States Civil Service Commission in accordance with section 6 to serve for such period of time and for such political subdivisions as the court shall determine is appropriate to enforce the guarantees of the fifteenth amendment (1) as part of any interlocutory order if the court determines that the appointment of such examiners is necessary to enforce such guarantees or (2) as part of any final judgment if the court finds that violations of the fifteenth amendment justifying equitable relief have occurred in such State or subdivision: *Provided,* That the court need not authorize the appointment of examiners if any incidents of denial or abridgement of the right to vote on account of race or color (1) have been few in number and have been promptly and effectively corrected by State or local action, (2) the continuing effect of such incidents has been eliminated, and (3) there is no reasonable probability of their recurrence in the future.

(b) If in a proceeding instituted by the Attorney General under any statute to enforce the guarantees of the fifteenth amendment in any State or political subdivision the court finds that a test or device has been used for the purpose or with the effect of denying or abridging the right of any citizen of the United States to vote on account of race or color, it shall suspend the use of tests and devices in such State or politicial subdivisions as the court shall determine is appropriate and for such period as it deems necessary.

(c) If in any proceeding instituted by the Attorney General under any statute to enforce the guarantee of the fifteenth amendment in any State or political subdivision the court finds that violations of the fifteenth amendment justifying equitable relief have occurred within the territory of such State or political subdivision. the court, in addition to such relief as it may grant, shall retain jurisdiction for such period as it may deem appropriate and during such period no voting qualification or prerequisite to voting, or standard, practice, or procedure with respect to voting different from that in force or effect at the time the proceeding was commenced shall be enforced unless and until the court finds that such qualification, prerequisite, standard, practice, or procedure does not have the purpose and will not have the effect of denying or abridging the right to vote on account of race or color: *Provided,* That such qualification, prerequisite, standard, practice, or procedure may be enforced if the qualification, prerequisite, standard, practice, or procedure has been submitted by the chief legal officer or other appropriate official of such State or subdivision to the Attorney General and the Attorney General has not interposed an objection within sixty days after such submission, except that neither the court's finding nor the Attorney General's failure to object shall bar a subsequent action to enjoin enforcement of such qualification, prerequisite, standard, practice, or procedure.

SEC. 4. (a) To assure that the right of citizens of the United States to vote is not denied or abridged on account of race or color, no citizen shall be denied the right to vote in any Federal, State, or local election because of his failure to comply with any test or device in any State with respect to which the determinations have been made under subsection (b) or in any political subdivision with respect to which such determinations have been made as a separate unit, unless the United States District Court for the District of Columbia in an action for a declaratory judgment brought by such State or subdivision against the United States has determined that no such test or device has been used during the five years preceding the filing of the action for the purpose or with the effect of denying or abridging the right to vote on account of race or color: *Provided,* That no such declaratory judgment shall issue with respect to any plaintiff for a period of five years after the entry of a final judgment of any court of the United States, other than the denial of a declaratory judgment under this section, whether entered prior to or after the enactment of this Act, determining that denials or abridgments of the right to vote on account of race or color through the use of such tests or devices have occurred anywhere in the territory of such plaintiff.

An action pursuant to this subsection shall be heard and determined by a court of three judges in accordance with the provisions of section 2284 of title 28 of the United States Code and any appeal shall lie to the Supreme Court. The court shall retain jurisdiction of any action pursuant to this subsection for five years after judgment and shall reopen the action upon motion of the Attorney General alleging that a test or device has been used for the purpose or with the effect of denying or abridging the right to vote on account of race or color.

If the Attorney General determines that he has no reason to believe that any such test or device has been used during the five years preceding the filing of the action for the purpose or with the effect of denying or abridging the right to vote on account of race or color, he shall consent to the entry of such judgment. . . .

SEC. 10. (a) The Congress finds that the requirement of the payment of a poll tax as a precondition to voting (i) precludes persons of limited means from voting or imposes unreasonable financial hardship upon such persons as a precondition to their exercise of the franchise, (ii) does not bear a reasonable relationship to any legitimate State interest in the conduct of elections, and (iii) in some areas has the purpose or effect of denying persons the right to vote because of race or color. Upon the basis of these findings, Congress declares that the constitutional right of citizens to vote is denied or abridged in some areas by the requirement of the payment of a poll tax as a precondition of voting.

(b) In the exercise of the powers of Congress under section 5 of the fourteenth amendment and section 2 of the fifteenth amendment, the Attorney General is authorized and directed to institute forthwith in the name of the United States such actions, including actions against States or political subdivisions, for declaratory judgment or injunctive relief against the enforcement of any requirement of the payment of a poll tax as a precondition to voting, or substitute therefor enacted after November 1, 1964, as will be necessary to implement the declaration of subsection (a) and the purposes of this section.

(c) The district courts of the United States shall have jurisdiction of such actions which shall be heard and determined by a court of three judges in accordance with the provisions of section 2284 of title 28 of the United States Code and any appeal shall lie to the Supreme Court. It shall be the duty of the judges designated to hear the case to assign the case for hearing at the earliest practicable date, to participate in the hearing and determination of, and to cause the case to be in every way expedited. . . .

SEC. 11. (a) No person acting under color of law shall fail or refuse to permit any person to vote who is entitled to vote under any provision of this Act or is otherwise qualified to vote, or willfully fail or refuse to tabulate, count, and report such person's vote.

(b) No person, whether acting under color of law or otherwise, shall intimidate, threaten, or coerce, or attempt to intimidate, threaten, or coerce any person for voting or attempting to vote, or intimidate, threaten, or coerce, or attempt to intimidate, threaten, or coerce any person for urging or aiding any person to vote or attempt to vote, or intimidate, threaten, or coerce any person for exercising any powers or duties under section 3(a), 6, 8, 9, 10, or 12(e).

(c) Whoever knowingly or willfully gives false information as to his name, address, or period of residence in the voting district for the purpose of establishing his eligibility to register or vote, or conspires with another individual for the purpose of encouraging his false registration to vote or illegal voting, or pays or offers to pay or accepts payment either for registration to vote or for voting shall be fined not more than $10,000 or imprisoned not more than five years, or both: *Provided, however,* That this provision shall be applicable only to general, special, or primary elections held solely or in part for the purpose of selecting or electing any candidate for the office of President, Vice President, presidential elector, Member of the United States Senate, Member of the United States House of Representatives, or Delegates or Commissioners from the territories or possessions, or Resident Commissioner of the Commonwealth of Puerto Rico.

(d) Whoever, in any matter within the jurisdiction of an examiner or hearing officer knowingly and willfully falsifies or conceals a material fact, or makes any false, fictitious, or fraudulent statements or representations, or makes or uses any false writing or document knowing the same to contain any false, fictitious, or fraudulent statement or entry, shall be fined not more than $10,000 or imprisoned not more than five years, or both.

SEC. 12. (a) Whoever shall deprive or attempt to deprive any person of any right secured by section 2, 3, 4, 5, 7, or 10 or shall violate section 11 (a) or (b), shall be fined not more than $5,000, or imprisoned not more than five years, or both.

(b) Whoever, within a year following an election in a political subdivision in which an examiner has been appointed (1) destroys, defaces, mutilates, or otherwise alters the marking of a paper ballot which has been cast in such election, or (2) alters any official record of voting in such election tabulated from a voting machine or otherwise, shall be fined not more than $5,000, or imprisoned not more than five years, or both.

(c) Whoever conspires to violate the provisions of subsection (a) or (b) of this section, or interferes with any right secured by section 2, 3, 4, 5, 7, 10, or 11 (a) or (b) shall be fined not more than $5,000, or imprisoned not more than five years, or both.

(d) Whenever any person has engaged or there are reasonable grounds to believe that any person is about to engage in any act or practice prohibited by section 2, 3, 4, ,5, 7, 10, 11, or subsection (b) of this section, the Attorney General may institute for the United States, or in the name of the United States, an action for preventive relief, including an application for temporary or permanent injunction, restraining order, or other order, and including an order directed to the State and State or local election officials to require them (1) to permit persons listed under this Act to vote and (2) to count such votes.

(e) Whenever in any political subdivision in which there are examiners appointed pursuant to this Act any persons allege to such an examiner within forty-eight hours after the closing of the polls that notwithstanding (1) their listing under this Act or registration by an appropriate election official and (2) their eligibility to vote, they have not been permitted to vote in such election, the examiner shall forthwith notify the Attorney General if such allegations in his opinion appear to be well founded. Upon receipt of such notification, the Attorney General may forthwith file with the district court an application for an order providing for the marking, casting, and counting of the ballots of such persons and requiring the inclusion of their votes in the total vote before the results of such election shall be deemed final and any force or effect given thereto. The district court shall hear and determine such matters immediately after the filing of such application. The remedy provided in this subsection shall not preclude any remedy available under State or Federal law. . . .

Questions

1. What does the act outlaw?
2. What are the enforcement provisions? Given the history of Reconstruction, why are they important?
3. Why would so many white southerners feel threatened by this legislation?

30-6 *The Other America* (1962)

Michael Harrington

Like Walter Rauschenbusch (Document 21-2), Michael Harrington (see text p. 944) found that religious conviction led to social action. When he belonged to the Catholic Worker Movement, Harrington (1928–1989) learned to see Christ even in "the pathetic, shambling, shivering creature who would wander in off the street." Where others saw only prosperity, Harrington focused his attention on the "millions who are poor in the United States [and who] tend to become increasingly invisible."

Source: Reprinted with the permission of Simon & Schuster from *The Other America: Poverty in the United States* by Michael Harrington, pp. 158–162. Copyright © 1962, 1969, 1981 by Michael Harrington.

The United States in the sixties contains an affluent society within its borders. Millions and tens of millions enjoy the highest standard of life the world has ever known. This blessing is mixed. It is built upon a peculiarly distorted economy, one that often proliferates pseudo-needs rather than satisfying human needs. For some, it has resulted in a sense of spiritual emptiness, of alienation. Yet a man would be a fool to prefer hunger to satiety, and the material gains at least open up the possibility of a rich and full existence.

At the same time, the United States contains an underdeveloped nation, a culture of poverty. Its inhabitants do not suffer the extreme privation of the peasants of Asia or the tribesmen of Africa, yet the mechanism of the misery is similar. They are beyond history, beyond progress, sunk in a paralyzing, maiming routine.

The new nations, however, have one advantage: poverty is so general and so extreme that it is the passion of the entire society to obliterate it. Every resource, every policy, is measured by its effect on the lowest and most impoverished. There is a gigantic mobilization of the spirit of the society: aspiration becomes a national purpose that penetrates to every village and motivates a historical transformation.

But this country seems to be caught in a paradox. Because its poverty is not so deadly, because so many are enjoying a decent standard of life, there are indifference and blindness to the plight of the poor. There are even those who deny that the culture of poverty exists. It is as if Disraeli's famous remark about the two nations of the rich and the poor had come true in a fantastic fashion. At precisely the moment in history where for the first time a people have the material ability to end poverty, they lack the will to do so. They cannot see; they cannot act. The consciences of the well-off are the victims of affluence; the lives of the poor are the victims of a physical and spiritual misery.

The problem, then, is to a great extent one of vision. The nation of the well-off must be able to see through the wall of affluence and recognize the alien citizens on the other side. And there must be vision in the sense of purpose, of aspiration: if the word does not grate upon the ears of a gentile America, there must be a passion to end poverty, for nothing less than that will do.

In this summary chapter, I hope I can supply at least some of the material for such a vision. Let us try to understand the other America as a whole, to see its perspective for the future if it is left alone, to realize the responsibility and the potential for ending this nation in our midst.

But, when all is said and done, the decisive moment occurs after all the sociology and the description is in. There is really no such thing as "the material for a vision."

After one reads the facts, either there are anger and shame, or there are not. And, as usual, the fate of the poor hangs upon the decision of the better-off. If this anger and shame are not forthcoming, someone can write a book about the other America a generation from now and it will be the same, or worse.

I

Perhaps the most important analytic point to have emerged in this description of the other America is the fact that poverty in America forms a culture, a way of life and feeling, that it makes a whole. It is crucial to generalize this idea, for it profoundly affects how one moves to destroy poverty.

The most obvious aspect of this interrelatedness is in the way in which the various subcultures of the other America feed into one another. This is clearest with the aged. There the poverty of the declining years is, for some millions of human beings, a function of the poverty of the earlier years. If there were adequate medical care for everyone in the United States, there would be less misery for old people. It is as simple as that. Or there is the relation between the poor farmers and the unskilled workers. When a man is driven off the land because of the impoverishment worked by technological progress, he leaves one part of the culture of poverty and joins another. If something were done about the low-income farmer, that would immediately tell in the statistics of urban unemployment and the economic underworld. The same is true of the Negroes. Any gain for America's minorities will immediately be translated into an advance for all the unskilled workers. One cannot raise the bottom of a society without benefiting everyone above.

Indeed, there is a curious advantage in the wholeness of poverty. Since the other America forms a distinct system within the United States, effective action at any one decisive point will have a "multiplier" effect; it will ramify through the entire culture of misery and ultimately through the entire society.

Then, poverty is a culture in the sense that the mechanism of impoverishment is fundamentally the same in every part of the system. The vicious circle is a basic pattern. It takes different forms for the unskilled workers, for the aged, for the Negroes, for the agricultural workers, but in each case the principle is the same. There are people in the affluent society who are poor because they are poor; and who stay poor because they are poor.

To realize this is to see that there are some tens of millions of Americans who are beyond the welfare state. Some of them are simply not covered by social legislation: they are omitted from Social Security and from minimum wage. Others are covered, but since they are so poor they do not know how to take advantage of the opportunities, or else their coverage is so inadequate as not to make a difference.

The welfare state was designed during that great burst of social creativity that took place in the 1930's. As previously noted its structure corresponds to the needs of those who played the most important role in building it: the middle third, the organized workers, the forces of urban liberalism, and so on. At the worst, there is "socialism for the rich and free enterprise for the poor," as when the huge corporation farms are the main beneficiaries of the farm program while the poor farmers get practically nothing; or when public funds are directed to aid in the construction of luxury housing while the slums are left to themselves (or become more dense as space is created for the well-off).

So there is the fundamental paradox of the welfare state: that it is not built for the desperate, but for those who are already capable of helping themselves. As long as the illusion persists that the poor are merrily freeloading on the public dole, so long will the other America continue unthreatened. The truth, it must be understood, is the exact opposite. The poor get less out of the welfare state than any group in America.

This is, of course, related to the most distinguishing mark of the other America: its common sense of hopelessness. For even when there are programs designed to help the other Americans, the poor are held back by their own pessimism.

On one level this fact has been described in this book as a matter of "aspiration." Like the Asian peasant, the impoverished American tends to see life as a fate, an endless cycle from which there is no deliverance. Lacking hope (and he is realistic to feel this way in many cases), that famous solution to all problems—let us educate the poor—becomes less and less meaningful. A person has to feel that education will do something for him if he is to gain from it. Placing a magnificent school with a fine faculty in the middle of a slum is, I suppose, better than having a run-down building staffed by incompetents. But it will not really make a difference so long as the environment of the tenement, the family, and the street counsels the children to leave as soon as they can and to disregard schooling.

On another level, the emotions of the other America are even more profoundly disturbed. Here it is not lack of aspiration and of hope; it is a matter of personal chaos. The drunkenness, the unstable marriages, the violence of the other America are not simply facts about individuals. They are the description of an entire group in the society who react this way because of the conditions under which they live.

In short, being poor is not one aspect of a person's life in this country; it is his life. Taken as a whole, poverty is a culture. Taken on the family level, it has the same quality. These are people who lack education and skill, who have bad health, poor housing, low levels of aspiration and high levels of mental distress. They are, in the language of sociology, "multiproblem" families. Each disability is the more intense because it exists within a web of disabilities. And if one problem is solved, and the others are left constant, there is little gain.

One might translate these facts into the moralistic language so dear to those who would condemn the poor for their faults. The other Americans are those who live at a level of life beneath moral choice, who are so submerged in their poverty that one cannot begin to talk about free choice. The point is not to make them wards of the state. Rather, society must help them before they can help themselves.

Questions

1. Why is Harrington critical of the welfare state?
2. What does he mean by saying that "poverty is a culture"?
3. What is the difference between helping the poor and making them wards of the state?

30-7 Barry Goldwater's Acceptance Speech, Republican National Convention (1964)

Like Michael Harrington (Document 30-6), Senator Barry Goldwater (see text p. 942) believed that there was another, ignored America. But Goldwater (b. 1909) was not talking about the poor. Instead, he championed blue-collar and middle-class taxpayers, who he thought were at risk from an expanding and unresponsive federal government. The Arizona senator hoped that those people would put a conservative Republican in the White House. They did, but sixteen years too late to help his 1964 presidential bid.

Source: Excerpted by permission of the Republican National Committee from "Acceptance Speech by Senator Barry Goldwater, Republican National Convention, San Francisco, California," in Barry Goldwater, *Where I Stand* (New York: McGraw-Hill, 1964), pp. 9–16.

From this moment, united and determined, we will go forward together—dedicated to the ultimate and undeniable greatness of the whole man.

I accept your nomination with a deep sense of humility. I accept the responsibility that goes with it. I seek your continued help and guidance.

Our cause is too great for any man to feel worthy of it.

Our task would be too great for any man, did he not have with him the hearts and hands of this great Republican Party.

I promise you that every fibre of my being is consecrated to our cause, that nothing shall be lacking from the struggle that can be brought to it by enthusiasm and devotion—and hard work!

In this world, no person—no party—can guarantee anything. What we *can* do, and what we *shall* do, is to *deserve* victory.

The good Lord raised up this mighty Republic to be a home for the brave and to flourish as the land of the free—*not* to stagnate in the swampland of collectivism—*not* to cringe before the bullying of Communism.

The tide has been running against freedom. Our people have followed false prophets. We must and we *shall* return to proven ways—*not* because they are old, but because they are *true*. We must and we shall set the tides running again in the cause of freedom.

This Party, with its every action, every word, every breath, and every heartbeat, has but a single resolve:

Freedom!

Freedom—made orderly for this nation by our Constitutional government.

Freedom—under a government limited by the laws of nature and of nature's God.

Freedom—balanced so that order, lacking liberty, will

not become the slavery of the prison cell; balanced so that liberty, lacking order, will not become the license of the mob and the jungle.

We Americans understand freedom. We have earned it, lived for it, and died for it.

This nation and its people *are* freedom's model in a searching world. We *can be* freedom's missionaries in a doubting world. But first we *must renew* freedom's vision in our own hearts and in our own homes.

During four futile years, the Administration which we shall replace has distorted and lost that vision.

It has talked and talked and talked the *words* of freedom. But it has failed and failed and failed in the *works* of freedom

Failures cement the wall of shame in Berlin. Failures blot the sands of shame at the Bay of Pigs. Failures mark the slow death of freedom in Laos. Failures infest the jungles of Vietnam. Failures haunt the houses of our once great alliances, and undermine the greatest bulwark ever erected by free nations—the NATO community.

Failures proclaim lost leadership, obscure purpose, weakening will, and the risk of inciting our sworn enemies to new aggressions and new excesses.

Because of this Administration, we are a world divided—we are a nation becalmed.

We have lost the brisk pace of diversity and the genius of individual creativity. We are plodding at a pace set by centralized planning, red tape, rules without responsibility, and regimentation without recourse.

Rather than useful jobs, our people have been offered bureaucratic make-work. Rather than moral leadership, they have been given bread and circuses, spectacle and even scandal.

There is violence in our streets, corruption in our highest offices, aimlessness among our youth, anxiety among our elders. There is virtual despair among the many who look beyond material success for the inner meaning of their lives.

Where examples of morality should be set, the opposite is seen. Small men, seeking great wealth or power, have too often and too long turned even the highest levels of public service into mere personal opportunity.

Certainly, simple honesty is not too much to demand of men in government. We find it in most. Republicans demand it from everyone—no matter how exalted or protected his position.

The growing menace to personal safety, to life, limb, and property, in homes, churches, playgrounds, and places of business, particularly in our great cities, is the mounting concern of every thoughtful citizen. Security from domestic violence, no less than from foreign aggression, is the most elementary and fundamental purpose of any government. A government that cannot fulfill this purpose is one that cannot long command the loyalty of its citizens. History demonstrates that nothing prepares the way for tyranny more than the failure of public officials to keep the streets safe from bullies and marauders.

We Republicans see all this as more, *much* more than the result of mere political differences, or mere political mistakes. We see this as the result of a fundamentally and absolutely wrong view of man, his nature, and his destiny.

Those who seek to live your lives for you, to take your liberties in return for relieving you of your responsibilities—those who elevate the state and downgrade the citizen—must see ultimately a world in which earthly power can be substituted for divine will. This nation was founded upon the rejection of that notion and upon the acceptance of God as the author of freedom.

Those who seek absolute power, even though they seek it to do what they regard as good, are simply demanding the right to enforce *their* version of heaven on earth. They are the very ones who always create the most hellish tyrannies.

Absolute power *does* corrupt. And those who seek it must be suspect and must be opposed.

Their mistaken course stems from false notions of equality.

Equality, rightly understood, as our Founding Fathers understood it, leads to liberty and to the emancipation of creative differences.

Wrongly understood, as it has been so tragically in our time, it leads first to conformity and then to despotism.

It is the cause of Republicanism to resist concentrations of power, *private* or *public*, which enforce such conformity and inflict such despotism.

It is the cause of Republicanism to ensure that power remains in the hands of the people. And, so help us God, that is exactly what a Republican President will do—with the help of a Republican Congress.

It is the cause of Republicanism to restore a clear understanding of the tyranny of man over man in the world at large. It is our cause to dispel the foggy thinking which avoids hard decisions in the delusion that a world of conflict will mysteriously resolve itself into a world of harmony—if we just don't rock the boat or irritate the forces of aggression.

It is the cause of Republicanism to remind ourselves and the world that only the strong *can* remain free—that only the strong *can* keep the peace!

Republicans have shouldered this hard responsibility and marched in this cause before. It was Republican leadership under Dwight David Eisenhower that kept the peace and passed along to this Administration the mightiest arsenal for defense the world has ever known.

It was the strength and believable will of the Eisenhower years that kept the peace by using our strength—by using it in the Formosa Straits and in Lebanon, and by showing it *courageously* at all times.

It was during those Republican years that the thrust of Communist imperialism was blunted. It was during those years of Republican leadership that this world moved closer to *peace* than at any other time in the last three decades.

It has been during *Democratic* years that our strength to deter war has stood still and even gone into a planned decline.

It has been during *Democratic* years that we have weakly stumbled into conflict—*timidly* refusing to draw our own lines against aggression—*deceitfully* refusing to tell even our own people of our full participation—and *tragically* letting our finest men die on battlefields unmarked by purpose, pride, or the prospect of victory.

Yesterday it was Korea. Today it is Vietnam.

We are at war in Vietnam—yet the President who is the Commander in Chief of our forces refuses to say whether or not the objective is victory. His Secretary of Defense continues to mislead and misinform the American people.

It has been during *Democratic* years that a billion persons were cast into Communist captivity and their fate cynically sealed. Today, we have an Administration which seems eager to deal with Communism in every coin known—from gold to wheat, from consulates to confidences, and even human freedom itself.

The Republican cause demands that we brand Communism as the principal disturber of peace in the world today—indeed, the only significant disturber of the peace. We must make clear that until its goals of conquest are absolutely renounced, and its relations with all nations tempered, Communism and the governments it now controls are enemies of every man on earth who is or wants to be free. . . .

I can see, and I suggest that all thoughtful men must contemplate, the flowering of an Atlantic civilization: the *whole* of Europe reunified and freed, trading openly across its borders, communicating openly across the world.

This is a goal more meaningful than a moon shot—a truly inspiring goal for all free men to set for themselves during the latter half of the twentieth century.

I can see, and all free men must thrill to, the advance of this Atlantic civilization joined by its great ocean highway to the United States. What a destiny can be ours—to stand as a great central pillar linking Europe, the Americas, and the venerable and vital peoples and cultures of the Pacific.

I can see a day when all the Americas, North and South, will be linked in a mighty system, a system in which the errors and misunderstandings of the past will be submerged, one by one, in a rising tide of prosperity and interdependence. We know that the misunderstandings of centuries are not to be wiped away in a day or an hour. But we pledge that human sympathy—what our neighbors to the South call an attitude that is *simpatico*—no less than enlightened self-interest, will be our guide.

I can see this Atlantic civilization galvanizing and *guiding* emergent nations everywhere. . . .

During Republican years this again will be a nation of men and women, of families proud of their roles, jealous of their responsibilities, unlimited in their aspirations—a nation where all who *can*, *will* be self-reliant. . . .

We see, in private property and an economy based upon and fostering private property, the one way to make government a durable ally of the whole man, rather than his determined enemy. We see, in the sanctity of private property, the only durable foundation for Constitutional government in a free society.

And beyond that, we see and cherish diversity of ways, diversity of thoughts, of motives and accomplishments. We do not seek to live anyone's life for him—we seek only to secure his rights, guarantee him opportunity to strive, with government performing only those needed and Constitutionally-sanctioned tasks which cannot otherwise be performed.

We seek a government that intends to its inherent responsibilities of maintaining a stable monetary and fiscal climate—encouraging a free and competitive economy, and enforcing law and order.

Thus do we seek inventiveness, diversity, and creative difference within a stable order. For we Republicans define government's role, where needed, at *many* levels, preferably the one *closest* to the people involved.

Our towns and our cities, then our counties and states, then our regional compacts—and *only then* the national government! *That* is the ladder of liberty built by decentralized power. On it, also, we must have balance *between* branches of government at *every* level.

Balance, diversity, creative difference—*these* are the elements of the Republican equation. Republicans agree on these elements and they heartily agree to disagree on many, many of their applications.

This is a party for free men—*not* for blind followers and *not* for conformists. . . .

Any who join us in all sincerity, we welcome. Those who do not care for our cause we do not expect to enter our ranks in any case.

And let our Republicanism, so focused and so dedicated, not be made fuzzy and futile by unthinking labels.

Extremism in the defense of liberty is no vice. Moderation in the pursuit of justice is no virtue. . . .

Questions

1. What is Goldwater's definition of freedom?
2. Is his speech partisan or accurate in its treatment of the Democrats? Explain.

3. What are the enemies of freedom at home and abroad? Can they be fought with the same weapons?

Questions for Further Thought

1. To what extent does Michael Harrington's treatment of poverty in the 1960s (Document 30-6) apply to the 1990s?
2. How would you expect Harrington to react to Barry Goldwater's vision for American society (Document 30-7)? To what extent does Goldwater acknowledge Harrington's concerns?
3. How do Goldwater's views compare to Theodore Roosevelt's (Document 21-8)?

The Continuing Struggle for Civil Rights

Many African-Americans in the 1960s believed that progress toward equality was too slow. Stokely Carmichael and the Student Nonviolent Coordinating Committee (SNCC) were influenced by the speeches and writings of Malcolm X (see text p. 947) and the philosophy of black nationalism (Document 30-8). Urban riots were another manifestation of African-American dissatisfaction. Each summer between 1964 and 1968 cities suffered outbreaks of rioting. After the devastating Detroit riot in 1967, President Johnson appointed Otto Kerner, governor of Illinois, to head a commission to investigate the causes of urban violence (see text pp. 948–949). The commission found that patterns of racism characterized life in America's cities. On April 4, 1968 (shortly after the Kerner commission issued its report), Martin Luther King, Jr., was assassinated in Memphis, depriving the civil rights movement of its undisputed leader (see text pp. 949).

The ideas of equality and justice that King so eloquently presented spread to other groups in American society, which adopted the direct action tactics King and his followers had developed. Hispanics and native Americans were among the first groups to follow King's example (see text pp. 950–951). César Chávez's United Farm Workers and the American Indian Movement provided opportunities for these groups to protest inequality in America and to call attention to their distinctive cultures. Hispanics and native Americans showed that they too belonged (Documents 30-9 and 30-10). Soon other ethnic groups, homosexual men and women, and the poor organized as well (see text p. 952).

30-8 Malcolm X, "To Mississippi Youth" (1964)
Yusef Iman, "Love Your Enemy"

The Black Muslim leader Malcolm X (1925–1965) became the major spokesperson for black nationalism, a viewpoint that appealed especially to young urban African-Americans (see text pp. 946–948). Some elements of Malcolm X's views are expressed in a speech he gave to Mississippi students visiting New York in 1964. Malcolm X had a tremendous impact on Stokely Carmichael and others associated with black power. The ideas expressed in Yusef Iman's poem "Love Your Enemy" are clearly influenced by Malcolm X's philosophy.

Source: Malcolm X, "To Mississippi Youth," December 31, 1964. In *Malcolm X Speaks: Selected Speeches and Statements*, ed. George Breitman, pp. 137–146. Reprinted by permission of Pathfinder Press. Copyright © 1965 and 1989 by Betty Shabazz and Pathfinder Press. Yusef Iman, "Love Your Enemy," in *Black Fire: An Anthology of Afro-American Writing*, ed. LeRoi Jones and Larry Neal (New York: Morrow , 1968), pp. 387–388.

One of the first things I think young people, especially nowadays, should learn is how to see for yourself and listen for yourself and think for yourself. Then you can come to an intelligent decision for yourself. If you form the habit of going by what you hear others say about someone, or going by what others think about someone, instead of searching that thing out for yourself and seeing for yourself, you will be walking west when you think you're going east, and you will be walking east when you think you're going west. This generation, especially of our people, has a burden, more so than any other time in history. The most important thing that we can learn to do today is think for ourselves. . . .

I myself would go for nonviolence if it was consistent, if everybody was going to be nonviolent all the time. I'd say, okay, let's get with it, we'll all be nonviolent. But I don't go along with any kind of nonviolence unless everybody's going to be nonviolent. If they make the Ku Klux Klan nonviolent, I'll be nonviolent. If they make the White Citizens Council nonviolent, I'll be nonviolent. But as long as you've got somebody else not being nonviolent, I don't want anybody coming to me talking any nonviolent talk. I don't think it is fair to tell our people to be nonviolent unless someone is out there making the Klan and the Citizens Council and these other groups also be nonviolent. . . .

If the leaders of the nonviolent movement can go into the white community and teach nonviolence, good. I'd go along with that. But as long as I see them teaching nonviolence only in the black community, we can't go along with that. We believe in equality, and equality means that you have to put the same thing over here that you put over there. And if black people alone are going to be the ones who are nonviolent, then it's not fair. We throw ourselves off guard. In fact, we disarm ourselves and make ourselves defenseless. . . .

[W]e of the Organization of Afro-American Unity realized that the only time the black man in this country is given any kind of recognition, or even listened to, is when America is afraid of outside pressure, or when she's afraid of her image abroad. So we saw that it was necessary to expand the problem and the struggle of the black man in

this country until it went above and beyond the jurisdiction of the United States. . . .

And today you'll find in the United Nations, and it's not an accident, that every time the Congo question or anything on the African continent is being debated, they couple it with what is going on, or what is happening to you and me, in Mississippi and Alabama and these other places. In my opinion, the greatest accomplishment that was made in the struggle of the black man in America in 1964 toward some kind of real progress was the successful linking together of our problem with the African problem, or making our problem a world problem. Because now, whenever anything happens to you in Mississippi, it's not just a case of somebody in Alabama getting indignant, or somebody in New York getting indignant. The same repercussions that you see all over the world when an imperialist or foreign power interferes in some section of Africa—you see repercussions, you see the embassies being bombed and burned and overturned—nowadays, when something happens to black people in Mississippi, you'll see the same repercussions all over the world.

I wanted to point this out to you because it is important for you to know that when you're in Mississippi, you're not alone. As long as you think you're alone, then you take a stand as if you're a minority or as if you're outnumbered, and that kind of stand will never enable you to win a battle. You've got to know that you've got as much power on your side as that Ku Klux Klan has on its side. And when you know that you've got as much power on your side as the Klan has on its side, you'll talk the same kind of language with that Klan as the Klan is talking with you. . . .

I think in 1965, whether you like it, or I like it, or they like it, or not, you will see that there is a generation of black people becoming mature to the point where they feel that they have no more business being asked to take a peaceful approach than anybody else takes, unless everybody's going to take a peaceful approach.

So we here in the Organization of Afro-American Unity are with the struggle in Mississippi one thousand percent. We're with the efforts to register our people in

Mississippi to vote one thousand per cent. But we do not go along with anybody telling us to help nonviolently. We think that if the government says that Negroes have a right to vote, and then some Negroes come out to vote, and some kind of Ku Klux Klan is going to put them in the river, and the government doesn't do anything about it, it's time for us to organize and band together and equip ourselves and qualify ourselves to protect ourselves. And once you can protect yourself, you don't have to worry about being hurt. . . .

You get freedom by letting your enemy know that you'll do anything to get your freedom; then you'll get it. It's the only way you'll get it. When you get that kind of attitude, they'll label you as a "crazy Negro," or they'll call you a "crazy nigger"—they don't say Negro. Or they'll call you an extremist or a subversive, or seditious, or a red or a radical. But when you stay radical long enough, and get enough people to be like you, you'll get your freedom. . . .

Brought here in slave ships and pitched over board.
Love your enemy.
Language taken away, culture taken away.
Love your enemy.
Work from sun up to sun down.
Love your enemy.
Work for no pay.
Love your enemy.
Last hired, first fired.
Love your enemy.
Rape your mother.
Love your enemy.
Lynch your father.
Love your enemy.
Bomb your churches.
Love your enemy.
Kill your children.
Love your enemy.
Forced to fight his wars.
Love your enemy.
Pay the highest rent.

Love your enemy.
Sell you rotten foods.
Love your enemy.
Sell dope to your children.
Love your enemy.
Forced to live in the slums.
Love your enemy.
Dilapidated schools.
Love your enemy.
Puts you in jail.
Love your enemy.
Bitten by dogs.
Love your enemy.
Water hose you down.
Love your enemy.
   Love.
   Love.
   Love.
   Love.
   Love.
   Love, for everybody else.
But when will we love ourselves?

Questions

1. What is Malcolm X's opinion of the philosophy of nonviolence?
2. What strategy does Yusef Iman use to convey his message, and what is that message? How is Malcolm X's advice reflected in the poem "Love Your Enemy"?
3. What emotions do you believe Malcolm X and Yusef Iman hope to stir in their readers?

30-9 "Para Teresa"[1]

Inés Hernández

Like African-Americans, Chicanos experienced feelings of being treated like outsiders and interlopers in American society. As was true for all minority groups, there were differences in the Hispanic community as to what strategy would best overcome this prejudice and discrimination. Inés Hernández's poem about a confrontation with a schoolmate illustrates some of those differences.

[1]For Teresa. [Author's note]

Source: Inés Hernández, "Para Teresa," in *Con Razon, Corazon: Poetry*, rev. ed. (San Antonio: Texas: M & A Editions, n.d.).

A tí-Teresa Compean
Te dedico las palabras estás
que explotan de mi corazón[2]

That day during lunch hour
at Alamo which-had-to-be-its-name
Elementary
my dear raza
That day in the bathroom
Door guarded
Myself cornered
I was accused by you, Teresa
Tú y las demás de tus amigas
Pachucas todos
Eran Uds. cinco.[3]

Me gritaban que porque me creía tan grande[4]
What was I trying to do, you growled
Show you up?
Make the teachers like me, pet me,
Tell me what a credit to my people I was?
I was playing right into their hands, you challenged
And you would have none of it.
I was to stop.
I was to be like you
I was to play your game of deadly defiance
Arrogance, refusal to submit.
The game in which the winner takes nothing
Asks for nothing
Never lets his weakness show.

But I didn't understand.
My fear salted with confusion
Charged me to explain to you
I did nothing *for the teachers*.
I studied for my parents and for my grandparents
Who cut out honor roll lists
Whenever their nietos'[5] names appeared
For my shy mother who mastered her terror
to demand her place in mother's clubs

For my carpenter-father who helped me patiently with my
    math.
For my abuelos que me regalaron lápices en la Navidad[6]
And for myself.

Porque reconocí en aquel entonces
una verdad tremenda
que me hizo mi un rebelde
Aunque tú no te habías dado cuenta[7]
We were not inferior
You and I, y las demás de tus amigas
Y los demás de nuestra gente[8]
I knew it the way I knew I was alive
We were good, honorable, brave
Genuine, loyal, strong

And smart.
Mine was a deadly game of defiance, also.
My contest was to prove
beyond any doubt
that we were not only equal but superior to them.
That was why I studied.
If I could do it, we all could.

You let me go then.
Your friends unblocked the way
I who-did-not-know-how-to-fight
was not made to engage with you-who-grew-up-fighting
Tu y yo, Teresa[9]
We went in different directions
Pero fuimos juntas.[10]

In sixth grade we did not understand
Uds. with the teased, dyed-black-but-reddening hair,
Full petticoats, red lipsticks
and sweaters with the sleeves
pushed up
Y yo conformándome con lo que deseaba mi mama[11]
Certainly never allowed to dye, to tease, to paint myself
I did not accept your way of anger,

---

[2]To you, Teresa Compean, I dedicate these words that explode from my heart. [Author's note]

[3]You and the rest of your friends, all Pachucas, there were five of you. [Author's note]

[4]You were screaming at me, asking me why I thought I was so hot. [Author's note]

[5]Grandchildren's [Author's note]

[6]Grandparents who gave me gifts of pencils at Christmas [Author's note]

[7]Because I recognized a great truth then that made me a rebel, even though you didn't realize it [Author's note]

[8]And the rest of your friends/And the rest of our people [Author's note]

[9]You and I [Author's note]

[10]But we were together [Author's note]

[11]And I conforming to my mother's wishes [Author's note]

Your judgements
You did not accept mine.

But now in 1975, when I am twenty-eight
Teresa Compean
I remember you.

Y sabes—
Te comprendo,
Es más, te respeto.
Y, si me permites,
Te nombro—"hermana."[12]

[12]And do you know what, I understand you. Even more, I respect you. And, if you permit me, I name you my sister. [Author's note]

Questions

1. What did the poem's speaker do to combat racism, and what did Teresa advocate?
2. How did the speaker's attitude toward Teresa change and how do you account for this change?
3. Which position do you think was most effective—Teresa's or the poem's speaker's?

30-10 The Consequences of Termination for the Menominees of Wisconsin (1965)

In the 1950s Congress endorsed a new policy for native Americans. It was called termination and was intended to end "the legal standing of native tribes and move their members off reservations" (see text p. 951). But what looked good in Washington did not necessarily work for people such as the Menominees of Wisconsin. A Menominee advocacy group helped win reversal of the policy in 1965.

Source: DRUMS Committee, Menominee, chronology from DRUMS testimony, Hearings on Senate Concurrent Resolution Number 26, Senate Committee on Interior and Insular Affairs, July 21, 1971; in Peter Nabokov, ed., *Native American Testimony: A Chronicle of Indian-White Relations from Prophecy to the Present, 1492–1992* (New York: Viking Penguin, 1991), pp. 344–347.

Early in 1953, we Menominee wanted a portion of our 1951 settlement—about $5,000,000—distributed among ourselves on a $1,500 per capita basis. Since Congressional approval was required for such disbursement of our assets, [then] Representative Melvin Laird and Senator Joseph McCarthy introduced in Congress on behalf of our Tribe a bill to authorize the payment of *our* money to us.

This bill passed the House, but in hearings before the Senate Committee on Interior and Insular Affairs, it ran up against an amendment sponsored by the late Senator Arthur V. Watkins (R. Utah) calling for "termination" of federal supervision and assistance to the Menominee. Watkins and the Committee refused to report the bill favorably, calling upon us Menominee to submit a termination plan *before* we would be given *our* money! "Termination!" What did *that* mean? Certainly at that time, none of us Menominee realized what it meant! . . . In June, 1953,

we Menominee invited Senator Watkins to visit the Reservation and explain "termination" to us.

Senator Watkins badly wanted our termination. He was firmly convinced that factors such as our status as Reservation Indians, our tribal ownership of land, and our tax exemption were blocking our initiative, our freedom, and our development of private enterprise. He wished to see us rapidly assimilated into the mainstream of American society—as tax paying, hard working, "emancipated" citizens. . . .

One June 20, 1953, Senator Watkins spoke for 45 minutes to our General Council. He told us that Congress had already decided on terminating us, and that at most we could have three years before our "affairs would be turned over to us"—and that we would not receive our per capitas until *after* termination.

After he left, our Council had the opportunity to vote

on the "principle of termination!" Some opportunity! What little understanding we had of what termination would mean! The vote was 169 to 5 in favor of the "principle of termination." A mere 5 percent of the 3,200 Menominee people participated in this vote. Most of our people chose to be absent from the meeting in order to express their negative reaction to termination. Many who did vote affirmatively that day believed that termination was coming from Congress whether the Menominee liked it or not. Others thought that they were voting *only* in favor of receiving their per capitas. . . .

We then set about preparing a termination plan, which the BIA subsequently emasculated, and we received word that Senator Watkins was pressing ahead with his *own* termination bill. *Another* general council meeting was called, one which is seldom mentioned, but at which the Menominee voted 197 to 0 to *oppose and reject* termination. But our feelings did not matter—and although the Watkins bill met a temporary defeat on technical grounds in the House in late 1953, Senator Watkins re-introduced it in 1954.

We became convinced that there was *no* alternative to accepting termination. Therefore, all we pleaded for was adequate time to plan this sudden and revolutionary change in our lives! On June 17, 1954, the Menominee Termination Act was signed into law by President Eisenhower. . . .

Termination represented a gigantic and revolutionary *forced* change in the traditional Menominee way of life. Congress expected us to replace our Indian way of life with a complicated corporate style of living. Congress expected immediate Menominee assimilation of non-Indian culture, values, and life styles. . . .

The immediate effect of termination on our tribe was the loss of most of our hundred-year-old treaty rights, protections, and services. No amount of explanation or imagination prior to termination could have prepared us for the shock of what these losses meant.

Congress withdrew its trusteeship of our lands, transferring to MEI [Menominee Enterprises, Inc., the corporation which was to supervise Menominee holdings after termination] the responsibility for protecting these lands, our greatest assets. As we shall explain, far from being able to preserve our land, MEI has been forced to sell it. And because our land is now being sold to non-Menominee, termination is doing to us what allotment has done to other Indian tribes.

Congress also extinguished our ancient system of tribal "ownership" of land (under which no individual had separate title to his home) and transferred title to MEI. Consequently, we individual Menominee suddenly discovered that we would be forced to buy from MEI the land which had always been considered our own, and to pay title to our homesites. Thus began the tragic process of our corporation "feeding off" our people.

We Menominee lost our right to tax exemption. Both MEI and individual Menominee found themselves saddled with tax burdens particularly crushing to a small tribe struggling to develop economically.

BIA health, education and utility services ceased. We lost all medical and dental care within the Reservation. Both our reservation and hospital were closed because they failed to meet state standards. Individual Menominee were forced to pay for electricity and water that they previously received a no cost. Our county found it had to renovate at high cost its substandard sewerage system.

Finally, with termination and the closing of our tribal rolls, our children born since 1954 have been legally deprived of their birthright as Menominee Indians. Like all other Menominee, they have lost their entitlement to United States Government benefits and services to Indians. . . . The only major Menominee treaty right which the government has allowed us to retain has been our hunting and fishing right. Wisconsin had tried to deprive us of this right, but in 1968, after costly litigation, the United States Supreme Court ruled that this treaty right had "survived" termination. . . .

We hope you can appreciate the magnitude of these treaty losses to us. Visualize a situation similar to ours happening in one of your home states. Imagine the outrage of the people in one of your own communities if Congress should attempt to terminate their basic property, inheritance, and civil rights. . . .

Today Menominee County is the poorest county in Wisconsin. It has the highest birthrate in the state and ranks at or near the bottom of Wisconsin counties in income, housing, property value, education, employment, sanitation and health. The most recent figures available (1967) show that the annual income of nearly 80 percent of our families falls below the federal poverty level of $3,000. The per capita annual income of our wage earners in 1965 was estimated at $881, the lowest in the state. . . .

This lack of employment opportunities, combined with our high birthrate, forced nearly 50 percent of our county residents to go on welfare in 1968. Welfare costs in the country for 1968 were over $766,000 and our per capita welfare payment was the highest in the state. The majority of Menominee who have left our county to seek work in the cities have become trapped in poverty there also.

With the closing of the BIA hospital, we lost most of our health services, and most Menominee continue to suffer from lack of medical care. There have been no full-time doctors or dentists in Menominee County since termination. Shortly before termination, our people were stricken by a TB epidemic which caused great suffering and hardship because of the lack of local medical facilities. . . .

The loss of the BIA school required that our youth be sent to Shawano County for their high school training. The Shawano school system had assumed that Menominee children possess the same cultural and historical background as [children from the] middle-class white community. . . . Since 1961, our high school drop-out rates have increased substantially, absenteeism has soared, and our children apparently are suffering a downward trend in achievement. . . .

We have told story which is very tragic, yet it is a true story of the Menominee people since termination. We have told how termination has meant the loss of treaty benefits, has pushed our already poor community further into the depths of poverty, forced our sale of assets; and denied us a democratic community.

DRUMS COMMITTEE, *Menominee*

Questions

1. Who decided on termination?
2. What were the consequences of this policy?
3. How would Michael Harrington (Document 30-6) and Barry Goldwater (Document 30-7) react to this situation?

Questions for Further Thought

1. What similarities and differences are there among the groups that generated Documents 30-8 through 30-10?
2. Do these documents indicate that the United States is an intolerant society or one that is open to change? Explain your answer.
3. Are there any dangers involved when a group begins to focus on its position in society? Is backlash a great problem than a sense of victimization? Why or why not?

CHAPTER 31

The Vietnam Experience 1961–1975

★   ★   ★

Into the Quagmire, 1945–1968

The Vietnam War was the formative event in the lives of many Americans who came of age in the 1960s. Vietnam encompassed all the key concerns they expressed when they looked at their rapidly changing nation. There was the war itself, but there was more: civil rights issues related both to racial minorities and to the place of students in society (free speech on college campuses), the role of the university in supporting the military through weapons research, and the need for social and economic reforms that were stalled by the rising costs of the war. While the war in Vietnam dominated the 1960s, its roots had been planted many years earlier.

For centuries the people of Vietnam had lived under foreign domination (see text pp. 960–961). By the twentieth century France had become the dominant outsider in Southeast Asia and the target of nationalist forces that wanted Vietnamese independence. At the close of World War II, on V-J Day, Ho Chi Minh—who was Vietnamese, nationalist, and communist—declared Vietnam independent of France (Document 31-1). The United States refused to support Ho, instead siding with France in its efforts to hold on to its colonies in Southeast Asia (see text pp. 960–962). Harry Truman believed that a strong France—and colonies were seen as a sign of strength—was vital in the postwar world to help contain communism. By 1954, well into the Eisenhower administration, France had lost all hope of keeping Vietnam. Citing what came to be known as "the domino theory," American policy makers committed the United States to supporting a noncommunist South Vietnam in what had become a divided country (Document 31-2).

Under President John F. Kennedy (see text p. 962) the United States stepped up its presence in Vietnam by increasing the number of American military advisers assisting the political and military forces of South Vietnam. Then, under Lyndon Johnson, America's involvement began to escalate in gradual stages. Johnson asked for and received the nearly unanimous support of Congress to take whatever steps he wanted, including the use of military force, to defend Southeast Asia against communism (Document 31-3). By early 1965, ostensibly to protect Americans already in Vietnam, Johnson authorized Operation Rolling Thunder, a bombing program against North Vietnam, and then committed ground troops that became actively involved in the fighting (see text pp. 963–965).

The escalation of the American role in Vietnam generated controversy. By the spring of 1965 an antiwar movement had appeared in the United States, at first on college campuses, prompting the president to respond directly to his critics (Document 31-4). Between 1965 and 1968 President Johnson remained steadfast in his defense of South Vietnam, even in the face of rapidly growing criticism (see text pp. 967–969). The Tet offensive launched by North Vietnam and the Vietcong against South Vietnam in January and February 1968 caused a serious rethinking of American policies in Vietnam. The war appeared to be going badly for the United States, the president was under siege at home, and his Great Society had been checked by the costs of the war. The United States found itself in the quagmire of Vietnam with no way to win and no way to get out.

31-1 Ho Chi Minh and Vietnam's Declaration of Independence (1945)

After surviving for centuries under foreign domination, in 1945 Vietnam declared itself independent, hoping to chart its own course in the future (see text p. 960). The main architect of this independence movement was a Vietnamese nationalist, Ho Chi Minh, who had adopted communism as his governing philosophy during travels to Russia and France. On V-J Day, September 2, 1945, Ho spoke to his people, but the message he conveyed was directed to a much wider audience.

Source: Ho Chi Minh, *Ho Chi Minh: Selected Writings, 1920–1969* (Hanoi: Foreign Languages Publishing House, 1977), pp. 53–56.

All men are created equal: they are endowed by their Creator with certain unalienable Rights: among these are Life, Liberty, and the pursuit of Happiness.

This immortal statement was made in the Declaration of Independence of the United States of America in 1776. In a broader sense, this means: All the peoples on the earth are equal from birth, all the peoples have a right to live, to be happy and free.

The Declaration of the French Revolution made in 1791 on the Rights of Man and the Citizen also states: "All men are born free and with equal rights, and must always remain free and have equal rights."

Those are undeniable truths.

Nevertheless, for more than eighty years, the French imperialists, abusing the standard of Liberty, Equality, and Fraternity, have violated our Fatherland and oppressed our fellow citizens. They have acted contrary to the ideals of humanity and justice.

In the field of politics, they have deprived our people of every democratic liberty.

They have enforced inhuman laws: they have set up three distinct political regimes in the North, the Center, and the South of Vietnam in order to wreck our national unity and prevent our people from being united.

They have built more prisons than schools. They have mercilessly slain our patriots; they have drowned our uprisings in rivers of blood.

They have fettered public opinion; they have practiced obscurantism against our people.

To weaken our race they have forced us to use opium and alcohol.

In the field of economics, they have fleeced us to the backbone, impoverished our people and devastated our land.

They have robbed us of our rice fields, our mines, our forests, and our raw materials. They have monopolized the issuing of bank notes and the export trade.

They have invented numerous unjustifiable taxes and

reduced our people, especially our peasantry, to a state of extreme poverty.

They have hampered the prospering of our national bourgeoisie; they have mercilessly exploited our workers.

In the autumn of 1940, when the Japanese fascists violated Indochina's territory to establish new bases in their fight against the Allies, the French imperialists went down on their bended knees and handed over our country to them.

Thus, from that date, our people were subjected to the double yoke of the French and the Japanese. Their sufferings and miseries increased. The result was that, from the end of last year to the beginning of this year, from Quang Tri Province to the North of Vietnam, more than two million of our fellow citizens died from starvation. On March 9 [1945], the French troops were disarmed by the Japanese. The French colonialists either fled or surrendered, showing that not only were they incapable of "protecting" us, but that, in the span of five years, they had twice sold our country to the Japanese.

On several occasions before March 9, the Vietminh League urged the French to ally themselves with it against the Japanese. Instead of agreeing to this proposal, the French colonialists so intensified their terrorist activities against the Vietminh members that before fleeing they massacred a great number of our political prisoners detained at Yen Bay and Cao Bang.

Notwithstanding all this, our fellow citizens have always manifested toward the French a tolerant and humane attitude. Even after the Japanese *Putsch* of March, 1945, the Vietminh League helped many Frenchmen to cross the frontier, rescued some of them from Japanese jails, and protected French lives and property.

From the autumn of 1940, our country had in fact ceased to be a French colony and had become a Japanese possession.

After the Japanese had surrendered to the Allies, our whole people rose to regain our national sovereignty and to found the Democratic Republic of Vietnam.

The truth is that we have wrested our independence from the Japanese and not from the French.

The French have fled, the Japanese have capitulated. Emperor Bao Dai has abdicated. Our people have broken the chains which for nearly a century have fettered them and have won independence for the Fatherland. Our people at the same time have overthrown the monarchic regime that has reigned supreme for dozens of centuries. In its place has been established the present Democratic Republic.

For these reasons, we, members of the Provisional Government, representing the whole Vietnamese people, declare that from now on we break off all relations of a colonial character with France; we repeal all the international obligation that France has so far subscribed to on behalf of Vietnam, and we abolish all the special rights the French have unlawfully acquired in our Fatherland.

The whole Vietnamese people, animated by a common purpose, are determined to fight to the bitter end against any attempt by the French colonialists to reconquer their country.

We are convinced that the Allied nations, which at Teheran and San Francisco have acknowledged the principles of self-determination and equality of nations, will not refuse to acknowledge the independence of Vietnam.

A people who have courageously opposed French domination for more than eighty years, a people who have fought side by side with the Allies against the fascists during these last years, such a people must be free and independent.

For these reasons, we, members of the Provisional Government of the Democratic Republic of Vietnam, solemnly declare to the world that Vietnam has the right to be a free and independent country—and in fact it is so already. The entire Vietnamese people are determined to mobilize all their physical and mental strength, to sacrifice their lives and property in order to safeguard their independence and liberty.

Questions

1. In what ways does Ho Chi Minh make a direct appeal to the United States to support independence for Vietnam? How accurate is his comparison of the American colonies in 1776 and Vietnam in 1945?

2. What specific charges does Ho level against France to justify his call for an independent Vietnam?

3. Why does Ho expect the Western states to turn against one of their own to support him and the Vietnamese people?

31-2 Senator John F. Kennedy on the Importance of Vietnam (1956)

In 1956 a young Democratic senator from Massachusetts who hoped for his party's nomination for vice-president began to speak out on a variety of domestic and foreign policy issues. In this speech John F. Kennedy discussed the role of the United States in Vietnam and Southeast Asia. He played off the domino theory, using a variety of similar analogies to underscore his belief that the United States had committed itself to support South Vietnam. These views reappeared in his own presidency when he came to the White House in 1961 (see text p. 962).

Source: John F. Kennedy, "America's Stake in Vietnam: The Cornerstone of the Free World in Southeast Asia," delivered at a conference sponsored by the American Friends of Vietnam, Washington, D.C., June 1, 1956. In *Vital Speeches of the Day* 22 (August 1, 1956), pp. 617–619.

It is an ironic and tragic fact that this Conference is being held at a time when the news about Vietnam has virtually disappeared from the front pages of the American press, and the American people have all but forgotten the tiny nation for which we are in large measure responsible. This decline in public attention is due, I believe, to three factors: (1) First, it is due in part to the amazing success of President Diem in meeting firmly and with determination the major political and economic crises which had heretofore continually plagued Vietnam. (I shall say more about this point later, for it deserves more consideration from all Americans interested in the future of Asia).

(2) Secondly, it is due in part to the traditional role of American journalism, including readers as well as writers, to be more interested in crises than in accomplishments, to give more space to the threat of wars than the need for works, and to write larger headlines on the sensational omissions of the past than the creative missions of the future.

(3) Third and finally, our neglect of Vietnam is the result of one of the most serious weaknesses that has hampered the long-range effectiveness of American foreign policy over the past several years—and that is the overemphasis upon our role as "volunteer fire department" for the world. Whenever and wherever fire breaks out—in Indo-China, in the Middle East, in Guatemala, in Cyprus, in the Formosan Straits—our firemen rush in, wheeling up all their heavy equipment, and resorting to every know method of containing and extinguishing the blaze. The crowd gathers—the usually successful efforts of our able volunteers are heartily applauded—and then the firemen rush off to the next conflagration, leaving the grateful but still stunned inhabitants to clean up the rubble, pick up the pieces and rebuild their homes with whatever resources are available.

The role, to be sure, is a necessary one, but it is not the only role to be played, and the others cannot be ignored. A volunteer fire department halts, but rarely prevents, fires. It repeals but rarely rebuilds, it meets the problems of the present but not of the future. And while we are devoting our attention to the Communist arson in Korea, there is a smoldering in Indo-China, we turn our efforts to Indo-China until the alarm sounds in Algeria—and so it goes.

Of course Vietnam is not completely forgotten by our policy makers today—I could not in honesty make such a charge and the facts would easily refute it—but the unfortunate truth of the matter is that, in my opinion, Vietnam would in all likelihood be receiving more attention from our Congress and Administration, and greater assistance under our aid programs, if it were in imminent danger of Communist invasion or revolution. Like those peoples in Latin America and Africa whom we have very nearly overlooked in the past decade, the Vietnamese may find that their devotion to the cause of democracy, and their success in reducing the strength of local Communist groups, have had the ironic effect of reducing American support. Yet the need for the support has in no way been reduced. (I hope it will not be necessary for the Diem Government—or this organization—to subsidize the growth of the South Vietnam Communist Party in order to focus American attention on the nation's critical needs!) . . .

Let us briefly consider exactly what is "America's Stake in Vietnam":

(1) First, Vietnam represents the cornerstone of the Free World in Southeast Asia, the keystone to the arch, the finger in the dike. Burma, Thailand, India, Japan, the Philippines and obviously Laos and Cambodia are among those whose security would be threatened if the Red Tide of Communism overflowed into Vietnam. In the past, our policy makers have sometimes issued contradictory statements on this point—but the long history of Chinese invasions of Southeast Asia being stopped by Vietnamese warriors should have removed all doubt on this subject.

Moreover, the independence of Free Vietnam is crucial to the free world in fields other than the military. Her economy is essential to the economy of all of Southeast Asia; and her political liberty is an inspiration to those seeking to obtain or maintain their liberty in all parts of

Asia—and indeed the world. The fundamental tenets of this nation's foreign policy, in short, depend in considerable measure upon a strong and *free Vietnamese nation*.

(2) Secondly, Vietnam represents a proving ground of democracy in Asia. However we may choose to ignore it or deprecate it, the rising prestige and influence of Communist China in Asia are unchallengable facts. Vietnam represents the alternative to Communist dictatorship. If this democratic experiment fails, if some one million refugees have fled the totalitarianism of the North only to find neither freedom nor security in the South, then weakness, not strength, will characterize the meaning of democracy in the minds of still more Asians. The United States is directly responsible for this experiment—it is playing an important role in the laboratory where it is being conducted. We cannot afford to permit that experiment to fail.

(3) Third and in somewhat similar fashion, Vietnam represents a test of American responsibility and determination in Asia. If we are not the parents of little Vietnam, then surely we are the godparents. We presided at its birth, we gave assistance to its life, we have helped to shape its future. As French influence in the political, economic and military spheres has declined in Vietnam, American influence has steadily grown. This is our offspring—we cannot abandon it, we cannot ignore its needs. And if it falls victim to any of the perils that threaten its existence—Communism, political anarchy, poverty, and the rest—then the United States, with some justification, will be held responsible, and our prestige in Asia will sink to a new low.

(4) Fourth and finally, America's stake in Vietnam, in her strength and in her security, is a very selfish one—for it can be measured, in the last analysis, in terms of American lives and American dollars. It is now well known that we were at one time on the brink of war in Indo-China—a war which could well have been more costly, more exhausting and less conclusive than any war we have ever known. The threat of such war is not now altogether removed from the horizon. Military weakness, political instability or economic failure in the new state of Vietnam could change almost overnight the apparent security which has increasingly characterized that area under the leadership of Premier Diem. And the key position of Vietnam in Southeast Asia, as already discussed, makes inevitable the involvement of this nation's security in any new outbreak of trouble.

It is these four points, in my opinion, that represent America's stake in Vietnamese security. And before we look to the future, let us stop to review what the Diem Government has already accomplished by way of increasing that security. Most striking of all, perhaps, has been the rehabilitation of more than 3/4 of a million refugees from the North. For these courageous people dedicated to the free way of life, approximately 45,000 houses have been constructed, 2,500 wells dug, 100 schools established and dozens of medical centers and maternity homes provided.

Equally impressive has been the increased solidarity and stability of the Government, the elimination of rebellious sects and the taking of the first vital steps toward true democracy. Where once colonialism and Communism struggled for supremacy, a free and independent republic has been proclaimed, recognized by over 40 countries of the free world. Where once a playboy emperor ruled from a distant shore, a constituent assembly has been elected. Social and economic reforms have likewise been remarkable. The living conditions of the peasants have been vastly improved, the wastelands have been cultivated, and a wider ownership of the land is gradually being encouraged. Farm cooperatives and farmer loans have modernized an outmoded agricultural economy; and a tremendous dam in the center of the country has made possible the irrigation of a vast area previously uncultivated. Legislation for better labor relations, health protection, working conditions and wages has been completed under the leadership of President Diem.

Finally, the Vietnamese army—now fighting for its own homeland and not its colonial masters—has increased tremendously in both quality and quantity. . . .

But the responsibility of the United States for Vietnam does not conclude, obviously, with a review of what has been accomplished thus far with our help. Much more needs to be done, much more, in fact, than we have been doing up to now. Military alliances in Southeast Asia are necessary but not enough. Atomic superiority and the development of new ultimate weapons are not enough. Information and propaganda activities, warning of the evils of Communism and the blessings of the American way of life, are not enough in a country where concepts of free enterprise and capitalism are meaningless, where poverty and hunger are not enemies across the 17th parallel but enemies within their midst. As Ambassador Chuong has recently said: "People cannot be expected to fight for the Free World unless they have their own freedom to defend, their freedom from foreign domination as well as freedom from misery, oppression, corruption."

I shall not attempt to set forth the details of the type of aid program this nation should offer the Vietnamese—for it is not the details of that program that are as important as the spirit with which it is offered and the objectives it seeks to accomplish. We should not attempt to buy the friendship of the Vietnamese. Nor can we win their hearts by making them dependent upon our handouts. What we must offer them is a revolution—a political, economic and social revolution far superior to anything the Communists can offer—far more peaceful, far more democratic and far more locally controlled. Such a Revolution will require much from the United States and much from Vietnam. We must supply capital to replace that drained by the centuries of colonial exploitation; technicians to train those handicapped by deliberate policies of illiteracy; guidance to assist a nation taking those first feeble steps toward the complexities of a republican form of government. We must assist the inspiring growth of Vietnamese democracy and economy, including the complete integration of those refugees who gave up their homes and their belongings to seek freedom. We must provide military assistance to rebuild the new Vietnamese Army, which every day faces the growing peril of Vietminh Armies across the border.

And finally, in the councils of the world, we must never permit any diplomatic action adverse to this, one of the youngest members of the family of nations—and I include in that injunction a plea that the United States never give its approval to the early nationwide elections called for by the Geneva Agreement of 1954. Neither the United States nor Free Vietnam was a party to that agreement—and neither the United States nor Free Vietnam is ever going to be a party to an election obviously stacked and subverted in advance urged upon us by those who have already broken their own pledges under the Agreement they now seek to enforce.

All this and more we can offer Free Vietnam, as it passes through the present period of transition on its way to a new era—an era of pride and independence, an era of democratic and economic growth—an era which, when contrasted with the long years of colonial oppression, will truly represent a political, social and economic revolution.

This is the revolution we can, we should, we must offer to the people of Vietnam—not as charity, not as a business proposition, not as a political maneuver, nor simply to enlist them as soldiers against Communism or as chattels of American foreign policy—but a revolution of their own making, for their own welfare, and for the security of freedom everywhere. The Communists offer them another kind of revolution, glittering and seductive in its superficial appeal. The choice between the two can be made only by the Vietnamese people themselves. But in these times of trial and burden, true friendships stand out. As Premier Diem recently wrote a great friend of Vietnam, Senator Mansfield, "It is only in winter that you can tell which trees are evergreen." And I am confident that if this nation demonstrates that is has not forgotten the people of Vietnam, the people of Vietnam will demonstrate that they have not forgotten us.

Questions

1. In the mid-1950s Vietnam seemed to be fading from public view. According to Senator Kennedy, why was that happening?
2. According to Kennedy, what exactly was "America's stake in Vietnam"? Why did he see Vietnam as "the cornerstone of the Free World" in Southeast Asia? How do Kennedy's words indicate his belief in the domino theory?
3. What did Kennedy think the United States could do to help South Vietnam maintain its independence?

31-3 The Gulf of Tonkin Resolution (1964)

In accepting the Gulf of Tonkin resolution from Congress, which passed with only two dissenting votes, President Johnson claimed that the Senate's unanimity reflected a public consensus in favor of his administration's policy. Yet the administration was unwilling to explain exactly what had happened in the Gulf of Tonkin, suggesting that Johnson knew no such public consensus existed (see text p. 963). What is more impressive about the resolution is the ease with which the Senate surrendered its important constitutional privilege of declaring war. Wayne Morse, one of the two dissenters, warned against this "historic mistake" that effectively subverted the Constitution. But the resolution passed nonetheless, and it permitted Johnson to conduct the war largely on his terms.

Source: Department of State Bulletin, August 29, 1964, p. 268.

Whereas naval units of the Communist regime in Vietnam, in violation of the principles of the Charter of the United Nations and of international law, have deliberately and repeatedly attacked the United States naval vessels present in international waters, and have thereby created a serious threat to international peace;

Whereas these attacks are part of a deliberate and systematic campaign of aggression that the Communist regime in North Vietnam has been waging against its neighbors and the nations joined with them in the collective defense of their freedom;

Whereas the United States is assisting the peoples *of southeast Asia to protect their political freedom and has not territorial, military or political ambitions in that area, but desires only that these peoples should be left in peace to work out their own destinies in their own way: Now, therefore, be it*

Resolved by the Senate and House of Representatives of the United States of America in Congress assembled, That the Congress approves and supports the determination of the President, as Commander in Chief, to take all necessary measures to repel any armed attack against the forces of the United States and to prevent further aggression.

SEC. 2. The United States regards as vital to its national interests and to world peace the maintenance of international peace and security in southeast Asia. . . . The United States is, therefore, prepared, as the President determines, to take all necessary steps, including the use of armed force, to assist any member or protocol state of the Southeast Asia Collective Defense Treaty requesting assistance in defense of its freedom.

SEC. 3. This resolution shall expire when the President shall determine that the peace and security of the area is reasonably assured. . . .

Questions

1. What are the North Vietnamese accused of in this resolution?
2. What are the American interests in the region, according to the resolution?
3. In what ways does the resolution grant a free hand to the president?

31-4 Lyndon Johnson, "Peace without Conquest" (1965)

From the outset of the war Johnson coupled escalation in Vietnam with a public relations campaign at home. His strategy was to accompany increases in troop strength and bombing campaigns with pledges to seek diplomatic solutions with more determination. His first major speech after sending the first group of American ground troops was just such an effort. Most scholars agree that this address, given at Johns Hopkins University early in the war, was intended to stem the growth of dissent among opponents (see text pp. 967–969). The speech was vintage Johnson. He spoke of his dream for world order, expressed his sympathies for the "ordinary men and women of North Viet-Nam," and disavowed any aggressive intentions. He invoked the memory of the New Deal of the 1930s when he mused about turning the Mekong River into a TVA (see Chapter 26). Yet he gave no clear indication of American military intentions or specific ideas about how he planned to provide stability for South Vietnam.

Source: Public Papers of the Presidents of the United States: Lyndon Johnson, 1965 (Washington, D.C.: U.S. Government Printing Office, 1966), pp. 394–399.

Our objective is the independence of South Viet-Nam, and its freedom from attack. We want nothing for ourselves—only that the people of South Viet-Nam be allowed to guide their own country their own way.

In recent months attacks on South Viet-Nam were stepped up. Thus, it became necessary for us to increase our response and to make attacks by air. This is not a change of purpose. It is a change in what we believe that purpose requires. . . .

We hope that peace will come swiftly. But that is in the

hands of others besides ourselves. And we must be prepared for a long continued conflict. It will require patience as well as bravery, the will to endure as well as the will to resist. . . .

These countries of southeast Asia are homes for millions of impoverished people. Each day these people rise at dawn and struggle through until the night to wrestle existence from the soil. They are often racked by disease, plagued by hunger, and death comes at the early age of 40.

Stability and peace do not come easily in such a land. Neither independence nor human dignity will ever be won, though, by arms alone. It also requires the work of peace. The American people have helped generously in past times. Now there must be a much more massive effort to improve the life of man in that conflict-torn corner of the world. . . .

The task is nothing less than to enrich the hopes and existence of more than a hundred million people. And there is much to be done.

The vast Mekong River can provide food and water and power on a scale to dwarf even our own TVA.

The wonders of modern medicine can be spread through villages where thousands die every year from lack of care.

Schools can be established to train people in the skills that are needed to manage the process of development.

The ordinary men and women of North Viet-Nam, and South Viet-Nam . . . are brave people. They are filled with the same proportions of hate and fear, of love and hope. Most of them want the same things for themselves and their families. Most of them do not want their sons to die in battle, or to see their homes . . . destroyed.

Well, this can be their world yet. Man has the knowledge . . . to make this planet serve the real needs of the people who live on it.

Questions

1. What are the American objectives in Vietnam as Johnson defines them?
2. What is Johnson's impression of the sort of life the Vietnamese lead?
3. What kind of world does Johnson envision for the people of Southeast Asia?

Questions for Further Thought

1. How do the visions for Vietnam expressed by Ho Chi Minh (Document 31-1) and John F. Kennedy (Document 31-2) differ? Why was Ho's Vietnam unacceptable to the United States and American policy makers?
2. Comparing Documents 31-2, 31-3, and 31-4, what was America's purpose in Vietnam? What national interests were at stake? What motives impelled the American effort?
3. How might John F. Kennedy have reacted to Lyndon Johnson's speech (Document 31-4) at Johns Hopkins University?

The Challenge of Youth, 1962–1970

In the 1960s the children of the baby boom came of age. Their youthful energy and commitment to improving the quality of life in the United States—answering the challenge in John Kennedy's inaugural address to "ask what you can do for your country"—drove them to action both in the streets and in the halls of power. A variety of causes mobilized them into action: the civil rights movement, the war in Vietnam, and the impersonal character of colleges and universities.

The activism of the boomers blossomed on college campuses (see text pp. 969–971), where their presence reflected the greater prosperity that allowed more young people to attend college. In 1962 a group of students from major universities met to form the Students for a Democratic Society. Their proclamation, the Port Huron Statement, outlined their indictment of the status quo (Document 31-5). By 1965 SDS (see text pp. 969–970) had added American prosecution of the war in Vietnam to its list of grievances.

An early part of the youth protest was directed at major universities and their failure to respond to changes in society. Mario Savio, one of the leaders of the Free Speech Movement at the University of California at Berkeley, eloquently expressed that sentiment when he compared the university to a machine: "There is a time when the operation of the machine becomes so odious, makes you so sick at heart, that you can't take part; you can't even passively take part; and you've got to put your bodies upon the gears and upon the wheels, upon the levers, upon all the apparatus and you've got to make it stop."

As more young Americans engaged in these criticisms of traditional society, their movement became a full-blown counterculture (see text pp. 971–973), with all the trappings of a new social order: dress and hairstyles, drugs and free love, communal living and protest music. The music of the 1960s (see text p. 972) reflected the rising unhappiness of young people with their country. They gathered on campuses, in coffeehouses, and at music festivals such as Woodstock in 1969 to sing and chant and call for change (Document 31-6). In time, many elements of the counterculture were absorbed by the majority and continue as characteristics of American culture.

31-5   The Port Huron Statement (1962)

The Students for a Democratic Society (SDS) played a leading role in the youth movement. In 1962 two University of Michigan activists, Al Haber and Tom Hayden, organized the founding meeting of SDS, held at a United Auto Workers center in Port Huron, Michigan (see text pp. 969–970). The students approved the following manifesto.

Source: Students for a Democratic Society, *Port Huron Statement*, 1962. Reprinted by permission of Senator Tom Hayden. A copy of the third printing is available in the Labadie Collection, Hatcher Graduate Library, University of Michigan.

INTRODUCTION: AGENDA FOR A GENERATION

We are people of this generation, bred in at least modest comfort, housed now in universities, looking uncomfortably to the world we inherit.

When we were kids the United States was the wealthiest and strongest country in the world; the only one with the atom bomb, the least scarred by modern war, an initiator of the United Nations that we thought would distribute Western influence throughout the world. Freedom and equality for each individual, government of, by, and for the people—these American values we found good, principles by which we could live as men. Many of us began maturing in complacency.

As we grew, however, our comfort was penetrated by events too troubling to dismiss. First, the permeating and victimizing fact of human degradation, symbolized by the Southern struggle against racial bigotry, compelled most of us from silence to activism. Second, the enclosing fact of the Cold War, symbolized by the presence of the Bomb, brought awareness that we ourselves, and our friends, and millions of abstract "others" we knew more directly because of our common peril, might die at any time. We might deliberately ignore, or avoid, or fail to feel all other human problems, but not these two, for these were too immediate and crushing in their impact, too challenging in the demand that we as individuals take the responsibility for encounter and resolution.

While these and other problems either directly oppressed us or rankled our consciences and became our own subjective concerns, we began to see complicated and disturbing paradoxes in our surrounding America. The declaration "all men are created equal . . ." rang hollow before the facts of Negro life in the South and the big cities of the North. The proclaimed peaceful intentions of the United States contradicted its economic and military investments in the Cold War status quo. . . .

Not only did tarnish appear on our image of American virtue, not only did disillusion occur when the hypocrisy of American ideals was discovered, but we began to sense that what we had originally seen as the American Golden Age was actually the decline of an era. The worldwide outbreak of revolution against colonialism and imperialism, the entrenchment of totalitarian states, the menace of war, overpopulation, international disorder, supertechnology—these trends were testing the tenacity of our own commitment to democracy and freedom and our abilities to visualize their application to a world in upheaval.

Our work is guided by the sense that we may be the last generation in the experiment with living. But we are a minority—the vast majority of our people regard the temporary equilibriums of our society and world as eternally-functional parts. In this is perhaps the outstanding paradox: we ourselves are imbued with urgency, yet the message of our society is that there is no viable alternative to the present. Beneath the reassuring tones of the politicians, beneath the common opinion that America will "muddle through," beneath the stagnation of those who have closed their minds to the future, is the pervading feeling that there simply are no alternatives, that our times have witnessed the exhaustion not only of Utopias, but of any new departures as well. Feeling the press of complexity upon the emptiness of life, people are fearful of the thought that at any moment things might be thrust out of control. They fear change itself, since change might smash whatever invisible framework seems to hold back chaos for them now. For most Americans, all crusades are suspect, threatening. The fact that each individual sees apathy in his fellows perpetuates the common reluctance to organize for change. The dominant institutions are complex enough to blunt the minds of their potential critics, and entrenched enough to swiftly dissipate or entirely repel the energies of protest and reform, thus limiting human expectancies. Then, too, we are a materially improved society, and by our own improvements we seem to have weakened the case for further change. . . .

The search for truly democratic alternatives to the present, and a commitment to social experimentation with

them, is a worthy and fulfilling human enterprise, one which moves us and, we hope, others today. On such a basis do we offer this document of our convictions and analysis: as an effort in understanding and changing the conditions of humanity in the late twentieth century, an effort rooted in the ancient, still unfulfilled conception of man attaining determining influence over his circumstances of life.

VALUES

Making values explicit—an initial task in establishing alternatives—is an activity that has been devalued and corrupted. The conventional moral terms of the age, the politician moralities—"free world," "people's democracies"—reflect realities poorly, if at all, and seem to function more as ruling myths than as descriptive principles. But neither has our experience in the universities brought us moral enlightenment. Our professors and administrators sacrifice controversy to public relations; their curriculums change more slowly than the living events of the world; their skills and silence are purchased by investors in the arms race; passion is called unscholastic. The questions we might want raised—what is really important? can we live in a different and better way? if we wanted to change society, how would we do it?—are not thought to be questions of a "fruitful, empirical nature," and thus are brushed aside. . . .

Men have unrealized potential for self-cultivation, self-direction, self-understanding, and creativity. It is this potential that we regard as crucial and to which we appeal, not to the human potentiality for violence, unreason, and submission to authority. The goal of man and society should be human independence: a concern not with image of popularity but with finding a meaning in life that is personally authentic; a quality of mind not compulsively driven by a sense of powerlessness, nor one which unthinkingly adopts status values, nor one which represses all threats to its habits, but one which has full, spontaneous access to present and past experiences, one which easily unites the fragmented parts of personal history, one which openly faces problems which are troubling and unresolved; one with an intuitive awareness of possibilities, an active sense of curiosity, an ability and willingness to learn.

This kind of independence does not mean egotistic individualism—the object is not to have one's way so much as it is to have a way that is one's own. Nor do we deify man—we merely have faith in his potential.

Human relationships should involve fraternity and honesty. Human interdependence is contemporary fact; human brotherhood must be willed, however, as a condition of future survival and as the most appropriate form of social relations. Personal links between man and man are needed, especially to go beyond the partial and fragmentary bonds of function that bind men only as worker to worker, employer to employee, teacher to student, American to Russian. . . .

We would replace power rooted in possession, privilege, or circumstance by power and uniqueness rooted in love, reflectiveness, reason, and creativity. As a *social sys-* *tem* we seek the establishment of a democracy of individual participation, governed by two central aims: that the individual share in those social decisions determining the quality and direction of his life; that society be organized to encourage independence in men and provide the media for their common participation. . . .

Questions

1. What indictments does the Port Huron Statement bring against mainstream American society?
2. How does the Port Huron Statement address generational differences?
3. What does the statement say about civil rights? What does it say about academia?

31-6 "The Times They Are A-Changin'" (1963)

Bob Dylan

Bob Dylan's "The Times They Are A-Changing'" (1963) forecast alterations in American society that very much reflected the direction of the youth movement (see text p. 972). The lyrics capture the essence of what became known as the "generation gap" in the United States. Dylan established himself as one of the leading musicians and social critics of the 1960s.

Source: Bob Dylan, "The Times They Are A-Changin.'" Copyright © 1963, 1964 by Warner Bros. Rider Music. Copyright renewed 1991 by Special Rider Music. All rights reserved. International copyright secured. Reprinted by permission.

Come gather 'round people
Wherever you roam
And admit that the waters
Around you have grown
And accept it that soon
You'll be drenched to the bone.
If your time to you
Is worth savin'
Then you better start swimmin'
Or you'll sink like a stone
For the times they are a-changin'.

Come writers and critics
Who prophesize with your pen
And keep your eyes wide
The chance won't come again
And don't speak too soon
For the wheel's still in spin
And there's no tellin' who
That it's namin'
For the loser now
Will be later to win
For the times they are a-changin'.

Come senators, congressmen
Please heed the call
Don't stand in the doorway
Don't block up the hall
For he that gets hurt
Will be he who has stalled
There's a battle outside
And it is ragin'
It'll soon shake your windows
And rattle your walls
For the times they are a-changin'.

Come mothers and fathers
Throughout the land
And don't criticize
What you can't understand
Your sons and your daughters
Are beyond your command
Your old road is
Rapidly agin'.
Please get out of the new one
If you can't lend your hand
For the times they are a-changin'.

The line it is drawn
The curse it is cast
The slow one now
Will later be fast
As the present now
Will later be past
The order is
Rapidly fadin'.
And the first one now
Will later be last
For the times they are a-changin'.

Questions

1. To whom is the song addressed? Which institutions does Dylan target for criticism?
2. According to Dylan, what will be the fate of those people and institutions if they do not heed his warning?
3. Dylan sang, "For the loser now will be later to win" and "The first one now will later be last." Has this prophecy come true?

Questions for Further Thought

1. Were Tom Hayden (Document 31-5) and Bob Dylan (Document 31-6) predicting a revolution or warning that it was already under way? Cite examples from these documents to explain your answer.
2. How much significance did Hayden and Dylan place on the role of young people in American society? Explain your answer.
3. What actions were Dylan and Hayden urging their peers to take?

The Long Road Home, 1968–1975

"Coming home" from Vietnam proved to be a difficult task for both the United States government and the men and women who had worn American military colors in Vietnam. In 1968 the American people elected Richard Nixon to the presidency (see text p. 978), hoping that a Republican president might be able to end a war that had been tied to the Democrats by Lyndon Johnson. Nixon said that he would end the war through a program of "Vietnamization" (Document 31-7) but did not give any specific timetable for American withdrawal. As the war continued and then became wider with American troops dispatched into Cambodia in 1970 (Document 31-8), the mood of the country grew uglier. Antiwar protests heated up again and, after the Cambodian invasion, turned deadly when four students at Kent State University were killed by gunfire from National Guardsmen during an antiwar rally (see text p. 980).

President Nixon stayed faithful to Vietnamization despite the rising tide of criticism, pledging that he would end the war "with honor". Early in 1973, in the first days of his second term, Nixon announced that an American diplomatic team had signed a peace accord in Paris (see text pp. 981, 984). By April of that year American prisoners of war had been released from captivity, clearing the way for the withdrawal of U.S. ground forces. The war in Vietnam continued for two more years without an active American presence, ending in the spring of 1975 when North Vietnamese and Vietcong forces won a final campaign against South Vietnam.

On one level, for the United States the war in Vietnam ended in April 1973. On another, the war continued to be a painful experience for the American people, who had paid a high cost at home and abroad for the lost war (see text pp. 984–985). But no group paid a higher price than the men and women who had fought in Vietnam. For those who came home alive there remained the physical and emotional pains of war and resentment that some Americans directed against returning veterans (Document 31-9). For each of the Americans who died in Vietnam there were grieving families who mourned their losses (Document 31-10). The country that had been torn apart by its longest war finally began to heal when the Vietnam Veterans Memorial, popularly known as "the Wall," was dedicated in November 1982. The 58,000 men and women listed on the black granite wall and the veterans who had been ridiculed and resented were at last coming home.

31-7   Richard Nixon on "Vietnamization" (1969)

In this address to the American people from the White House on November 3, 1969, a year after he won the election, Nixon explained his plan to "Vietnamize" the war. Vietnamization did not bring the war to a quick end, and for several months it did not reduce the number of American soldiers in Vietnam (see text p. 979). In this speech Nixon tried to explain the need for a continuing American presence. All too aware that protests against continuing American involvement were stronger than ever, especially on college and university campuses, he also sought to rally what he called the "great silent majority" to support his new policy. Unmentioned in this speech is the companion policy to troop withdrawal, a dramatic (and secret) increase in American bombing raids over North Vietnam.

Source: Department of State Bulletin, November 24, 1969.

Let me briefly explain what has been described as the Nixon doctrine—a policy which not only will help end the war in Viet-Nam but which is an essential element of our program to prevent future Viet-Nams.

We Americans are a do-it-yourself people. We are an impatient people. Instead of teaching someone else to do a job, we like to do it ourselves. And this trait has been carried over into our foreign policy.

In Korea and again in Viet-Nam, the United States furnished most of the money, most of the arms, and most of the men to help the people of those countries defend their freedom against Communist aggression.

Before any American troops were committed to Viet-Nam, a leader of another Asian country expressed this opinion to me when I was traveling in Asia as a private citizen. He said: "When you are trying to assist another nation defend its freedom, U.S. policy should be to help them fight the war, but not to fight the war for them."

Well, in accordance with this wise counsel, I laid down in Guam three principles as guidelines for future American policy toward Asia:

—First, the United States will keep all of its treaty commitments.

—Second, we shall provide a shield if a nuclear power threatens the freedom of a nation allied with us or of a nation whose survival we consider vital to our security.

—Third, in cases involving other types of aggression, we shall furnish military and economic assistance when requested in accordance with our treaty commitments. But we shall look to the nation directly threatened to assume the primary responsibility of providing the manpower for its defense. . . .

The defense of freedom is everybody's business—not just America's business. And it is particularly the responsibility of the people whose freedom is threatened. In the previous administration we Americanized the war in Viet-Nam. In this administration we are Vietnamizing the search for peace.

The policy of the previous administration not only resulted in our assuming the primary responsibility for fighting the war but, even more significantly did not adequately stress the goal of strengthening the South Vietnamese so that they could defend themselves when we left.

The Vietnamization plan was launched following Secretary [of Defense Melvin R.] Laird's visit to Viet-Nam in March. Under the plan, I ordered first a substantial increase in the training and equipment of South Vietnamese forces.

In July, on my visit to Viet-Nam, I changed General Abrams' orders so that they were consistent with the objectives of our new policies. Under the new orders, the primary mission of our troops is to enable the South Vietnamese forces to assume the full responsibility for the security of South Viet-Nam. . . .

We have adopted a plan which we have worked out in cooperation with the South Vietnamese for the complete withdrawal of all U.S. combat ground forces and their replacement by South Vietnamese forces on an orderly scheduled timetable. This withdrawal will be made from strength and not from weakness. As South Vietnamese forces become stronger, the rate of American withdrawal can become greater. . . .

If the level of infiltration or our casualties increase while we are trying to scale down the fighting, it will be the result of a conscious decision by the enemy.

Hanoi could make no greater mistake than to assume that an increase in violence will be to its advantage. If I conclude that increased enemy action jeopardizes our remaining forces in Viet-Nam, I shall not hesitate to take strong and effective measures to deal with that situation.

This is not a threat. This is a statement of policy which as Commander in Chief of our Armed Forces I am making in meeting my responsibility for the protection of American fighting men wherever they may be.

My fellow Americans, I am sure you can recognize from what I have said that we really only have two choices open to us if we want to end this war:

—I can order an immediate, precipitate withdrawal of all Americans from Viet-Nam without regard to the effects of that action.

—Or we can persist in our search for a just peace, through a negotiated settlement if possible or through continued implementation of our plan for Vietnamization if necessary—a plan in which we will withdraw all of our forces from Viet-Nam on a schedule in accordance with our program, as the South Vietnamese become strong enough to defend their own freedom.

I have chosen this second course. It is not the easy way. It is the right way. It is a plan which will end the war and serve the cause of peace, not just in Viet-Nam but in the Pacific and in the world.

In speaking of the consequences of a precipitate withdrawal, I mentioned that our allies would lose confidence in America.

Far more dangerous, we would lose confidence in ourselves. Oh, the immediate reaction would be a sense of relief that our men were coming home. But as we saw the consequences of what we had done, inevitable remorse and divisive recrimination would scar our spirit as a people. . . .

If [the plan for peace] does succeed, what the critics say now won't matter. If it does not succeed, anything I say then won't matter.

I know it may not be fashionable to speak of patriotism or national destiny these days. But I feel it is appropriate to do so on this occasion.

Two hundred years ago this nation was weak and poor. But even then, America was the hope of millions in the world. Today we have become the strongest and richest nation in the world. The wheel of destiny has turned so that any hope the world has for the survival of peace and freedom will be determined by whether the American people have the moral stamina and the courage to meet the challenge of free-world leadership.

Let historians not record that when America was the most powerful nation in the world we passed on the other side of the road and allowed the last hopes for peace and freedom of millions of people to be suffocated by the forces of totalitarianism.

And so tonight—to you, the great silent majority of my fellow Americans—I ask for your support.

I pledged in my campaign for the Presidency to end the war in a way that we could win the peace. I have a initiated a plan of action which will enable me to keep that pledge.

The more support I can have from the American people, the sooner that pledge can be redeemed; for the more divided we are at home, the less likely the enemy is to negotiate at Paris.

Let us be united for peace. Let us also be united against defeat. Because let us understand: North Viet-Nam cannot defeat or humiliate the United States. Only Americans can do that.

Questions

1. How does Nixon generalize his Vietnamization policy into the "Nixon doctrine"?
2. According to Nixon, how does his Vietnamization policy differ from the policy followed by President Johnson?
3. What arguments does he use to persuade Americans to support Vietnamization?

31-8   Richard Nixon on Sending U.S. Troops to Cambodia (1970)

On April 30, 1970, just five months after announcing the "Nixon doctrine" and his plan to "Vietnamize" the war, President Nixon again spoke to the nation on television directly from the White House. This time he announced that U.S. troops would attack North Vietnamese and communist South Vietnamese forces across the border in officially neutral Cambodia (see text p. 979). Antiwar protests reached perhaps their highest level in 1970 (see text p. 980). In this speech Nixon tried to provide a rationale for the American incursion into Cambodia, denounce and isolate antiwar protesters, and increase public support for his approach to the Vietnam conflict. His effort to achieve these three distinct and somewhat conflicting purposes led Nixon to use both complicated reasoning and strikingly pungent language in this speech.

Source: Department of State Bulletin, May 18, 1970.

Ten days ago, in my report to the Nation on Viet-Nam, I announced a decision to withdraw an additional 150,000 Americans from Viet-Nam over the next year. I said then that I was making that decision despite our concern over increased enemy activity in Laos, in Cambodia, and in South Viet-Nam.

At that time, I warned that if I concluded that increased enemy activity in any of these areas endangered the lives of Americans remaining in Viet-Nam, I would not hesitate to take strong and effective measures to deal with that situation.

Despite that warning, North Viet-Nam has increased its military aggression in all these areas, and particularly in Cambodia.

After full consultation with the National Security Council . . . and my other advisers, I have concluded that the actions of the enemy in the last 10 days clearly endanger the lives of Americans who are in Viet-Nam now and would constitute an unacceptable risk to those who will be there after withdrawal of another 150,000.

To protect our men who are in Viet-Nam and to guarantee the continued success of our withdrawal and Vietnamization programs, I have concluded that the time has come for action. . . .

For the past 5 years . . . North Viet-Nam has occupied military sanctuaries all along the Cambodian frontier with South Viet-Nam. Some of these extend up to 20 miles into Cambodia. The sanctuaries . . . are on both sides of the border. They are used for hit-and-run attacks on American and South Vietnamese forces in South Viet-Nam.

These Communist-occupied territories contain major base camps, training sites, logistics facilities, weapons and ammunition factories, airstrips, and prisoner of war compounds. . . .

Tonight American and South Vietnamese units will attack the headquarters for the entire Communist military operation in South Viet-Nam. This key control center has been occupied by the North Vietnamese and Viet Cong for 5 years in blatant violation of Cambodia's neutrality.

This is not an invasion of Cambodia. The areas in which these attacks will be launched are completely occupied and controlled by North Vietnamese forces. Our purpose is not to occupy the areas. Once enemy forces are driven out of these sanctuaries and once their military supplies are destroyed, we will withdraw.

These actions are in no way directed at the security interests of any nation. Any government that chooses to use these actions as a pretext for harming relations with the

United States will be doing so on its own responsibility and on its own initiative, and we will draw the appropriate conclusions.

Now, let me give you the reasons for my decision.

A majority of the American people, a majority of you listening to me, are for the withdrawal of our forces from Viet-Nam. The action I have taken tonight is indispensible for the continuing success of that withdrawal program.

A majority of the American people want to end this war rather than to have it drag on interminably. The action I have taken tonight will serve that purpose.

A majority of the American people want to keep the casualties of our brave men in Viet-Nam at an absolute minimum. The action I take tonight is essential if we are to accomplish that goal.

We take this action not for the purpose of expanding the war into Cambodia, but for the purpose of ending the war in Viet-Nam and winning the just peace we all desire. We have made and we will continue to make every possible effort to end this war through negotiation at the conference table rather than through more fighting on the battlefield. . . .

My fellow Americans, we live in an age of anarchy, both abroad and at home. We see mindless attacks on all the great institutions which have been created by free civilizations in the last 500 years. Even here in the United States, great universities are being systematically destroyed. Small nations all over the world find themselves under attack from within and from without.

If, when the chips are down, the world's most powerful nation, the United States of America, acts like a pitiful, helpless giant, the forces of totalitarianism and anarchy will threaten free nations and free institutions throughout the world.

It is not our power but our will and character that is being tested tonight. The question all Americans must ask and answer tonight is this: Does the richest and strongest nation in the history of the world have the character to meet a direct challenge by a group which rejects every effort to win a just peace, ignores our warning, tramples on solemn agreements, violates the neutrality of an unarmed people, and uses our prisoners as hostages?

If we fail to meet this challenge, all other nations will be on notice that despite its overwhelming power the United States, when a real crisis comes, will be found wanting.

During my campaign for the Presidency, I pledged to bring Americans home from Viet-Nam. They are coming home.

I promised to end this war. I shall keep that promise.

I promised to win a just peace. I shall keep that promise.

We shall avoid a wider war. But we are also determined to put an end to this war. . . .

Questions

1. How does President Nixon seek to persuade Americans that the attack was "not an invasion of Cambodia"?
2. How does Nixon try to persuade his listeners that he is avoiding a "wider war"?
3. What does Nixon mean by his reference to "the forces of totalitarianism and anarchy"?

31-9 Lynda Van Devanter on Coming Home to "the World" (1983)

Many of the young men and women who volunteered for Vietnam were answering President Kennedy's call to service for their country. Lynda Van Devanter, fresh out of nursing school, wanted to do what she could for her country, and going to Vietnam seemed an appropriate step. During her time "in country" her views changed dramatically: she came to resent President Nixon and the American policy makers who promoted the war, detested the "Saigon warriors" who pushed papers in the safety of their offices but never entered the field of fire, and hated the "lily-livered" South Vietnamese troops who gave too little support to the American forces. But what hurt her most was the reception she received when she came back home to "the world" and discovered that many Americans did not want to be reminded of the lost war (see text pp. 984–985).

Source: Excerpted from Lynda Van Devanter, with Christopher Morgan, *Home Before Morning: The Story of an Army Nurse in Vietnam* (New York: Beaufort Books, 1983), pp. 209–212.

When the soldiers of World War II came home, they were met by brass bands, ticker-tape parades, and people so thankful for their service that even those who had never heard a shot fired in anger were treated with respect. It was a time when words like honor, glory, and duty held some value, a time when a returning GI was viewed with esteem so high it bordered on awe. To be a veteran was to be seen as a person of courage, a champion of democracy, an ideal against which all citizens could measure themselves. If you had answered your country's call, you were a hero. And in those days, heroes were plentiful.

But somewhere between 1945 and 1970, words like bravery, sacrifice, and valor had gone out of vogue. . . . When I returned to my country in June of 1970, I began to learn a very bitter lesson. The values with which I had been raised had changed; in the eyes of most Americans, the military services had no more heroes, merely babykillers, misfits, and fools. I was certain that I was neither a babykiller nor a misfit. Maybe I was a fool. . . .

Perhaps if I hadn't expected anything at all when I returned to the States, I would not have been disappointed. Maybe I would have been contented simply to be on American soil. Maybe all of us who arrived at Travis Air Force Base on June 16 had unrealistic expectations.

But we didn't ask for a bass band. We didn't ask for a parade. We didn't even ask for much of a thank you. All we wanted was some transportation to San Francisco International Airport so we could hop connecting flights to get home to our families. We gave the Army a year of our lives, a year with more difficulties than most Americans face in fifty years. The least the Army could have done was to give us a ride.

At Travis we were herded onto buses and driven to the Oakland Army Terminal where they dumped us around 5 A.M. with a "so long, suckers" from the driver and a feeling that we were no more than warm bodies who had outlived their usefulness. Unfortunately, San Francisco International was at least twenty miles away. Since most of us had to get flights from there, wouldn't it have been logical to drop us at the airport? Or was I expecting too much out of the Army when I asked it to be logical?

I checked into commercial buses and taxis, but none were running. There was a transit strike on, and it was nearly impossible to get public transportation of any kind. So I hung one of my suitcases from my left shoulder, hefted my duffel bag onto my right shoulder, grabbed my overnight case with my left hand and my purse with my right, and struggling under the weight, walked out to the highway, where I stuck out my thumb and waited. I was no stranger to hitchhiking. It was the only way to get around in Vietnam. Back in 'Nam, I would usually stand on the flight line in my fatigues, combat boots, jungle hat, pigtails, and a smile. Getting a ride there was a cinch. In fact, planes would sometimes reach the end of the runway, then return to offer me a lift.

But hitchhiking in the real world, I was quickly finding out, was nowhere near as easy—especially if you were wearing a uniform. The cars whizzed past me during rush hour, while I patiently waited for a good Samaritan to stop. A few drivers gave me the finger. I tried to ignore them. Some slowed long enough to yell obscenities. One threw a carton of trash and another nearly hit me with a half-empty can of soda. Finally, two guys stopped in a red and yellow Volkswagen bus. The one on the passenger side opened his door. I ran to the car, dragging the duffel bag and other luggage behind me. I was hot, tired, and dirty.

"Going anywhere near the airport?" I asked.

"Sure am," the guy said. He had long brown hair, blue eyes framed by wire-rimmed glasses, and a full curly beard. There was patches on his jeans and a peace sign on his T-shirt. His relaxed, easy smile was deceptive.

I smiled back and lifted my duffel bag to put it inside the van. But the guy slammed the door shut. "We're going past the airport, sucker, but we don't take Army pigs." He spit on me, I was stunned. . . .

[The driver] floored the accelerator and they both laughed uncontrollably as the VW spun its wheels for a few seconds, throwing dirt and stones back at me before it roared away. The drivers of other passing cars also laughed.

I looked down at my chest. On top of my nametag sat a big glob of brownish-colored saliva. I couldn't touch it. I didn't have the energy to wipe it away. Instead, I watched as it ran down my name tag and over a button before it was absorbed into the green material of my uniform.

I wasn't angry, just confused. I wanted to know why. Why would he spit on me? What had I done to him? To either of them? It might have been simple to say I had gone to war and they blamed me for killing innocent people, but didn't they understand that I didn't want this war any more than the most vocal of peace marchers? Didn't they realize that those of us who had seen the war firsthand were probably more antiwar than they were? That we had seen friends suffer and die? That we had seen children destroyed? That we had seen futures crushed?

Where they that naive?

Or were they merely insensitive creeps who used the excuse of my uniform to vent their hostility toward all people?

I waited a few more hours, holding my thumb out until I thought my arm would fall off. After awhile, I stopped watching people as they hurled their insults. I had begun noticing the people who didn't scream as they drove by. I soon realized they all had something in common. It was what I eventually came to refer to as "the look." It was a combination of surprise at seeing a woman in uniform, and hated for what they assumed I represented. Most of them never bothered to try to conceal it. "The look" would start around the eyes, as if they were peering right through me. Their faces would harden into stone. I was a pariah, a nonperson so low that they believed they could squash me underfoot. . . .

While I stood there alone, I almost wished I was back in 'Nam. At least there you expected some people to hate you. That was a war. But here, in the United States, I guess I wanted everything to be wonderful. I thought that life would be different, that there would be no more pain. No more death. No more sorrow. It was all going to be good again. It had to be good again. I had had enough of fighting, and hatred, and bitterness.

Around 10:30 A.M., when I had given up hope and was sitting on my duffel bag. . . . an old black man in a beat up '58 Chevy stopped and got out of his car. He walked with a limp and leaned forward as if he couldn't stand straight. His clothes were frayed and his face deeply lined. He ran his bony fingers through his gray-black hair, then shook his head and smiled. "I don't know where you're going, little girl," he said. "But I been by here four times since early morning and you ain't got a ride yet. I can't let you spend your whole life on this road." He was only headed for the other side of Oakland, but he said he'd rather go out of his way than see me stranded. He even carried my duffel bag to the trunk. As we drove south on 101, I didn't say much other than thank you, but my disillusionment was obvious.

"People ain't all bad, little girl," he said. "It's just some folks are crazy mixed up these days. You keep in mind that it's gotta get better, cause it can't get any worse."

Questions

1. Compare the different homecomings of veterans returning from World War II and Vietnam veterans coming home to "the world." How do you explain these differences?

2. Why was Lynda Van Devanter so surprised at the "welcome" she received? Why did she wish she was back in Vietnam rather than home?

3. The "old black man" who picked up Van Devanter assured her that things "can't get any worse." In fact, for many Vietnam veterans life got much worse after their return home. What kinds of problems did Vietnam veterans suffer after coming home?

31-10 A Mother Remembers Her Son at "the Wall" (1984)

Eleanor Wimbish

For some families who lost sons and daughters in Vietnam the pain and suffering of the war continue to be part of daily life (see text pp. 984–985). They anguish over the loss of a loved one and wonder why their nation did not mourn with them during the war. A few find comfort in the healing powers of the Vietnam Veterans Memorial that commemorates all the men and women who served in Vietnam as well as the 58,000 who died during the war. In this letter from Mrs. Eleanor Wimbish to her son Billy at "the Wall," a mother expresses both grief and love for her child who did not come home from the war. Sergeant William R. Stocks died in Vietnam on February 13, 1969, at age twenty-one years. To date, Billy's mother has sent him more than two dozen letters at the Wall.

Source: Reprinted from *Dear America: Letters Home from Vietnam*, pp. 299–300, edited by Bernard Edelman for the New York Vietnam Veterans Memorial Commission; published originally by W. W. Norton & Company, 1985.

Dear Bill,

Today is February 13, 1984. I came to this black wall again to see and touch your name, and as I do I wonder if anyone ever stops to realize that next to your name, on this black wall, is your mother's heart. A heart broken 15 years ago today, when you lost your life in Vietnam.

And as I look at your name, William R. Stocks, I think of how many, many times I used to wonder how scared and homesick you must have been in that strange country called Vietnam. And if and how it might have changed you, for you were the most happy-go-lucky kid in the world, hardly ever sad or unhappy. And until the day I die, I will see you as you laughed at me, even when I was very mad at you, and the next thing I knew, we were laughing together.

But on the past New Year's Day, I had my answer. I talked by phone to a friend of yours from Michigan, who spent your last Christmas and the last four months of your life with you. Jim told me how you died, for he was there and saw the helicopter crash. He told me how you had flown your quota and had not been scheduled to fly that day. How the regular pilot was unable to fly, and had been replaced by someone with less experience. How they did not know the exact cause of the crash. How it was either hit by enemy fire, or they hit a pole or something unknown. How the blades went through the chopper and hit you. How you lived about a half hour, but were unconscious and therefore did not suffer.

He said how your jobs were like sitting ducks. They would send you men out to draw the enemy into the open and *then* they would send in the big guns and planes to take over. Meantime, death came to so many of you.

He told me how, after a while over there, instead of a yellow streak, the men got a mean streak down their backs. Each day the streak got bigger and the men became meaner. Everyone but *you*, Bill. He said how you stayed the same, happy-go-lucky guy that you were when you arrived in Vietnam. How your warmth and friendliness drew the guys to you. How your [lieutenant] gave you the nickname of "Spanky," and soon your group, Jim included, were all known as "Spanky's gang." How when you died it

made it so much harder on them for you were their moral support. And he said how you of all people should never have been the one to die.

Oh, God, how it hurts to write this. But I must face it and then put it to rest. I know that after Jim talked to me, he must have relived it all over again and suffered so. Before I hung up the phone I told Jim I loved him. Loved him for just being your close friend, and for sharing the last days of your life with you, and for being there with you when you died. How lucky you were to have him for a friend, and how lucky he was to have had you.

Later that same day I received a phone call from a mother in Billings, Montana. She had lost her daughter, her only child, a year ago. She needed someone to talk to for no one would let her talk about the tragedy. She said she had seen me on [television] on New Year's Eve, after the Christmas letter I wrote to you and left at this memorial had drawn newspaper and television attention. She said she had been thinking about me all day, and just had to talk to me. She talked to me of her pain, and seemingly needed me to help her with it. I cried with this heartbroken mother, and after I hung up the phone, I laid my head down and cried as hard for her. Here was a mother calling me for help with her pain over the loss of her child, a grown daughter. And as I sobbed I thought, how can I help her with her pain when I have never completely been able to cope with my own?

They tell me the letters I write to you and leave here at this memorial are waking others up to the fact that there is still much pain left, after all these years, from the Vietnam War.

But this I know, I would rather to have had you for 21 years, and all the pain that goes with losing you, than never to have had you at all.

Mom

Questions

1. In Vietnam there was great camaraderie between soldiers. How does this fact come home to Billy's mother?
2. How has Eleanor Wimbish been able to help other parents who have lost children? What does she think of this new role
3. How has "the Wall" helped families come to terms with the loss of a loved one?

Questions for Further Thought

1. Compare and contrast Richard Nixon's rationale for continuing American involvement in Vietnam (Documents 31-7 and 31-8) with Lyndon Johnson's rationale (Document 31-4).
2. Did Nixon's decision to send troops into Cambodia in 1970 (Document 31-8) violate his pledge to the American people that he was going to wind down America's role in Vietnam? Do you think Lynda Van Devanter would have supported Nixon's move?

3. Compare the views on coming home from Vietnam described by Linda Van Devanter (Document 31-9) and those expressed in Eleanor Wimbish's letter to her
son (Document 31-10). How can you account for these differences?

CHAPTER 32

The Lean Years 1969–1980

★　　　★　　　★

The Nixon Years and *Lowered Expectations and New Challenges*

Richard M. Nixon dominated American political and social debate between 1968 and 1976. In 1968 Nixon was elected president after pledging to end the war in Vietnam, heed the "silent majority" of citizens who were appalled by the civil rights and anti-Vietnam protests, and bring the nation "together again" (see text p. 990). The Watergate scandal of his reelection campaign in 1972 led to his near impeachment and then resignation in 1974 (see text pp. 992–995). His successor, Gerald Ford, lost the 1976 presidential election in part because he had pardoned Nixon for any crimes he might have committed in the Watergate scandal.

Nixon's politics were as difficult to characterize as those of any president in American history. Nixon presented a complex array of views and actions in domestic affairs. He spoke of reducing the size of government but also sponsored initiatives in welfare, environmental reform, and aid to the states (see text pp. 990–991 and Document 32-1). In foreign affairs Nixon emphasized the need for a hard line in the Cold War but traveled to Beijing to open relations with China for the first time since the communists had seized power there in 1949. He proposed to "Vietnamize" the war by shifting the fighting to the Vietnamese but authorized the biggest and most far-reaching U.S. bombing raids of the war, as well as the invasion of Cambodia (p. 979). Nixon opposed government interference in the daily lives of American citizens but did not hesitate to use federal agencies such as the FBI and the Internal Revenue Service against people he considered his political "enemies" (Document 32-2) or to assert that the president should enjoy more freedom from accountability to Congress or the federal courts than any of his predecessors had ever sought (see text pp. 993–994). He spoke of bringing the nation together but also tried to win office by emphasizing differences between the "silent majority" and "protesters" of all kinds. It appeared to at least one observer that Nixon wanted an imperial presidency (Document 32-3); instead, he got Watergate.

Watergate by itself would have been difficult for the American public to accept, but there was more. Postwar prosperity had begun to stall in the late 1960s, and with the OPEC oil price increases of the 1970s the very nature of the national economy was forever changed (see text pp. 996–998). Spiraling oil prices meant inflation, which was accompanied by rising unemployment as other nations challenged the United States for domestic and foreign markets.

The story of economic decline had a number of elements. A rise in energy prices (Document 32-4) was one; the closing of a plant in Homestead, Pennsylvania (Document 32-5), where steel had once been king, was another.

32-1   Memorandum on "Benign Neglect" (1970)

Daniel Patrick Moynihan

Daniel Patrick Moynihan (see text p. 990) served in both Democratic and Republican administrations in the 1960s. As a domestic adviser to Richard Nixon in 1970, Moynihan (b. 1927) promoted a racial policy of "benign neglect." The memorandum reprinted here quickly became controversial when it was leaked to the press in March 1970.

Source: Daniel Patrick Moynihan, "Memorandum for the President" (1970). In "Text of the Moynihan Memorandum on the Status of Negroes," *New York Times,* March 1, 1970.

Following is the text of a "Memorandum for the President" by Daniel P. Moynihan, counselor to President Nixon, on the position of Negroes:

As the new year begins, it occurs to me that you might find useful a general assessment of the position of Negroes at the end of the first year of your Administration, and of the decade in which their position has been the central domestic political issue.

In quantitative terms, which are reliable, the American Negro is making extraordinary progress. In political terms, somewhat less reliable, this would also appear to be true. In each case, however, there would seem to be countercurrents that pose a serious threat to the welfare of the blacks and the stability of the society, white and black.

1. Employment and Income

The nineteen-sixties saw the great breakthrough for blacks. A third (32 per cent) of all families of Negro and other races earned $8,000 or more in 1968 compared, in constant dollars, with 15 per cent in 1960.

The South is still a problem. Slightly more than half (52 per cent) of the Negro population lived in the South in 1969. There, only 19 per cent of families of Negro and other races earned over $8,000.

Young Negro families are achieving income parity with young white families. Outside the South, young husband-wife Negro families have 99 per cent of the income of whites! For families headed by a male age 25 to 34 the proportion was 87 per cent. Thus, it may be this ancient gap is finally closing.

Income reflects employment, and this changed dramatically in the nineteen-sixties. Blacks continued to have twice the unemployment rates of whites, but these were down for both groups. In 1969, the rate for married men of Negro and other races was only 2.5 per cent. Teenagers, on the other hand, continued their appalling rates: 24.4 per cent in 1969.

Black occupations improved dramatically. The number of professional and technical employees doubled in the period 1960–68. This was two and a half times the increase for whites. In 1969, Negro and other races provided 10 per cent of the other-than-college teachers. This is roughly their proportion of the population (11 per cent).

2. Education

In 1968, 19 per cent of Negro children 3 and 4 years old were enrolled in school, compared to 15 per cent of white children. Forty-five per cent of Negroes 18 and 19 years old were in school, almost the equal of the white proportion of 51 per cent. Negro college enrollment rose 85 per cent between 1964 and 1968, by which time there were 434,000 Negro college students. (The total full-time university population of Great Britain is 200,000.)

Educational achievement should not be exaggerated. Only 16 per cent of Negro high school seniors have verbal test scores at or above grade level. But blacks are staying in school.

3. Female-Headed Families

This problem does not get better, it gets worse. In 1969, the proportion of husband-wife families of Negro and other races declined once again, this time to 68.7 per cent. The illegitimacy ratio rose once again, this time to 29.4 per cent of all live births. (The white ratio rose more sharply, but was still only 4.9 per cent.)

Increasingly, the problem of Negro poverty is the problem of the female-headed family. In 1968, 56 per cent of Negro families with income under $3,000 were female-headed. In 1968, for the first time, the number of poor Negro children in female-headed families (2,241,000) was greater than the number in male-headed families (1,947,000).

4. Social Pathology

The incidence of antisocial behavior among young black males continues to be extraordinarily high. Apart from white racial attitudes, this is the biggest problem black Americans face, and in part it helps shape white racial attitudes. Black Americans injure one another. Because blacks live in de facto segregated neighborhoods and go to de facto segregated schools, the socially stable elements of the black population cannot escape the socially pathological ones. Routinely, their children get caught up in the antisocial patterns of the others.

You are familiar with the problem of crime. Let me draw your attention to another phenomenon, exactly parallel, and originating in exactly the same social circumstances: Fire. Unless I mistake the trends, we are heading for a genuinely serious fire problem in American cities. . . .

Many of these fires are the result of population density. But a great many are more or less deliberately set. (Thus, on Monday, welfare protestors set two fires in the New York State Capitol.) Fires are in fact a "leading indicator" of social pathology for a neighborhood. They come first. Crime, and the rest, follows. The psychiatric interpretation of fire-setting is complex, but it relates to the types of personalities which slums produce. (A point of possible interest: Fires in the black slums peak in July and August. The urban riots of 1964–1968 could be thought of as epidemic conditions of an endemic situation.)

5. Social Alienation

With no real evidence, I would nonetheless suggest that a great deal of the crime, the fire-setting, the rampant school violence and other such phenomenon in the black community have become quasi-politicized. Hatred—revenge—against whites is now an acceptable excuse for doing what might have been done anyway. This is bad news for any so-ciety, especially when it takes forms which the Black Panthers seem to have adopted.

This social alienation among the black lower classes is matched and probably enhanced, by a virulent form of anti-white feeling among portions of the large and prosperous black middle class. It would be difficult to overestimate the degree to which young, well-educated blacks detest white America.

6. The Nixon Administration

As you have candidly acknowledged, the relation of the Administration to the black population is a problem. I think it ought also to be acknowledged that we are a long way from solving it. During the past year, intense efforts have been made by the Administration to develop programs that will be of help to the blacks. I dare say, as much or more time and attention goes into this effort in this Administration than any in history. But little has come of it. There has been a great deal of political ineptness in some departments, and you have been the loser.

I don't know what you can do about this. Perhaps nothing. But I do have four suggestions.

First. Sometime early in the year, I would gather together the Administration officials who are most involved with these matters and talk out the subject a bit. There really is a need for a more coherent Administration approach to a number of issues. (Which I can list for you, if you like.)

Second. The time may have come when the issue of race could benefit from a period of "benign neglect." The subject has been too much talked about. The forum has been too much taken over to hysterics, paranoids and boodlers on all sides. We may need a period in which Negro progress continues and racial rhetoric fades. The Administration can help bring this about by paying close attention to such progress—as we are doing—while seeking to avoid situations in which extremists of either race are given opportunities for martyrdom, heroics, histrionics or whatever. Greater attention to Indians, Mexican-Americans and Puerto Ricans would be useful. A tendency to ignore provocations from groups such as the Black Panthers might also be useful. (The Panthers were apparently almost defunct until the Chicago police raided one of their headquarters and transformed them into culture heroes for the white—and black—middle class. You perhaps did not note on the society page of yesterday's Times that Mrs. Leonard Bernstein gave a cocktail party on Wednesday to raise money for the Panthers. Mrs. W. Vincent Astor was among the guests. Mrs. Peter Duchin, "the rich blonde wife of the orchestra leader," was thrilled, "I've never met a Panther," she said. "This is a first for me.")

Third. We really ought to be getting on with research on crime. We just don't know enough. It is a year now since the Administration came to office committed to doing something about crime in the streets. But frankly, in that year I don't see that we have advanced either our understanding of the problem, or that of the public at large. (This of course may only reveal my ignorance of what is going on.)

At the risk of indiscretion, may I put it that lawyers are not professionally well-equipped to do much to prevent crime. Lawyers are not managers, and they are not researchers. The logistics, the ecology, the strategy and tactics of reducing the incidence of certain types of behavior in large urban populations simply are not things lawyers think about often.

We are never going to "learn" about crime in a laboratory sense. But we almost certainly could profit from limited, carefully done studies. I don't think these will be done unless you express a personal interest.

Fourth. There is a silent black majority as well as a white one. It is mostly working class, as against lower middle class. It is politically moderate (on issues other than racial equality) and shares most of the concerns of its white counterpart. This group has been generally ignored by the Government and the media. The more recognition we can give to it, the better off we shall all be. (I would take it, for example, that Ambassador [Jerome H.] Holland is a natural leader of this segment of the black community. There are others like him.)

Questions

1. What does Moynihan mean by "benign neglect"?
2. Which advances in race relations and which problems does he note?
3. Given the text of the memorandum, why did it generate controversy?

32-2 White House Conversations (1972)

On June 17, 1972, seven men were arrested in connection with a break-in at the headquarters of the Democratic National Committee in the Watergate hotel and apartment complex in Washington, D.C. The arrests led to revelations that forced Richard Nixon to resign his presidency on August 9, 1974.

Nixon had arranged to have all conversations in the Oval Office secretly taped, in part so that he could use the tapes to write a history of his administration. When one of his junior aides told a Congressional committee about the existence of the tapes, the Watergate investigation focused exclusively on this source (see text pp. 993–994). Nixon fiercely resisted pressure to release the tapes for as long as possible: he knew they would provide the "smoking gun," the incontrovertible evidence that he had committed several crimes, including the suppression of evidence and the obstruction of justice by ordering officials in the White House, the CIA, and the FBI to participate in the cover-up.

In the first conversation excerpted here, six days after the Watergate break-in, Nixon met in the Oval Office with his chief of staff, H. R. Haldeman, to discuss the early progress of the FBI's investigation of the event (see text p. 993). The second conversation is with John Dean, the White House counsel (the official lawyer to the president). Reference is also made to the former U.S. attorney general, John Mitchell, campaign director of the Committee to Re-Elect the President (CREEP); Maurice Stans, the finance chairman of CREEP; John Ehrlichman, the domestic affairs assistant to the president; and E. Howard Hunt and G. Gordon Liddy, former CIA agents and private security consultants to the Nixon White House.

Source: White House transcripts of conversations between H. R. Haldeman and Richard Nixon in the Oval Office of the President, June 23, 1972; and between John Dean and Richard Nixon, September 15, 1972. U.S. Congress, House, *Hearings before the Committee on the Judiciary,* 93rd Cong., 2nd sess., 1974.

JUNE 23, 1972

HALDEMAN: Now, on the investigation, you know the Democratic break-in thing, we're back in the problem area because the FBI is not under control, because [Director Patrick] Gray doesn't exactly know how to control it and they have—their investigation is now leading into some productive areas. . . . They've been able to trace the money—not through the money itself—but through the bank sources—the banker. And it goes in some directions we don't want it to go. Ah, also there have been some [other] things—like an informant came in off the street to the FBI in Miami who was a photographer or has a friend who is a photographer who developed some films through this guy [Bernard] Barker and the films had pictures of Democratic National Committee letterhead documents and things. So it's things like that that are filtering in. . . . [John] Mitchell came up with yesterday, and John Dean analyzed very carefully last night and concludes, concurs now with Mitchell's recommendation that the only way to solve this . . . is for us to have [CIA Assistant Director Vernon] Walters call Pat Gray and just say, "Stay to hell out of this—this is ah, [our] business here. We don't want you to go any further on it." That's not an unusual development, and ah, that would take care of it.

PRESIDENT: What about Pat Gray—you mean Pat Gray doesn't want to?

HALDEMAN: Pat does want to. He doesn't know how to, and he doesn't have any basis for doing it. Given this, he will then have the basis. He'll call [FBI Assistant Director] Mark Felt in, and the two of them—and Mark Felt wants to cooperate because he's ambitious—

PRESIDENT: Yeah.

HALDEMAN: He'll call him in and say, "We've got the signal from across the river to put the hold on this." And that will fit rather well because the FBI agents who are working the case, at this point, feel that's what it is.

PRESIDENT: This is CIA? They've traced the money? Who'd they trace it to? . . .

HALDEMAN: Ken Dahlberg.

PRESIDENT: Who the hell is Ken Dahlberg?

HALDEMAN: He gave $25,000 in Minnesota and, ah, the check went directly to this guy Barker.

PRESIDENT: It isn't from the Committee though, from [Maurice] Stans?

HALDEMAN: Yeah. It is. It's directly traceable and there's some more through some Texas people that went to the Mexican bank which can also be traced to the Mexican bank—they'll get their names today.

PRESIDENT: Well, I mean, there's no way—I'm just thinking if they don't cooperate, what do they say? That they were approached by the Cubans? That's what Dahlberg has to say, the Texans too.

HALDEMAN: Well, if they will. But then we're relying on more and more people all the time. That's the problem and they'll [the FBI] . . . stop if we could take this other route.

PRESIDENT: All right.

HALDEMAN: [Mitchell and Dean] say the only way to do that is from White House instructions. And it's got to be to [CIA Director Richard] Helms and to—ah, what's his name? . . . Walters. . . . And the proposal would be that . . . [John] Ehrlichman and I call them in, and say, ah—

PRESIDENT: All right, fine. How do you call him in—I mean you just—well, we protected Helms from one hell of a lot of things.

HALDEMAN: That's what Ehrlichman says.

PRESIDENT: Of course; this [Howard] Hunt [business.] That will uncover a lot of things. You open that scab there's a hell of a lot of things and we just feel that it would be very detrimental to have this thing go any further. This involves these Cubans, Hunt, and a lot of hanky-panky that we have nothing to do with ourselves. Well, what the hell, did Mitchell know about this?

HALDEMAN: I think so. I don't think he knew the details, but I think he knew.

PRESIDENT: He didn't know how it was going to be handled though—with Dahlberg and the Texans and so forth? Well who was the asshole that did? Is it [G. Gordon] Liddy? Is that the fellow? He must be a little nuts!

HALDEMAN: He is.

PRESIDENT: I mean he just isn't well screwed on, is he? Is that the problem?

HALDEMAN: No, but he was under pressure, apparently, to get more information, and as he got more pressure, he pushed the people harder.

PRESIDENT: Pressure from Mitchell?

HALDEMAN: Apparently. . . .

PRESIDENT: All right, fine, I understand it all. We won't second-guess Mitchell and the rest. Thank God it wasn't [special White House counsel Charles] Colson.

HALDEMAN: The FBI interviewed Colson yesterday. They determined that would be a good thing to do. To have him take an interrogation, which he did, and the FBI guys working the case concluded that there were one or two possibilities—one, that this was a White House (they don't think that there is anything at the Election Committee) they think it was either a White House operation and they had some obscure reasons for it—non-political, or it was a—Cuban [operation] and [involved] the CIA. And after the interrogation of Colson yesterday, they concluded it was not the White House, but are now convinced it is a CIA thing, so the CIA turnoff would—

PRESIDENT: Well, not sure of their analysis, I'm not going to get that involved. I'm (unintelligible).

HALDEMAN: No, sir, we don't want you to.

PRESIDENT: You call them in.

HALDEMAN: Good deal.

PRESIDENT: Play it tough. That's the way they play it and that's the way we are going to play it. . . .

PRESIDENT: O.K. . . . Just say (unintelligible) very bad to have this fellow Hunt, ah, he knows too damned much. . . . If it gets out that this is all involved, the Cuba thing, it would be a fiasco. It would make the CIA look bad, it's going to make Hunt look bad, and it is likely to blow the whole Bay of Pigs thing which we think would be very unfortunate—both for CIA, and for the country, at this time, and for American foreign policy. Just tell him to lay off. Don't you [think] so?

HALDEMAN: Yep. That's the basis to do it on. Just leave it at that. . . .

SEPTEMBER 15, 1972

PRESIDENT: We are all in it together. This is a war. We take a few shots and it will be over. We will give them a few shots and it will be over. Don't worry. I wouldn't want to be on the other side right now. Would you?

DEAN: Along that line, one of the things I've tried to do, I have begun to keep notes on a lot of people who are emerging as less than our friends because this will be over some day and we shouldn't forget the way some of them have treated us.

PRESIDENT: I want the most comprehensive notes on all those who tried to do us in. They didn't have to do it. If we had had a very close election and they were playing the other side I would understand this. No—they were doing this quite deliberately and they are asking for it and they are going to get it. We have not used the power in this first four years, as you know. . . . We have not used the Bureau, and we have not used the Justice Department, but things are going to change now. And they are either going to do it right or go.

DEAN: What an exciting prospect.

PRESIDENT: Thanks. It has to be done. We have been (adjective deleted) fools for us to come into this election campaign, and not do anything with regard to the Democratic Senators who are running, et cetera. And who the hell are they after? They are after us. It is absolutely ridiculous. It is not going to be that way any more.

Questions

1. According to these transcripts, how much did President Nixon know about the financial and security operations of his reelection campaign?
2. According to the transcripts, what did Nixon know on June 23, 1972, about the Watergate break-in and related matters? What evidence do the transcripts provide that Nixon ordered the CIA and the FBI to participate in the cover-up?
3. Do the transcripts reveal other matters that Nixon might not have wished to have made public or that might have affected public respect for government?

32-3 *The Imperial Presidency* (1973)

Arthur M. Schlesinger, Jr.

Arthur M. Schlesinger, Jr., did more than study the presidency as a historian; he also worked as a special assistant to President Kennedy. During Watergate (see text pp. 992–995) Schlesinger (b. 1917) released this study charting the exploding growth of the powers of the presidency since World War II. Schlesinger warned that "unless the American democracy figures out how to control the Presidency in war and peace without enfeebling the Presidency across the board, then our system of government will face grave troubles."

The scheme of presidential subordination could easily be pressed to the point of national folly. But it was important to contend, not for a strong Presidency in general, but for a strong Presidency within the Constitution. The Presidency deserved to be defended on serious and not on stupid points. In 1973 Watergate produced flurries of near hysteria about the life expectancy of the institution. Thus Charles L. Black, Jr., Luce Professor of Jurisprudence at the Yale Law School, argued that, if Nixon turned over his White House tapes to Congress or the courts, it would mean the "danger of degrading or even destroying the Presidency" and constitute a betrayal of his "successors for all time to come." The republic, Professor Black said, could not even risk diluting the "symbolism" of the office lest that disturb "in the most dangerous way the balance of the best government yet devised on earth"; and it almost seemed that he would rather suppress the truth than jeopardize the symbolism.

Executive privilege was not the issue. No Presidents cherished the Presidency more than, say, Jackson or Polk; but both readily conceded to Congress the right in cases of malversation to penetrate into the most secret recesses of the executive department. Nor, in the longer run, did either [Sam] Ervin's [Chairman of the Senate Watergate committee] hope of presidential subordination or Black's fantasy of presidential collapse have real substance. For the Presidency, though its wings could be clipped for a time, was an exceedingly tough institution. Its primacy was founded in the necessities of the American political order. It had endured many challenges and survived many vicissitudes. It was nonsense to suppose that its fate as an institution was bound up with the fate of the particular man who happened to be President at any given time. In the end power in the American order was bound to flow back to the Presidency.

Congress had a marvelous, if generally unfulfilled, capacity for oversight, for advice, for constraint, for chastening the Presidency and informing the people. When it really wanted to say No to a President, it had ample means of doing so; and in due course the President would have no choice but to acquiesce. But its purpose was, as Wilson said, "watchful criticism, talk that should bring to light the whole intention of the government and apprise those who conducted it of the real feeling and desire of the nation . . . in order that nothing which contravened the common understanding should be let pass without comment or structure, in order that measures should be insisted on which the nation needed, and measures resisted which the nation did not need or might take harm from." It was inherently incapable of conducting government and providing national leadership. Its fragmentation, its chronic fear of responsibility, its habitual dependence on the executive for ideas, information and favors—this was life insurance for the Presidency.

Both Nixon and Ervin were wrong in supposing that the matter could be settled by shifting the balance of power in a decisive way to one branch or the other. The answer lay rather in preserving fluidity and re-establishing comity. Indeed, for most people—here Ervin was a distinguished exception—the constitutional and institutional issues were make-believe. It was largely a matter, as Averell Harriman said, "of whose ox is getting gored: who is in or out of power, and what actions either side may want." When

Nixon was in the opposition, there had been no more earnest critic of presidential presumption. Each side dressed its arguments in grand constitutional and institutional terms, but their contention was like that of the two drunken men described long ago by Lincoln who got into a fight with their greatcoats on until each fought himself out of his own coat and into the coat of the other. To aficionados of constitutional controversy, this doubtless seemed reductionism; but history, in this case as in the case of the war-making power, sustained the proposition. Neutral principles! Neutral principles!

The supreme neutral principle, as vital in domestic policy as in foreign policy, was that all great decisions of the government must be shared decisions. The subsidiary principle was that, if the Presidency tried to transform what the Constitution saw as concurrent into exclusive authority, it must be stopped; and, if Congress tried to transform concurrent into exclusive authority, it must be stopped too. If either the Presidency or Congress turned against the complex balance of constitutional powers that had left room over many generations for mutual accommodation, then the ensuing collision would harm both branches of government and the republic as well. Even together Congress and the Presidency were by no means infallible; but their shared decisions, wise or foolish, at least met the standards of democracy. And, shared, the decisions were more likely to be wise than foolish. "I never came out of a committee meeting or a conference," Wilson once said, "without seeing more of the question that was under discussion than I had seen when I went in. And that to my mind is an image of government." He summed up the essential spirit of the constitutional republic: "The whole purpose of democracy is that we may hold counsel with one another, so as not to depend upon the understanding of one man, but to depend upon the counsel of all."

Easier to say than to do, of course, as Wilson's subsequent career attested. All Presidents affected a belief in common counsel, but most after a time preferred to make other arrangements. Still, the idea was right, and the process of accountability had to begin inside the President himself. A constitutional President could do many things, but he had to believe in the discipline of consent. It was not enough that he personally thought the country in trouble and genuinely believed he alone knew how to save it. In all but the most extreme cases, action had to be accompanied by public explanation and tested by public acceptance. A constitutional President had to be aware of what Whitman called "the never-ending audacity of elected persons" and had to understand the legitimacy of challenges to his own judgment and authority. He had to be sensitive directly to the diversity of concern and conviction in the nation, sensitive prospectively to the verdict of history, sensitive always to the decent respect pledged in the Declaration of Independence to the opinions of mankind.

Yet Presidents chosen as open and modest men were

not sure to remain so amid the intoxications of the office; and the office grew steadily more intoxicating in the later twentieth century. A wise President, having read George Reedy and observed the fates of Johnson and Nixon, would take care to provide himself, while there still was time, with passports to reality. Presidents in the last quarter of the twentieth century might, as a beginning, plan to rehabilitate (I use the word in almost the Soviet sense) the executive branch of government. This does not mean the capitulation of the Presidency to the permanent government; nor should anyone forget that it was the unresponsiveness of the permanent government that gave rise to the aggressive White House of the twentieth century. But it does mean a reduction in the size and power of the White House staff and the restoration of the access and prestige of the executive departments. The President will always need a small and alert personal staff to serve as his eyes and ears and one lobe of his brain, but he must avoid a vast and possessive staff ambitious to make all the decisions of government. Above all, he must not make himself the prisoner of a single information system. No sensible President should give one man control of all the channels of communication; any man sufficiently wise to exercise such control properly ought to be President himself.

As for the cabinet, while no President in American history has found it a very satisfactory instrument of government, it has served Presidents best when it has contained men strong and independent in their own right, strong enough to make the permanent government responsive to presidential policy and independent enough to carry honest dissents into the Oval Office, even on questions apart from their departmental jurisdictions. Here again, Franklin Roosevelt, instead of being the cause of it all, was really a model of how a strong President fitted the cabinet into the constitutional order. In his first term he recognized that his reform program needed support from the progressive wings of both parties. Accordingly he brought two progressive Republicans, Wallace and Ickes, into his cabinet and took special care to work with progressive Republicans in Congress. Toward the end of his second term Roosevelt saw that foreign policy posed a different set of political problems. He now reorganized his cabinet to include internationalist Republicans like Stimson and Knox. In this way FDR gained some of the objectives and advantages of cabinet government, using the cabinet both to broaden his base of support and to reassure the people that there was no risk of his taking momentous decisions without the counsel of men in whom the nation reposed trust. His idea of government was to gather round him independent and opinionated men and, up to a point, give them their head.

While no President wants to create the impression that his administration is out of control, FDR showed how a masterful President could maintain the most divergent range of contacts, surround himself with the most articulate and positive colleagues and use debate within the executive branch as a means of clarifying issues and trying out people and policies. Or perhaps FDR was in a way the cause of it all, because he alone had the vitality, flair and cunning to be clearly on top without repressing everything underneath. In a joke Henry Wallace, not usually a humorous man, told in my hearing in 1943, FDR could keep all the balls in the air without losing his own. Some of his successors tried to imitate his mastery without understanding the sources of his strength.

But not every President is an FDR, and FDR himself, though his better instincts generally won out in the end, was a flawed, willful and, with time, increasingly arbitrary man. When Presidents begin to succumb to delusions of grandeur, when the checks and balances inside themselves stop operating, external checks and balances may well become necessary to save the republic. The nature of an activist President in any case, in Sam Lubell's phrase, was to run with the ball until he was tackled. As conditions abroad and at home nourished the imperial Presidency, tacklers had to be more than usually sturdy and intrepid.

How to make external checks effective? Congress could tie the Presidency down by a thousand small legal strings, but, like Gulliver and the Lilliputians, the President could always break loose. The effective means of controlling the Presidency lay less in law than in politics. For the American President ruled by influence; and the withdrawal of consent, by Congress, by the press, by public opinion, could bring any President down. The great Presidents understood this. The President, said Andrew Jackson, must be "accountable at the bar of public opinion for every act of his Administration." "I have a very definite philosophy about the Presidency," said Theodore Roosevelt. "I think it should be a very powerful office, and I think the President should be a very strong man who uses without hesitation every power that the position yields; but because of this fact I believe that he should be sharply watched by the people [and] held to a strict accountability by them."

Holding a President to strict accountability required, first of all, a new attitude on the part of the American people toward their Presidents, or rather a return to the more skeptical attitude of earlier times: it required, specifically, a decline in reverence. An insistent theme in Nixon's public discourse was the necessity of maintaining due respect for the Presidency. The possibility that such respect might be achieved simply by being a good President evidently did not reassure him. He was preoccupied with 'respect for the office' as an entity in itself. Can one imagine Washington or Lincoln or the Roosevelts or Truman or Kennedy going on in public, as Nixon repeatedly did, about how important it was to do this or that in order to maintain 'respect for the office'? But the age of the imperial Presidency had in time produced the idea that run-of-the-mill politicians, brought by fortuity to the White House, must be treated thereafter as if they had become superior and perhaps god-like beings.

The Nixon theoreticians even tried to transform reverence into an ideology, propagating the doctrine, rather novel in the United States, that institutions of authority were entitled to respect *per se*, whether or not they had done anything to earn respect. If authority were denied respect, the syllogism ran, the whole social order would be in danger. "Your task, then, is clear," my friend Pat Moynihan charged his President in 1969: "To restore the authority of American institutions." But should institutions expect obedience they do not, on their record of performance, deserve? To this question the Nixon ideologues apparently answered yes. An older American tradition would say no, incredulous that anyone would see this as a question. In that spirit I would argue that what the country needs today is a little serious disrespect for the office of the Presidency; a refusal to give any more weight to a President's words than the intelligence of the utterance, if spoken by anyone else, would command; an understanding of the point made so aptly by Montaigne: "Sit he on never so high a throne, a man still sits on his own bottom."

And what if men not open and modest, even at the start, but from the start ambitious of power and contemptuous of law reached the place once occupied by Washington and Lincoln? What if neither personal character, nor the play of politics, nor the Constitution itself availed to hold a President to strict accountability? In the end, the way to control the Presidency might have to be not in many little ways but in one large way. In the end, there remained, as Madison said, the decisive engine of impeachment.

Questions

1. Why does Schlesinger think Americans should show less reverence for the presidency?
2. How did the Nixon administration react to the threat presented by a skeptical public?
3. According to Schlesinger, what is the ultimate defense against a renegade president?

32-4 Consumer Energy Prices, 1960–1990

After more than two decades of low inflation, consumer prices—led by dramatic increases in the price of oil—rose sharply in the 1970s (see text pp. 996–997). High oil prices and the expectation that they would remain high fueled a construction boom in Houston, Denver, and other centers of the U.S. petroleum industry through the early 1980s. These cities would be among the hardest hit by the economic hard times of the late 1980s and early 1990s.

Source: U.S. Bureau of the Census, *Statistical Abstract of the United States 1991*, 111th ed. (Washington, D.C.: U.S. Government Printing Office, 1991), p. 478.

Questions

1. In which years did the increase in energy prices significantly outstrip the rise in consumer prices generally?
2. In which years was the rise in energy prices less than the increase in overall consumer prices? What do you think the benefits and/or disadvantages of comparatively low energy prices have been?
3. Examine the level and trend of energy and overall consumer prices in the presidential election years 1968, 1972, 1976, and 1980. Is there any correlation between high inflation and the defeat of the incumbent president?

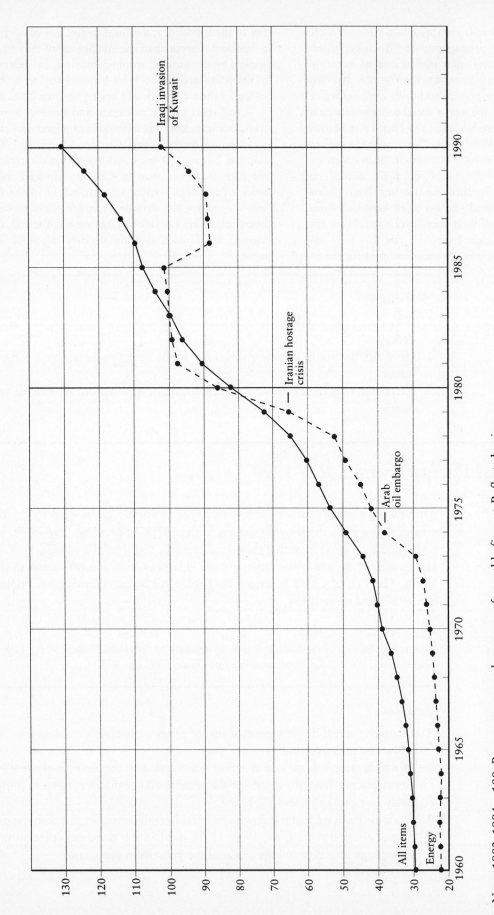

CONSUMER PRICE INDEXES: ALL ITEMS AND ENERGY, 1960–1990

Note: 1982–1984 = 100. Represents annual averages of monthly figures. Reflects buying patterns of all urban consumers.

32-5 *Homestead*

William Serrin   Homestead, Pennsylvania, was a hardscrabble community that owed much of its existence to the steel industry (see text pp. 998–999). The Homestead Works opened in 1881 and remained in operation for the next 105 years. William Serrin found the story of the people, place, and industry so compelling that he left the *New York Times* to write it.

Source: From *Homestead: The Glory and Tragedy of an American Steel Town* by William Serrin, pp. 392–398. Copyright © 1992 by William Serrin. Reprinted by permission of Times Books, a division of Random House, Inc.

II

Eighth Avenue continued to run down, and now the once-bustling street was a tatterdemalion thoroughfare made up of the few old stores that were hanging on and the Goodwill, Salvation Army, and Saint Vincent de Paul thrift shops. One of Chief Kelly's last fights had been to attempt to persuade the managers of the thrift shops to stop putting their collections of junk—worn-out toys, skates, sleds, books, kitchenware, clothes, shoes—on the sidewalk. He was not successful. But there was little market for such items. In the end, even Goodwill closed, and the windows were boarded up with plywood.

The borough building, constructed in 1909, the place where Mother Jones had been jailed and Frances Perkins had been refused permission by Burgess Cavanaugh to speak in Frick Park, was also closed. The building had not been maintained and was getting run-down. One day Chief Kelly was going down to the basement. A rotten step gave way, and he fell and wrenched his ankle. He was on crutches for several days. A half-dozen people who worked there came down with cancer, and it was thought that the building contained some carcinogen—asbestos perhaps—although this was never proven. Council meetings were moved to the old high school. The fire department was moved to a garage across the street, and the police department was moved into the old post office, which the country [sic] remodeled for the borough in exchange for the borough's agreeing to house a number of work-release prisoners in the building.

In June 1990, Saint Mary Magdalene's School closed. It was the last Roman Catholic school in Homestead. In the fall, it would have begun its one hundredth year. The students knew that they would miss their school enormously. "Everybody cares about you," Jackie Piskor said. "If you have a problem, you can go to any of the teachers, and they will help you, or to your friends, and they will help you." The students, even at their young age, knew that hard times had fastened on Homestead. They could not go across the street to play in Frick Park because they feared they would be bullied. There were often drugs being sold there, they said. Even Saint Mary Magdalene's Roman Catholic Church was locked, day and night.

Most of the students were enrolling in public schools. They said that they would especially miss their prayers. "How many times a day do you pray?" I asked. They counted the prayers, some using their fingers. "Seven," they said. The last day, the children came for half a day, and there was much crying in the halls and on the asphalt playground. A second-grade teacher, Nancy Stanich, tearfully embraced her students. Dave Lasos, a seventh grader, sat disconsolately in the hall, his head buried in his arms. Sister Marie Margaret, the principal, said "We have met our Waterloo."

The town government continued to face enormous problems. The borough's deficit increased from $30,000 in 1989 to $300,000 in 1990, and the population continued to fall. It was 4,179 in the 1990 census, down 17.9 percent from 5,092 in 1980. In 1988, the corporation sold the Homestead Works to the Park Corporation for $14 million—$2.5 million for the land and $11.5 million for the equipment and machinery. Soon, demolition crews arrived, and one by one the old mills came down. For a time, Mayor Simko continued to believe that the Valley Machine Shop would be purchased from Park and reopened, but the letter of intent that he had been expecting the day we had toured the works had not come through. The investors said that reopening the mill would not be feasible, in view of the depressed condition of the steel industry.

In 1990, Allegheny County reduced the assessed value of the mill site from $30 million to $14 million. In November, Homestead, Munhall, West Homestead, and the Steel Valley School District reached an agreement with Park to reduce the assessed value of the site from $14 million to $9.5 million. The agreement entitled Park to a refund on 1989 real estate taxes of $67,000 from the boroughs and $45,500 from the school district, which Park agreed to apply to future tax bills.

The town had become a place for small-time speculators. Wayne Laux, a man whom almost no one in Homestead knew anything about, began to buy buildings near the mill site—including the one that had housed Rufus "Sonnyman" Jackson's Skyrocket Lounge and Manhattan Music Club—and then sold them to Park. Many were demolished. Half a century after the demolition that had preceded the wartime expansion of the works, lower Homestead was again being razed.

The corporation and the union continued the missteps that had helped to bring about their downfall. In June 1990, the corporation agreed to pay $34 million in costs and penalties for the cleanup of waste water that had been illegally dumped into the Calumet River, in Indiana, by its Gary plant. In September 1990, a federal district court judge in Birmingham, Alabama, fined the corporation $4.1 million and gave prison terms to two union officials, Thermon Phillips and E. B. Rich, found guilty of conspiring with the corporation to obtain lucrative pensions for themselves in exchange for agreeing to concessions during contract negotiations in December 1983. This was the agreement that the corporation had used to persuade local unions across the country to grant similar concessions. In December 1990, the corporation agreed to pay a $3.2 million fine levied by the Occupational Safety and Health Administration for hundreds of violations the administration said had occurred at its Pennsylvania plants.

The corporation's interest in steel continued to shrink. In early 1991, its steel operations became an independent subsidiary. In May, its stock was split into two—one for energy, one for steel—and the steel stock was dropped from the Dow Jones Industrial Average and replaced by the stock of the Walt Disney Company.

By this time, the national union's membership had dropped to 490,000, one-third of the 1.4 million who had belonged in 1979. In 1991, a plan to organize white-collar workers was announced, and a woman organizer with substantial experience in the field was hired. But the effort failed.

III

The local union meetings continued until the summer of 1987, and the union hall remained open after that to assist laid-off workers. No dues had come in from Homestead since the mill had been closed, and the national union had been helping the local with its bills. But the bad blood between the national union leaders and Weisen had continued, and finally the union saw an opportunity to close the hall. In December, Weisen had gone to the Soviet Union with his wife and their son Bobby for an operation on the broken vertebra in Bobby's neck. A drive to raise money for the trip had been started by Weisen's old supporters, but everyone wanted Bobby to get well, and Lynn Williams, the new president of the national union, stopped by the Weisens' home to give them a thousand dollars.

In February 1988, while Weisen was still in the Soviet Union, the national union ordered the Homestead union

hall closed. Mike Stout, the grievance man, was furious, and to keep him quiet the union reluctantly allowed him to set up a local headquarters in an empty, ramshackle orange building, once a restaurant, on McClure Street, at the top of the hill. He put a sign on the door of the old hall that said: "The international has shut our union hall down and moved us to a storefront on the corner of Seventeenth Street and McClure Street (orange building). We should have the same number, but if you have any problems with TRA or SUB [Training and Relocation Allowance and Supplemental Unemployment Benefits], call me at home."

The orange building was run-down and hot and stuffy. There was no longer much spirit among the men who sat there in front of fans at desks trucked up from the old union hall. The place smelled like old hamburgers and french fries. Occasionally, unemployed workers came by for assistance, but soon they stopped coming. Not even Weisen came by much anymore. He was unemployed, like most others, and was looking for work. In November 1988 the orange building was closed. There had been eight union lodges in Homestead at the time of the 1892 strike. An Amalgamated Association lodge, the Spirit of Ninety-two, had been established in Homestead with the passage of the National Industrial Recovery Act, in June 1933. The steelworkers' union had had a local in Homestead since 1936, for more than half a century. Now there was no union in Homestead.

IV

Most of the men who lost their jobs when the mill went down accepted their fate and settled in, living on part-time work or on pensions. Many had trouble sleeping and finding things to do with the time on their hands. They dropped children or grandchildren off at school, helped around the house, worked on the lawn. After a time, their wives and children got used to having them around. Sometimes the men drove down by the works and watched the demolition crews taking it down. The men would have reunions at one of the firehouses or social clubs, but those were not much fun. One by one they stopped going, and soon no one planned reunions anymore.

"I still think about that damn place," Bob Krovocheck said. He had worked in the mill for thirty-eight years and was fifty-six years old when he lost his job. His highest pay was twenty-seven thousand dollars in 1985. He tried working as a janitor for four dollars an hour, but he was overweight and had bad knees, and the work was too demanding, so he had to quit. His wife had been seriously injured in an automobile accident on the Pennsylvania Turnpike in 1981, and he spent much of his time taking care of her. They lived on his pension of $1,100 a month, $876 after taxes and medical deductions.

Krovocheck missed the mill enormously. "I dream about it every once in a while," he said. "I miss going to work, being around the guys, the eight-hour turn, the routine. I miss the money, too. It was a good living. I wasn't living from payday to payday. It's funny. I remember that every once in a while one of us in the mill would say, 'Let's get our pension and get out of here.' But pensioneering ain't all that great, especially if you've got somebody sick you're taking care of.

"During the day, I take care of the wife, get the meals, keep the house halfway decent. It ain't like she would keep it. I do the cooking and laundry. I read quite a bit. I go up the street and have a couple of beers. I go to the store and get the groceries. I come home and make supper. I watch TV. I go to bed. I get rather depressed, especially when I drive up past where we worked, the structural mill. I'm okay, if you want to call me okay."

Richard Holoman, a craneman, had worked in the mill for thirty-two years and was fifty-one when he lost his job. His highest pay was $22,500 a year. After the mill went down, he had a job as a security guard for three months and worked for a short time cleaning an industrial garage, three and a half hours a night, for fourteen dollars a night. Then he got a job as a janitor at Saint Agnes's Roman Catholic Church, in West Mifflin. He changed light bulbs, mopped floors, cut the grass, fixed the sisters' car. It wasn't bad, as work goes. He could set his own hours, but mostly he worked 6:00 A.M. to 2:00 P.M., five days a week—good hours for an old steelworker, steady daylight.

Denny Wilcox, a roller, got a part-time job as a bank courier, twenty-five hours a week at $6.10 an hour. He received a pension of $1,100 a month. "We're not living high off the hog, but we're making it," he said. "It's hard. You start looking down on yourself. You'd think, if you put on an application that you have thirty five years of service, an employer would know that you are dedicated. You'd think they'd grab you in a minute. But they discriminate against you because of age. They all do. I think that's why I'm not full-time now, because they discriminate because of age. They know I get a pension."

Ray McGuire, a repairman, had worked in the mill for thirty-six years and had taken only two sick days. He got a pension of $1,000 a month and caught on as an electrician, going from one shop to another, wherever he was needed. Sometimes a temporary agency found him work, or else he would hear of something himself. He worked for a while at the machine company that now occupied part of the old Mesta Machine plant. One day he had to go to the Homestead Works to pick up some tools. "I went to the exact place where I worked, and I got so nauseated I thought I was going to throw up," he said. "I thought: 'I worked here. What are you people doing to this place? What are you doing to my cranes?' And then I thought: 'Wait a minute. This wasn't my place. These weren't my cranes.' But that's the way I thought—that it was my place." He lived in Pleasant Hills, not far from Homestead, but he no longer went to Homestead at night. He was afraid of crime

there, and besides, he got despondent when he went to Homestead, even when he just drove through the town. "The place looks like a morgue," he said.

Bob Todd, a craneman and grievance man, was unemployed for a year. Then he was called to the Edgar Thomson Works, where he got a job as a safety man in the slab mill, making seventeen thousand dollars a year. It was not as much as he had been making at Homestead, but it was a job. About two hundred Homestead workers were given jobs there, and another few dozen were hired by the Irvin Works.

Bill Brennan, a millwright, had worked in the mill for thirty-nine years and was sixty-four when he retired on his pension of $775 a month after deductions. He also got Social Security, and his house was paid for. His father had worked at the Homestead Works, and so had his three brothers. In 1984, when he had a heart-bypass operation, he was on sickleave for six months. His heart was now okay, though he had to take three pills a day. When he went back into the mill after his bypass, the other millwrights carried him, hid him out, for six months—they did the heavy work that he had done and did not tell the supervisors. He would pick up a sledgehammer or a big crescent wrench, and the others would take it from him and tell him to go somewhere, get lost, and they would do the job. "I miss guys like that, good working people," he said.

Bobby Schneider, a roller, got a part-time job tending bar at the Slovak Club in Munhall. He had worked in the mill for thirty-one years and had earned $35,000 in his best year. The bartender's job wasn't much, though it got him out of the house and gave him something to do. He lived on a pension check of $1,077 a month after deductions. His wife worked as a secretary in a real-estate company. His section of the last beam rolled at the Homestead Works was still in the trunk of his car, four years after the mill went down. He had intended to shine it up and put it in the house, but he never got around to it. His two pals, Red Hrabic and Jimmie Sherlock, both lived on pensions of about $900 a month and were doing okay. The three of them met at Hess's Bar in Hunkie Hollow almost every afternoon at about four, or maybe at the Slovak Club, in Munhall, if Schneider was tending bar there.

There was much crying in Homestead. Men and women often went to wakes and funerals, for there were many deaths among the men from the works. I knew or heard of three dozen men who died or committed suicide. That's a lot of men gone, and at an early age, too. I think that many of them died because the mill closed, though I can't prove it. But it's a lot of dead guys, isn't it?

There was one man I never got out of my mind—Rich Locheer, the hooker from Number Two Structural who had denounced the government's retraining programs at the meeting with the two men in the pinstripe suits from Senator Heinz's staff. I had planned to meet with Locher, but time passed, and I was busy. One winter day, preparing for a trip to Homestead, I wrote down his telephone number, thinking I would go see him. When I got to Homestead, I ran into Mike Stout, the former grievance man. When I told him that I was going to call Locher, he said: "Don't bother. Locher is dead. He finished the retraining program but couldn't get a nursing job, so he took a gun and killed himself—shot half his head away, in his garage." Stout continued with his paperwork and did not look up. One more death was not much to him. He knew too many stories like this.

I liked Locher. He was a good man. He had a temper and often used profane language, but don't many of us? He was an excellent father and husband, and he probably deserved more out of life than to take two brief vacations at hot trailer parks in Virginia and go out to eat once a month at McDonald's or Long John Silver's, to lose his job as a craneman and not get a job as a nurse. One more thing. Locher was right about the training programs. They were bullshit.

Questions

1. How does the plant's closing affect community institutions?
2. Why does the mill exert such a strong influence on its former workers?
3. What program is supposed to help unemployed steelworkers get back into the economy? Why is Serrin so critical of it?

Questions for Further Thought

1. Americans have lost their reverence for the presidency, as Arthur Schlesinger urged (Document 32-3). How has that change affected the American government?
2. Do the excesses of Watergate (Document 32-2) vindicate Barry Goldwater's criticism of big government (Document 30-7)? Why or why not?
3. What, if anything, can the government do to control energy prices and avert plant closings (Documents 32-4 and 32-5)? Keep in mind the international component of each issue.

Social Gridlock: Reform and Reaction in the 1970s and Post-Watergate Politics: Failed Leadership

The energy crisis was not the only challenge to American confidence in the 1970s. As people learned more about the dangers of pesticides and hazardous waste and grew more skeptical about governmental officials, a broad-based environmental movement grew (see text pp. 1000–1001, 1004), often through the efforts of women (Document 32-6). Women failed, however, in their efforts to secure ratification of the Equal Rights Amendment, championed by, among others, Gloria Steinem (Document 32-7).

During the 1970s urban racial conflict intersected with deindustrialization and economic restructuring to produce fiscal crises in many cities (see text pp. 998–999). Partly because of the continuing influence of the counterculture, the 1970s featured a growing emphasis on personal fulfillment (see text pp. 999–1000). The growing social and political conservatism of the decade was manifested by opposition to busing, affirmative action, the Equal Rights Amendment, and abortion (see text pp. 1005–1006). Phyllis Schlafly (see text p. 1006) was an articulate if controversial advocate of these and other causes (Document 32-8).

The nation's leaders were unable to meet all these challenges. Nixon understood

The nation's leaders were unable to meet all these challenges. Nixon understood many of the issues as well as anyone, but his abuse of power had led to his disgrace. Gerald Ford never established himself as an effective leader, partly because Congress was determined to assert its constitutional authority in the aftermath of Watergate (see text p. 1011). Jimmy Carter campaigned for a new open and moral foreign policy but allowed himself to be imprisoned by the Iranian hostage crisis (see text pp. 1011–1014). Carter was no more effective in domestic affairs: unable to find solutions to serious economic and oil supply problems, he decided that the real problem was a national "crisis of confidence" (Document 32-9). The public agreed—and turned to Ronald Reagan (see text pp. 1014–1015 and Document 32-10).

32-6 "And No Birds Sing"

Rachel Carson

The environmental movement of the 1960s and 1970s (see text pp. 1000–1001, 1004) was strongly influenced by the publication of Rachel Carson's *Silent Spring* in 1962. Carson (1907–1964) condemned the notion "that nature exists for the convenience of man" as she detailed the effects of the insecticide DDT on the environment.

Source: Excerpted from Rachel Carson, *Silent Spring* (Boston: Houghton Mifflin, 1962), pp. 103–110.

Over increasingly large areas of the United States, spring now comes unheralded by the return of the birds, and the early mornings are strangely silent where once they were filled with the beauty of bird song. This sudden silencing of the song of birds, this obliteration of the color and beauty and interest they lend to our world have come about swiftly, insidiously, and unnoticed by those whose communities are as yet unaffected.

From the town of Hinsdale, Illinois, a housewife wrote in despair to one of the world's leading ornithologists, Robert Cushman Murphy, Curator Emeritus of Birds at the American Museum of Natural History.

Here in our village the elm trees have been sprayed for several years [she wrote in 1958]. When we moved here six years ago, there was a wealth of bird life; I put up a feeder and had a steady stream of cardinals, chickadees, downies and nuthatches all winter, and the cardinals and chickadees brought their young ones in the summer.

After several years of DDT spray, the town is almost devoid of robins and starlings; chickadees have not been on my shelf for two years, and this year the cardinals are gone too; the nesting population in the neighborhood seems to consist of one dove pair and perhaps one catbird family.

It is hard to explain to the children that the birds have been killed off, when they have learned in school that a Federal law protects the birds from killing or capture. "Will they ever come back?" they ask, and I do not have the answer. The elms are still dying, and so are the birds. *Is* anything being done? *Can* anything be done? Can *I* do anything?

A year after the federal government had launched a massive spraying program against the fire ant, an Alabama woman wrote: "Our place has been a veritable bird sanctuary for over half a century. Last July we all remarked, 'There are more birds than ever.' Then, suddenly, in the second week of August, they all disappeared. I was accustomed to rising early to care for my favorite mare that had a young filly. There was not a sound of the song of a bird. It was eerie, terrifying. What was man doing to our perfect and beautiful world? Finally, five months later a blue jay appeared and a wren." . . .

One story might serve as the tragic symbol of the fate of the birds—a fate that has already overtaken some species, and that threatens all. It is the story of the robin, the bird known to everyone. To millions of Americans, the season's first robin means that the grip of winter is broken. Its coming is an event reported in the newspapers and told eagerly at the breakfast table. And as the number of migrants grows and the first mists of green appear in the woodlands, thousands of people listen for the first dawn chorus of the robins throbbing in the early morning light. But now all is changed, and not even the return of the birds may be taken for granted.

The survival of the robin, and indeed of many other species as well, seems fatefully linked with the American elm, a tree that is part of the history of thousands of towns from the Atlantic to the Rockies, gracing their streets and their village squares and college campuses with majestic archways of green. Now the elms are stricken with a disease that afflicts them throughout their range, a disease so serious that many experts believe all efforts to save the elms will in the end be futile. It would be tragic to lose the elms, but it would be doubly tragic if, in vain efforts to save them, we plunge vast segments of our bird population into the night of extinction. Yet this is precisely what is threatened.

The so-called Dutch elm disease entered the United States from Europe about 1930 in elm burl logs imported for the veneer industry. It is a fungus disease; the organism invades the water-conducting vessels of the tree, spreads by spores carried in the flow of sap, and by its poisonous secretions as well as by mechanical clogging causes the branches to wilt and the tree to die. The disease is spread from diseased to healthy trees by elm bark beetles. The galleries which the insects have tunneled out under the bark of dead trees become contaminated with spores of the invading fungus, and the spores adhere to the insect body and are carried wherever the beetle flies. Efforts to control the fungus disease of the elms have been directed largely toward control of the carrier insect. In community after community, especially throughout the strongholds of the American elm, the Midwest and New England, intensive spraying has become a routine procedure.

What this spraying could mean to bird life, and especially to the robin, was first made clear by the work of two ornithologists at Michigan State University, Professor George Wallace and one of his graduate students, John Mehner. When Mr. Mehner began work for the doctorate in 1954, he chose a research project that had to do with robin populations. This was quite by chance, for at that time no one suspected that the robins were in danger. But even as he undertook the work, events occurred that were to change its character and indeed to deprive him of his material. . . .

During 1954, the year of the first light spraying, all seemed well. The following spring the migrating robins began to return to the campus as usual. Like the bluebells in Tomlinson's haunting essay "The Lost Wood," they were "expecting no evil" as they reoccupied their familiar territories. But soon it became evident that something was wrong. Dead and dying robins began to appear on the campus. Few birds were seen in their normal foraging activities or assembling in their usual roosts. Few nests were built; few young appeared. The pattern was repeated with monotonous regularity in succeeding springs. The sprayed area had become a lethal trap in which each wave of migrating robins would be eliminated in about a week. Then new arrivals would come in, only to add to the numbers of doomed birds seen on the campus in the agonized tremors that precede death.

"The campus is serving as a graveyard for most of the robins that attempt to take up residence in the spring," said Dr. Wallace. But why? At first he suspected some disease of the nervous system, but soon it became evident that

"in spite of the assurances of the insecticide people that their sprays were 'harmless to birds' the robins were really dying of insecticidal poisoning; they exhibited the well-known symptoms of loss of balance, followed by tremors, convulsions, and death."

Several facts suggested that the robins were being poisoned, not so much by direct contact with the insecticides as indirectly, by eating earthworms. Campus earthworms had been fed inadvertently to crayfish in a research project and all the crayfish had promptly died. A snake kept in the laboratory cage had gone into violent tremors after being fed such worms. And earthworms are the principal food of robins in the spring.

A key piece in the jigsaw puzzle of the doomed robins was soon to be supplied by Dr. Roy Barker of the Illinois Natural History Survey at Urbana. Dr. Barker's work, published in 1958, traced the intricate cycle of events by which the robins' fate is linked to the elm trees by way of the earthworms. The trees are sprayed in the spring (usually at the rate of 2 to 5 pounds of DDT per 50-foot tree, which may be the equivalent of as much as *23 pounds per acre* where elms are numerous) and often again in July, at about half this concentration. Powerful sprayers direct a stream of poison to all parts of the tallest trees, killing directly not only the target organism, the bark beetle, but other insects, including pollinating species and predatory spiders and beetles. The poison forms a tenacious film over the leaves and bark. Rains do not wash it away. In the autumn the leaves fall to the ground, accumulate in sodden layers, and begin the slow process of becoming one with the soil. In this they are aided by the toil of the earthworms, who feed in the leaf litter, for elm leaves are among their favorite foods. In feeding on the leaves the worms also swallow the insecticide, accumulating and concentrating it in their bodies. Dr. Barker found deposits of DDT throughout the digestive tracts of the worms, their blood vessels, nerves, and body wall. Undoubtedly some of the earthworms themselves succumb, but others survive to become "biological magnifiers" of the poison. In the spring the robins return to provide another link in the cycle. As few as 11 large earthworms can transfer a lethal dose of DDT to a robin. And 11 worms form a small part of a day's rations to a bird that eats 10 to 12 earthworms in as many minutes.

Not all robins receive a lethal dose, but another consequence may lead to the extinction of their kind as surely as fatal poisoning. The shadow of sterility lies over all the bird studies and indeed lengthens to include all living things within its potential range. There are now only two or three dozen robins to be found each spring on the entire 185-acre campus of Michigan State University, compared with a conservatively estimated 370 adults in this area before spraying. In 1954 every robin nest under observation by Mehner produced young. Toward the end of June, 1957, when at least 370 young birds (the normal replacement of the adult population) would have been foraging over the campus in the years before spraying began,

Mehner could find *only one young robin*. A year later Dr. Wallace was to report: "At no time during the spring or summer [of 1958] did I see a fledgling robin anywhere on the main campus, and so far I have failed to find anyone else who has seen one there."

Part of this failure to produce young is due, of course, to the fact that one or more of a pair of robins dies before the nesting cycle is completed. But Wallace has significant records which point to something more sinister—the actual destruction of the birds' capacity to reproduce. He has, for example, "records of robins and other birds building nests but laying no eggs, and others laying eggs and incubating them but not hatching them. We have one record of a robin that sat on its eggs faithfully for 21 days and they did not hatch. The normal incubation period is 13 days . . . Our analyses are showing high concentrations of DDT in the testes and ovaries of breeding birds," he told a congressional committee in 1960. "Ten males had amounts ranging from 30 to 109 parts per million in the testes, and two females had 151 and 211 parts per million respectively in the egg follicles in their ovaries."

Soon studies in other areas began to develop findings equally dismal. Professor Joseph Hickey and his students at the University of Wisconsin, after careful comparative studies of sprayed and unsprayed areas, reported the robin mortality to be at least 86 to 88 per cent. The Cranbrook Institute of Science at Bloomfield Hills, Michigan, in an effort to assess the extent of bird loss caused by the spraying of the elms, asked in 1956 that all birds thought to be victims of DDT poisoning be turned in to the institute for examination. The request had a response beyond all expectations. Within a few weeks the deep-freeze facilities of the institute were taxed to capacity, so that other specimens had to be refused. By 1959 a thousand poisoned birds from this single community had been turned in or reported. Although the robin was the chief victim (one woman calling the institute reported 12 robins lying dead on her lawn as she spoke), 63 different species were included among the specimens examined at the institute.

The robins, then, are only one part of the chain of devastation linked to the spraying of the elms, even as the elm program is only one of the multitudinous spray programs that cover our land with poisons. Heavy mortality has occurred among about 90 species of birds, including those most familiar to suburbanites and amateur naturalists. The populations of nesting birds in general have declined as much as 90 per cent in some of the sprayed towns. . . .

It is only reasonable to suppose that all birds and mammals heavily dependent on earthworms or other soil organisms for food are threatened by the robins' fate. Some 45 species of birds include earthworms in their diet. Among them is the woodcock, a species that winters in southern areas recently heavily sprayed with heptachlor. Two significant discoveries have now been made about the woodcock. Production of young birds on the New Brunswick breeding grounds is definitely reduced, and adult birds that have been analyzed contain large residues of DDT and heptachlor.

Already there are disturbing records of heavy mortality among more than 20 other species of ground-feeding birds whose food—worms, ants, grubs, or other soil organisms—has been poisoned. These include three of the thrushes whose songs are among the most exquisite of bird voices, the olive-backed, the wood, and the hermit. And the sparrows that flit through the shrubby understory of the woodlands and forage with rustling sounds amid the fallen leaves—the song sparrow and the white-throat—these, too, have been found among the victims of the elm sprays.

Questions

1. Why is Carson's opening sentence particularly effective?
2. What is the connection between Dutch elm disease and the poisoning of robins?
3. How does Carson use the robins' plight as a metaphor?

32-7   Statement in Support of the Equal Rights Amendment (1970)

Gloria Steinem

In 1972 Gloria Steinem and other journalists founded *Ms.* magazine, which became the most successful mass-circulation feminist publication. She is an acknowledged leader of the modern feminist movement. Her testimony to the Senate Subcommittee on Constitutional Amendments, given in support of the Equal Rights Amendment (see text p. 972), includes the major tenets of the feminist position.

Source: U.S. Congress, Senate, *The Equal Rights Amendment: Hearings Before the Subcommittee on Constitutional Amendments of the Committee on the Judiciary*, 91st Cong., 2d. sess., 1970.

During 12 years of working for a living, I have experienced much of the legal and social discrimination reserved for women in this country. I have been refused service in public restaurants, ordered out of public gathering places, and turned away from apartment rentals; all for the clearly-stated, sole reason that I am a woman. And all without the legal remedies available to blacks and other minorities. I have been excluded from professional groups, writing assignments on so-called "unfeminine" subjects such as politics, full participation in the Democratic Party, jury duty, and even from such small male privileges as discounts on airline fares. Most important to me, I have been denied a society in which women are encouraged, or even allowed to think of themselves as first-class citizens and responsible human beings.

However, after 2 years of researching the status of American women, I have discovered that in reality, I am very, very lucky. Most women, both wage-earners and housewives, routinely suffer more humiliation and injustice than I do.

As a freelance writer, I don't work in the male-dominated hierarchy of an office. (Women, like blacks and other visibly different minorities, do better in individual professions such as the arts, sports, or domestic work; anything in which they don't have authority over white males.) I am not one of the millions of women who must support a family. Therefore, I haven't had to go on welfare because there are no day-care centers for my children while I work, and I haven't had to submit to the humiliating welfare inquiries about my private and sexual life, inquiries from which men are exempt. I haven't had to brave the sex bias of labor unions and employers, only to see my family subsist on a median salary 40 percent less than the male median salary.

I hope this committee will hear the personal, daily injustices suffered by many women—professionals and day laborers, women house-bound by welfare as well as by suburbia. We have all been silent for too long. But we won't be silent anymore.

The truth is that all our problems stem from the same sex based myths. We may appear before you as white radicals or the middle-aged middle class or black soul sisters, but we are all sisters in fighting against these outdated myths. Like racial myths, they have been reflected in our laws. Let me list a few.

That women are biologically inferior to men. In fact, an equally good case can be made for the reverse. Women live longer than men, even when the men are not subject to business pressures. Women survived Nazi concentration camps better, keep cooler heads in emergencies currently studied by disaster-researchers, are protected against heart attacks by their female sex hormones, and are so much more durable at every stage of life that nature must conceive 20 to 50 percent more males in order to keep the balance going.

Man's hunting activities are forever being pointed to as tribal proof of superiority. But while he was hunting, women built houses, tilled the fields, developed animal husbandry, and perfected language. Men, being all alone in the bush, often developed into a creature as strong as women, fleeter of foot, but not very bright.

However, I don't want to prove the superiority of one sex to another. That would only be repeating a male mistake. English scientists once definitively proved, after all, that the English were descended from the angels, while the Irish were descended from the apes; it was the rationale for England's domination of Ireland for more than a century. The point is that science is used to support current myth and economics almost as much as the church was.

What we do know is that the difference between two races or two sexes is much smaller than the differences to be found within each group. Therefore, in spite of the slide show on female inferiorities that I understand was shown to you yesterday, the law makes much more sense when it treats individuals, not groups bundled together by some condition of birth. . . .

Another myth, that women are already treated equally in this society. I am sure there has been ample testimony to prove that equal pay for equal work, equal chance for advancement, and equal training or encouragement is obscenely scarce in every field, even those—like food and fashion industries—that are supposedly "feminine."

A deeper result of social and legal injustice, however, is what sociologists refer to as "Internalized Aggression." Victims of aggression absorb the myth of their own inferiority, and come to believe that their group is in fact second class. Even when they themselves realize they are not second class, they may still think their group is, thus the tendency to be the only Jew in the club, the only black woman on the block, the only woman in the office.

Women suffer this second class treatment from the moment they are born. They are expected to be, rather than achieve, to function biologically rather than learn. A brother, whatever his intellect, is more likely to get the family's encouragement and education money, while girls are often pressured to conceal ambition and intelligence, to "Uncle Tom."

I interviewed a New York public school teacher who told me about a black teenager's desire to be a doctor. With all the barriers in mind, she suggested kindly that he be a veterinarian instead.

The same day, a high school teacher mentioned a girl who wanted to be a doctor. The teacher said, "How about a nurse?"

Teachers, parents, and the Supreme Court may exude a protective, well-meaning rationale, but limiting the individual's ambition is doing no one a favor. Certainly not this country; it needs all the talent it can get.

Another myth, that American women hold great economic power. Fifty-one percent of all shareholders in this country are women. That is a favorite male-chauvinist statistic. However, the number of shares they hold is so small that the total is only 18 percent of all the shares. Even those holdings are often controlled by men.

Similarly, only 5 percent of all the people in the country who receive $10,000 a year or more, earned or otherwise, are women. And that includes the famous rich widows.

The constantly repeated myth of our economic power seems less testimony to our real power than to the resentment of what little power we do have.

Another myth, that children must have full-time mothers. American mothers spend more time with their homes and children than those of any other society we know about. In the past, joint families, servants, a prevalent system in which grandparents raised the children, or family field work in the agrarian systems—all these factors contributed more to child care than the labor-saving devices of which we are so proud.

The truth is that most American children seem to be suffering from too much mother, and too little father. Part of the program of Women's Liberation is a return of fathers to their children. If laws permit women equal work and pay opportunities, men will then be relieved of their role as sole breadwinner. Fewer ulcers, fewer hours of meaningless work, equal responsibility for his own children: these are a few of the reasons that Women's Liberation is Men's Liberation too.

As for psychic health of the children, studies show that the quality of time spent by parents is more important than the quantity. The most damaged children were not those whose mothers worked, but those whose mothers preferred to work but stayed home out of the role-playing desire to be a "good mother."

Another myth, that the women's movement is not political, won't last, or is somehow not "serious."

When black people leave their 19th century roles, they are feared. When women dare to leave theirs, they are ridiculed. We understand this; we accept the burden of ridicule. It won't keep us quiet anymore.

Similarly, it shouldn't deceive male observers into thinking that this is somehow a joke. We are 51 percent of the population; we are essentially united on these issues across boundaries of class or race or age; and we may well end by changing this society more than the civil rights

movement. That is an apt parallel. We, too, have our right wing and left wing, our separatists, gradualists, and Uncle Toms. But we are changing our own consciousness, and that of the country. Engels noted the relationship of the authoritarian, nuclear family to capitalism; the father as capitalist, the mother as means of production, and the children as labor. He said the family would change as the economic system did, and that seems to have happened, whether we want to admit it or not. Women's bodies will no longer be owned by the state for the production of workers and soldiers; birth control and abortion are facts of everyday life. The new family is an egalitarian family.

Gunnar Myrdal noted 30 years ago the parallel between women and Negroes in this country. Both suffered from such restricting social myths as: smaller brains, passive natures, inability to govern themselves (and certainly not white men), sex objects only, childlike natures, special skills, and the like. When evaluating a general statement about women, it might be valuable to substitute "black people" for "women"—just to test the prejudice at work.

And it might be valuable to do this constitutionally as well. Neither group is going to be content as a cheap labor pool anymore. And neither is going to be content without full constitutional rights.

Finally, I would like to say one thing about this time in which I am testifying.

I had deep misgivings about discussing this topic when National Guardsmen are occupying our campuses, the country is being turned against itself in a terrible polarization, and America is enlarging an already inhuman and unjustifiable war. But it seems to me that much of the trouble in this country has to do with the "masculine mystique;" with the myth that masculinity somehow depends on the subjugation of other people. It is a bipartisan problem; both our past and current Presidents seem to be victims of this myth, and to behave accordingly.

Women are not more moral than men. We are only uncorrupted by power. But we do not want to imitate men, to join this country as it is, and I think our very participation will change it. Perhaps women elected leaders—and there will be many of them—will not be so likely to dominate black people or yellow people or men; anybody who looks different from us.

After all, we won't have our masculinity to prove.

Questions

1. What comparisons does Steinem make between women and African-Americans?
2. What arguments involving the family does Steinem indicate were used by ERA opponents? What is Steinem's response to those arguments?
3. According to Steinem, in what ways are women different from men? Why is this significant?

32-8 *The Power of the Positive Woman* (1977)

Phyllis Schlafly

By the late 1970s many Americans had grown frustrated with what seemed to be a constant litany of social criticism. Increasingly, they were attracted to views such as those expressed by the conservative activist Phyllis Schlafly (b. 1924). For Schlafly and others the problem was the critics, not American society (see text pp. 1006–1007).

In the following excerpt, Schlafly outlines what she thinks the women's movement should entail.

Source: Excerpted from Phyllis Schlafly, *The Power of the Positive Woman* (New Rochelle, N.Y.: Arlington House Publishers, 1977), pp. 16–19.

The women's liberationists and their dupes who try to tell each other that the sexual drive of men and women is really the same, and that it is only societal restraints that inhibit women from an equal desire, an equal enjoyment, and an equal freedom from the consequences, are doomed to frustration forever. It just isn't so, and pretending cannot make it so. The differences are not a woman's weakness but her strength. . . .

The new generation can brag all it wants about the new liberation of the new morality, but it is still the woman who is hurt the most. The new morality isn't just a "fad"—it is a cheat and a thief. It robs the woman of her virtue, her youth, her beauty, and her love—for nothing, just nothing. It has produced a generation of young women searching for their identity, bored with sexual freedom, and despondent from the loneliness of living a life without commitment. They have abandoned the old commandments, but they can't find any new rules that work.

The Positive Woman recognizes the fact that, when it comes to sex, women are simply not the equal of men. The sexual drive of men is much stronger than that of women. That is how the human race was designed in order that it might perpetuate itself. The other side of the coin is that it is easier for women to control their sexual appetites. A Positive Woman cannot defeat a man in a wrestling or boxing match, but she can motivate him, inspire him, encourage him, teach him, restrain him, reward him, and have power over him that he can never achieve over her with all his muscle. How or whether a Positive Woman uses her power is determined solely by the way she alone defines her goals and develops her skills.

The differences between men and women are also emotional and psychological. Without woman's innate maternal instinct, the human race would have died out centuries ago. There is nothing so helpless in all earthly life as the newborn infant. It will die within hours if not cared for. Even in the most primitive, uneducated societies, women have always cared for their newborn babies. They didn't need any schooling to teach them how. They didn't need any welfare workers to tell them it is their social obligation. Even in societies to whom such concepts as "ought," "social responsibility," and "compassion for the helpless" were unknown, mothers cared for their new babies.

Why? Because caring for a baby serves the natural maternal need of a woman. Although not nearly so total as the baby's need, the woman's need is nonetheless real.

The overriding psychological need of a woman is to love something alive. A baby fulfills this need in the lives of most women. If a baby is not available to fill that need, women search for a baby-substitute. This is the reason why women have traditionally gone into teaching and nursing careers. They are doing what comes naturally to the female psyche. The schoolchild or the patient of any age provides an outlet for a woman to express her natural maternal need.

This maternal need in women is the reason why mothers whose children have grown up and flown from the nest are sometimes cut loose from their psychological moorings. The maternal need in women can show itself in love for grandchildren, nieces, nephews, or even neighbors' children. The maternal need in some women has even manifested itself in an extraordinary affection lavished on a dog, cat, or a parakeet.

This is not to say that every woman must have a baby in order to be fulfilled. But it is to say that fulfillment for most women involves expressing their natural maternal urge by loving and caring for someone.

The women's liberation movement complains that traditional stereotyped roles assume that women are "passive" and that men are "aggressive." The anomaly is that a woman's most fundamental emotional need is not passive at all, but active. A woman naturally seeks to love affirmatively and to show that love in an active way by caring for the object of her affections.

The Positive Woman finds somebody on whom she can lavish her maternal love so that it doesn't well up inside her and cause psychological frustrations. Surely no woman is so isolated by geography or insulated by spirit that she cannot find someone worthy of her maternal love. All persons, men and women, gain by sharing something of themselves with their fellow humans, but women profit most of all because it is part of their very nature. . . .

Most women's organizations, recognizing the preference of most women to avoid hard-driving competition, handle the matter of succession of officers by the device of a nominating committee. This eliminates the unpleasantness and the tension of a competitive confrontation every year or two. Many women's organizations customarily use a prayer attributed to Mary, Queen of Scots, which is an excellent analysis by a woman of women's faults:

Keep us, O God, from pettiness; let us be large in thought, in word, in deed. Let us be done with fault-finding and leave off self-seeking. . . . Grant that we may realize it is the little things that create differences, that in the big things of life we are at one. . . .

Finally, women are different from men in dealing with the fundamentals of life itself. Men are philosophers, women are practical and 'twas ever thus. Men may philosophize about how life began and where we are heading; women are concerned about feeding the kids today. No woman would ever, as Karl Marx did, spend years reading political philosophy in the British Museum while her child starved to death. Women don't take naturally to a search for the intangible and the abstract. The Positive Woman knows who she is and where she is going, and she will reach her goal because the longest journey starts with a very practical first step.

Questions

1. Why does Phyllis Schlafly refer to psychology in three instances?
2. How does Schlafly compare to reformers such as Frances Willard (Document 19-4) and Jane Addams (Document 21-5)?
3. Does Schlafly see men and women as true equals? Why or why not?

32-9   Jimmy Carter on the National "Crisis of Confidence" (1979)

By the summer of 1979, President Carter and the nation faced a wide range of economic problems, including spiraling inflation and unemployment (see text pp. 1011–1012). International oil prices had risen rapidly after the "oil shock" of 1973, while the output of oil fields in the United States had fallen (see text pp. 996–997). Temporary shortages produced long lines at gasoline stations, and the prices of hydrocarbon fuels—oil, gasoline, and natural gas—rose to new highs. High fuel prices led in turn to higher prices for goods, transportation, and the storage and merchandising of goods. Carter worked hard to find legislative solutions to these problems but was unable to find any that satisfied many members of Congress, and his popularity with the American people fell. In this speech he argues that the problem lies more in a national "crisis of confidence" than in a failure of his leadership.

Source: Public Papers of the Presidents of the United States: Jimmy Carter, 1979 (Washington, D.C.: U.S. Government Printing Office, 1980), pp. 1235–1241.

. . . I want to speak to you first tonight about a subject even more serious than energy or inflation. I want to talk to you right now about a fundamental threat to American democracy.

I do not mean our political and civil liberties. They will endure. And I do not refer to the outward strength of America, a nation that is at peace tonight everywhere in the world, with unmatched economic power and military might.

The threat is nearly invisible in ordinary ways. It is a crisis of confidence. It is a crisis that strikes at the very heart and soul and spirit of our national will. We can see this crisis in the growing doubt about the meaning of our own lives and in the loss of a unity of purpose of our Nation.

The erosion of our confidence in the future is threatening to destroy the social and the political fabric of America.

The confidence that we have always had as a people is not simply some romantic dream or a proverb in a dusty book that we read just on the Fourth of July. It is the idea which founded our Nation and has guided our development as a people. Confidence in the future has supported everything else—public institutions and private enterprise, our own families, and the very Constitution of the United States. Confidence has defined our course and has served as a link between generations. We've always believed in something called progress. We've always had a faith that the days of our children would be better than our own.

Our people are losing that faith, not only in government itself but in the ability as citizens to serve as the ultimate rulers and shapers of our democracy. As a people we know our past and we are proud of it. Our progress has been part of the living history of America, even the world. We always believed that we were part of a great movement of humanity itself called democracy, involved in the search for freedom, and that belief has always strengthened us in our purpose. But just as we are losing our confidence in the future, we are also beginning to close the door on our past.

In a nation that was proud of hard work, strong families, close-knit communities, and our faith in God, too many of us now tend to worship self-indulgence and consumption. Human identity is no longer defined by what one does, but by what one owns. But we've discovered that owning things and consuming things does not satisfy our longing for meaning. We've learned that piling up material goods cannot fill the emptiness of lives which have no confidence or purpose.

The symptoms of this crisis of the American spirit are all around us. For the first time in the history of our country a majority of our people believe that the next 5 years will be worse than the past 5 years. Two-thirds of our people do not even vote. The productivity of American workers is actually dropping, and the willingness of Americans to save for the future has fallen below that of all other people in the Western world.

As you know, there is a growing disrespect for government and for churches and for schools, the news media, and other institutions. This in not a message of happiness or reassurance, but it is the truth and it is a warning.

These changes did not happen overnight. They've come upon us gradually over the last generation, years that were filled with shock and tragedy. We were sure that ours was a nation of the ballot not of the bullet, until the murders of John Kennedy and Robert Kennedy and Martin Luther King, Jr. We were taught that our armies were always invincible and our causes were always just only to suffer the agony of Vietnam. We respected the presidency as a place of honor until the shock of Watergate. . . .

Energy will be the immediate test of our ability to unite this Nation, and it can also be the standard around which we rally. On the battlefield of energy we can win for our Nation a new confidence, and we can seize control again of our common destiny.

In little more than two decades we've gone from a position of energy independence to one in which almost half the oil we use comes from foreign countries, at prices that are going through the roof. Our excessive dependence on OPEC has already taken a tremendous toll on our economy and our people. This is the direct cause of the long lines which have made millions of you spend aggravating hours waiting for gasoline. It's a cause of the increased inflation and unemployment that we now face. This intolerable dependence on foreign oil threatens our economic independence and the very security of our Nation.

The energy crisis is real. It is worldwide. It is a clear and present danger to our Nation. These are facts and we simply must face them. . . .

In closing, let me say this: I will do my best, but I will not do it alone. Let your voice be heard. Whenever you have a chance, say something good about our country. With God's help and for the sake of our Nation, it is time for us to join hands in America. Let us commit ourselves together to a rebirth of the American spirit. Working together with our common faith we cannot fail.

Questions

1. What evidence does Carter offer to support his argument that the American people are experiencing a "crisis of confidence"?
2. In his view, why is the crisis of confidence a much deeper problem than the shortage of energy, inflation, and the recession?
3. What does Carter propose to do to resolve the crisis of confidence? How do you think the American people—and American voters—responded to this speech?

32-10 Acceptance Speech, Republican National Convention (1980)

Ronald Reagan

When Ronald Reagan (see text pp. 1014–1015) accepted the Republican nomination for the presidency, he attacked the record of the Carter presidency, which he held responsible for "this unprecedented calamity which has befallen us." Government, he declared, "should go on a diet." Hard work, low taxes, strong families, and military spending would restore American greatness.

Source: Excerpted by permission of the Republican National Committee from Ronald Reagan, acceptance speech, Republican National Convention, Detroit, Michigan, August 15, 1980, in *Vital Speeches of the Day* 46 (August 15, 1980).

This convention has shown to all America a party united, with positive programs for solving the nation's problems; a party ready to build a new consensus with all those across the land who share a community of values embodied in these words: family, work, neighborhood, peace and freedom.

Now I know we've had a quarrel or two but only as to the method of attaining a goal. There was no argument here about the goal. As President, I will establish a liaison with the 50 Governors to encourage them to eliminate, wherever it exists, discrimination against women. I will monitor Federal laws to insure their implementation and to add statutes if they are needed.

More than anything else, I want my candidacy to unify our country; to renew the American spirit and sense of purpose. I want to carry our message to every American, regardless of party affiliation, who is a member of this community of shared values.

Never before in our history have Americans been called upon to face three grave threats to our very existence, any one of which could destroy us. We face a disintegrating economy, a weakened defense and an energy policy based on the sharing of scarcity.

The major issue of this campaign is the direct political, personal, and moral responsibility of Democratic Party leadership—in the White House and in the Congress—for this unprecedented calamity which has befallen us. They tell us they've done the most that humanly could be done. They say that the United States has had its day in the sun, that our nation has passed its zenith. They expect you to tell your children that the American people no longer have the will to cope with their problems; that the future will be one of sacrifice and few opportunities.

My fellow citizens, I utterly reject that view. The American people, the most generous on earth, who created the highest standard of living, are not going to accept the notion that we can only make a better world for others by moving backward ourselves. And those who believe we can have no business leading this nation. . . .

Isn't it once again time to renew our compact of freedom; to pledge to each other all that is best in our lives; all that gives meaning to them—for the sake of this, our beloved and blessed land?

Together, let us make this a new beginning. Let us make a commitment to care for the needy; to teach our children the virtues handed down to us by our families; to have the courage to defend those values and virtues and the willingness to sacrifice for them.

Let us pledge to restore, in our time, the American spirit of voluntary service, of cooperation, of private and community initiative; a spirit that flows like a deep and mighty river through the history of our nation.

As your nominee, I pledge to you to restore to the Federal Government the capacity to do the people's work without dominating their lives. I pledge to you a Government that will not only work well but wisely, its ability to act tempered by prudence, and its willingness to do good balanced by the knowledge that government is never more dangerous than when our desire to have it help us blinds us to its great power to harm us. . . .

The head of a Government which has utterly refused to live within its means and which has, in the last few days, told us that this coming year's deficit will be $60 billion, dares to point the finger of blame at business and labor, both of which have been engaged in a losing struggle just trying to stay even.

High taxes, we are told, are somehow good for us, as if, when government spends our money it isn't inflationary, but when we spend it, it is.

Those who preside over the worst energy shortage in our history tell us to use less, so that we will run out of oil, gasoline and natural gas a little more slowly. Well, now, conservation is desirable, of course. We must not waste energy. But conservation is not the sole answer to our energy needs.

America must get to work producing more energy. The Republican program for solving economic problems is based on growth and productivity.

Large amounts of oil and natural gas lay beneath our land and off our shores, untouched because the present

Administration seems to believe the American people would rather see more regulation, more taxes and more controls than more energy.

Coal offers a great potential. So does nuclear energy produced under rigorous safety standards. It could supply electricity for thousands of industries and millions of jobs and homes. It must not be thwarted by a tiny minority opposed to economic growth which often finds friendly ears in regulatory agencies for its obstructionist campaigns.

Now make no mistake. We will not permit the safety of our people or our environmental heritage to be jeopardized, but we are going to reaffirm that the economic prosperity of our people is a fundamental part of our environment. . . .

It is essential that we maintain both the forward momentum of economic growth and the strength of the safety net between those in our society who need help. We also believe it is essential that the integrity of all aspects of Social Security be preserved.

Beyond these essentials, I believe it is clear our Federal Government is overgrown and overweight. Indeed, it is time our Government should go on a diet. Therefore, my first act as chief executive will be to impose an immediate and thorough freeze on Federal hiring. Then, we are going to enlist the very best minds from business, labor and whatever quarter to conduct a detailed review of every department, bureau and agency that lives by Federal appropriation. . . .

Our instructions to the groups we enlist will be simple and direct. We will remind them that Government programs exist at the sufferance of the American taxpayer and are paid for with money earned by working men and women and programs that represent a waste of their money—a theft from their pocketbooks—must have that waste eliminated or that program must go. . . .

Everything that can be run more effectively by state and local government we shall turn over to state and local government, along with the funding sources to pay for it. We are going to put an end to the money merry-go-round where our money becomes Washington's money, to be spent by states and cities exactly the way the Federal bureaucrats tell us it has to be spent.

I will not accept the excuse that the Federal Government has grown so big and powerful that it is beyond the control of any President, any administration or Congress. We are going to put an end to the notion that the American taxpayer exists to fund the Federal Government. The Federal Government exists to serve the American people and to be accountable to the American people. On January 20, we are going to reestablish that truth.

Also on that date we are going to initiate action to get substantial relief for our taxpaying citizens and action to put people back to work. None of this will be based on any new form of monetary tinkering or fiscal sleight-of-hand. We will simply apply to government the common sense that we all use in our daily lives.

Work and family are at the center of our lives, the foundation of our dignity as a free people. When we deprive people of what they have earned, or take away their jobs, we destroy their dignity and undermine their families. We can't support families unless there are jobs; and we can't have jobs unless the people have both money to invest and the faith to invest it. . . .

The American people are carrying the heaviest peacetime tax burden in our nation's history—and it will grow even heavier, under present law, next January. We are taxing ourselves into economic exhaustion and stagnation, crushing our ability and incentive to save, invest and produce.

This must stop. We must halt this fiscal self-destruction and restore sanity to our economic system.

I've long advocated a 30 percent reduction in income tax rates over a period of three years. This phased tax reduction would begin with a 10 percent "down payment" tax cut in 1981, which the Republicans in Congress and I have already proposed.

A phased reduction of tax rates would go a long way toward easing the heavy burden on the American people. But we shouldn't stop there. . . .

For those without skills, we'll find a way to help them get new skills.

For those without job opportunities we'll stimulate new opportunities, particularly in the inner cities where they live.

For those who've abandoned hope, we'll restore hope and we'll welcome them into a great national crusade to make America great again.

When we move from domestic affairs, and cast our eyes abroad, we see an equally sorry chapter in the record of the present Administration. . . .

—Soviet combat brigade trains in Cuba, just 90 miles from our shores.

—Soviet army of invasion occupies Afghanistan, further threatening our vital interests in the Middle East.

—America's defense strength is at its lowest ebb in a generation, while the Soviet Union is vastly outspending us in both strategic and conventional arms.

—Our European allies, looking nervously at the growing menace from the East, turn to us for leadership and fail to find it.

—And incredibly, more than 50, as you've been told from this platform so eloquently already, more than 50 of our fellow Americans have been held captive [in Teheran] for over eight years—eight months—by a dictatorial foreign power that holds us up to ridicule before the world. . . .

Who does not feel a growing sense of unease as our allies, facing repeated instances of an amateurish and confused Administration, reluctantly conclude that America is unwilling or unable to fulfill its obligations as leader of the free world?

Who does not feel rising alarm when the question in any discussion of foreign policy is no longer, "Should we do something?" but "Do we have the capacity to do anything?"

The Administration which has brought us to this state is seeking your endorsement for four more years of weakness, indecision, mediocrity and incompetence. No. No. No American should vote until he or she has asked: Is the United States stronger and more respected now than it was three-and-a-half years ago? Is the world safer, a safer place in which to live?

It is the responsibility of the President of the United States, in working for peace, to insure that the safety of our people cannot successfully be threatened by a hostile foreign power. As President, fulfilling that responsibility will be my No. 1 priority. . . .

Of all the objectives we seek, first and foremost is the establishment of lasting world peace. We must always stand ready to negotiate in good faith, ready to pursue any reasonable avenue that holds forth the promise of lessening tensions and furthering the prospects of peace. But let our friends and those who may wish us ill take note: the United States has an obligation to its citizens and to the people of the world never to let those who would destroy freedom dictate our future course of life on this planet. I would regard my election as proof that we have renewed our resolve to preserve world peace and freedom. That this nation will once again be strong enough to do that. . . .

[A]n American President told the generation of the Great Depression that it had a "rendezvous with destiny." I believe this generation of Americans today also has a rendezvous with destiny.

Tonight, let us dedicate ourselves to renewing the American compact. I ask you not simply to "trust me," but to trust your values—our values—and to hold me responsible for living up to them. I ask you to trust that American spirit which knows no ethnic, religious, social, political, regional or economic boundaries; the spirit that burned with zeal in the hearts of millions of immigrants from every corner of the earth who came here in search of freedom. . . .

I have thought of something that's not a part of my speech and worried over whether I should do it. Can we doubt that only a Divine Providence placed this land, this island of freedom, here as a refuge for all those people in the world who yearn to breathe free? Jews and Christians enduring persecution behind the Iron Curtain; the boat people of Southeast Asia, Cuba and of Haiti; the victims of drought and famine in Africa, the freedom fighters in Afghanistan, and our own countrymen held in savage captivity.

I'll confess that I've been a little afraid to suggest what I'm going to suggest. I'm more afraid not to. Can we begin our crusade joined together in a moment of silent prayer?

God bless America.

Thank you.

Questions

1. As outlined in this speech, what was Ronald Reagan's view of the proper relationship between the federal government and the American people?

2. What was Reagan's prescription for curing the ills of the American economy?

3. Candidate Reagan charged the Democratic administration with "weakness, indecision, mediocrity and incompetence." He also spoke positively of the need for a revival of the "American spirit." Do you think Reagan's appeal to the voters had more to do with the perceived failings of the Democrats or the Republican party's conservative agenda?

Questions for Further Thought

1. How does the work of Rachel Carson (Document 32-6) compare to that of early twentieth-century muckrakers (see Documents 21-2–21-5)?

2. Was the unpopularity Jimmy Carter experienced after his "Crisis" speech (Document 32-9) part of the fallout from Watergate? Why or why not?

3. Using Documents 32-9 and 32-10, consider what Americans want from their leaders. Are those expectations consistent? Why or why not?

CHAPTER **33**

A New Domestic and World Order 1981 to the Present

★　　　★　　　★

The Reagan Presidency, 1981–1989 and **The Bush Presidency and the End of the Cold War, 1989–1993**

Ronald Reagan's election to the presidency ushered in an era of dramatic political change. Reagan promised to curb government spending on social welfare, increase spending on defense, cut taxes, and balance the budget. The personal qualities Reagan brought to the White House defined the 1980s in much the same way that Franklin Roosevelt's personality defined the 1930s. Reagan invoked the memory of FDR in his acceptance speech to the Republican convention in the summer of 1980 by declaring, as his Democratic predecessor had in 1936, that "this generation of Americans . . . has a rendezvous with destiny." After the disillusionment of Vietnam and Watergate, the economic hard times of the 1970s, and the humiliation of the Iran hostage affair, voters found Reagan's optimism reassuring.

During his first term in office Reagan enjoyed enormous, though not universal, popularity. Although some Americans felt he was prone to respond to complex issues with simplistic platitudes (see text pp. 1020–1021), many more saw him as embodying American virtues such as fortitude and self-reliance, which Reagan would have said came from his small-town upbringing (Document 33-1). Even his cabinet officers, who admired Reagan's policies, were sometimes uneasy about his preoccupation with image making (Document 33-2).

President Reagan identified government as the problem, not the solution. He called for reducing federal taxes, repealing federal regulations, and eliminating wasteful federal spending. Social welfare programs were targeted for sharp cuts, partly in response to the ideas of conservative theorists such as George Gilder (Document 33-3). Supply-side economic theory, which was popular among Reagan's economic advisers, held that cutting tax rates on the wealthy and on corporations would lead to a higher level of investment, improved productivity, and the creation of more and better-paying jobs, all of which would ultimately increase tax revenues and reduce the federal deficit (see text pp. 1021–1022).

In the early 1980s the Reagan White House successfully pushed through Congress its legislative agenda of reducing taxes and cutting back on social programs; this program came to be known as Reaganomics. Reaganomics enjoyed some successes. Inflation was brought under control, and starting in his third year in office, Reagan presided over the longest period of peacetime economic expansion in American history.

Contributing to this economic prosperity was the administration's decision to increase defense spending significantly. Conservatives argued that since the end of the Vietnam War America had lagged dangerously behind its Soviet opponent (see text p. 1022). But larger defense budgets helped drive up the budget deficit. And Reagan's commitment to rolling back Soviet influence wherever he could, particularly in Central America, mired his administration in scandal during his second term. In 1986 it was revealed that the president had approved a secret program of selling U.S. arms to Iran in an effort to secure the release of American hostages in Lebanon. Lieutenant Colonel Oliver North, a staff member of Reagan's National Security Council, then used the profits from the arms sales to supply military aid to the Nicaraguan Contras (see text p. 1023). The Iran-Contra affair prompted a Senate investigation, although North's spirited defense of his role made him a folk hero to some Americans (Document 33-4).

George Bush was elected to the presidency in 1988 after promising a "kinder, gentler" country; some understood this as an indirect criticism of the domestic policies of President Reagan. But as president Bush never developed a clearly defined domestic policy (see text pp. 1025–1027). Instead, his administration focused primarily on foreign affairs.

By the end of the 1980s it was apparent that the world was changing in dramatic ways. The rise of Mikhail Gorbachev to power in the Soviet Union led to the defusing of cold war tensions, the collapse of communism in Eastern Europe, and finally the collapse of the Soviet Union (see text pp. 1027–1028). After more than forty years the United States had "won" the Cold War, but the meaning of that victory for America's future at home and abroad was not clear.

Bush's greatest triumph came in his leadership of the United Nations–endorsed coalition against Iraq in the Persian Gulf War of 1991 (Document 33-5). By driving Iraqi dictator Saddam Hussein's forces out of Kuwait, Bush offered a dramatic demonstration of the military prowess of the United States in the "new world order." But the war had huge environmental costs and served as a timely reminder of America's continued dependence on imported oil.

In the aftermath of the war Bush's popularity soared to such heights that many Democrats despaired of unseating him in the 1992 election. But Bush's apparent inability or unwillingness to counter the effects of the severe recession that hit the economy in 1990 (see text p. 1026) was his undoing. In addition, many nagging economic problems that had been swept under the rug during the "Morning in America" euphoria of the Reagan years came back to haunt Reagan's successor, including the spiraling federal deficit.

33-1 *An American Life* (1990)

Ronald Reagan   Although Ronald Reagan (b. 1911) sometimes seemed to treat public office as another acting role (see text p. 1020), he did possess firmly grounded political views that were the product of his upbringing. These excerpts from Reagan's autobiography, *An American Life*, describe his youth in Dixon, Illinois, and his perceptions of the effect government had on townspeople during the Great Depression. Those experiences helped shape his views on the role of government in society.

Source: Excerpted from Ronald Reagan, *An American Life* (New York: Simon & Schuster, 1990), pp. 27–29, 66–69.

With nearly ten thousand people, Dixon was more than ten times larger than Tampico. We arrived there in 1920 when I was nine years old, and to me it was heaven.

Dixon had a busy main street lined with shops, several churches, an elementary and a high school, a public library, a post office, a wire screen factory, a shoe factory, and a cement plant. At the outskirts of town, dairy farms stretched as far as you could see. It was a small universe where I learned standards and values that would guide me for the rest of my life.

Almost everybody knew one another, and because they knew one another, they tended to care about each other. If a family down the street had a crisis—a death or serious illness—a neighbor brought them dinner that night. If a farmer lost his barn to a fire, his friends would pitch in and help him rebuild it. At church, you prayed side by side with your neighbors, and if things were going wrong for them, you prayed for them—and know they'd pray for you if things went wrong for you.

I grew up observing how the love and common sense of purpose that unites families is one of the most powerful glues on earth and that it can help them overcome the greatest of adversities. I learned that hard work is an essential part of life—that by and large, you don't get something for nothing—and that America was a place that offered unlimited opportunity to those who did work hard. I learned to admire risk takers and entrepreneurs, be they farmers or small merchants, who went to work and took risks to build something for themselves and their children, pushing at the boundaries of their lives to make them better.

I have always wondered at this American marvel, the great energy of the human soul that drives people to better themselves and improve the fortunes of their families and communities. Indeed, I know of no greater force on earth.

I think growing up in a small town is a good foundation for anyone who decides to enter politics. You get to know people as individuals, not as blocs or members of special interest groups. You discover that, despite their differences, most people have a lot in common: Every individual is unique, but we all want freedom and liberty, peace, love and security, a good home, and a chance to worship God in our own way; we all want the chance to get ahead and make our children's lives better than our own. We all want the chance to work at a job of our own choosing and

to be fairly rewarded for it and the opportunity to control our own destiny. . . .

Later in life I learned that, compared with some of the folks who lived in Dixon, our family was "poor." But I didn't know that when I was growing up. And I never thought of our family as disadvantaged. Only later did the government decide that it had to tell people they were poor.

We always rented our home and never had enough money for luxuries. But I don't remember suffering because of that. Although my mother sometimes took in sewing to supplement my dad's wages and I grew up wearing my brother's clothes and shoes after he'd outgrown them, we always had enough to eat and Nelle was forever finding people who were worse off then we were and going out of her way to help them.

In those days, our main meal—dinner—was at noon and frequently consisted of a dish my mother called "oatmeal meat." She'd cook a batch of oatmeal and mix it with hamburger (I suspect the relative portions of each may have varied according to our current economic status), then serve it with some gravy she'd made while cooking the hamburger.

I remember the first time she brought a plate of oatmeal meat to the table. There was a thick, round patty buried in gravy that I'd never seen before. I bit into it. It was moist and meaty, the most wonderful thing I'd ever eaten. Of course, I didn't realize oatmeal meat was born of poverty.

Nowadays, I bet doctors would say it was healthy for us, too.

Dixon straddles the Rock River, a stretch of blue-green water flanked by wooded hills and limestone cliffs that meanders through the farmland of northwestern Illinois on its way to the Mississippi.

The river, which was often called the "Hudson of the West," was my playground during some of the happiest moments of my life. During the winter, it froze and became a skating rink as wide as two football fields and a long as I wanted to make it. In the summer, I swam and fished in the river and ventured as far as I dared on overnight canoe trips through the Rock River Valley, pretending with playmates to be a nineteenth-century explorer.

In my hand-me-down overalls, I hiked the hills and cliffs above the river, tried (unsuccessfully) to trap muskrats at the river's edge, and played "Cowboys and Indians" on hillsides above the river.

When we first moved to Dixon, we lived on the south side of the river. When we could afford it, we moved across the river to a larger house on the north side. As I look back on those days in Dixon, I think my life was as sweet and idyllic as it could be, as close as I could imagine for a young boy to the world created by Mark Twain in *The Adventures of Tom Sawyer*. . . .

For a twenty-one-year-old fresh out of college, broadcasting the Big Ten games was like a dream, and as the end of the season approached, I prayed the people at WOC would offer me a permanent job. But after the final game, Pete told me the station didn't have an opening. He said if something came up, he'd call me, but with the Depression growing worse daily, he sounded as if there wasn't much hope.

Once again, disappointed and frustrated, I headed for home.

Back in Dixon, Jack [Reagan's father] reminded me that while I'd been talking about forward passes and quarterback sneaks, events a lot more important than football games had been occurring: Franklin D. Roosevelt had been elected the thirty-second president of the United States by a landslide and Jack predicted he would pull America out of its tailspin.

There weren't many Democrats in Dixon and Jack was probably the most outspoken of them, never missing a chance to speak up for the working man or sing the praises of Roosevelt.

I had become a Democrat, by birth, I suppose, and a few months after my twenty-first birthday, I cast my first vote for Roosevelt and the full Democratic ticket. And, like Jack—and millions of other Americans—I soon idolized FDR. He'd entered the White House facing a national emergency as grim as any the country has ever faced and, acting quickly, he had implemented a plan of action to deal with the crisis.

During his Fireside Chats, his strong, gentle, confident voice resonated across the nation with an eloquence that brought comfort and resilience to a nation caught up in a storm and reassured us that we could lick any problem. I will never forget him for that.

With his alphabet soup of federal agencies, FDR in many ways set in motion the forces that later sought to create big government and bring a form of veiled socialism to America. But I think that many people forget Roosevelt ran for president on a platform dedicated to reducing waste and fat in government. He called for cutting federal spending by twenty-five percent, eliminating useless boards and commissions and returning to states and communities powers that had been wrongfully seized by the federal government. If he had not been distracted by war, I

think he would have resisted the relentless expansion of the federal government that followed him. One of his sons, Franklin Roosevelt, Jr., often told me that his father had said many times his welfare and relief programs during the Depression were meant only as emergency, stopgap measures to cope with a crisis, not the seeds of what others later tried to turn into a permanent welfare state. Government giveaway programs, FDR said, "destroy the human spirit," and he was right. As smart as he was, though, I suspect even FDR didn't realize that once you created a bureaucracy, it took on a life of its own. It was almost impossible to close down a bureaucracy once it had been created.

After FDR's election, Jack, as one of the few Democrats in town, was appointed to implement some of the new federal relief programs in Dixon. It removed him from the ranks of the unemployed and also gave me my first opportunity to watch government in action.

As administrator of federal relief programs, Jack shared a small office in Dixon with the County Supervisor of Poor. Every week, people who had lost their jobs came to the office to pick up sacks of flour, potatoes, and other food and pieces of scrip they could exchange for groceries at stores in town.

Occasionally, I dropped into the office to wait for Jack before we walked home together. I was shocked to see the fathers of many of my schoolmates waiting in line for handouts—men I had known most of my life, who had had jobs I'd thought were as permanent as the city itself.

Jack knew that accepting handouts was tough on the dignity of the men and came up with a plan to help them recover some of it. He began leaving home early in the morning and making rounds of the county, asking if anyone had odd jobs available, then, if they did, persuaded the people to let him find somebody to do the work. The next week when the men came in for their handouts, Jack offered the work he'd found to those who'd been out of work the longest.

I'll never forget the faces of these men when Jack told them their turn had come up for a job: They brightened like a burst of neon, and when they left Dad's office, I swear the men were standing a little taller. They wanted *work*, not handouts.

Not long after that, Jack told several men he had found a week's work for them. The responded to this news with a rustling of feet. Eventually, one broke the silence and said: "Jack, the last time you got me some work, the people at the relief office took my family off welfare; they said I had a job and even though it was temporary, I wasn't eligible for relief anymore. I just can't afford to take another job."

Later on, thanks again to his party connections, Jack was placed in charge of the Works Progress Administration office in Dixon. The WPA was one of the most productive elements of FDR's alphabet soup of agencies because it put people to work building roads, bridges, and other projects. Like Jack's informal program, it gave men and women a chance to make some money along with the satisfaction of knowing they *earned* it. But just as Jack got the program up and running, there was a decline in the number of people applying for work on the projects. Since he knew there hadn't been a cure for unemployment in Dixon, he began asking questions and discovered the federal welfare workers were telling able-bodied men in Dixon that they shouldn't take the WPA jobs because they were being taken care of and didn't need help from the WPA.

After a while, Jack couldn't get any of his projects going; he couldn't get enough men sprung from the welfare giveaway program. I wasn't sophisticated enough to realize what I learned later: The first rule of a bureaucracy is to protect the bureaucracy. If the people running the welfare program had let their clientele find other ways of making a living, that would have reduced their importance and their budget.

Questions

1. What political values did Reagan learn from growing up in a small town?
2. How do his observations on the depression compare with those in Chapters 25 and 26 of the textbook?
3. Was the world of 1920s and 1930s America relevant to social problems a half century later? Why or why not?

33-2 *For the Record* (1988)

Donald T. Regan

Ronald Reagan's treasury secretary and chief of staff, Donald Regan, offered a surprisingly unflattering portrait of his boss in this memoir of his White House years. Reagan's "preoccupation," Regan revealed, was with image, not with the substance of policy decisions (see text pp. 1020–1021).

Source: Excerpted from Donald T. Regan, *For the Record: From Wall Street to Washington,* pp. 246–250, 266–268. Copyright © 1988 by Donald T. Regan. Reprinted by permission of Harcourt Brace, Inc.

Ronald Reagan seemed to be regarded by certain members of his inner circle not as the powerful and utterly original leader that he was, but as a sort of supreme anchorman whose public persona was the most important element of the Presidency. According to the rules of this school of political management, controversy was to be avoided at nearly any cost: every Presidential action must produce a positive public effect. In practice, this meant stimulating a positive effect in the media, with the result that the press, not the people, became the President's primary constituency. . . .

It was [deputy chief of staff Michael] Deaver's job to advise the President on image, and image was what he talked about nearly all the time. It was Deaver who identified the story of the day at the eight o'clock staff meeting and coordinated the plans for dealing with it, Deaver who created and approved photo opportunities, Deaver who alerted the President to the snares being laid by the press that day. Deaver was a master of his craft. He saw—designed—each Presidential action as a one-minute or two-

minute spot on the evening network news, or a picture on page one of the *Washington Post* or the *New York Times*, and conceived every Presidential appearance in terms of camera angles. . . .

Every moment of every public appearance was scheduled, every word was scripted, every place where Reagan was expected to stand was chalked with toe marks. The President was always being prepared for a performance, and this had the inevitable effect of preserving him from confrontation and the genuine interplay of opinion, question, and argument that form the basis of decision. . . .

The President is possessed of a philosophical agenda based on a lifetime of experience and thought. He is a formidable reader and a talented conversationalist with a gift for listening. It was precisely this gift that led to many of his gaffes and misstatements in encounters with the press: Ronald Reagan remembered nearly everything that was said to him. If someone told him (to use a wholly fictitious example) that there had been 35,987 hairs in Stalin's mustache, this fact would go into the Presidential memory bank, possibly to emerge weeks or months later in the middle of a press conference. It never seemed to occur to him that anyone would give him incorrect information. His mind was a trove of facts and anecdotes, something like the morgue of one of his favorite magazines, *Reader's Digest,* and it was impossible to guess when or why he might access any one of these millions of bytes of data. . . .

Reagan shunned the abstract, the theoretical, the cold and impersonal approach to problems. His love of stories was connected to this same tendency to see everything in human terms. Although even some of his intimates scoffed (ever so discreetly) at his bottomless fund of anecdotes about it, Reagan's experience as governor of California constituted a unique body of executive and political experience. He had a formidable gift for debate when he was allowed to debate in a spontaneous way. His problems in these matters, as in the first debate with Walter Mondale in 1984, nearly always resulted from his being overprogrammed. His briefers, forgetting that a President has a cast of thousands to remember facts for him, had crammed his mind with so many bits of information that he tried to rely on data instead of explaining the issue and defending his policy. I had seen him defend his ideas and critique the proposals of other heads of state with the best of them at six international economic summits, and it was not uncommon for him to render courageous decisions on domestic economic questions in the face of nearly unanimous advice and pressure to do the opposite. . . .

[Regan describes giving the president a working paper in August 1985 outlining what he thought the White House's priorities should be for the following year.]

Ronald Reagan read the paper while he was at the ranch and handed it back to me on his return without spoken or written comment.

"What did you think of it?" I asked.

It's good, the President replied, nodding in approval. It's really good, Don.

I waited for him to say more. He did not. He had no questions to ask, no objections to raise, no instructions to issue. I realized that the policy that would determine the course of the world's most powerful nation for the next two years and deeply influence the fate of the Republican party in the 1986 midterm elections had been adopted without amendment. It seemed, also, that I had been authorized as Chief of Staff to make the necessary arrangements to carry out the policy. It was taken for granted that the President would do whatever was asked of him to make the effort a success. We went on to the next item on the agenda.

I confess that I was surprised that this weighty matter was decided so quickly and with so little ceremony. In a way, of course, it was flattering; it is always gratifying to

anticipate the boss's wishes with acceptable accuracy. Still, I was uneasy. Did the President really want us to do all these things with no more discussion than this? I decided that this must be the case, since always in the past, if he did not say no, the answer was yes. By now I understood that the President did not share my love of detail and my enthusiasm for planning. I knew that he was not an aggressive manager. Perhaps I should have quizzed him on tax policy or Central America or our approach to trade negotiations; certainly my instincts and the practice of a lifetime nudged me in that direction. But I held my tongue. It is one thing brashly to speak your mind to an ordinary mortal and another to say, "Wait a minute!" to the President of the United States. The mystery of the office is a potent inhibitor. The President, you feel, has his reasons.

Another President would almost certainly have had his own ideas on the mechanics of policy, but Reagan did not trouble himself with such minutiae. His preoccupation was with what might be called "the outer Presidency." He was content to let others cope with the inner details of running the Administration. . . . Reagan chose his aides and then followed their advice almost without question. He trusted his lieutenants to act on his intentions, rather than on his spoken instructions, and though he sometimes asked what some of his less visible Cabinet officers were doing with their departments, he seldom spontaneously called for a detailed status report. The degree of trust involved in this method of leadership must be unprecedented in modern American history. Sometimes—as was inevitable given that many of his closest aides, including almost all of the Cabinet, were virtual strangers to him—this trust was betrayed in shocking fashion. When that happened Reagan seldom criticized, seldom complained, never scolded. Not even the Iran-Contra debacle could provoke him into harsh words, much less subordinates who had let him down.

Never—absolutely never in my experience—did President Reagan really lose his temper or utter a rude or unkind word. Never did he issue a direct order, although I, at least, sometimes devoutly wished that he would. He listened, acquiesced, played his role, and waited for the next act to be written. From the point of view of my own experience and nature, this was an altogether baffling way of doing things. But my own style was not the case in point. Reagan's method had worked well enough to make him President of the United States, and well enough for the nation under his leadership to transform its mood from pessimism to optimism, its economy from stagnation to steady growth, and its position in the world from weakness to strength. Common sense suggested that the President knew something that the rest of us did not know. It was my clear duty to do things his way.

Questions

1. What does Donald T. Regan see as Ronald Reagan's greatest strengths in his years in office?
2. What does Regan see as Reagan's greatest weaknesses?
3. What relation, if any, do you see between Reagan's strengths and weaknesses as a political leader?

33-3 *Wealth and Poverty*

George Gilder

In *Wealth and Poverty* (1981), a book that strongly influenced the Reagan administration, the conservative theorist George Gilder argued that it was the immoral and irresponsible behavior of the poor themselves rather than any structural defects in the economy that perpetuated poverty in the United States.

The only dependable route from poverty is always work, family, and faith. The first principle is that in order to move up, the poor must not only work, they must work harder than the classes above them. Every previous generation of the lower class has made such efforts. But the current poor, white even more than black, are refusing to work hard. Irwin Garfinkel and Robert Haveman, authors of the ingenious and sophisticated study of what they call *Earnings Capacity Utilization Rates*, have calculated the degree to which various income groups use their opportunities—how hard they work outside the home. This study shows that, for several understandable reasons, the current poor work substantially less, for fewer hours and weeks a year, and earn less in proportion to their age, education, and other credentials (even *after* correcting the figures for unemployment, disability, and presumed discrimination) than either their predecessors in American cities or those now above them on the income scale. (The study was made at the federally funded Institute for Research on Poverty at the University of Wisconsin and used data from the census and the Michigan longitudinal survey.) The findings lend important confirmation to the growing body of evidence that work effort is the crucial unmeasured variable in American productivity and income distribution, and that current welfare and other subsidy programs substantially reduce work. The poor choose leisure not because of moral weakness, but because they are paid to do so.

A program to lift by transfers and preferences the incomes of less diligent groups is politically divisive—and very unlikely—because it incurs the bitter resistance of the real working class. In addition, such an effort breaks the psychological link between effort and reward, which is crucial to long-run upward mobility. Because effective work consists not in merely fulfilling the requirements of labor contracts, but in "putting out" with alertness and emotional commitment, workers have to understand and feel deeply that what they are given depends on what they give—that they must supply work in order to demand goods. Parents and schools must inculcate this idea in their children both by instruction and example. Nothing is more deadly to achievement than the belief that effort will not be rewarded, that the world is a bleak and discriminatory place in which only the predatory and the specially preferred can get ahead. Such a view in the home discourages the work effort in school that shapes earnings capacity afterward. As with so many aspects of human performance, work effort begins in family experiences, and its sources can be best explored through an examination of family structure.

Indeed, after work the second principle of upward mobility is the maintenance of monogamous marriage and family. Adjusting for discrimination against women and for child-care responsibilities, the Wisconsin study indicates that married men work between two and one-third and four times harder than married women, and more than twice as hard as female family heads. The work effort of married men increases with their age, credentials, education, job experience, and birth of children, while the work effort of married women steadily declines. Most important in judging the impact of marriage, husbands work 50 percent harder than bachelors of comparable age, education, and skills.

The effect of marriage, thus, is to increase the work effort of men by about half. Since men have higher earnings capacity to begin with, and since the female capacity-utilization figures would be even lower without an adjustment for discrimination, it is manifest that the maintenance of families is the key factor in reducing poverty.

Once a family is headed by a woman, it is almost impossible for it to greatly raise its income even if the woman is highly educated and trained and she hires day-care or domestic help. Her family responsibilities and distractions tend to prevent her from the kind of all-out commitment that is necessary for the full use of earning power. Few women with children make earning money the top priority in their lives.

A married man, on the other hand, is spurred by the claims of family to channel his otherwise disruptive male aggressions into his performance as a provider for a wife and children. These sexual differences alone, which manifest themselves in all societies known to anthropology, dictate that the first priority of any serious program against poverty is to strengthen the male role in poor families.

These narrow measures of work effort touch on just part of the manifold interplay between family and poverty. Edward Banfield's *The Unheavenly City* defines the lower class largely by its lack of an orientation to the future. Living from day to day and from hand to mouth, lower class individuals are unable to plan or save or keep a job. Banfield gives the impression that short-time horizons are a deep-seated psychological defect afflicting hundreds of thousands of the poor.

There is no question that Banfield puts his finger on a crucial problem of the poor and that he develops and documents his theme in an unrivaled classic of disciplined social science. But he fails to show how millions of men, equally present oriented, equally buffeted by impulse and blind to the future, have managed to become far-seeing members of the middle classes. He also fails to explain how millions of apparently future-oriented men can become dissolute followers of the sensuous moment, neglecting their jobs, dissipating their income and wealth, pursuing a horizon no longer than the most time-bound of the poor.

What Banfield is in fact describing in his lower-class category is largely the temperament of single, divorced, and separated men. The key to lower-class life in contemporary America is that unrelated individuals, as the census calls them, are so numerous and conspicuous that they set the tone for the entire community. Their congregation in ghettos, moreover, magnifies greatly their impact on the black poor, male and female (though, as Banfield rightly observes, this style of instant gratification is chiefly a male trait).

The short-sighted outlook of poverty stems largely from the breakdown of family responsibilities among fathers. The lives of the poor, all too often, are governed by the rhythms of tension and release that characterize the sexual experience of young single men. Because female sexuality, as it evolved over the millennia, is psychologically rooted in the bearing and nurturing of children, women have long horizons within their very bodies, glimpses of eternity within their wombs. Civilized society is dependent upon the submission of the short-term sexuality of young men to the extended maternal horizons of women. This is what happens in monogamous marriage; the man disciplines his sexuality and extends it into the future through the womb of a woman. The woman gives him access to his children, otherwise forever denied him; and he gives her the product of his labor, otherwise dissipated on temporary pleasures. The woman gives him a unique link to the future and a vision of it; he gives her faithfulness and a commitment to a lifetime of hard work. If work effort is the first principle of overcoming poverty, marriage is the prime source of upwardly mobile work.

It is love that changes the short horizons of youth and poverty into the long horizons of marriage and career. When marriages fail, the man often returns to the more primitive rhythms of singleness. On the average, his income drops by one-third and he shows a far higher propensity for drink, drugs, and crime. But when marriages in general hold firm and men in general love and support their children, Banfield's lower-class style changes into middle-class futurity.

The key to the intractable poverty of the hardcore American poor is the dominance of single and separated men in poor communities. Black "unrelated individuals" are not much more likely to be in poverty than white ones. The problem is neither race nor matriarchy in any meaningful sense. It is familial anarchy among the concentrated poor of the inner city, in which flamboyant and impulsive youths rather than responsible men provide the themes of aspiration. The result is that male sexual rhythms tend to prevail, and boys are brought up without authoritative fathers in the home to instill in them the values of responsible paternity: the discipline and love of children and the dependable performance of the provider role. "If she wants me, *she*'ll pay," one young stud assured me in prison, and perhaps, in the welfare culture, she can and will. Thus the pattern is extended into future generations.

Questions

1. What does Gilder see as the primary cause of poverty?

2. What does he see as the solution to poverty?

3. Why should Gilder's ideas have appealed so strongly to Ronald Reagan?

33-4 Oliver North Testifies before Congress (1987)

Lieutenant Colonel Oliver North was a principal figure in the Iran-Contra scandal that broke in 1986 (see text p. 1023). North was accused of using the profits from the secret sale of arms to Iran to provide aid to the Contra guerrillas in Nicaragua. In this statement before the House-Senate investigative committee North depicted himself as a loyal soldier carrying out the wishes of his superiors to the best of his ability. He contrasted his own patriotic devotion to the "fickle, vacillating, unpredictable, on-again off-again" policies of the legislators who were scrutinizing his actions.

Source: Oliver L. North, testimony before Congress. U.S. Congress, *Joint Hearings before the Senate Select Committee on Secret Military Assistance to Iran and the Nicaraguan Opposition and the House Select Committee to Investigate Covert Arms Transactions with Iran*, 100th Cong., 1st sess., pt. 1, 1987.

As you all know by now, my name is Oliver North, Lieutenant Colonel, United States Marine Corps. My best friend is my wife Betsy, to whom I have been married for 19 years, and with whom I have had four wonderful children, aged 18, 16, 11 and 6.

I came to the National Security Council six years ago to work in the administration of a great president. As a staff member, I came to understand his goals and his desires. I admired his policies, his strength, and his ability to bring our country together. I observed the President to be a leader who cared deeply about people, and who believed that the interests of our country were advanced by recognizing that ours is a nation at risk and a dangerous world, and acting accordingly. He tried, and in my opinion succeeded, in advancing the cause of world peace by strengthening our country, by acting to restore and sustain democracy throughout the world, and by having the courage to take decisive action when needed. . . .

The National Security Council is, in essence, the President's staff. It helps to formulate and coordinate national security policy. . . . While at the NSC, I worked most closely with three people: Mr. Robert C. McFarlane, Admiral John Poindexter, and CIA Director, William Casey. . . .

Over time, I was made responsible for managing a number of complex and sensitive covert operations that we have discussed here to date. I reported directly to Mr. McFarlane and to Admiral Poindexter. I coordinated directly with others, including Director Casey. My authority to act always flowed, I believe, from my superiors. My military training inculcated in me a strong belief in the chain of command. And so far as I can recall, I always acted on a major matter with specific approval, after informing my superiors of the facts, as I knew them, the risks, and the potential benefits. I readily admit that I was action-oriented, that I took pride in the fact that I was counted upon as a man who got the job done. And I don't mean this by way of criticism, but there were occasions when my superiors, confronted with accomplishing goals or difficult tasks, would simply say, "Fix it, Ollie," or, "Take care of it." Since graduating from the Naval Academy in 1968, I have tried to be the best Marine officer that one can be. In combat, my goal was always to understand the objective, follow orders, accomplish the mission, and to keep alive the men who served under me. . . . I honestly believed that any soldier who has ever been to a war truly hopes he will never see one again. . . .

During 1984, '85, and '86, there were periods of time when we worked two days in every one. My guess is that the average workday lasted at least 14 hours. To respond to various crises, the need for such was frequent, and we would often go without a night's sleep, hoping to recoup the next night or thereafter. . . . My only real regret is that I virtually abandoned my family for work during these years. . . .

I worked hard on the political military strategy restoring and sustaining democracy in Central America and in particular, El Salvador. We sought to achieve the democratic outcome in Nicaragua that this administration still supports, which involved keeping the contras together in both body and soul. We made efforts to open a new relationship with Iran, and recover our hostages. We worked on the development of a concerted policy regarding terrorists and terrorism and a capability for dealing in a concerted manner with that threat. . . .

There were many problems. I believed that we worked as hard as we could to solve them, and sometimes we succeeded, and sometimes we failed, but at least we tried, and I want to tell you that I, for one, will never regret having tried.

I believe that this is a strange process that you are putting me and others through. Apparently, the President has chosen not to assert his prerogatives, and you have been permitted to make the rules. You called before you the officials of the Executive Branch. You put them under oath for what must be collectively thousands of hours of testimony. You dissect that testimony to find inconsistencies and declare some to be truthful and others to be liars. You make the rulings as to what is proper and what is not proper. You put the testimony which you think is helpful to your goal up before the people and leave others out. It's sort of like a baseball game in which you are both the player and the umpire. It's a game in which you call the balls and strikes and where you determine who is out and who is safe. And in the end you determine the score and declare yourselves the winner.

From where I sit, it is not the fairest process. One thing is, I think, for certain—that you will not investigate yourselves in this matter. There is not much chance that you will conclude at the end of these hearings that the Boland Amendments and the frequent policy changes therefore were unwise or that your restrictions should not have been imposed on the Executive Branch. You are not likely to conclude that the Administration acted properly by trying to sustain the freedom fighters in Nicaragua when they were abandoned, and you are not likely to conclude by commending the President of the United States who tried constantly to recover our citizens and achieve an opening that is strategically vital—Iran. I would not be frank with you if I did not admit that the last several months have been difficult for me and my family. It has been difficult to be on the front pages of every newspaper in the land day after day, to be the lead story on national television day after day, to be photographed thousands of times by bands of photographers who chase us around since November just because my name arose at the hearings. It is difficult to be caught in the middle of a constitutional struggle between the Executive and legislative branches over who will formulate and direct the foreign policy of this nation. It is difficult to be villified by people in and out of this body, some who have proclaimed that I am guilty of criminal conduct even before they heard me. . . . And, as I indicated yesterday, I think it was insensitive of this committee to place before the cameras my home address at a time when my family and I are under 24-hour armed guard by over a dozen government agents of the Naval Investigative Service because of fear that terrorists will seek revenge for my official acts and carry out their announced intentions to kill me.

It is also difficult to comprehend that my work at the NSC—all of which was approved and carried out in the best interests of our country—has led to two massive par-

allel investigations staffed by over 200 people. It is mind-boggling to me that one of those investigations is criminal and that some here have attempted to criminalize policy differences between co-equal branches of government and the Executive's conduct of foreign affairs.

I believe it is inevitable that the Congress will in the end blame the Executive Branch, but I suggest to you that it is Congress which must accept at least some of the blame in the Nicaraguan freedom fighters' matter. Plain and simple, the Congress is to blame because of the fickle, vacillating, unpredictable, on-again off-again policy toward the Nicaraguan Democratic Resistance—the so-called Contras. . . .

Armies need food and consistent help. They need a flow of money, of arms, clothing and medical supplies. The Congress of the United States allowed the executive to encourage them, to do battle, and then abandoned them. The Congress of the United States left soldiers in the field unsupported and vulnerable to their communist enemies. When the executive branch did everything possible within the law to prevent them from being wiped out by Moscow's surrogates in Havana and Managua, you then had the investigation to blame the problem on the executive branch; It does not make sense to me.

In my opinion, these hearings have caused serious damage to our national interests. Our adversaries laugh at us and our friends recoil in horror. I suppose it would be one thing if the intelligence committees wanted to hear all of this in private and thereafter pass laws which in the view of Congress make for better policies or better functioning of government. But, to hold them publicly for the whole world to see strikes me as very harmful. Not only does it embarrass our friends and allies with whom we have worked, many of whom have helped us in various programs, but must also make them very wary of helping us again.

I believe that these hearings, perhaps unintentionally so, have revealed matters of great secrecy in the operation of our government. And sources and methods of intelligence activities have clearly been revealed to the detriment of our security. . . .

I don't mind telling you that I'm angry that what some have attempted to do to me and my family [*sic*]. I believe that the committee hearings will show that you have struck some blows. But, I am going to walk from here with my head high and my shoulders straight because I am proud of what we accomplished. I am proud of the efforts that we made, and I am proud of the fight that we fought. I am proud of serving the administration of a great president. . . . In closing, Mr. Chairman, and I thank you for this opportunity, I would just simply like to thank the tens of thousands of Americans who have communicated their support, encouragement and prayers for me and my family in this difficult time. Thank you, sir.

Questions

1. How does North justify his role in the Iran-Contra affair?
2. Why does North maintain that Congressional scrutiny of decisions by the executive branch of government is unwise and unjustified?
3. Why do you think many Americans were persuaded by Colonel North's defense? Are you persuaded by his arguments?

33-5   George Bush on Aggression in the Gulf (1990)

Speaking before the United Nations General Assembly in New York on October 1, 1990, as communism crumbled in Eastern Europe and the Soviet Union (see text pp. 1027–1028), President George Bush called on the international community to roll back Iraqi aggression in Kuwait (see text p. 1028) and help define a "new world order."

Source: George Bush, speech to the United Nations General Assembly, New York, October 1, 1990. In *Vital Speeches of the Day 57* (October 15, 1990).

The founding of the United Nations embodied our deepest hopes for a peaceful world. And during the past year, we've come closer that ever before to realizing those hopes. We've seen a century sundered by barbed threats and barbed wire, give way to a new era of peace and competition and freedom. . . .

Not since 1945 have we seen the real possibility of using the United Nations as it was designed, as a center for international collective security. . . .

Can we work together in a new partnership of nations? Can the collective strength of the world community expressed by the United Nations unite to deter and defeat aggression? Because the cold war's battle of ideas is not the last epic battle of this century.

Two months ago, in the waning weeks of one of history's most hopeful summers, the vast, still beauty of the peaceful Kuwaiti desert was fouled by the stench of diesel and the roar of steel tanks. And once again, the sound of distant thunder echoed across a cloudless sky. And once again, the world awoke to face the guns of August.

But this time, the world was ready. The United Nations Security Council's resolute response to Iraq's unprovoked aggression has been without precedent. Since the invasion on August 2, the Council has passed eight major resolutions setting the terms for a solution to the crisis. The Iraqi regime has yet to face the facts. But as I said last month, the annexation of Kuwait will not be permitted to stand. And this is not simply the view of the United States. It is the view of every Kuwaiti, the Arab League, the United Nations. Iraq's leaders should listen. It is Iraq against the world.

Let me take this opportunity to make the policy of my Government clear. The United States supports the use of sanctions to compel Iraq's leaders to withdraw immediately and without condition from Kuwait. We also support the provision of medicine and food for humanitarian purposes, so long as distribution can be properly monitored. Our quarrel is not with the people of Iraq. We do not wish for them to suffer. The world's quarrel is with the dictator who ordered that invasion.

Along with others, we have dispatched military forces to the region to enforce sanctions, to deter and if need be defend against further aggression. And we seek no advantage for ourselves, nor do we seek to maintain our military forces in Saudi Arabia for one day longer than is necessary. U.S. forces were sent at the request of the Saudi Government.

The American people and this President want every single American soldier brought home as soon as this mission is completed.

Let me also emphasize that all of us here at the U.N. hope that military force will never be used. We seek a peaceful outcome, a diplomatic outcome. And one more thing: in the aftermath of Iraq's unconditional departure from Kuwait, I truly believe there may be opportunities for Iraq and Kuwait to settle their differences permanently, for the states of the gulf themselves to build new arrangements for stability and for all the states and the peoples of the region to settle the conflicts that divide the Arabs from Israel.

But the world's key task, now, first and always, must be to demonstrate that aggression will not be tolerated or rewarded. . . .

The United Nations can help bring about a new day—

a day when these kinds of terrible weapons and the terrible despots who would use them, or both, were a thing of the past. It is in our hands to leave these dark machines behind, in the dark ages where they belong, and to press forward to cap a historic movement towards a new world order, and a long era of peace.

We have a vision of a new partnership of nations that transcends the cold war; a partnership based on consultation, cooperation and collective action, especially through international and regional organizations; a partnership united by principle and the rule of law and supported by an equitable sharing of both cost and commitment; a partnership whose goals are to increase democracy, increase prosperity, increase the peace and reduce arms. . . .

I see a world of open borders, open trade and, most importantly, open minds, a world that celebrates the common heritage that belongs to all the world's people, taking pride not just in hometown or homeland but in humanity itself. I see a world touched by a spirit like that of the Olympics, based not on competition that's driven by fear, but sought out of joy and exhilaration and a true quest for excellence.

And I see a world where democracy continues to win new friends and convert old foes, and where the Americas—North, Central and South—can provide a model for the future of all humankind, the world's first completely democratic hemisphere. And I see a world building on the emerging new model of European unity, not just Europe, but the whole world whole and free.

This is precisely why the present aggression in the gulf is a menace not only to . . . one region's security, but to the entire world's vision of our future. It threatens to turn the dream of a new international order into a grim nightmare of anarchy in which the law of the jungle supplants the law of nations. And that's why the United Nations reacted with such historic unity and resolve. And that's why this challenge is a test that we cannot afford to fail. . . .

Questions

1. What does President Bush see as the role of the United Nations in the new world order?
2. What role does he hope the Soviet Union will play in this order?
3. Why do you think Bush saw the Iraqi invasion of Kuwait as such a dangerous threat to the new world order he envisioned?

Questions for Further Thought

1. Given Reagan's criticisms of the overbearing reach of the federal government during the 1980 campaign and Donald Regan's description of him as "not an aggressive manager" of administration policies (Document 33-2), it seems ironic that the Reagan White House encountered serious political difficulties because of the alleged abuse of executive authority in the Iran-Contra affair. How do you explain this apparent contradiction?

2. Although he was America's oldest president, Ronald Reagan seemed to have an intuitive grasp of the requirements of presidential politics in the modern media-dominated era. Judging from the documents you have just read, how were Reagan's policies and public statements crafted to meet these requirements?

3. How successful was Ronald Reagan in achieving his conservative agenda in domestic and foreign policy?

4. Is there a contradiction between the Reagan revolution's belief in small government and George Bush's response to Iraqi aggression against Kuwait? Explain your answer.

An Age of Anxiety and Restructuring the Domestic Order: Public Life since 1993

Many of the premises of Reaganomics turned out to be flawed. Tax cuts for the wealthy did not produce the expected reinvestment in American industry and subsequent increased tax revenues. Manufacturing jobs continued to disappear at an alarming rate throughout the 1980s. Although the economy provided great opportunities for some people, many others were left behind. Laid-off factory workers in the shrinking steel, automobile, and other manufacturing industries found that low-paying service jobs did not match the wages or benefits of their previous jobs. Wealth was redistributed upward in the 1980s, with the best off increasing their share, the worst off losing ground, and the middle class struggling (see text pp. 1030–1032).

In the 1980s and early 1990s America became a more diverse society as millions of immigrants, mostly from Central America, the Caribbean, and southeast Asia, entered the country (see text pp. 1032–1035). In 1994, voters in California tried to attack the problems of illegal immigration through Proposition 187 (Document 33-6). One of the most visible symbols of the social distress of the 1980s was the dramatic increase in poverty and homelessness (Document 33-7). Poverty was especially widespread among families headed by women and in the black community. Also troubling was the spread of acquired immune deficiency syndrome (AIDS) (see text pp. 1038–1040). Critics charged that the federal government was slow to respond with funds for research on and treatment of this deadly disease, which by the early 1990s had killed more Americans than had died in fighting the Korean and Vietnam wars combined (Document 33-8).

More than ever, Americans felt that they were living in a technology-dominated culture, with the spread of personal computers, fax machines, cellular phones, and cable networks (see text pp. 1040–1041). These were exciting developments for some (Document 33-9) but unsettling for others. Many Americans yearned for simplicity amid the complexity. Republicans responded to that kind of anxiety in 1994 by offering the Contract with America (see text pp. 1046–1047 and Document 33-10).

33-6   Proposition 187 (1994)

Anxiety about immigration often occurs during periods of economic stress (see text p. 1035), and California in the mid-1990s was no exception. As a bulwark of the military-industrial complex, the state might have suffered more than any other from the end of the Cold War. The "peace dividend" seemed to be a combination of high unemployment and taxes.

Such was the environment in 1994, when Californians passed Proposition 187. The referendum sought to deny government services to illegal immigrants.

Source: California Secretary of State's Office, *1994 California Voter Information: Proposition 187, Text of Proposed Law.*

SECTION 1. Findings and Declaration.

The People of California find and declare as follows:

That they have suffered and are suffering economic hardship caused by the presence of illegal aliens in this state.

That they have suffered and are suffering personal injury and damage caused by the criminal conduct of illegal aliens in this state.

That they have a right to the protection of their government from any person or persons entering this country unlawfully.

Therefore, the People of California declare their intention to provide for cooperation between their agencies of state and local government with the federal government, and to establish a system of required notification by and between such agencies to prevent illegal aliens in the United States from receiving benefits or public services in the State of California.

SECTION 2. Manufacture, Distribution or Sale of False Citizenship or Resident Alien Documents: Crime and Punishment.

Section 113 is added to the Penal Code, to read:

113. Any person who manufactures, distributes or sells falso documents to conceal the true citizenship or resident alien status of another person is guilty of a felony, and shall be punished by imprisonment in the state prison for five years or by a fine of seventy-five thousand dollars ($75,000).

SECTION 3. Use of False Citizenship or Resident Alien Documents: Crime and Punishment.

Section 114 is added to the Penal Code, to read:

114. Any person who uses false documents to conceal his or her true citizenship or resident alien status is guilty of a felony, and shall be punished by imprisonment in the state prison for five years or by a fine of twenty-five thousand dollars ($25,000).

SECTION 4. Law Enforcement Cooperation with INS.

Section 834b is added to the Penal Code, to read:

834b. (a) Every law enforcement agency in California shall fully cooperate with the United States Immigration and Naturalization Service regarding any person who is arrested if he or she is suspected of being present in the United States in violation of federal immigration laws. . . .

SECTION 5. Exclusion of Illegal Aliens from Public Social Services.

Section 10001.5 is added to the Welfare and Institutions Code, to read:

10001.5. (a) In order to carry out the intention of the People of California that only citizens of the United States and aliens lawfully admitted to the United States may receive the benefits of public social services and to ensure that all persons employed in the providing of those services shall diligently protect public funds from misuse, the provisions of this section are adopted.

(b) A Person shall not receive any public social services to which he or she may be otherwise entitled until the legal status of that person has been verified as one of the following:

(1) A citizen of the United States.

(2) An alien lawfully admitted as a permanent resident.

(3) An alien lawfully admitted for a temporary period of time.

(c) If any public entity in this state to whom a person has applied for public social services determines or reasonably suspects, based upon the information provided to it, that the person is an alien in the United States in violation of federal law, the following procedures shall be followed by the public entity:

(1) The entity shall not provide the person with benefits or services.

(2) The entity shall, in writing, notify the person of his or her apparent illegal immigration status, and that the person must either obtain legal status or leave the United States.

(3) The entity shall also notify the State Director of Social Services, the Attorney General of California, and the United States Immigration and Naturalization Service of the apparent illegal status, and shall provide any additional information that may be requested by any other public entity.

SECTION 6. Exclusion of Illegal Aliens from Publicly Funded Health Care.

Chapter 1.3 (commencing with Section 130) is added to Part 1 of Division 1 of the Health and Safety Code, to read:

Chapter 1.3. Publicly-Funded Health Care Services

130. (a) In order to carry out the intention of the People of California that, excepting emergency medical care as required by federal law, only citizens of the United States and aliens lawfully admitted to the United States may receive the benefits of publicly-funded health care, and to ensure that all persons employed in the providing of those services shall diligently protect public funds from misuse, the provisions of this section are adopted.

(b) A person shall not receive any health care services from a publicly-funded health care facility, to which he or she is otherwise entitled until the legal status of that person has been verified as one of the following:

(1) A citizen of the United States.

(2) An alien lawfully admitted as a permanent resident.

(3) An alien lawfully admitted for a temporary period of time.

(c) If any publicly-funded health care facility in this state from whom a person seeks health care services, other than emergency medical care as required by federal law, determines or reasonably suspects, based upon the information provided to it, that the person is an alien in the United States in violation of federal law, the following procedures shall be followed by the facility:

(1) The facility shall not provide the person with services.

(2) The facility shall, in writing, notify the person of his or her apparent illegal immigration status, and that the person must either obtain legal status or leave the United States.

(3) The facility shall also notify the State Director of Health Services, the Attorney General of California, and the United States Immigration and Naturalization Service of the apparent illegal status, and shall provide any additional information that may be requested by any other public entity. . . .

SECTION 7. Exclusion of Illegal Aliens from Public Elementary and Secondary Schools.

Section 48215 is added to the Education Code, to read:

48215. (a) No public elementary or secondary school shall admit, or permit the attendance of, any child who is not a citizen of the United States, an alien lawfully admitted as a permanent resident, or a person who is otherwise authorized under federal law to be present in the United States. . . .

SECTION 8. Exclusion of Illegal Aliens from Public Post-secondary Educational Institutions.

Section 66010.8 is added to the Education Code, to read:

66010.8. (a) No public institution of postsecondary education shall admit, enroll, or permit the attendance of any person who is not a citizen of the United States, an alien lawfully admitted as a permanent resident in the United States, or a person who is otherwise authorized under federal law to be present in the United States. . . .

SECTION 9. Attorney General Cooperation with the INS.

Section 53069.65 is added to the Government Code, to read:

53069.65. Whenever the state or a city, or a county, or any other legally authorized local governmental entity with jurisdictional boundaries reports the presence of a person who is suspected of being present in the United States in violation of federal immigration laws to the Attorney General of California, that report shall be transmitted to the United States Immigration and Naturalization Service. The Attorney General shall be responsible for maintaining ongoing and accurate records of such reports, and shall provide any additional information that may be requested by any other government entity. . . .

Questions

1. To what extent are these findings and declarations convincing? What, if any, facts are missing?
2. Which provisions appear reasonable and which appear unfair? Why?
3. Imagine writing a state referendum on immigration. How would it compare to Proposition 187?

33-7 *Rachel and Her Children* (1988)

Jonathan Kozol

The social critic Jonathan Kozol described the world of the "welfare hotel" in his 1988 study *Rachel and Her Children*. Such institutions were the only shelter available for many homeless families in New York City in the 1980s.

Source: From *Rachel and Her Children* by Jonathan Kozol, pp. 51–55. Copyright © 1988 by Jonathan Kozol. Reprinted by permission of Crown Publishers, Inc.

There are families in this building whose existence, difficult though it may be, still represents an island of serenity and peace. Annie Harrington's family has a kind of pained serenity. Gwen and her children live with the peace of resignation. I think of these families like refugees who, in the midst of war, cling to each other and establish a small zone of safety. Most people here do not have resources to create a zone of safety. Terrorized already on arrival, they are quickly caught up in a vortex of accelerating threats and are tossed about like bits of wood and broken furniture and shattered houses in an Arkansas tornado. Chaos and disorder alternate with lethargy and nearly absolute bewilderment in face of regulations they cannot observe or do not understand.

Two women whom I meet in the same evening after Christmas, Wanda and Terry, frighten me by their entire inability to fathom or to govern what is going on inside and all around them.

Terry is pregnant, in her ninth month. She's afraid that, when she gives birth, she may not be able to bring home her baby from the hospital because she is not legally residing here.

Wanda, curled up like a newborn in a room no larger than a closet, is three months pregnant, planning an abortion.

Would doctors say these women are emotionally unwell? They might have no choice. Were these women sick before they came here? I don't see how we could possibly find out. What startles me is not that they have difficulty coping but that neither yet has given up entirely.

Terry: twenty-eight years old. She has three kids. She graduated from a school in Flushing and has worked for eight years as a lab assistant. Burnt out of her home, she stayed for two years with her sister's family: three adults, eight children, crowded into four unheated rooms. Evicted by her sister when the pressure on her sister's husband and their kids began to damage their own marriage, she had to take her children to the EAU at Church Street in Manhattan. Refusing to accept a placement at a barracks shelter, she's been sleeping here illegally for several nights in a small room rented to her cousin.

When we meet, she's in the corridor outside the crisis center, crying and perspiring heavily. She sits on a broken chair to talk to me. She's not on Medicaid and has been removed from AFDC. "My card's being reprocessed," she explains, although this explanation explains nothing. She's not on WIC. "I've got to file an application." Her back is aching. She is due to have her child any day.

This is the reason for her panic: "If I can't be placed before the baby's born, the hospital won't let me take the baby. They don't let you take a newborn if you haven't got a home." As we will see, this is not always so, but the possibility of this occurrence is quite real. Where are her kids? "They're here. I've got them hidden in the room."

She takes me to her cousin Wanda's room. I measure

it: nine feet by twelve, a little smaller than the room in which I store my files on the homeless. Wanda's been here fifteen months, has four kids, no hot plate, and no food in the refrigerator. She's had no food stamps and no restaurant allowance for two months. I ask her why. (You ask these questions even though you know the answer will be vague, confused, because so many of these women have no possible idea of why they do or don't receive the benefits they do or don't deserve.) She's curled up in a tattered slip and a torn sweater on a mattress with no sheet. Her case was closed, she says. Faintly, I hear something about "an application." Her words are hard to understand. I ask her whether she was here for Christmas. The very few words she speaks come out in small reluctant phrases: "Where else would I go?" She says her children got some presents from the fire department. There's a painting of Jesus and Mary on the wall above the bed. "My mother gave it to me."

A week later I stop by to visit. She's in the same position: drowsy and withdrawn. I ask her if she celebrated New Year's Eve. "Stayed by my lonesome" is all that I understand. She rouses herself enough to ask me if I have a cigarette. In the vacuum of emotion I ask if she ever gets to do something for fun. "Go to a movie . . ." But when I ask the last time she's been to a movie she says: "1984." What was the movie? *"Dawn of the Living Dead."*

When she says she's pregnant and is planning an abortion I don't care to ask her why, but she sits up halfway, props herself against a pillow, looks at Terry, shrugs, and mumbles this: "What you want to bring another baby into this place for? There ain't nothin' waitin' for them here but dirty rooms and dyin'."

Her children, scattered like wilted weeds around her on the floor, don't talk or play or move around or interrupt. Outside in the corridor I ask her cousin if the kids are sick. Terry says: "They're okay. They just didn't have no food to eat today." So I ask: "Did you?" She shakes her head. I go down to Herald Square, buy french fries and chicken at a fast-food store, milk and cookies at a delicatessen, and return. The minute I walk in Wanda sits up, clearheaded and alert. Her kids wake from their stupor. Fifteen minutes later, every bit of chicken, all the french fries, cookies, milk have been consumed. There is a rush of energy and talking in the room. The kids are pestering the adults, as they ought to.

"I have a problem," Wanda says. "My blood sugar goes down. It is called [pronounced very precisely] hypoglycemia."

I meet Terry one year later by sheer chance outside Grand Central Station. She's in a food line for the sandwiches distributed by a charitable group at 10:00 P.M. Her kids are with her. She's holding a baby in her arms. She tells me she's in another hotel near the Martinique. "Don't have no refrigerators there . . ."

I lose her in the crowd of people waiting for a meal.

In the subway station under Herald Square a woman who has seen me coming from the Martinique follows me and stops me by the stairs. Her hair is disheveled. Words spill from her mouth. She says that she was thrown out of the Martinique. Her children were sick with diarrhea. Someone "reported" her; for what I do not ask. After the Martinique she says that she was in a place I've never heard of called the Brooklyn Arms. Her youngest child, one year old, became much sicker there. City workers finally persuaded her to give up all three kids to foster care. She's living now in a crowded women's shelter where, she says, there are twelve women in a room. She shrieks this information at me on the platform not far from the shrieking trains.

"There's no soap, no hygiene. You go to the desk and ask for toilet paper. You get a single sheet. If you need another sheet you go back down and ask them for some more. I sleep on an army cot. The bathroom's flooded."

Is she telling me the truth? Is she on drugs? Is she unwell? Why did she elect to tell me this? Why do the words come out so fast? I feel unkind to cut her off, but I am frightened by her desperation. I leave her there, pouring out her words into the night.

The nurse in the Martinique says this: "A mother gave birth last week to a baby that weighed just over a pound. She was in her seventh month. Her children rubbed her belly while she cried. I called an ambulance."

The nurse is kind, compassionate, and overwhelmed. "People are fractured by this system. I'm responsible for 500 families, here and in another building. Custody cases. Pregnant women. Newborn children. I can get them into WIC. I'm snowed . . ." She's on the telephone, buried in papers, talking with women, hearing their questions, trying to come up with answers. There are others like her in the crisis center who create a tiny zone of safety in the larger zone of fear. But twenty-five hardworking nurses like this woman would be scarcely equal to the miseries that flood across her desk out of this factory of pain and tears. . . .

Questions

1. How does Kozol challenge the belief that a "safety net" was in place to protect the welfare of the neediest?
2. As an opponent of current government social welfare policies, why does Kozol focus on the experiences of families?
3. Why do the families depicted in Kozol's account seem incapable of improving their lot in life?

33-8 "A Week on Ward 5A" (1989)

Ed Wolf

Ed Wolf was a volunteer counselor in a privately funded support group for AIDS patients (see text pp. 1038–1040) and their families and friends known as the Shanti Project. His matter-of-fact description of a typical week in San Francisco General Hospital conveys some of the human cost of the AIDS epidemic. (Some terms in this account may be unfamiliar: PWA stands for People with AIDS; ARC stands for AIDS-Related Complex, a condition in which a patient tests HIV-positive and displays some of the symptoms of AIDS without having the full-blown symptoms of the disease; and PWARC stands for People with AIDS-Related Complex.)

Source: Ed Wolf, "A Week on Ward 5A," *Eclipse*, the Shanti Project, Spring 1989. In Nancy F. McKenzie, ed., *The AIDS Reader: Social, Political, and Ethical Issues* (New York: Penguin USA, 1991), pp. 528–533. Reprinted by permission of the Shanti Project, San Francisco, CA 94102.

(All client names have been changed to maintain confidentiality.)

Seven days a week, every day of the year, there are Shanti counselors on Ward 5A to offer support to all who come here—patient, visitor and staff alike. We are counselor, advocate, educator, hand-holder, masseur, facilitator, and mediator all rolled into one.

There are currently seven of us, offering our services throughout the hospital. Together we are gay and straight, male and female, HIV-positive and HIV-negative, black, brown, and white. As a team we speak Spanish, French, Greek, and English. Some of us are raising kids, one is a grandparent, some take dance classes, some go kayaking and camping. Some have their own private practice, some are planning to go back to school. We keep journals, we cook, and some of us do volunteer work for other organizations.

Together we work as a team. Two, three, or four of us on the ward at any one time. We know we can lean on each other, learn from each other, and rely on each other. The days here can be very intense, and we use each other to unload, to enliven, to comfort.

SUNDAY

Ann spoke to me this evening about her brother, who is dying of AIDS. Ken was able to speak to her several days ago, but is now incoherent. Ann is from out of town and is filled with feelings of grief and loss. The doctors told her last week that Ken wouldn't live past Friday, and now, two days later, he's still alive. We spoke about the dying process and why it might be taking him so long to die. Is he ready yet? Has he said his goodbyes? Has she said hers?

She spoke tenderly, of how her brother's impending death has reopened for her an old wound, the death of her infant daughter several years ago.

We discussed together her ability to deal, and to cope, and to find ways to carry the immeasurable sadness she is experiencing.

Earlier this evening I spoke with a young man who had recently been diagnosed with pneumocystis. He described how his "journey" with AIDS was progressing, of his KS [Karposi's sarcoma] diagnosis last year, of the day he was first told he was HIV-positive. He asked me if I had taken the HIV-antibody test. I told him that I had, and that I had tested negative. I told him one of my first reactions had been "why me?" He told me he had the same reaction to his test results. Together we explored the randomness of things and the importance of separating judgment from the events that come into our lives. Before I left his room, he said he had recently stopped asking "why me?" "Nowadays," he said, "I ask 'what's next'"?

MONDAY

This morning, as I get ready to go to work, I wonder if Ken and his sister will still be at the hospital. Has he died during the night?

As Shanti counselors at San Francisco General Hospital, we are privileged to come into people's lives while they are experiencing extraordinary circumstances. We may become involved with a patient and his or her loved ones for several days or several weeks; often there's only enough time for a single visit. We are constantly opening up to new people and letting go of familiar faces. During my two

days off-duty this past week, half of the ward was discharged and an equal number of patients were admitted. We often have feelings of incompleteness, of unfinishedness, with the rapid comings and goings of the patients and the visitors with whom we work. I am always reminded that life on the ward magnifies the larger picture—how we are all constantly walking in and out of each other's lives.

Every morning at 11 o'clock the Shanti counselors, social workers, and the charge nurse come together for report. Together we go over every patient with AIDS or ARC in the hospital and assess their varying needs. These patients are going home today; someone's being transferred to 5A from the Intensive Care unit. Someone's mom has come to see him for the first time since his diagnosis—can one of the Shanti counselors be sure to check in on them later today? Ken is still alive; his sister needs help finding a chaplain.

There are three Shanti counselors on duty today and we divide and prioritize the patients to be seen. I will follow up on Ken and his sister, but first there's someone a nurse wants me to talk with.

He's not a patient here. He's sitting in a chair in the corridor, a young black man who has just recently arrived in San Francisco. Jim tells me he has little money and needs a place to stay, says that he is HIV-positive, feels weak and tired all the time, and is having trouble keeping his food down. He has not been diagnosed with either AIDS or ARC—can I help him?

I explain how without an actual AIDS/ARC diagnosis he cannot receive the services he's requesting through Shanti. I suggest some of the emergency shelters in San Francisco, some of the food lines, where to go for food stamps and general assistance. I encourage him to make an appointment at Ward 86, the outpatient clinic here at SFGH. Jim tells me the horrific story of his past year, of his enlistment in the military, of the standard blood tests they now require, and the shock he felt when he was rejected by the local board because he was HIV-positive.

Shunned by family and friends, he has come to San Francisco because "I heard how they help people here." As we part in the hallway, I am filled with a sense of helplessness and concern.

As I go in to see Ken, I am struck by the sound of his breathing. It is loud and labored, and the oxygen coming from the wall fills the room with a harsh hissing. He lies on his side; he cannot speak. His sister is not in the room, but his lover, Bill, is at his bedside, looking very tired and very sad. We talk about the death of his father and the similarity of the pain of losing a dad and a lover, the pain of losing anyone we love, of being left behind. I gently touch Ken's arm as Bill tells me a little about their seven years together; a special trip one summer, a mountain they had climbed. He has been wondering if Ken can still hear. As we talk he decides he probably can, and that these bittersweet sharings of their life together are like a memorial service. We wonder what it would be like to hear one's own memorial service, and decide it would be okay to know that you are missed, that you had left many loving memories behind. The sadness in the room swells up and as Bill cries, I gently move my hand and place it on the heart of the man in the bed.

As the day draws to a close, I check in with one of my coworkers. He listens as I describe the sadness that I felt in Ken's room, and how difficult it was for me to let the young HIV-positive man walk away down the hall, unable to do more for him. He tells me of an especially good connection he made with one of his patients, and how happy he is that another went home today.

TUESDAY

As I enter through the main lobby of the hospital this morning, I find myself wondering if Ken is still alive.

The day began in a rush as I encounter Ken's sister in the hallway. Ann has already extended her stay here in San Francisco for two days—she must get to the bus station and return home to her children and other responsibilities. But Ken is still alive. How can she leave him? We move into an empty room on 5A and sit together. Her eyes are swollen from all the crying she has done in the last few days. She says to me, "I must go and I can't go."

At first I am struck with the seeming impossibility of this dilemma. I experience a growing sense of my own inadequacies in trying to help in some way. I also know that this woman has her own answers and that she doesn't need me to tell her what to do. She sought me out to be a supportive presence, to be a sounding board perhaps, to discuss and explore her own options. As she tells me of her situation at home, it becomes increasingly clear that she must return to her children as soon as possible.

I ask her if she can tell Ken what she is telling me, how much it hurts to be leaving him now. We begin to talk about permission and the startling similarities between her need for permission to go home and Ken's need for permission to die in his own time, on his own terms.

She decides that she can do this. I ask her if she'd like me to come with her to Ken's room, and she softly says, "Thank you, no." As we return to the hallway, I give her a parting hug and know that I will not be seeing her again.

The tone of this interaction seems to reverberate through the rest of the day. I have lunch in the hospital cafeteria with one of the chaplains, and as he tells me about a recent weekend retreat he attended, I know that several floors above us Ken and his sister are gently parting.

Later in the day I meet with Alfredo, who is here visiting his brother Ramon. Ramon has pneumocystis, is from Mexico, and is far from his family. I listen as Alfred speaks of life in Mexico City and the AIDS epidemic there, and for just a moment I see Ann looking out a bus window, heading home.

WEDNESDAY

The first half of every Wednesday is devoted to getting together with the other counselors. We alternate, from week to week, between support group and case presentation. This morning one of the counselors discussed an especially difficult series of interactions he had with a patient who was having problems with the nursing staff. We then had a business meeting and a short support group. Through these first four hours of the day, I repeatedly thought of Ken.

Wednesday is also discharge planning day, when many outside AIDS service agencies come together with the in-house staff to discuss the discharge plans for all PWAs and PWARCs currently in the hospital. It is here that I find out that Ken is still alive. The medical team reports that his "deep pain reflex" is gone and he is now comatose.

When the meeting ends, I go to see Ken. There is no one visiting. The room is filled with balloons, flowers, and get-well cards. Someone has placed a small teddy bear on the pillow near his head. Ken seems peaceful His breaths are very short and far between as I place my hand on his chest and breathe with him for a while. I tell of some of my interactions with his sister and his lover, and that they have told me they will be all right. I tell him it's okay to let go. I become aware of my own wish that his suffering will end soon, today, now. I am aware then of the necessity of my having to let go, of respecting the mystery of how and when any of us die.

The day is quickly coming to a close as I leave Ken's room and go to see one more patient. He was here a year ago and I remember him well. I have pulled our old chart on him and read through some of the previous conversations we had.

As I enter his room, I perceive how much Marvin has changed since we last met. His body is extremely thin; he is too weak to stand on his own. But the biggest change is in his mental status. He has been diagnosed with HIV dementia and is here awaiting placement.

Five of the sixteen patients on 5A this week are here because of dementia and the placement problems it creates. Because of the level of difficulty experienced in trying to connect with someone who is demented and the anguish it can cause the visitor, demented patients often spend a lot of time alone.

Today as I sit with Marvin, I find myself working hard to connect in any possible way. I ask about the television show he is watching; the lunch he has just been fed. I read all his get-well cards out loud and ask him about each of the senders.

Because his responses are minimal, I feel I have not connected. As I begin to leave his vacant eyes follow me and he asks, "You're not leaving yet, are you?"

I sit down and tell him I can stay a little longer. I am touched and moved by his question. I sit with him in silence now as he gazes blankly at the television, and I hold his hand. I assumed that my presence had not been felt and, in dong so, had almost missed the connection we were so clearly sharing.

THURSDAY

Today is my last day on the ward before a three-day weekend, my birthday weekend as a matter of fact, and I have made plans to go to the mountains. After 2 ½ years on 5A, I have found it very important to take care of myself, especially on my days off. As I get ready for work, I think of the full week I've already had.

When I get to the hospital I see that Ken is still alive.

Morning report runs longer than usual because the census is very large.

All 16 beds on 5A are full and another 16 patients are on other wards. There are 14 patients with pneumocystis, many newly diagnosed. There will be a lot for the weekend counselors to do.

I go and say good-bye to Ken. A friend is visiting, and so is Ken's Shanti volunteer. Ken's breathing seems very faint, too delicate and weak to be keeping him alive. As I leave, I know I will not see him again. . . .

Questions

1. How does Ed Wolf react to the pain he describes in Ward 5A? Does he seem involved with or detached from it?
2. What is the significance of his repeated thoughts of the patient named Ken?
3. What does the scrapbook reveal about the scale of the epidemic?

33-9 "The Electronic Cottage" (1980)

Alvin Toffler

As the historian Frederick Jackson Turner suggested, Americans are forever looking to the frontier and the better future that may accompany it. The critic and futurist Alvin Toffler fits into that tradition. Toffler sees the communications revolution of the second half of the twentieth century as the Third Wave of change in human history, following the development of agriculture and the Industrial Revolution. The frontier is cyberspace, and changes ushered in by the computer (see text pp. 1040–1041), Toffler believes, promise a great future. Here Toffler discusses how the Third Wave will make work once again a cottage industry.

Source: Excerpted from Alvin Toffler, *The Third Wave* (New York: Morrow, 1980), pp. 218–223.

THE HOME-CENTERED SOCIETY

If the electronic cottage were to spread, a chain of consequences of great importance would flow through society. Many of these consequences would please the most ardent environmentalist or techno-rebel, while at the same time opening new options for business entrepreneurship.

Community Impact: Work at home involving any sizeable fraction of the population could mean greater community stability—a goal that now seems beyond our reach in many high-change regions. If employees can perform some or all of their work tasks at home, they do not have to move every time they change jobs, as many are compelled to do today. They can simply plug into a different computer.

This implies less forced mobility, less stress on the individual, fewer transient human relationships, and greater participation in community life. Today when a family moves into a community, suspecting that it will be moving out again in a year or two, its members are markedly reluctant to join neighborhood organizations, to make deep friendships, to engage in local politics, and to commit themselves to community life generally. The electronic cottage could help restore a sense of community belonging, and touch off a renaissance among voluntary organizations like churches, women's groups, lodges, clubs, athletic and youth organizations. The electronic cottage could mean more of what sociologists, with their love of German jargon, call *gemeinschaft*.

Environmental Impact: The transfer of work, or any part of it, into the home could not only reduce energy requirements . . . but could also lead to energy decentralization. Instead of requiring highly concentrated amounts of energy in a few high-rise offices or sprawling factory complexes, and therefore requiring highly centralized energy generation, the electronic cottage system would spread out energy demand and thus make it easier to use solar, wind, and other alternative energy technologies. Small-scale energy generation units in each home could substitute for at least some of the centralized energy now required. This implies a decline in pollution as well, for two reasons: first, the switch to renewable energy sources on a small-scale basis eliminates the need for high-polluting fuels, and second, it means smaller releases of highly concentrated pollutants that overload the environment at a few critical locations.

Economic Impact: Some businesses would shrink in such a system, and others proliferate or grow. Clearly, the electronics and computer and communications industries would flourish. By contrast, the oil companies, the auto industry, and commercial real estate developers would be hurt. A whole new group of small-scale computer stores and information services would spring up; the postal service, by contrast, would shrink. Papermakers would do less well; most service industries and white-collar industries would benefit.

At a deeper level, if individuals came to own their own electronic terminals and equipment, purchased perhaps on credit, they would become, in effect, independent entrepreneurs rather than classical employees—meaning, as it were, increased ownership of the "means of production" by the worker. We might also see groups of home-workers organize themselves into small companies to contract for their services or, for that matter, unite in cooperatives that jointly own the machines. All sorts of new relationships and organizational forms become possible.

Psychological Impact: The picture of a work world that is increasingly dependent upon abstract symbols conjures up an overcerebral work environment that is alien to us and, at one level, more impersonal than at present. But at a different level, work at home suggests a deepening of face-to-face and emotional relationships in both the home and the neighborhood. Rather than a world of purely vicarious human relationships, with an electric screen interposed between the individual and the rest of humanity, as imagined in many science fiction stories, one can postulate a world divided into two sets of human relationships—one

real, the other vicarious—with different rules and roles in each.

No doubt we will experiment with many variations and halfway measures. Many people will work at home part-time and outside the home as well. Dispersed work centers will no doubt proliferate. Some people will work at home for months or years, then switch to an outside job, and then perhaps switch back again. Patterns of leadership and management will have to change. Small firms would undoubtedly spring up to contract for white-collar tasks from larger firms and take on specialized responsibilities for organizing, training, and managing teams of home-workers. To maintain adequate liaison among them, perhaps such small companies will organize parties, social occasions, and other joint holidays, so that the members of a team get to know one another face-to-face, not merely through the console or keyboard.

Certainly not everyone can or will (or will want to) work at home. Certainly we face a conflict over pay scales and opportunity cost. What happens to the society when an increased amount of human interaction on the job is vicarious while face-to-face, emotion-to-emotion interaction intensifies in the home? What about cities? What happens to the unemployment figures? What, in fact, do we mean by the terms "employment" and "unemployment" in such a system? It would be naïve to dismiss such questions and problems.

But if there are unanswered questions and possibly painful difficulties, there are also new possibilities. The leap to a new system of production is likely to render irrelevant many of the most intractable problems of the passing era. The misery of feudal toil, for example, could not be alleviated within the system of feudal agriculture. It was not eliminated by peasant revolts, by altruistic nobles, or by religious utopians. Toil remained miserable until it was altered entirely by the arrival of the factory system, with its own strikingly different drawbacks.

In turn, the characteristic problems of industrial society—from unemployment to grinding monotony on the job, to overspecialization, to the callous treatment of the individual, to low wages—may, despite the best intentions and promises of job enlargers, trade unions, benign employers, or revolutionary workers' parties, be wholly unresolvable within the framework of the Second Wave production system. If such problems have remained for 300 years, under both capitalist and socialist arrangements, there is cause to think they may be inherent in the mode of production.

The leap to a new production system in both manufacturing and the white-collar sector, and the possible breakthrough to the electronic cottage, promise to change all the existing terms of debate, making obsolete most of the issues over which men and women today argue, struggle, and sometimes die.

We cannot today know if, in fact, the electronic cottage will become the norm of the future. Nevertheless, it is worth recognizing that if as few as 10 to 20 percent of the work force as presently defined were to make this historic transfer over the next 20 to 30 years, our entire economy, our cities, our family structure, our values, and even our politics would be altered almost beyond our recognition.

It is a possibility—a plausibility, perhaps—to be pondered.

It is now possible to see in relationship to one another a number of Third Wave changes usually examined in isolation. We see a transformation of our energy system and our energy base into a new *techno-sphere*. This is occurring at the same time that we are demassifying the mass media and building an intelligent environment, thus revolutionizing the *info-sphere* as well. In turn, these two giant currents flow together to change the deep structure of our production system, altering the nature of work in factory and office and, ultimately, carrying us toward the transfer of work back into the home.

By themselves, such massive historical shifts would easily justify the claim that we are on the edge of a new civilization. But we are simultaneously restructuring our social life as well, from our family ties and friendships to our schools and corporations. We are about to create, alongside the Third Wave techno-sphere and info-sphere, a Third Wave *socio-sphere* as well.

Questions

1. What is the appeal of this kind of look at the future?
2. According to Toffler, what will workers demand?
3. What problems might working at home involve that Toffler ignores? What advantages are there to working outside the home?

33-10   The Contract with America (1994)

Republican strategists conceived of the Contract with America (see text pp. 1046–1047) as a campaign tool during the 1994 Congressional elections. This statement of principles and intentions also proved effective after the election, with Republicans in control of both houses and eager to demonstrate how they differed from the opposition.

Source: Rep. Newt Gingrich, Rep. Dick Armey, and the House Republicans, *The Contract with America*, 1994.

The Contract's Core Principles. The Contract with America is rooted in 3 core principles:

Accountability - The government is too big and spends too much, and Congress and unelected bureaucrats have become so entrenched to be unresponsive to the public they are supposed to serve. The GOP contract restores accountability to government.

Responsibility - Bigger government and more federal programs usurp personal responsibility from families and individuals. The GOP contract restores a proper balance between government and personal responsibility.

Opportunity - The American Dream is out of the reach of too many families because of burdensome government regulations and harsh tax laws. The GOP contract restores the American dream.

The Contract

As Republican Members of the House of Representatives and as citizens seeking to join that body we propose not just to change its policies, but even more important, to restore the bonds of trust between the people and their elected representatives.

That is why, in this era of official evasion and posturing, we offer instead a detailed agenda for national renewal, a written commitment with no fine print.

This year's election offers the chance, after four decades of one-party control, to bring to the House a new majority that will transform the way Congress works. That historic change would be the end of government that is too big, too intrusive, and too easy with the public's money. It can be the beginning of a Congress that respects the values and shares the faith of the American family.

Like Lincoln, our first Republican president, we intend to act "with firmness in the right, as God gives us to see the right." To restore accountability to Congress. To end its cycle of scandal and disgrace. To make us all proud again of the way free people govern themselves.

On the first day of the 104th Congress, the new Republican majority will immediately pass the following major reforms, aimed at restoring the faith and trust of the American people in their government:

- FIRST, require all laws that apply to the rest of the country also apply equally to the Cóngress;

- SECOND, select a major, independent auditing firm to conduct a comprehensive audit of Congress for waste, fraud or abuse;

- THIRD, cut the number of House committees, and cut committee staff by one-third;

- FOURTH, limit the terms of all committee chairs;

- FIFTH, ban the casting of proxy votes in committee;

- SIXTH, require committee meetings to be open to the public;

- SEVENTH, require a three-fifths majority vote to pass a tax increase;

- EIGHTH, guarantee an honest accounting of our Federal Budget by implementing zero base-line budgeting.

Thereafter, within the first 100 days of the 104th Congress, we shall bring to the House Floor the following bills, each to be given full and open debate, each to be given a clear and fair vote and each to be immediately available this day for public inspection and scrutiny.

1. THE FISCAL RESPONSIBILITY ACT
A balanced budget/tax limitation amendment and a legislative line-item veto to restore fiscal responsibility to an out-of-control Congress, requiring them to live under the same budget constraints as families and businesses.

2. THE TAKING BACK OUR STREETS ACT
An anti-crime package including stronger truth-in-sentencing, "good faith" exclusionary rule exemptions, effective death penalty provisions, and cuts in social spending from this summer's "crime" bill to fund prison construction and additional law enforcement to keep people secure in their neighborhoods and kids safe in their schools.

3. THE PERSONAL RESPONSIBILITY ACT
Discourage illegitimacy and teen pregnancy by prohibiting welfare to minor mothers and denying increased AFDC for additional children while on welfare, cut spending for welfare programs, and enact a tough two-years-and-out provision with work requirements to promote individual responsibility.

4. THE FAMILY REINFORCEMENT ACT
Child support enforcement, tax incentives for adoption, strengthening rights of parents in their children's education, stronger child pornography laws, and an elderly dependent care tax credit to reinforce the central role of families in American society.

5. THE AMERICAN DREAM RESTORATION ACT
A $500 per child tax credit, begin repeal of the marriage tax penalty, and creation of American Dream Savings Accounts to provide middle class tax relief.

6. THE NATIONAL SECURITY RESTORATION ACT
No U. S. troops under U.N. command and restoration of the essential parts of our national security funding to strengthen our national defense and maintain our credibility around the world.

7. THE SENIOR CITIZENS FAIRNESS ACT
Raise the Social Security earnings limit which currently forces seniors out of the work force, repeal the 1993 tax hikes on Social Security benefits and provide tax incentives for private long-term care insurance to let Older Americans keep more of what they have earned over the years.

8. THE JOB CREATION AND WAGE ENHANCEMENT ACT
Small business incentives, capital gains cut and indexation, neutral cost recovery, risk assessment/cost-benefit analysis, strengthening the Regulatory Flexibility Act and unfunded mandate reform to create jobs and raise worker wages.

9. THE COMMON SENSE LEGAL REFORM ACT
"Loser pays" laws, reasonable limits on punitive damages and reform of product liability laws to stem the endless tide of litigation.

10. THE CITIZEN LEGISLATURE ACT
A first-ever vote on term limits to replace career politicians with citizen legislators.

Further, we will instruct the House Budget Committee to report to the floor and we will work to enact additional budget savings, beyond the budget cuts specifically included in the legislation described above, to ensure that the Federal budget deficit will be less than it would have been without the enactment of these bills.

Respecting the judgment of our fellow citizens as we seek their mandate for reform, we hereby pledge our names to this Contract with America.

Questions

1. How does the Contract with America demonize government?
2. What public sentiments does the contract capitalize on? How did those sentiments arise?
3. What are the advantages and dangers in using this kind of election strategy?

Questions for Further Thought

1. In 1980 American voters turned a Democratic incumbent out of the White House in favor of a Republican challenger. Twelve years later they turned a Republican incumbent out of the White House in favor of a Democratic challenger (while an independent third candidate attracted nearly 1 in 5 votes). What changed in those twelve years in terms of the major domestic and foreign policy concerns which shaped the response of American voters?
2. How do you explain the gulf between public support for Proposition 187 (Document 33-6) and the experiences of Inés Hernández (Document 30-9)?
3. Although their contents differ greatly, the Contract with America (Document 33-10) and the Progressive party platform of 1912 (Document 21-9) both struck a chord with voters. What do these documents share that might explain their popularity?
4. As Americans confront the end of the twentieth century, what issues seem likely to shape the politics of the early twenty-first century?

Credits and Acknowledgments